Legalising Land Righ

Law, Governance, and Development

The Leiden University Press series on Law, Governance, and Development brings together an interdisciplinary body of work about the formation and functioning of legal systems in developing countries, and about interventions to strengthen them. The series aims to engage academics, policy makers and practitioners at the national and international level, thus attempting to stimulate legal reform for good governance and development.

General Editors:
Jan Michiel Otto (Leiden University)
Benjamin van Rooij (Leiden University)

Editorial Board:
Abdullahi Ahmed An-Naím (Emory University)
Keebet von Benda Beckman (Max Planck Institute for Social Anthropology)
John Bruce (Land and Development Solutions International)
Jianfu Chen (La Trobe University)
Sally Engle Merry (New York University)
Julio Faundez (University of Warwick)
Linn Hammergren (World Bank)
Andrew Harding (University of Victoria)
Fu Hualing (Hong Kong University)
Goran Hyden (University of Florida)
Martin Lau (SOAS, University of London)
Christian Lund (Roskilde University)
Barbara Oomen (University of Amsterdam and Roosevelt Academy)
Veronica Taylor (University of Washington)
David Trubek (University of Wisconsin)

Legalising Land Rights

Local Practices, State Responses and Tenure
Security in Africa, Asia and Latin America

Edited by

Janine M. Ubink,
André J. Hoekema,
and Willem J. Assies

Leiden University Press

This book has been made possible by a grant from the Netherlands Organisation for Scientific Research (NWO MAGW SaRO).

Cover design: Studio Jan de Boer, Amsterdam
Layout: The DocWorkers, Almere

ISBN   978 90 8728 056 7
e-ISBN   978 90 4850 669 9
NUR   759 / 828

Contents

1 Legalising land rights in Africa, Asia and Latin America: An introduction

Janine Ubink

The potential of legalisation of land assets

Millions of people live and work on land that they do not legally own in accordance with enforceable state law. Secure land rights are a basis for household food security and shelter, and provide a safety net in case of unemployment or retirement. The absence of state recognition for local property rights is considered to affect people's tenure security, which in turn impinges on people's social-economic security and impedes development. People who are not secure in their property rights will not invest labour and other resources in the fertility and productivity of their agricultural land, the improvement of their houses built on the land, and the infrastructure of their neighbourhood. Tenure insecurity also hinders the provision of services and infrastructure by the government. Furthermore, people are unable to acquire formal loans, as they cannot use their land or houses as collateral. The lack of state-guaranteed documents moreover inhibits the ability to make transactions of land and houses with strangers who are not familiar with local ownership structures, which will restrict the land market.

Traditionally, endeavors to legalise or formalise extra-legal land tenure have focused on state-led individual titling and registration.[1] This was based on the assumption that individual property rights would improve access to credit and thus increase the ability of landholders to invest in their land. Furthermore, individual titles would remove disincentives to invest through an increase of landholders' confidence that they would not be deprived of their land. This paradigm was broadly supported by legal scholars as well as by those in other disciplines as diverse as economics and land surveying.

There has been some success with titling and registration. Feder et al. (1988) and Li, Rozelle, and Brandt (1998) argue on the basis of data from Thailand and China that private property increased security, investment, and productivity. Deininger (2003:47) has reported increases in land values and agricultural investment following registration programmes in Nicaragua, Ecuador, and Venezuela. However, in several other countries, especially but not exclusively in Africa, no significant relationship was found between tenure regimes on the one hand and

security, credit use, and productivity on the other (Atwood 1990; Bruce
and Migot-Adholla 1994; DFID 1999; Gerschenberg 1971; Migot-Adholla et al. 1993; Ouédraogo et al. 1996; Varley 2002). Registration
programmes have proved to be 'slow, expensive, difficult to keep up-to
date and hard for poor people to access' (Cotula, Toulmin, and Quan
2006:20). As a result, very little land has been registered, and 'where
titling and registration have been implemented, greater agricultural investment has not necessarily materialised' (id.). Empirical evidence
shows that land titling and registration of private property can create,
rather than reduce, uncertainty and conflict over land rights (Atwood
1990:663). 'Latent disputes can flare up when local actors realise that
registration will bring about final adjudication of land rights' (Cotula,
Toulmin, and Quan 2006:20). Unsuccessful attempts to substitute
state titles for customary entitlements – and according to Cousins not
one attempt has been fully successful – may even reduce security by
creating normative confusion, which the powerful may take advantage
of (Cousins 2000:171; cf. Atwood 1990:663-5; Bruce, Migot-Adholla,
and Atherton 1994:260; Coldham 1979:618-9; DFID 1999:11; Lanjouw
and Levy 2002). 'Many registration programmes had negative distribu-
tive effects, as those with more contacts, information and resources
were able to register land in their names, to the detriment of poorer
claimants', and holders of secondary land rights are often expropriated
(Cotula, Toulmin, and Quan 2006:20. See also Atwood 1990; Lund
1998; Migot-Adholla and Bruce 1994:20-1; Nyamu-Musembi 2006:19-
22; Platteau 2000; Van den Brink et al. 2006:12).[2] Research has also
shown that registration does not improve access to credit where high
transaction and other costs hinder credit supply, and that many poor
families are unwilling to borrow for risk of being unable to repay and
losing the land through foreclosure (Cotula, Toulmin, and Quan
2006:20; Durand-Lasserve and Selod 2007:10, 12; Gilbert 2002:14-20;
Home and Lim 2004; Van den Brink et al. 2006:13). Field and Torero
even suspect that titling may reduce the banks' ability to foreclose as
the latter could anticipate that governments who promote titling will
also protect borrowers. This would deter them from lending (Field and
Torero 2006, quoted in Durand-Lasserve and Selod 2007:25).
    The failures of state-led individual titling and registration (ITR) pro-
jects coincided with research showing that some property rights which
are only informally agreed on and enforced can be very secure (Bruce
and Migot-Adholla 1994). This is a recurring theme in more recent literature. Gilbert (2002:7) for instance states that in urban squatter areas
in Latin America, evictions are only likely to occur when settlements
threaten powerful vested interests, for example through their geographical proximity to elite residential areas, or when military or authoritarian governments are in power. In sub-Saharan Africa, according to

Durand-Lasserve (2006:3-4), communal or customary land systems guarantee a reasonably good level of security, even when these are not formally recognised by the state. At the same time, many authors also stress the limitations of this security. Durand-Lasserve (*id.*) points out that the customary arrangement can deteriorate due to, for instance, conflicts between those who allocate the land and other members of the group, or when a major conflict arises between customary owners and public authorities about the ownership and the use of the land, or about the legitimacy of the customary claim. Other research and policy papers point to the decreasing security of tenure in the face of land shortage and competition and express new worries about increasing in-equity of informal, including customary, land tenure. They emphasise issues of unequal power relations within communities and point out that local institutions are vulnerable to power plays of elites, as well as to politics of exclusion (Amanor 2001:11-20; Carney and Watts 1990; Cousins 2002:77; Lavigne Delville 1999; Moore 1998:42; Oomen 2002; Peters 2002:48; Toulmin, Lavigne Delville, and Traoré 2002:15).

The disappointment with ITR approaches to formalisation, together with the realisation that some state regulation is desirable to prevent the usurpation of rights by local power holders – whether customary leaders, local politicians, or criminal big men such as mafiosi – have led to a widely supported search for 'a third way' or 'a new paradigm' which 'does not prescribe a specific approach to land reform' but is based on pluralism (Toulmin and Quan 2000b:5). According to this new approach, existing property rights often do not seem to be in need of a wholesale replacement with new property rights regimes. Alternative policies from titling are needed to strengthen security of tenure, and must build on local concepts and practice rather than importing one-size-fits-all models (Otto 2004:8). This entails, among other things, recognition by the state of local land rights and increased formalisation of those systems (Bruce and Migot-Adholla 1994; Cotula, Toulmin, and Quan 2006:21; Van den Brink et al. 2006:5). 'Land registration may still be a useful component of a broader tenure security strategy, particularly where customary systems have collapsed, where land disputes are widespread', and in areas with high competition for land (Cotula, Toulmin, and Quan 2006:21. See also Bruce, Migot-Adholla, and Atherton 1994:262; Van den Brink et al. 2006:13-15).

Probably the most prominent proponent of legalisation is Hernando de Soto. In 'The Mystery of Capital' (2000) he recommends that to combat poverty, the poor should quickly move their assets from an un-productive extra-legal sphere into the legal sphere where these assets could turn into 'capital'. He heavily criticises the standard legalisation projects and the lack of progress in land tenure reform. In a chapter on 'the mystery of legal failure', De Soto blames lawyers for being un-

willing and unable to construct the 'bridges' that would enable the poor
to enter the realm of law and capital. He proposes a twofold alternative
strategy for legalisation: first, the 'discovery' and analysis of informal
'social contracts' that presently regulate human-land relations; and second, a legal and political strategy for designing 'bridges' to connect, harmonise and integrate those rules with the formal legal system. He
claims that this twofold strategy will speed up the legalisation of land
tenure. The ease with which De Soto promotes 'discovering' the informal 'social contracts' suggests a limited awareness with the many well-
documented difficulties of doing so. Unfortunately, his writing does not
answer the question of how such exercises should be undertaken (Otto
2004:9, 2009, forthcoming). De Soto's choice of wording, referring to
the building of bridges between customary, informal, or illegal assets
and the formal legal system – although it remains largely an abstract
notion – seems to fit well at face value with the 'new paradigm' noted
by Toulmin and Quan. On second look, however, it becomes clear that
he sees titling and registration of individual property rights as the only
way to reach his goal of transforming property into collateral, collateral
into credit, and credit into income (Woodruff 2001:1219).

Most people are glad to receive a title deed. It is this popularity that
explains why many governments have taken up this option, especially
in urban areas (cf. Gilbert 2002). Recently, however, as a result of the
shift in thinking and the 'new paradigm', several land policies and laws
present important innovations compared to their predecessors. A number of countries have provided for the registration of customary rights
(e.g. Uganda, Mozambique, Tanzania, Niger, and Namibia). In Mozambique, customary use rights are even protected when they are not registered. And several titling programmes have issued titles not only to individuals but also to families (e.g. Nicaragua and Brazil) and to groups
or communities (e.g. South Africa, Mozambique, Kenya, and the Philippines) in rural as well as urban areas (Cotula, Toulmin, and Quan
2006:21. See also Durand-Lasserve 2006:10; IIED 2006:7-8).

This book hopes to contribute to the ongoing quest for a new paradigm in land tenure regulation that will reconcile state perspectives of
a programmatic, national and legal nature with local land rights and allocation processes. The material in this book arises from an international, comparative research project on the potential of legalisation of
land assets.[3] The main objective of the book is to obtain an overview
and in-depth insight into legalisation policies that have evolved in Africa, Latin America, and Asia. It contains eleven case studies in eight different countries that deal with urban, peri-urban, and rural land, and
focus on agricultural as well as residential land use. These case studies
examine the different designs of land tenure legalisations, the justifications and objectives for the legalisation processes, and their effects on

tenure security and on the vulnerability of smallholders to losing their land rights. They furthermore identify the winners and losers of the legalisation processes and the challenges that need to be addressed to improve the tenure security of smallholders.

Only with sufficient knowledge of both the local socio-legal contexts and the particularities of the various land tenure regimes can the documented attempts at legalisation be understood.[4] Given the broad scope of countries studied and the great diversity within and between countries and continents, it was considered necessary to supplement the case studies of legalisation projects and programmes with overview studies of the land tenure regimes of the countries in which they were situated. Land law often forms an arena for struggle between different ideologies and interests, including: enabling a free market for land, providing security for the poor, keeping government agents in control, democratic decentralisation, and respecting the customary traditions of the region (McAuslan 1998). National regimes vary according to the priority attached to these goals (Otto 2004:9). The countries selected for this book include various degrees of recognition of customary law, of democratic decentralisation, of state interventionist control as well as different colonial legal backgrounds. These criteria, combined with the backgrounds of the research group, have led to the selection of the following countries: Ethiopia, Ghana, Namibia, Senegal, Bolivia, Mexico, China, and Indonesia.

The integration of extra-legal tenure

Land tenure may be defined as the terms and conditions on which land is held, used and transacted (Adams, Sibanda, and Turner 1999:135). It designates the rights individuals and communities have with regard to land, and should thus primarily be viewed as a social relation involving a complex set of rules that governs land use and land ownership (Durand-Lasserve and Selod 2007:4). In practice, a continuum in land tenure rights can be observed, especially in developing countries where different sources of law and different ownership patterns may coexist (Payne 2002, quoted in Durand-Lasserve and Selod 2007:4). There is thus a diversity of tenure situations, ranging from the most informal types of possession and use to full ownership (Durand-Lasserve and Selod 2007:4).

From the viewpoint of the state, three main situations of 'extra-legal' land tenure can be distinguished. First, many people have rights in land on the basis of customary law; when customary law and customary rights are not recognised by the state, this creates an extra-legal situation (according to state law). Second, a large number of people occupy public or private land against the wishes of the legal owner. Third, there are a number of people who have acquired land from a legal or customary owner but reside on unauthorised land developments, for instance where land is subdivided and sold illegally by informal developers – because the required permission for land subdivision was not obtained or because it violates zoning or planning regulations. This situation can also occur when the new occupants of the land have not gone through the compulsory procedures for registration or titling or have not acquired the right permits for settling or building (see also Gilbert 2002:6-7). Rural areas mainly display the first type of extra-legality, based on customary rights in land that are not recognised by the state. This is not an exclusively rural affair, though. Research shows that also in urban and peri-urban areas, land transfers and acquisitions often depend on customary rights and relations (see Hesseling and Eichelsheim, this volume; Reerink, this volume). The second and third types of extra-legality are mainly urban and peri-urban occurrences.[5]

Legalisation is a process by which extra-legal tenure is integrated into the national legal system.[6] Obviously, this can be done in many different ways. Tenure legalisation programmes are influenced by the approaches and orientations to legalisation as defined by governments, funding agencies, and implementing agencies. They also depend on a set of legal, social, administrative, and political factors that include the constitutional, legal, and regulatory framework, the political balance of power at the central and local government levels, the state of demand for tenure formalisation, political will and commitment, pressures from civil society, the perception of the legitimacy of the extra-legal tenure situation by governmental institutions and the population, the financial and human resources available for implementing tenure formalisation, the administrative apparatus available for implementation including checks and balances and accessible administrative justice to control the abuse of administrative powers, and the extent of legal empowerment of local stakeholders (cf. Durand-Lasserve and Selod 2007:15). The local diversity of these factors results in a range of different legalisation policies. These policies can for instance be geared towards any of the three categories of extra-legal land tenure mentioned above (customary tenure, occupation against the wishes of the legal owner, or unauthorised land developments); they can aim to deliver personal rights or real rights to individuals or collectives; and they can focus on rural, peri-urban, or urban areas, and on residential or agricultural land. Together these policies form a whole spectrum ranging from recognition of land administration of certain groups to individual titling and registration of extra-legal property. The case studies described in this book deal with legalisation projects and programmes throughout this whole spectrum, and include the recognition of customary land rights and communal land management rights, administrative recognition of occupation, often in the form of permits to occupy or short-term leaseholds, and the delivery of property rights through titling and registration.

Tenure security

One of the main stated objectives of legalisation programmes is the enhancement of tenure security. Various definitions of tenure security circulate in the literature.[7] Some of these definitions focus on the element of certainty of land rights. Certainty is mostly seen as a function of two elements: (1) assurance in exerting rights, and (2) the costs of enforcing these rights, which should not be inhibiting (Place, Roth, and Hazell 1994:19-21). Durand-Lasserve and Selod (2007:6), for instance, define tenure security in urban areas as the right of all individuals and groups to effective protection by the state against forced eviction. In contrast, insecure tenure should be viewed as a risk of forced eviction (cf. UN Habitat 2004:31).[8] FAO, in a study on rural land tenure, defines tenure security as 'the certainty that a person's rights to land will be recognised by others and protected in cases of specific challenges' (FAO 2002:18). Other definitions not only encompass the certainty of land rights, but also the extent or breadth of these rights – which refers to the quantity and quality of the land rights held – and their duration – the length of time for which these rights are valid.[9] For instance, Migot-Adholla and Bruce (1994:3) have defined tenure security as the perceived right by the possessor of a land parcel to manage and use the parcel, dispose of its produce, and engage in transactions, including temporary or permanent transfers, without hindrance or interference from any person or corporate entity, on a continuous basis. Place et al. (1994:19) have in similar fashion defined land tenure security as existing when an individual perceives that he or she has rights to a piece of land on a continuous basis, free from imposition or interference from outside sources, as well as the ability to reap the benefits of labour and capital invested in the land, whether in use or upon transfer to another holder.

Most authors agree that, rather than defining land tenure security as something that either exists or does not exist, it is more accurate to think of it as a continuum. The first group of authors then posits that it can be measured by the amount of certainty. The second group claims that it can be measured by three criteria: extent or breadth, duration, and certainty. This second definition of tenure security, with its three elements, provides more details with regard to the position of the landholder. As such it is a valuable instrument of measurement and information. On the other hand, Van Rooij (this volume) shows that higher values of land resulting from increases in breadth and duration might lead to intensified struggles over land and therefore to decreased certainty of the bundle of rights. This poses the question of how to weigh these various factors. Has tenure security increased or decreased when farmers hold bigger bundles of rights for longer periods but with less certainty? Besides, as Lund cautions, when the extent and duration of rights determine the measure of tenure security, this seems to imply that private property has the highest tenure security possible. However, while increasing exclusivity may produce more tenure security for the excluding party, the opposite will be the case for the one who is being excluded. Thus, increasing tenure security for one usually correlates with decreasing tenure security for another (Lund 2000:16). In individual titling programmes of communal lands, for example, claims of subordinate right-holders to conditional, partial, or common access tend to be neglected (Atwood 1990:661; Cotula, Toulmin, and Hesse 2004:2; Lund 2000:16; Shipton and Goheen 1992:316). In the same vein, individual titling of family lands can lead to the exclusion of vulnerable family members such as women, youth, and the elderly (cf. Hesseling and Eichelsheim, this volume). When talking about increasing tenure security, one should thus always ask whose security is increasing. Safitri (this volume) furthermore shows that in her case-study area in Indonesia, the willingness to invest and the effects on poverty reduction were not so much determined by the extent of rights bestowed in the legalisation scheme, but rather by the kind of lands targeted and especially the level of their productivity. FAO (2002:19) points out that 'equating security with transfer rights to sell and mortgage is true for some parts of the world but it is not true in many others. People in parts of the world where there are strong community-based tenure regimes may enjoy tenure security without wishing to sell their land, or without having the right to do so, or having strictly limited rights to transfer'. A restriction of transfer rights may even protect people from distress sales. The provision of full private title might in such cases rather lead to loss of land than to higher tenure security. Finally, the predilection for private property rights ignores the preferences of households, who may value some tenure category above freehold tenure (Payne 2002, quoted in Durand-Lasserve and Selod 2007:29). It might be for instance that the lack of formal titles is a price which the poor pay to gain access to plots which they could otherwise not afford (Payne 2000:9). Or it might be that the members of a community fear the loss of communal cohesion when community members can individually determine to transact their rights to outsiders (see Duhau, this volume).

Two of the four definitions above mention that tenure security is a perceived quality. Other definitions do not incorporate people's perceptions, but distinguish between people's real tenure security and their perceived tenure security. There is no consensus, however, among researchers about the correct indicators of this real tenure security. In empirical studies, researchers therefore often rely on perceptions of tenure security. For instance, research may report that households seeking legalisation state that their motivation is to increase their security of tenure, or that legalised households tend to believe their tenure is more secure than that of extra-legal households. Even researchers using definitions focusing on some kind of concrete element, such as the extent of protection against eviction, often have no choice but to focus on people's perceptions in their empirical research. They might for instance be unable to measure the threat of eviction but can ask people whether they believe they are at risk of being evicted. The incorporation of perception in the definition of tenure security can thus partly be explained by the methodological difficulties of measuring real tenure security. A second explanation can be found in the often supposed relationship between tenure security and willingness to invest in land. This link indeed presupposes that the people perceive their tenure situation to be secure; it is their perception that will make people act. On the other hand, the relationship between tenure security and the collateralisation of land rather depends on the perception of the money-lender with regard to the security of tenure of the borrower, and the willingness of governments to upgrade settlement areas depends on their perception of the permanency of the settlement.

Besides a distinction between real and perceived tenure security, another valuable division is the one between *de jure* and *de facto* tenure security. People's perceptions of the security of their tenure are not only formed by their legal position, they are equally formed by the practical situation they find themselves in. Have there been many evictions and demolitions of buildings or destruction of crops lately? Has their land occupation been acknowledged by the local authorities, for instance through the payment of taxes to local government[10] or tribute to traditional authorities, or through the servicing of residential areas? Have local authorities made any statements about the security, legitimacy, or legality of their occupation? When the *de facto* tenure security of an informal tenure situation is high, legalisation may be 'a less efficient engine of change' than its supporters suppose (Varlcy 2002:455).

The above discussions of the literature pose the question of where this book stands. With regard to the various defining elements of tenure security – certainty, extent, and duration – the studies in this book make an effort to combine a focus on the element of certainty of land rights with careful attention to the possible existence of restrictions with regard to the elements of extent and duration of rights. Where relevant, they discuss the latent consequences of the existence or otherwise of such restrictions. In many case studies, the extent of *de jure* tenure security and of *de facto* tenure security are distinguished, compared, and explained. Most case studies in this book focus largely on the local perceptions of tenure security, which they regard either as a defining part of tenure security or as an indicator of tenure security. In this book, we do not take the relationship between formalisation and tenure security as a given, but rather regard it as the main object of study. The various case studies explicitly pose the question 'tenure security for whom?' and include an analysis of the effects of legalisation programmes on smallholders and urban/peri-urban poor. Notwithstanding its focus on the link between legalisation and tenure security, this book also recognises that tenure formalisation may have a series of objectives other than that of providing security of tenure to households living on informal land. These other objectives – which often include improving the efficiency of land and housing land markets, promoting private investment through the use of land as collateral, improving the property tax base, and increasing public sector influence over land and housing markets (Payne 2000:6-9) – are also an object of study in this book.

In the following section I shall describe the legalisation programmes and policies that are analysed in the case studies, and the lessons that can be drawn from their implementation. As stated before, this book also contains overview studies of the land tenure regimes in the eight countries in which these legalisation policies are found. These rich and detailed country studies not only add value to and offer a necessary background for understanding the case studies, they are also valuable instruments for comparing state land tenure regimes. However, as their level of detail and diversity do not easily allow for short descriptions, I shall limit myself in the following section to a discussion of the case studies, and focus on the main debate in this book: the relationship between legalisation on the one hand, and tenure security, legal security, investment, marketisation, and productivity on the other.

The scope of the case studies in this book

Ethiopia

Dessalegn Rahmato (chapter 3) describes a programme of rural land registration that has been undertaken in Ethiopia since 2003, with the goal of issuing every rightful holder of farmland a certificate of use rights and having his/her plots recorded in a registry. The registration programme was expected to enhance tenure security and reduce the number of land disputes. The author shows that although the number of land cases in the Social Courts has declined, the number of disputes in the localities has not. It seems that they have rather been rerouted to other dispute settlers, mainly the Land Administration Committees. It cannot be concluded therefore that land registration has allayed the prevalence of rural conflict and antagonism on account of land disputes. An additional argument the author makes is that the employment of local techniques and familiar methods of measurement and demarcation – often considered a success due to their low costs – in fact has not delivered accurate, consistent, and reliable results, and is therefore likely to lead to disputes and conflicts. Additionally, the local authorities do not have the capability to update the information in the land registry, which makes the whole undertaking far from sustainable. With regard to conflicts between peasants and the government, the average peasant feels that there is no legal mechanism for the redress of grievances. Despite the registration programme a majority of the peasants still believe that the government can take away their land if it wants to, for development projects for instance or to redistribute land to accommodate the increasing numbers of landless people. Although most peasants believe that they will receive some governmental compensation in such cases, they worry that it will not be adequate. As peasants attribute their tenure insecurity to a large extent to actions by the government and believe that these actions cannot be challenged in court, the author concludes that the peasants' perception of tenure insecurity cannot be removed merely by issuing user certificates. The construction of strong tenure security for peasants needs to involve measures in the political sphere and the sphere of governance, including empowerment of the poor. At the moment it is only rarely that peasants contest the decision of local officials. Empowerment cannot come about without rights awareness, which includes not only knowledge about land and property regulations but also about political-juridical rights and ways to use them in the interest of the poor.

Ghana

Kojo Amanor (chapter 5) focuses on the impact of new wealth created in the cashew and timber sectors in the Brong Ahafo Region of Ghana. In the first sector, the Forestry Service has developed a programme of informal mechanisms for registering teak plantations. However, the costs of registration are high, and the benefits of registering are not clear or tangible, as government has not been able to develop a programme of loans to support the development of teak plantations. These factors, combined with an unwillingness to take long-term risks, are important factors which presently hinder the capitalisation of teak

plantations. In contrast, within the cashew sector an institutional framework for the disbursement of loans to small farmers has been developed, which eschews linking land to collateral, since this would result
in high transaction costs resulting from poorly developed land markets
and information systems. The loans programme for cashew forces
farmers to bear the transaction costs of a tedious programme of farmer
group monitoring which combines peer group pressure, threats of removal of extension, and financial support with more coercive measures
including police action. This does not translate into the easy capitalisation of assets by independent farmers developing their own investment
strategies, but into forms of dependent accumulation in which support
to farmers is conditional upon them following the prescriptions of agricultural banks, agricultural extension services, and agribusiness. Discussion of agricultural policies in these two sectors shows that security
in land does not necessarily translate into collateral, unless particular
types of land can be capitalised and the risk of investment in these sectors is low. When the assets of farmers are not easily capitalised, the
disbursement of loans may occur through other forms that do not use
land as security. Thus, the assumed relationship between registration,
tenure security, and capitalisation are not supported by this evidence
from Ghana. Amanor's case study furthermore points to the intricacies
of legalising customary tenure situations. Customary relations are often contested and subject to power struggles over the control and definition of land rights. When the contested nature of customary relations
and power relations is not recognised by the state, attempts to legalise
informal arrangements frequently accommodate the interests of the local elite, and in the process the rights of the poor are eroded. Additionally, the pressures of commodification within customary systems often
result in conflicts between notions of user rights and fungible assets.
Since processes of legalisation are often concerned with the creation of
clearly defined rights in fungible property, this easily results in the erosion of forms of property based on dynamic land use and the strengthening of fungible assets, which transforms the nature of customary
property. This becomes particularly clear in the case of tree plantations.
A first example lies in the requirement that the documentation needed
for the registration of teak plantations be signed by chiefs and family
elders, which opens up potential avenues for monies to be exacted
from planters by chiefs for recognition of their land rights and acquisition of documentation. A second example can be found in the undermining of the bush fallowing system of small food farmers with the
development of tree plantations that permanently remove land from
the recycling system of bush fallowing. This expansion of tree planters
with registered holdings often ultimately undermines and erodes the
base of the food crop farmers and of their system of land use. While

tree planters usually constitute the richer segments of the population with surplus capital to invest in hiring labour, they paradoxically constitute a major clientele for poverty reduction programmes concerned with security of customary land tenure and securing land rights for the poor, since tree plantations are fungible assets, which are easily mapped and demarcated, unlike the mobile resource base of bush fallow cultivators. This shows that notions of customary tenure are selectively constructed to mould and fashion the customary to fit contemporary policy agendas, and exclude elements that are not considered compatible. This process is carried out through the legalisation, formalisation, and recognition of customary land tenure.

The second chapter on Ghana, by Janine Ubink, similarly stresses the intricacies of legalising customary tenure situations (chapter 6). Her case study deals with quite an indirect form of legalisation, through constitutional recognition of customary land management and of the position of chiefs. She describes how in peri-urban areas the new value of land has triggered a multitude of struggles and negotiations, mainly between chiefs on the one hand and villagers on the other, for the rights to allocate land and share in the revenue. Despite high local resistance, the chiefs in a number of case-study villages persisted in their style of land management, which was highly lucrative for themselves and sometimes for other selected members of the community – such as elders or royal family members – but extremely detrimental to the livelihoods of the poor majority. The farmers' tenure security was severely corroded by the chiefs' actions. Practices such as multiple sales and allocation of land unsuitable for residential purposes also threaten the tenure security of the new lessees. The author points to the behaviour of government to explain how chiefs are able to continue acting contrary to the wishes of the majority of the villagers, both old and new. Despite the constitutional provision that customary land should be managed on behalf of and in trust for the people, the government hardly steps into local land management issues. State institutions established to check upon chiefly land administration do not in reality exercise effective control. They currently provide hardly any checks and balances on local land administration. Their discourse as well as their actions rather point towards the existence of an informal 'policy of non-interference', inspired by the political power of the chiefs and the alliance between traditional and state elites. The fact that the government continually emphasises the sovereignty of the chiefs and that land administration rests exclusively in their hands gives additional legitimacy to the chiefs and provides them with ample leeway to administer land the way they please. The National Land Policy and the Land Administration Programme (LAP) do not seem to promise any change in this respect in the near future. On the contrary, despite the formulation of goals like equity and accountability, the government has not actually imposed any such requirements on the chiefs in the implementation process of the LAP so far. In combination with a progressive erosion of local checks and balances, the chiefs have a free hand to determine their own position in customary land management. It seems that this has given chiefs the power to overstretch the somewhat dynamic nature of customary law by manipulating it to suit their needs and legitimise their claims, resulting in the described detrimental effects on the tenure security of the people. Any substantial change in this situation requires two intimately connected transformations: the organisation and empowerment of local farmers, and a different attitude of the government towards chiefly rule and customary land management. Similar to Amanor's chapter, Ubink's chapter thus brings to the fore that legalisation of customary tenure arrangements without attention to the contested nature of customary relations often furthers the interests of the traditional elite and damages the rights of the poor.

Namibia

Marco Lankhorst and Muriël Veldman (chapter 8) analyse the Flexible Land Tenure Bill, an innovative form of legalisation of extra-legal land tenure, which for some years now has been awaiting passage into law in Namibia. This bill is innovative in two ways. First, recognising that the executive branches of most developing countries lack the capacity and resources to manage the complex procedures involved in legalisation and subsequent upkeep of the registration system, this bill simplifies and thus reduces the costs of the registration process. Second, acknowledging the financial constraints of the target group, it allows those who seek to acquire title to share the costs of registration amongst each other, as members of a group. The study focuses on the town of Otjiwarongo, and compares the costs and benefits of both flexible titling and extra-legality for its inhabitants, as these factors will together determine whether flexible titling provides settlers incentives to join in a scheme and to continue to respect its regulations. The main cost of extra-legality lies in the threat of future relocation without compensation. Such relocations of extra-legal settlers have occurred with some frequency. One of the central objectives of the bill is to provide secure tenure. In the two neighbourhoods studied in Otjiwarongo, however, the majority of the plots do not adhere to the provision in the National Housing Development Act prescribing that plots have a minimum size of 300 square metres. Another problem is that in the current layout of these settlements, there is no room for public services to be provided. To remove the need for further relocations and thereby enhance tenure security of its inhabitants, the registration scheme should be supplemented with the design of a layout for the area. According to the authors, however, the same result could be achieved by (1) designing a layout, or requesting central government for dispensation from the problematic layout requirements, whilst postponing titling, or (2) dropping the prospect of titling altogether. Put differently, the same results can be achieved under extra-legality. Another expected benefit of the Flexible Land Tenure Bill is that it enables registered landholders to engage in transactions such as sale or rental. The data reveal, however, that plots are already sold and sub-rented with some frequency by extra-legal holders. The absence of third-party-encroachment problems, which is related to the existence of a registry and the fact that plots are pegged and fenced, suggests that current arrangements enable such transactions in a way that would appear to fairly effectively shield buyers from competing claims. Therefore, the provisions in the Flexible Land Tenure Bill that enable holders of a title to engage in transactions neither constitute an advantage or a drawback. In fact, if we include in the analysis (1) the fees incurred in registering transactions, and (2) the various limitations on the freedom to engage in such transactions that the bill makes, we see that extra-legality may even constitute the more attractive alternative. With respect to the third expected benefit of the bill, *viz.* the opening up of access to credit, the chapter also states it as unlikely that landhold titles will in practice be used as collateral. Micro-financing programmes and saving groups may offer settlers better prospects. The authors therefore conclude that it is doubtful whether the Flexible Land Tenure Bill could achieve its objectives, at least in Otjiwarongo's extra-legal settlements. They plead for a careful selection of zones where conditions for implementation are more favourable than in Otjiwarongo and for implementation of the registration scheme in those areas only. It is crucial that policymakers take into account the perspective of the settlers because their cooperation is indispensable to the success of legalisation. Settlers' lack of interest will lead to non-compliance and continued extra-legality. In areas where cooperation cannot be expected, bolstering existing extra-legal arrangements might provide a more promising way of improving tenure security.

Senegal

In their chapter Gerti Hesseling and John Eichelsheim describe re-allocation programmes that have been undertaken since the 1970s in the Senegalese town of Ziguinchor (chapter 10). These programmes were intended to replace the earlier land tenure situation based on Diola customary law. In reality, they created a new, hybrid system that combined a continued emphasis on the Diola patron-client (*adjiati-ad-*

jaoura) relationship with a role for new actors involved in municipal town planning. In this new urban constellation, the position of the patron became more and more politicised. This expansion of his role was acceptable for the members of the traditional society as long as the political ambitions of the patron did not result in him neglecting his obligations towards his indigenous clients in favour of the interests of his other, 'immigrant', followers. When the patron starts to answer to political demands that hurt his inner circle, he loses his authority, and his clients turn against him and his political associates. In Ziguinchor, this resulted in high tensions between locals and 'outsiders' and even in violent clashes. The authors discuss the effect of this new hybrid system on people's tenure security. They show that most people in the study area feel quite secure in their tenure. This is partly based on an erroneous belief that their 'tickets' or other documentary evidence provide a legally sound title. However, people who know that they do not possess a valid legal title still have quite a strong perception of tenure security. This is based on their experiences with administrative agents, who rarely tear down houses without state compensation. People trust this state of laissez-faire to continue and expect to be protected by political strong men, through their relationship with their patrons, or with people involved in the municipal land planning system. This chapter also brings to the fore the effect of the individualisation of family land on marginal family members. The case of the Sagan plots shows that the issuance of personalised 'tickets' enhances tenure security of some people – the people whose names appear on the 'tickets' – but usually coincides with the erosion of that of others. In this way, the drive for individualisation of tenure can significantly increase the vulnerability of people who lack knowledge of urban legislation and who are dependent on family relations. The authors therefore end with the warning that when the effects of re-allocation programmes on tenure security are discussed, one should thus always ask the question, whose tenure security?

Bolivia

Diego Pacheco discusses two areas in the Bolivian department of Santa Cruz where local indigenous/*originary* groups have demanded formalisation of their rights to common-property areas (chapter 12). Following the 1995 constitutional mandate of recognising legal pluralism and certain territorial rights in order to ensure collective tenure security for indigenous peoples, Bolivia has constructed new legal arrangements for indigenous territorial autonomy allowing indigenous peoples to govern themselves, within a certain territory and to a specific extent, according to their own cultural patterns, social institutions, and legal systems.

Despite these official arrangements, the two cases in this chapter show that such formalisations involve lengthy and complicated procedures riddled with uncertainty. The chapter analyses the contextual, motivational, and informational hurdles obstructing the titling of common-property areas, and the effects of the regularisation processes on people's tenure security. In the cases studied, indigenous people's tenure security, in areas that were considered to be in their *de facto* possession, actually decreased as a result of the starting of the titling process. In both case-study areas, the land regularisation seems to have triggered a more rapid expansion of non-indigenous individual land owners into the areas because they saw it as a last chance to claim ownership rights in those areas which in their view were 'open access areas', despite their *de facto* use and occupation by indigenous people. This process of last minute land-grabbing by 'third parties' can largely be explained by three factors: power asymmetries between medium- and large-scale non-indigenous landowners claiming forestland and indigenous people claiming communal property rights; limited capacity of indigenous peoples to develop relationships of trust with the technicians involved in the regularisation processes; and the inadequate supervision of professionals operating at the local level by their principals. Tenure security is also affected by the actions of the indigenous people themselves, through land transactions between indigenous people's leaders and illegal intruders which are then ratified by the government. In particular, indigenous people located in well-endowed natural resources areas are more often inclined to follow their own self-interest, which erodes the tenure security of the community as a whole. Conversely, indigenous people with less incentive to resign the common good may gain some local power as a result of the regularisation process. In cases of both externally induced tenure insecurity and internally caused tenure insecurity, the problems are intertwined with the lack of control on the implementation bureaucracy, which delays and distorts the titling process through mismanagement and corruption.

Mexico

In Mexico, more than half of the national territory is held by *ejidos* and *comunidades agrarias* (agrarian communities), agrarian property institutions regulated by the Agrarian Law involving collective as well as individual property rights. They were created in the context of agrarian reform and the process of land redistribution, which was one of the main outcomes of the Mexican Revolution (1910-1917). The exercise of *ejidal* or communal property rights implies the mediation of a collective entity or corporation made up by the group of duly recognised and registered *ejidatarios* or *comuneros* in each agrarian nucleus (i.e. each *ejido* or comunidad). While two-thirds of lands granted to *ejidos* and *comuni-dades* are held collectively, individuals in most *ejidos* and many *comuni-dades* have long-term use rights to particular parcels that they cultivate independently. Prior to the 1992 constitutional reform, rights over *eji-dal* lands were non-transferable and largely inalienable. Despite these legal rules of non-marketability, irregular/illegal transactions of *ejidal* rights were common. These transactions created a class of landholders that did not have formally recognised agrarian rights and therefore were in a precarious tenure condition. In chapter 14, Emilio Duhau fo-cuses on an *ejido* in a peri-urban area of Mexico City's Metropolitan Zone and analyses the impacts of the post-1992 legal reforms that lar-gely removed the restrictions on transfer and alienability of *ejidal* lands and that included the legalisation of some of the property rights that have arisen out of formerly illegal transactions. The author shows that the current agrarian legislation has considerably enhanced the certainty and protection of *ejidatario's* property rights. Mexican peasants have seized without much reticence the advantages offered in those respects by the agrarian rights certification process and the possibilities opened to them by the enhancement of their property rights. At the same time, however, just like in the great majority of the *ejidos*, the *Ejidal Assembly* in Duhau's case study has so far not opted to adopt a regime of free-hold tenure. Although many younger and better informed *ejidatarios* desire such a change, older *ejidatarios* fear that this will invoke specific burdens such as the payment of property taxes and drinkable water fees, and that this will change their way of life and their ability to de-fine and adopt collective strategies and in general to form a meaningful local community. This brings to the fore that farmers' interest in en-hancing the security of their tenure does not always run parallel with their interest in acquiring full individual property. The author explicitly stresses the limited knowledge and awareness among *ejidatarios* of the existing legislation and the competences of the municipality on the one hand and the autonomy and jurisdiction of the *Ejidal Assembly* on the other. These generalised confusions and misunderstandings ex-plain why many *ejidatarios* fail to comply with and also fail to profit from the optimal strategies within their reach. Additionally, it makes them susceptible to manipulation by their better informed colleagues.

China

Benjamin van Rooij (chapter 16) describes two recent Chinese laws, the 1998 Land Management Law and the 2003 Rural Land Contract Law, that have increased the breadth (more rights of transfer) and the duration (from fifteen to 30 years) of land use rights. Although the awareness of the new laws is high and many land contracts have been signed and land certificates issued, farmers' security in exercising their new rights is threatened by the widespread and often illegal taking of their land without satisfactory compensation. The sharp rise in such land loss conflicts warns that Chinese land tenure still lacks certainty. These conflicts find their roots in unclear legislation, weak checks and balances on local governments and Village Committees, and the resultant weak implementation of law. Changes in legislation alone will thus not be sufficient to decrease current land loss conflicts. It seems rather that legislative changes should be combined with measures that help to enhance implementation. Such measures should be a combination of improving state law enforcement action against violations of the law and increasing possibilities for access to justice for aggrieved farmers. Behind the weak checks and balances are not so much legal or socio-legal problems, but rather political problems related to the existing power relations. At its heart, the current land loss crisis is thus one of power, involving weak farmers and strong elites. Future reforms should be directed at such power imbalances and, as with any institutional change adopted, the risk of elite co-optation should be considered. Enhancing land tenure security in China therefore involves empowerment of the weak and poor. Such empowerment first requires enhancing their access to the legal system, strengthening the role of civil society, while work should also focus on general development activities such as literacy training, strengthening community organisation, and legal awareness promotion.

The second case study on China, by Jianping Ye and Jian Wu (chapter 17), also reports the increasing amount of illegal land use and land loss conflicts. The authors blame these occurrences on the existing dualist tenure system, with government-regulated collective land and market-based, state-owned land tenure regimes, which necessitates a tedious land conversion process to legally change farmland into land for residential or commercial construction. The case study describes two different responses of the Chinese government to the irregularities. The first part of the chapter portrays a programme to formalise and recognise illegal land use and constructions in Shenzhen city, Bao'an District. Due to the large profits to be made through illegal land uses and to the ineffectiveness of the state regulatory apparatus, illegal land use and illegal buildings have become a permanent feature of the peri-urban landscape over a period of more than a decade. The high administrative and social costs of demolition have made it virtually impossible to re-convert the land to agriculture. The Bao'an government felt it had no other alternative than to recognise the illegal land use. This is done under certain strict conditions, to prevent encouragement of further illegal behaviour. The second part of the chapter refers to a 'Land Exchange Programme' in Tianjin Municipality, Dongli District.

Rather than a restorative response after the creation of illegal land use
and buildings, this programme entails a pro-active strategy to avoid the
creation of such illegal land use and construction. The main plan is to
move farmers out of their rural houses into high-rise buildings that allow for a much more intensive land use. As a result, the total cultivated
land area can be maintained while more construction land can be released. As the Land Exchange Programme converts all land at once, it
prevents commercial land users from circumventing the tedious land
conversion process, and thus decreases the incidence of illegal land
use. This programme does not change the total agricultural land area,
therefore tenure security of farmers' agricultural land is guaranteed.
Nevertheless, the authors opine that the ease with which the government unilaterally decides to requisition collective Rural Residential
Land (RRLS) and rural houses in the Land Exchange Programme may
serve as an alarm bell for tenure security, as there is no reason to believe that agricultural land may not one day also be requisitioned by
the government for one reason or another. One of the supposed benefits of the programme lies in the capitalisation of residential land.
Whereas the sale of rural residential land to non-members was prohibited, the new high-rise apartments can be transacted freely, thus bringing dead capital alive. However, an important comment is made in this
regard by the authors when they explain that rural housing was only a
'dead' asset because of the legal prohibition of free circulation. It is
therefore nothing but the state and the property rights arrangement it
imposes that make rural houses illiquid. The authors furthermore criticise the lack of participation from farmers in this top-down administrative programme, and the fact that they are largely excluded from sharing the economic benefits arising from economic development taking
place on the formerly collective peri-urban land. Despite these criticisms, the authors acknowledge the innovation of the programme and
its attempts to dismantle institutional rigidities and barriers that have
bred illegal land use.

Indonesia

Gustaaf Reerink discusses a systematic registration programme under
the Land Administration Programme (LAP) Indonesia (chapter 19). He
shows that although systematic titling programmes such as LAP have
been able to overcome financial, bureaucratic, and time constraints of
sporadic registration programmes and related negative perceptions of
the people regarding the registration process, they nonetheless fail to
reach the *kampong* dwellers with the lowest incomes. This limited
reach can be explained by the fact that the LAP is only implemented in
locations where registration is relatively easy, which means that loca-

tions where many low-income dwellers reside are ignored. Besides, some of the same obstacles occurring in cases of sporadic land registration remain in place, namely the stringent evidence requirements for initial registration and a lack of political will to grant new rights to informal landholders. The author draws two important conclusions from his case study with regard to tenure security. First, that registration does not always enhance the legal security of the landholders. Land registration programmes in Bandung contributed little to the legal security of *kampong* dwellers, due to the fact that they often do not meet other legal requirements such as the obligation to obtain spatial planning related permits or to perform derivate registration after a change in the legal status of the land. Additionally, registration of land only offers limited legal security for two reasons: first, a land certificate is not regarded as conclusive but only offers strong evidence regarding a land right which can be disputed by a third party during the five years after the certificate has been issued, and second, the issuing of double land certificates by the NLA – due to maladministration and corruption – affects the reliability of the land register and the extent of protection a certificate offers. In his second main conclusion, Reerink challenges the fact that legal security is often equated with tenure security. Further data from his research show that in Post-New Order Bandung, both the *de facto* tenure security (measured by interference from third parties) of low-income *kampong* dwellers holding land certificates (but often not fulfilling other legal requirements) and the perceived tenure security of these people are stronger than among those who do not have such documents. This for instance also means that the former invest more in their land and housing than the latter. These data thus show that legal security is not always a determining factor for *de facto* and perceived tenure security.

In the second Indonesian case study Myrna Safitri describes the effects of two different legalisation processes in Langkawana, a village in the forest frontier of Lampung (chapter 20). The first involved the registration of individual property rights in residential non-forest land. Although this legalisation enhanced the legal status and the tenure security of the land, it did not lead to an increased use of the land as collateral for loans, nor to a higher number of land transactions. Despite the legalisation, Langkawana villagers considered their residential land as an asset that needed to be held onto at all costs, not as a marketable commodity. This legalisation did not enhance investment in the land and did not change the people's level of poverty. The second legalisation process involved the granting of a community forestry license on forest land. Although this did not provide the villagers with individual titles, it did enhance their (perception of) tenure security, i.e. the extent to which the villagers felt assured of their ability to access their land, to manage and use it, and to effectively exclude others. As a result, people invested more time and labour in their forest gardens, diversified their crops, and planted more perennial and cash-producing crops. This led to a significant improvement in the people's quality of life. After the granting of the community forestry license, the number of market transactions decreased, which contradicts the theory that enhanced tenure security will lead to more land transactions. This case on the contrary shows that villagers prefer not to sell secure and productive land. The greater the profits that can be expected from land, the less willing people are to transfer their land. The less tenure security, the less one can count on profits from the land in the future, and the more willing people will be to transfer the land. This case thus shows that legalisation of land rights does not always lead to marketisation. People's decisions to take part in land transactions are determined by their perception of the value of the land and the contribution of the land to their household economy. The legal status of land is merely one factor, but not the major one, in determining land transactions. This case furthermore shows that the relationship between legalisation of land tenure and poverty reduction will be determined not only by the kind and extent of rights – individual or communal rights, ownership or use rights – granted to the people but also by the kind of lands on which these rights are granted. In other words, it will have a greater effect on poverty reduction to target lands that are highly productive than to target lands that are unproductive.

Concluding remarks

The case-study chapters of this book provide rich descriptions of projects and programmes of legalisation of extra-legal tenure ranging from the recognition of communal ownership to the creation of full private title and various forms in between. They draw grounded conclusions on the relationship between legality, tenure security, investments, and marketisation. This section does not aim to produce a full enumeration of all the lessons learnt, but wishes to stress some of them with regard to the book's main object of study, *viz.* the relationship between the various programmes of legalisation and tenure security. The tendency of several scholars to equate extra-legality and tenure insecurity and presuppose a causal link between tenure legalisation and tenure security improvement has already been criticised in the literature. This book provides additional scientific underpinning for this refutation, and provides new details of the circumstances under which certain kinds of formalisation may fail to increase tenure security and may sometimes even decrease it. Some of the lessons to be learnt from the case studies in this regard include the following:

1) The *de facto* tenure security/insecurity of informal land varies considerably. It depends on a multitude of factors including the normative basis of the land interest, the legitimacy of the informal claims, the identity of the land user and of the original owner, the location and market value of the land, the alternative uses of the land, the nature and attitude of the government and of the local power holders, and their relationship. When the *de facto* tenure security of informal land is high, a programme of formalisation may not have the effect of increasing it. Additionally, when people have a highly limited legal awareness – as many poor people do – changes in the legal situation may not have much effect on people's perception of their tenure security (see Dessalegn Rahmato; Hesseling and Eichelsheim; and Reerink, all this volume; cf. Gilbert 2002:8; Varley 2002:455).

2) When threats to tenure security find their roots not only in weak legal positions but also in the weak implementation of legislation, changes in legislation alone will not be sufficient to enhance tenure security. When the tenure insecurity is caused by political problems, the response needs to involve the creation of effective checks and balances on implementing bureaucrats, improving state law enforcement action against violations of the law, and increasing possibilities for access to justice for aggrieved farmers, and in general the empowerment of the weak and poor (see Dessalegn Rahmato; Pacheco; Reerink; and Van Rooij, all this volume).

3) Certain formalisation processes can create conflict over land rights, due to the finality of the process (Pacheco, this volume). Similarly, the enhanced value of the land expected to result from the legalisation process may raise the number of conflicts about such land (Van Rooij, this volume).

4) Limited awareness of the poor of legislation, procedures for legalisation, and division of regulating competences can lead to easy manipulation by the better informed, whether local elite, street-level bureaucrats, or national politicians (see Duhau, this volume; cf. Cotula, Toulmin, and Quan 2006:20; Cousins 2000; Durand-Lasserve 2006:10; Migot-Adholla and Bruce 1994:20-21; Van den Brink et al. 2006:12).

5) When the contested nature of local (customary) relations and power relations are not recognised by the state, attempts to legalise informal arrangements frequently accommodate the interests of the local elite and erode the rights of the poor (Amanor; Ubink, this volume).

6) When legalisation processes are too complex for the bureaucracy or too complicated, time-consuming and costly for the intended beneficiaries, formalisations will only occur sporadically, and mainly by the wealthier section of communities. The poorest households in particular may not have the means to pay their share of the formalisation costs. Additionally, these households may not be entitled or eligible for tenure formalisation (Reerink, this volume; cf. Durand-Lasserve and Selod 2007:10).

7) The regularisation of urban or peri-urban plots may not always lead to legally secure positions due to the fact that the newly formalised households often cannot comply with additional regulation involving planning and construction norms and standards (Lankhorst and Veldman; Reerink, this volume).

8) Formalisation can give incentives to landowners to try and evict secondary rights holders, usufructuaries, or tenants in order to value their land in a more profitable way (Amanor; Ubink, this volume; cf. Durand-Lasserve 2006:7; Durand-Lasserve and Selod 2007:11; Payne 2000:9).

9) Registration and titling in the name of an individual will create higher tenure security for this individual but can simultaneously decrease the tenure security of people dependent on this person (Hesseling and Eichelsheim, this volume).

10) When the insecurity of extra-legal property or the restrictions on transactions of such property are caused by the state, the state could as easily remove them in a different way than through legalisation. Lankhorst and Veldman (this volume), for instance, state that the main threat of relocation comes from the fact that the settlers in their study areas do not conform with certain stringent lay-out requirements and plead that a change of those requirements would have a greater impact on the tenure security of the settlers than a registration scheme. Similarly, Ye and Wu (this volume) stress that the restrictions on transactions of rural residential land result from state legislation, which could be changed without the whole process of 'Land Exchange' that the Chinese government is now piloting.

Notes

1   See for an overview of the main international publications and policy statements concerning land tenure legalisations, Assies 2007.
2   Several ex post evaluations of the state-imposed tenure conversion program in Kenya have observed that individualisation has led to land concentration, increased marginalisation and landlessness as people in positions of economic and political power take advantage of the less powerful, deepening tenure insecurity instead of lessening it (Coldham 1979; Okoth-Ogendo 1976; Quan 2000:35-7).

3   This project was originally entitled 'The Mystery of Legal Failure? A critical, comparative examination of the potential of legalisation of land assets in developing countries
for achieving real legal certainty'. It was funded by the Dutch Council for Scientific
Research (NWO/WOTRO), and managed jointly by the Universities of Leiden, Amsterdam, and Nijmegen, and the African Study Centre (Leiden), see Otto 2004.

4   The project will also produce a second book, entitled *"Legalising Land Rights: Law, tenure security and development"*. This book will discuss the more general and theoretical
debates surrounding the issue of legalisations. It will also compare the lessons from
the case and country studies presented in this book. Publication is expected in 2010.

5   Whereas we use the term 'extra-legal' to denote all property rights that are not recognised by the state, FAO (2002:11) uses it only for property rights that are not recognised by the law but also not against the law.

6   Instead of legalisation, many authors use the term formalisation, which refers to
changing a situation of 'informality'. We wish to avoid using this term as it is unclear
and inherently confusing. According to some authors, it carries with it a vision of
squatters on urban lands. Such a situation can often easily be formalised, especially
when the landowner is the state, which can agree to give land to squatters with zero
or low compensation. Unlike urban squatters, many customary landholders do not
hold land informally, but according to an alternative, community-based formality.
This makes formalisation – in the sense of replacing this situation of community-
based formality with state-based formality – a completely different exercise (Van den
Brink et al. 2006:12). Others rather understand informal as customary or traditional
rights and formal as statutory rights, but this distinction ignores the fact that in some
countries customary rights have been given formal legal recognition (FAO 2002:11).
Additionally, formalisation seems to imply a linear evolution from informal to formal
situations, ignoring the fact that in reality situations of informality are often the result of new laws, as people who cannot or do not want to observe them are thereby
brought into a situation of informality. As Durand-Lasserve and Selod (2007:6) put
it, tenure informality is the end result of legal, political, and economic exclusion mechanisms. Formalisation thus creates new situations of informality. Admittedly, this
last critique could also be waged against the term legalisation. See for a critique on
the distinction between legality and illegality, Varley 2002.

7   For an overview of donor understandings of what defines land tenure security, see International Land Coalition 2006:6-7.

8   They distinguish four interrelated factors that together determine the level of tenure
security: tenure status (unauthorised commercial developments or squatter settlements); the primary tenure rights of the land (public, private, or customary-owned
land); the occupancy status of the dwelling (owners, tenants, etc.); and the political
and legal context (Durand-Lasserve and Selod 2007:6).

9   In general, as duration lengthens, tenure security improves. However, duration need
not be perpetual to create an adequate incentive framework for land investments and
improvements; see Ping et al., this volume.

10 In many countries, including Egypt, India, and Columbia, tenure security is achieved
over time through the accretion of various documents relating to property taxes and
other formal documents (Durand-Lasserve 2006:10).

2 Peasants and agrarian reforms: The unfinished quest for secure land rights in Ethiopia

Dessalegn Rahmato

Introduction

The last 50 years of the twentieth century were momentous years for Ethiopia, particularly regarding its political and agrarian history. The period was marked by revolutionary changes in state and class structure and in tenure relations and agrarian institutions. In these turbulent and often bloody years, the country experienced far more radical changes than at any time in its recent history, and nowhere were these transformations more profound than in the agrarian sector. From feudal monarchy to military-communist dictatorship, to ethnic-based federalism: such were the major political changes that succeeded each other in this short half-century, each accompanied by radical agrarian and economic reforms.

The populist uprising of the mid-1970s, initially spearheaded by militant elements from the urban population, and subsequently led by military officers who came to be known as the *Derg*, brought down the government of Emperor Haile Selassie and put an end to the centuries-old institution of crown and monarchy. The military regime of the *Derg* replaced imperial rule rapidly and successfully carried out one of the most radical land reforms in the world, and won for a time a great deal of popularity among the peasantry as well as the urban population. But the honeymoon between the state and the peasants lasted only a brief period and was replaced by increasingly bitter resentment on the part of the latter on account of the damaging and unpopular policies pursued by the *Derg*, including collectivisation, forced resettlement and villagisation, and grain requisitioning. As the *Derg* turned the country into a hard-line Communist state, opposition to it intensified, culminating in the second half of the 1980s in a full-scale civil war which engulfed the greater part of the country. The seventeen years of military-communist rule, lasting from 1974 to 1991, were one of the bloodiest periods in the country's history, and the civil war, which was fought in the countryside, took a heavy toll on peasant lives and property (Andargachew Tiruneh 1993; Dessalegn Rahmato 1996). The *Derg* was finally overthrown by a mélange of insurgent forces, some of whom had been fighting for independence since the 1960s.

The end result was the secession of Eritrea, the province on the Red Sea coast which had been incorporated into Ethiopia in the second part of the 1950s, and the establishment of an ethnic-based federalist state in the rest of the country.

Yet, despite all the political upheaval and social and agrarian transformations, some significant institutions and practices remained unchanged; chief among them, and of particular relevance to us here, are the relationship between the peasant and the state on the one hand, and the nature of property rights – especially peasants' rights to land – on the other. Neither the revolution of the 1970s and the radical agrarian reforms that accompanied it, nor the rural engineering attempted by the current federalist state, has succeeded in satisfying the deeply held aspirations of the country's peasantry for secure rights to land. Thus, while the particulars have changed and the terms of the discourse are different, the central problem of the land system today remains the same as in the past, namely secure rights of access to land for smallholders and the poor.

In this study I shall examine the land reforms that were attempted by the three successive governments and their intended and unintended consequences, taking land tenure security as my focal point for analysis and focusing only on land rights among settled farmers in the highlands.[1] To this end, I present the results of land reforms in each particular period. I briefly discuss, first, the modernisation of land legislation during the Imperial period, and second, the radical land reforms under the *Derg*. The third part of the study will be devoted to the land laws and policies of the present government. In the conclusion, I try to point out why land reform in the three periods under discussion failed to serve the basic interests of smallholder farmers.

The imperial regime: Tax and tenancy reforms (1942-1972)

Let me begin with a brief outline of the land tenure system before the Revolution and of the reform initiatives attempted at the time.[2] The distinctive aspect of the tenure system during the imperial regime was that the tenure holder, indeed the land itself, was encumbered with a bundle of obligations, contrasting sharply with modern land systems where tenure confers on the holder a bundle of rights. While the imperial regime did bring about some significant changes, the legacy of the past was still strong and continued to define a great many aspects of the system throughout the lifetime of the regime (see Crummey 2000 for a historical review). Tenure rights were predominantly conditional rights of use and not of ownership in the capitalist sense of the term, and the obligations in question included tax, tribute, and labour on the one hand, and personal, military, administrative, political, and ecclesiastical service on the other. Tenure rights conferred mostly limited rights of transfer (e.g. to siblings by inheritance, to tenants for temporary use), and absolute transfer rights such as sale or purchase were not widespread. In the case of transfer to siblings, the heirs inherited not so much the land *per se* but the obligations on it. In the southern regions of Ethiopia a different system existed, marked by the co-existence of forms of individual ownership, free from many of the obligations noted here, along with tenancy; such forms of tenure also existed, in pockets, elsewhere. Most of the lands in question were small in size and worked by owner-cultivators, but local landowners, members of the local gentry, owned larger tracts of land which they rented out in parcels to tenant farmers.

The imperial land system began to undergo fundamental but limited changes from the 1960s, when conditional tenure based on tribute, personal, and military service was abolished (at least by law), and there was a gradual evolution towards rights of private and transferable ownership. This shift was spearheaded by the state itself, which encouraged holders of land it had granted as a reward for loyal service, which ordinarily was held under conditional tenure, to convert part of it to freehold. At the same time, side by side with changes in the tenure regime came reforms in the rural tax regime, and this had two major implications: one was that new taxes were added to existing ones (education and health tax), and second was that the tax burden fell, in practice, not on the landholder but on the cultivator of the holding in cases where the two were not one and the same, which was often the case.

We may classify tenure rights under the imperial regime broadly into three categories: land under what I call reversionary rights, land under private ownership, and state domain land. I submit that the greater part of the land in the country at the time was held under reversionary and usufruct rights, which were rights of temporary use in which the final decision rested with someone other than the user or immediate holder. Tenancies, *semon* (Church) lands, many of the various forms in which state domain land was operated, and some of the land held by members of the landed nobility fall under reversionary tenure. Even land under the *rist* system may be described as reversionary, since the individuals had only use rights over their holdings, which they could not transfer to others by sale. The *rist* system, in its generic form, was a system in which land was held by a descent or village group whose members had equal use rights to the land, and in which, in some localities, there was periodic reallocation of holdings.

A common approach in the literature has been to view the system on the basis of a North/South divide, where *rist* tenure was said to be prevalent in the north of the country and tenancy widespread in the

south. This approach, while adequate for some purposes and often favoured by the imperial government's own agency, the Ministry of Land
Reform and Administration (MLRA), hides some of the complex aspects of the land system, and in particular tends to leave out the size-
able population of small owner-cultivators and the immense holdings
under government control frequently described as state domain land.
The main sources of tenancy were lands held by the nobility, the local
gentry, and the state. It was also not uncommon for owner-cultivators
to rent out some of their land to tenants, but this form of tenancy did
not pose a significant problem, because ultimately it was a tenancy
among equals or almost equals and was largely free of relations of
domination and subordination that characterised the relationship between tenants on the one hand and the landed nobility and local gentry
on the other. The nobility, who were almost always absentee owners,
held large tracts of land, particularly in the southern provinces, almost
all of which were parcelled out for rent to tenant cultivators. The local
gentry, by contrast, owned much less land in comparison and often resided in the vicinity of their property.

Tenancy was an onerous institution, putting immense burdens on
tenant cultivators, siphoning off their surplus and causing a great deal
of uncertainty among them. It was common for tenants to hand over
half, or more, of their harvest to the landlord in the form of rent, and
to provide labour and personal services to him or her as part of their
obligations. What made matters worse was the fact that, for most peasants, the terms of their obligations were not contractual but based on
oral agreements which were subject to arbitrary interpretations favourable to the landlord. More than 50 per cent of all holdings in the country as a whole were operated by tenant farmers, while in some of the
southwestern provinces the figure was much higher.[3]

A significant aspect of the imperial land system was the decisive
power of the state, both as a landlord in its own right and in the
authority vested in it by the Constitution, to claim land that was
deemed to be 'ownerless' by the laws of the country. Such land included land held by pastoralists and others under customary ownership. Article 130 of the 1955 Constitution holds that 'all property not
held in the name of any person, natural and juridical, including all
land in escheat, and all abandoned properties, as well as all forests and
grazing lands' are state domain. Article 31 states that the 'Emperor also
makes grants from abandoned properties, and properties in escheat,
for the purpose of recompensing faithful service to the Crown' (Consolidated Laws of Ethiopia 1972). On the basis of this, all land utilised by
pastoralists in the country fell under state domain which, according to
Wetterhall (1972), would give the state control over nearly 65 per cent
of the land area of the country. Wetterhall estimates that, excluding the

nomadic areas, the government held nearly 17 million hectares of land, of which 11 million was considered arable, which was equal to 57 per cent of the arable land of the country. Of the total arable land under state domain, some twenty per cent was committed, consisting in the main of land occupied by tenants and squatters, land allocated to large-scale mechanised concessions, and land given out in the form of imperial land grants. It is clear that while the tenure regime here cannot be described as one based on state ownership, as it was to become following the Revolution (and still is), the imperial state was a powerful landlord and had a strong influence in shaping the land system at the time.

State domain was to be a cause of insecurity and resentment among a large population of pastoralists and peasants alike, especially from the second half of the 1960s, because of large-scale evictions of customary users. Many of the beneficiaries of imperial land grants either evicted the peasants and herders already on the land or turned them into tenants subject to the payment of rent. The threat of eviction hung over not only such peasants but others as well because many landlords were encouraged by the government policy promoting mechanised agriculture at the time. Tenants on government land faced the same difficulties and the same kind of exactions as other tenants. Insecurity was also a serious problem in other reversionary forms of land rights, in particular for peasants in the *rist* system. Hoben (1973) has shown the high degree of insecurity among land users in his study of the system in Gojjam. He argued that the system fostered endemic competition, conflict, and litigiousness among *rist* holders; it was, he says, a socially disintegrative force. Litigation to get access to more land both by the lowly holder and by the local gentry was rife – indeed, Joireman (2001) suggests that litigation was the chief means of getting access to more land for the gentry, as the existing judicial environment favoured the well-to-do over the poor and the disadvantaged.

There were many voices urging the imperial government to carry out reforms to modernise the land system. These included not just radical students, progressive elements within the civil service, businessmen, and professionals, but also donor agencies, international organisations, and foreign friends of the country. There was, however, strong opposition from the landed classes to any measure that would threaten their property, and they considered reform of the tenure structure as anathema. Such was the power and influence of these classes that the regime turned a deaf ear to the demand for change. But while the result was far from adequate, a number of initiatives to change aspects of the agrarian system were undertaken with varying degrees of success during the lifetime of the imperial regime, the principal one being the reform of land taxation.

Haile Selassie had been a reformist in the past, and on three different occasions he had taken measures aimed at restructuring land taxation and revenue collection. Historically, it was the form of tax and other obligations attached to the land that defined the tenure system. In other words, the tenure regime was a tax regime, and therefore land tax reform was considered to be equivalent to land reform. In the pre-reform period, i.e. the period before the 1940s, the cultivator was burdened with a wide variety of taxes, corvee labour, and personal service to the state and the landlord. The cultivators' burden was made more onerous because taxes were determined arbitrarily, and the demand for corvee labour and personal service was unlimited. The more burdensome taxes and corvee obligations were abolished in the 1920s and 1930s. However, in the circumstances of the second half of the twentieth century, the tax reform was woefully inadequate in meeting the needs of economic development or the demands of social equity.

The country's traditional land tax system was noted for its great diversity and complexity. It was a cause of conflict between the landlord and the tenant cultivator on the one hand, and the landlord and the state on the other. In the latter case, the conflict arose in part because much of the land in the country was unmeasured and unregistered, giving rise to disputes over how much tax the governors of the various provinces and sub-provinces had raised, since they were responsible for collecting taxes which they were obliged to transfer to the imperial treasury after retaining a given percentage for their own administrative expenses, and how much they had transferred to the state.

The main effort at tax reform was in the post-Italian period when several pieces of legislation were initiated, the most important of which for our purposes being the land tax proclamation of 1942, which was repealed by another proclamation issued in 1944 (*Consolidated Laws of Ethiopia* 1972 for this and what follows). These reforms introduced a relatively improved tax system that was centrally administered. Agricultural land in the southern provinces, which were the predominantly tenancy areas, was classified into three categories depending on the fertility of the soil (fertile, semi-fertile, and poor), and a uniform rate of land tax and tithe was levied on each class of land. In the north, the *rist* areas, the tax system was based on the tribute system in which villages and communities were responsible for collecting a fixed tax from their residents and members and handing it over to the government. Two additional taxes, the education tax of 1947 and the health tax of 1959, were introduced later. In 1967, a new legislation abolished the tithe (rather tax-in-lieu of tithe) and replaced it by the agricultural income tax. This legislation was to be responsible for the rural revolts in Gojjam and Wollo provinces in northern Ethiopia (Dessalegn Rahmato 1996). On paper, the tax regime that evolved out of these reforms appeared to be equitable and modern, but in practice it was anomalous and a burden on the very cultivator it was meant to benefit. The land-owner who was legally responsible for paying all taxes levied on the land (and there were several) escaped paying by shifting the burden onto the tenants and others (Lawrence and Mann 1966).

The tax reforms introduced in the 1940s remained largely un-changed for almost 35 years. The World Bank considered the tax re-forms as 'Ethiopia's most successful single land reform measure' (1973:Annex 12:20), but as Lawrence and Mann (1966) and others more knowledgeable about the imperial land system have argued, tax reform kept many aspects of the land system intact with all its ineffi-ciencies and injustices and was not able to address the strong aspira-tions of the labouring peasant for secure rights to land. Considering three and half decades of uninterrupted rule, the effort of the imperial regime in the sphere of agrarian change was woefully inadequate.

I now turn to the story of the moderate land and tenancy reform in-itiative that was prepared and presented for legislation to Parliament in the 1960s, but which, after much delay, was defeated in the legislature by the combined weight of the landed classes and the monarchy in the waning years of the imperial regime. The beginning of the reform in-itiative goes back to 1961, when a proposal for improvement of the landlord-tenant relationships was presented to the government for con-sideration by a special inter-governmental committee set up for the purpose. The proposal also recommended a cadastral survey and land registration on the one hand, and the imposition of a surtax on large holdings on the other. This was shelved without serious debate, and in-stead the MLRA was charged with preparing a land reform proposal that would be acceptable to the decision-makers, as well as the power-ful landed elements in Parliament. MLRA was strongly in favour of smallholder farming, as opposed to large-scale agriculture, which it be-lieved would lead to greater eviction of peasants from the land. The re-form measures it was keen to promote from the last quarter of the 1960s consisted of the following: a) tenancy reform to lighten the bur-den of the tenant and to provide tenure security; b) allocation of gov-ernment land to small cultivators, rather than to civil servants, military officers, and the well-to-do, as was the case at the time, with plots not exceeding two to five hectares; c) land registration to promote security of holding; and d) limiting the size of land held by big landlords and distributing the excess to the landless and the needy. Of these, only te-nancy reform was presented to Parliament for enactment (MLRA 1972).

The tenancy reform was drafted in 1968, revised in 1970 and 1971, and finally presented to Parliament in 1972. The most important provi-sions in the original draft were the introduction of written agreements between landlord and tenant, the payment of a fixed rent instead of the customary share rent, rent control, and compensation by the landlord for improvements made on the land by the tenant in the event of termination of tenancy. The final draft bill submitted to Parliament was a watered down version, and only the compensation provision was retained, thus leaving the tenant in the same inferior bargaining position as before (MLRA 1968, 1972; see also Stahl 1974). Nevertheless, MLRA lobbied hard among MPs in the Chamber of Deputies (the Lower House) to get the reform approved, and according to Zegeye Asfaw, former senior expert in MLRA,[4] the great majority of them were willing to vote in favour. However, the bill was not brought to a vote because of the strong opposition of some of the powerful landlords in Parliament and the personal intervention of the Emperor. Such was the ignominious end to the one and only 'land reform' initiative ever attempted during the imperial regime. Both monarchy and landlordism were to perish two years later following the popular uprising and the seizure of power by the *Derg*.

Radical land reform under military-communism (1975-1990)

In early 1974 the Imperial regime was shaken by a series of mass popular protests, occurring first in the major urban areas, but later spreading to the countryside. These protests were accompanied by unrest in the armed forces, leading to a number of mutinies by soldiers and junior officers in several military camps. The committee of officers that emerged through these agitations, known widely as the *Derg*, eventually assumed the leadership of what came to be the Ethiopian Revolution. The aging Emperor was deposed in September of that year, and the *Derg* assumed power without much serious opposition. One of the *Derg*'s thorough-going measures to dismantle the political and economic power and institutions of the old regime was the radical land reform of March 1975. I have dealt with the land reform, its implementation and consequences at some length elsewhere, and I shall not repeat the arguments here (Dessalegn Rahmato 1984, 1993). I shall try instead to examine some aspects of the radical land reform which are relevant for my purposes here, and which have not received much treatment so far.

The radical land reform was launched on 4 March 1975, but the legislation did not appear in the *Negarit Gazeta* (the official legal gazette) until the end of April. Formal implementation began in some areas in May, but in others this was several months later; in some of the more remote areas implementation was delayed for a year or more. There is very little information about how the legislation was drafted and took its final form. We have no evidence that the military officers who assumed the leadership had any plans to undertake a redistribution of rural property before they had deposed the Emperor and assumed power. Moreover, the *Derg* did not promote any public debate on land reform, nor did they seriously seek expert opinion or the views of interest groups or peasant representatives. In fact, for the entire period the *Derg* was in power, it was secretive about most of its reform legislations, on the grounds that prior knowledge would, it believed, give the losers of the reforms opportunities to sabotage the measures. One of the most radical measures of agrarian restructuring in the country's history was thus legislated in circumstances that can only be described as secretive. Nevertheless, when the legislation was formally announced, it was received with great enthusiasm by a cross-section of society, with a great number of peasants participating in demonstrations of support in subsequent weeks and months.

The land reform was one of the most radical measures undertaken anywhere in the developing world at the time and may be compared in thoroughness and impact to the Chinese and Vietnamese reforms of the 1950s. The reform abolished all customary and formal rights to land and vested in the state the power to redefine property rights and access to land. The core of the legislation is the provision that gives the state, as the trustee of the people, the right of ownership of all rural land and other resources and that prohibits private ownership of land. Rights holders were allowed only use rights over the land they were cultivating, which they could not sell, mortgage, lease or contract out. Moreover, only under certain circumstances could the holder pass it on to siblings, as the legislation provided that young peasants who came of age had the right to a plot of land in their *kebelle*.[5] Rights to land thus came to be rights of usufruct. Tenancy and other forms of subordination based on land ownership were done away with. The reform put great emphasis on the self-labouring peasant household and prohibited tenancy or the hiring of labour. The reform abolished landlordism, and this, in my view, is its enduring legacy and its greatest achievement. All property belonging to landlords, gentry, and landed nobility alike was expropriated without compensation. The smallholding peasant thus came to constitute the sole social force of the rural class structure. Reform also swept away all customary tenure arrangements, though local dispute settlement, land transaction, and mutual aid institutions remained resilient and continue to function to this day.

Land distribution took place among households organized in Peasant Associations (PAs) in each *kebelle*. Political power at the local level was restructured, with the PA assuming authority at the *kebelle* level, and 'progressive' minded officials newly appointed by the *Derg* replacing the gentry at the level of the *woreda* and above. Membership in the PAs was open to peasants only, and landlords were barred from participation, thus closing off any chances such persons may have had of getting control of the organisations and using them for their own purposes. A Judicial Tribunal consisting of peasant lay 'judges' was also established at the *kebelle* level (later at the level of the *woreda*) whose task was to resolve disputes – especially disputes arising from land matters – within peasant communities; this undercut the authority of the judiciary, enabling peasants to deal with their own problems in their own way.

This radical reform was implemented under rather unusual circumstances. At the time of implementation, the new regime had no strong presence in the rural areas, and it is a measure of the political euphoria of the time that such a far-reaching reform was initiated without giving serious thought to the practicalities of its implementation. Very little thought was given to the problems that would arise in implementing it under the diverse and complex circumstances of the country at the time. There was ample evidence that the landed classes would try to undermine the reform. While many of the powerful nobility were quickly neutralised through arrests and executions at the outset of the Revolution, the local gentry were firmly entrenched in the rural areas and were a force to be reckoned with. However, all through the first two years of the Revolution, the new regime conducted a virulent political campaign against what it termed 'counter-revolution elements', which at this time was a reference to the landed classes. Members of the aristocracy, retired generals, and wealthy personages were arrested in large numbers, and their property was confiscated. Some of these men were later executed. The nationalisation of urban land and rental houses in July 1975, a reform aimed primarily at humbling the propertied classes, including the gentry, further sealed the fate of these classes.

When reform came to the countryside, it came together with what I have called 'rural activators' elsewhere (Dessalegn Rahmato 1996), consisting of *zemach* students (i.e. students from higher educational institutions deployed in the rural areas to spread the gospel of the new regime), local development agents, and newly appointed public servants at the district and lower level. These were the principal reform agents of the *Derg*. In place of the disciplined and experienced party cadres who played such a critical role in the successful implementation of the radical land reforms in China and Vietnam (see Moise 1983), the *Derg* had to make do with a young, inexperienced, and ill-disciplined but zealous force of rural activators, hastily assembled and deployed in the countryside. These agents of the *Derg* were different from anyone the peasants were familiar with: they spoke a different 'language' and expressed solidarity with peasants, the poor, and the down-trodden – something previously unheard of in rural communities. However, they had no coherent guidelines for the tasks they shouldered, and no clear objectives to aim for. In consequence, the implementation of the reform was a chaotic affair for the first two years. But it is my view that without the energetic efforts of these activators, it is doubtful whether the reform process in the countryside would have been successfully undertaken. Indeed, I submit that though not quite aware of it themselves, these activators succeeded in drawing the peasantry into the agrarian struggle and fanned the flames of the Revolution. It was these rural activators who organised the peasantry, and who enabled it to carry out land redistribution.

Although the *Derg*'s reform possessed a good number of positive elements, it was flawed in several respects that undermined its overall benefits to the peasantry. First, reform had a selective impact; that is, not all peasants benefited equally. For landless peasants the reform provided access to land, while for tenants it removed the burden of exploitation by landlords; but small owner-cultivators, who made up a quarter of all rural households, lost some of their land during distribution. Second, as was noted above, landholders had restricted rights over their plots, and this had a dampening effect on peasant initiative and entrepreneurship.[6] Third, rights to land was based on residency, i.e. peasants' access to land was conditional on continued residence in their *kebelle*, and absence from their land, except for a very short period, would jeopardise their rights. Reform thus blocked rural out-migration because of peasants' fear of losing their allotments, and this gave rise to growing pressure on the land and the diminution of household plots through fragmentation and sub-division. But the most damaging impact was the insecurity of holding that it gave rise to. The promise of land to all meant that periodic redistribution was unavoidable to accommodate new claimants. In the 1980s, there were three to four redistributions in many rural communities in which those said to hold larger plots were deprived of some of their land, which was given to others. Reform thus brought with it a dynamic process of levelling down.

The initial legislation was soon followed by a number of new legislations and policy directives. In the second half of the 1970s, there were several laws to restructure PAs and redefine their tasks and responsibilities. Thereafter, new laws and directives to launch collectivisation, justify grain requisition, promote villagisation, and undertake resettlement were issued in quick succession. The 1980s was thus a decade of increasing institutional instability which created uncertainty and mistrust among the rural population. Due to space limitations, I shall not discuss these programmes in-depth but will look briefly at collectivisation, which came to pose a major threat to peasant enterprise and individual rights to land.[7]

The earlier reform legislation was driven by what may be called radical populism. At this early stage, the overriding concern of the *Derg* was to break the back of the old order and its supporting pillars, namely the monarchy, the landed classes, the exploitive system of property relations in the rural areas, and what was broadly referred to as feudalism and underdevelopment. The language of the government at this time was pitched to the 'popular masses' with a strong appeal to nationalism and justice to the poor. The ideal society in the countryside was viewed as being made up of self-labouring peasant farmers who had sufficient means (land, livestock, and income) for a livelihood based on the rustic values of hard work, honesty, and cooperation. But this populist phase was short-lived, soon replaced by the doctrinaire ideology of Soviet-style communism accompanied by hard-line rural policies, including agricultural socialisation.

The shift to collectivisation was decided upon soon after the radical land reform, with heavy investment in state farms, followed by the push for what were known as peasant producer cooperatives. The government's ambitious plan was that the 'transition to socialist agriculture' would be largely completed by the first half of the 1990s, i.e. some fifteen years after the process of collectivisation was launched. By then, the socialist agricultural sector was to become dominant, operating over 60 per cent of the cultivable land. Decision-makers favoured producer cooperatives, in particular, which were expected to cultivate 50 per cent of the farm land in the country in this period, because they were believed to be more efficient and more cost-effective. The government's justification for accelerating collectivisation was that it would greatly increase agricultural production and thus promote food security, pave the way for the modernisation of farming, particularly the introduction of new technology, and improve the livelihood of the rural people. All through the 1980s thousands of peasants were forced into hastily organised producer cooperatives, thereby losing their individual rights to land, and state agriculture was encouraged to expand its operations through increased investment. However, both enterprises continued to perform poorly, frequently below the smallholder sector, and to absorb a disproportionate share of state revenue. In the end, collectivisation failed to achieve any of the goals expected of it and instead wasted immense resources, remaining a cause for resentment and insecurity among individual smallholding peasants. By the close of the 1980s, the drive for collectivisation was halted as the government came to realise that the high cost of collectivisation was unsustainable, and the programme was finally brought to an end in 1990 with the announcement of the Mixed Economy reforms, a dramatic turnaround which was forced on the *Derg* as much by the failure of the programme as the escalation of the war by insurgents against the government. Producer cooperatives were thoroughly dismantled by peasants, and individual rights to land were restored immediately following the announcement of the new policy.

I conclude this brief review by noting that the radical rural reforms of the military regime were a success in some respects and a dismal failure in others, especially from the standpoint of secure rights to land. The initial land reform transformed rural Ethiopia into a society of self-labouring peasants whose livelihood became increasingly precarious on account of the dynamics of the reform itself, which undermined peasant confidence and exacerbated tenure insecurity. The legislation redefined the land system in a radical way, but in doing so, and in its practicalities, it made insecurity of property rights an enduring element. It replaced the landlord with the state and provided the latter greater hegemony over the peasant.

Reforming the reform: Land rights and legislation since 1995

Following the overthrow of the military government in 1991 and the seizure of power by the insurgent forces, united in a coalition of ethnic-based parties called the Ethiopian People's Revolutionary Democratic Front (EPRDF), the country was divided into what are called *killils* (regions or states) drawn along ethnic lines. The Constitution that was subsequently adopted established a federal political system with the *killils* as the component elements. The administrative structure of the country currently consists of the *killil,* below which is the zone (comparable to a province), the *woreda* (district) and the *kebelle* (sub-district). As part of the devolution of power within the federal framework, the *killils* were given wide administrative and legislative powers, including the power to issue legislation to administer land and natural resources. This and other legislation issued by the *killils* is expected to conform to federal laws.

The federal government's land policy is quite similar to that of the *Derg* described above, and hence the discussion of the details of the current legislations will have to be brief.[8] There are, however, a number of differences and several new initiatives which I shall note below. Federal and *killil* legislations pertaining to land include the Constitution issued in 1995, the federal law of 1997, which was repealed and replaced by a similar law issued in 2005, and a law on land expropriations and payment of compensation (FDRE 2005a). *Killil* legislations on land, the most recent of which were issued in 2002 (by Oromia) and 2004 (Southern *killil*), have been superseded by the latest federal law, and all *killils* are now in the process of preparing new laws as a consequence. At present, government land policy is enshrined in the

Constitution, which promises each adult in the rural areas who wishes
to live by farming 'land sufficient' for his/her livelihood; access to land
for rural persons is thus a right. Land is here defined as the property
of the people but is administered on their behalf by the state. This
principle is reproduced in all *killil* constitutions. In effect, land is state
property, and peasants thus have only use rights over plots they have
in their possession which cannot be sold, exchanged, or mortgaged.[9]

There are several factors that have added to tenure insecurity among
landholders. The first is the absence of a clear justice system for settling land disputes. During the imperial regime, the local courts were
the only authority (outside traditional institutions) that had the competence to hear cases involving land disputes. The main criticism of these
courts at the time was that they were thoroughly corrupt and almost invariably ruled against the poor and in favour of the rich and privileged.
The *Derg* deprived these courts of the power to try land cases and
vested such powers in the newly created Judicial Tribunals, which were
a part of Peasant Associations and consisted of peasant lay 'judges'. All
land matters at the *kebelle* level were brought before the Judicial Tribunals (Dessalegn Rahmato 1984). The present government has abolished these tribunals and established what are called Social Courts –
formal state courts at the *kebelle* level comprised of official judges.
These courts are empowered to hear land cases. However, land or other
disputes that are beyond their competence are frequently referred to
the *woreda* courts. To the average peasant, the *woreda* is too far away
from his/her locality, and taking one's case there is inconvenient, time-
consuming, and costly. Moreover, peasants have little confidence in
either the Social Courts or *woreda* courts, and instead prefer to take
their cases to customary dispute settlement institutions (Dessalegn
Rahmato 2004).

The second factor is the authority given to different government
agencies to intervene in land matters. The local Development Agent
(DA),[10] the *kebelle* council, and officials from the Offices of Agriculture
and of Environment Protection can make decisions that may threaten
an individual household's rights and access to land. This has given
state officialdom at the local level immense power over the peasant. In
fact, a recent federal law (FDRE 2005a) gives the local authority additional discretionary power to dispossess peasants of their land. Under
this law, the *woreda* administration is empowered to expropriate farm
land if it deems the land will be more useful if allotted to a public or
private investor, cooperative society, or others, or if it is needed for public purposes. Once the landholder is served with an eviction order by
the *woreda*, he/she has no recourse to appeal and must vacate the land
within 90 days. The holder is offered compensation, but this is often
far below the market price of the property involved.

The third factor is what I call the lack of legislative awareness by both peasants and local officials. Copies of legislation and policy documents are rarely provided to the local DA, the *kebelle,* or *woreda* authorities, nor are these officials adequately briefed about government decisions. Thus, officials who have the closest contact with the peasant farmer interpret the law or government policy not according to what it actually says, but what they think it says, and there is often a big gap between one and the other. At the same time, peasants are equally ignorant of the law and their rights, and consequently are powerless to voice their dissent or defend their rights. A fourth factor is the frequent revisions of the law, which as in the case of the *Derg*, has given rise to institutional instability. Frequent changes to the law have created greater uncertainty among peasants who have come to lose faith in the legal system and in government policies.[11]

I noted earlier that the factors that exacerbated tenure insecurity during the *Derg* were periodic land redistribution, as well as the fact that land rights were tied to continuous residence in one locality. The latest federal legislation has removed neither the threat of redistribution nor the residency requirement (FDRE 2005b, see art. 9). While the *Derg* did not, by law, expressly provide for periodic redistribution, this legislation and other federal policy instruments include provisions that do so, though they are hedged with a number of conditionalities. In this respect, the Oromia *killil*'s land law of 2002, which expressly put an end to both periodic redistribution and the residency requirement, is much better, and revising it to work in harmony with the new federal law will be a step backward for peasants in this *killil*. An improvement on earlier legislation is that holders can now pass on their rights to their heirs freely and without conditions; in some *killils* the right to inherit was formerly subject to a number of conditions. Land renting is allowed but, as previously, is subject to conditions, including approval and registration at the local government office. There are several new measures that have been introduced by the latest federal legislation (FDRE 2005b), and one of them provides for land measurement, topographical mapping, and registration as part of a measure of user certification. Another is the requirement that in the event of land reallocations, inheritance, and land rentals, the size of the land in question should not fall below the minimum plot size, though what exactly the minimum size should be is not specified. A third is the choice of resettlement and villagisation as new programme options to promote improved land use and management practices. Land users are still obligated to 'use the land properly' and are liable to penalties, including the loss of their rights to the land, in the event of improper use, resulting in what the document calls 'damage to the land' (FDRE 2005b). In brief, while some improvements have been introduced, the new federal law has still not adequately addressed the root causes of tenure insecurity hanging over all rights holders.

The government's justification for its land policy is based on what may be described as social equity. The Constitution and all other government documents pertaining to land declare that every rural individual has a right to a plot of land sufficient for his/her livelihood and should claim the right in his/her *kebelle* when he/she reaches the age of maturity. Moreover, the government argues that private ownership will give rise to peasant dispossession through distress sale or evictions, high concentration of rural property in the hands of a few – in particular, in the hands of the urban bourgeoisie – and widespread poverty and landlessness. These arguments are based on unsubstantiated fears, and very little hard evidence is available to support them. There is no evidence in this country or elsewhere to show that in the absence of the restraining hand of the state, peasants will readily sell their land at the first opportunity. Though flawed in many respects, the recent study by the Ethiopian Economic Association found that most peasants were not keen to sell their land if they were given the chance (EEA 2002; see also Dessalegn Rahmato 1994).

A result of the equity principle is the expectation that state ownership will do away with the problem of landlessness, but the reality on the ground is the reverse. Since the initial land reform of the *Derg* in the mid-1970s, landlessness has become a problem of the young. Young people who were not old enough to benefit from the last redistribution end up landless when they become adults. The main instrument employed to deal with landlessness so far has been periodic redistribution. Other means include the expropriation of landholders who fail to meet the obligations specified in each *killil's* land legislation, and the distribution of their plots to the landless. A recent measure that has also been employed for the same purpose is the 'privatisation' of hillsides. In both Amhara and Tigrai *killils*, degraded hillside has been divided up and distributed to members of the surrounding community. This was originally an environmental rehabilitation measure, but officials are now using it as a measure to tackle the problem of landlessness. Under present circumstances, landlessness is a dynamic problem: each generation that comes of age is landless and demands rights to land. In some localities the end result of accommodating its demands is increasing land fragmentation and the progressive levelling down of holdings. In others, these measures do not generate enough land and not all young people receive land.

A third element of the equity principle is the promotion of social equality in rural society. State ownership, it is argued, will ensure that the gap between the rich and the poor is narrowed and that inequalities of wealth and property leading to social antagonism and class conflict will be minimised. True, the existing land system discourages rural differentiation based on land size. As a result of periodic redistribution and other measures imposed by the dictates of the land system, differences in land ownership among households is narrowing. Equality of holdings is being achieved in a two-fold process: a) larger holders are losing some of their land through a process of unilateral levelling down; what is taken from them does not lift smaller holders up but goes to benefit some of the landless; b) larger holders are losing some of their land, and smaller holders are gaining as a result. The term 'large' and 'small' holder should be taken in its relative sense: compared to the situation in other African countries, the largest holder in Ethiopia would be a small holder elsewhere in the continent. At any rate, social equality has come at a heavy price, in that the equality that is unfolding in the countryside is equality of poverty.

As we can see from the distribution of holdings in the country, shown in Table 2.1, more than a third of households operate what can only be described as micro-holdings, namely 0.5 hectare (ha) or less. The majority, i.e. nearly 56 per cent, hold 0.1 to one ha, and 87 per cent operate two ha or less. Medium-sized holders, i.e. those farming two to five ha, constitute a little under twelve per cent of households, while only one per cent may be considered large holders with over five ha of land. The distribution of micro-holdings is more severe in the Southern *killil*, where the figure for those holding 0.1 to 0.5 ha is 56.4 per cent, followed by Tigrai with 40.5 per cent. All farmers in the country except those in the Southern *killil* are engaged predominantly in the cultivation of cereal crops, and an average family would, under normal circumstances, require between 2.5 to 3.5 ha of good quality land to produce enough food to feed itself for one harvest year. By this yardstick, only about thirteen per cent of holdings are capable of sustaining their owners, and the rest face food shortages on a regular basis. The figures in Table 2.1 show quite clearly the depth of poverty and land hunger in the rural areas. It may be worth noting here that under circumstances of shrinking land resources and high population pressure, the promise of the right to land given in the law to any citizen in the rural areas can only be described as misguided and counterproductive.

Table 2.1 *Percentage distribution of holdings by size (in ha)*

Killil	< 0.1	0.1 – 0.5	0.51-1.00	1.01-2.00	2.01-5.00	<5.01
Tigrai	7.0	33.5	29.9	21.4	7.6	0.4
Amhara	7.6	22.0	25.8	30.5	13.6	0.5
Oromia	5.9	24.6	25.3	26.2	16.1	1.9
Southern	9.9	46.5	25.4	14.2	3.8	0.2
National	7.6	29.5	25.7	24.3	11.9	1.0

Source: (CACC 2003)

A brief discussion of informal land transactions is in order here. Despite restrictions and prohibitive legislations, peasants have continued to engage in the informal 'land market'. Even at the time of the *Derg*, when almost all forms of land transfer were prohibited, peasants found ways to bend the rules to suit their needs. The informal land market, although at the time severely circumscribed, continued to play a vital role in helping peasants cope under the most difficult circumstances.

There were numerous forms of land transfer during the *Derg*. Though these differed from one locality to another, they included land rentals, sharecropping, joint use, short-term contracts, and occasionally mortgages – all of course undertaken clandestinely. If we add to these the numerous arrangements which peasants employed to get access to oxen or labour (for example short-term 'leases', land loans, exchange, etc.), the diversity of the practice becomes obvious. Land was also transferred through inheritance and marriage endowment.

Current land policy allows short-term land transfers, although in some cases these are encumbered by conditionalities. Nevertheless, the present system is more flexible in this regard than the previous one. Land transfer practices are just as complex at present as they were in the past. Currently, the most common forms of short-term land transfer are sharecropping, rentals, land loans, and limited 'leases' (Ahmed et al. 2002). Long-term transfers include inheritance and endowments. There are several kinds of endowments, the most common of which is the marriage endowment. Since land cannot be sold, mortgaged or exchanged on long-term bases, these forms of transfer are not part of the land market, although there is some evidence to suggest that peasants are engaging surreptitiously in such transfers, including land sales, in some areas (Bruce, Hoben, and Dessalegn Rahmato 1994).

As noted above, the government has embarked on new measures to try to promote greater tenure security and to address, in part, the serious food crises that the country continues to face despite increased food aid and new agricultural development programmes. These measures, as we saw, include land certification and registration on the one hand and resettlement on the other. In view of space limitations, I shall briefly examine certification and registration only, leaving out the subject of resettlement for now (see Dessalegn Rahmato 2004 on this).

The Ethiopian government has pinned its hopes on land certification to provide tenure security to peasant farmers and to deflect criticism of its rural development policies by local civil society groups, academics, and the donor community. Land certification and registration, which were launched cautiously in a limited number of localities a few years ago, have been turned into a massive programme undertaken at an accelerated rate throughout the country since the beginning of 2003. In a recent paper, a government official claims that by the end of 2005 over six million of the country's 13 million-plus rural households had received what is known as first-level user certificates. I believe this figure is somewhat inflated, and the true figure may be a good deal less.[12] The paper goes on to note that the remaining households will receive similar certificates in the next five years (Solomon Abebe 2006). The programme has been implemented, for the most part, without the use of modern surveying, mapping, and cadastre technology, and the registration system in place at the moment is cumbersome and does not allow timely updating and efficient management, both of which are of crucial importance if the goal of an effective and secure system of land administration is to be achieved. There are a few pilot schemes, supported by donor agencies, in which high or intermediate cadastral and registration technology has been employed; in the next three years a quarter of a million households are expected to receive certificates accompanied by cadastral maps of their plots in the pilot areas supported by donor agencies (USAID 2006a). But the cost and technical and institutional capacity implications are currently being assessed to determine whether or not, and how soon, this approach will be standard practice in the next phase of the certification programme.

Government officials and their supporters expect land certification and registration to achieve the following objectives: provide secure rights of tenure and protect the rights of vulnerable groups such as women; reduce land disputes and litigation; facilitate land use planning and management of community and state lands; and increase smallholders' investment in, and output from, their plots. It will be some time before we have sufficient evidence to assess whether or not these objectives have been achieved.

The evidence indicates that certification has been undertaken with a great deal of haste, and that there have been considerable difficulties faced by implementing authorities. Nevertheless, it has been given a good deal of support by donor organisations and seems to be well received by many peasants at the moment. But these are early days, and it would be unrealistic to base one's judgment on current opinion. Future plans include introducing dramatic improvements by employing modern methods of plot identification, boundary demarcation, and registration through the use of high or intermediate technologies for land surveying, index mapping, and establishing a land information system (LIS) to enable the efficient updating of land registers. While a number of donors (including the World Bank and USAID) have shown a willingness to support the new initiative, the cost implications and the institutional capacity of the public offices at the local level where the land registers are to be maintained are major hurdles whose short- or long-term impact has not been seriously considered as yet.

Many peasants interviewed in several *killils* for an earlier study were happy to receive land certificates, though a few were uncertain and cautious in their comments (Dessalegn Rahmato 2004). There is a feeling among many that the documents will provide holders with greater security than was possible in the past. Many of those who gave favourable opinions pointed to numerous conservation practices that peasants have been forced to abandon because of tenure insecurity – such as fallowing, soil protection measures, crop rotation and green manuring – which they thought would be resumed now. However, certification has been undertaken under the existing legal and policy framework, and holders thus do not have any more rights than they had before. While the measure may have helped reduce some problems, new problems and hence new conflicts will arise in the future unless modern techniques are employed to improve the system now in use.

My recent review of the available documentation on the country's brief experience in land certification and registration reveals a mixed picture (Dessalegn Rahmato 2006a). The works discussed were divided on the question of whether certification has led to greater tenure security. While some were positive, others were sceptical (Berhanu Adenew and Fayera Abdi 2005; Mitiku Haile et al. 2005). A work commissioned by USAID (2004) notes that landholders do not have strong tenure security even with certification, as this would not prevent the government from undertaking periodic land redistribution. The 2005 federal land legislation discussed above, which provides for land certification and which was issued while certification was being undertaken in many parts of the country, includes a provision for land redistribution, though there are conditions attached to it. As far as land disputes are concerned, the findings are even more disturbing: it appears that certification has either had no discernable impact on land conflicts or, as in the Amhara case, has aggravated conflicts (Berhanu Adenew and Fayera Abdi 2005). The World Bank (2005) says that the *kebelle* Social Courts reported a decrease of cases of land conflict after certification, but we need a more careful study of the results of the programme before concluding that land disputes have indeed become less frequent now. In many parts of the country, land disputes are often handled through customary dispute settlement mechanisms rather than through the Social Courts. With regard to the impact on women's land rights, the recent evidence reviewed in my earlier work shows mixed results, some works noting that women were at risk during the process of certification, others arguing that women were one of the main beneficiaries of the programme (Askale Teklu 2005; Berhanu Adenew and Fayera Abdi 2005; see discussion in Dessalegn Rahmato 2006a). Evidence was not available as to whether certification has led to increased opportunities for credit services or increased incentives for investment.

On the other hand, there is broad agreement that there is insufficient institutional capacity at the local level, where certification and registration are processed and managed. The efficient management of land registers and the constant updating of land information require not only the installation of a modern information system but a well trained and motivated staff, without which certification and registration can become counter-productive and a cause of increased conflict (Solomom Bekure et al. 2006).

One area which has not been given sufficient attention is the impact of population pressure on secure rights to land. The agricultural population of the country has been growing at a high rate for many decades, with the current rate estimated to be more than three per cent per year. The evidence suggests that the rural population has more than doubled in the last three decades: it was put at 26.3 million in 1970 but grew to 52.7 million in 2001 (CACC 2003; Marcos Ezra 1990). Moreover, the demographic movement out of the rural areas is fairly limited, far less than the rate of population growth, which means that the land resources of the countryside are under extreme pressure. There is a high rate of land fragmentation and sub-division, and land which is marginal and was used in the past mainly for grazing purposes has been brought under cultivation. For this and other reasons, environmental degradation is taking place at an alarming rate. These conditions can ultimately neutralise the benefits of certification.

To sum up, while the programme of land certification and registration is a step in the right direction, its implementation and the approach that has been adopted leave a lot to be desired. Moreover, such a programme does not rule out the need for a more sound legislation on the one hand and greater rights awareness on the part of the poor and labouring peasants on the other. The literature on African land tenure suggests that even under the best of circumstances, certification by itself will not be sufficient to ensure full tenure security (Bruce and Migot-Adholla 1994), and the Ethiopian case is not expected to be an exception.

Conclusions

Despite the radical reforms of the past and the significant changes that have occurred, there are also close similarities in the land systems of the pre- and post-Revolution periods. First, in both systems, the state had immense power over landed property: in the past the state was both a landlord in its own right and had a strong say over land not formally under its control. At present, the state has power over *all* landed property. Second, a majority of peasants in the past had only use rights over the land they cultivated, and such land was not transferable in any form on a long-term basis except through inheritance by siblings; this is almost identical to the rights peasants have under the present system. In brief, the tenure system in this country over the last 50 years may be described as one in which, in one way or another, the state has defined or has had a decisive say over rights of access to and disposal of rural land. This power became total with the nationalisation of land after the Revolution and in the period since then. Under both sets of circumstances, the cultivator remained subordinate and dependent on public authority for his/her very livelihood.

Moreover, both in the imperial past and at the present time, the land system has failed to provide land users with secure rights of tenure that are robust and not subject to arbitrary revocation by others, including the state. In the past, the tenant, the *rist* holder, as well as the owner-cultivator, were all subject, in one form or another, to the loss of their holdings or restrictions in their use. As noted above, the problem of the first two categories of cultivators is obvious, but while better off in many ways, the owner-cultivator was not free from uncertainty and fear. First, there were a number of powerful landlords who held high positions in government and who were notorious for engrossing land by unscrupulous methods. Such landlords often used their authority to expropriate land belonging to owner-cultivators with minimal compensation. The courts at the time were so thoroughly corrupt that redress of grievances through the justice system was out of the question for the average cultivator. Second, due in part to the fact that there was no cadastral survey and that only a small portion of the land in the country was measured and registered, there were frequent land disputes especially over plot boundaries, but also over inheritance and transfer rights. Such disputes could drag on through the courts for many years and could cause financial ruin and even family breakups among litigants on occasion. Finally, in the past, before Haile Selassie's land tax reforms, the owner-cultivator, known as *gebbar* (literal meaning: tribute payer), was burdened with many of the same obligations as the tenant, including dues in the form of labour, personal service, and duty during military campaigns.

The degree and extent of land insecurity thus varied from one political (and ownership) regime to another; nevertheless, it is widely recognised that it was a threat hanging over a majority of peasant cultivators in the imperial period which also became a danger affecting all peasants in the period since then. While before the radical land reform over 50 per cent of the farming population was under tenancy and dependent on the landed classes and the state, at present all peasants are 'tenants' of the state (though not in the full sense of the word) and all of them suffer a high degree of tenure insecurity. Insecurity of tenure was responsible, in the past as well as today, for the lack of long-term investment on the land and of effective environmental measures, and this, coupled with other factors too numerous to deal with here, continued to aggravate the poverty of rural society (Dessalegn Rahmato and Taye Assefa 2006).

Yet there are other factors that have a strong bearing on the question I wish to deal with here, *viz.* the effect and effectiveness of land reforms. These include state-society power relations and the process of reform legislation itself. The relation between the state and the peasant has always been an unequal one and reflects, at each particular occasion, the hegemony of the ruling power. Despite differences in a number of important aspects, the three regimes under discussion share many things in common, and may be described as intrusive. Each in its own way has been driven by the desire to regulate, manipulate and mobilise rural society for its own ends. As we have seen already, one important weapon in this endeavour has been the control of land resources. The modern state has always made strenuous efforts to intervene in and exercise control over the rural sector, and agrarian change has taken place within this overriding concern. It has narrowed the gap between the public and private sphere and succeeded in becoming virtually the only active force in rural society, with all other actors merely shadows. The peasant has thus been left little room for independent initiative and self-actualisation.

Over the years, Ethiopian peasants have expressed their dissatisfaction with the existing form of property and power relations in various ways, though unlike Latin America or pre-modern China, peasant uprisings have not been part of the country's agrarian history[13]. The massive show of support by the rural population for the new military state and its overthrow of the imperial regime, and later for the proclamation of land reform, was a clear statement of peasant alienation from the imperial system, which they saw as one based on exploitation, and their acceptance of the present order of things. One is doubtful if the reform would have been successfully implemented, or the military state itself would have survived for long, without the active participation of the peasantry in reform implementation and in the struggle against landlord opposition. The *Derg* lost the support of the peasantry in subsequent years with its unpopular and ruinous rural policies; the result was that the rural population either refused to come to the aid of the state in its hour of need, or gave its tacit backing to the insurgent forces fighting against it, which paved the way for the eventual collapse of the *Derg*. Under the current government, millions of peasants expressed discontent with existing policies and practices by casting their vote against the ruling party and in favour of opposition candidates in the national elections of 2005.

The process of legislating changing itself that was briefly noted earlier has a significant bearing on the final outcome and is thus important to examine. All the reforms we have examined, whether conservative, radical, or moderate, have been reforms from above, relying for the most part on the instrumentality of the law to effect change. They reflect a technocratic approach to social or agrarian transformation. The legislations in question were formulated without consultation or the participation of either the intended beneficiaries or the wider stakeholders. They were implemented in most cases by technocratic and civil servants except in the case of the *Derg*'s land reform of 1975, which was issued under exceptional circumstances. But legislating reform from above is undemocratic and, as is clear from the Ethiopian experience, invariably fails to satisfy the intended beneficiaries or to meet its stated objectives. The decision-making process in all the three regimes has been undemocratic, with the power to initiate and shape policy concentrated in a few hands at the top. Laws and policies were prepared by a few technocrats and sometimes, as in the case of the *Derg*, in complete secrecy. All the political leaders in question viewed participatory decision-making as a challenge to their authority and were hostile to any effort to democratise the institutions of policy-making (Andargachew Tiruneh 1993; Pausewang, Tronvoll, and Aalen 2002).[14] Thus, all through the period under review, the Ethiopian peasant has been the object of reform and a passive recipient of state 'beneficence'.

Reform from above often reflects the assumptions, values, ideological orientation, and class and political interests of the authors in power. The law is not a neutral instrument of change, at least not in matters of property and agrarian relations in the Ethiopian context. The agrarian issue in this country, as in many others, has always been a political issue. The chief resource of the country still remains the land, and access to it has invariably been fiercely contested both by the land user and by hegemonic forces that have often sought the economic benefits, as well as social and political dominance, this would confer. The control of the land and its products has been the source of class power and the basis of the hegemony of the state. In all three regimes, the state employed its hegemony to redefine rights of property, to siphon off the rural surplus, to manage or manipulate rural production, and to ensure peasant subordination. Reform from above, undertaken in particular in circumstances where the intended beneficiaries have not been involved in its formulation nor have been given the instruments by which to defend the benefits contained in the reform, will neither serve their interests nor be sustainable in the long run.

Notes

1   Ethiopia has a fairly large pastoral population located in the lowlands of the country. Land tenure in pastoralist communities is, however, different and complex. For an extensive literature on pastoralist land rights see Helland 2006. This study will also not encompass a discussion of urban land tenure for the same reasons.

2   See for a more detailed examination of the imperial land system, Dessalegn Rahmato 1984 and references in it.

3   There are conflicting figures on the extent of tenancy. Dessalegn Rahmato (1984) givers lower figures; CSO (1967) suggests that 55 per cent of peasants in the country were tenants; Bahru Zewde (1991) argues that 50-65 per cent of holdings in the country was operated by tenants.

4   Interviewed in 2000.

5   The *kebelle* here is equivalent to a sub-district and the *woreda* to a district.

6   Dessalegn Rahmato 1984, 1993.

7   For discussion of all these programmes, particularly collectivisation, see Dessalegn Rahmato 1993.

8   For an extended discussion see Dessalegn Rahmato 2004.

9   The key articles in the Constitution regarding land tenure are: article 40, sub-articles 3, 4, 6, and 7; and article 52, sub-article (d) (FDRE 1995).

10 The DA is the government's rural extension agent found in each *kebelle*.

11 For the magnitude of institutional instability since the 1970s, see Annex in Dessalegn Rahmato 2004.

12 The World Bank (2005) puts the number of households which have received certificates at between five and six million. Yet, at the end of 2004, in Amhara, one of the largest *killils*, where registration was begun much earlier than in Oromia and the Southern *killil*, registration had been completed in only 30 per cent of the *kebelles*.

13 See Dessalegn Rahmato 1996 for a discussion of this.

14 For more references on the authoritarian political tradition in Ethiopia, see Dessalegn Rahmato 1996.

3 Land rights and tenure security: Rural land registration in Ethiopia

Dessalegn Rahmato

Introduction[1]

In 2003, the Ethiopian government undertook a programme of rural land registration, and by 2006 more than half the country's farm households had received what are commonly referred to as land certificates. Initially, land certification was expected to be completed by the year 2010, but the implementation of the programme was greatly accelerated following the elections of 2005, and it now appears that the completion date will be much earlier. The goal is to issue every rightful holder of farm land a certificate of use rights and to have his/her plots recorded in a registry kept at the local *kebelle* office. The main objective of the programme is to address the problem of tenure insecurity and to establish an effective framework for land administration at the local level. Land registration is expected to reduce land disputes and litigation, to bring about the empowerment of women, and to lead to increased investments in the land (see Solomon Abebe 2006). The documents issued vary in form from one *killil* to another: in Tigrai, landholders are given a piece of paper which resembles a certificate, while in Amhara, the documents issued look like a bank book and are referred to as 'user books'. It is arguable whether the programme in progress can be called title registration, but for the purposes of this study I shall assume that what is being undertaken in rural Ethiopia is a form of title registration.

This study explores the relationship between land rights and title registration and the extent to which the latter has contributed to peasants' security of rights to land. It is based on the findings of field investigation in two locations in the north and south of the country undertaken in 2006 and early 2007. The analysis presented will rely mainly on the information gathered in Dessie Zuria *woreda*, South Wollo zone, Amhara *killil*, northern Ethiopia, but for the purpose of comparison I shall make use of the results of my field work in several *woreda*s in Wollaita zone, southern Ethiopia. The two locations are very different in most respects, such as agrarian history, farming systems, and cultural practices; but the most important difference, which has a bearing on the subject under study and which has not been given sufficient attention in the relevant literature, has to do with demographic pressure. Wollaita is perhaps the most vulnerable area in southern Ethiopia, due in large part to high demographic pressure and acute land shortage. The demographic stress in the area has been increasing in severity for well over half a century and is responsible to a great extent for high levels of rural destitution and frequent food and health crises. In the rural communities where we conducted our interviews, the population density is over 500 persons per km^2, and a household which has 0.25 ha of land here is considered fortunate. In contrast, Dessie Zuria, while very populous by the standards of Amhara *killil*, has a population density of about one-third that of Wollaita, and average land holdings measure over 0.70 ha.

The extent and variety of the instruments I used to gather information in the two locations differed. In Dessie Zuria, the instruments consisted of the following: a field survey undertaken on a selected sample of certificate holders in two *kebelles*; interviews with key peasant informants and about a dozen local public officials; case histories gathered from a number of household heads; and information relevant to land certification collected from public records (including police and court records) and the *woreda* databases. In contrast, the field work in Wollaita was less extensive: though I did not conduct a field survey here, I held the same kind of interviews, though with a smaller number of peasants and local officials. I was unable to gather information from public records about the certification programme but did collect socio-economic data useful for the study.

The different approaches in my field work are partly due to differences in the scope of implementation of the certification programme in the north and south of the country. In the two *kebelles* in Dessie Zuria *woreda*, land certification is almost complete, having been launched in 2003 and implemented with a good deal of care and resource expenditure. More than 90 per cent of landholders have received certificates. The *woreda* as a whole has been designated by the authorities as one of two pilot *woredas* in the *killil* selected for special attention through the support of Sida, the Swedish donor organisation, as well as to serve as a model for other *woredas*. By contrast, in Wollaita the certification programme got under way very recently, and in 2006 when I did the field work, less than half the rural households had received their documents. In Wollaita and the Southern *killil* in general, the programme has been dogged with difficulties, delays, and a shortage of resources.

Land certification has aroused a great deal of enthusiasm and has raised considerable expectations among the population in the rural areas, although this varies in degree from one part of the country to another. Compared to the situation in the recent past, i.e. before the certification programme was launched, there has been considerable improvement in peasant attitudes with respect to tenure security and land transactions. Most peasants say they now have a greater sense of security in their holdings than in the past. A majority of the respondents in our sample survey in the north of the country said they were more confident in renting out their land to others. A surface reading of the evidence suggests that there are relatively fewer land disputes at present, and certification is given as the main reason for this apparent decrease. In all, land certification is seen by a majority of peasants as a welcome measure, although neither the beneficiaries nor the public officials at the local level had any say in its inception, planning, or method of implementation.

The initiative has also raised considerable interest among the country's major donors as well as within academic circles. Donor groups such as USAID and the World Bank, in particular, are favourably impressed and are quite keen to provide support to the programme in one form or another.[2] A new survey report prepared by a World Bank team makes a highly positive assessment of the registration programme. It argues that large-scale land certification has been undertaken rapidly and successfully, with low cost, in a participatory manner, and with positive results. It suggests that 'elements of Ethiopia's certification process, with modification as needed, could serve as a model for other African countries' (Deininger et al. 2007). There is now less criticism than previously of the government's land policy, and the government itself is quite satisfied that it has finally addressed the problem of tenure insecurity for the rural population.

And yet, a careful and more nuanced reading of the evidence from the field clearly indicates that the issue is much more complex than it appears at first glance or is made out to be. As I shall show in the pages that follow, land certification is certainly a step in the right direction; nevertheless, the kind of robust tenure security that would allow individuals greater freedom of choice and action with respect to their property and livelihoods still eludes the country's hard pressed peasants. Security of rights to land in the proper sense of the term is an important basis for peasant empowerment, but there was no evidence to suggest that the peasants in our study had gained any sense of empowerment and autonomy or that their subordinate attitudes towards the state and state officials had changed in any way. Indeed, it was evident from our field experience that some of the institutional changes at the grassroots level that accompanied land certification have enhanced the authority of the state over the farm household.

Formalisation of property rights: A brief review

There is a considerable body of recent works on law, property rights, and economic development, and both academics and donor groups have drawn attention to the importance of these concepts and their relationship to tenure security and poverty reduction (De Soto 2000; Mwangi 2006; Toulmin and Quan 2000b; World Bank 2003d). The basic argument is that economic pursuits and relationships require an effective and inclusive legal system with clearly defined rules securing rights to property, determining the obligations of state and individuals, and governing commercial and contractual relations. Such a legal system promotes efficiency, increased investment, and entrepreneurial drive.

The work of Hernando de Soto, in particular, places greater emphasis on the poor, on the one hand, and formalisation of property law as an instrument of poverty reduction, on the other. De Soto holds that property rights codified in law, and the recognition of such rights made manifest in the form of title and registration, provide full security for disadvantaged populations in both rural and urban settings, and are essential conditions for poverty reduction and broad-based economic development. His work has stimulated considerable debate and interest among academics and the donor community, as well as international organisations. Though his ideas have been enthusiastically received within some donor circles, they have aroused strong criticism from within the property rights school, as well as among practitioners and scholars engaged in the development field. De Soto contends that to be poor does not mean to be asset-less; on the contrary, he shows that the poor hold immense assets and wealth in the form of land, houses, buildings, and small businesses, which if properly recognised would enable them to pull themselves out of poverty. The problem is that these assets are not valued because they are neither properly documented nor provided legal protection. Giving formal property rights to the poor transforms these assets into living capital, enabling them to access credit and allowing them to invest in their business and improve their earnings. De Soto is convinced that once their immense wealth is 'unlocked' through an inclusive property law and adequate formalisation, such as title registration, the entrepreneurial drive of the poor will energise the formal economy, leading to high rates of growth and development.

De Soto's work has been criticised for many shortcomings and from a variety of perspectives, and I shall briefly look at those relevant to this study.[3] In the first instance, his conception of property law is said to be narrowly constructed: he recognises only formal written law and individual/private property and leaves out other legal forms and property systems. In the African context, especially, land rights are subject to multiple legal systems, since both customary and private/individual tenure is accepted in many countries in the continent. There are those who argue that legal pluralism is not well suited to formalisation measures such as title and registration, while others suggest that customary tenure does not require formalisation to ensure protection of rights and security of holdings. De Soto and his supporters would argue that customary legal and property institutions, and the social and cultural network in which they are embedded, make formalisation a futile exercise, and that hence there is a strong need for institutional reform. Second, the argument that formalisation of property rights opens up opportunities for access to institutional credit is not supported by the empirical evidence. In fact, in Ethiopia as well as in many African countries, the poor as well as non-poor rely to a large extent on customary saving and credit institutions rather than the formal financial sector because the former are easy to access, do not require collateral, and provide quick and efficient service. The issue of collateral is frequently not the main reason that the formal sector is shunned, even by those who can provide collateral. Third, formalisation of land rights has been highly unsuccessful in Kenya and other African countries where titling and registration programmes have been undertaken since the 1950s and 1960s. As Sara Berry (1993) and others have shown, the enduring strength of customary tenure and the practice of ensuring claims to land through systems of social, political, and kin networks and negotiations have meant that formal records and title play an insignificant role in either access to land or dispute settlement.

To these arguments I will add the following three points which I believe are significant in light of the Ethiopian experience, and which the critical literature has either ignored or given much less attention than they deserve. To begin with, by over-emphasising the determinant role of property law and its legalisation, de Soto adopts a state-centric view of property rights and its guarantee for the poor. But, as we shall see later, formalisation of the law by itself provides no robust guarantee, and where such guarantee has been achieved, it has been the result of struggles by the poor themselves and non-state agents. Moreover, formal property law, he argues, and the conversion process in the law allow the poor to convert their assets into capital. Under capitalism, he states, the legal infrastructure is hidden in the property system, and the formal property system converts assets into value (De Soto 2000:45-46). But de Soto fails to recognise that the formal property system of capitalist societies is a product of a long historical process and the outcome of competing (often warring) economic interests, social classes, political parties, and sectional groupings.[4] Hidden in the formal property law of a capitalist country is a small slice of its social

history. Where this kind of pluralist struggle is absent or weakly manifested, as is the case in many developing countries, property law comes
to reflect the interests of one dominant group or, as in Ethiopia, those
of the state and its mandarins. Here property law is not inclusive but
restrictive, prohibiting disadvantaged populations the freedom and opportunity to get the full value of their assets. It is enough to cite apartheid South Africa as an extreme example of legal exclusion, and the
'feudal' imperial state of Ethiopia as a case of restrictiveness. As we
shall see in the discussion below, title registration in such circumstances at best only formalises the restrictive rights in question and
does not expand their scope.

Second, de Soto reflects a narrow conception of property rights in
two particular respects. First, he anchors such rights in property law,
and thus covers them in legalist costume; and second, he does not
make allowances for rights protection outside the statutory framework.
The legalist approach is inadequate because property rights will be of
limited value if they exist in isolation, and must rather be part of a political legal system incorporating rights to justice, human rights, and
good governance. Property rights should thus be understood in the
broader, political legal sense, since only then can we measure the real
significance of formalisation and registration. On the other hand, as
the contemporary and historical experience shows, where the poor are
concerned, property as well other rights have to be continually defended, otherwise there is the danger that they will be eroded or nulli-
fied by powerful forces, including the state itself seeking to maximise
its own interests. Rights protection outside the formal legal system,
through poor people's own organisations or through political and
rights advocacy groups, has made it possible for the poor to benefit
from existing formalisation programmes, as has been shown by a
number of recent works on Asian and African countries.[5]

Third, de Soto has very little to say about rights awareness and the significance of this to the poor. In fact, the literature on property rights in
general has not paid sufficient attention to this subject except for brief
references here and there to the 'accessibility' of the law, by which is
meant whether the law is written in comprehensible language and
whether it is in the public domain. By rights awareness I mean knowledge and voice: knowledge of rights through some form of rights education or advocacy, and the ability of the poor to voice their demands in defence of their rights. Since the state is frequently not a disinterested
party, the transmission of such awareness is best accomplished either directly by individuals having access to the sources in question, through
poor people's organisations or rights advocacy groups. I hold that rights
awareness is an important element of the empowerment of the poor,
and a reference to customary institutions illustrates this point. Where

customary institutions function effectively, they do so because individuals have clear and direct knowledge of the rules and responsibilities, they are able to voice their views when disputes arise, and there is direct access to dispute settlement mechanisms. There have been many examples where tenure reform implementation and land rights formalisation measures have failed because public agents and others paid scant attention to the importance of legal awareness (Palmer 2000).

While not directly addressing de Soto's arguments, the 'legal empowerment' school may be cited as one example where legal literacy and the provision of legal support services to the poor has been employed as an instrument of empowerment in programmes of agrarian reform, poverty reduction, and improvement of women's rights in a number of Asian countries (Golub 2003; Manning 1999). Legal empowerment here means knowledge of the relevant law and is slightly less inclusive than the concept of rights awareness which I have defined above. In this connection, mention must be made of the recently established international forum called the Commission on Legal Empowerment of the Poor,[6] which holds that the institutionalisation of a legal system that is inclusive of the poor provides empowerment and is an important condition for poverty reduction. It views functioning property rights as an important element of good governance. The legalist approach that is evident here as well as in the works noted earlier puts strong emphasis on the poor using the law to improve their economic interests and to hold secure rights to property.

The political legal framework

The political setting

The year 2005, when the federal government issued an important land law in which land certification featured prominently, was also the year when the country held its most hotly contested parliamentary elections. The 2005 elections were different from previous elections because for the first time in the country's electoral history, a large number of opposition candidates were allowed to participate, some running as independents and others under the umbrella of loosely formed coalitions and united fronts. Significantly also, the state-controlled media were opened up, allowing access to the opposition as well as the party in power. The opposition was able to contest nearly 80 per cent of the 523 seats in Parliament, competing vigorously not just in the urban centres but also in the rural areas. For the first time ever, peasants all over the country with access to the radio were able to listen to live debates between the government and the opposition and to campaign speeches by candidates highly critical of government policies and programmes.

There was thus a massive grassroots interest, as well as high expectations within rural areas in particular, that had not been apparent in any of the preceding elections. Figures provided by the country's National Electoral Board (NEB), a government body, shows that nearly 80 per cent of the population eligible to vote registered, of which 90 per cent turned out to cast their ballots on Election Day. Measured by voter registration and the turnout on ballot day, Election 2005 was a resounding success. The final results of the elections were fiercely contested by the opposition, as well as some international observer groups, both claiming that the government lost the elections by a good margin, while figures released by the NEB some three months after the ballots were cast gave the victory to the government. Even if we go by the official results, it is quite clear that the opposition faired immensely better in this election than at any time in the past. In 2000, it was able to win only twelve per cent of the seats in the House of Representatives of the Federal Parliament, whereas the official count declared by NEB shows that it won 40 per cent of the seats in this election, with the Coalition for Unity and Democracy (CUD) as the strongest contending party winning twenty per cent. Opposition successes in the *killil* elections were equally impressive.[7] Significantly enough, this success resulted from massive support by urban and, more importantly, rural voters.

There are a number of issues and events connected with the elections that are significant for our purposes, and I would like to go over them briefly here. First is the fact that the land issue, while not considered a burning issue in the campaign, was taken up for debate by a number of candidates and some of the bigger political parties. The government came in for some strong criticism on its land policy, and some of the front runner candidates let it be known that if they were elected to Parliament they would propose changing the policy in favour of a more secure form of ownership. This greatly concerned the government, for whom the existing system of state ownership was almost sacrosanct and one of the main pillars of its political and economic strategy for the country. The government's strong commitment to state ownership had ideological roots, but it was also an instrument which enabled it to have greater leverage over land allocations and greater hegemonic intervention in rural society.

The second issue had to do with the government's expectations regarding the outcome of the elections. State officials were confident that the ruling party would win the elections handsomely but conceded that Parliament after the elections would be different from the outgoing one and that a good number of the seats in it would be taken by the opposition. Their assessment was that in large measure they would lose the urban vote, while the rural vote would be massively behind them. As ballot day approached, however, and the turn of the electorate towards the opposition became apparent, the confidence of the authorities came under severe strain; nevertheless, they still remained convinced that victory was theirs, even though the massive majority they had expected would not materialise. This led to a spate of decisions by the government, and in its dying days a series of legislations were rushed through Parliament, which was to be a cause of bitterness and recrimination between the governing party and the opposition. Since they have a bearing on our discussion, we shall look at two of these decisions.

The first was the passing of two important land laws in July 2005, nearly two months after the elections were held. The public was so agitated following the elections – by what they regarded as undue delay in the announcement of the results – that not many voices were raised to question the propriety of the old Parliament continuing to sit and pass laws weeks after the people had voted in new legislators. The most important act was the rural land administration law, but another law was also passed in the same month, which dealt with land expropriation and the payment of compensation; a law that has not received much attention in the debate here. The other decision worth noting was the passing of legislation to change the Parliamentary rules of procedure, which was rushed through the House about a month later. One of these approved rule changes made it impossible for any party in Parliament, except a party with a majority seat, to initiate legislation, replacing the old rule in which it was sufficient for twenty MPs to propose legislation for it to be considered by the House. The aim of the government was to effectively paralyse the opposition in Parliament and remove any risk that some of its cherished policies, including those on land, would be reversed in the post-election period.

The post-election period was marked by high political and social tension, and there were a good number of protests and strikes in the urban areas. These protests were forcibly put down by the security forces, culminating in the death of scores of protesters and the arrest and detention of thousands of people. Most of the leadership of CUD, a large number of its campaigners, as well as journalists and civil society activists were arrested and charged with attempting to overthrow the Constitution by violent means and genocide.[8] In the rural areas the situation was different, and here the government adopted what may be described as a carrot and stick approach. On the one hand, many local authorities conducted considerable harassment of peasants suspected of voting for the opposition, and on a few occasions, peasants who resisted harassment were reported to have lost their land allocations. On the other hand, land certification programmes were accelerated, covering a large number of households in a short time. Respondents in the two localities in the north and south of the country where we did field work informed us that many in their communities had voted for the opposition, but while they themselves had not suffered any serious consequences, they had heard of such harassment in other localities.

The aim of speeding up land certification was to win back the support of the rural population and to undermine the chances of the opposition. This was important for the governing party, because elections for *kebelle* and *woreda* assemblies, which were planned for 2006 but postponed, would soon be taking place. These local elections are critical for the governing party, because losing them would erode its power base in the countryside and, given that the urban areas are a hotbed of opposition, this would mean running the risk of losing the general elections scheduled for 2010. The ruling party is now busy in the rural areas, holding numerous meetings for political and organisational purposes, involving both active and non-active peasants. It is quite evident that the party is conscious of the latent power of the peasantry and that it needs to gain its support if it is to stay in power. This is where the land question assumes immense significance.

Institutional setting

The most important institutional change in the last half decade is the *woreda* (or district) level decentralisation, which was initiated in 2001 and is now almost complete. Decentralisation here is aimed at bringing development programme management closer to the community and to make service delivery more efficient and effective. Under this new system, *woredas* will receive block grant transfers from the government which they are expected to manage themselves. They also have the power to prepare their own budgets and annual plans, to generate income from their own resources and use the income for their own purposes, and to recruit and hire staff (see Tegegne Gebre-Egziabher and Kassahun Berhanu 2006). In effect, the *woreda* has now become the focal point of local-level planning and programme implementation. Below the *woreda* is the *kebelle*, which is responsible for needs assessment and service delivery, as well as law and order; it is expected to establish close and direct links with the rural household. Both structures are governed by elected councils and thus are expected to be democratic institutions. Local-level democracy, which is the other objective of decentralisation, obviously opens up immense opportunities for all community-directed programmes. Such an institutional set-up is supposed to enable peasant communities and individual households to express their preferences, needs, and demands. In turn, programme planning and implementation will benefit by greater bottom-up participation and better opportunities for monitoring and evaluation.

On the other hand, there are at present considerable hurdles that need to be overcome. The decentralisation programme has been largely completed, including the shifting of staff from both the *killil* and zones to the *woreda*s. However, the institutional capacity of a great majority of the *woreda*s is a cause for great concern at present. Many *woreda*s lack basic infrastructure, capable and trained staff, proper equipment, and resources, and so their capacity falls short of the duties and responsibilities they have been burdened with. As a result, decentralised planning and programming has been severely constrained, and the opportunities for local-level democracy have been limited. Weak institutional, resource, and staff capacity has been aggravated by high rates of staff turnover and institutional instability. Public employees who have higher qualifications are especially less likely to stay in the *woreda*. Staff turnover has badly impacted programme planning and implementation, raising issues of sustainability and programme quality. Also, changes and reforms in government bodies have been quite numerous, and this has contributed to institutional weakness.

There are important institutional changes at the *kebelle* and lower levels, and as we observed in Dessie Zuria *woreda*, this has come about partly as a consequence of land certification. The *kebelle* is divided into three sub-*kebelles* and ten *gotts* (which are large precincts); below these are 'communes' which are development units of 35 to 50 households. These lower units have direct links to the executive leadership of the *kebelle*, thus lines of communication as well as control now extend to the household level. The elected *kebelle* council, which is the decision-making power in the *kebelle*, elects several standing committees, of which the Executive, Land Administration, and Crime Prevention committees are the most important ones. There are ad-hoc 'task forces' formed from time to time, such as the Food Security and Environment task forces, but they are temporary bodies and are disbanded when they complete their tasks. In each particular case, it is the Executive which selects the committee members (as well as magistrates to the local Social Courts) and presents them to the Council for approval. In both *kebelles* we studied, the Executive leadership consisted of members of the ruling party, and party membership is a factor, though not an overriding one, in being elected to committee posts. All officials elected were male, but in one of our study *kebelles* we found one woman who was a member of the 14-strong Executive Committee.

A word is in order here on the status of the Social Courts. Social Courts were established by law in all *killils*, and their competence extends only to minor cases with a pecuniary value not exceeding 1000 *Birr* (see Amhara National Regional State (ANRS) 1997). These are in effect 'community' courts and in a sense a replacement for the Judicial Tribunals of the *Derg*. The magistrates of the courts are selected from the *kebelle* and have no legal training, and their formal education does not extend beyond the rudimentary level. The magistrates my team interviewed in Dessie Zuria *woreda* were all members of the ruling party. While the choice of magistrates from within the community is a positive measure, there is cause for concern with regard to the independence of the courts and impartiality of the magistrates. The Social Court has not been established as an independent body, and this may in the long term compromise its credibility. The change of magistrates every five years that is required by the law is ill-advised, since this will mean losing valuable experience and knowledge gained through the training given to the magistrates. While most peasants interviewed in Dessie Zuria as well as Wollaita were quite satisfied with the work of the Social Courts, the courts are reported to be corrupt and unpopular in some parts of the country.

An important issue that needs to be raised here is the dominant role of the ruling party in local affairs. The structure of rural governance is in fact much more complicated than meets the eye. While there has been administrative decentralisation, providing the *woreda* and to some extent the *kebelle* more responsibility and authority than in the past, in terms of 'party politics' there is a strong system of centralisation and upward accountability. The ruling party operates on the principle of what in the old Soviet communist system used to be called 'democratic centralism'. At the local level, party and government are closely linked with little or no separation between the two. As was noted above, the leadership of the *kebelles*, including active members in committees, are members of the party; this is also more or less true in the *woreda*. The members of the elected Councils in both cases are either party members or have been supported by the party. Thus, there is very little opportunity for alternative voices to be heard. Local officials depend on instructions from above, and there is a hierarchical cadre system, and as a result, the party has immense influence in decision-making and programme management.

The practice in many local communities during the certification process was to elect from among the participating households an ad hoc committee called the Land Administration Committee (or LAC) to be entrusted with the task of recording the boundaries of individual holdings, measuring them, and registering the owners and their household members. The LAC was intended to be a temporary body and was to disband once the certification process was over. This situation has changed, and the LAC has become a standing committee elected by the Council whose responsibilities now include serving as a first instance body for hearing and resolving land disputes. The LAC consists of seventeen members, but at each weekly sitting four members of the Executive Committee attend the deliberations. LAC members are a mix of peasant party activists and local elders who are known to have a good reputation in the community. There is thus an attempt to combine modern and customary dispute resolution practices. We shall return to this presently.

The legal framework

Here I am concerned more with the process of legalisation of the federal laws noted above than their contents, since I have discussed the laws in an earlier work (Dessalegn Rahmato 2006b). As was noted above, the federal legislation was submitted to Parliament and approved under contentious political circumstances. The land administration law, which was prepared by the Ministry of Agriculture and Rural Development, was submitted to Parliament at the end of March 2005. The Ministry says that the draft was sent for comments to senior government officials both at the federal and *killil* level, but there was no attempt to invite public debate on it nor to solicit the opinions of particular stakeholders, such as NGOs and civil society organisations, the academic and research community, or rural development experts. The draft was not accessible to the public. The government-controlled media noted only the submission of the draft law to Parliament but was careful not to seem to encourage public discussion of it. There was at the time widespread understanding among government bodies, the donor community in the country, and informed opinion that the land issue was almost taboo, and senior government officials were known to have discouraged any public debate on the subject (see Dessalegn Rahmato 2004). The draft law was sent to the Rural Development Standing Committee of the House in April, with the Committee returning the draft to the full House in June with suggestions for some minor revisions which were mainly of an editorial and non-substantive nature. At the time of the final debate in the House, a dozen or so representatives from civil society organisations as well as officials from concerned government departments and other guests were invited to attend the proceedings. Since the ruling party controlled more than 90 per cent of the seats in the House, the draft law was approved without any serious debate by MPs; it was finally published in the official gazette in late July. This law replaces the federal law issued in 1997 and requires all *killil* land laws to be revised to be in harmony with it, since federal law supersedes all legislation issued by lower bodies.

Before turning to the revised Amhara *killil* land law which came out in May 2006, I would like to say a few words about the frequency of changes to the law having to do with rural land, its administration, and use. While the basic principle defining land rights is contained in the Federal Constitution of 1995, there have been numerous laws issued at both the federal and *killil* level pertaining to tenure, administration, and use, and this has contributed to the problem of institutional/legal instability noted above. In the Amhara *killil* in particular, laws to provide for land redistribution were issued in 1996 and 1997; the land use and environmental protection authority, which is responsible for land matters in the *killil*, was established by law in August 2000; and the law to define land administration and use was issued in October 2000. It is this latter law which has now been revised following the federal law of 2005. Policy directives on land use and environmental protection, which are as binding on landholders as the formal laws, have been issued on a number of occasions in between these laws. There are at the time of writing only two *killils* which have issued land laws to harmonise with the federal law, Amhara and Tigrai, both of which published their legislation in 2006. Oromia, whose land law was issued in 2002, and the Southern *killil*, which brought out a similar law as recently as 2004, are in the last stages of completing their respective revisions; however, we cannot discuss either one because they have not been officially published. We should note here that all four of these *killils* are territorially extensive, having large peasant populations mostly found in areas inaccessible by modern transport. The dissemination of the contents of any law to the peasantry is thus a long and difficult process. Many peasants in the South, for instance, do not have knowledge of the 2004 land law which is now being revised.

The Amhara land law draws heavily on the federal law; it is thus sufficient to present here the main provisions that are relevant for our study (Amhara National Regional State (ANRS) 2006). As in the federal case, the *killil* law affirms the principle of state ownership of land which prohibits its sale, mortgage, or exchange, with the holder having only the right of use, a right dependent on residency in the rural area and engagement in agricultural pursuits. Use rights are also dependent on a host of conditions, of which most have to do with what is described as 'proper' land and environmental management practices. Holders who do not follow these practices are subject to a variety of penalties, including the loss of their right to the land. What these 'proper' practices consist of is not stated precisely, such that they might be legally challenged; they are only broadly stated and thus provide ample discretionary power to state officials. Holders may also lose their right if they are absent from their farms and the land is left idle for three consecutive years or more. The right to rent out land is allowed but only for a short period of time; longer periods have to be registered in the *kebelle*. Future land redistribution has not been entirely ruled out but now is subject to the consent of a majority of the landholders in a given locality. Articles 22 to 24 (with 21 sub-articles combined) describe the process of land titling and registration. The *kebelle* plays a significant role, since it is empowered to administer land in its jurisdiction and to issue land certificates and maintain a land registry.

The settlement of land disputes is left vague, but a previous law issued in 1997 defines the powers, duties and responsibilities of the *kebelle*-based Social Courts (Amhara National Regional State (ANRS) 1997). This is the lowest court in the country's judicial system and is empowered to hear and decide on a wide variety of petty cases brought before it by *kebelle* residents, including land cases. Its power extends to cases where the monetary claims in any decision do not exceed 1000 *Birr* (a little over 100 US dollars). The judges to the court are selected from the community and approved by the Council upon recommendation by the *kebelle* executive; they have the same term of office as both the Council and the executive. While the choice of judges from within the community is a positive measure, there is cause for concern with regard to the independence of the courts and impartiality of the magistrates. The Social Court has not been established as an independent body, and this may in the long term compromise its credibility. Disputants may either take their case to the higher, *woreda* court directly, if they think the case is beyond the competence of the Social Court, or may appeal to the *woreda* court if they are not satisfied with the decision of the Social Court.

A brief examination of the legal landscape in the rural areas is in order here to place the arguments presented in this study in their proper perspective. The federal and *killil* constitutions provide the broad basis for human, democratic, and property rights. On paper, rural as well as other citizens enjoy a wide variety of such rights, though in practice the reality is much different. The variety of land laws noted above determine rights of access to land, and set out the legal framework for the administration, registration, and management of farm and non-farm land. Peasants do not have direct access to the constitutional or legal instruments, however; indeed, in the urban areas also, legal documents are hard to come by for most citizens. Even if they have access to them, peasants often have no education and cannot read and understand legal documents. More than two-thirds of our sample in Dessie Zuria, for instance, were illiterate and only ten per cent had enough formal education to be able to understand such documents. Moreover, there are no voluntary organisations or individuals in the rural areas that provide free legal service to peasants, neither are there active peasant organisations that farmers can turn to if they wish to get legal advice or aid. Indeed, there are hardly any independent legal service organisations in the country, though a few human rights groups based in Addis Ababa, the capital, are now beginning to provide legal aid to a limited number of poor people. Ethiopia is far behind in this respect compared with other countries in Africa and Asia (Manning 1999).

The agricultural cooperatives that are active in most rural areas are handmaidens of the government and are engaged primarily in the purchase and distribution of farm inputs to farmers. They do not undertake legal advocacy work, although they would be best placed to provide legal services were they to become free of government tutelage. There were 27 people who had been issued with permits to practise law in Dessie Zuria *woreda*, but they are professional lawyers based in Dessie and mostly inaccessible to peasants because of the high fees they charge. Most rural *woredas* do not have as many professional lawyers, and the high number here was due to the fact that Dessie is a large and important regional town.

Thus, in brief, the state acts both as a player and the referee. The task of determining land rights and interpreting the laws rests with local public officials, but – and this is an important point – since the government is both the juridical owner of the land as well as the source of the laws, officials are more prone to present a positive interpretation and to give a favourable reading of the law, and the chances that such a reading may hide as much it reveals are quite high. In a politicised environment, such as we have at present, the law is more likely to be read less objectively and less accurately by local authorities.

Land certificates and registration

The local context: Dessie Zuria woreda

With Dessie, one of the largest and oldest towns in northeast Ethiopia at its centre, Dessie Zuria *woreda*, the district in which our main research was undertaken, is the most populous district in South Wollo; it has a population of 261,000 inhabitants. Aba Sokotu and Gelsha, the two *kebelles* where we conducted field work, are located close to Dessie on the main east-west highway, and peasants here have benefited from the economic and market opportunities the town provides. The town has now expanded into the rural areas, and in the west, two of the rural *kebelles* adjacent to Aba Sokotu, which were the site of the first pilot certification programme, were incorporated into it. This caused considerable conflict between the peasants, the land administration authorities, as well as the town officials. We shall return to this shortly.

Peasants in our two sites are quite atypical in a great many respects: their proximity to a major urban centre, relatively better transport services, and their frequent travels to Dessie have opened up opportunities for improved employment and income on the one hand, and for greater social and political awareness on the other – opportunities denied to other peasants in more remote and less urban surroundings. Peasants here sell a wide variety of agricultural goods, as well as livestock, timber, and firewood in the Dessie market, from which they purchase in return a range of basic goods and services. Some peasants are half farmers and half traders, and as individual plots have shrunk and the land available for farming has decreased more and more, peasants turn to petty trading to earn income and maintain their families. But the town also provides many other benefits: greater chances for social interaction, for increased access to information and the media, and the expansion of one's horizon and experience.

Proximity to a major provincial and district capital also means that rural communities are more accessible and hence benefit from increased visits by development officials, both from the public and voluntary sector, and improved service delivery. Schools, improved health facilities, veterinary posts, farmer training centres, and agricultural extension posts have been constructed and function in both sites. Because of the special nature of the *woreda*, peasants here have also received more attention than those in other locations. In addition, peasants benefit from micro-finance institutions, the services of the main farmers' cooperative (which is now the main channel through which farm inputs are distributed), and access to half a dozen or so development NGOs which run a variety of health, education, and environmental rehabilitation programmes in the *woreda*.

An important public support programme recently launched in many parts of the rural areas, called the productive safety net programme (SNP), has been underway in Dessie Zuria and the two research sites since 2005, and in the district as a whole nearly 30 per cent of households are beneficiaries of the programme. The programme identifies chronically food-insecure households, predominantly in the rural areas, and provides them with employment and the opportunity to earn income on a regular basis. Designed to be part of the government's food security strategy and planned to run for at least five years, the programme was initially aimed at benefiting some 5 million chronically poor households in the country, but the number has gone up to 7 million at present. The main employment schemes are public works, environmental rehabilitation, and construction of service-giving institutions. Beneficiary households are also eligible under the programme for a variety of assistance schemes delivered through a package approach to help them diversify their sources of income and to build up their assets. SPN is an on-going programme in which considerable resources are transferred to participating households (to the tune of nearly USD 200 million a year nationwide) through the employment schemes, the package approach, or both (MOFED 2005). Local officials are responsible for selecting beneficiary households, preparing the employment and package schemes, managing the programme, and distributing resources. This has been an unexpected 'windfall', as it were, to local authorities because it gives them considerable power and influence over peasant farmers.

A major event that has shaped public opinion in the area is the land redistribution programme carried out in Amhara *killil* in 1997, in which many peasants who were considered large owners by the authorities were stripped of large portions of their holdings and the land distributed to the landless or land poor. While it was welcomed by those who stood to gain, redistribution caused a good deal of turmoil in the rural areas, was bitterly resented by those who lost their property, and became a source of anxiety to others (Ege 1997). The programme was carried out in full in many areas, but there were a few districts where it was either not implemented at all or implemented only partially. Both Aba Sokotu and Gelsha fall in the latter category, in which a small number of households lost their land and a few landless peasants received small allotments.

Land certification

Among the first recipients of land certificates[9] issued by Amhara *killil* in early 2005 were peasants in two *kebelles* in Dessie Zuria located adjacent to our research sites. This was a pilot scheme and the culmination of a long process of preparation, going back to 2003, both in the office and on the ground. The purpose of the scheme was to test the feasibility and cost of using modern technology, and the experiment employed GPS techniques to demarcate *kebelle* and individual plot boundaries. However, the certification process was halted halfway through, when the land administration authorities realised that the two locations in the programme had been absorbed into Dessie town as a result of a decision by higher authorities to allow urban expansion in the *killil* to a fifteen km radius. This was poor planning on the part of all public officials concerned, and the pilot scheme in the district was abandoned with considerable wastage of resources. The decision caused a good deal of disquiet among the peasant households involved: those who had received their certificates did not know how secure they would be in the new circumstances, and those who did not, and they were many, were afraid of being dispossessed without fair compensation by the urban authorities since they did not have any proof of rights to their land. Urbanisation poses a serious risk of land expropriation, as service infrastructure, housing, and other buildings will be constructed as part of the process of urban growth. It will also mean peasants will have to give up farming and face the risk of unemployment, since there will be few opportunities for alternative livelihoods available to them. Angry protestations were made by peasants to the authorities concerned, including to the visiting Minister of State for Agriculture and Rural Development, but without any results, and at the time of our field work the case was still unresolved.

Another cause of peasant disquiet that accompanied certification was the road building project that is being undertaken in the west of Dessie Zuria district. The highway linking the town of Dessie with the western part of South Wollo zone is being upgraded and expanded to accommodate much heavier traffic, but in the process many peasants have lost their farm land, houses, and some common land which was used by the surrounding community for grazing and other purposes. The authorities responsible were willing to pay compensation to some but not to others, on the grounds that the land adjacent to the highway was by law the property of the highway department; as justification they cited an old and obscure law issued in 1944, which few people outside the highway bureaucracy were aware of. They also argued that the commons were no man's land and not eligible for compensation. Peasants were angry because they felt cheated: they had been farming those lands for over a generation and had their certificates as proof of ownership, yet they were denied the fair treatment that they were promised by the certification programme. The compensation offered for the houses and buildings on the land was seen as quite adequate, but holders were offered only small payments for the land itself, because the authorities argued it was public property. I should note here that the certification programme excluded common lands, which was a cause of dissatisfaction among many peasants.

These incidents may be seen as minor glitches in the certification programme, caused largely by poor planning and the incompetence of local officials, rather than as inherent flaws in the programme itself. This is true in part, but it does show that peasant insecurity is more deep-rooted and cannot be removed merely by issuing user certificates. Peasants are dependent on local officials for interpreting the law, and interpretation is frequently made to suit the given circumstance. This is one of the factors for peasant subordination, and insecurity cannot be cured without addressing the causes of subordination.

Before we turn to the full story of land certification, we need to look at the issue of compensation and its payment. The right to compensation for land taken away by public authorities or private interests has priority in the minds of peasants we interviewed in Dessie Zuria. The most important benefit that land certification has brought with it, according to most respondents, is the right to compensation. In the past, land was taken away for public purposes without adequate compensation. The justification public officials use when they wish to take someone's land is *limat*, which may be loosely rendered as 'development'. There have been and still are numerous *limat* initiatives under way (too numerous to list here) in the rural areas, and each initiative re-

quires its own *limat* office in the *kebelle* and at times in sub-divisions of
the *kebelle* as well. For instance, water harvesting is one of the *limats*
underway all over the district, and this has its own office in the *kebelle*.
There are two kinds of compensation: in kind (i.e. a plot equal in size
to the one lost is offered in return), or in cash. Peasants often note that
compensation in kind often means ending up with a plot poorer in
quality and frequently more distant than the plot taken away. Land is a
scarce commodity, and there are no unused plots that are of good quality anywhere.

The compensation payment in cash on the other hand may be relatively better, but it has its own faults. First, it was only in 2005 that a
compensation law was issued by the federal government; to date there
are no comparable laws at the *killil* level, and local officials on the
ground simply make ad hoc improvisations, and as result there is a
good deal of inconsistency. Strictly speaking, the compensation that the
federal law provides is compensation for displacement and does not include the value of the land, hence it is not fair payment for those who
lose their holdings. The justification is that land is public property and
is not subject to compensation. A second cause for concern for peasants, particularly in peri-urban areas, is the expropriation of their land
for investment purposes. This is not a particularly pressing problem in
either Dessie Zuria or Wollaita at present, although we have seen the
repercussions on peasants resulting from the decision to allow urban
expansion into the rural areas. The federal law provides that the local
authorities have the power to remove any peasant from the land if that
land is required by a private investor to establish an agricultural or industrial enterprise (see Dessalegn Rahmato 2006b for details). In this
case, the government pays compensation, and the landholder does not
negotiate directly with the private investor; he/she would have gained
more if he/she had the right to do so.

Let us now examine the process and outcome of land certification
based on our findings from our research sites.[10] For peasants, the process begins with an announcement in the *kebelle* calling on all landholders to attend a meeting on a specific date to discuss land and tenure issues. This was true in Dessie Zuria as well as in Wollaita. In Gelsha, one of our survey sites, the formal announcement was preceded
by rumours that individual plots were to be measured and land reallocation would take place. At the meeting, *woreda* and *kebelle* officials
give a briefing about the purpose of the meeting. Peasants are then
asked to elect four individuals from each of the ten *gotts* (or precincts)
of the *kebelle* to the Land Administration Committee (LAC). In both
our sites, there were no women elected to the Committees, which consisted of 40 members each. After a brief training, the LAC, supported
by *kebelle* and *woreda* officials, assumes responsibility for the main pre-

paratory tasks of certification and registration, which include identification of individual plots, demarcation and boundary marking, measurement of plots, and recordings of personal details to be included in the land registry and certificate, such as the holder's name and that of his/her spouse, names of siblings and heirs, and other pertinent facts. Disputes may arise at each stage of this process, and the LAC either attempts to resolve them on the spot or refers the case to the *kebelle* office. Four LAC members and two to three officials from the *woreda* and the *kebelle* office are deployed in each *gott* (or precinct) to undertake the preparatory tasks.

The first order of business is to identify the *kebelle* boundary. In the absence of maps or permanent boundary markings, and due to the fact that *kebelle* boundaries have been redrawn on numerous occasions, this is not an easy task and has been the cause of conflict among peasants as well as among officials of different *kebelles*. In our case, the *kebelles'* area and boundary coordinates were determined using GPS techniques, which is not common practice, and was only possible here because Dessie Zuria is a pilot district and has benefited from donor support. This was the only stage in which modern technology was employed; all the other tasks were carried out with the use of traditional techniques and crude tools. In Wollaita, some *kebelle* boundaries had trees and shrubs planted on them, and these were accepted as being adequate to demarcate one *kebelle* from another. Each landholder had to be present on his/her plots during individual demarcation and boundary marking. The identity of one's land is determined in relation to the adjacent plots owned by other peasants. This is the most contentious stage of the process, as farm plots in Ethiopia do not customarily have permanent boundary markings, and there are often disputes among adjacent holders about the exact extent of each other's plots. While the dispute may be settled during the demarcation process, this is often temporary, and the dispute frequently flares up soon after.

In the steeper lands in Wollo as a whole and in Dessie Zuria as well, peasants use a traditional structure called *wober* as a plot boundary. This is a bund constructed along the contour and allowed to build up over several years, employed also as a soil conservation measure. The structure is temporary, however, and peasants plough it over to get access to the soil collected underneath which they think is rich in nutrients. The *wober* is then constructed elsewhere, and since it is not uncommon for peasants to encroach on the neighbours' plots in doing so, this has become a cause of constant conflict among farmers. A common method of demarcation used by the LAC was to place stones and lumps of soil on the boundaries, but these are moveable objects and in many cases proved to be inadequate to prevent disputes.

The measurement of individual plots was the most unsatisfactory part of the certification process, and many peasants interviewed were critical of the manner in which their plots were measured. Plot measurement is fraught with difficulties in many parts of the country, because even the simplest measuring tape is not available in most places, and different traditional methods are used by different officials in different places, thus giving rise to inaccuracies and inconsistencies. Two different methods of measurement were employed in the two *kebelles* in our study. In Aba Sokotu, LAC officials used what may be described as visual measurement to determine the size of farm plots. This consisted of the head of the Committee estimating the size of a plot by sight: no measuring tools were employed, and some peasants considered it as no better than guess work. Surprisingly enough, there were no protests during the measurement, as the results rarely went against peasant expectations; nevertheless, this was to cause disputes among holders after the certificates were handed out. In Gelsha, LAC officials employed ropes, strings, and sticks to measure plots. A piece of rope or stick, measured by the arm, was taken to be equivalent to a given length in the metric system, and this was the chief measuring tool in the *kebelle*. At each precinct the arm measurement was carried out by the head of the LAC for that precinct, thus no two measuring ropes were of the same size. This was to be a cause of discontent here because, as we shall see later, land measurement was accompanied by land reallocation. In Wollaita, in contrast, regular tape measures were used to measure plots, though I have been informed that in some of the lowland areas, traditional methods were employed. However, informants here noted that a good number of plots were neither demarcated nor measured because of the disputes over them involving claims and counter-claims.

The final task for the LAC in each precinct is the recording of the personal details of landholders and their families. Each certificate should contain the names and addresses of the household head, his/her spouse, and siblings or other relations in the household, in addition to the physical and positional details of the land. While there are no specific rules on the matter, peasants have been told by local officials that relations whose names do not appear in the certificate will not have the right to inherit the land. These same details are recorded in the land registry, copies of which are kept in the *kebelle* and *woreda* office. The certificate also contains brief summaries of the rights and obligations of landholders and the conditions under which certificates may be withdrawn. In most cases it took about a year from the time the preparatory tasks were completed to the time the user certificates were finally distributed to individual holders. In contrast, landholders in Wollaita got their certificates one or two months after the end of the process.

It has been argued by some that the country's land titling and registration programme was a success in part because local authorities employed low cost techniques and familiar methods to complete the preparatory tasks (Deininger et al. 2007; World Bank 2005). But this is a misunderstanding of the whole point of the programme: title registration is meant to provide security and to minimise disputes, and this can only be possible if the programme is credible in the eyes of the beneficiaries concerned. The use of low cost traditional tools and techniques is not a problem in itself, but such techniques do not deliver accurate, consistent, and reliable results and are therefore liable to give rise in the end to disputes and even bitter conflicts. Moreover, the system that has been employed is a static rather than a dynamic one because it is not designed to be sustainable in the long run. This fundamental flaw will, in my opinion, seriously undermine its credibility among peasants. Sustainability means the capability by local authorities, particularly at the *kebelle* level, not only to physically maintain the land registry, but to update the information in it, as well as in the certificates in the hands of landholders. All records must be updated and kept current, as changes in land holdings, plot boundaries, and land transfers occur in the *kebelle*. This requires considerable capacity both in terms of investment in modern equipment and trained human resources, none of which was visible on the ground. Moreover, there are costs to be incurred to manage a sustainable record system, but the land administration authorities do not seem to have given sufficient attention to this matter.

Land rights and tenure security

Rights awareness

I shall discuss here the significance of the main findings from my field survey undertaken in the north of the country. The findings are based mainly on data gathered from 110 questionnaires administered on a randomly selected sample of certificate holders in Aba Sokotu and Gelsha, but I shall supplement this information with data from in-depth interviews with key peasant informants as well as with *kebelle* and *woreda* officials. The in-depth interviews add flesh to the bare bones of the questionnaires and give better insights about many of the issues of concern to us here. Readers are reminded of the point raised earlier in this study, namely that the peasants of Dessie Zuria have had the benefit of economic, social, and political interaction with the urban world and are therefore more aware than the average peasant.

As was noted earlier in this study, property rights will provide security that is robust when they are an integral part of other basic political and democratic rights enjoyed by citizens and when they can be defended through the instrumentality of these rights. In our case, the legal instruments having to do with property and basic rights consist of the constitutions (federal and *killil*) and the various land laws issued and currently in force. Rights awareness is an important element contributing to the robustness of security of tenure and is the basis for the empowerment of the poor. De Soto has very little to say on this subject and its significance.

One of the aims of our field investigation was to try to find out the extent to which peasants were aware of their rights under the law. Peasants in Dessie Zuria were asked if they were aware of the existence of the constitution and laws that defined basic political, human, and property rights and governed access to land and other property. The intent was not to test peasants' legal knowledge in the deeper sense of the term but to find out about legal literacy at the primary level. What we thought were simple questions in the survey, however, proved to be quite involved, since many peasants were not quite clear what a constitution actually was or that rights to land were also governed by specific land laws. Even after careful explanation, quite a number of respondents failed to understand the terms adequately. One of our key peasant informants, for instance, who has more formal education (fifth grade) than most peasants, listed five constitutions that he was aware of: the federal, *killil*, zonal, and *woreda* constitutions, and the constitutions of lower and higher courts. He obviously mistook 'constitution' for administrative rules or rules of procedure. Some of the peasant informants interviewed thought many peasants in their community had a good deal of legal awareness, while the others were of the opinion that this was not the case and that there was only limited awareness in the community. The former opinion is based on the fact that the land certificates contain a few statements setting out the benefits of the documents and the obligations holders have in respect of their land. These are by no means the full extent of rights to land contained in the relevant legal documents.

The findings from our survey provide a different picture. A little over 28 per cent of our sample had not heard about any of the country's constitutions, only twenty per cent knew about the existence of the Federal Constitution, and 34 per cent were aware of the *killil* constitution. On the other hand, nearly 32 per cent of our sample did not know of any laws governing rights to land, only twelve per cent were aware of the federal land law, and 28 per cent were aware of the *killil* land law. For all practical purposes, peasants' rights to land are governed by the *killil* law, and it is quite revealing that 72 per cent of our respondents were not aware of it. Table 3.1 gives a breakdown of the figures regarding peasant awareness of existing land laws. In Wollaita, on the other hand, all except one informant said they had no knowledge of the laws or constitutions or knew any specific rights provided in either document.

Women, who made up 30 per cent of our sample, were proportionally more ignorant of the law than men, but the margin of difference between the two, ten per cent, was not very wide, considering the fact that both communities were predominantly Muslim. Peasants were asked how they came to be aware of the law, and the majority stated that it was through local state officials, with a significant number pointing to friends and relatives as their source of information, and a lesser number to the mass media.

Given that there are no rights advocacy organisations in the rural areas, the task of raising rights awareness poses difficult problems. For reasons that I have noted above, this task cannot be left to the government if the goal is the empowerment of the peasantry. The NGOs based in the area – and there are over 30 of them in South Wollo as a whole – are engaged in service delivery and *limat* programmes and do not undertake advocacy work. They play no role either in the legislative effort or the certification process. Since the great majority of peasants here (as well as in Wollaita) are not literate, providing copies of the relevant laws to individual households would not only be too costly but would be counter-productive. Public officials at the *kebelle* level themselves did not have access to all the relevant legal documents, except for a few photocopies of the recent *killil* land law. They usually get to learn about new *killil* or federal policies and legislations through periodic training workshops and briefings at the *woreda* office or occasionally at the *killil* capital in Bahr Dar. When we arrived for our fieldwork in Dessie, a team from the Amhara *killil* land administration authority had just completed a briefing programme in Dessie for *kebelle* and *woreda* officials on the new *killil* land law. This kind of briefing is not common practice in all localities; the exception in Dessie Zuria *woreda* resulted from its special status, as noted above. Amhara is quite large, made up of 106 *woredas* and over 2900 *kebelles*, and to hold regular

Table 3.1   *Peasant awareness of land laws (Dessie Zuria)*

	Yes		No	
	No.	%	No	%
Federal law	13	11.8	97	88.2
Killil law	31	28.2	79	71.8
Federal & *Killil* laws	28	25.5	82	74.5

training sessions in all these localities and for all these officials would be a costly undertaking.

Peasants in both Dessie Zuria and Wollaita expressed a strong faith in the law as an instrument of security of property and of tenure. Nearly 94 per cent of respondents in our field survey believed that laws can provide a guarantee for rights to land. Moreover, many believed that knowledge of the law was as important as the law itself. Peasants with whom we held extended interviews in both locations were of the opinion that raising rights awareness and providing legal literacy would help to empower title holders, enabling them to defend their rights and to promote their interests. A number of the informants in Dessie Zuria thought it would be best to employ, for this purpose, the services of community organisations and religious leaders who have a good reputation among the people, since they would be less costly and more accessible to them.

Land disputes and dispute settlement

It is often argued that the three most important benefits of title registration are guarantee of ownership and security of tenure, reduction of land disputes, and improved access to credit from financial institutions (Marquardt 2006). The World Bank (2005) found that the immediate benefit of land certification in the country was the reduction of land cases in the *kebelle* courts, which are known as Social Courts. To what extent does the evidence we collected in our survey support these claims?

At one level, it does appear that land disputes and the burden on the Social Courts have been reduced. To the question about land disputes in our questionnaire, a great majority of respondents answered that there have been fewer land disputes in the community since the certificates were distributed. The chief judge of the Social Court in Aba Sokotu, who was interviewed for this study, stated that there had been fewer land cases brought before his court now than before certification. Almost all *woreda* and *kebelle* officials interviewed were of the opinion that land certification has succeeded in reducing disputes among farm households. The most frequently cited causes of disputes were conflicts over plot boundaries, inheritance, divorce, blocking access paths or transit corridors, planting certain tree species on boundary lines, and crop damage. The argument of those interviewed was that the land certificate clearly defines the boundaries of each holder, and there is thus documentary evidence to make going to court irrelevant or unwise. But as we noted earlier, the boundary markings that were employed were for the most part movable objects and not permanent ones, hence this has not ruled out boundary conflict. The second point is that many of the cases of conflict that were cited are not directly related to the records that appear in the certificates or land registry; they do not, in other words, carry documentary evidence.

A closer examination shows that the issue is quite complex, and there is ample cause for concern. To begin with, there are two kinds of land dispute that are relevant to our subject: disputes among peasants on the one hand, and disputes between peasants and the government on the other. In terms of incidence and court case load, the first form of dispute is by far the most pervasive. There are a number of options available to disputants. At the simplest level, they can come to a settlement through the intervention of close friends and relatives; however, the most common practice is to take the case to customary dispute settlement institutions, i.e. elders, religious leaders, etc. When asked where they would take their case first if there were land disputes, 80 per cent of respondents said they would first approach local elders and community leaders. As a second option, 94 per cent said they would take their case to the *kebelle* office, and as a third option, 67 per cent chose the local court. There is thus a strong tendency to avoid formal institutions in favour of customary ones. Aware of this preference for community institutions, decision-makers are now attempting to incorporate these institutions into the formal sector. The new *killil* land law now recognises customary dispute settlement mechanisms as first-line options for disputants.

However, as was noted above, there have been significant institutional changes that have accompanied land certification, one of which has been to give the land administration committees the additional responsibility of resolving land disputes. LAC members include local elders who are selected specifically for this purpose. Thus, at the grassroots level, there are now initiatives to combine the formal and the informal. The new procedure followed when parties to a land dispute bring their case to the *kebelle* is to send the case not to the Social Court but to the LACs which are established at the *gott* level. If the dispute is settled there, that ends the matter; if not, the committee transfers the case with its written decisions to the Social Court. This has reduced the case load of the local courts, but it does not necessarily mean that there are fewer disputes now than before. The chief judge referred to above noted that even now, land disputes constitute the largest number of cases in his court.

Our findings in Wollaita present a slightly different picture. Prior to certification, peasants sought the services of traditional elders to settle land disputes. At present, however, all informants said disputants take their case to the LACs that have been established in each sub-*kebelle*. If the dispute is not resolved here, the case is referred to the *kebelle* Social Court, and from here it may be taken to the *woreda* court. The evidence suggests that fewer people now rely on customary institutions to handle land disputes.

On the other hand, the information we gathered from the Dessie Zuria *woreda* court and police station in Dessie, the *woreda* capital, reveals a more troubling picture. The court is responsible for civil cases, while the police handle criminal cases. Cases are brought before the district court from all 31 *kebelles* directly by litigants or are referred, or sent on appeal, by the Social Courts. The chief officer of the district court, whom we interviewed in his office in Dessie, said he was very distressed by the high and growing number of cases coming before his court from the rural areas. He noted that in the great majority of instances these are cases in which land disputes play an important role in one form or another. The two most important land-related cases were marital disputes and inheritance (of land) disputes. In the last one and half years alone, that is in the period when land registration and titling were taking place in the district, the court heard nearly 1,250 such cases, which is much higher compared with a similar period in the past. He pointed out the increasing number of appeal cases brought to the court from the *kebelles*. Our investigation at the district police station tallied more or less with the information from the district court. The chief inspector of police, whom we interviewed, thought there was a rise in land cases brought to the attention of police. In the year 2005/2006, there were 1,153 criminal cases involving land disputes recorded at the station, and this, according to the chief inspector, was a high figure for one year. In the last six months of 2006 alone, land cases numbered 550. Thus, if we add up the case loads in the district police station and court, the number of cases in which land was at the centre of the dispute is very high for one district.

Both the court officer and the chief inspector pointed out that in cases originating from the rural areas, the line separating the criminal and the civil is a thin one. If you scratch a criminal case, they wanted to say, you will find a civil cause for it. Both officials were quite concerned by it, and they gave us several examples to illustrate the complicated nature of rural cases. For example: a case of assault involving two peasants is brought to the police station because it is a criminal offence. Upon investigation it turns out that the cause is a dispute over land. The court officer in fact believed that almost all rural cases, whether criminal or civil, are at bottom caused by land disputes.

Thus, the picture that emerges here is of a rural society rife with conflict and antagonism primarily on account of disputes over land which title registration has not allayed. These disputes and their prevalence are indicative of a deeper social malaise and confirm the widely held view that resource conflict is more common among disadvantaged populations than among the better-off. They reveal profound insecurities about basic livelihoods and property rights, insecurities which have been aggravated by growing rural poverty, population pressure, and scarcity of land, and limited opportunities for alternative sources of income. In these circumstances, one can speak of the structural embeddedness of land disputes and their pernicious effect on community relations. From time to time such disputes turn into violent conflict, taking on a religious, ethnic, or clan form, as is happening in some parts of rural Wollaita at present. There has been a spate of violence that has flared up between clan groups here in which lives have been lost and property damaged. The initial cause was minor disputes over land among individual peasants or neighbours.

The second type of conflict, i.e. between the peasant and the government, is of a different nature altogether. Peasant displeasure with the government may arise due to decisions that lead to the expropriation of peasant land, to the imposition of an unpopular cropping, land management or environmental regime, or forced labour or financial contributions for public schemes – all of which are not uncommon. The average peasant knows that there is no mechanism, legal or constitutional, for redress of grievances when the government is a party to the dispute. The government is too powerful to be challenged, and besides, all magistrates and judges are government employees, and there are few opportunities for a fair hearing. There is an old saying which reveals the state's unchallenged power in the minds of the poor: just as one cannot touch the sky, so one cannot take the 'king' to court (the king here means the state). We did ask all persons we interviewed whether they thought the government should be taken to court if peasants felt aggrieved by its decisions. Many did think the government should be taken to court, but upon closer scrutiny we realised that many of these people understood the government to be the public servants who hold government posts rather than the government as an institution. There have been a few cases in which government officials have been taken to court by peasants, but the disputes were between the two individuals rather than between a peasant and a government agency. In Wollaita, on the other hand, almost all informants thought the government could not be taken to court. As one informant put it: land is held by the government, and the government is also responsible for issuing the laws and appointing the judges to the courts, so what is the meaning of taking the government to court? The chief judge of the Social Court of one *kebelle* interviewed for this study agreed: he thought it was not possible to take the government to court.

Access to free legal services was a subject on which we had extended discussions with key informants, peasants, and public officials. In the survey, we asked respondents whether access to free legal services would help peasants defend their rights better, and 71 per cent answered in the affirmative, but 26 per cent thought it would not. The provision of free legal service to the poor was considered by all informants as a capital idea, but there were differences among them with regard to who should provide it and whether or not it would be accepted by the courts. Some thought the service would be acceptable by the courts if it was provided by the government, with a few suggesting that it should be provided only by the public sector. Some of the higher officials on the other hand thought there would be difficulties and that the courts would not be willing to accept it if such a service were provided by the voluntary sector. Some peasant informants, who did not have a positive view of the courts, and who considered them as corrupt and biased in favour of the privileged, thought legal services, especially legal representation on behalf of the poor by advocacy organisations, would be strongly resisted by the courts as well as local government bodies because it would be a challenge to their authority.

Land certificates and tenure security

As was noted above, peasants do not have rights of ownership over the land, they have only use rights. Land rights here, in other words, are rights of usufruct only. Land registration and certification merely confirm the right of use of the land for the households' livelihood, and the documents handed out to peasants are strictly speaking user certificates and not land certificates in the proper sense of the term.

While land registration has been well received by peasants in both our research sites in the north and south of the country, and there are changed attitudes regarding land renting and leasing as a result, a good deal of uncertainty and insecurity remains, and this becomes evident when one probes the matter a little deeper. Everyone is certain that they will receive compensation in the event they lose their land; however, not everyone is sure whether the compensation will be fair and commensurate. When land is expropriated by local authorities for public purposes or *limat* – and this is not infrequent – compensation is often paid in kind, i.e. the peasant receives land which is supposed to be of equal value to the land he/she has lost. Local authorities simply do not have the financial resources to be able to pay compensation in cash. However, there is scarcely any farm land to distribute in either of our research sites, hence peasants are offered land which is of poor quality and in some cases not really suitable for farming. Cash payments for compensation are offered only if land expropriation is undertaken at the request of a private investor, or if the land is needed for large-scale public projects such as roads, dams, or urban housing, etc.

Peasants are also not sure of future government intentions and plans: whether there will be new land redistributions or new infrastructure projects that may involve land alienation are questions that are on the minds of many. There is no tradition of consultation with rural communities when new initiatives are planned; on the contrary, the common practice under the present and previous governments has been for new programmes to be imposed from above, frequently without even local authorities concerned being informed or adequately prepared. Peasants are almost always the last to know, and they are informed only when implementation is to be undertaken. Almost all peasants in our two research locations said they heard about land registration when they were called to attend a general meeting to elect the committee that was to be responsible for implementing it. Administrative decentralisation, briefly noted above, has given local authorities a little more freedom to act in terms of programme management and implementation, budget preparation, and use; nevertheless, it has not done away with top-down decision-making, because lower-level officials are still dependent on higher authorities for development and other programme initiatives as well as financial resources.

There is another issue that is important but is often ignored, namely demographic growth and resource scarcity. The subject of population pressure as a factor in aggravating insecurity of rights to land, with or without formalisation, has not been given sufficient attention in the current debate. Unrelenting population growth and increasing scarcity of land, which are really two sides of the same coin, is a serious concern to many peasants in the country, but it is an immediate and pressing danger in Wollaita, in particular where the severity of the demographic stress is approaching catastrophic levels. Here, household plots are shrinking in size, the fertility of the soil is declining steadily, and farm incomes are getting smaller – but at the same time there are more mouths to feed every year (Bush 2002; Eyasu Elias 2002). Hunger is widespread, and starvation is a constant danger but has been averted thanks to timely interventions by the government and the voluntary sector (in the form of food aid and safety net schemes). The threat of the loss or erosion of rights to land hangs over most peasants in Wollaita on account of poverty made worse by micro-holdings and decreasing household income. This fear has not been mitigated in any significant way by land certification. Distress sales of agricultural produce, including the harvest, are widespread; similarly, distress sales of land, which are carried out surreptitiously, are known to take place occasionally. Distress land transactions, not uncommon in the past, still persist, where the poor are driven to give up a good deal of their rights to the land for a small return. There are strong pressures on holders with small plots to transfer their land to others either temporarily or for longer periods. The size of the landless population is higher here than in many other places, and this is a cause of apprehension and insecurity for landholders, because they fear that the government will impose land redistribution on them to accommodate the landless.

Partly as a result of the demographic danger, peasants in Wollaita are less enthusiastic about land certification than those in Dessie Zuria. Asked about the most pressing problems in their community, Wollaita peasants cited population pressure and land shortage on the one hand, and soil fertility decline on the other as being paramount. While all are in favour of title registration, some are sceptical about its long-term benefits in the light of the demographic stress and the increasing vulnerability of households. A few of our informants here were apprehensive that the benefits of the certificates would soon be eroded by demographic pressure. The problem is compounded by customary inheritance rules. In most parts of Wollaita, partible, pre-mortem inheritance is the rule: i.e. household heads divide up their land equally and distribute it to male siblings during their own lifetime (and not after their death). This means a family may divide its possessions to four or more male heirs and end up landless in the process. In this situation, land certificates are of little value.

We asked respondents in our survey in Dessie Zuria whether they thought future land redistribution was likely now that they had received their certificates and the registration programme had been completed. The answers we received were quite revealing of their apprehensions: more than 44 per cent thought redistribution was likely, while 29 per cent were of the opposite mind. The details are given in Table 3.2 below. It could be argued that those who said they were not sure were not expressing full confidence, and if we add this group to those who said redistribution is likely, we find a very high degree of uncertainty among peasants in the survey. On the other hand, many *kebelle* and *woreda* officials believed land redistribution was unlikely, though a significant minority, including higher officials, thought that redistribution could take place in the future if there were good grounds for it. In Wollaita, despite title registration, nearly half of our informants thought the government would take away their land if it wanted to.

Table 3.2 *Peasant views on future land redistribution (Dessie Zuria)*

Views	Number	Percentage
Not Applicable	1	0.9
Redistribution likely	49	44.5
Redistribution unlikely	32	29.1
Do not know/Not sure	28	25.5
Total	**110**	**100.0**

Land redistribution did in fact take place along with land certification in Gelsha *kebelle*, one of our survey sites. There was no legal basis for it, nor was it an integral part of title registration; on the contrary, it was undertaken at the discretion of local officials. The *kebelle* authorities here decided that no household should possess land that was more than sufficient for its subsistence, which was determined by adopting a minimum holding size of 0.49 ha. A household's land size was based on this minimum, with allowances made for the number of registered members in it, and any land in excess was taken away and distributed to the needy. The size of the land of each household was measured using the crude methods described earlier. While we do not have exact figures, it was clear that a good number of households were dispossessed. There were also land relocations: households said to have large holdings and in distant locations were offered land nearer to their homes in exchange for giving up their distant plots. On occasions, however, the land offered in exchange was of poorer quality. One of our peasant informants in Gelsha told us that he had two ha of land before registration, but the authorities took away half of it and gave him one hectare of land near his homestead. He was disappointed but did not complain and thanked his stars because the land he was offered was of good quality. He said others were not as fortunate.

Another important question that was included in our survey had to do with the likelihood of land expropriations. We asked respondents if they thought their land would or would not be taken away from them. Table 3.3 shows the answers we received. Half of our respondents were of the opinion that their land may be taken away from them in the future, even with the certificates, but 42 per cent were more confident this would not happen. There have been frequent instances when peasants had given up their land on the authority of local officials, accepting the decisions without much protest. On a few occasions, however, such decisions have been contested by peasants. The following case is interesting because it combines many issues together: land expropriation, improper use of authority, and gender discrimination.

The case involves a peasant woman and an official of the land administration unit in Aba Sokotu *kebelle* whom we shall call TA. TA ear-

Table 3.3 *Peasant views on whether land will be taken away (Dessie Zuria)*

Views	Number	Percentage
Not applicable	1	0.9
Likely to be taken	55	50.0
Unlikely	46	41.8
Do not know/Not sure	8	7.3
Total	**110**	**100.0**

lier gave up his land because the authorities said it was needed for the
school being built in the *kebelle*. In return, he was offered land which
was taken away from a peasant woman who was declared to be in possession of more land than she needed for her subsistence. Her plot
was chosen for expropriation, according to the officials, not only because she was a large holder but because it was as good as the land TA
had given up. This reallocation took place after land certification,
which meant the authorities took back the woman's certificate and
gave her another one. The woman formally complained to the *kebelle*
office which ruled that TA was justly compensated, and she had no
case to pursue. The woman then took the case to the district court in
Dessie. At the time of our field work, the case was pending in the
court, and TA was called on one occasion to give evidence. We were unable to interview the woman because she was not available, but we
were given to understand that she would appeal to a higher court in
the event the district court's decision was unfavourable to her.

This was an unusual case for several reasons. There is a great deal
of discrimination against women in the rural areas. There were no women in any of the important committees or offices in the *kebelle* in
either Dessie Zuria (except one) or in Wollaita. It is not infrequent for
women household heads to lose part of their land on the grounds that
they cannot manage it adequately; women are not supposed to plough
the land, or do any of the more strenuous physical work. In most
cases, women accept decisions that are discriminatory because of
strong cultural pressures. The population in Dessie Zuria is predominantly Muslim, and women are not expected to shoulder public roles
or engage in argument with men in public. In practice, however, women are quite active and often participate in public gatherings. The
head of the district Women's Association based in Dessie interviewed
for this study bitterly complained about the treatment of rural women
by both local officials and the courts. She said women-headed households were unfairly treated during land reallocations, and the courts
are known to be partial to men in cases involving divorce and property
settlement. What makes this case exceptional is that in the first place it
is only rarely that peasants contest the decision of local officials. The
common practice is to accept government decisions with at best some
verbal complaints and show of disappointment. In the second place,
the persistence of the woman to see the case through the courts, despite the odds against her and the costs involved, makes it worthy of
note.

Finally, a word on tenure security. I have argued elsewhere that real
and full security of tenure is affirmed when: a) the landholder has a
right to the land on a continuous basis for good or for long enough to
have an incentive to improve or invest on it; b) the landholder feels as-

sured that his/her rights are not arbitrarily overridden by others, including the state; c) the holder has the freedom to use, dispose of, or transfer the land free from interference by others, including the state (Dessalegn Rahmato 2004:35). Measured in these terms, land certification has failed to assure peasants the robust security for which they have been searching for generations.

Conclusion

What I have attempted to argue in the preceding pages is that land rights go beyond the legal construct and extend into the political sphere and the sphere of governance. The formalisation of land rights, in the form of registration and title, as in our case, cannot by itself guarantee robust security, especially for the poor who are severely disadvantaged in economic, social and political terms, and who do not have visibility, voice, or negotiating power. The relationship between the state, which is responsible for formalisation, and the poor is a relationship of hegemony and subordination, and this relationship will have to change to enable the poor to secure and defend rights to property. The first step in this direction is the empowerment of the poor through their own effort and, as has been shown in some Asian and Latin American countries, the effort of social movements and advocacy organisations.

Empowerment cannot come about without rights awareness: this is not just knowledge about the law having to do with land and other property but also about political-juridical rights and ways to make use of them to ensure poor people's interests. Rights awareness must help the poor to enhance their visibility and voice: it must enable them to speak for themselves, to contest unfavourable decisions and to defend their rights. Such awareness can be promoted not by government agencies but by the poor themselves and by independent third parties. The enhancement of rights awareness cannot be left to the government because, as we have argued above, that would in the end be counter-productive.[11]

What is missing in de Soto and the conventional property law debate is the connection between rights on the one hand and the empowerment of the poor on the other. Without the latter, legalisation will be a remedy without effect because it will not address the special circumstances of the poor; if secure property rights are to be guaranteed, legalisation must go hand in hand with empowerment. In Ethiopia, as we have seen, the subordination of the peasant to state authority is manifest in many forms and has been an enduring element of the relationship between the one and the other; it was in this context that land certification was undertaken. Formalisation has not questioned the basis of the relationship but has assumed it to be normal and justified, hence its failure to guarantee security of tenure.

Moreover, there is no sign that the empowerment of the rural poor is underway or is even a possibility in the near future in the communities we studied; the same may be said of peasant communities in other parts of the country. As I showed earlier, the level of rights awareness, even of rudimentary legal literacy, is very low. Since peasants have barely any legal representation and are hardly capable of negotiating or lobbying, they continue to be voiceless and excluded from the decision-making process. In these circumstances, land certification can only be of limited benefit, and indeed, as some of the general literature on land titling indicates, it may even be counter-productive in the long run (see Dessalegn Rahmato 2006a).

Notes

1   The meaning of local administrative terms is given in the appendix at the end.
2   For a review of works on land certification and donor attitudes, see Dessalegn Rahmato 2006a.
3   See Nyamu-Musembi 2006 for the range of De Soto criticisms. For the legal pluralism argument in the African context, see articles and references in Mwangi 2006.
4   See the classic study of Moore (1966) for the historical perspective; Aston and Philpin (1985) for the debate.
5   See Franco 2005 for the Philippines; the experience of Land Alliances in supporting the rural poor in some African countries appears in Mwangi 2006; on legal advocacy groups in Africa and Asia, see Golub 2003, Manning 1999.
6   De Soto is joint chairman of the Commission; visit http://legalempowerment.org. undp for publications.
7   For comparison with earlier elections see Dessalegn Rahmato and Meheret Ayenew 2004; for the 2005 elections see Dessalegn Rahmato and Meheret Ayenew 2006. For figures from NEB, visit www.electionsethiopia.org. I should note that the ruling party is made up of a coalition of ethnic parties in power in each of the *killils*.
8   Several western governments and a number of international human rights groups condemned the government for the use of excessive force in suppressing the protests. An inquiry committee set up by the government to investigate the events concluded that 196 people were shot and killed by the security forces.
9   The documents are known here as holders' books because they look like bank books, but we shall refer to them as certificates for convenience.
10 See Solomom Bekure et al. 2006 for articles about experiences in other parts of the country.
11 USAID in Ethiopia is trying to support a program of public information and awareness, the aim being to inform landholders 'of their land use rights and obligations'. It appears the program will rely on state agencies to achieve its end (USAID 2006b).

Appendix

Administrative terms

Killil: Autonomous administrative unit, often inhabited by one eth-
             nic group, making up the country's federal system. *Killils* (fre-
             quently rendered as Regions or Regional States in official
             documents) are large units: the Amhara *killil*, in which our
             main study was undertaken, has a population of 18.6 million.

Zone: Unit within *killil* equivalent to a province; the *woreda* where
             we conducted our main field work is found in South Wollo
             zone which has eighteen *woredas*, and the zonal and *woreda*
             capital is the town of Dessie.

Woreda: Unit within zone, comparable to a district. The *woreda* is
             governed by an elected Council and manages its own budget
             and development programmes. Our research *woreda* is called
             Dessie Zuria which has 31 *kebelles* within it.

Kebelle: Unit within *woreda*, comparable to a sub-district. The average
             kebelle in our study *woreda* contains 900 to 1000 households.
             The *kebelle* is governed by an elected Council. (See text for
             sub-divisions of the *kebelle*.) The two *kebelles* where we
             conducted fieldwork are Aba Sokotu (15 km from Dessie) and
             Gelsha (30 km from Dessie).

4 Securing land rights in Ghana

Kojo Sebastian Amanor

Introduction

Land in Ghana has not been nationalised, and the national constitution recognises the rights of customary authorities in land administration. Nevertheless, the notion of customary authority has been redefined by the state in many instances since the colonial period, and what constitutes the customary system and customary chiefs is really a modern arrangement that arises from an alliance between state and 'traditional authorities', particularly since in some areas chieftaincy was created in the colonial period.

There are three types of land in Ghana, which are classified as customary, state, and vested. Customary land comes under the authority of paramount chiefs, sub-chiefs, earth priests, and clan or extended family heads, depending upon the relative power of these different sections, their relationship with the state, and the ways in which they have been historically incorporated into district administration since the colonial period. Customary systems of tenure are often highly contested, with different authorities claiming to be the original and authentic 'traditional authority'. Customary land has also been subject to increasing interference from government agencies, which have assumed responsibility for the allocation of timber concessions and for the collection of revenues and rents, such as rents from migrant farmers and timber revenues. The collected revenues are shared between central government agencies, local government, and customary authorities.[1] In effect, customary land becomes subject to revenue-sharing arrangements and joint management between state and customary authorities. Thus, the customary system really consists of a hybrid system of accommodation between customary authorities and state institutions.

State lands consist of lands that have been acquired by the state for the purposes of national development. This includes land acquired for public works, national development projects, state economic enterprises, and concessions allocated by government to the corporate sector. The state has acquired land through the creation of a legal framework of eminent domain, which enables the state to acquire land compulsorily for the national interest, which extinguishes the previous interests in land subject to payment of compensation. Vested lands are subject to dual ownership in which the land is vested in the president in trust for the chiefly stools or for the landholding communities in areas where land does not come under the authority of chiefs. The government neither pays compensation for the land nor expropriates the land to other parties, but assumes responsibility for its management and for the collection of revenues. A portion of the collected revenues is retained by government, and a portion is disbursed to the chiefs or landowners and local government, according to a revenue-sharing formula.[2]

There has been considerable abuse of the notion of public or national interest since the 1960s, with the state using notions of eminent domain to extract rents for bureaucratic and political elites, and to expropriate land for the wealthy and for allies of the political regime. Chiefs have also abused the notions of their customary custodianship on land to promote narrow and selfish interests and accumulate wealth. They have expropriated existing land users without providing them with compensation or alternative land. They often engage in multiple sales of the same land to different parties, and they fail to comply with contracts to which they originally agreed. They redefine customary norms to satisfy their whims and self-interest with impunity (Abudulai 2002; Alden Wily 2003; Amanor 1999; Boni 2005; Ubink 2006). This has resulted in highly inefficient land markets, which lack transparency and are characterised by many social injustices.

In recent years, there have been major attempts to introduce administrative land reforms and to promote the regularisation and harmonisation of land management within the state and customary sectors. The aims of the reforms are to create a more comprehensive land documentation system which links the formal and customary systems, and creates a more transparent and efficient system of land administration. Reform within the land management sector has also been influenced by economic liberalisation, the cutting back of the state, the divestiture of state enterprises, and the promotion of free markets and private investment. This has resulted in attempts to devolve land administration to the customary authorities. However, this strengthening of the customary occurs in the context of social upheaval and rapidly changing social and economic relations. It occurs in a period of increasing commoditisation of land and growing demand for land among corporate sectors and the wealthy. It is associated with the increasing shortage of land and landlessness in rural and peri-urban areas, increasing migration to urban areas, and a serious problem of homelessness in urban areas. In attempting to make sense of the changing framework of land administration, this chapter examines land tenure policy within a historical context. It locates the changing framework of land policies and policy instruments within the broader context of changing paradigms of economic and social development.

In Ghana, three different phases in the land question can be identified that have occurred since the Gold Coast became incorporated into the modern world economy as a colony with a modern administrative framework:

1. The early colonial phase, in which there was minimal state intervention in economic production, from the early twentieth century to the 1940s. Rural administration was carried out through Indirect Rule and the establishment of Native Authorities;
2. The late colonial phase and early postcolonial phase, in which the state intervened in economic activities and development planning and established state economic enterprises, from the late 1940s to 1983;
3. The neoliberal phase characterised by economic liberalisation and the rolling back of state interventions in the economy and social welfare provisioning, which started with the introduction of structural adjustment in the early 1980s.

This chapter traces the framework of land management as it evolved in different epochs, contextualising the changing frameworks for land administration in the changing paradigms of economic development policies. It also examines the framework for the management of land and natural resources within different economic sectors, including agriculture, forestry, mining, and real estate, showing how the changing relationships between the state, private capital, and international markets and finance impact on land administration and the concept of land tenure and land reform. After a general introduction to different tenure and administrative regimes in Ghana, this chapter examines the impact of the colonial administration on land tenure, in the context of indirect rule. During the 1940s a major transformation in agricultural policy occurred in the context of state-led development which had major ramifications on land tenure and the role of the state in land management. The following section traces the relationship between land policy and agricultural development from the 1940s through the early independence period, and to the era of structural adjustment and the introduction of neoliberal policies. This is followed by an analysis of land relations within the forestry and mining sectors, and within urban and peri-urban real estate. The changing relationships of various groups to land are examined in these various sectors, documenting the impact of policies on land users, land purchasers, developers and investors, and the control of the state and traditional authorities over the alienation, appropriation, regulation, and sale of land. The final section examines recent land administrative reform initiatives and their impact on security in the use of land and security in the purchase of land and creation of land markets.

The regional divide: North and south

Ghana can be divided into two distinct areas: the south and the north. The south was incorporated into the colonial economy as a primary commodity-producing area of cocoa, gold and timber, and the north as a labour reserve for the export economy of the south. In the south, under colonial rule, land ownership was retained by customary chiefs under a system of Indirect Rule. In contrast, in the north, the Lands and Native Rights (Northern Territories) Ordinance of 1931 placed the management of land in the post of Governor to administer on behalf of the people in accordance with their customs. The north was largely integrated into British colonial rule as a labour reserve for the south, chiefs being appointed firstly to recruit forced labour and then during the 1920s to impose taxes on men, which forced them to migrate to the south to earn wages to meet tax obligations. Minimal investments were made in the development of the north, and controls over the emergence of land markets prevented wealthy investors from the south acquiring large tracts of land for agricultural purposes (Benning 1996). Thus, the development of the north was hindered until after independence. It continues to be less developed than the south.

In 1979 the land in northern Ghana was eventually returned to customary custodians as a result of a sustained campaign of northern elites and chiefs, and a unitary land administration system was created for the whole country. The 1979 Constitution established that land in Northern Ghana was no longer public land and was to be vested in the original owners of the land (Danaa 1996). This has not been easy to implement since notions of customary rights have often been contested in the north. In many parts of the north, the colonial government created and invented chiefs and their administrative boundaries, particularly in those societies that did not have unitary paramount chiefs, where land originally came under the authority of ritual earth priests. With the recognition of customary rights of ownership, land in the north has often been transferred to invented chieftaincies, which never controlled land before the colonial administration, rather than to earth priests who maintained ritual control over land. Control over land has become increasingly contested between chiefs and earth priests, but also among chiefs at different levels of the (invented) hierarchy (Benning 1996; Lund 2006).

Because of the different histories of incorporation of the north and south into the colonial economy, land in the south is more commodified. Land has been widely sold in the south since the early nineteenth century. Land markets have been constrained and restricted in the north, although there is some evidence that land transactions did occur before colonial rule was consolidated, particularly during periods of famine when the poor sold plots for cowries to purchase food (Benning 1996).

By the 1970s, the economy of the north began to be transformed from a labour reserve to a food production area. Government invested in large rice and vegetable irrigation projects, and many aspiring commercial farmers from the south invested in developing rice. However, commercial food crop farming has had mixed success in the north, and by the early 1980s many of the commercial rice estates collapsed (Konings 1986). Cocoa continues to be the main crop produced in the south, although there is increasing diversification into other crops for urban food markets and export.

Land and colonial rule

Export crop production began in the southeastern Gold Coast in the early nineteenth century, when the Krobo and Akuapem area began producing palm oil for exports. The rapid expansion of oil palm cultivation led to the development of a moving land frontier in which farmers began purchasing virgin land from neighbouring peoples and chiefs (Amanor 1994). An institutional framework developed for the sale of land (Hill 1963). By the late nineteenth century, land sales intensified as farmers in the southeast replaced oil palm with cocoa and moved into the moist forests of southern Akyem. The town chiefs in Akyem alienated considerable areas of land to these migrant farmers, a movement which has been well documented by Polly Hill (1963).

Considerable investment in gold concessions occurred in the gold boom of the 1870s and 1880s on the Gold Coast (Dumett 1998; Howard 1978; Kimble 1963). The scramble for gold assumed geopolitical dimensions. Fear that Asante would sign a treaty with France for the exploitation of gold led to the British occupation of Kumasi, the capital of the Ashanti Empire, in 1895, and the annexation of the Gold Coast as a British colony. One of the early concerns of British colonial rule was to bring land under the control of the colonial government by vesting all 'waste land' or unoccupied land in the Crown. However, control of land in the south by the colonial state was eventually rejected for a policy based on Indirect Rule, which vested the allodial title to land in paramount authorities organised in Native Authorities.[3] In this framework only paramount rulers could transact land with outsiders and foreign investors. This effectively constrained the development of free land markets and speculation in land by preventing land users (the holders of 'usufruct') and other groups from selling land.

British colonial policy claimed to support the retention of customary values against the onslaught of modernity. However, the customary values retained were often inventions of tradition that suited the objectives of colonial rule (Ranger 1993). The history of most African societies in the nineteenth century was characterised by rapid transformation, conflicts and social turmoil, rather than the stable traditions depicted by colonial rule. Chiefs often exploited the constructs of stable homogeneous traditions and customs to further their own interests and build their power base. This was often contested under Indirect Rule, by groups who felt their rights violated by chiefs. Dissension was expressed in numerous petitions to the colonial authority, demonstrations, violent conflicts, the 'destoolment' (dethronement) of chiefs, and legal litigation, which were all the hallmark of life under British colonial rule.

The concept of custom was often manipulated by chiefs to further their own narrow interests (Rathbone 1993, 1996). As long as this furthered the objectives of colonial rule, this was tolerated by the colonial authority. In many instances, the customary was associated with privilege for the rural political elite and a corresponding denial of human rights for the majority of rural people through the imposition of coercion by the chiefs. Rural dwellers were subject to forced labour for public works and the extraction of numerous revenues. Chiefs became responsible for appropriating land for public works, forest reserves, mining and timber concessions, and allocating land to farmers for export crop production.

The new economic interests that chiefs acquired in land assured that there was a conversion of land to new values and land uses. As Field (1948:7) commented:

> The new income from mines and land sales means that the land, originally valueless to the *oman* [local state] and quite independent of it, has become *linked* to the *oman*. The *oman* does not control or own it, but has acquired a very acute interest (in the non legal sense) in it.

While chiefs had powers to sell land and negotiate concessions, they could only transact land and natural resources with outsiders. Indigenes had rights to use land freely in the areas in which they belonged. Lands that they developed were usually converted into lineage lands and claimed by their descendants. Farmlands usually came under the administration of the extended lineages that had developed the land rather than under chiefs. Thus, chiefs could only get revenues by transacting land with people from outside the locality and by transacting lands which were not already occupied by farming people. They could only gain revenues from land that lay beyond those occupied by rural communities for residential and farming purposes (Boni 2005). Thus, the notion arose that lands beyond those used by farming communities belonged to the stool, which had the right to sell them.

The development of cocoa farming was accompanied by a rapid scramble for land in which chiefs attempted to sell as much undeveloped forestland as possible to migrants before local farmers could convert it into farm. During the 1920s and 1930s, colonial policies of creating labour reserves in northern Ghana and in the neighbouring Sahelian countries resulted in a large influx of migrant labour into the forest. In addition to selling land to migrant farmers, the chiefs could also allocate land to migrant labourers or sharecroppers, who were responsible for delivering a portion of the plantations they created or a portion of the harvest they reaped to the chiefly stool.

Between the 1920s and 1950s most of the land within the high forest zone was converted into cocoa plantation, as a process of rapid accumulation of land assets for cocoa farming took place. Much of this land was converted into cocoa plantations by migrant capitalist farmers and migrant labourers (Hill 1956, 1963). By the 1940s, the dominant population within the rural areas of the forest consisted of migrants. However, this was not recognised within the framework of Indirect Rule, which conceived of rural areas as consisting of homogenous tribes with a common custom and tribunals that tried cases according to the local tribal customs (Macmillan 1946).

As a larger influx of migrant farmers and labourers entered the cocoa districts, land became increasingly scarce in relation to labour. The prices of land and the tenure arrangements were increasingly modified in favour of the landlords. Boni (2005) shows how the conditions of land ownership became transformed in the Sefwi Wiawso area of the Western Region. Originally, before the development of cocoa farming, land had a low commodity value, and migrants gained land freely. In the early years of the development of cocoa in the Western Region, chiefs sought to encourage migrants to develop cocoa and released land to them on highly favourable terms. As the cocoa industry began to expand, land was transacted through outright sales, in which migrants purchased freehold. As land became scarcer, these were replaced by land leases and sharecropping arrangements in which in addition to making payments of money to chiefs for land, migrants had to provide the chiefs with a proportion of the crop or a proportion of the cocoa plantation they created. The payments, which the farmers originally understood they had made for the land, were later reinterpreted by chiefs as customary prestations to request the granting of land. Boni (2005) shows how these customary payments changed over time, reflecting the growing value of land. Chiefs developed and created new 'customary' tenure arrangements, clauses and conditions, and they were often made to apply retrospectively to all previous agreements. Migrant farmers increasingly experienced deteriorating conditions and terms under which they held rights to land. This often led to increasing friction between chiefs and migrants as migrants attempted to resist changes in their contracts.

The alienation of land to migrants also created land shortage for local youth, particularly among poorer families, who no longer had the option to clear unclaimed forestland, since chiefs had alienated all these lands to migrants. This resulted in increasing frictions between local youth and the chiefs and between local youth and migrants, since the youth perceived the migrants as having occupied their land to their detriment. In some instances, local youth organised against their chiefs to destool them for abusing their privileges. However, the colonial authority would often mobilise the police to defend chiefs against youth who were portrayed as troublemakers (Rathbone 1993). By the late 1940s and 1950s discontent with the system of Indirect Rule had spread and became manifest in the riots and lootings of 1948. During the 1950s, many chiefs were 'destooled' by youth and commoners (Amamoo 1958). A commission of enquiry into the riots of 1948 found considerable discontent among commoners and 'young men' with the system of Native Authorities and chiefs. The Watson Commission made recommendations for replacement of the native authority system by democratically elected local councils. However, the introduction of a system of elected local government did not completely overhaul the influences of the chieftaincy institutions, and chiefs were allowed to appoint one-third of the members of local councils. Since then, local government in Ghana has been characterised by arrangements in which one-third of the councillors are appointed by chiefs, central government, or an alliance of the two. This is justified in terms of allowing people with expertise and competence to be appointed to local government but has tended to hinder downward accountability and ensures that political elites and central government dominate local government.

Post-war agricultural restructuring and state-led development

During the 1940s, laissez-faire policies of minimum government interventions in the economy were replaced by a new framework rooted in state intervention in the economy to promote development. The state began to take an active role in rural development and agricultural development. In post-war policy circles, it was argued that trusteeship under Native Administration had failed to produce the impetus for agricultural development (Hailey 1943). Food production had stagnated, and food imports had increased to meet the needs of the rapidly expanding urban population. Oil palm production was a frequently cited example of the inadequacies of policy. Oil palm production had originated in West Africa, which had been the major export palm oil-producing centre in the nineteenth century. It had been displaced by modern plantation production in Southeast Asia in the twentieth century, and now could not even meet domestic oil demands. It was argued that agricultural development required large investments from the state. Left to the private sector this investment was unlikely to occur.

During the 1950s, the colonial government began to introduce large-scale agricultural development schemes. These schemes were based upon developing modern smallholder agriculture, new infrastructure, and mechanised agriculture. These new developments were articulated within a framework of community development, in which the whole community was mobilised to participate in local development projects through mass education, the forerunner of community participation. The early attempts of the colonial government to establish large agricultural development schemes, such as the Gonja Development Project, were largely a failure (Konings 1986). Nevertheless, this created the legacy for agricultural development projects, which was taken forward in the 1960s and 1970s in state irrigation and other schemes.

Three distinct mechanised agricultural sectors were created: state farms; private estate agriculture provided with loans and subsidised inputs by government; and large-scale development and irrigation schemes, which incorporated small farmers on a contractual basis. These initiatives were based on promoting large-scale estate agriculture and required the expropriation of considerable areas of land. To achieve this, the state needed to transform its relationship with chiefs, as had been developed under Indirect Rule. It now established an eminent domain, through which it controlled the allocation of land to productive sectors and development projects in accordance with a framework of national planning. To be able to regulate production on the large-scale rural development projects of this period, the state needed to own these schemes, and regulate production and marketing. However, the state did not nationalise the land and remove it from the administration of chiefs. It sought the compliance of chiefs in this process of expropriation. It recognised the allodial powers of chiefs and gained their collaboration in expropriating land for national development. In return, the rights of chiefs to a compensation payment for the expropriated land were recognised. In contrast, farmers were only compensated for the

crops on the land, unless they had registered title to the land. This caveat enabled expropriation to be carried out without negotiation with
the individual farmers, who were only recognised as owning crops
rather than land. Negotiation for expropriation in the national interest
was carried out between the state and chiefs. The economic benefits
that chiefs could gain from expropriation, in the form of compensation
and concession fees once the land had been transferred to new economic enterprises, ensured their support for expropriation. Chiefs
would collaborate with government in finding suitable areas for expropriation, particularly since they were unable to gain revenues from local communities who held rights to occupy land freely. Thus, expropriation of peasant farmers through eminent domain became a device
used by the state in collaboration with the chiefs to further their mutual interests.

This resulted in a new alliance between the state and chiefs, in
which the chiefs facilitated the expropriation of land for development
projects and saw that their 'subjects' complied with the directives of
state and parastatal development projects. Konings (1986) documents
many instances of chiefs using coercive powers to ensure the compliance of their subjects in state projects. He claims that the authority of
the chiefs on irrigation projects in northern Ghana in the 1980s had
been so well consolidated by the state that none of their directives
could be challenged by the peasantry. The chiefs had at their command
an array of 'traditional' sanctions, which were supported by the state,
and this made it dangerous for farmers to question their authority.
Konings narrates instances of farmers who were evicted from their villages by the chiefs for daring to question their decisions. Similar developments occurred in modern oil palm estates that were created in the
1970s. The Ghana Oil Palm Development Project (GOPDC) was created on land that was expropriated with the agreement of chiefs: 7,000
families farming on 9,000 hectares of land were expropriated (Amanor
1999; Gyasi 1992).

While some land was often redistributed to farmers on these agricultural projects after the creation of new infrastructures, this redistribution was often highly skewed, favouring the wealthy, commercial farmers, and men over women. In the Weija Irrigation Project, irrigated
land was redistributed to male household heads, with the assumption
that women would help their husbands in farming (Botchway 1993).
The men were obliged to sell their produce to the project parastatal
marketing company. However, prior to the creation of the irrigation
project, women had farmed independently. They also marketed their
husbands' crops from which they derived significant incomes. The
creation of the irrigation project deprived them of land and of income,
since the project monopolised the marketing of irrigated crops. Mar-

ginalised from the project, women refused to work on their husbands' irrigated plots and focused on farming beyond the perimeter of the irrigation project. Konings (1986) describes how irrigation projects in northern Ghana deprived women of land. Women were deliberately recreated as cheap farm labour which large-estate rice farmers exploited.

During the 1970s, the state increasingly used the pejorative of eminent domain to expropriate land for commercial farmers and bureaucrats, often with close links to the political administration. Much of the land in irrigation projects was allocated to aspiring commercial farmers with close links to the political administration, including military officers and bureaucrats, rather than to members of the community. Konings (1986) also describes how, independently of the state, chiefs would expropriate local farmers and sell off land to commercial farmers. They often mimicked the rhetoric of the state, claiming to reallocate the land in the 'national interest' or the interest of 'development'.

Institutional framework for land administration in the postcolonial period

The new developments in agriculture during the post-war and early independence period were reflected in institutional and legislative reforms. The first significant legislation was the 1952 State Councils Ordinance, which regulated the sale of land by chiefs by requiring this to be conducted with the consent of State Councils. State Councils were district councils constituted by representation of all the chiefs within the district, with the Paramount Chief or Head Chief as the President of the Council. This represented the first stages of reform of the Native Authority system, which introduced checks on the powers of paramount chiefs. Without the consent of the State Council, all transactions in land by chiefs were invalid.

In 1952, elected local government was introduced, and the Municipal Councils Ordinance was enacted. The management of stool lands was vested in the local councils who were responsible for collecting the revenues from stool land and depositing them with the Accountant General, who divided them between the local council and the stools according to a sharing agreement worked out between the stools and the local council. In the event of failure to agree upon the distribution of revenues, the matter was to be referred to the Minister of Land for resolution. The Municipal Councils Ordinance did not affect the ownership of stool land, which remained under the jurisdiction of the chiefs. However, transfer of stool land to other owners required the approval of the local councils. Land purchasers needed to approach both the local councils and the State Council to get transactions recognised. While local councils became responsible for the management of stool lands, there was no provision made for systematically recording land transactions and registering title at the district level.

Subsequent development of land legislation emerged in the context of party political conflicts. The Convention People's Party (CPP) won the first general election in the newly independent republic of Ghana. However, several prominent paramount chiefs supported the main opposition Union Party (UP). This included the Asantehene, Prempeh II, and the Okyenhene of Akim Abuakwa, Ofori Atta II. The CPP accused these chiefs of misappropriating stool revenues and using them to fund the UP party, rather than using them for the benefit of the communities in which their stool lands were vested. In 1958, the Ashanti Stool Lands Act and the Akim Abuakwa (Stool Revenue) Act were introduced, which placed the land of these stools in the hands of the President to manage on behalf of the stools and the communities. These acts effectively established the state as the trustee of the lands of these two stools, and central government became the administrator of revenues accruing from the stool lands. The acts also established a sharing arrangement for the revenues from the stools, which were to be disbursed between the central government, the local district authorities, and the stool. In 1960, the Stool Lands Act extended this arrangement to all customary stool lands in the country, which vested the administration of land in the president as a trustee of the public interest. This not only curtailed the power of the chiefs over land, but also led to the replacement of the newly created framework for decentralised land management within local districts with centralised state administration of land.

The Administration of Stool Land Act 1962 made the collection of stool land revenue the responsibility of the state and made the state responsible for overseeing and regulating transactions in stool land. The act empowered the state to authorise occupation and use of stool land for public interest, and to determine the amount of compensation for land and the value derived from the land by the people.[4] The combination of the Stool Lands Act and the Administration of Stool Lands Act served to establish an eminent domain for the state. They vested in the President the right of compulsory acquisition of land in the national interest. They gave the Office of the President the sole right to determine the national interest, and to expropriate land for this purpose (Amankwah 1989).

The reforms to the system of land administration in the 1960s strengthened state control over land. The establishment of eminent domain enabled the state to alienate land whenever it needed to and in relation to its development objectives. It enabled the state to expropriate land and convert customary land into state land. Beyond this, there was little attempt to interfere within customary relations, to strengthen the rights of land users, or check the existing abuses by customary authorities. The only attempt to regulate land relations was the introduction of the 1962 Rent Restrictions Act, which prevented stools from leasing land to migrants on share arrangements and forced them to convert share contracts into monetary rents. However, after the violent overthrow of the CPP government in 1966, the Rent Restriction Act was repealed and a tribute system reintroduced, in which farmers had to provide the stools with one-tenth of their crop as rent. This has subsequently been changed, reverting in some areas to a one-third share of the yield.

While there was little interference with the nature of customary tenure systems, the state was able to insert its land administration institutions directly into the management of customary land. An accommodation was reached between the state and customary authorities. The state recognised the rights of chiefs to control land and revenues, and the chiefs consented to the state gaining a share of these revenues and actively participating in the management of stool revenues. The chiefs also complied with facilitating the expropriation of land for the 'national interest' and for commercial sectors and investors supported by the state. This arrangement has served to undermine the rights in land of farmers and other land users. The most that land users could gain was compensation for the crops they had planted on the land. However, if they had registered the land and gained title deeds, they could claim compensation for the land as their personal property. Land titling is largely confined to wealthy commercial farmers and corporate firms, since it is a complex and expensive process that is beyond the means of most peasant farmers. This caveat has protected the rights of the commercial and corporate sector to their investments in land, while allowing small farmers to be expropriated with impunity. It has enabled an alliance of the state, chiefs, and private sector investors to capture rents from the expropriation of smallholder farmers. Registration merely emphasised the favoured status of commercial interests groups, who were more likely to register land and to protect the interests they often gained through the expropriation of the less fortunate.

Transformations in peasant agricultural holdings

Although considerable expropriation of land has occurred for the allocation of land to commercial and high-input mechanised agriculture, this comprises a relatively small sector. The majority of land is under peasant holdings in both the export agricultural and food-producing sectors. Within this sector, there is significant social differentiation and change in both the productive relations and the nature of holdings. However, this varies between different areas and regions, and the most commodified rural areas occur in the forest zone.

The most significant transformations in agriculture arise in the context of the decline of frontier land. In the past, farmers had alternatives between farming on existing family land and expanding into new, uncultivated forest areas. At present, this option has largely disappeared in the high forest zone, where farmers increasingly depend upon family land. Since there is insufficient family land to meet the requirements of all members of the lineage, this leads to growing conflicts over family land.

In the past, when land was plentiful, elders allocated land to their children and to members of their extended family who had served them well, to help them develop their farm enterprises. Labour was highly valued, and land used to attract labour. At present, land has acquired a higher scarcity value than labour, and attempts to allocate land to junior kin are often disputed by other relatives within the extended family. Shortage of land also results in a large number of people looking to hire or sharecrop land. Family elders are often interested more in the potential immediate income that can be generated by the land rather than in redistributing it to dependent kin. Young family members who wish to develop commercial tree crops, such as oil palms or cocoa, are often frustrated in their attempt to get family land from elders. The elders argue that the farmers are removing land from the family for long periods for their own personal benefits. In some instances, family elders have destroyed the plantations of those who have been given land by their parents, after the death of the one who granted the land. Youth, children, and wives who have worked on the farms of an uncle or father find that after his death junior brothers claim the farms without allocating them a portion in recognition of their inputs into these farms (Amanor 2001; Okali 1983). As a consequence, many young farmers prefer to farm independently on sharecrop contracts rather than work on family land (Amanor 2001; Gyasi 1994).

In some areas, sharecropping is becoming the dominant mode of transferring land. In the Kwae area, Amanor and Diderutuah (2001) found that around 50 per cent of plots were farmed on sharecropping arrangements, and that land was being given out to close kin on a sharecrop basis. The rise of sharecropping and other tenancy arrangements as dominant tenure arrangements complicates land ownership. Security of tenure and security of ownership have become distinct issues, and a strengthening of customary forms of ownership, as defined by family elders and chiefs, could undermine the remaining rights that youth and women possess in land.

Increasingly, farming is an individual activity, in which cultivators hire land and labour, and landowners contract their land out to share-croppers. Elders with insufficient capital to hire labour frequently sharecrop the land. Land is also sharecropped for tree crops such as oil palm, which incur high costs in purchasing seeds and inputs and hiring labour. The tenants have the responsibility to create the tree plantations using their own capital. The plantations are divided between the landowner and the tenant when they start bearing. The tenant has rights to continue managing their share of the plantation until it stops bearing, which can be 25 years for oil palm and 50 years for citrus.

In some areas the customary payments associated with the allocation of land to extended family members have been inflated to exclude poorer family members from gaining family land for planting food crops. The high costs of the customary payments ensure that they must invest in high value commercial crops to recoup their expenditure on gaining access to land (Amanor and Diderutuah 2001). In these areas, agriculture is increasingly commodified, and the process of commodification has transformed customary land tenure arrangements and social relations within families.

Constraints in state-led agricultural land reform

The post-war system of land administration was established to create greater accountability in the transaction of land, to hold chiefs accountable and to facilitate the development of agricultural modernisation. In practice, there has been an accommodation between chiefs and state, which has led to the expropriation of many small farmers with derisory compensation payments. While this expropriation is carried out in the national interest, a significant proportion of expropriated land has ended up in the private commercial sector. This has resulted in increasing bureaucratic and chiefly abuse.

Within the customary sector, land transactions continue to lack transparency and accountability. The high demand for land results in a growing contestation of customary tenure norms and increasing insecurity in rights to use and own land. Chiefs seek to benefit from the growing demand for land by reinventing customary tenure arrangements to suit their interests. They find ways of increasing exaction on migrant farmers, and ways of expropriating local farmers without compensation (Boni 2005). In some areas, the growing value of agricultural investment in land is resulting in the breakdown of family inheritance systems, with family elders preferring to accumulate capital by allocating land to sharecroppers rather than redistributing it within the extended family. There is a trend for family land to be allocated to richer farmers and to rich tenants with capital to develop the land. The least powerful members within extended families, including women, youth, and the poor, frequently suffer the effects of this process of capital accumulation (Amanor 1999; Amanor and Diderutuah 2001). These developments result in increasing inequity in rural holdings and increasing contestation of land ownership and land rights. Customary relations are frequently being redefined by power.

A fiction is being maintained that customary relations continue to exist independently of the changing economic, social, and political relations. This enables the rich and powerful to claim customary privilege and to use land to further their ambitions. Poorer farmers are losing land rights and become vulnerable to exploitative relations, which are justified as the elaboration of customary 'norms' and privileges under modern conditions (Boni 2005; Ubink 2006).

Segments of the corporate and commercial sector have benefited from the expropriation of land. However, the dominant processes of compulsory acquisition of land and expropriation of the poor through the manipulation of concepts of customary privilege do not facilitate the development of well-functioning land markets. It creates tedious processes through which access to land is dependent upon political and bureaucratic interventions. Without these interventions, land transactions become highly risky. The recent expansion of private sector investment requires the growth of transparent markets and clearly defined concepts of ownership rather than the improvisation of customary norms and privilege by the powerful in a changing economy. Thus, the existing land administration system fails to create an adequate and transparent framework to inspire confidence in land transactions and to cater for the increasing demand for land. The problems within the existing framework have also been created by the demands of the corporate sector and international investment for access to land resources. This becomes apparent when developments in the control of resources in the forestry and mining sector are examined.

The forestry sector

Many of the developments in land administration in the agriculture sector are mirrored in the forestry sector. The timber industry in Ghana expanded rapidly in the post-war period, when large supplies of export timber were required for post-war construction in Europe. This resulted in the rapid expansion of expatriate timber companies in Ghana, in the late 1940s and 1950s, and the rapid growth of timber exports (Amanor 1999, 2005a). Prior to this, timber had largely been produced by small-scale pitsaw operators within the cocoa farming belt. These pitsawyers purchased timber trees from farmers. The dominant arrangement was for the sawyers to convert trees into beams and allocate farmers one-third of these or a third of the proceeds. During the early colonial period, stools did not claim ownership of timber resources on farms. However, with the expansion of timber concessions in farming areas, a new legal framework was required, which secured timber resources outside of forest reserves for concessionaires.

The expansion of timber exports coincided with the movement of cocoa farmers into the new frontier areas in the Western Region. Attempts to redefine timber tenure began to emerge in the context of the opening up of the cocoa frontier by migrant farmers in the Western Region. New 'customary arrangements' were created in which the trees on the lands into which migrant farmers were moving were recognised as the property of chiefs (Amanor 2005a). In signing Memorandums of Agreements for transactions in land with migrant farmers, clauses were introduced that specified that the timber resources on the farms belonged to the chiefs. The timbers on these lands were allocated as concessions, and the chiefs benefited from the timber royalties. The timber royalties were often worth more than the sale of land to migrants, and chiefs would often sell large areas of land at favourable prices to ensure they could gain control of the timber resources. The Protected Timber Lands legislation of the 1950s gave timber companies rights to fell all exploitable timber trees in their concessions before farmers were allowed to enter and clear the land (Amanor 2005a).

In this period, a distinct set of practices developed in different parts of the colony in relation to rights in timber. In the Eastern and Ashanti regions, timber on existing farms was largely extracted by small-scale operators who entered into negotiation with farmers for individual trees. In the frontier areas of the Western Region in which most timber resources were concentrated, timber trees were recognised as the property of chiefs, who had sole rights to transact the timber on farmlands with concessionaries.

With independence, new legislation was enacted to reflect the changing status of the former colony, and the changing relationship between chiefs and state. The Concession Ordinance of 1962 vested all timber trees within the nation in the President to manage on behalf of their owners, the chiefs. This legislation extended the new arrangements developed in the Western Region to the whole country, introducing the fiction that timber trees customarily belonged to chiefs. Since there was no timber industry in the pre-colonial era, timber tenure is essentially a modern phenomenon, which is not prescribed by customary norms.

During the 1960s and 1970s, timber concessionaires continued to focus on the new frontier areas of the Western Region, which were rich in timber species, and to ignore the more patchy timber resources of the older frontier areas in the Eastern and Western Regions. However, as these resources began to decline, concessionaires began to focus on extracting the remaining timber in other farming areas, to which the Forest Service extended concessions during the late 1980s and 1990s. Timber concessionaires began to encroach on the timber resources on farms, creating considerable damage to the farms. This resulted in growing conflicts between the Forestry Service and concessionaires on one side, and farmers and chainsaw operators (who had replaced the pitsawyers) on the other.

New legislation was created in 1994 to facilitate the monopolisation of farm timber resources for timber companies. The 1994 Forest Policy removed the management of off-reserve forest resources from district councils and placed them under the Forestry Service, redefining timber as a strategic national resource that should not be decentralised. After gaining control of the off-reserve areas, one of the first legislations introduced by the Forestry Service was to introduce a national ban on the use of chainsaws in processing timber (Amanor 2005a). Paradoxically, these changes were introduced within a framework of participatory forest management. However, the Forestry Service has largely confined its consultations to chiefs, whom it recognises to be the legitimate representatives of communities. Chiefs have benefited from the new legislation. They receive part of the royalties from the exploitation of farm timber, while the farmers who have tended and preserved the trees receive nothing.[5] The empowerment of chiefs in forest policy has resulted in an increasing loss of rights in timber for farmers. With the expansion of the concession system into farmland, the farming areas have been rapidly denuded of timber. Current projections estimate the complete decline of commercially exploitable timber resources in a few years. Plans for the future of the industry are based on the replacement of naturally occurring timber by plantation timber. Projects are now being developed in the transition zone of the forest for the development of plantation timber. These may lead to a further erosion of the resource base of small farmers, as increasingly land is given out by chiefs for the development of commercial timber plantations at the expense of small farmers.

The mining sector

Although the colonial state did not directly intervene in the control of land, it effectively monopolised gold resources for foreign mining companies by banning small-scale gold mining in 1905. With the attainment of independence, the Minerals Act of 1962 was introduced, which vested ownership and control of minerals in the President on behalf of the Republic of Ghana. This empowered the state to grant licenses for prospecting and mining and to prescribe the conditions of exploitation. While the state recognised the interests of the stools in minerals under their jurisdiction and their rights to royalties and concession rent, it reserved the right to manage minerals and negotiate concessions with foreign companies to the state. In 1972, the Minerals Operations (Government Participation) Decree was enacted to enable the state to gain controlling shares in mining companies. There was no attempt to readdress the banning of small-scale operators, who continued to operate illegally.

The rights of small-scale operators were not addressed until the 1980s when a Small-Scale Gold Mining Law was passed under the influence of economic liberalisation policies. This law made provisions for the registration of small-scale miners at the district level and the allocation of licenses for areas of 3-5 hectares for periods of 3-25 years. However, with the subsequent expansion of corporate mining concessions, local communities and informal sector miners experienced declining access to land. During the 1990s, corporate sector gold mining rapidly expanded in Ghana to become the most important export-oriented economic activity within the country. Gold mining technology also changed from deep pit mining to more expansive and environmentally destructive opencast cyanide heap-leach mining. In the Wassa district of the Western Region, 30,000 people were displaced from their communities to make way for mining operations.[6] Many people have lost access to farmland and suffered contamination of their water supplies by cyanide and other toxic wastes. This has resulted in a number of deaths from poisoning.

Expropriation has taken place without the provision of adequate compensation to the communities. This is justified with recourse to the familiar argument that the allodial rights belong to the chiefs, who are the rightful recipients of compensation. Many informal sector gold miners found their livelihood criminalised as gold-mining concessions are allocated in areas in which they have been exploiting gold. As security forces are deployed at the behest of the mining companies to evict small-scale mining in their concessions, this has resulted in a number of violent skirmishes and deaths. There has been an escalation in violence as communities attempt to protect their interests and resist expropriation. The law courts have also introduced harsh sentences against members of mining communities who resist expropriation. In December 2006, five activists of the Wassa Association of Communities Affected by Mining (WACAM), an organisation that seeks to defend the interests of communities against mining companies, were arrested for meeting with disaffected members of communities in a con-

cession recently allocated to Newmont in Brong Ahafo. When brought
before the court, the five activists were sentenced to two weeks prison
custody. The judge stated: 'in recent times, the mining communities
had been disturbing the foreign companies' and he would use this case
to set an example so that the community people would stop harassing
the mining companies.[7] The expansion of investments in mining concessions has resulted in declining access to land, natural resources and
livelihoods for the rural communities in the areas. The rule of law has
served to protect the interests of the powerful and undermine the basic
human rights of the poor.

Real estate: Urban and peri-urban areas

In recent years, land has been rapidly commodified in urban and peri-
urban areas for building property. This is due to the rapid expansion of
the urban population; the growth of a business and middle class with
money to invest; the expansion of corporate investment in Ghana; and
the willingness of private companies to pay high prices for prime properties in central Accra for business premises and residences for their
cosmopolitan managerial and technocratic employees. A property in
the Osu, Ridge, or Labone areas of Accra can now sell in excess of
USD 500,000.[8] Rents for houses in these areas mount up to USD
6,000 per month.

The rapid growth of the urban population in recent years has resulted in overcrowding in the poorer areas of Central Accra. The combination of overcrowded housing and high rents results in many urban
dwellers searching for rental housing and building plots on the outskirts of the city and in peri-urban areas. This in turn has resulted in
the rapid conversion of farming land into residential plots. This process of expansion of residential areas is poorly regulated, since the institutional structure for urban land administration has not been developed to cope with the present scale of transactions. The consequences
are highly insecure land ownership, disputes over land, and poor land
planning procedures. Portions of land are not often allocated for important community services, such as schools and recreational facilities,
and areas are not demarcated for future use (Gough and Yankson
2000). The growing urban sprawl contributes to poor infrastructure
development, and houses are frequently located in unsuitable areas.

Within the urban area, land for housing is mainly sold by chiefs or
the central government on land acquired for public purposes. The acquisition of land in urban areas is usually carried out by people who
are not indigenes of the area, since urbanisation results in the develop-

ment of a heterogeneous population emanating from all regions in the country.

Indigenes originally had the right to build houses in their settlements and to farm lands over which their extended families claimed ownership or which lay in uncultivated areas that were not claimed by anyone. The usual practice for indigenes wanting land for building purposes was to approach the family head or chiefs and elders with a request for land. The recipients usually made a presentation of drinks and sheep before witnesses to the family elders to seal the transaction after land was allocated to them (Gough and Yankson 2000).

Migrants wanting land for building purposes usually approached the chief and elders of the community and provided them with drink and some money. A sum was paid annually to the landowners, who acknowledged the secondary rights of the migrant and the rights of the chiefs as the original landowners (Gough and Yankson 2000). This customary framework was retained alongside the drawing up of indentures and site plans by surveyors hired by the customary authorities. The state defines these transactions as land leases, and the 1992 Constitution prohibits the creation of freehold interests in customary land and only allows for land leases. However, a normative structure for leases does not exist in practice (Antwi and Adams 2003), and most buyers are not clear about what will happen when their leases expire. Gough and Yankson (2000) found that only 25 per cent of land purchasing households they interviewed had paid ground rent to the municipal authority.

Chiefs often use notions of customary rights in land to evade accountability. This often occurs in the context of competition between the government and chiefs to gain control over land and revenues for land. Revenues from stool lands are constitutionally subject to a sharing arrangement, in which ten per cent of total revenues are taken by the state through the Administrator of Stool Lands for administrative purposes. The remaining 90 per cent are divided between the landowning stool (chief), which receives 25 per cent, the paramount stool (with ultimate political authority over the area), which receives twenty per cent, and the local council, which receives 45 per cent of revenues. By presenting land sales as customary 'drink' money, the chiefs are able to evade the declaration of monies they receive from land sales and evade the collection of revenues by the Administrator of Stool Lands (Antwi and Adams 2003; Ubink 2008). They are able to use the money they receive as they please, since it is not documented or subject to scrutiny.

The lack of transparency in the transaction of land and the ambiguous status of land sales enable chiefs to engage in fraudulent practices. They frequently sell the same plot of land to different people. Multiple sales occur in three contexts. First, they occur because of disputed own-ership of land or rights to sell lands between rival factions of chiefly lineages (such as two brothers), who sell the same plots to different parties. Second, they occur when land purchasers fail to develop their plots in a timely fashion. As infrastructure within the areas develops and property values increase, chiefs are tempted to capture the price differential by reselling undeveloped plots. Third, multiple sales occur intentionally, by fraudulent chiefs with the sole goal of making more money. The original purchasers may lose their land altogether and the payments they made. However, if they persist in gaining redress, they may be allocated an alternative plot in an undeveloped area. Chiefs are able to engage in these fraudulent practices with impunity since there is only a weak legal framework for the redress of multiple land sales, and since chiefly rule is often highly contested by a number of differ-ent factions. Real estate developers also engage in corrupt practices. They buy large areas from chiefs, but then bribe surveyors and bureau-crats in the land agencies to register much larger areas than they pur-chased. This often includes areas in which individuals have purchased plots from the chiefs.

Because of the lack of transparency in land markets, land purchasers seek to protect their investment by physically occupying the plot. They often give the plots to tenants to occupy and farm. They erect tempor-ary dwellings on the land, place sand and blocks on the plot, and begin building as soon as possible. Physically developing the plot is regarded as a safer investment in securing the plot than attempting to register it, particularly since the land may be given out to others before the cumbersome process of registration is completed. Investment in devel-oping the land is seen as creating more security than gaining the title before expending capital on the land.

Insecure land markets result in unregulated and unplanned build-ings in residential areas and increasing conflicts over land, particularly as land prices rise. Chiefs have taken to hiring armed land guards to protect what they consider to be their land, land subject to dispute with other stools and rival factions of chiefly lineages, and to physically re-move land developers who have purchased land from rival factions. Conflicts sometimes result in the loss of life.

The rapid increase in land prices and demand for land has resulted in an erosion of the rights of indigenes to land as farmland in peri-ur-ban areas is increasingly transformed into residential estates. Fre-quently, the expansion of residential areas results in the expropriation of farmers within the area, as chiefs attempt to capture the new value in the land. In a study of peri-urban Kumasi, Ubink (2006) found that chiefs were expropriating farmers of land without compensation, which they then sold to property developers. The chiefs attempted to

reinvent customary land to justify expropriation. For instance, at Besease, the chief claimed that the land his subjects (indigenes) were
farming on 'was only "given out" for farming purposes and that when
the village expands and reaches it, the land falls back into chiefly administration, giving chiefs the right to allocate land to outsiders for
more lucrative residential purposes' (Ubink 2006:4). This claim was
disputed by the inhabitants of the village, who insisted on their rights
to their land. They often attempt to sell their land to outside purchasers before the chief can lay claim to it. However, the chiefs are often
able to expropriate the lands of farmers successfully and sell them to
property developers. The land buyers often belong to more powerful
sections of society than the farmers, and the state is reluctant to intervene in controlling the powers of chiefs over the alienation of land
(Ubink 2008, in press) since this often benefits the state and the national elite who exercise state power. The chiefs frequently use the
funds they obtain from land sales for their own personal use rather
than for the development of the community. Gough and Yankson
(2000) find similar developments within peri-urban areas of Accra, in
which farmlands are sold by chiefs to purchasers requiring building
plots, and little of this revenue finds its way back into community development. Abdullai (2002) reports that during the structural adjustment era, many villagers lost their farmland in Tamale, which was converted by chiefs into building plots. In one village the chief was accused of 'selling our children [i.e. their birth right] to buy that car as
well' (Abdullai 2002:81). With the development of sales of residential
land, the abilities of community members to gain land for property development are also curtailed. Community members wanting land to develop housing often have to prove that they have the means to develop
the property before they are allocated land (Gough and Yankson 2000).
The intention is to prevent community members speculating in land,
gaining access to land that they later sell to make a profit. However,
this also serves to limit the access of indigenes to land. Most of the
chiefs in peri-urban areas have failed to reserve lands around the existing community for its future needs. There are differences in the responses of chiefs. Both Gough and Yankson (2000) and Ubink (2008)
document instances of more enlightened chiefs who invest in the future development of the community or reserve land for the future
needs of the community. However, the few examples of enlightened
chiefs only serve to highlight the lack of accountability of chiefs in general, and their ability to use land to serve their immediate selfish
needs. Youth often suffer the most from this allocation of building
plots by chiefs and elders, and often end up without housing or land to
farm. This often leads to growing resentment on the part of the youth,
who feel that their elders have sold out their inheritance (Abudulai

2002; Gough and Yankson 2000). These grievances are often aggravated by high rates of unemployment among the youth.

Significant areas of urban land have also been acquired by the government in the public interest. Larbi (1996) estimates that thirteen per
cent of Accra land has been acquired by the government. Much of this
land has been used to provide residential properties for the rich rather
than meet the objectives for which it was originally acquired. In Accra,
this includes areas of Ridge, which were acquired for housing government administrative staff in the colonial period, and East Legon, which
was acquired for the development of the airport. Lands acquired by
Tema Development Corporation have also been used to develop housing estates for the wealthy, with houses costing in the region of USD
100,000. In the early independence period, state corporations were created to develop housing for workers. They now largely cater to the
needs of the wealthy. State expropriation of land for the creation of
these wealthy estates has been carried out without providing adequate
compensation to the chiefs or the affected communities, particularly in
relation to the extent of the value these lands now command. There is
a large backlog of outstanding compensation claims dating back to the
1970s, which are in excess of the equivalent of USD 110 million. These
claims attract no interest, despite the very high rates of inflation in
Ghana (Kasanga and Kotey 2001). Given the wide disparities between
the luxury of these housing estates and the relative poverty of the pre-
existing communities, this has produced considerable discontentment
within the communities about the expropriation of land. This is often
exploited by chiefs in their bid to gain greater control over land from
the government, although they are often equally as guilty in the misuse
of land.

The expansion of population and growing demand and values for
land has resulted in an urban housing crisis, particularly in Accra. Little low-cost housing is being created to cater to the needs of the urban
poor. Many landlords in Accra require advance payments of up to three
years' rent from tenants, which many people cannot afford. This has
resulted in increasing homelessness. A tour of the streets of Accra by
night reveals many people and families sleeping on the streets, particularly around the markets and in the central commercial districts. The
main markets and lorry parks are often surrounded by densely habited
shacks, stalls and other wooden structures in which many recent migrants to the city dwell. Some of these informal shack settlements have
a population in excess of 30,000, such as in Old Fadama. Apart from
the lack of sanitary facilities, these communities are also highly vulnerable to outbreaks of fire resulting from the high density of roughly assembled wooden structures. The urban councils frequently attempt to
evict these squatters, who have nowhere to go. However, the extent of

the squatting problem means that eviction is usually an unsuccessful strategy. In recent years a number of NGOs have begun working in these areas, negotiating with the urban councils on behalf of the inhabitants, initiating community development, sanitation, slum upgrading, savings, and low-cost housing initiatives. These include Slum Dwellers International, People's Dialogue Ghana, a partner of Homeless International Ghana, and the Ghana Homeless People's Federation.[9]

The existing policy for land administration in urban areas is characterised by a poor regulatory framework and a lack of transparent and accountable land markets. Existing land markets fail to meet the needs of a large part of society for land and housing. The existing framework enables chiefs to alienate land with impunity, without meeting the present and future needs of their communities and without addressing the livelihood needs of those they expropriate. The land administration bureaucracy has also been characterised by a lack of accountability and rent-seeking behaviour. Similarly, the state has abused compulsory acquisition of land to allocate choice urban plots for the development of wealthy residential areas. Chiefs and bureaucrats frequently collude to maximise their benefits from the lack of transparency in land markets. This results in a highly inefficient land administration system in which few purchasers of land have confidence. Consequently, most members of urban society attempt to secure land and housing outside the formal sector and outside the rule of law. This, however, creates glaring problems for an economy that has become increasingly dependent upon foreign investment, since foreign investors expect to be able to secure land through property markets and legally enforced transactions.

Contemporary land reform initiatives in an era of neo-liberalism

The development of new paradigms of development, based on promoting free markets and divestiture of state organisation, has created pressures for reform of the institutional framework of land administration. However, deregulated markets also create problems and can reinforce the lack of accountability. The current policy framework for administrative land reform proceeds from the premise that to function efficiently, land markets require improved information on land holdings and ownership, greater transparency and efficiency in land registration and management, and the ability to enforce contractual agreements through legal provisions.

The first step taken in reforming the land administration system was the enactment of the Land Title Registration Act of 1986. While land registration enactments have existed in Ghana since 1843, they have only provided for the voluntary registration of deeds. The purpose of the Land Title Registration Act was to facilitate the recognition of transactions in land and the maintenance of comprehensive records of land transactions by prescribing compulsory registration of title. The Land Title Registration Act aimed to minimise disputes and regulate fraud in land transactions. It was argued in policy circles that the development of a comprehensive land-titling scheme would create the necessary information on land holdings to provide for greater transparency and secure forms of private property ownership that could provide adequate incentives for investment in land resources. However, land title registration has had a limited impact. Registration has only been implemented in Accra, Tema, and Kumasi. Twenty years after the enactment of the Land Title Registration Act, only 111,784 applications had been received for registration, and only 16,829 title certificates had been issued (Dowuona-Hammond 2003). Registration has been constrained by high transaction costs, large 'rents' extracted by the bureaucracy, slow processing procedures, poor integration between the different land administration agencies, and disputes over land ownership, as customary authorities and rival factions within chiefly lineages engage in multiple sales of land. The high costs and frustration result in many people not registering their land. In a survey conducted in 1995/6 of 233 land-purchasing households within peri-urban Accra, Gough and Yankson (2000) found that 60 per cent of the sample had not registered their land because they considered it too difficult or unnecessary. In a survey conducted in 1999 of 286 land-purchasing households in Accra, Antwi and Adams (2003) found that nearly 78 per cent of the sample had not formally registered their land. A considerable proportion of those with registered plots had spent more than five years to get land titles.

The second strategy to attain administrative land reform revolved around the creation of a National Land Policy (Ministry of Lands and Forestry 1999), which defined the main aims and objectives of land administration. The National Land Policy attempted to create a framework for the harmonisation of land management between different government agencies and between government agencies and the customary sector. A major objective of the National Land Policy was to promote greater equity in access to land by strengthening and modernising customary land tenure. The mechanisms that were identified to achieve this included:

– collaborating with traditional rulers and other land stakeholders to review, harmonise, and streamline customary practices;
– facilitating the land administration skills of traditional authorities and family land owners to create a system of proper record-keeping and to establish customary land secretariats;

- developing digital databases within government departments and agencies involved in land service delivery, and harmonised information systems linking national agencies with decentralised customary secretariats (Ministry of Lands and Forestry 1999:16).

The National Land Policy sought to promote a system of land tenure reform by recognising and documenting all the different existing rights in land. This included allodial title, customary freehold, leasehold, and secondary rights associated with use and customary tenancy agreements, including sharecropping. However, by recognising all possible rights within the customary system – and not, for example, deliberating on the contradictions between user rights and allodial rights, or the ways in which the claims of chiefs to allodial rights have been used to expropriate the poor – the Land Policy merely reaffirms the existing status quo. It reaffirms the unwillingness of the state to intervene in checking abuses of power. The Land Policy has failed to initiate a much-needed dialogue in society about democratic land reform and the role of chiefs in land administration (Alden Wily and Hammond 2001; Ubink 2006).

The recommendations of the National Land Policy are being implemented within the Land Administration Project (LAP) (Ministry of Lands and Forestry 2003; World Bank 2003b). One of the major components of this project is establishing Pilot Customary Land Secretariats (CLS) within all regions of Ghana, with appropriate governance structures to assure institutionalised community-level participation and accountability in the use of stool land and the revenue it generates. However, from the inception of the LAP, it has been the government's clear political choice that CLSs should fall under the aegis of traditional authorities rather than opting for more community-based approaches to the management of customary land. By placing the customary land secretariats under the authority of the chiefs, the LAP ignores the fact that the notions of the 'customary' powers and rights of chiefs are loaded with political inventions and endorses the roles that chiefs were accorded in land administration in the colonial period, as if there were a timeless principle of customary tenure.

Ten pilot land secretariats have now been established. Plans exist to scale this up to 50 CLSs in the next five years. In policy circles, it is envisaged that the CLSs will facilitate the development of transparency and equity, strengthen the accountability of customary authorities in land management, open up a debate at the local level regarding the procedures and norms which should guide land administration – including clarification of the nature of usufructuary rights and protection of these rights against the chiefs' conversion drive – and, eventually, provide comprehensive documentation of local land-holdings. However, this overlooks the desire of powerful chiefs and rural elites to protect and enhance their economic interests in land. According to Ubink and Quan (2008), chiefs are resisting attempts to record their incomes from land sales, land leases, and tenancy agreements. In addition, they are trying to use the CLSs to facilitate transactions of agricultural and residential plots to outsiders, to enlarge their control of land revenues, and to change long-standing land allocations to strangers. In the implementation of the LAP, the government has been highly reluctant to interfere with the disposal of land by the chiefs and impose pressure for greater accountability and equity. This creates the risk that traditional authorities may use enhanced and equipped CLSs to further their tendencies of dispossessing community members who have obtained land through informal arrangements without adequate compensation. This will have the perverse effect of further eroding popular rights in land while claiming to empower the poor.

The concept of traditional authorities maintaining records and registers of landholding is not particularly new. Since the 1940s, various chiefs have attempted to maintain registers of landholdings, particularly of migrant farmers who are subject to various customary payments for land. This registration of land has been used to transform the conditions under which migrants hold land, and to facilitate further extraction of revenues by chiefs, redefinition of contractual relations, and the appropriation of land. Boni (2005) documents an attempt by the paramount chief of Sefwi to register migrant farmers' lands land during the 1980s. Surveyors were instructed to map out the existing portions of migrant cocoa farms and confiscate existing site plans. This was interpreted by migrant farmers as an attempt to expropriate the areas they had not planted under cocoa, and to extort money from them. The migrants refused to comply, and the paramount chiefs attempted to mobilise their supporters and local youth to dispossess the migrants of their land. Government was forced to intervene with the escalation of violence and a commission of enquiry was set up which found in favour of the migrants. However, all too frequently, the government fails to intervene and allows chiefs to appropriate land (Ubink 2008, in press). As Boni (2005:242) comments:

> Local power holders – rather than state bureaucrats – have enforced 'custom' in villages; the title of the tenant, the taxes to be paid, the definition of farm boundaries underwent continuous negotiation that saw in the chiefly establishment and the leaders both the judge and the interested parties. Those recognised as the rightful interpreters of 'tradition' wittingly capitalised on the ambiguity and transformability of custom. The government's ac-

ceptance of this mode of land tenure administration represented
the – yet unresolved – legalisation of extortion.

Many chiefs have close family ties and affinities with business interests
and are often businesspersons and professionals in their own right (Arhin Birempong 2001). These interests often define the ways in which
they interact with their communities. Thus, the contemporary framework, which presents the sphere of customary relations as undifferentiated and representing subaltern rural interests or civil society interests in opposition to a corrupt state, is over-simplistic. Chiefs often represent distinct elite interests and are often willing to expropriate local
community interests for pecuniary reward. Chiefs have sacrificed the
future interests of their subjects to gain revenues from migrant farmers, property developers, timber concessionaires, and foreign investors.
Both state and customary authorities have colluded in the dispossession of the poor to further the interests of foreign investment in the
agricultural, forestry, and mining sectors. The expansion of the market
has resulted in the displacement of peasant cultivators to make way for
new corporate sectors.

The combination of empowering traditional rulers to administer customary land relations and the expansion of land markets results in a
dangerous alliance. This increasingly dispossesses the poor while
claiming to promote 'efficiency with equity'. The contemporary framework for land reform fails to address the underlying contradictions and
lack of accountability within customary tenure systems, which arises
from the insecurity of ownership for land users deriving from the concept of the allodial rights of chiefs. This empowers chiefs to alienate
land and redefine customary values at the expense of existing customary (or informal sector) land users, who are not given a voice. However,
this redefinition of the customary is taking place in a period of rapid
social change and increasing commodification of land. The redefinition
of the customary under these circumstances serves to sanction the privatisation and accumulation of land, the rise of individual sales and expropriation, and the conversion of family lands into market commodities. This is particularly dangerous in the present period when frontier
land has been extinguished, and chiefs have sold all existing lands under their control. The increasing empowerment of chiefs is in danger
of opening up a new phase of land expropriations in which the state,
chiefs, rural elites, and the corporate sector collaborate in redefining
customary land to expropriate land at the expense of the poor and marginalised. The strengthening of customary land tenure under neo-liberal management serves to undermine customary tenure arrangements
and facilitates the transformation of communal and family land resources into private, commercial, and corporate property.

In 2002 the Foundation for Building the Capital of the Poor (FBCP) was launched in Accra, an initiative developed by the Ghanaian Ministry of Justice with Hernando de Soto's Institute for Liberty and Democracy, with the support of the United Nations Development Programme (UNDP). The FBCP was launched in September 2002 at a high profile event attended by the President of Ghana, J.A. Kufuor, the former US President, Bill Clinton, and Hernando de Soto. The FBCP aims to establish a regional training centre in Accra for the benefit of other African countries and devise the legal means and reforms to assist in mobilising the assets held by the poor to facilitate their economic development. The programme hopes to bring all lands and assets into the formal economic sector through registration, which should give titleholders access to credit and collateral. Helping poor people register their land and property is supposed to facilitate their access to loans for development of their businesses. However, since its launch in 2002, the FBCP has made little visible progress. The underlying rationale of the programme is not much different from those that informed the Land Title Registration Act of 1986. It fails to address the underlying constraints that have prevented people from titling land, and the constraints on the development of credit markets for the rural poor (Bruce 1993; Bruce, Migot-Adholla, and Atherton 1994). The framework assumes the existence of a multitude of undifferentiated and aspiring business people within the informal sector, all with clearly defined property rights within the informal sector, who are frustrated by legal conventions in registering their land. In reality, land relations are constrained by multiple claims on land, numerous family members with competing rights to land, and power relations that enable the privileged to appropriate and redefine customary or informal land regimes.[10] This results in contested rights and ownership of land, and struggles for the appropriation of land and the defence of livelihoods and user rights in land. This reality is recognised by the Land Administration Project, which attempts to document all the different types of rights. However, the failing (or disingenuity) of LAP is that it presumes that a just and equitable solution can be worked out between the various actors in the different domains with differing access to power. It accords rights of administration to the most powerful actors within the process – those who claim customary privileges and the rights to redefine customary relations in their own interest and to extinguish the rights of others. It confuses rights and privilege and divorces land reform from the conditions under which people make their livelihood. While present land reform programmes claim to promote equity and efficiency and 'pro-poor market policies', they are being implemented in the context of growing deprivation and impoverishment and lack of vision of the future security of the poor. A large gap exists between the extravagant claims of the development policy to be 'pro-poor' and the conditions under which large sections of the population live. The main policy concerns are with carrying out reforms that will attract external investors and promote the accumulation of capital. This chapter has shown that in the context of increased external investment and expansion of global markets, the land rights of the rural poor have consistently been destabilised.

Conclusion

Within Ghana three distinct phases can be distinguished in land administration and its reform. These different phases are closely associated with the changing framework of economic and development policy, and the limitations resulting from previous policy frameworks. In the first phase of colonial rule up to the 1940s, economic policy was based on limited government intervention in economic production, and government controls were largely established over revenue collection in the import and export trade. The economic base of the colony was founded on peasant production in agriculture, with expatriate mercantile firms controlling the marketing of produce. Large European agricultural plantations were not encouraged. The mining sector was controlled by expatriate mining companies with concessions, and small-scale mining was banned. Export timber production was limited in this period and confined to areas near the coast with accessible transport to the ports. The dominant paradigms for development were based on limited government interventions in transforming the economic basis of the colony and forms of administration based on indirect rule and an alliance with 'traditional rulers' and paramount chiefs willing to collaborate with the colonial administration. In return for building the foundations of colonial rural administration, these chiefs were empowered to control land, which they could sell and extract various forms of revenues from, and to impose taxation and labour services on the population. This enabled a rural administration to be effected without heavy investment in administration, and the rural population to be controlled by the chiefs through customary rights and privileges. The chiefs had powers to make bylaws, but these were ratified and monitored by the colonial administration. Early attempts to place land under the colonial authority were abandoned in the light of popular discontent, and land was placed under the authority of paramount chiefs. During the nineteenth century a land market began to emerge. Colonial administration sought to hinder the development of land markets by only recognising the ability of chiefs to sell land and negotiate concessions with expatriate companies and by defining land relations in terms of customary codes elaborated by the paramount authority. This resulted in a definition of customary tenure in which chiefs owned allodial rights to land, and the peasantry only held user rights in land. While chiefs had rights to sell land, they could only sell it to non-locals without user rights. This led to a large influx of migrants into the main cocoa-producing areas. The main developments in this period were the rapid expansion of export agriculture into new frontier areas and the conversion of forest into farmland.

By the 1940s this framework was found wanting, and a new development framework was created which had important ramifications on land administration. The system of Native Administration resulted in growing discontent in the anti-colonial movement against the autocratic rule of chiefs. Reforms were introduced which replaced chiefly rule with democratically elected district councils. Economic policy was transformed, and the state began directly investing in economic enterprises. Agricultural development policies were initiated which were based on the promotion of mechanised and high-input agriculture and irrigation. Since the major paradigms for development in the post-war period were based on increasing state intervention in the economy and major state investments in production, this led to the creation of state-led development projects and state agricultural enterprises. These required the alienation of considerable land for the state, which necessitated the creation of a framework of eminent domain through which the state could gain access to land for development projects. An uneasy alliance was built between the state and the chiefs, in which the chiefs participated in the alienation of land for national development. In return, the chiefs continued to be recognised as the owners of the land with allodial title and gained access to royalties, rents, and concession fees for land they expropriated. This frequently led to the expropriation of farmers to make way for large development projects. The state also engaged in joint enterprises with international capital and promoted an echelon of large-scale estate farmers, who often formed part of the state elite. Land was expropriated for these three sectors in the national interest or in the interest of development. The articulation of a customary sector based on the allodial rights of the chiefly classes and the user rights of the peasantry was maintained and formed the basis through which the state exercised eminent domain and expropriated land with the chiefs for national development or the development of capitalism. Land administration became increasingly centralised, and national land cadastres and land title registers were introduced. These largely catered for large estate farmers, corporations, and agribusiness.

During the 1980s neo-liberal policies were introduced, which divested state enterprises, decentralised administration, and encouraged free markets and foreign investment. Economic recovery resulted in the rapid expansion of investment in urban real estate and foreign investment in the mining and agricultural sectors. The framework for land administration, developed in the early independence period, proved to be cumbersome, since it was largely adapted to enabling state expropriation of land rather than multiple market transactions. Thus, reforms were introduced which attempted to streamline land markets, make transactions more transparent and efficient, and facilitate land registration and records management. Attempts are also being initiated to decentralise land administration, which will enable a more efficient maintenance of records covering customary claims of ownership. However, the notions of customary ownership based on chiefly allodial rights and user rights for their subjects has been maintained. In the present period there are large pressures on land emanating from an expanding population and increasing demands on lands for livelihoods, accommodation and accumulation. In contrast to earlier periods, large areas of frontier lands no longer exist, and urban areas are rapidly expanding into rural areas, creating a peri-urban fringe. These growing demands for land result in increasing displacement of certain categories of land users, usually the most disempowered, marginalised and poor. Expansion of urban areas results in the displacement of small farmers by wealthier urbanites investing in real estate and the creation of new commercial agricultural sectors, and agricultural accumulation results in the displacement of small food crop farmers. The new pressures on land result in rapidly increasing values for land. The demand for land increasingly results in friction over land within the customary sector as different groups attempt to capture the new values in land. To meet the new market demands for land, chiefs frequently attempt to appropriate the land of users to sell to commercial sectors and real estate developers, and family elders transact the land of their lineages without providing for the needs of the members of their lineages. This often leads to the reinvention of custom to justify such appropriations as within customary norms. The tendencies are reinforced by the state, which increasingly recognises the rights of chiefs but does little to protect the rights of land users. It fails to problematise the nature of customary tenures, along with the power relations which define it and justify privilege and injustices, and which do not allow the chiefs to exercise accountability. Thus, chiefs are able to continually reinvent customary tenure to suit their interests and gain more revenues from land. This results in a situation in which the customary is increasingly redefined within parameters concerned with rights to sell and alienate land as private property. Increasingly within the customary sector, people gain access to land through market transactions rather than inheritance. Growing numbers of people experience difficulty in gaining land for their livelihoods in rural areas and for accommodation in urban areas, leading to increasing impoverishment and growing grievances and conflicts around land. Increasingly, the poor within the informal sector are being displaced by real estate and new forms of agricultural property. Thus, contemporary reforms of land tenure and administration revolve around the interests and demands of markets and investors in property, and the creation of security and an enabling environment for these sectors. They are less concerned with creating security for those who gain access to land based on customary user rights and informal sectors which do not result in the alienation of land and its capitalisation. Although there is a focus on regularising customary arrangements, the process of regularisation transforms the nature of customary rights and converts them from user rights into private property leases. It does not strengthen the security of existing land users, but frequently erodes it by empowering chiefs to control and sell land to external investors. There is a tendency in contemporary policy frameworks to associate the customary with the rights and privileges of chiefs to transact land rather than the user rights of the people. This leads to a focus on strengthening the customary rights and privileges of chiefs rather than the user rights of the people. There are dangers in these developments, since the growing powers of chiefs over land is not checked by processes to assure accountability, transparency, and propriety or ethical codes of conduct. In examining security in land, it is important to differentiate security of user rights from security in market purchases. In the present period, market-based policies and processes of accumulation of land and wealth are tending to result in the sacrifice of user rights to meet demands for the commodification of land.

Notes

1   According to section 8(1) of the Office of the Administrator of Stool Lands Act, 1994 (Act 481) ten per cent of the revenue shall be paid to the Office to cover administrative expenses. The remaining revenue shall be disbursed in the following proportions: 25 per cent to the stool; twenty per cent to the traditional authority; and 55 per cent to the District Assembly.

2   *Ibid.*

3   As stated above, a different situation prevailed in the Northern Territories, particularly in those areas lacking an organised system of chieftaincy. Here land was vested in the colonial state to manage on behalf of the people according to their customary norms, and the colonial administration attempted to create and build systems of chieftaincy.

4   This was often estimated at rates well below the actual market value.

5   In off-reserve areas, ten per cent of the royalties are taken by the government for administrative charges, and the remainder is divided 25 per cent to the local chief, twenty per cent to the paramount stool, and 55 per cent to the district council.

6   Oxfam International 'WACAM: a powerful voice for mining communities in Ghana'
    http://www.oxfam.org/en/programs/development/wafrica/ghana_mining.htm.
7   Mining Violations in Ghana 5th December 2006, http://www.blacklooks.org/2006/
    12/mining_violations _ in_ghana.html).
8   'House prices in Accra too high' *Business News* of Monday, 22 January 2007,
    http://www.ghanaweb.com/GhanaHomePage/NewsArchive/artikel.php?ID=117694.
9   See http://www.sdinet.org/reports/rep44.htm for a report on the activities of NGOs
    in Ghana working with the homeless and urban squatters.
10 Nyamu-Musembi (2006) addresses some of the shortcoming of de Soto's theory and
    raises some of these issues, particularly in relation to women's property rights in
    Kenya.

5 Tree plantations, agricultural commodification, and land tenure security in Ghana

Kojo Sebastian Amanor[1]

Within contemporary policy circles it is assumed that the registration of land leads to increasing security and facilitates long-term investment. Secure rights in land enable land assets to be capitalised through collateral. However, the major impediment to land registration is assumed to be institutional structures, which result in expensive processes of registration. Thus, contemporary land administration reform seeks to create innovative and decentralised institutional processes that reduce the cost of registration and enable informal or customary rights to land to be registered. This chapter argues that the processes of legalising or formalising the land holdings of peasant farmers does not necessarily lead to increasing security of tenure among the poor, but frequently creates more insecurity. The process of securing rights through legalisation usually creates new avenues for investment and the accumulation of land and wealth, which frequently undermines the land rights of the poor.

Legalisation can be carried out by extending formal title to individual farmers or by creating avenues through which customary relations are recognised by government agencies and then registered. However, customary relations are often contested and subject to power struggles over the control and definition of land rights. When the contested nature of customary relations and power relations are not recognised by the state, attempts to legalise informal arrangements frequently accommodate the interests of the rural elite, and in the process the rights of the poor are eroded. Additionally, the pressures of commodification within customary systems often result in conflicts between notions of user rights and fungible assets. Since processes of legalisation are often concerned with the creation of clearly defined rights in fungible property, this often results in the erosion of forms of property based on dynamic land use and the strengthening of fungible assets, which transforms the nature of customary property.

This chapter furthermore argues that security in land does not necessarily translate into collateral, unless particular types of land can be capitalised and the risk of investment in these sectors is low. When the assets of farmers are not easily capitalised, the disbursement of loans may occur through other forms that do not use land as security. Thus, the constraints on the capitalisation of assets are not only confined to institutions, but also to the nature of the markets, transaction costs and market risk.

De Soto (1989) argues that the poor in developing countries have considerable assets worth trillions of US dollars, which they have developed through their productive endeavours. However, the legal framework and institutional structures in their respective nations do not enable them to capitalise these assets. Large investments are made in building housing and small businesses without the registration of property. Focussing on the newly arrived migrant from rural to urban areas in the informal sector, De Soto argues that the 'informals' (as he categorises them) constitute emerging entrepreneurs who work outside the legal system. He explores institutional reforms that will enable this extra-legal sector to be incorporated within economic policies and integrated with the formal sector, in which relevant support can be provided which will enable 'informals' to capitalise their assets and obtain mortgages, loans and collateral. De Soto argues that the vibrancy of a nation's economic system is determined by the ways in which its legal institutions operate:

> The more people are able to participate in the economy and detect opportunities, the greater the potential development. The great strength of a market economy is that it relies on the people's ingenuity and capacity for work, instead of on the limited contribution of an arbitrarily chosen elite. What is needed is to make the transition from a system in which individuals are subordinated to the aims of the state, to one in which the state is at the service of individuals and community (De Soto 1989:244).

De Soto largely focusses on the informal housing, trade, and transport sectors, and shows their considerable contribution to the economy, bringing together economic approaches developed in studying the informal sector with a new institutional economics framework approach to property rights. He dismisses notions that poverty in developing countries arises from cultural dimensions and the lack of individualistic entrepreneurial spirit. However, De Soto tends to over-exaggerate the entrepreneurial base within the informal sector. While he is right to point to the considerable value in economic wealth generated in the informal sector and its contribution to the national economy, he fails to examine social differentiation within this sector. Not all 'informals' own their own houses, run their own businesses, and have their own transport. Significantly large numbers of 'informals' rent premises, use public transport, and hire out their own labour. Many people within the informal sector also invest considerable amounts of time and money in social redistribution, providing social safety networks for the diminishing social services provided by the state.

By focussing on recent migrants to urban areas and those with businesses, De Soto is able to overlook certain problems which relate to the ways in which land becomes transformed from communal and family property into individual property and the implications of the commodification of land for community solidarity (Manji 2006b) and for more marginalised groups, such as women (Nyamu-Musembi 2006). Similar issues concerned with finding ways of harmonising the formal sector with the informal or customary sector have been addressed by a number of other researchers, working within a framework largely focussed on agricultural development (Lavigne Delville 2000; Toulmin and Quan 2000b). This framework questions the value of formal land titling programmes. Bruce (1993), for instance, examines the relationship between formal titling and collateral. He argues that land titling programmes that aim to create collateral and the mortgaging of land will not have positive effects unless other critical institutions exist for supporting agricultural development. This includes rural land markets, support services that encourage agricultural innovation, and prices for agricultural produce that permit the recovery of the costs of investment. Collateral is only effective in well developed land markets, which will enable banks to reconvert default loans into capital through sale of the land held as collateral. In the absence of favourable conditions for agricultural investment, loans obtained against agricultural land as collateral will tend to be invested in sectors other than agriculture. Security of land for credit and tenure security are different entities (id.). Thus, security of ownership is only one of a number of preconditions which will enable land to be used as security for loans.

The ability to capitalise land is based upon a number of market factors and risk factors which go beyond land tenure legalisation and the rule of law. Within African countries, capital is scarce, and agricultural investments are highly risky. This results in high rates of interest on loans, which in Ghana are often between twenty and 30 per cent per annum in the formal banking sector. Given difficulties in realising profits, which would enable these interest rates to be met in the agricultural sector, most loans are given to traders or diverted into commodity trading, where a much faster turnover can be achieved, not dependent upon the rhythm and vagaries of the seasons.

The creation of an institutional framework for agricultural loans and collateral does not necessarily enhance the productive abilities of farmers. Loans can often create dependency and result in farmers adopting technological prescriptions that may not necessarily be in their long-term interest. Van der Ploeg (1990) distinguishes between two different farming strategies or calculi, which he calls the intensive (I-calculi) and the extensive (E-calculi) styles. The I-calculi farmer attempts to gain the highest yield and quality of agriculture by perfecting the craft of farming. The E-calculi farmer is more concerned with maximising cost-benefit to achieve the highest returns to investments in labour and inputs. The I-calculi farmers are concerned with maintaining control and autonomy over their production and prefer to produce their own inputs such as fodder and rear their own livestock rather than purchase livestock and concentrate feed. The E-calculi farmers are more concerned with immediate profit and integration into agricultural markets. Agricultural services and agribusiness often provide loans which undermine the independence of farmers and lock them into commodity chains and agribusiness prescriptions. Increasingly, the majority of agricultural value is appropriated by large agribusiness firms who supply inputs to farmers and purchase crops from farmers for processing. In modern agribusiness only about ten per cent of agricultural value accrues to the farmer; the remainder is absorbed by the chains of input production and food processing (Watts 1994). Increasingly, the large supermarket chains drive down the profit margins of farmers as they find new sources of cheap supplies to source (Young 2004). While modern agriculture is dependent upon loans, this frequently results in a technological treadmill in which the farmer is increasingly forced to increase expenditure on inputs to maintain existing levels of production. This results in periodic farm crises and the bankruptcy of many small farmers. Thus, the final outcomes of the capitalisation of agricultural production and assets do not necessarily result in general economic security. It frequently leads to increasing economic insecurity for a large section of the population, ultimately resulting in bankruptcy and land loss (Amanor 1999).

In examining land reform and the legalisation or formal recognition of customary tenure, it is important to link land tenure security with economic systems and economic development. However, we should not assume, as De Soto tends to, that the accumulation of wealth is not problematic, or that all actors at the local level possess clear individual rights in assets and aspire to be entrepreneurs. The process of wealth accumulation usually creates social differentiation, resulting in both increasing wealth in some strata and growing impoverishment among the poor.

Customary and communal relations should not be idealised and assumed to represent just and egalitarian social values. Social relations within communities are influenced by social change and by processes of commodification and capital accumulation. Thus, in an agricultural setting, we need to focus on the process of agricultural commodification and the influences of these processes on social relations, production relations, and the land tenure system.

This chapter focuses on the impact of new wealth created in exotic fruit trees and timber plantations in the Brong Ahafo Region of Ghana. Tree plantation cultivation is being actively encouraged by the Ghanaian government, which is attempting to provide support services and loans to plantation farmers. This study examines the impact of plantation development and the accumulation of new wealth on land tenure systems and conflicts over land. It explores the major constraints on development programmes that attempt to capitalise farm assets, register land and plantations, and provide access to loans for farmers investing in plantations. It investigates the relationship between registration and legalisation of customary holdings, the commodification of agriculture, and the security of land tenure.

Site and survey

A study was carried out in four settlements situated in three neighbouring traditional chieftaincies, examining how the recent development of tree plantations affected land tenure relations. The settlements included:
- Banda Ahenkro, the main town in the Banda traditional state, situated in the newly created Tain district;
- Weila, a town of Banda migrants who settled a long time ago in the Mo traditional state, in the North Kintampo district;
- Asantekwa, a Mo settlement in the Kintampo North district;
- Nante, a Brong settlement in the Nkoranza traditional state in Kintampo South district.

These settlements are situated in the northern transition zone of Brong Ahafo, which is characterised by low population densities and readily available land. Over the last twenty years there has been a large influx of migrants from northern Ghana into this area, mainly engaged in food farming. As a result of the availability of land in this area, it is being promoted by the government for large-scale plantation development. This has resulted in an influx of large-scale plantation developers. Many local farmers are also taking up small plantation development. The vegetation consists of guinea savanna woodland, characterised by many small trees and grassland, and transitional environments consisting of mosaics of high forest and savanna woodland vegetation. The Mo and Banda settlements are characterised by savanna woodland, while that of Nante is transitional.

This study is based on a survey of 181 tree crop farmers in the four settlements, consisting of 120 men and 61 women. This gender disparity emerges because tree crop planters are relatively wealthy farmers

Figure 5.1 *The Brong Ahafo Transition Zone*

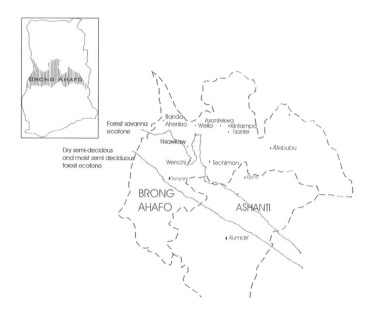

who are predominantly men. Few young farmers and migrants are re-presented in the survey for the same reasons. However, the gender constraints vary between different settlements, reflecting pressures on land and division of labour in farming. It is most pronounced at Asan-tekwa, where only nine per cent of interviewed planters were women, while it is much less pronounced in the other settlements. Thus, 50 per cent of the respondents at Weila were women, as were 38 per cent at Nante and 37 per cent at Banda Ahenkro. To examine the social con-straints on plantation development, a second survey of 209 farmers was conducted at Asantekwa, which attempted to discover the distribu-tion of plantations within the general population and the reasons which prevented particular categories of farmers from creating planta-tions.

Agriculture in northern Brong Ahafo

During the colonial period, agricultural policies were largely concerned with the promotion of cocoa as the major export crop in the forest zone. The agricultural potential of the Brong Ahafo Region (or northern Ashanti as it was called in the colonial period) was, by contrast, hindered by poor infrastructure. It was only in the 1950s that agricultural modernisation began to be promoted in the area. The low population density and availability of land attracted large-scale agricultural projects to the area, which became a major zone of state farms followed by modern private estate mechanised agriculture. By the mid-1970s and early 1980s, subsidised inputs and mechanised land clearing began to be adopted by small farmers in the vicinity of the state farms and agricultural service centres established by the government (Amanor and Pabi 2007). The development of a transport network linking these agricultural centres to the main urban centres facilitated the expansion of smallholder sector agriculture within the region. By the 1970s the major wholesale food markets in Ghana emerged in the Brong Ahafo Region, which became the major food-producing area for the urban markets (Amanor and Pabi 2007). The main food crops produced in the northern area of Brong Ahafo are yam and groundnut, and in the southern, more-forested areas, maize and vegetables.

With the introduction of structural adjustment measures in 1983, mechanised high input agriculture collapsed as government subsidies were removed. With the collapse of mechanised agriculture, more commercially oriented farmers moved into tree crop production, which is seen as a viable commercial sector. Increasingly, tree crops are being promoted in this zone by government services and a number of NGOS as part of a programme of export-oriented agriculture initiated under structural adjustment. These developments have created increasing pressures on land within the Brong Ahafo Region as commercial farmers seek large plots of land on which to establish plantations.

The main tree crops include cashew, mango and teak. Cashew is the dominant tree crop, as can be seen in Tables 5.1 and 5.2, which show the distribution of these tree crops in the various settlements in the sample. Teak is largely grown as a timber crop, for electricity poles, and as fuelwood for the curing of tobacco. It has been heavily promoted by the Forestry Service in recent years, as naturally occurring timber is becoming increasingly scarce, and the timber industry is looking to a future based on plantation production of timber. It has also been promoted among the more prosperous smallholder farmers by NGOs. The northern sections of the Brong Ahafo Region have become a major zone for tree crop production because of the lack of development of pre-existing export crops, the comparatively low density of population, and the availability of land. Tree plantations have expanded in this zone from the 1980s. Cashew was largely disseminated through farmer networks from the late 1970s in settlements bordering the Côte d'Ivoire, such as at Banda, and has only been taken up in the last ten years by the agricultural services in Ghana. During the 1980s

Table 5.1 *Mean acreages under tree crop plantations*

Plantation crop	Banda	Weila	Asantekwa	Nante	Total
Cashew	9.5	2.2	2.9	2.8	5.0
Teak	0.1	1.0	4.4	1.8	1.6
Oil palm	.	.	0.2	0.6	.
Mango	.	.	0.3	0.2	.
No. of farmers	62	38	41	40	181

Table 5.2 *Percentage of farmers cultivating tree crops*

Plantation crop	Banda (%)	Weila (%)	Asantekwa (%)	Nante (%)	Total (%)
Cashew	100	97	90	85	94
Teak	13	20	32	52	28
Oil palm	.	3	9	20	9
Mango	2	8	27	12	9
No. of farmers	62	38	41	40	181

NGOs also played important roles in promoting tree cultivation in farming communities, particularly the Adventists Development and Relief Services (ADRA). In recent years there have been a number of donor-sponsored organisations promoting the development of an infra-structure for the export promotion of tree crops and enhanced quality control, including Technoserve and the USAID-sponsored Trade and Investment Programme Competitive Export Economy (TIPCEE).

These developments have resulted in a significant number of com-mercial farmers seeking large tracts of land on which to develop large plantations, and a significant number of richer farmers within settle-ments investing in the development of small tree plantations. Small-holder farmers take up plantation development for a number of rea-sons including the following:

− To provide an investment for the future or for their old age, when they do not have the strength to go clear land and make new farms. A number of elderly farmers, in their seventies and eighties were interviewed, whose only source of income came from their cashew plantations.

− To create an 'inheritance' (*agyapadee*) from which their children can benefit in the future.

− To create an investment in a farm which will provide capital from year to year from the same plot of land; in the case of cashew a var-iant of this answer is that plantations help to look after the family and pay for children's school fees.

Many tree farmers view the different types of farms as contributing towards an investment portfolio. Food crops provide the basic food for feeding the family. Cashew and mango provide a medium-term investment, providing capital for further farm investment and for meeting the major family expenditures, such as school fees. Teak provides a long-term investment, which provides a large lump sum when it is eventually sold.

While many farmers see plantation crops as providing more profitable investments than food crops, food cropping is important in the area, since it is a major food basket for the urban areas, particularly for yams, maize and vegetables. Tree crops are usually integrated with food crop production. Tree seedlings are planted in food plots and food crops are cultivated among them for up to three or four years, until the trees begin to establish a canopy. In many instances, farmers plant tree crops in areas with poor soil fertility, or in old farming areas in which the fertility of the land has declined through continual cultivation. At Weila, most women planting cashew used old groundnut farms with declining fertility. These are usually situated around the perimeters of the settlement, since these were the first areas to have been cultivated.

Tree plantations, in their early years, require considerable labour in management. Fire is a big hazard in tree plantations. If they are not kept free of weeds they are prone to being burnt, and so a fire belt is cleared around the plantation. Farmers gradually extend their tree plantations, by cultivating adjacent areas from year to year and planting trees in the old plots. The cost of weeding is the major constraint on the extent to which they establish their plantation. Farmers who overextend their plantations beyond their capacities and hire labour usually end up with burnt plantations. In the Nante area, farmers often hire out their young cashew plantations to migrants to cultivate food crops, on the condition that they weed around and maintain the young trees in the plantations. While some farmers hire out land to the migrant farmers, some give out this land freely (i.e. expect no monetary payment in addition to labour). Some farmers also give out land to migrant farmers provided they plant trees in the plot. After a three-year period of cultivation, they release new adjacent land to the migrants to extend the plantation. This enables them to develop their plantation while minimising the outlays of hiring labour.

Some farmers also plant their food crops around the plantation to minimise the incidence of fire. The plantation will be extended into these areas at a later date, and a new food cropping perimeter will be created. Since the cultivation of plantations results in the occupation of land by pure stands of trees (which will remain for many years), this disrupts fallowing strategies and removes land from recycling between annual crop cultivation and fallow restoration. Thus, the expansion of plantations can result in inadequate land for food cropping within a system of fallow restoration. To ensure that food cropping is not disrupted by the expansion of plantations, the most fertile land is frequently reserved for yams, which require good soils, and so plantations are established beyond the main food cropping area or in areas characterised by less fertile soil. Thus, the expansion of tree crops has engendered considerable debate about appropriate and sustainable land management practices.

Size of tree plantations and social composition of tree farmers

An extensive survey of 209 farmers was conducted at Asantekwa in early 2008 to investigate the prevalence and size of plantations. The sample consisted of 112 men and 97 women. Some 63 per cent of men and 26 per cent of women had tree plantations. Of the total sample 45 per cent had tree plantations. The most common reason given by women for their lack of tree plantations was lack of land, often because their husbands had created a tree plantation, and this left insufficient land for their needs. Married women usually depend on their husband to provide them with land. Thus, the expansion of male acreages under plantation at Asantekwa negatively impacts on women's access to land.

The men interviewed in this survey consisted of 88 locals and 24 migrants. Some 76 per cent of local men created tree plantations as compared to thirteen per cent of migrants. Migrants do not usually create plantations since land is only released to them for food crop cultivation, unless they apply specifically for land for plantation development from the chief. Migrants are usually temporary residents, and plantations are a long-term investment, so many migrants are not interested in obtaining land for plantation development.

Within the four communities of Banda, Weila, Asantekwa, and Nante, most of the cashew plantations are relatively small. However, since most plantations are recent – with the exception of those at Banda – they are in a process of expansion, and farmers usually extend the cultivation of tree crops over their land from year to year. It is difficult to determine the ultimate extent of these plantations at present. The survey shows that 75 per cent of cashew plantations were less than five acres.[2] The median size was about three acres. However, Banda plantations tended to be larger than in the other settlements, not surprising given the longer periods farmers have been involved in cashew cultivation. Thus, the median size (i.e. half the farmers have plantations under this size) of cashew plantations was six acres at Banda compared with two acres for the other settlements. The largest plantation at Banda was estimated at 100 acres, compared to thirteen acres at Weila, sixteen acres at Asantekwa, and fifteen acres at Nante. Men usually had significantly larger plantations than women. The average size of planta-tions owned by males was 6.1 acres, while the average for women was 2.8 acres. The largest woman's cashew plantation was twelve acres. The largest five per cent of male plantations ranged from eighteen to 100 acres, while the largest five per cent of female plantations were be-tween eight and twelve acres. Some 75 per cent of women's cashew plantations were less than three acres compared to six acres for men.

The median size of teak plantations in the survey was three acres. Some 75 per cent of plantations were under one acre at Banda, under two acres at Asantekwa, under 2.5 acres at Nante, and under 7.5 acres at Weila. The largest plantation was estimated to be about 150 acres. This was cultivated by a caretaker chief for satellite settlements in the Asantekwa area. He gave out land to migrants to cultivate crops in re-turn for planting, weeding, and tending his teak plantation. The largest teak plantation at Banda was only two acres, as compared to fifteen acres at Weila, and seventeen acres at Nante. Around 50 per cent of male plantations were two acres or less, while the median for women's plantations was one acre. The largest women's teak plantation was two acres. Some ten percent of male teak growers had plantations exceed-ing ten acres.

Within Brong Ahafo teak and cashew plantations are also created by large-scale commercial planters who originate from outside the area and are attracted by the cheap but suitable land. An example of a com-mercial plantation is Vicdoris Farms, a large cashew plantation situated in Dawadawa No. 2, north of Kintampo. The owner of Vicdoris Farms is a wealthy Ashanti pharmaceutical distributor with branches in Accra and Kumasi and other towns. Vicdoris Farms is more than 1,500 acres, of which 800 acres has already been developed into cashew plantation. The land was acquired from the paramount chief and registered as a lease with the Regional Land Commission.

The development of the smallholder and commercial tree crop sec-tors creates significant pressures of commodification on land, agricul-ture, and land-based assets. This results in a number of struggles that attempt to redefine customary land relations, land management strate-gies, and investment patterns in agriculture. This further results in the development of plantation agriculture as a means of securing claims on land, as well as in a growing interest in various types of land regis-tration as a means of securing the increasing investment of capital and labour in land. Such development of agricultural accumulation results in the redefinition of customary land relations and attempts to seek ex-ternal legitimation from the state and development agencies of both contemporary patterns of agricultural accumulation and their asso-ciated land tenure practices.

The land tenure system and dynamics of change

Within the transitional zone there are two distinct land tenure systems: a communal system which is found at Banda Ahenkro, Weila, and Asantekwa, and a family tenure system, which is found at Nante. Under the communal system, all citizens can farm anywhere on the land of their settlement, provided no one else is farming it or making claims to managing the land in a system of rotational bush fallowing. In the family system, land that has been cleared by members of extended lineages is claimed by their descendants, and the land comes under the authority structure within the extended lineage, whether it is actively farmed or preserved as fallow.

The family land system is characteristic of the high forest zone and the communal system of the more savanna-like areas in the high forest zone. The clearance of high forest is a major undertaking involving considerable labour. Secondary forest is characterised by fast-growing softwood trees which are often easier to clear and which often create higher soil fertility than primary forests, which store many of the nutrients in biomass. Farmers in the high forest zone frequently maintain their lands as secondary forests, returning to farm them before they regenerate into primary forest. Youth often prefer to work on the land that their ancestors cleared rather than going out to clear new land, although ambitious and enterprising farmers will extend their areas of cultivation by clearing new forest areas. The family rights in land arise out of claims to being descendants of those who originally cleared the land.

In contrast, in the savanna woodlands, there is no such clear division between primary and secondary forest. Savanna woodlands consist of many small, rapidly regenerating trees and grassland. Fire is endemic within the woodland savanna and frequently disrupts the regeneration of fallow vegetation. The population density is also very low. Rather than managing contingent plots of land within a rotational bush-fallowing system, farmers tend to move around, cultivating suitably regenerated areas. The majority of the labour is often expended in weeding and tilling the land rather than removing large primary forest trees. Thus, farmers have less incentive to continue managing areas in which they have invested less labour in clearing the trees. Farming in the savanna areas usually consists of a combination of moving forward and backwards within one area, and locating to new areas when the opportunities to expand farming become constrained by other people moving to farm in the area, or by decreasing soil fertility.

In practice, the differences between the family farming system and the communal system are not so distinct and often blur into each other, particularly as the systems become increasingly commodified, and available land becomes less abundant. Farmers within family lands often clear new plots within unclaimed forest. Farmers within the communal tenure system often work abreast of their relatives. Thus, children often begin farming by helping their parents, who then allocate them a piece of land to work adjacent to them, and in this way they can keep a watchful eye on them and offer them farming advice. As their children grow up, they work alongside each other, offering each other mutual advice. When the grandparents die, their land is often given over to their grandchildren. With increasing population and the influx of migrants, more people within the communal tenure system become dependent upon receiving lands from their parents and grandparents, since unclaimed lands by this point lie at a distance from the settlement. Thus, the communal land system begins to acquire the characteristics of family land. At Nante, where the family land system prevails, 83 per cent of the respondents gained land from close relatives, as compared to 52 per cent of those at Banda and Weila, and 28 per cent at Weila.

In both systems women usually get land from their husbands or, when they are single or divorced, from close male relatives. Some 36 per cent of women at Weila, 27 per cent at Nante, and 26 per cent at Banda got land from their husbands.[3] Also, 27 per cent of Nante women got land from their fathers, and another 27 per cent from their mothers. About 38 per cent of Banda women got land from their parents, as compared to 26 per cent of women at Weila.

Within both these systems, land is not allocated as a demarcated area. Farmers can clear as much land as they are able based on their strength and ability to hire labour, until they meet other farmers clearing from their farms. To avoid crossing each other's land and path of farming, farmers usually work abreast. In the communal system, a farmer wishing to relocate to a new area will discuss his/her intentions with neighbouring farmers with the intention of working out a mutually beneficial direction of farming that prevents farmers crossing each other unnecessarily. Farmers with more capital and labour resources will be able to clear larger tracts of land than those with a lesser capacity to mobilise labour.

This arrangement also extends to land that is allocated to migrants in the communal system. They usually make annual payments for farming rights to chiefs, rather than payments for specific plots of land. They are usually shown an area to clear and allowed to extend their farms on the basis of their own strength, rather than on the basis of making payments for a particular area of land. In contrast, in the more heavily populated forest zone, land is usually hired out to migrants for monetary rents or as sharecrop arrangements on demarcated plots.

Rights of chiefs and of local farmers

Rights to land are also constructed within a political and administrative system of control over land, which defines the land relations between chiefs and their 'subjects'. The political relations of land originate from the colonial period of Indirect Rule, when a system of customary land tenure was articulated by the colonial administration in collaboration with the chiefs. The state recognises the allodial rights as being vested in the chief and the user rights in their subjects. This enables citizens to use land freely for farming purposes but does not allow them to sell their land, since it is recognised as ultimately belonging to the stool. Chiefs can transact land and natural resources with migrants, but not with their subjects who have rights to use the land.

Since chiefs cannot gain revenues from local farmers, they are often interested in transacting natural resources and land with migrants and with commercial investors. This frequently leads to conflicts, as locals try to protect their own use of local resources, and chiefs attempt to transact land and natural resources and prevent locals extending their use over them. Three incidents, narrated below, illustrate the conflicts that arise over the control and commodification of land and agriculture at Weila, Asantekwa, and Banda.

The chief of Chaara claims ultimate ownership of the land of Weila. The Weila people originally migrated from Banda and sought permission to settle on land under Chaara. In 1996 a commercial teak farmer approached the Chaara chief for land on which to create a large teak plantation. The Chaara chief decided to allocate land at Weila. He consulted with the Weila chief, but not with the farmers and people of Weila. The farmers of Weila only became aware of this transaction when the commercial farmer came with labourers to Weila to begin demarcating the land. The youth of Weila were extremely concerned about this, since a large area on the immediate east of the town had been allocated to the developer. This was the main area in which they could find uncultivated land, and the development would create a serious land shortage for them. They protested against the demarcation of the land and took the matter up with the paramount chief at New Longoro. The paramount chief found in their favour and agreed that the lease of land to the contractor would result in a serious land shortage for the people of Weila. The contract with the commercial farmer was annulled. Later, under the influence of Ghana-Canada in Concert, an NGO promoting tree planting in the Mo area, the leader of the youth at Weila began to develop his own teak plantations, as did other youth. The Weila chief began to complain about the inconsistencies of his actions, alleging that while he had opposed the investor appropriating land, he was now appropriating land from the community and ordered a halt to his plantation. The youth leader now had to come before the chiefs and elders to request permission to create the plantations and provide drink, money, and a sheep to propitiate them.

At Asantekwa, the chief and youth have been locked in disputes over access and control over land and natural resources. Asantekwa is a relatively recent settlement, which has been developed in the last 50-60 years, with its inhabitants coming from the surrounding Mo settlements. The land of Asantekwa comes under the jurisdiction of the chief of Mansra. During the early 1990s the Mansra chief gained revenue from migrant Sissala charcoal burners. However, the youth of Asantekwa took up charcoal burning and forced the Sissala to move elsewhere. This loss of revenue resulted in increasing friction between the Mansra chief and the youth. When farmers began to move into tree plantations, the Mansra chief attempted to establish greater control over land. He argued that the development of plantations on yam farming land was creating a problem of land shortage for food crops and that farmers should establish their tree plantations beyond the food-producing area. He advised cashew and teak farmers to register their plantations with him. In his bid to extend his control over the land, the Mansra chief appointed a caretaker chief to look after the land at Asantekwa. This appointment of a chief was a controversial decision, for there are two sections within Asantekwa who claim to be the original setters of the land. They originate from the settlements of Banaatwi and Ahenakrom. The appointed chief came from the Banaatwi section. The Ahenakrom section (which has stronger credentials in the claim to being the original settlers and more support among the townspeople) complained that this was not right, and that the chief should have consulted with the townspeople before appointing a chief. The Mansra chief responded that the land belonged to him, and he could appoint anyone he chose as chief. The Ahenakrom section referred the case to the elders at Mansra, who were divided on the matter but criticised the chief for his actions. He was considered to have behaved arrogantly. Increasingly frustrated, the chief abdicated.

In Banda, there are also conflicting interpretations of the rights of citizens, chiefs, and migrants to land. The presence of migrants is very important for tree crop and yam production, since they provide most of the hired labour. The townspeople attract migrants by providing them with land for food cultivation. Migrants usually have a landlord within the town, whom they work for, and who provides them with land. The migrants are also registered with the chief, who provides them with a permit to farm in his domain. This permit includes a photograph of the migrant, defines the economic rights of the migrant, and records the sums they pay annually for farming rights. In 2007, the migrants paid ¢200,000 (about USD 22) for an annual farming permit. Several of the migrants have been able to establish cashew plantations after seeing the chief. Some of them confided that the chief advised them to go into cashew production. In contrast with this, many of the townspeople claim that by custom migrants do not have the right to cultivate cashew unless they marry a local woman and have children with her, who will inherit the plantation.[4] These various positions on migrants emanate out of the different interests in the conflict over land between chiefs and local citizens. Limiting the access of migrants to land for tree crop production prevents the chief from transacting large areas of land with outsiders and retains a large supply of land for local farmers. If marriage is the condition for access to a plantation, then access to plantations is negotiated with families with marriageable daughters rather than with chiefs. On the other hand, if the chief is able to release land to migrants for tree crop cultivation by encouraging migrants to go into cashew production, the chief can create a demand for land for commercial agriculture from which he can gain large revenues in the future.

The large-scale commercial farmers gain land by approaching chiefs to lease land. They purchase the land from the chief. However, the chiefs usually represent this as a customary arrangement to evade control and interference from state agencies. In contrast to transactions with migrant peasant farmers, a specific area of demarcated land is transacted and a site plan drawn up by surveyors. The chiefs sign the site plan which is then registered with the Regional Land Commission. While it is difficult to get information on the amounts of money involved in these transactions, one source indicated that around Kintampo a commercial mango farmer was recently offered a one square mile (2.5 km sq) plot by a chief for ¢75 million (about USD 8,000). While this is a large sum by rural standards, this is relatively cheap for commercial developers given the large extent of the land and the potential returns from investment in tree crops. Chiefs are often willing to transact large tracts of land with commercial developers since they cannot gain land revenues from local farmers.

Commodification of agriculture

The development of tree crop plantations disrupts the redistribution of land through bush fallowing and cultivation. Plantations take land out of cultivation for many years and give their developers new rights in land. The land now acquires a value it did not hold previously. Tree plantations enable investors to store capital in land and to invest in labour to acquire land, although this investment has considerable risk from the hazards of fire. The overextension of the enterprise beyond the ability to intensively manage and weed the plantation often results in burnt plantations that have to be replanted or abandoned. The claims on land established by investing in plantations have been secure, since in the customary system of land tenure, the ability to point to trees that one has planted on fallow land is used as evidence of rights to the land established through occupation.

However, the new wealth that arises from the creation of plantations creates new concerns about the long-term security of investments in land and the risk of this investment for prosperous farmers within the communities. The ease with which plantation owners can accumulate land and wealth creates worries among those with the new wealth that this wealth will lead to future sources of dispute. Thus, bush fires on plantations become interpreted as the deliberate work of jealous neighbours. Tree planters begin to harbour concerns that their children will not be able to inherit their wealth since this will be challenged by the elders, and that the chiefs will introduce new bylaws and establish claims on their land that will undermine and nullify their investments, or that the government will introduce new legislation that will undermine their rights in the land (see Table 5.3). These fears arise out of a concern that the world is changing rapidly, that customary relations are also changing, and the best strategy for the future, for a world we do not know, is to gain formal recognition of ownership of land through documents, which the government and legal sector respect. Thus, the backdrop to the changes brought about by investment in plantations is not a customary world of stable land, moral, and social values, but a customary world which is being transformed by economic change, continually struggling to adapt its frameworks and rules to the processes of commodification. Processes of social differentiation are beginning to erode the conventions through which user rights in land are established.

In this context, farmers become increasingly interested in securing the land outside of informal arrangements within the family and customary system. Registration of land favours plantation owners. It is not possible to register land within the customary bush-fallowing system, since rights are established through clearance and labour rather than through demarcation of particular areas. However, it is possible to register plantations, particularly since farmers usually stop extending them after a period and concentrate on their management. On average, 90 per cent of the farmers interviewed in the survey expressed an interest in registering their plantations. This ranged from 95 per cent of respondents at Asantekwa to 85 per cent at Banda. Most farmers were interested in registering land to make claims on the land rather than to secure access to loans, collateral, and government services (see Table 5.3). Some farmers at Banda stated that they had several plots of land

Table 5.3 *Main reasons for wanting to register land*

Reason for wanting to register land	Frequency	Percentage
In case of disputes within the family or with farming neighbours/chief	82	52
The world is changing, and you cannot be sure what future disputes will come over land. The safest bet is to get formal documents	8	6
So that children can inherit it without difficulty	45	29
To be able to get a loan, advice and support from government agencies	20	13
Total	155	100

in different places. They had to keep these plots under constant cultivation to maintain their claims over the land and to prevent other farmers who needed land from encroaching upon these plots. They envisaged that a land document expressing their ownership of these plots would be a viable way of securing the land. Registration of customary claims on land in this context brings security to those who are overstretched in their management of land, rather than to those looking to extend their existing lands. It breaks down the redistributive features in the land management system, which arises from allowing people to make claims on land on the basis of their command over the necessary labour to maintain management over the land.

A dominant concern underlying much of the thinking of many of these farmers was that the world is changing, and in the new commodified world documents are important. The Queenmother at Banda was adamant that registering of land contravened the spirit of customary land relations, since the land did not belong to the farmer as a possession but could only be used. But then she stated with great authority and certainty, 'but things are about to change'. At the time when research was conducted at Banda Ahenkro, a Lands Officer had just been appointed by the Tain District Assembly to register lands in Banda Ahenkro. Similarly at Asantekwa, there was an expectation of impeding change in land tenure matters, with many farmers believing that the chief had issued a proclamation that farmers should register their plantations. However, as narrated above, the subsequent political disputes that had arisen around this resulted in the chief 'abdicating' his stool. Many farmers are concerned that they and their children will lose their claims to land if they do not register their plots and others do, particularly if others make claims to their land in the registration process. Paradoxically, by claiming that land ownership can be made increasingly more secure, national land policy and registration programmes introduce an element of insecurity into existing tenure relations. They make farmers anxious to secure what was already considered secure, in case other people are able to use the new procedures to make claims on their land.

While the overwhelming majority of farmers expressed interest in registering their land, very few farmers have been able to register their land 'formally' or 'informally' with state agencies. In the survey, only one farmer had a site plan (the caretaker chief of satellite settlements around Asantekwa with a 150-acre teak plantation). Another five farmers had registered their teak plantation with the Forestry Service, and another four were in the process of registering their teak plantation with the Forestry Service. Some 88 per cent of the respondents did not know the procedures for registering land or plantations.

In most instances, the cost involved in registering land is the main constraint. Formal land registration is beyond the means of most farmers. At the Town and Country Planning Office of the Kintampo District Office, one officer estimated that the cost of providing a registered site plan for farmers would be ¢2.5 million (about USD 265) for a two-acre plot, ¢3.5 million (USD 370) for ten acres, and ¢7 million (USD 740) for a 30-acre plot. The major expenditure involved in this process is getting a licensed surveyor in Kumasi to sign the site plan. There are no licensed surveyors in Kintampo. While most farmers were interested in registering their land, very few were willing to pay amounts commensurate with the cost of registering land formally (see Table 5.4). Very few farmers were willing to spend more than ¢500,000 (about USD 50) to register their land.

Land registration, regularisation and loans

Formal registration of land leases or plantations in Ghana is beyond the means of the majority of farmers. It has essentially been developed to meet the needs of the commercial sector. However, in recent years

Table 5.4 *Amount farmers are prepared to pay to register their plantation*

Amount willing to pay to register land (cedis)	Frequency	Percentage
cannot pay anything	1	0.8
Up to 20,000	10	7.8
21-50,000	24	18.6
51,000-100,000	20	15.5
101,000-200,000	19	14.7
201,000-500,000	33	25.6
501,000-1 million	8	6.2
Between 1 and 2 million	5	3.9
Over 2 million	9	7.0
Total	129	100.0

administrative reforms in a number of sectors have attempted to create
new institutional structures to enable the registration of customary
rights in land or the land of small farmers. The Land Administration
Project (LAP) is developing a number of pilot Customary Land Secretariats to document customary land holdings. Within the research area,
there were no operational Customary Land Secretariats, and the LAP
project has had little influence on land tenure issues. However, there
are a number of sector-based initiatives which attempt to create more
accessible processes of land registration or access to loans for plantation owners.

In the forestry sector, with the growing focus on plantation timber,
the Forestry Service has become increasingly concerned with regularising tenure arrangements and registering owners of timber plantations.
New legislation in the forestry sector seeks to clarify and regularise
ownership and benefit-sharing within forest reserves and in private
plantations. Increasingly, forest reserve land is being allocated to the
commercial sector for development. Arrangements have been worked
out between chiefs, the commercial sector, and the Forestry Service
and translated into benefit-sharing arrangements. The commercial sector is responsible for developing the plantations. The Forestry Service
is responsible for protecting the reserves, supervising reforestation
plans, and monitoring developments. The chiefs are responsible for
guaranteeing the security of the land on which the project occurs and
ensuring that the community does not encroach on the reserves. The
commercial developers receive 90 per cent of the stumpage value of
the timber. The chiefs receive 'drink money' or customary payments
for the land, annual rent payments, and six per cent of the stumpage
value of the timber. The forestry commission receives two per cent of
the stumpage value, and the communities on whose land the forest reserve stands receive two per cent for community development projects.

On individually owned private sector plantations, the legal framework for timber rights has clarified that 100 per cent of the value of
the timber belongs to the farmer, subject to the local land tenure arrangements under which the land was negotiated by the planter. This
means that chiefs cannot claim a portion of the planted timber as custodians of the land, unless this constituted a prior agreement under
which the land was released to the farmer. Levies and conveyance fees
on the timber are paid by the purchaser of the timber.

The Forestry Commission[5] has declared its intent to register all individual timber plantations in Ghana. This intent largely arises from the
need to monitor sources of timber and to control the legality of production, since there are concerns about the present proliferation of illegal
logging. Given the extent of timber plantations, which are now being
established within forestry reserves, it is important for the Forestry Ser-

vice to be able to monitor the sources of timber conveyed along roads to prevent illegal harvesting of forest reserves and theft from private plantations. Registration of owners enables the origins of timber to be checked against conveyance documents. Registration of ownership also enables the Forestry Service to maintain a record of the volumes of timber being cultivated and their state of maturity, in order to forecast trends in timber production. It enables the Forestry Service to identify potential sources of timber for timber contractors, and to provide management services, recommendations for plantation developers, and loans or access loans against plantations.

Two systems of plantation registration have been developed in the Forestry Sector. The first comprises the formal registration of the plantation as a lease with title deeds and a site plan. The site plan is usually drawn up by the Town and Country Planning Department of the local District Assembly, sent to a registered surveyor to sign, and then registered with the regional branch of the Lands Commission. A copy of the site plan is registered with the Forestry Service and sent to the Forestry Commission in Accra. The formal registration of the plantation enables the owner to apply for loans.

The second process involves the 'informal' registration of the plantation with the district Forestry Service Division. This is a 'free' service provided by the Forestry Service. The plantation is not measured, demarcated or mapped. However, a forestry officer visits the plantation to verify its existence, and the owner fills in a form to register it with the Forestry Service. The form has fields for the family head, village chief and paramount chief to sign and substantiate that the plantation is the property of the owner and that his ownership is recognised by the family and chief. Clearly, much thought has gone into the preparation of this document. The objective is to involve all the important stakeholders in verifying the legitimacy of the property of the plantation owner, and thus harmonising the institutional structures of the customary system with registration by the Forestry Service. However, this opens avenues for chiefs to begin to demand payments from farmers, since chiefs do not sign land documents without receiving a payment and 'customary drinks'. In many areas, chiefs attempt to extract payments from local farmers for creating plantations, and farmers are resisting these demands. As discussed above, in Asantekwa, recent political conflicts between the Mansra chief and the townspeople arose from the attempts by the chiefs to regularise the use of land for plantations and to gain greater control over land. Where these types of disputes occur, the attempts of the Forestry Service to create a 'harmonisation' between the formal and informal systems may enable chiefs to extract revenues from plantation farmers and further inflame disputes and increase the insecurities in land holding.

A second major constraint in the registration of plantations within the Forestry Service arises out of the lack of logistical support and insufficient staff to implement this programme, a point that the Plantations Officer at Kintampo woefully conceded. In the course of carrying out interviews at Nante, I informed some teak farmers about the free registration of land carried out by the District Forestry Service and advised them to go and register their plantations at Kintampo. The sceptical farmers laughed politely at my suggestion. One of them pointed out: 'If we go to Kintampo to register our land the forestry officer will tell us that they do not have money for transport to come here. So before they come here we will have to pay for their *transport and allowance.*' This was borne out at Banda Ahenkro where we found a teak farmer with an incomplete form, which a Forestry Officer from the regional capital had sold him for ¢100,000. The Forestry Officer had convinced him that he was 'favouring' him, since the real price of the form was ¢200,000. However, what was of concern to this teak planter was that he had been waiting for more than a year for the officer to come back to help him complete the filling of the form.

Poor logistical support not only prevents programmes from being implemented, the frustration it brings breeds lack of accountability and encourages staff to engage in corrupt practices. Thus, the combination of local political interests in land, poor logistical support within the Forestry Service, and the farmers' distrust of forestry officers is likely to undermine the attempts of the Forestry Service to comprehensively register the teak plantations of smallholder farmers. However, if planters absorb the transaction costs in registering their plantation, the Forestry Service largely gains from its extended ability to monitor timber without absorbing the costs of the information – particularly since there is little benefit for planters in registering their plantations.

Within the cashew farming sector no attempts have been made to register the plantations of farmers, although this capacity exists within some of the Agricultural Departments, such as the one at Kintampo. The Trade and Investment Programme for Competitive Export Economy (TIPCEE) is mapping cashew farms, using district extension services to carry out the programme with GPS devices. However, as is common with many national and donor initiatives, the information being generated is not shared with the district. According to the Director of Agriculture, the software for the programme uses a special dongle key, which prevents the information being accessed and used by the Kintampo District Agricultural Department.

While registration of cashew plantations does not have the same priority as the registration of teak plantations, loans for farmers are much more prevalent in the cashew sector. Loans to cashew farmers are given out in the Tain, Kintampo North and Kintampo South districts by the Agricultural Development Bank (ADB) in Techiman. The applications are made through the Agricultural Department. Loans are not made against collateral of land or plantations. Collateral in this case is replaced by the solidarity of social groups. Before farmers can receive a loan, they must join a cashew farmers group, which consists of between eight to twelve farmers. If any member of a group defaults on repayment, all other members of the group will be penalised and excluded from future loans. If a significant number of groups default, then the settlement will be excluded from receiving loans. The loans are given to assist farmers in planting food crops in young cashew plantations and in weeding the plantations to ensure the survival of the young cashew plants from fire. Before loans are given, the cashew plantations of the group members are first inspected by an agricultural officer to certify that they exist and are suitable for granting loans. The group members then need to open a bank account with ADB, deposit an initial sum for opening the account, and get their photograph taken for an identity card. The amount given to all farmers for the loan is ¢ 1.5 million (about USD 160). This has to be repaid with twenty per cent interest within one year. However, the transaction costs that farmers have to bear on the loan are quite high in relation to the loan, which include the costs of opening the bank account, transport to Techiman on a number of occasions, or paying for the transport expenses of representatives of the group. Many farmers estimated that they spent at least ¢300,000 on 'going up and down' to get the loan, which substantially reduced the amount available for expenditure on their farms (and increases the interest rate on the actual amount available for farm expenditure to about 50 per cent if they receive 1.2 million after the deduction of costs in getting the loan). Not surprisingly, a large number of farmers fail to repay their loans on time. The amount of the loan was also considered to be modest in relation to the expense involved in managing cashew (see Table 5.5). The total amount of the loan enables a farmer to hire labour to weed three acres of cashew, or more realistically, if the costs of purchasing seeds for food crop production are ta-

Table 5.5 *Cost of hired labour*

Labour task	Cost (cedis)
Clearing one acre	150,000-200,000
Raising yam mounds	200,000
First weeding	150,000-200,000
Second weeding	150,000-20000
Weeding an existing 1-acre cashew plantation	400,000
Cultivating 1 acre of yam with cashew (excluding cost of planting material)	800,000

ken into consideration, an approximate maximum of two acres. However, it does not take into consideration the cost of clearing new land if the farmers wish to expand their acreage, nor of using pesticides on established cashew.

In the survey, 32 per cent of cashew farmers received loans. This varied from 63 per cent of the cashew farmers interviewed at Weila to only eighteen per cent at Banda Ahenkro (see Table 5.6). Fewer loans are given to farmers in the Tain district than in Kintampo North and South, ostensibly because of a high failure rate in repayment. In Banda Ahenkro, only one cashew farmers' group received loans in 2006, and one individual in that group has failed to honour his repayment of the loan in time. At present, no farmers are receiving loans. Most of the farmers receiving loans are those who plant seeds recommended by the Agricultural Department. Some 70 per cent of the farmers receiving loans planted seeds provided by the Agricultural Department. However, in Banda most cashew plantations have been established with seeds acquired outside the agricultural extension system. Thus, it is likely that the Ministry of Agriculture uses the promise of loans to promote its extension recommendation, only recommending farmers for loans who plant their seeds and follow their recommendations.

Most of the farmers who have received loans are highly critical of the loan programme. Some 70 per cent of farmers felt that it was excessively difficult to get the loan, and that it required an excessive waste of time and energy on 'go and come' (*ko ne bra*). And 86 per cent of the cashew farmers felt that they had to spend an excessive amount of money on the logistics of applying for and following the loan through. However, 76 per cent of the cashew farmers said they would still apply for another ADB loan, since there was no viable alternative source of institutional capital loans. A total of 90 per cent of all loans to cashew farmers originated from ADB. The remaining farmers obtained loans from cashew-buying companies or credit unions. Although these loans were easier to get than the ADB loans, they were for much smaller amounts, often under ¢500,000. Cashew-buying agents may often use small loans to engage in forward buying to secure future supplies, deducting the loan from the future sale of the crop.

Table 5.6 *Proportion of cashew farmers receiving loans*

	Banda (%)	Weila (%)	Asantekwa (%)	Nante (%)	Total (%)
Percentage of farmers receiving loan from ADB	18	63	34	20	32
No. of farmers	60	38	41	40	179

Although the bank could easily use the cashew plantations as collateral against the loan, and take measures to possess the farm until the loan and interest are paid off, the management costs of this would most likely be higher than the value of the loan. Thus, the bank prefers to place the transaction costs on the farmers through the organisation of farmers' groups with a collective responsibility towards loan repayment. The relatively low value of the cashew in relation to the high interest rates and the small amounts of capital loaned prevent the cashew plantations of small farmers being used as collateral by banks. The value of the plantation can only be capitalised through working it and harvesting the cashew, since the land has little value beyond the comparatively high investments in labour and crop, which can be destroyed by bush fires when it is relaxed. Thus, by possessing cashew plantations against defaults on loans, the banks assume a high-risk investment which requires considerable investment in labour to yield dividends. Markets for existing cashew plantations are limited, and thus default on the loans cannot be immediately capitalised.

Conclusion

Within Brong Ahafo the Forestry Service has developed a programme of informal mechanisms for registering teak plantations. However, it has not developed a programme of loans to support the development of teak plantations to complement the registration of land and enable farmers to gain land for collateral. Although the plantation registration programme claims to facilitate the 'free' registration of teak plantations for farmers, the lack of logistical support means that farmers largely have to absorb the transaction costs of registering their plantations, which may include payments to forestry officers. Moreover, the benefits of registering are not clear or tangible. The requirements that the documentation be signed by chiefs and family elders are concerned with establishing community legitimacy and transparency for land registration, but they fail to take into account political struggles over the control of land which often divide the interests of chiefs and community elders from cultivators. It opens up potential avenues for money to be exacted from planters by chiefs for recognition of their land rights and acquisition of documentation. These requirements create high transaction costs, which deter most farmers from pursuing land registration. Thus, informal registration becomes an avenue pursued by only a few determined teak planters, mainly those who seek an active client relationship with the Forestry Service.

While the government has attempted to gain support from the private sector and foreign investors for financial support to teak planters

in the form of loans, this has not been successful. The main constraints result from the reluctance of the private sector and international capital to invest in plantation development, given the high risks.
Nevertheless, the government continues to invest in developing public
sector plantations within the forest reserves and in creating favourable
incentives for private sector investment, hopeful of eventually attracting
foreign investment. The teak plantation registration programme of the
Forestry Service is largely concerned with the gradual building up of
an information system on the location of existing plantations, which
can be used to link buyers and sellers in the present, gradually developing conditions for when capital investors become more interested in investing in the future development of teak. The programme is constrained by a failure to attract private sector investment in financing
loans for teak farmers commensurate with the value of investment in
teak. It mainly offers farmers who register their plantations state recognition of their ownership of teak, information on potential buyers and
price, and technical advice for teak production. Scarcity of capital for
loans and unwillingness to take long-term risks are important factors
which presently hinder the capitalisation of teak plantations. However,
the registration of teak plantations also has the ulterior objective of
meeting the needs of the Forestry Service to monitor legal timber and
track the origins of felled timber. By actively registering their plantations teak farmers help the Forestry Service to build up low cost information. As capital becomes available for teak development, it is likely
that institutional innovations for the recognition of teak plantations
will take place, but alongside political struggles to gain control over
teak and extract revenues from it, which are likely to undermine some
of the interests of the poorest and most marginal sections of society

In contrast with this, within the cashew sector an institutional framework for the disbursement of loans to small farmers has been developed by the agricultural services in collaboration with the ADB. However, this eschews linking land to collateral, since this would result in
high transaction costs resulting from poorly developed land markets
and information systems, which are incommensurate with the size of
the loans and the management costs of capitalising debt through collateral. While the Ministry of Agriculture is involved with TIPCEE in the
mapping and digitising of cashew plantations, the results of this are
not made public within the districts or used in registering farmers'
plantations, nor are they officially used against the provisions of loans
at present. While many cashew farmers have received small loans, the
transaction costs of linking loans to the registration of land are higher
than the value of the loans. Cashew is also a high-risk crop, which is
vulnerable to fire. The ADB loans programme for cashew thus attempts to minimise risk by forcing farmers to bear the transaction

costs of a tedious programme of farmer group monitoring which transforms them into bank clients with mandatory accounts. This combines peer group pressure, threats of removal of extension and financial support with more coercive measures including police action. This does not translate into the easy capitalisation of assets by independent farmers developing their own investment strategies, but into forms of dependent accumulation in which support to farmers is conditional upon them following the prescriptions of agricultural banks, agricultural extension services, and agribusiness. Thus, even in the agricultural sectors with fungible assets and the most secure delineation of property rights, farmers are not easily able to capitalise their assets, since the capitalisation of assets is subject to political control and the desire of capital to reorganise markets in specific directions. It is extremely unlikely that smallholder food crop farmers will be able to capitalise their land through community-based land registration programmes, given the constraints that this richer echelon of commercially aspiring rural farmers experience in attempting to capitalise their farm assets.

In the present global policy frameworks for land administration, much is made of harmonisation between customary and formal systems. This chapter has shown that in the transitional zone of Ghana, this concept is highly problematic in the context of agricultural change occurring within farming systems. The smallholder/peasant farming sector now contains two different sectors with diametrically different principles of farm use, although the same farmers use both systems. The food-producing sector is based on a bush-fallowing system rooted in perpetual movement over land, as well as the recycling of land. Farmers use land as they require it but are only allowed to claim rights in land that they use and manage. If they extend their farms in one direction, and leave land unmanaged in another direction, a new farmer can legitimately move into that land. There is no attempt to demarcate the area that a single individual can cultivate or to limit the maximum area they can cultivate. Everyone cultivates according to his or her strength. As labour becomes commoditised, strength comes to denote the ability to hire labour. The system is well adapted to the conditions of expanding farming frontiers, in which the overriding ideology is one of encouraging everyone to develop as much land as they can.

With the development of tree plantations, this ideology is transferred into plantation development, and planters are encouraged to develop as much land as they can. This ultimately begins to undermine the pre-existing tenure system. The tree plantations permanently remove land from the recycling system of bush-fallowing. External investors become interested in developing large plantations and acquiring land, and land begins to acquire a commodity value that the chiefs attempt to exploit. However, attempts by the chiefs to allocate large tracts of land to inves-

tors is frequently opposed by local people when it threatens their livelihood and land use interests, and disrupts their system of bush-fallowing (as occurred at Weila). Conflicts may develop between neighbours
or within families over the alienation and accumulation of land by tree
planters, which may result in attempts to limit plantations and demarcate areas in which plantations cannot be developed by local farmers.
With external investors expressing interest in plantations, chiefs may
attempt to contain the expansion of plantations by locals, to be able to
sell remaining areas of land or attempt to force local plantation developers to pay revenues for the privilege of creating plantations. Thus,
both internal processes of accumulation and social differentiation and
external investments by commercial planters create pressures that
transform existing land relations.

The land rights of tree planters have been highly secure within the
customary system of land use, since this accords rights to fallow land
based on the evidence of management of the land, including the planting or tending of trees. However, the new wealth that plantations create
and their potential disruption of bush-fallowing strategies result in conflicts. Tree planters develop anxieties over the value of the plantations
they create. They become worried that elders in the family will prevent
their children from inheriting their plantations. These anxieties translate into an interest in titling their plantations to secure their wealth
further. Tree planters tend to be highly amenable to programmes concerned with land titling and extending secure property rights to those
who have acquired their land in the customary sector. Various donor-
supported programmes are assisting new export sector tree crops.
While tree planters usually constitute the richer segments of the population with surplus capital to invest in hiring labour, these programmes
are promoted as poverty reduction programmes. They frequently develop components concerned with security of customary land tenure and
securing land rights for the poor. Paradoxically, these tree planters will
constitute a major clientele for these programmes in years to come,
since tree plantations are fungible assets, which are easily mapped and
demarcated, unlike the mobile resource base of bush-fallow cultivators.
This expansion of tree planters with registered holdings will ultimately
serve to undermine and erode the base of the food crop farmers and
their system of land use. In policy circles, this is likely to be promoted
as facilitating community-based land management and harmonisation
of customary and formal systems, without any hint of the complex debates, discourses, and conflicts that occur around these competing land
uses. It may also be presented as the march of progress, as more valuable cash crops replace food crops and permanent cultivation bush-fallowing. However, within the system of bush-fallowing without clearly
demarcated land ownership, food farmers have managed to create con-

siderable value in crops, which rivals the leading export crops, as alluded to by the comparison between the value of the contribution of yam and cocoa to the agricultural economy. This only goes to show that notions of customary tenure are selectively constructed to mould and fashion the customary to fit contemporary policy agendas and exclude elements that are not considered compatible. This process is carried out through the legalisation, formalisation, and recognition of customary land tenure.

In reality, a large gulf exists between the dynamic land use systems based on use rights and recycling of land, and the visions of a customary system based on clearly defined and fungible property rights. The transition from the one system to the other is unlikely to occur without considerable appropriation of land from the poorer sections of farmers. It is perhaps this appropriation of common property and family user rights that will redefine land assets and create the basis for individualised land tenure security based on legalisation and the rule of law, so loved by De Soto and advocates of the new institutional economics.

Notes

1   I particularly wish to thank Patrick Nsiah of Asantekwa who was of great assistance in helping to carry out fieldwork for this research and contributed to my understanding of the issues in this area. Eric Osei and Kofi Gyampoh also helped in the initial field research.
2   1 acre is equivalent to 0.4 hectares.
3   Fifty per cent of women at Asantekwa also got land from their husbands, but the number of women was too small in the sample to be statistically significant.
4   The Banda have a matrilineal inheritance system, so the children of a Banda woman and a migrant are recognised as Banda.
5   The Forestry Commission is responsible for formulating forestry policy in Ghana, and the Forestry Service implements these policies.

6 Legalising customary land tenure in Ghana: The case of peri-urban Kumasi[1]

Janine Ubink

Introduction

Ghana has legalised customary tenure indirectly, through constitutional recognition of customary land management and of the position of chiefs. The 1992 Constitution continues the practice started in the colonial period to vest all customary lands – which constitute approximately 80 per cent of the land in Ghana (Alden Wily and Hammond 2001:46-8; Kasanga and Kotey 2001:13; Larbi, Odoi-Yemo, and Darko 1998:1) – in the appropriate stool, skin or land-owning family[2] on behalf of and in trust for their people, and confirms that such lands be managed according to the fiduciary duty of the traditional authorities towards their people (articles 267(1) and 36(8)). The Constitution furthermore guarantees the 'institution of chieftaincy, together with its traditional councils as established by customary law and usage' (art. 270(1)). Article 270(2) stipulates that Parliament cannot interfere in the recognition process of chiefs. This power lies exclusively with the Traditional Councils and Houses of Chiefs, with a final appeal to the Supreme Court (articles 273 and 274, 1992 Constitution and sections 15, 22, 23, Chieftaincy Act, 1971 (Act 370)).

The fact that in Ghana customary land is managed by traditional authorities, does not preclude the fact that the government is to a certain extent also involved in this realm. Over the years various Land Sector Agencies have been involved in land use planning, land title registration, issuance of formally registered leases, stool land revenue collection, and adjudication of land disputes. In 1999, after decades of piecemeal legislative and state management measures, the government of Ghana formulated its first comprehensive National Land Policy in 1999 (Ministry of Lands and Forestry 1999) and has embarked, with multi-donor support, upon a Land Administration Project intended to reform land institutions and develop land policy so as to provide greater certainty of land rights for ordinary land users and enable greater efficiency and fairness in the land market (Ministry of Lands and Forestry 2003; World Bank 2003b).

This chapter studies customary land management in peri-urban Kumasi. Peri-urban areas form tenure hotspots where property relations are subject to intense contestation and where access to wealth and authority is undergoing rapid change. Due to the expansion of urban centres and population growth, peri-urban areas are witnessing a high demand for residential and sometimes commercial land, which triggers struggles over the rights to convert farmland, now cultivated by community members, and to sell it for other purposes. Since traditional authorities have a strong position with regard to land, they play a prominent role in these conversions. Peri-urban Kumasi, the zone around the capital of the Ashanti Region, is a case in point. Kumasi is a bustling city and an important transportation hub and houses the still vibrant royal court of the Asantehene,[3] the powerful king of all Asante. Its number of inhabitants has grown by 4.2 per cent annually since 1960, to 1,400,000 at present. This has led to the abovementioned pressure on land in the peri-urban area. Increasingly, farmland is being converted to other uses, especially alongside the major roads to Kumasi, where access to the city is easy and electricity is available. Many peripheral villages have now become fully encapsulated by Kumasi. This chapter is based on fieldwork in nine peri-urban villages, at a range of ten to 40 kilometres from Kumasi.[4]

In this chapter we will study the case of 'tenure hotspot' peri-urban Kumasi to provide an insight into an example of long-term, indirect legalisation of customary tenure. The following questions will be asked: (1) How is customary land managed by traditional authorities in peri-urban Kumasi? (2) To what extent and how is the government involved in customary land management, both before and after the new National Land Policy and its implementing Land Administration Project? (3) What are the effects of this constellation on the tenure security of the indigenous[5] farmers?

Customary land management by traditional authorities

Chiefs

In the Ashanti Region it is the chiefs who are the caretakers of all customary land or stool land. According to representations of customary law in case law, textbooks and legal discourse, Ashanti convention holds that the ultimate title, also called the allodial title, of every piece of land is held in common by the members of a community,[6] and the chief is the custodian of such land. Chiefs are customarily and constitutionally obliged to administer and develop the land in the interests of the whole community (articles 36(8) and 267(1), 1992 Constitution). Stool lands, therefore, are communal property. As long as there is vacant land, each member of a community has the right to farm and build on part of it, which gives the member a usufructuary title[7], also called customary freehold, to the land.[8] The usufructuary interest can be inherited[9] and is extinguished only through abandonment, forfeiture[10] or with the consent and concurrence of the interest holder. The usufructuary cannot be deprived of any of the rights constituting the interest, and not even the chief can make an adverse claim (Asante 1969:105-106; Danquah 1928:197-200, 206, 221; Ollennu 1962:29, 55-56; Ollennu 1967:252-255; Pogucki 1962:180; Sarbah 1968:64-67; Woodman 1996:53, 66, 107).[11]

These customary rules date from the days when communities were involved in subsistence farming in land-abundant areas, when not land but people were of value to the chief and the community. Now that market production, population growth, and urbanisation have enhanced the economic value of land, many chiefs in peri-urban Kumasi claim that these rules are outdated and need to be adjusted to modern circumstances. They argue that communal land that can be used in a more productive way should be brought back under chiefly administration. Or, as the Beseasehene (the chief of Besease) said: 'It is a law that when the town[12] is growing and it comes to your farm, you do not have any land.'[13] These claims have seriously weakened the value and security of the usufructuary interest: when there is a demand to change the use of land from agricultural to residential, individual farmers lose the security of their usufructuary rights, and the chief claims the power to reallocate these lands.

Some chiefs, however, are taking the argument much further and are venturing to manipulate and shift the meaning of communal land ownership.[14] They claim that their rights to administer stool land do not derive from their function as caretakers on behalf of the community but instead assert that 'land belongs to the royal family, since it was members of the royal family who fought for the land' and the chief has administrative powers over the land as the leader of the royal family.[15] According to these chiefs, the royal family had only given the land out for farming purposes to temporary caretakers and can reclaim it when its use is changed without any need for compensation. 'The farmer does not lose any land since he did not own any land. The farmer is only the caretaker for the chief. The land was given to him free of charge, so how can he claim part of the money when it has been sold?'[16] This narrowing down of the land-owning community weakens the security of usufructuary rights even more as it degrades the nature of the customary rights of usufruct. The customary freehold is transformed into a permissive right of tenant-like character, based on the leniency of the chief instead of on the communal ownership of the land. The allodial title proportionally gains in weight and shifts from the community as a whole to the royal family, on whose behalf the chief claims outright ownership.

The argument of the first group of chiefs – that communal land which can be used in a more productive way should be brought back into chiefly administration – is only convincing if the proceeds of the conversion are used for community development such as infrastructure, education and alternative livelihood projects, which might help inhabitants of the village to make a living after the loss of their agricultural land. Although all the chiefs interviewed – even the ones who claim that land ownership lies with the royal family and not with the whole community – acknowledged that they have at least a moral obligation to use part of stool land revenue to compensate the farmer and/or for community development, actual practice differs considerably. The neighbouring villages of Jachie and Tikrom offer two extreme examples. In Jachie, the chief demarcated a large part of the village farmland for residential plots and allowed members of the community to buy this land at a very low price. The remaining plots were leased to outsiders for residential purposes. All the revenue generated has been used for community development. In the four years of his reign, the Jachiehene has built a library, a school, and a palace, and has allocated part of his land to a technical school in exchange for scholarships. The neighbouring Tikromhene provides the opposite example. He has converted and leased most of the farmland in his village without giving the community members any part of the demarcated land or any financial compensation. When a member wants a residential plot, he has to pay the market price. Out of the revenue from stool land leases, almost nothing has left the chief's palace.[17] As the above-mentioned examples of Tikrom and Jachie illustrate, practices regarding the division of land and revenue differ enormously. On average, however, chiefs receive unsatisfactory marks from most villagers for their administration of the land. 'So much money goes to the chief, and so little to development'[18] and 'Due to the greedy nature of landowners (i.e. chiefs) there is not much development in this town'[19] are utterances heard regularly in the villages.

The effects of the two kinds of discourses – more productive use or landownership lies with the royal family – are not that different in peri-urban Kumasi.[20] Chiefs from both groups are rapidly converting farmland, in which indigenous community members or families have usufructuary rights, into residential land which they allocate to outsiders through customary leases. This is leading to increasing tenure insecurity among indigenous farmers. As a result of the allocations, poor and marginalised families frequently lose their agricultural land, their employment and their income base. Apart from some positive exceptions, traditional authorities display little accountability for any money generated, and most indigenous land users are seeing little or no benefit from the leases. They are only rarely – and then very inadequately –

compensated for the loss of their farmland, and in most villages only a meagre part of the money is used for community development. Although the new lessees are benefiting from the land conversions, they are also affected by the lack of community improvement, since the areas they are building their houses in are seldom serviced with electricity, roads and sewers. Furthermore, the numerous accounts of multiple sales of the same piece of land to different buyers and of sales of alleged residential plots on land unsuitable for residential purposes show the buyer's vulnerable tenure security. In sum, the practice of customary land management in peri-urban Ghana differs widely from the constitutional provision that puts the interest of the community first (article 36(8), 1992 Constitution).

Local negotiations, struggles and debates

Local land administration practices result from continuing processes of negotiation and are not only shaped by the ideology, claims, and actions of the chief but also by the extent to which these are accepted or contested locally and nationally. The chiefs' actions in peri-urban Kumasi and their severe effects on the tenure security and livelihoods of the people are causing a great deal of turmoil among community members. Individuals, families, and other groups of people are challenging the chiefs' actions.[21] In some villages, people have tried to resist the reallocation of land by the chief *per se*, while in other villages the reallocation itself was accepted but the way it was done was contested, especially the division of the financial returns from the reallocation. In the following examples, both categories of resistance are discussed.

(i) Resistance against the chiefs' reallocation of land

Outsiders started to look for residential land in the village of Brofoyeduru about fifteen years ago. 'At first it was the chief selling[22] these plots, but the farmer did not get his right percentage', i.e. the chief paid no compensation to the farmer.[23] After a while, the chief's sisters went to talk to him, and he allowed first one and then all of his siblings to sell their own land. When word got out, other people also started selling. 'The chief is letting it go. He signs the papers after the sale for some money.'[24] Although the people in Brofoyeduru successfully resisted the actual sale of their land by the chief, they do not in general deny the chief's right to sell. Some villagers explained their behaviour as follows: 'The right thing would be for the chief to sell it. But if the chief does that, the farmer does not get much money. Since everyone is poor here, the chief has to allow it.'[25]

In Besease, unlike in Brofoyeduru, many people deny outright their chief's claim that he can reallocate their land. The majority of the villagers acknowledged the chief's right to be informed about a sale, to sign the land allocation papers, and to receive a signing fee for this service – although some said it should be the buyer who takes care of these issues and not the seller – but they claimed the farmers were the only ones to initiate a sale and to receive the money paid for the land: 'When the town reaches my land, I can sell it. The *abusua panin*[26] and the chief have no say in that;'[27] 'If the chief wants a third of the money when I sell land, I will take the case to court.'[28] Land transactions in Besease thus display ongoing struggles between the four land-owning chiefs and their people. 'If you are very persistent, the chief cannot take your land away,' a farmer explains. 'You can sell it and give part (of the money) to the chief. But if you are unlucky, the chief will take the land, and if you don't fight it, you won't get anything.'[29]

Struggles over land can sometimes lead to violent incidents between villagers and the chief. For instance, the Beseasehene sold land that did not belong to his family. When the buyer started to develop the land, the family that had the customary freehold in the land stopped him. After the buyer applied to the chief to recover his losses, the chief 'went to the land-owing family to plead, but he nearly got beaten up'.[30] In some villages there have even been large-scale violent uprisings of commoners against the chief. For instance in Pekyi No. 2, where the chief sold a large part of the village land to the Deeper Life Christian Ministry and then pocketed the money, the commoners chased both the chief and the church representatives out of the village, killing one of the latter in the process.

Of the nine villages studied in depth, only in Boankra – where there has not been a chief for the last fourteen years – did the royal family seem to acknowledge the families' rights to initiate the sale of land: 'When the new chief comes, the clans can still sell their own land, but with the consent of the chief, who will 'take something' for the stool.'[31] However, it remains to be seen what position the royal family will take in land negotiations when a new chief is enstooled.

(ii) Resistance against the way chiefs reallocate land

In a number of the case-study villages, people did generally accept the fact that chiefs were reallocating community land, but they vehemently opposed the procedure and the division of revenues. The previously mentioned village of Tikrom presents a worst-case scenario with regard to community development. According to a Unit Committee member, 'the Tikromhene is selling land without consulting anyone, compensating the farmer, or giving part of the revenue to the town', and part of the remaining land has been degraded or even destroyed as a result of sandmining.[32] Furthermore, the chief does not abide by the planning scheme and has, for instance, sold land that was reserved for the school.

A long process of consultation took place between the chief and the community. At a series of village meetings, the people requested a substantial percentage of land revenues for community development, but to no avail. They then tried to involve the chief from their place of origin, but this chief did not want to come and talk to his 'son'. As the Tikromhene comes directly under the Asantehene, the former assemblyman[33] then wrote a petition to the Asantehene in May 2002. However, the case has never been called before the Asantehene, and it is assumed by some that the Tikromhene has encouraged the secretary of the Asantehene to remove the petition from the files. In addition, the former assemblyman has brought in the Environmental Protection Agency (EPA) to investigate the chief's sandmining close to streams. The EPA came, looked and reproached the chief, but does not have the power to prosecute. Such power lies with the District Assembly, but it is rarely used. A local radio station discussed the sandmining problem in Tikrom in one of its programmes, in which the assemblyman appealed to the Asantehene for help, but there has been no response.

As the example of Tikrom shows, local assembly members often play an important role in challenging misadministration by chiefs. In many villages, the same role is played by members of the Unit Committee, the lowest level of local government in Ghana. One of their popular procedural solutions to the misadministration of stool land is the establishment of a village committee, usually called a Plot or Land Allocation Committee, to oversee the proper allocation of village land. Such a committee usually consists of representatives of the chief and his elders and representatives of the village, often Unit Committee members. The Plot Allocation Committee checks that the site plan is in accordance with the planning scheme, and it has to sign the allocation papers. The existence of such a committee normally coincides with the transfer of a fixed portion of the revenue to the community for development. Although many chiefs pay lip service to such committees, they usually work with a committee made up solely of elders and the chief himself, and popular attempts to set up committees with a broader representation have often been frustrated by the chiefs.

The kinds of activities undertaken in Tikrom to challenge the chief's style of stool land administration were also found in many other villages and appear to be a common response to misadministration by chiefs. Their success is often limited, leaving the people with feelings of desperation or resignation that they have been left to their own devices. The following statements by two former assemblymen aptly illustrate these feelings: 'In Europe, if a government is criticised three times, the government goes. But here people come to beat you up in-

stead';[34] 'People who lose their land to the chief usually don't go to a
chief or to court, normally they give up.'[35]

Because of this lack of success in negotiations with the chief, many
people do not aim their anger and resistance at the chief who is selling
the land but at the buyer. Both my fieldwork and a study of pending
cases at the High Court of Kumasi show that the farmer, who is angry
that his land has been sold by the chief, often tries to restrain the buyer
from going onto the land and building there. For instance in Adadeentem, the former chief sold substantial portions of the community's
land. This aroused a lot of dissatisfaction amongst the people, but no
concrete actions were taken against the chief. One of the villagers, however, sued the buyer of a vast tract of land in the High Court of Kumasi. Another example of the 'buyer loses out' principle is found in Besease, where the Beseasehene sold two plots of land belonging to his
subchief, the Kontihene. On finding out about the sale, the Kontihene
first 'caused trouble with the Beseasehene', but 'we enstooled him, so
(...) we don't want to quarrel with him. But the buyer can't come and
work on it. If you come to work you will meet the Konti.'[36]

Traditional controls on chiefly administration

Chiefs often reject people's suggestions and claims about adjusting
stool land administration and continue to rule as they always have
done. This poses the question of how is it possible that these chiefs
cannot be steered away from their devastating track? Are there no
checks and balances on their administration? A literature survey of
some of Ghana's 'grand old men' in the field of customary land tenure
yields the following quotes: '(T)he occupant of the stool can only bind
the stool, i.e., the town or community, if he acts with the consent and
concurrence of the whole town or community represented by the subchiefs, and the principal councillors from the various sections' (Ollennu 1962: 130). 'Hereditary[37] councillors, or elders as they are called in
the lower councils, and chiefs or sub-chiefs in the higher ones, are the
heads of houses, families, or towns who have been elected by members
of a house, family, or town to be their respective head, patriarch, or
chief. (...) They hold their offices in the pleasure not of the Chief or
head Chief, but by the sufferance of the people who have elected them
to the Council. (...) It is of utmost importance, in view of our form of
government, for the Chief, who is always the President of his Council,
to give due weight and make full allowance of the expressed opinion of
these councillors' (Danquah 1928:57). 'The chief was bound by his oath
to consult the elders on all matters, and to obey their advice' (Busia
1951:14). To supplement these authoritative but not too recent writers[38]
with a contemporary influential voice, I turn to Kasanga who, less spe-

cifically but equally romantically, states that 'there are reasonable checks at the local level on almost everybody' (Kasanga 2000a:72; cf. Kasanga and Kotey 2001: 31).

According to these writers, traditional responsibility for village chiefs thus rests on two pillars. The first pillar is made up of a council of elders, selected by and representing all major factions of the community, without whose consent the chief cannot make any decisions. The second pillar consists of the possibility to destool seriously malfunctioning chiefs. Leaving aside whether traditional rule was ever so equitable and well-balanced as these authors claim – which has been convincingly refuted in the extensive oeuvre of McCaskie (including McCaskie 1992, 1995, 2000a) – the current performance of chiefs in peri-urban Kumasi at least disabuses us of the idea that the two pillars function effectively in present-day village practice.

To begin with, in a number of case-study villages, the council elders are primarily or even entirely selected from the royal family and not from the important families in the community, as in Kotwi. The Kotwi stool was originally carved out of the Asampong stool, and the Kotwihene was like a subchief to the Asamponghene and thus did not have his own subchiefs. Later, the Kotwihene was upgraded, and he now swears his oath directly to the Asantehene. Although he could now have subchiefs, he has not installed any. He has continued to discuss village affairs with the elders from his family, and when there is a public ceremony, the Asamponghene and his subchiefs will join the Kotwihene and his elders. The absence of a council representing the whole community was encountered in a number of the other case-study villages as well. Furthermore, the rule that elders hold their offices not in the pleasure of the chief but to serve the family that has elected them also seems to be under strain. For instance in Nkoransa, where the secretary of the chief explained that 'it is not the rule that a certain family always brings a subchief. It is the chief who picks them. When one dies, he can choose a new one'.[39] This is underpinned by the abundance of conflicts between elders and their own family, who can no longer dismiss them when unsatisfied.[40] Regardless of the composition of the council, the chief often co-opts his elders by sharing the benefits from land administration with them, removing their incentives to effectively check the use of power and, if necessary, to stand up against the chief (cf. Abudulai 2002:83). According to a UC member of Tikrom, 'the subchiefs support the chief because they get a share of the money. If they argue with him, they won't get anything'.[41] Even at the Asantehene's Land Secretariat it is acknowledged that 'in many villages the elders connive with the chief'.[42] And those elders that are not co-opted are often simply ignored by the chief, as is aptly illustrated by the following statement: 'Beseasehene is a new chief. He doesn't mind the rules,' says his Kontihene subchief, 'I tried to talk to him, but he didn't take my advice. If I wasn't educated, he would try to cheat me as well.'[43]

When the people of a community want to destool their chief, a case has to be brought before the Traditional Council, which is made up of the paramount chief and his subchiefs.[44] A first hurdle is that destoolment charges cannot be brought by commoners but only by the 'kingmakers', i.e. those subchiefs and members of the royal family who can also make or enstool a chief (Hayford 1970:36). As discussed above, these subchiefs are often co-opted and are therefore not likely to take the lead in actions against the chief. And if they do dare to do so, according to one of the subchiefs of the Ejisuhene, this is only 'after many years of wrongdoing, the chief will first be given the benefit of the doubt'; to explain why they have waited so long to start a destoolment case against the chief, he adds: 'The kingmakers have deposed the previous Ejisuhene and installed this one, of whom they had high expectations. They now lose part of their legitimacy when they want to destool the one they selected.'[45] If those years of waiting are added to the years the destoolment procedure itself may take, it is obvious that a chief can easily come to sell a considerable amount of stool land and spend the proceeds as well. A second obstacle lies in the fact that the paramount chief, who chairs the Traditional Council, often has a direct interest in who occupies the village stool, mainly because of his claims to a share in the villages' land revenues. The paramount chief of Ejisu, for instance, favoured those chiefs who sold large amounts of stool land and shared the proceeds with him. The fact that this did not usually leave much land or revenue for the community did not seem to bother him. Furthermore, to mention a third hindrance, the members of the Traditional Council consist of direct colleagues of the chief-on-trial. Many of the current destoolment charges are to do with land administration in one way or another. And often the charges against the chief-on-trial, such as selling farmland and not using enough stool land revenue for community development, are also points of discussion in the villages of the judging chiefs. Clearly, their personal interests in such cases may stand in the way of objective and impartial judgment.

The main customary checks and balances on chiefs – ruling in council with subchiefs and the possibility of destoolment – are not very effective therefore. One can add to this the fact that chiefly accountability is extremely low. Most land administration is concealed due to a lack of registration. A good chief may account for his administration of his own accord, but this is an exception rather than the rule. Some elders and chiefs claim that 'nobody has the right to ask the chief to account',[46] and 'if it goes wrong, there is nothing to do about it'.[47] They explain this by the fact that the chief also has his professional income, and it is impossible to know whether he is spending personal or stool money. Or they say that 'the chief does not receive any remuneration but does have job-related expenses, to which the people do not want to contribute'[48] and that the chief continues to have obligations for which customary provisions have ceased.[49] Others claim that to ask a chief to account for his expenditures is considered a vote of no confidence. 'If a chief does his work well, no one will bring him to account.'[50] Most people will not dare to do this unless there are clear indications of serious misconduct by the chief. And even then, 'who is to bell the cat?' The chief is still a powerful figure in most villages, and one is certain to encounter his wrath by highlighting irregularities in his actions. Moreover, taking action against a chief violates his traditional sanctity. Most people would consider it the task of the royal family, and if the royal family does not enact this task, how can commoners be expected to take it upon themselves? The only kind of functioning accountability is what I call 'end-term accountability'. During destoolment procedures, a chief has to account for all stool revenue, but by then most of the money has usually been spent and is very hard to recover. Besides, as noted, starting a destoolment procedure brings its own difficulties.

Colonial distortion of checks, balances and accountability

The current customary system lacks effective checks and balances and accountability, but this is not surprising when the historical development of the position of the chiefs is taken into account. During the colonial period, local checks and balances and accountability structures were severely distorted when the British government overrode the traditional rules of investiture and reserved for itself the right to appoint and dismiss chiefs (Annor 1985:153; Busia 1951:105-6; Toulmin and Quan 2000a:10; Van Rouveroy van Nieuwaal 1987:11). With this 'devolution', as Von Trotha (1996:81) calls it, the local attachment of the chief to some extent gave way to his responsibilities and loyalties towards the government. Where commoners tried to reassert local checks and balances, a chief who was on friendly terms with the British administrator was easily able to discredit the commoners by branding them as malcontents and troublemakers (Kumado 1990-1992:203; McCaskie 2000b).

The British gave the chiefs strong rights in land by accepting their claims that according to customary law, all land belonged to a customary community with the chief as the administrator. However, they did not give the chiefs free reign in all aspects. They regularly held them to account, monitored the bylaws they made, and intervened in local conflicts, thereby to some extent compensating for the lack of local checks and balances, at least in the field of land administration (Crook

1986:88; Dennis 1957). Post-colonial governments in Ghana have shown an ambivalent attitude to chieftaincy (Kofi-Sackey 1983; Kumado 1990-1992; Nugent 1994; Ray 1996; Van Rouveroy van Nieuwaal 1987, 1996), and the pendulum has swung between devolution and the prohibition of governmental interference. Although under the current Constitution the Ghanaian state is not permitted to exercise its sovereignty over chiefs regarding their enstoolment and destoolment (article 270(2), 1992 Constitution), the pre-colonial local checks and balances and accountability structures have not been rebuilt. A crucial question therefore is whether the current government can also impose state constraints on the administration of chiefs to compensate for the lack of local checks and balances.

State involvement

We have seen that the 1992 Constitution vests all customary or stool lands – which constitute approximately 80 per cent of the land in Ghana – in the appropriate stool on behalf of and in trust for their people, and confirms that such lands must be managed by traditional authorities (articles 267(1) and 36(8), 1992 Constitution). Notwithstanding these provisions, the state has sought to regulate certain aspects of stool land management. Over the years various governments have taken piecemeal measures in the areas of land use planning, land title registration, issuance of formally registered leases, stool land revenue collection, and adjudication of land disputes. This section of the chapter will first describe the mandate as well as the actual functioning of the principal state institutions involved in these fields to show the checks and balances they are able to place on chiefly administration. Then it will emphasise some of the political constraints state institutions face by looking at the government's policy of non-interference with regard to chieftaincy. Finally, it will discuss current policy efforts under the National Land Policy (Ministry of Lands and Forestry 1999) and the Land Administration Project (Ministry of Lands and Forestry 2003; World Bank 2003b).

Office of the Administrator of Stool Lands

The Constitution provides for an Office of the Administrator of Stool Lands (OASL), which was established by the OASL Act, 1994 (Act 481). This office is responsible for the establishment of a stool land account and for the collection of all 'rents, dues, royalties, revenue or other payments whether in the nature of income or capital from the stool lands' to be paid into this stool land account (article 267(2), 1992

Constitution and section 2, OASL Act, 1994 (Act 481)). Of the revenue accruing from stool lands, ten per cent is paid to the OASL to cover administrative expenses. The other 90 per cent is to be disbursed in the following proportions: 25 per cent to the stool for its maintenance; twenty per cent to the traditional authority; and 55 per cent to the District Assembly (Sections 3 and 8, OASL Act, 1994 (Act 481)). Although this could curb the appropriation of stool land revenue by chiefs for their personal use, there is no legal requirement that the 25 per cent of the revenue received by stools is reinvested in the community. Rather, the provisions encourage chiefs to retain the revenue 'for the maintenance of the stool in keeping with its status'. The use of the twenty per cent share to the Traditional Council is not specified. According to Alden Wily and Hammond (2001:118-119), the government in this way 'endorses the perception of chiefs of themselves that they are the owners, not merely trustees acting on behalf of the real owners, the community at large'.

This provision has a long history pre-dating the current 1994 Act. It dates back to the Local Government Ordinance, 1951 (Cap 64), and its original purpose was to be the first step in depriving the big chiefs of any role in land management and eventually of ownership and their claims to have the right to collect land 'rents' (Rathbone 2000:30). Chiefs, therefore, have always resisted handing over 'their' income to the OASL. Since in peri-urban areas the conversion from agricultural to residential land accounts for most land revenue, chiefs in these areas centre their resistance on the definition of stool land revenue. They claim that the money they receive for the allocation of land is not purchase money but 'drink money' or 'drinks'. They refer to the custom of bringing some drinks to the chief when acquiring land from him as an acknowledgement of the ownership of the land, to show allegiance towards the chief, and for the customary pouring of libations on the ground to seek the gods' blessings for the transaction. Where a bottle of Schnapps was sufficient in times of land abundance, when land became more valuable a small amount of cash money was added to the Schnapps. In peri-urban Ghana and other areas where land is highly valued and demand is increasing, the amount of cash demanded has gradually risen and now effectively constitutes a market price for the purchase of land leases (Alden Wily and Hammond 2001; Edusah and Simon 2001; Kasanga and Kotey 2001; McCaskie 2000b). The chiefs continue to call this payment 'drinks' and claim that it should therefore not be regarded as 'stool land revenue' in the sense of the OASL Act, and they resist the disclosure of the sums collected. In peri-urban areas, the only land revenues that flow to the OASL consist of ground rents – annual governmental fees payable on land leases – which are distributed according to the constitutional formula. These rents are small compared to the sums of 'drink money' collected directly by the chiefs in selling land leases. The total amount of ground rent on a 99-year residential lease adds up to about five per cent of the amount of 'drink money'. Because 'drink money' is portrayed by the chiefs as a ritual device rather than the means of exchange in a sales transaction, it is not collected by the OASL, and so not subject to distribution under the constitutional formula, and thus becomes, effectively, part of the chief's income.

Contrary to Kasanga and Woodman (2004:185), who for unclear reasons claim that 'it has been accepted by everyone concerned that those (sums in 'drinks') do not amount to revenue from stool lands within the meaning of the statute law', most officials interviewed consider that the law meant to include this 'drink money' in the definition of 'stool land revenue'.[51] This interpretation seems to square with the very broad definition of stool land revenues provided in the OASL Act, as quoted above. This issue has, however, never been tested in the courts. In the highly personalised society of Ghana, if a case were brought to court by an officer of the OASL, this would not be considered an action on behalf of the government, of the ruling political party, or even of the OASL in general, but as a personal action of that particular officer. Such an action would surely provoke the wrath of all of the chiefs. According to the District Chief Executive of Ejisu-Juaben district, 'The one who does it will become an enemy of the chiefs', and this can pose serious dangers to the career of the official concerned.[52] In a number of cases officials have been 'transferred' after standing up to a powerful paramount chief or the Asantehene. According to the District Chief Executive of Ejisu-Juaben district, 'careless statements by land officials could be dangerous. They may have to pay a price for discourtesy'.[53] Furthermore, as the Deputy Regional Lands Officer in Kumasi explains, every official is also 'subject of a stool and subordinate to the chief', and such an action would be considered an act of disloyalty towards him.[54] The one official we encountered who did want to go to court over a sum of 'drink money' of Cedis 3 billion (at the time of sale the equivalent of approximately € 300,000) claimed that he was stopped by 'the government', because 'the President does not want to pay for such an action'.[55]

The lack of an effective political mandate for the OASL to exercise the role intended by the constitution is only part of the story. A lack of funds, qualified staff, equipment, and vehicles on the one hand, and mismanagement, corruption, and lack of accountability in the OASL's own use of land revenues on the other (Grant 2004:20-21, 40-41; Kasanga and Kotey 2001:iii; Kasanga and Woodman 2004:185) also severely hamper the functioning of the OASL and affect its legitimacy in the eyes of the people. To date, the revenues collected and distributed by the OASL have never been publicly disclosed, and the use of land revenues received by all parties remains unaccounted for and non-transparent. Accusations of irregularities in both spheres are rampant.

Lands Commission

The Lands Commission (LC) first came into existence following the 1969 Constitution, under the Lands Commission Act, 1971 (Act 362), and operates under the Lands Commission Act, 1994 (Act 483), since the advent of the 1992 Constitution. The LC is responsible for the management of all public and vested lands,[56] is meant to advise and make recommendations on policies with respect to land use and development, and advise on and assist in the execution of the registration of land titles (section 2, Lands Commission Act, 1994 (Act 483)). With regard to stool land, section 4 of Act 483 states: 'There shall be no disposition or development of any stool land by any person unless the Regional Lands Commission (...) has certified that the disposition or development is consistent with the development plan drawn up or approved by the planning authority' (cf. art. 267(3) of the 1992 Constitution). This section continues the practice begun in 1962 by the Administration of Lands Act, 1962 (Act 123) to require the consent of the state to the alienation of stool land (Kasanga and Kotey 2001: 3). Thus, if a stool wants to dispose of land, it has to ask the LC for its consent and concurrence. This could enhance the tenure security of the indigenous farmers. However, in practice, consent before an allocation of stool land is never sought. Concurrence after the allocation is sometimes sought, although not by the chief but by lessees who want to formalise their acquisition, and this is still quite rare. Typically, only the more educated people or people with connections in the bureaucracy go through the long,[57] cumbersome, and expensive process of formalisation.[58] The provision of consent and concurrence is not enforced by the LC and therefore does not in practice provide an effective check upon the administration of lands by chiefs. Like the OASL, the LC is hampered by a shortage of trained and motivated staff, lack of basic logistics and support services, poor remuneration and incentive packages, low morale, and endemic corruption (Report on the Beneficiary Assessment Survey of the Lands Commission – Ghana, 1997, quoted in Hueber and de Veer 2001:195; Centre for Democracy and Development 2000:99-105; Grant 2004:21-21, 40-41, 95; Kasanga 2000b:14; Kasanga and Kotey 2001:iii, 8).[59]

District Assembly

The Local Government Act, 1993 (Act 462), designates District Assemblies (DA), which have been created since 1986 but only received constitutional backing in 1992, as the main planning authority charged with the overall development of the district. With regard to land administration, they have legislative powers to make bylaws with respect to construction, sanitation, and the environment. The preparation and approval of planning schemes, the granting of building permits, and the enforcement of regulations and sanctions for non-compliance all rest with the DA (Kasanga and Kotey 2001:9). Villages and towns are supposed to draw up a land use planning scheme with the help of the Town and Country Planning Department (TCPD) of the DA. Such a planning scheme designates the uses of the various areas, and shows the boundaries of the individual plots. When a prospective developer applies for a building permit, the TCPD has to check whether the site plan conforms to the planning scheme, and whether the allocation paper is signed by the local chief.

Ammissah et al. (1990:34, quoted in Hueber and de Veer 2001:19) argue that 'Since the main aim of the chiefs is to maximise financial returns within the shortest possible time, important land uses such as open spaces, playgrounds, schools, markets, refuse dumps, roads, etc. are sacrificed, in order to augment the supply of building plots. This is a major cause of haphazard and unauthorised development in all statutory planning areas'. By means of the land use planning process, the DA could provide some checks on the land administration by chiefs, preventing double allocations,[60] and reserve land for public purposes or even for agriculture. Chiefs can prevent the drawing up of a planning scheme, however, by withholding their cooperation and not providing any information. 'If a chief does not cooperate, you cannot make a planning scheme.'[61] According to the TCPD in Ejisu, 'It is to the benefit of the chief not to have an approved planning scheme. Therefore, the cooperation of chiefs is not very high. Most have their own unapproved planning scheme'.[62] Furthermore, although awareness of planning schemes, and building, permits is increasing, it is still low, and most people do not comply with the demand for a building permit, or partly due to the lengthy[63] bureaucratic procedures and the costs involved, the building precedes the formal planning process (Edusah and Simon 2001: section 4.4; Hueber and de Veer 2001:191; Toulmin and Longbottom 2001:29-30).[64] Finally, fieldwork showed that the implementation of planning regulation is often lacking, due to a lack of personnel, funds, and logistics (cf. DFID/Toulmin, Brown, and Crook 2004:12; Hueber and de Veer 2001:188-9; Kasanga and Kotey 2001: 9-10) and mismanagement and corruption (cf. Kasanga 1996:99; Kasanga and Kotey 2001:iii). And even when violations are found, severe sanctions, such as demolition of unauthorised structures, are avoided (cf. Hueber and de Veer 2001:191).

Furthermore, when the DA does not have a financial interest, it tries not to get involved in 'local affairs'. For instance, if there is more than one land-owning chief in a village, the TCPD will accept a signature of any one of the chiefs as a valid one. And if there is an agreement within a village that a Plot Allocation Committee – a locally initiated committee consisting of representatives of both the chief and the village that should sign all allocation notes and secure a percentage of the revenue for community development – should also sign the allocation papers, this is considered an internal village affair by the TCPD, and they do not check whether such a signature is found on the allocation paper. In this way, the locally agreed upon solution to problems of transparency and distribution of land revenue is not supported by the government.

While the land use planning system could in theory provide a check on chiefly land administration, it also provides chiefs with additional powers in local struggles over land. The formalisation of the land allocation process by the government, with the signature of the chief as a key element, gives chiefs an extra-official card to play, especially those higher up in the hierarchy of traditional authorities. For instance, Abudulai (2002) describes how in Tamale the sub-committee of the LC attributes most of the problems in the field of land administration to the lack of documentary evidence. It therefore decided that divisional chiefs must countersign allocation papers to bring some order into the system. Similar actions were encountered during fieldwork at the DA in Ejisu – where it was decided that building permits could be given only when the allocation papers bore the countersignature of the paramount chief, so as to prevent future land disputes and litigation, not least involving the paramount chief himself – and at the LC in Kumasi – where despite a court ruling that Kaase stool lands did not fall under the authority of the Asantehene, the LC tried to convince the Kaasehene to have all land allocations countersigned by the Asantehene at the cost of one-third of the purchase price.[65] A comparable example is found in the distribution of OASL revenues, which are usually paid to the paramount chief, who is supposed to redistribute them in his area according to the constitutional formula. These actions can be explained by a combination of 'administrative efficiency' – dealing with one big man instead of a whole group of people – and attempts to satisfy the person with the greatest troublemaking capacity.

Every electoral area has its own representative at the DA. In many villages, these local assembly members and the members of the Unit Committee (UC) – the lowest level of local government – are public figures, who are widely known, easily accessible, and often most actively involved in development of the community. They are aware of the fact that a lot of money for town development could be generated by stool land allocations. It is therefore not surprising that where chiefs are un-willing to distribute land revenues, UC and DA members are often in direct confrontation with the chief, or lead the public actions against him. Yet, while the UC and DA members are a local force to be reck-oned with, they are not often backed by the district authorities. The District Chief Executive (DCE) of Ejisu, for instance, while acknowled-ging the negative effects of chiefly land conversions in his district, went no further than the occasional public statement that chiefs should spend part of the land revenues on community development. When we proposed the idea to back up local Plot Allocation Committees (PACs) by providing building permits only when allocation papers carry the PAC's signature, he rejected the proposal because land revenue would then be spent by the UC and fall outside his own responsibility.[66] More generally, during the UC and DA inauguration ceremonies, members are often instructed to refrain from interfering in chieftaincy and land matters.[67]

State courts

As regards the position of state courts in the field of customary land management, chiefly re-appropriations and conversions of stool lands in which community members have a usufructuary interest are not supported by court decisions (Ubink 2002-2004). Although a trend can be discerned in judicial customary law – rules of customary law as set out by the courts – towards more power to the chief as administra-tor to ensure sound town planning and a more equal distribution of land, this cannot be interpreted to mean that the chief has the power to deal with land as he wishes, without regard for community interests or compensation for farmers. Customary law in the Ghanaian courts rather conveys an image of protection of usufructuary rights against the chiefs' attempts to re-appropriate stool lands for 'development' pur-poses. First, usufructuary rights are quite secure. Second, the transfer of the usufructuary title does not need the consent of the allodial title holder. This seems even to apply when farmland is transferred for non-farm purposes, such as housing or cemetery plots. And even if a chiefly grant were needed to change land use from agricultural to resi-dential, as was stated in one court case,[68] it seems that the community member has a right to receive this grant unless overriding communal interests prohibit it. Third, chiefs can be held accountable for the way they use stool land revenues, since there is a 'statutory imperative that moneys from stool land acquisitions should be lodged in a designated fund'.[69]

Although state courts protect the interests of indigenous farmers whose land is being re-appropriated by the chief, the effect of such court decisions on local land practices and tenure security is limited. Notwithstanding the large number of land cases in the courts, many more land conflicts never reach them, either because of the aggrieved parties' lack of access or interest, or because the land conflicts are embedded in 'chieftaincy affairs' for which state courts have no jurisdiction (section 15(1) Chieftaincy Act, 1971 (Act 370)). Moreover, court decisions seem to have little effect on land disputes beyond the specific cases on which the court decides. This can be explained by a number of factors: First, people have minimal knowledge of court decisions. During fieldwork, people hardly referred to case law or legislation, and when they did they often misunderstood it or invented their own provisions. Second, the existence of an arena for strong local chiefs, hardly constrained by local checks and balances and – as we will see in the next section – also barely controlled by the government, which explains why chiefs do not feel bound to comply with the rules of customary law as set out by the courts.[70]

A policy of non-interference

In the sections above a number of examples display a lack of political willingness to enhance the functioning of Land Sector Agencies (LSAs) such as the OASL and the LC and strengthen their checks on chiefly land management: the unwillingness of the political establishment to bring before the court the question of whether 'drink money' is stool land revenue in the sense of the OASL Act; the instructions to DA and UC members to abstain from chieftaincy affairs; and the refusal of the TCPD to check land allocation notes for a signature of the Plot Allocation Committee, where such committees exist.

This lack of political support – which results in large part from a deference to chiefly authority and power amongst local government officials – is also mirrored in the policy discourse of the present government. In the media, government officials at all levels regularly and vehemently proclaim that they will not 'meddle in chieftaincy affairs'.[71] According to Boafo-Arthur (2003:138), President Kufuor himself 'has made it clear that the current ruling party is not interested in meddling in chieftaincy affairs.' These 'non-interference' statements are sometimes made in reaction to chieftaincy disputes, over which section 15(1) of the Chieftaincy Act, 1971 (Act 370), declares the government has no jurisdiction, but also to express in more general terms that the government will not interfere in chiefly administration such as in the field of land management, which is not dictated by any legislative provision whatsoever. For instance, the former coordinator of the Land Administration Project at the Ministry of Lands and Forestry asked in an interview: 'Is it the business of the government to address the accountability of chiefs? Within the local system there exists accountability, they can 'destool' a chief, or remove his authority. We do not want to impose accountability on the chiefs, since land is essentially a chief's thing.'[72] And the former Minister of Lands and Forestry, Professor Kasanga, argued that 'The state should not attempt to enforce local checks and balances. This should be done by the citizens themselves'.[73] Obviously, such state discourse, together with what we refer to as the government's 'policy of non-interference', provides chiefs with ample room for manoeuvre and gives them little reason to fear state intervention in land matters.

The primary basis for the present government's policy of non-interference appears to be a deliberate political alliance with powerful chiefs, coupled with a recognition of the chiefs' considerable local political power and influence and their roles as the key vote-brokers, especially in the rural areas. In addition, the current tendency to fill chieftaincy positions with highly educated professionals blurs the traditional distinction between the governmental elite and the chiefs, and creates new alliances between these two groups (Ray 1992).[74] The elite of the party presently in power, the NPP, is especially closely connected to the chiefs. Not only does it have its stronghold in the Ashanti Region, with its powerful chiefs, but President Kufuor himself is connected through marriage to the royal family of the Asantehene. Many members of the current government, up to high levels, are chiefs or royal family members in their hometown. It should also be noted that rampant irregularities and mismanagement by state institutions in procedures of compulsory acquisition of land do not give the state a strong moral position from which to judge the quality of chiefly land administration (Kotey 1996; *Daily Graphic*, 22 August 2002, 17). Moreover, when the state needs to make new land acquisitions itself, a cooperative relationship with chiefs will be useful.

Chiefs seek to capitalise on the government's current support for chieftaincy by rekindling discussions on certain subjects, such as: the creation of a second chamber of parliament consisting of chiefs; the representation of chiefs on DAs; the referral of all proposals for legislation to the National House of Chiefs for comment as an integral part of the legislative process; the de-vesting and return of former stool lands vested in the President; and an increase in the percentage of stool land revenue to be disbursed by the OASL to the chiefs.[75] Chiefly statements and demands on these issues at workshops and policy meetings generally go unchallenged by government representatives.

The overall picture of governmental intervention in customary land throughout most of the post-independence period is one of piecemeal attempts to control the management of stool lands. We have seen that the government has constitutionally recognised customary land management and the position of chiefs. This indirect legalisation was supplemented by state institutions created and mandated to act as a check on stool land management. These institutions do not, however, in reality exercise effective control upon the chiefly administration of land due to a combination of factors: a lack of chiefly cooperation with the tasks and duties of LSAs; the LSAs' lack of funds, staff and material and their problems of mismanagement and corruption; and the difficulties for and unwillingness of officials to challenge chiefly behaviour. In this context, the lack of political interest by the present administration to contest the authority of the chiefs by tackling their frequent lack of co-operation in land matters is so pervasive that we can speak of a policy of non-interference.

Land Administration Project

Against this background of state institutions and discourse, the government of Ghana, after decades of piecemeal legislative and state management measures, formulated its first comprehensive National Land Policy in 1999 (Ministry of Lands and Forestry 1999) and has embarked, with multi-donor support, upon a Land Administration Project (LAP) intended to reform land institutions and develop land policy so as to provide greater certainty of land rights for ordinary land users and enable greater efficiency and fairness in the land market (Ministry of Lands and Forestry 2003; World Bank 2003b). Under the LAP the medium- to long-term plan is that government should divest itself of responsibility for the management of stool lands. This should proceed incrementally, on the basis of the satisfaction of certain criteria, including the setting up of Customary Land Secretariats (CLSs) with appropriate governance structures to assure institutionalised community-level participation and accountability in the use of stool land and the revenue it generates. CLSs were expected to improve record-keeping and strengthen the accountability of customary authorities in land management, which would in turn 'bring benefits in terms of: lower costs and simpler methods for confirming claims to land; easier public access to information regarding land use and holdings; improved boundary dispute resolution; and opening up of debate at local level regarding the procedures and norms which should guide land administration' (DFID/Toulmin, Brown, and Crook 2004: para 39). The principal beneficiaries were expected to be the majority of people for whom the current land administration system is effectively inoperable due to the lack of transparency in the land allocation process, uncertain tenure rights, high costs, and slow and complex bureaucratic procedures (DFID/Toulmin, Brown, and Crook 2004: para 6).

Guaranteeing tenure security of small land owners in peri-urban Ghana against powerful chiefs and elders requires a clarification of the nature of usufructuary rights and a protection of these rights against the chiefs' conversion drive (cf. DFID/Toulmin, Brown, and Crook 2004:19; Ministry of Lands and Forestry 2003:13; World Bank 2003b:37). Alden Wily and Hammond (2001:28, 54) show, however, that during the LAP conception and design process there was no wide and open discussion of the role of chiefs in the administration of stool land – including the tendency of chiefs to behave like private landlords – or of the possible checks and balances the state could place on stool land administration. Furthermore, from the inception of the LAP, it has been the government's clear political choice that CLSs should fall under the aegis of traditional authorities rather than opting for more community-based approaches to the management of customary land. By placing the CLSs under the aegis of the chiefs, the LAP ignores the fact that the notion of the 'customary' powers and rights of chiefs is loaded with political inventions and endorses the roles that chiefs were accorded in land administration in the colonial period as if this is a timeless principle of customary tenure (Amanor 2005b:110-1). This approach, which was not necessarily the donors' intention, enhances the risks of elite capture of increasing land revenues to the detriment of ordinary land users.

In the pilot phase of the CLSs, the government has displayed strong reserve in dealing with chiefly prerogatives and accountabilities (Ubink and Quan 2008). For example, through the CLS pilot process, LAP staff have opportunities to introduce Memoranda of Understanding (MoUs) between the Ministry and the chiefs, setting out the responsibilities on both sides and working towards the establishment of a wider regulatory framework for CLSs. However, the government has not as yet made efforts to clarify the nature of usufructuary rights or adapt model MoUs drafted by the CLS facilitation team and have them signed as formal agreements between the Ministry and the chiefs to govern the operations of the pilot CLSs. LAP staff has even advised against the use, in draft MoUs, of language which might be interpreted by the chiefs as imposing requirements of accountability, disclosure of revenues, or significant commitments of stool resources to supporting CLSs. The government has so far not introduced a clear policy on the purpose and responsibilities attached to CLSs, and the parameters for the establishment of each pilot CLS remain somewhat ad hoc. What is clear is that in order to secure the votes that the chiefs command, the government in the short to medium term is unlikely to risk antagonising the chiefs by requiring public disclosure of land revenues and accountability in their use.

Although the LAP includes provisions for strengthening civil society participation and advocacy in relation to land management, this has been slow to develop and remains problematic at the time of writing. On the one hand, Ghanaian civil society has limited pre-existing capacity and virtually none in place for the engagement and advocacy on land. It is difficult to induce this by external intervention because of widespread deference to chiefly authority and a history of co-option of civil society by both chieftaincy and political parties (Amanor 2001: 112-3). On the other hand, the Ministry has been reluctant to give up control over funds intended to support civil society partners or commission services from them, and there is a lack of alternative mechanisms such as independent trusts or programmes capable of managing funds to meet the donors' and government's requirements.

Conclusion

This chapter has described how the new value of peri-urban land has triggered a multitude of struggles and negotiations. Although actions, statements, and beliefs as to what is just vary between villages, families, and individuals, one main tug-of-war can be outlined: the struggle between chiefs on the one hand and villagers on the other for the rights to allocate land and share in the revenue. Despite high local resistance, the chiefs in a number of case-study villages persisted in their style of land management, which was highly lucrative for them and sometimes for other selected members of the community – such as elders or royal family members – but extremely detrimental to the livelihoods of the poor majority. Farmers' tenure security, especially the aspect of assurance,[76] was severely corroded by the chiefs' actions.[77] Practices such as multiple sales and allocation of land unsuitable for residential purposes also threaten the tenure security of the new lessees. This poses the question of how chiefs are able to continue acting contrary to the wishes of the majority of the villagers, both old and new. I will discuss three determining factors.

A first factor encountered in this chapter is the erosion of customary checks and balances on chiefly functioning. Customary responsibility should be guaranteed by the existence of a council of elders, consisting of representatives of all major sections of the community, whose permission a chief needs for any decision he wants to take. We saw, however, that in many villages in peri-urban Kumasi, the councillors no longer represent the major families of the community, are co-opted or ignored, and that the customary notion of ruling in council has thus been severely eroded. The second check on traditional rule, the possibility to destool a seriously malfunctioning chief, is also prone to difficulties. Charges have to be brought by the kingmakers, not by commoners, and will be judged by a council composed of other chiefs.

The second factor is found in the behaviour of government, which currently provides hardly any checks and balances on local land administration.[78] Their discourse as well as their actions point towards the existence of an informal 'policy of non-interference', inspired by the political power of the chiefs and the alliance between traditional and state elites. The fact that the government continually emphasises the sovereignty of the chiefs and that land administration rests exclusively in their hands gives additional legitimacy to the chiefs and provides them with ample leeway to administer land the way they please. The National Land Policy and the Land Administration Program do not seem to promise any change in this respect in the near future. On the contrary, the CLS pilot programme carries a significant risk that CLSs will strengthen the political and economic weight of the traditional authorities by providing formal recognition of their powers to administer and allocate land. If the government does not clearly spread the message of the legitimacy of communal interests in land and the need for accountability of the chiefs, then it will de facto allow traditional authorities to use enhanced and equipped CLSs to further tendencies of dispossessing community members of lands (cf. Antwi 2006:5)

The third explanatory factor lies in the fact that stool land management is characterised by a leading position for the chiefs and the prominence of customary law. This is the reality in most localities and has been recognised in the 1992 Constitution. On account of the prominence of customary law in the field of land administration, all actors in land struggles have to legitimise their actions and claims largely with appeals to customary law.[79] When circumstances change and new opportunities arise, they will try to use the unwritten and somewhat negotiable nature of customary law to construct norms in their own interest. Struggles over land will thus often take the form of interpretative struggles over meaning in which 'the power to name' can be a highly political issue (Bassett 1993:21; Shipton and Goheen 1992:309-311). The critical question is, which actor or group of actors has the power to issue definitions and is able to mobilise support – from community members, the traditional system, and the state – for its version of customary law? Since the chiefs are generally regarded as authorities in the field of customary law and as guardians of stool land, they are able to point to 'custom' to acquire and legitimate power over land in the local arena and to resist interference by the state.

In conclusion, the government of Ghana has indirectly legalised customary land tenure and the position of the chiefs as custodians of this land. Besides the provision that customary land should be managed on behalf of and in trust for the people, the government hardly steps into local land management issues. State institutions established to check upon chiefly land administration do not in reality exercise effective control, and the Land Administration Project, despite the formulation of goals like equity and accountability, has not actually imposed any such requirements on the chiefs in the implementation process so far. In combination with the eroded local checks and balances, the chiefs have a free hand to determine their own position in customary land management. It seems that this has given the chiefs the power to over-stretch the somewhat dynamic nature of customary law by manipulating it to suit their needs and legitimise their claims, resulting in the described detrimental effects on the tenure security of the people. Any substantial change in this situation requires two intimately connected transformations: the organisation and empowerment of local farmers, and a different attitude of the government towards chiefly rule and customary land management.

Notes

1   Field work in Ghana on which this research is based was supported by the Netherlands Organisation for Scientific Research (NWO/WOTRO), Mordenate College, the Leiden University Fund (LUF), and the *Adatrechtstichting* (Customary Law foundation).
2   In large parts of southern Ghana, customary land is referred to as stool land in reference to the carved wooden stool which is a traditional symbol of chieftainship and is believed to contain the souls of the ancestors. In the north of Ghana, customary land is defined as skin lands, for here the chiefs sit on a hide. In other areas, such as the Volta Region and Greater Accra, where family heads have jurisdiction over land, we speak of family lands.
3   *Ohene* is the word for king or chief in *(Ashanti-)Twi*, the language of the Asante. Within the Ashanti Region each village chief (*ohene* or *odikro*) is subordinate to a paramount chief (*omanhene*), who again is subordinate to the Asantehene.
4   My main village of study was Besease, situated approximately twenty-three kilometres from Kumasi on the road to Accra. Furthermore, I studied four other villages on or near this road – Jachie, Tikrom, Adadeentem, and Boankra – and four villages on the road to Obuasi – Ahenema Kokoben, Kotwi, Brofoyeduru, and Nkoransa.
5   The term indigenous refers to the non-migrant population of a locality. Inclusion in this category can be an issue of ongoing negotiation and contestation.
6   The customary 'community' does not include all people living within a geographical unit such as a village, but only the indigenous people.
7   This customary usufructuary right is broader and should not be confused with the British usufruct. This also comes to the fore in the use of the term customary freehold as a synonym for customary usufructuary rights.
8   Some authors claim that the rule that no express grant is needed to farm or build on vacant communal land has been eroded by the increased use of land, resulting in a

need to expressly apportion remaining vacant land (Ollennu 1962:32; Woodman 1996:91).

9   Under Ashanti customary law, individual property is inherited by the matrilineal family. Usufructuary titles thus become family property after the death of the usufructuary.

10 Forfeiture results from a denial by the usufructuary of the landlord's title.

11 See Ubink (2002-2004) for a description of case law regarding customary land management.

12 'Town' refers to the built-up area of the village.

13 Interview, 11 May 2003.

14 Such manipulation is facilitated by the varying ways in which certain words, such as stool, stool land and ownership, are used in different contexts. For instance, the fact that the allodial title holder is often defined as the owner, without referring to the usufructuary title holder as the owner, gives ample leeway for reinterpretation.

15 Interview with former Akyeamehene subchief of Tikromhene, 7 January 2004. The argument that the royal family fought for the land is also found in Rathbone (1996: 511).

16 Interview with former Akyeamehene subchief of Tikromhene, 7 January 2004.

17 When confronted with the many development projects in the neighbouring village of Jachie, the Tikromhene pointed out that he was building a primary school in his village. On further enquiry in the village, however, it turned out that this project was being financed by the EU.

18 Interview with Besease youngster, 15 June 2003.

19 Interview with Unit Committee Ahenema Kokoben, 11 November 2003. The Unit Committee forms the lowest level of local government in Ghana and is made up of five to fifteen people per village.

20 Peri-urban Kumasi is exemplary for the whole peri-urban arena. Alden Wily and Hammond (2001:44, 69-73) describe the 'curtailment of communal property rights, through a form of feudalisation of land relations' as a problem occurring in the entire peri-urban arena of Ghana. According to Kasanga and Kotey (2001:18) evidence from all ten regional capitals 'confirms that the displacement of poor and marginalised families from their land is a national disease'. See for more literature on land struggles in peri-urban Ghana Abudulai 1996, 2002; Berry 2002; DFID 2001:28-30, D13-14; Gough and Yankson 2000; Hammond 2005; Kasanga et al. 1996; Kasanga and Woodman 2004; Kotey and Yeboah 2003:3, 19, 21, 53; Maxwell et al. 1998:3; NRI (Natural Resources Institute) and UST (University of Science and Technology) 1997:91; Toulmin and Longbottom 2001:ii-iii, 30; Ubink 2007a; Wehrmann 2002.

21 During my fieldwork I did not find any NGO involved in land matters in peri-urban Kumasi. Discussions with church leaders in Besease revealed that these leaders were not in any way involved in land issues.

22 Although stool land is officially leased rather than sold because the Constitution prohibits the sale of customary land (article 267(5)), nearly everyone talks about the 'selling' of land, and many people, 'sellers' as well as 'buyers', seem to regard it as a definitive transfer.

23 Interview with members of the Unit Committee and the royal family of Brofoyeduru, 5 November 2003.

24 *Ibid.*

25 *Ibid.*

26 Head of the extended family.

27 Interview with farmer in Besease, 27 August 2003.

28 Interview with farmer in Besease, 29 August 2003.

29 Interview with farmer in Besease, 27 August 2003.

30 Interview with elder of Kontihene subchief of Beseasehene, 20 May 2003.

31 Interview with royal family members Boankra, 18 December 2003.

32 Interview, 15 April 2003.

33 The District Assembly is the second lowest level of local government in Ghana. An assembly member is the representative of an electoral area in the assembly.

34 Interview with former assemblyman Tikrom, 15 April 2003.

35 Interview with former assemblyman Feyiase, 8 April 2003.

36 Interviews with Kontihene subchief of Beseasehene and one of the Konti elders, 20 May and 1 July 2003.

37 The position of both chiefs and councilors is hereditary in the sense that it has to be filled by a person from a certain family – in the Ashanti region usually matrilinear. Within such a family, there are usually a number of people eligible to fill the position, of which the family will choose the most suitable candidate. Besides hereditary councilors, a chief can also appoint a number of non-hereditary councilors on the basis of their personal merit. When such a councilor dies, the position disappears, and the family will not be permitted to select a successor. See for a more elaborate discussion of election of chiefs and subchiefs Busia 1951:6-13; Danquah 1928:110; Hayford 1970:3; Kofi-Sackey 1983:66; Kumado 1990-1992; Obeng 1988:34-45.

38 See also Hayford 1970:73; Pogucki 1962:182; Sarbah 1968:66, 87.

39 Interview, 28 October 2003.

40 Interview with Unit Committee member Tikrom, 26 June 2003. Cf. Abudulai 1996; Kasanga 1996.

41 Interview, 26 June 2003.

42 Interview with Asantehene's Land Secretariat, 2 July 2003.

43 Interview with Kontihene subchief Besease, 1 July 2003.

44 Section 15 of the Chieftaincy Act, 1971 (Act 370), confers exclusive jurisdiction in any 'cause or matter affecting chieftaincy' – as defined at section 117 of the Courts Act, 1993 (Act 459), i.e. an action concerned with the nomination, appointment, election of a chief or destoolment – to the Traditional Council or, if a paramount chief is involved, to the Regional Houses of Chiefs. From such a case an appeal lies to the Regional Houses of Chiefs, then to the National House of Chiefs and finally even to the Supreme Court. This means that one cannot take such cases to the regular state courts, only to the Supreme Court in last instance. It must be noted, however, that the courts have not allowed for such a broad interpretation of the words 'cause or matter affecting chieftaincy', and thus the entire functioning of Traditional Councils falls outside their scope. For instance, land cases that are not concerned with the nomination, appointment, election or destoolment of a chief can be taken to the state courts.

45 Interview with Kontihene subchief of Ejisumanhene, 27 May 2003.

46 See, for instance, interview with elder of the Beseasehene, 5 June 2003.

47 Interview with Gyaasehene subchief of Ejisumanhene, 1 June 2003.

48 Interview, 29 June 2003.

49 Such as the chief's right to wild animal skins, tributes of fish, and communal work on his farm (Annor 1985:157; Busia 1951:44).

50 Interview with Okyeame subchief of Beseasehene, 12 June 2003.

51 Interviews at the Regional Lands Commission Kumasi, 9 April 2003; Regional OASL Kumasi, 27 June 2003; Ejisu Juaben District Assembly, 9 September 2003.

52 Interview, 9 September 2003.

53 Interview, 12 January 2004.

54 Interview, 9 April 2003.

55 Interview with District Chief Executive Ejisu-Juaben district, 9 September 2003.

56 Lands vested in the president in trust for a landholding community under the Administration of Lands Act, 1962 (Act 123).

57 It takes on average between six months and two years to process a document submitted to the Lands Commission (Grant 2004:95).

58 In a survey among 242 people in peri-urban Kumasi, 123 people (50.8 per cent) answered they had never heard of the LC. Of the 119 (49.2 per cent) who had heard of the LC, 65 (27 per cent) were not aware of its tasks and functions.

59 Cf. interviews with Deputy Regional Lands Officer Kumasi, 9 April 2003; and Technical Director Forestry, Ministry of Lands and Forestry, 15 August 2003.

60 Multiple sales of the same plot of land to several persons is a large and growing problem in peri-urban Accra, and is also described for peri-urban Kumasi (Edusah and Simon 2001; Oduro-Kwarteng 2003).

61 Interview director TCPD Ejisu-Juaben district, 27 May 2003, cf. planning officer TCPD Kuntanase district, interview 7 April 2003.

62 Chiefs can have their land demarcated by unofficial surveyors who do not interfere with planning and which leaves open the possibility of later changes in the plan. Such amendments were frequently encountered during fieldwork. In a DFID-sponsored project 34 of the 37 villages in peri-urban Kumasi possessed village layout plans, but the majority of these plans was prepared without reference to the statutory agencies responsible for planning (DFID 2001:D8, E13).

63 According to the law, the whole process of acquiring a building permit should not take longer than three months. But in 2003 the Ejisu-Juaben district had not seen a meeting of the Planning Committee in over two years (interview Director TCPD Ejisu-Juaben district, 27 May 2003).

64 Of 242 people surveyed in peri-urban Kumasi, 115 (47.5 per cent) had never heard of a building permit. The other 127 (52.5 per cent) had heard of it, but only 75 of them (31 per cent of the total) could actually explain what it is. When these same 242 people were asked whether they possessed any documents on the house, 85 answered yes, 83 no and the other 74 said that they did not know. Of the 85 that answered yes, 48 did not know what kind of documents, 29 said they did not have a building permit and eight said they did have a building permit. According to the deputy regional lands officer of Kumasi, 87 per cent of the people has no building permit and only ten per cent of the people tries to get a formal lease (interview, 20 September 2005).

65 Interview with Deputy Regional Lands Officer Kumasi, 16 December 2003.

66 Interviews with District Chief Executive Ejisu-Juaben district, 9 September 2003 and 12 January 2004.

67 Interview with District Chief Executive Ejisu-Juaben district, 9 September 2003.

68 Unreported judgment, no. 5/97 of 13 May 1997.

69 Owusu v. Agyei (1991) 2 G.L.R. 493, at 506.

70 See for an elaborate discussion of customary land law in Ghanaian courts, including access to courts and effects of court decisions, Ubink 2002-2004.

71 See for instance Daily Graphic 25 August 2003, p. 3; Ghanaian Times 5 August 2003, p. 1, 25 August 2003, p. 3.

72 Interview, 19 August 2003.

73 Interview, 3 December 2005.

74 Bierschenk 1993 describes the same phenomenon for Bénin.

75 See for instance paramount chief of Asante Asokore S.K.B. Asante 2003:9; president of the national house of chiefs Odeneho Gyapong Ababio II 2003:3.

76 Tenure security is often said to encompass three elements: extent, duration, and certainty. Certainty again is a function of two elements: (1) assurance in asserting rights, and (2) the costs of enforcing these rights, which should not be inhibiting (Migot-Adholla and Bruce 1994:3; Place, Roth, and Hazell 1994:19-21).

77 See Ubink 2007b for the effects of chiefly land (mis)management on popular percep-
    tions of chiefs, their other functions such as dispute settlement and stimulating local
    development, and the institution of chieftaincy.
78 Aside from the courts that do in individual cases protect the usufructuary rights of
    community members.
79 To some extent state legislation and statements by state officials are also used as a lo-
    cal resource, but in general, claims are legitimised by referring to customary law.

7 Land tenure reform and tenure security in Namibia

Marco Lankhorst[1]

Introduction

Land tenure in modern-day Namibia is still deeply influenced by its apartheid history. Under South African rule, the black population faced restrictions both in terms of the nature of the rights to land that could be held, and the parts of the country where such rights could be obtained. With some exceptions, they could access land only in the so-called homelands, where tenure was regulated by customary law. The white elite, on the other hand, appropriated almost all of the commercially attractive land, forcing many of the original inhabitants to resettle. Although formal restrictions on access have been removed, much of this pattern remains visible today. A few thousand settlers of European descent have freehold titles to approximately 4,500 farms, whilst the majority of Namibia's predominantly rural population continues to live in the former homelands, where land tenure is administered by traditional authorities. At the same time, however, the removal of pass-laws has unleashed hitherto repressed internal migration caused by demographic, economic, and ecological changes. This migration creates pressures on land in both urban and communal areas.

These circumstances have given rise to a number of land rights issues, which can be divided into two categories for the purpose of analysis (see Table 7.1). The first set of questions involves the distribution of land tenure rights amongst different groupings in Namibian society. Most important amongst these is the imbalance in commercial land holding between settlers of European descent and black Namibians in general. This is the primary focus of government attention when it comes to land reform. Ethnically specific historical claims on commercial land by the Herero, and (in more latent form) the San and Nama – the tribes most affected by the colonial dispossessions and displacements (in this regard, see Harring 2004 and Werner 1993) – can also be brought under this heading. It must be stressed, however, that such claims are not acknowledged by the government (Melber 2005:139).

The second set of questions is tenure security related.[2] The matter arguably affecting the largest group of people is that land tenure claims based on communal law appear to be poorly protected against government intervention. Relying on its ultimate ownership of unregistered land, the state has on a number of occasions attempted to resettle communities with land rights based on communal law, in order to make room for commercial and other activities. In the urban context, large numbers of slum dwellers live in comparable uncertainty. They generally occupy municipal land, and although this situation is condoned and in most places facilitated, forced resettlements occur with some regularity. Then there is the plight of many San, and to a lesser extent also of the Nama and Damara, who live without a lawful claim or effective legal protection on communal or commercial land owned by others. And lastly, there is the complex problem of encroachments of commonage in the communal areas. Particularly since independence, communal lands have witnessed a process of privatisation through illegal fencing that reduces access to grazing and water for those excluded, which in turn has led to encroachment on the commonage of neighbouring communities. An overview of these two sets of land rights problems is provided below, in Table 7.1.

Recent literature evaluating the government's redistributive policies shows that, although important as a symbol to redress past wrongs, these measures improve neither the economic situation of individual beneficiaries, particularly the poor amongst them, nor that of Namibia's agricultural sector as a whole. Two policy instruments exist to effectuate the redistribution process, the so-called Affirmative Action Loan Scheme (AALS) and the resettlement programmes. The AALS allows relatively well-off communal farmers – they must be in possession of a minimum of 150 heads of cattle – to obtain credit at favourable terms with which to buy commercial farms on the market. In practice, this requirement, intended to ensure the viability of larger capital-intensive agricultural enterprises, rules out participation by the poor.[3] They are targeted instead by the government's individual and collective resettlement programmes.

Resettlement programmes involve the purchase by the state of ranches used for extensive livestock farming, which are then either sub-divided in a large number of smaller units to be farmed intensively

Table 7.1   *Land rights issues in Namibia*

1.	**Redistributive**
a.	White minority vs. black majority in general
b.	Ethnically specific historical claims
2.	**Tenure security related**
a.	Communal rights holders vs. the state
b.	Informal settlers in urban areas
c.	Landless San in rural areas (commercial and communal)
d.	Encroachment in communal areas

or managed collectively. A parallel to this programme exists in the former homelands, which centres on unused communal land. There are clear indications that the results achieved in terms of poverty alleviation are unimpressive. To begin with, largely on account of the cost involved in purchasing commercial land, the scale of the programme is modest. In the first thirteen years of its operation, less than two per cent of white-held commercial farm land was transferred into the hands of the black community (Fuller 2006:7).[4] By 2001 just over 30,000 beneficiaries had been allocated a plot under these programmes, of whom more than 23,000 through the communal limb of the programme (Tapia Garcia 2004; Werner and Vigne 2000:49).[5] More importantly, the income that settlers derive from the land tends to be insufficient for subsistence purposes (Werner and Vigne 2000). As a general matter, agricultural output tends to be disappointing (Tapia Garcia 2004:50 provides an overview of studies into the functioning of these schemes).

Various explanations for this situation have been offered, including a lack of skills amongst the beneficiaries (Werner and Vigne 2000) and the climatic unsuitability of most of Namibia's agricultural land for small-scale intensive farming (Werner 2003:4). This combination offers little hope that, without an illusory significant increase in the amount of resources invested, the resettlement programme can be modified so as to effectively promote the interests of Namibia's poor.

Given the obstacles in the way of redistribution, the second set of land tenure problems, relating to tenure insecurity, emerges as worthy of more serious attention. The threat of state intervention on communal land, the uncertainty faced by extra-legal settlers in urban slums, the dependency of certain traditional communities on others for access to land, and the inter-related processes of privatisation of the commonage and encroachment of the commonage all adversely affect the livelihoods and/or the willingness to invest of some of the most disadvantaged segments of Namibian society. Targeting these problems, therefore, has the potential to remove significant obstacles to the development of the individuals and communities involved.

The objective of this contribution is to chart the scope for making such improvements to tenure security by: (1) systematically discussing the legal, social, economic, and historical circumstances that give rise to these problems; (2) critically examining recent legislation that aims to remedy them, including the Communal Land Reform Act (Act no. 5 of 2002), the Nature Conservation Amendment Act 1996 (Act no. 5 of 1996), and the Flexible Land Tenure Bill; and (3) by advancing more promising alternatives or complementary strategies. The discussion of these matters is organised as follows. The first section provides a number of summary statistics to familiarise the reader with the socio-economic conditions that provide the background to our discussion of land rights issues. The next section takes a historical perspective to bring the main features of Namibia's land tenure system into focus. The last section discusses in detail each of the tenure security-related land rights issues introduced above, as well as the related government initiatives. A final section concludes.

Some relevant indicators

This section provides a brief introduction to socio-economic conditions in Namibia, so as to begin to familiarise the reader with the situation of the various groups affected by the tenure security-related problems discussed below. As is clear from the discussion in the Introduction, three of these problems relate to the rural context and one occurs in the urban context. Therefore, after reviewing some general indicators, we look at conditions specific to these settings and also make comments on the status of the San and the Nama, which informs the discussion of their problems with accessing land. We start, however, by discussing climatic conditions.

To begin with, considering climatic conditions helps to explain why Namibia, which is 1.5 times as big as France but has fewer than two million inhabitants and is thus amongst the world's most sparsely populated countries, has a land problem at all. The extremely arid climate renders much of the available land only marginally fertile. In addition, the agriculturally most attractive terrains are predominantly held by a select group of white settlers. These matters are, of course, primarily important in understanding land redistribution policies and their impact. There is also, however, a more subtle implication for the tenure security-related problems addressed here. To make the exploitation of marginal lands viable, significant investments will generally be required. This applies to commercial farming, subsistence farming, and more traditional forms of land use.[6] Tenure security can be expected to have a major impact on the willingness to invest. Therefore, these climatic conditions, particularly when considered in combination with the conditions of poverty that are about to be discussed, underscore the need to address the problems of tenure security with which this contribution is concerned.

Turning to the socio-economic conditions, as well as the issue of poverty, we run into a second paradox. Namibia is a middle income country with a 2002 per capita income of USD 6,210 at PPP (UNDP 2004b:186), which is relatively high by African standards.[7] The distribution of income is highly skewed, however.[8] The richest 25 per cent of the population earns 66 per cent of national income, whereas the poorest 25 per cent can dispose of no more than 6.3 per cent (Republic of Namibia 2006b:38). Some 35 per cent of the population survives on less than USD1 a day (UN Habitat 2005:15), the World Bank threshold for extreme poverty. These facts are complemented by high levels of unemployment, at 31 per cent (Republic of Namibia 2001a), and a serious HIV/AIDS problem, with a HIV prevalence rate of 19.6 per cent in the year 2006 (UNAIDS 2006:18).

Poverty, in these and other manifestations, is concentrated in rural areas and in informal urban settlements. Namibia's rural population, which makes up roughly 65 per cent of the total, accounts for only 37 per cent of national consumption, reflecting much higher urban household and per capita income levels (Republic of Namibia 2006b). In addition, it can be gleaned from the Republic of Namibia (2006b) that in the countryside, where 48 per cent of the households rely on subsistence farming as their primary source of income, households are larger, literacy rates are lower, and there is less access to durable goods. By contrast, HIV prevalence in rural areas not close to main roads is generally considerably lower than in urban areas (Republic of Namibia 2001b).[9]

That conditions in rural areas are, on the whole, poorer than in the cities is also confirmed by a process of rapid internal migration from rural to urban areas.[10] In 2001, roughly 33 per cent of the population lived in urban centres, an increase of five per cent compared with 1991 (Republic of Namibia 2001a). Migration has resulted in an annual population growth rate of 3.9 per cent in the capital Windhoek (Gold and Mitlin 2001:22), for instance. These migrations away from the countryside appear to be predominantly motivated by a search to improve living conditions (Fjeldstad et al. 2005:14) and particularly for employment (LAC 2005a:10), which is confirmed by the fact that urban centres have more people in economically active age groups than rural areas (Republic of Namibia 2001a).

Having little means, many of these internal migrants end up in informal settlements on the fringes of towns. Fjeldstad et al. (2005:1) estimate that about 40 per cent of the urban population lives in such areas, while Christensen (2004:2) puts the number of households for the whole of Namibia at 100,000. As can be expected, conditions in these settlements, at least where income levels are concerned, are not much different from the situation in the countryside. Surveys conducted by Lankhorst and Veldman (this volume), for instance, suggest that income levels in informal settlements are much closer to the rural average reported by the Republic of Namibia (2006b:36) than the urban aggregate. Similarly, where some form of employment provides the main source of income for almost 77 per cent of the inhabitants of urban centres (*id.*:19), Lankhorst and Veldman (this volume) found that only 38 per cent of households in informal settlements could rely on salaries or wages.[11]

It will be shown below that the problems with tenure security in rural areas have a particularly strong impact on the San and, to a somewhat lesser extent, the Nama.[12] It is useful, therefore, that we very briefly discuss some aspects of the socio-economic situation of these groupings. This will provide the necessary background for understanding the specific land rights problems they face. The San,[13] who number around 30,000 and are spread out primarily over the northeast of the country, are beyond a doubt the most marginalised people of modern-day Namibia. Their 1998 Human Development Index (HDI, which assesses life expectancy, literacy, school enrolment, and income), for instance, was much lower than that of the population as a whole (around 0.30, as opposed to 0.77 – UNDP 1999), and significantly lower than that of other minorities. As Harring and Odendaal (2006) report, most San are unemployed. Those that do have jobs are farm labourers, working on both white- and black-owned farms, mostly under unfavourable conditions. In addition, the San stand out for their weak representation in government (Suzman 2002:23). The Nama,[14] who number around 60,000 and are concentrated in the southern and western parts of Namibia, fare considerably better in terms of HDI, although they are still around fifteen percentage points below the national average (UNDP 1999). A considerable number of them, however, live and work on the farms of others under conditions comparable to those of the San.

A background to land tenure in Namibia

Namibian property law is characterised by a duality inherited from the colonial period, consisting of a parallel freehold and communal system. The freehold system, based on a mixture of Roman Dutch law and English common law, will not be dealt with extensively in this section. Its Western origins allow for the assumption that its main features, in terms of individualisation and registration, are sufficiently well known. In addition, none of the new or recent legislative instruments affecting tenure security discussed below involve the granting of freehold titles. The main focus in this section is, therefore, on communal law. To understand the institutional, substantive, and spatial complexities of modern communal law, it is essential to place it in its historical context.

European occupation and settlement of South West Africa, as Namibia was known at the time, started relatively late with its annexation by Germany in 1885. Throughout the period of German occupation, the reach of the colonial administration never covered the whole of the colony, but remained confined to the central and southern parts of the country, known as the 'police zone'. Progressive settlement combined with the disruptive effect of a rinderpest epidemic soon brought the original inhabitants of this zone, the semi-pastoral Herero and the Nama, into conflict with the Germans. Brutal use of military force by the Germans led to very large losses of life and massive displacements for both tribes.

After the First World War, South West Africa became a British protectorate administered by South Africa. The new colonial government built upon the structures left by the Germans. It instituted a system of indirect rule in the outerlying regions, and encouraged white South Africans to settle in the police zone. While in 1913 the German colony had counted 1,331 white-owned farms, in 1938 this number had grown to 3,305 (Suzman 2002:8). Of the original populations most affected by these settlements, the Herero and Nama were relocated to so-called 'native reserves' outside the police zone, which for the most part consisted of marginal lands (Suzman 2002:8). The influence of white settlement on the position of the San peoples, which was considerably different but not less detrimental, will be discussed below.

Members of all native communities were only permitted to settle in the reserve allocated to their tribe (homeland).[15] Native authorities, who were appointed by the colonial administration, enjoyed a degree of autonomy in the administration of the reserves, which included powers to allocate land to their subjects according to customary laws. The reserve system further depended on severe restrictions on the movement of the native peoples. Travel between these reserves and the police zone was strictly regulated by the authorities. It is generally recognised that this constellation of measures was designed, at least in part, to assure white farms and industries of a large pool of cheap migrant labour (see e.g. Hendricks 1990 and Suzman 2002).[16]

Although restrictions on movement and the right to settle in the former police zone were removed when Namibia gained independence from South Africa, other important features of the homeland system have been preserved. As regards land tenure, it should be pointed out, first, that the country remains divided into a segment where land is held under freehold title (which accounts for approximately 43 per cent of its surface area) and the former home lands, now called communal areas (approximately 42 per cent).[17] There, the government has instituted tenure regulations that continue to give some room to customary practices. Significantly, also, post-apartheid legislation regulating the recognition and exercise of traditional authority has kept the ethnically based territorial divisions within the formal homelands in place (see Figure 7.1). Most important amongst this legislation are the Traditional Authorities Act (Act number 25 of 2000) and the previously mentioned Communal Land Reform Act.

Figure 7.1   *Communal lands in independent Namibia*

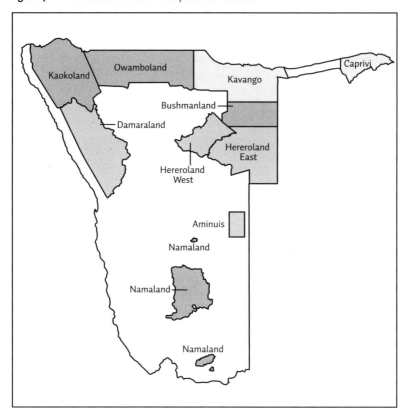

The Communal Land Reform Act legitimises and circumscribes the role of traditional authorities in the allocation of land to the members of their traditional communities. The legitimacy of the exercise of such powers, according to the Traditional Authorities Act, is subject to recognition of the traditional authority, and effectively of the traditional community he or she represents, by the central government.

This recognition process involves the identification of the area habitually inhabited by this community, over which the powers of the traditional authority extend. The nature of customary land rights that traditional authorities can grant, and the procedures to be followed, are to a considerable extent regulated by the Communal Land Reform Act. A primary provision of the act (section 17) determines, in accordance with the Constitution (see schedule 5), that ultimate ownership of communal land is vested in the state. Tenure claims in the communal areas (described in the act as customary land rights and leasehold rights) are therefore best classified as use rights. The implications thereof are discussed below. The act further provides that applications for land to chiefs or headmen have to be made in writing. The validity of land allocations by traditional authorities is dependent on the approval by the region's 'communal land board' and must be followed by registration.[18] In addition, the act contains rules regarding (1) the types of land use for which rights may be granted to individual community members, (2) the duration of customary land tenure rights, (3) the maximum size of plots, (4) transfer and inheritance, and (5) contains a prohibition on charging fees for the allocation of land tenure rights. Finally, the act confirms the powers of traditional authorities to regulate access to grazing on their community's commonage.

Tenure security-related land rights issues

Tenure insecurity hinders development.[19] It can easily be appreciated that it may inhibit investments, for example to improve housing in urban slums or to set up an income-generating tourism venture in communal areas. The consequences can be wider, however, as non-economic aspects of development may also be affected. Traditional communities will often feel a strong cultural link with the land they have historically occupied. A threat to this area may, thus, hinder the capacity of communities to negotiate a place in the modern world.[20]

This section discusses a number of causes of tenure insecurity in Namibia, and examines and evaluates the legal instruments that may be used to reduce these uncertainties. It starts by discussing uncertainty raised by incidents where the government, claiming its ultimate ownership of communal land, required rights holders to resettle in order to allow the land to be used for other purposes. It then moves on to consider the situation in urban informal settlements, where government-imposed relocations are also a frequently recurring problem. The last two sub-sections focus on insecurity caused not by government intervention but by the actions of other persons or communities.

State interventions in communal areas

On a number of occasions, well covered in the media and the literature, the post-independence Namibian government has taken or planned actions which substantially limit the use that certain traditional communities could make of their lands. In each of the cases that are about to be discussed, the administration's objective was to use these lands for a purpose that was considered to be of over-riding importance. In none of these cases was the community involved given a direct say in the process leading to the government's decision affecting their land, nor were serious and encompassing negotiations started after this decision had been made, nor was adequate compensation offered. This sub-section discusses some of the implications of such an approach.

The best-known of these incidents, due to its coverage in the international press, involves the planned construction of a hydropower dam at the Epupa Falls in the northwestern part of the country (Kaokoland on Figure 7.1); a project on which the Namibian government cooperates with Angola. The government sees the realisation of this project as crucial to the development of the region. The dam would provide both power and employment. At the same time, however, the lake that would form behind the dam would disrupt the lives of those members of the Himba people who live near the Kunene River. It is reported that around 1,000 Himba would be displaced, and as many as 5,000 would lose access to grounds for grazing, which would increase pressure on pastures further inland and would increase susceptibility to drought (Suzman 2002:20). Also, construction of the dam would submerge 160 ancestral graves, which many Himba consider significant, since burial sites form an anchor point in defining social relations and relations to the land (id.). Lastly, it has been suggested that the lake would increase health risks in the region by producing a higher incidence of insect-carried diseases such as malaria (Corbett 1999). However, the plans offered those immediately affected very little in terms of compensation. Cost estimates for the project included no provisions for the purchase of the land involved and noted that resettlement costs would be low because the Himba are poor and have little personal property (Harring 2004:75). The official consultation procedure started by the government in 1991 failed to inform the Himba of the lake formation until a later stage (in 1997). There appear to be strong indications, also, that the government obstructed the organisation of the protests that followed. Meetings have been dispersed (Daniels 2004:54), and members of the Owambo tribe, sympathetic to the government, have been resettled in the area to provide a counter-balance (Harring 2004:75). Nonetheless, a vocal international campaign was mounted,[21] which, together with complications on the Angolan side, led to the temporary suspension of the project.

The same reluctance on the side of the Namibian government to inform and involve the leadership and members of affected communities can be seen in other instances where the Namibian government laid claim to communal lands. These include its attempts to establish a refugee camp on !Kung San traditional land (see Pakleppa 2004) and its efforts to extend a prison farm into Khwe San territory (see Daniels 2004).[22]

The statutory basis for these (planned) interventions is to be found in the Communal Land Reform Act. This act empowers the president of the republic to withdraw terrain from communal land in the public interest on the condition that just compensation is paid. These incidents suggest that where withdrawal of communally held tenure is involved (as opposed to claims held by individuals in the communal areas), the government intends to offer very little in the way of compensation. In any case, it appears that the state relies on a method for calculating compensation that, from the perspective of the communities involved, may understate the value of their land

There are good arguments in favour of taking a more inclusive approach to compensability, even from the government's point of view. To begin with, it is certainly possible that the current restrictive stance has wider consequences. Creating a reputation for underestimating the value of communal land can be expected to affect the behaviour of communal rights holders other than those directly affected. To give an example, it may negatively influence the decisions of other communities who, like the Khwe and Himba, seek to expand their income base by investing in tourism. Second, a decision-making procedure that involves the affected community at an early stage can be expected more often to lead to a workable outcome. This is significant given that three of the four cases referred to above attest to the fact that even relatively small and, in the cases of the San, politically weak communities can be effective in blocking the implementation of the government's plans. Lastly, such a cooperative approach offers better prospects for minimising the negative impact of these plans.

Informal settlers in urban areas

Many inhabitants of the homelands who moved to the cities in search of work when the apartheid era pass laws were abolished ended up in extra-legal (informal) settlements. These are to be found in and around most towns, in both the former police zone and the communal areas. This sub-section briefly discusses instruments that could be used to increase the sense of security of persons occupying a plot in such areas.[23]

During apartheid, black people working in police zone towns either stayed in a sort of hostel, known as single quarters, or in townships (which were in most cases communal enclaves surrounded by freehold land). Illegal settlements in and around towns were vigorously combated during most of the apartheid period. Only in the second half of the 1980s, when some restrictions of the separate development policy were relaxed to allow freer movement, were modest informal settlements allowed to emerge near urban centres (Fjeldstad et al. 2005:5).

In the homelands, sizable urban centres emerged only from the 1960s onwards in response to the administrative and military requirements of the South African Defence Force. Like in the police zone, these towns were strictly segregated. There was no homeland equivalent to the government-planned townships of the police zone, however, so that all non-white settlement around these towns occurred in an unregulated fashion (*id.*).

As mentioned, after independence these informal settlements increased in size and number. In 1992, with the passing of the Local Authorities Act (Act no. 23 of 1992), all unregistered (i.e. non-freehold) lands falling within municipal boundaries, where the bulk of these informal settlements are to be found, were transferred to the newly established local authorities, both in the communal areas and in the former police zone. This land is meant to be subdivided, serviced, and sold to the public. In an attempt to regulate the growth of extra-legal settlements, so-called 'reception areas' have been designated in many towns. Newcomers are channelled towards these areas, where they enjoy a *de facto* permit to occupy a plot until a permanent solution is found.

The prospect of eventual relocation to a site that can be permanently settled is a primary reason why the inhabitants of reception areas experience insecurity. Lankhorst and Veldman (this volume) find that forced relocations to, within, and between reception areas – i.e. to another non-permanent location – constitute another important and more immediate reason for uncertainty. Such relocations can be motivated by reasons to do with public health, safety, or zoning, or by the desire to make space for other kinds of development. In general, slum dwellers receive no compensation in case of relocation other than help with the actual moving. To avoid having to do so, local authorities tend to prohibit the erection of permanent structures in these areas (Fjeldstad et al. 2005: 16). Lankhorst and Veldman (this volume) show that the resulting insecurity can be a cause of anxiety amongst a substantial portion of the inhabitants, and that it can have a tempering effect on household maintenance and the willingness to make improvements.

The Namibian government appears to be determined to address the problem of insecurity in urban slums by means of legalisation of tenure. As it has proven impossible to give a meaningful number of informal settlers access to freehold ownership under existing legislation,[24] a bill has been prepared that introduces new forms of low-cost statutory tenure. Although much effort was devoted by the drafters of this Flexible Land Tenure Bill to reduce the administrative costs of developing and registering new land (by creating local registries with simplified procedures), it remains to be seen whether sufficient resources will be made available to implement this programme. The long delay in signing this bill into law may well be explained by such funding problems.[25]

An alternative to improve legalisation, which could be relied on to improve tenure security in the intermediate period, would be to introduce a clear policy regarding urban relocations, obliging local authorities to pay compensation in conformity with prices formed on the informal market (in cases where no genuine public health or safety concerns are at issue). Such a policy would, of course, impose a cost on Namibia's local authorities and therefore limit their freedom of action.[26] But most local authorities, however strapped for cash they may be, have large reserves of land, so the effect need not be too quelling.

As Lankhorst and Veldman (*id.*) show in more detail, there are two further arguments for proceeding with caution in addressing the problems in Namibia's urban slums by means of the framework set up in the Flexible Land Tenure Bill. First, it is questionable whether flexible titling alone will allow for substantial improvements in tenure security. This can be explained as follows. To reduce the costs of legalisation for the settlers, the bill allows large numbers of them to register their land as a group in the local registry, initially without indicating the internal sub-divisions. On the administrative side, cost savings are made possible *inter alia* because group registration is not affected by the costly and time-consuming administrative requirements that come with developing new residential land under freehold tenure, notably those imposed by zoning regulations. Given, however, that the bill foresees that group tenure can, eventually, be individualised and turned into freehold tenure, application of these regulations is in reality postponed rather than circumvented. As a consequence, settlers may be certain of their ownership of the land they hold as a group, but the shape, dimensions, and even the location of their individual plot within it may later be changed. For this reason, group title-holders will be advised on their title certificate that they should not erect permanent structures before their rights have been upgraded, or a layout for the area has been approved by the local authority. [27]

A second reason to proceed with caution in implementing the Flexible Land Tenure Bill is the following. In addition to improving tenure security, the bill aims to improve the economic opportunities of Namibia's urban poor, notably by allowing them to sell, let, and mortgage their rights. As a general matter, it is not evident that the tenure forms introduced by the bill would indeed give settlers more freedom to dispose of their land than they currently enjoy. Lankhorst and Veldman (*id.*) show that selling and letting is quite common in the current situation of extra-legality. And it should be taken into account that the bill introduces a number of transaction costs for settlers that are absent under extra-legality (such as registration fees). Moreover, given the level and irregularity of income in these settlements, and the difficulties in establishing the limits of individual plots, it is unlikely that banks will be interested in extending credit to their inhabitants, suggesting that the ability to use flexible titles as collateral might well be meaningless.

Therefore, application of the bill – once signed into law – is not advisable unless sufficient resources become available to create and staff registries and to satisfy the necessary administrative requirements. Before that happens, a clear policy regarding relocations that obliges local authorities to pay compensation appears to be the best option to improve tenure security in Namibia's urban slums.

Landless San and other peoples without access to land in rural areas

The post-independence land tenure system in Namibia does not provide all formerly disadvantaged ethnicities equal access to land in rural areas. The San, in particular, remain at a disadvantage. Two factors have contributed to their situation. First, a substantial portion of San traditional land falls in the former police zone and is held under freehold title, mainly by white commercial farmers. Second, the vast majority of San communities in the communal areas have not seen their claims to traditional leadership recognised by government. San land use is therefore often dependent on the interests of commercial farmers or the leaders of other traditional communities. There are clear signs both in the commercial and the communal context that this hinders their development. The Nama and the linguistically related Damara people face similar problems. Given the importance of ethnicity, these problems are more political in nature than the other land issues dealt with in this section, and the discussion here is limited to charting some of the main features of the debate.

The history of the San over the past centuries is characterised by progressive marginalisation, brought about by the impact of migration and colonisation. Originally, the San were spread out thinly over most of modern-day Namibia, living a highly mobile life of hunting and gathering. Southward migrations into northern and central Namibia by the much more numerous and cattle-herding Bantu tribes (mainly Damara, Herero, Owambo, and Kavango) forced the San into retreat. Subsequent displacements of the Herero, Nama, and Damara tribes under the German colonial administration pushed them back further. During the South African mandate the San held a unique, but unenviable position. They were deemed to be a lesser expression of humanity insufficiently developed to be granted a reserve. Only at a late stage was Bushmanland (see Figure 7.1) constituted as the San homeland. It was, however, never given self-governing status, nor were serious attempts made to concentrate South West Africa's San within this area. The area was inhabited only by a few hundred members of two of the seventeen distinct San groupings present in Namibia (Harring and Odendaal 2006:1). As a result, the vast majority of the San found themselves either on white-owned commercial farms or, outside the police zone, in the native reserves of other tribes (*id.*). The problems in the former police zone are discussed first.

Many San living on commercial land face problems that in Namibia are referred to under the heading of the 'farm workers issue'. Given the size of commercial farms and the nature of the work, these labourers, who are amongst the worst paid of Namibia's work force, generally have no choice but to make their homes on their employer's estate. They come in two varieties. There are those whose roots lie elsewhere, often in communal areas, and then there are so-called generational workers, whose families have been living on the land for long periods. As follows from the historical account given above, the latter group includes many San. A considerable number of Damara, as well as a number of Nama, both also original inhabitants of the former police zone, are in the same position. The vulnerability of this group was highlighted after independence when, in anticipation of the passing of labour and social security laws, many commercial farmers dismissed and expelled a number of their workers (Suzman 2002:23). This process is still continuing and particularly affects the elderly (Fuller 2006:10). Changes in farm ownership, including those occasions when farms come into the hands of black owners by means of the government's redistributive policies, also frequently result in dismissal (Fuller 2006:11; Werner 2003:14). Often these landless workers move to form extra-legal settlements around neighbouring towns (Suzman 2002:23). This problem has increasingly caught the attention of the government. In 2002 the Ministry of Lands and Resettlement drafted a policy on farm workers' rights. The document has not been published, however, and to date no effective measures have been taken.

Most San living in the communal areas are also dependent on others for access to land. In the second half of the 1990s, the leaders of six San communities applied for recognition under the *Traditional Authorities Act*. Although at first none of their submissions were approved, the government finally recognised the leaders of the two San peoples living in Bushmanland, the !Kung in the West and the Ju|'hoansi in the East (see Harring 2004:72; Suzman 2002). They are said to constitute only fifteen per cent of Namibia's total San population (Harring and Odendaal 2006:2). As suggested, those communities who saw their claims rejected live under the traditional authority of other tribes, mainly Owambo and Kavango. The disadvantages of this dependence are illustrated by some events in the recent history of the Khwe San people.

The Khwe live in Namibia's Caprivi region. Their claim to traditional authority is contested by the Mkubushu. When this Bantu tribe entered the area several hundred years ago from what are now Angola and Zambia, the San were already there. Although their relation was not entirely hostile, the Mkubushu, a politically centralised, agricultural, and thus sedentary people, have dominated the Khwe for much of the ensuing period. Amongst others, the Khwe were forced to retreat from the fertile lands near the Okavango River into the dry interior. During apartheid, whilst the Mkubushu were resettled elsewhere so as to leave a buffer zone for operations of the South African Defence Force, many Khwe cooperated with the military and remained in the region. After independence, despite having what are generally recognised to be strong credentials (Harring 2004; Harring and Odendaal 2006; Suzman 2002), the Khwe leadership's application for recognition was rejected by the government in favour of the Mkubushu's claim that the Khwe fall under their chieftainship.

The point here is not to discuss the formal legal merit of the Khwe claim (in this regard, see, for example, Harring and Odendaal 2006), but rather to highlight some of the disadvantages of their unrecognised status. To begin with, the Khwe have been unable to exert influence on the post-independence resettlement of the Mkubushu in the area, a process in which their access to land was further reduced (Suzman 2002:24). The Khwe were also not consulted by the government about the conversion of a large portion of their traditional territory into the Bwabwata national park. There is opposition to the park because its regulations complicate food collection, and because it is considered less likely that the inhabitants will be allowed to share in the revenues generated, than if the area had been proclaimed a Khwe conservancy (Harring and Odendaal 2006:11).[28] Lastly, with the government seeking and obtaining consent from the Mkubushu chief, the Khwe have been unable to prevent the transformation of a defunct government farm on their traditional lands into the Divindu Rehabilitation Project, a prison farm, which they feared would adversely affect their business at the nearby n//goavaca tourist campsite. Only by seeking redress at the High Court in 1997 with the help of the Legal Assistance Centre have they managed to stall an extension of the prison farm (see Daniels 2004). Clearly, formal recognition would have enhanced the bargaining position of the Khwe's traditional leaders in each of these situations and would, therefore, have given the Khwe community more freedom to shape its future.

Encroachment on communal lands

Encroachment on communal rangeland has been a pervasive problem since independence. In many cases the intrusion is directly related to a process of privatisation of commonage by fencing. The results are reduced access to land for grazing, land degradation, and, ultimately, conflicts over land. This final sub-section traces the origins of these problems and investigates to what extent the instruments provided by the Communal Land Reform Act and the Nature Conservation Amendment Act may be relied upon to remedy them.

Encroachment of communal land often takes the form of members of one traditional community moving their cattle herds into the lands traditionally occupied by another community. For example, Herero and Kavango herds appear to be kept in Bushmanland on a permanent basis (see Harring and Odendaal 2006:25). Similarly, Owambo have moved into Western districts of the Kavango region (see Cox et al. 1998 and Fuller 2006:11). It may, however, also happen that members from another community move in to occupy land for permanent settlement, as Owambo from the Ohangwena and Oshikoto regions did in Ukwangali (Fuller 2006:10), or that members from the same community but from a different locality claim access, as happened, for instance, amongst the Herero at Okonyoka in the Aminuis communal area (Twyman et al. 2001).

Reduced access to land for grazing is what drives these migrations. Several developments have contributed to this reduction. After independence, wealth accumulated by blacks in the urban-based economy has increasingly been invested in commercial farming on communal lands. Taking advantage of weak oversight by traditional authorities or of good connections, many of these commercial farmers have closed off attractive portions of commonage (often including boreholes) in order to assure themselves of a good return on their investment (Cox et al. 1998; Verlinden and Kruger 2007). Subtractions from the commonage have also occurred due to population increases in towns and cattle posts. To feed the extra mouths, more fertile pasture in the surroundings is gradually turned into fields for cropping (Verlinden and Kruger 2007). Both processes have increased the pressure on the remaining rangeland, where the bulk of subsistence farmers are left to herd their livestock, resulting in widespread degradation.

The ensuing migrations in search of better grazing, as well as the process of illegal fencing, must be seen in light of a reduction in the effective level of control over access to rangeland after independence. Several arguments have been presented to explain this reduction. To begin with, Namibia's new constitution overturned two cornerstones of the homeland policy by giving every citizen the right to reside and settle in any part of the country (art. 21h). In addition, it vests ownership of communal lands in the state (schedule 5). In the immediate after-math of independence, these changes raised uncertainty about the scope of traditional leaders' powers to regulate access to land, particu-larly as regards the exclusion of members of other communities (Fuller 2006:4; Sullivan 2002:166). At the same time, part of the administra-tive support for traditional leaders provided by the colonial administra-tion temporarily fell away (Cox et al. 1998), while as has been sug-gested (Kakujaha Matundu 2002:10), their sense of responsibility for rangeland conservation had been eroded under apartheid by concen-trating management in the hands of white administrators. These fac-tors, together with the inherent difficulties of monitoring access on very large, remote, and not easily accessible terrains, and the fact that government attention has been focused on white ownership in the for-mer police zone, created an environment on communal rangeland that is qualified by many as presenting the characteristics of an open access regime (e.g. Kakujaha Matundu 2002; Verlinden and Kruger 2007: 190).

The Communal Land Reform Act (of 2002), which is the primary le-gal instrument regulating land use in Namibia's communal areas, ad-dresses the issue of fencing and the problem with enforcing customary common property principles. It contains a clear prohibition of fencing on communal land (art. 16) and provides rules by which to judge whether existing fences can be retained. In this regard article 28(8) re-quires that an existing fence was erected in accordance with customary law, and that it will not unreasonably interfere with the use of the com-monage by other members of the traditional community.[29] Article 29 (1) confirms the powers of traditional authorities to regulate and, thus, limit access to commonage, and article 29(5) makes the erection of fences, obstruction of access to water, permanent settlement, and culti-vation on such land punishable as an offence.

It is too early to assess whether these provisions allow for effective traditional rangeland management systems to be restored or rein-vented. The case study by Verlinden and Kruger (2007), which is based on data gathered in 2005, suggests that the tide has not yet turned. Much depends on how traditional leaders will make use of their discre-tionary powers, notably to enforce the prohibition on fencing. The risk remains that they will be co-opted by wealthy and politically well-con-nected individuals. A possible solution to such problems may lie in the creative use of conservancies.

A conservancy is a legal entity regulated by the Nature Conservation Amendment Act of 1996.[30] The foremost purpose of this act is to re-construct a common property regime for wildlife in order to fill a va-cuum created under apartheid that was closely related to the lack of rangeland control discussed earlier. Traditionally, the inhabitants of Na-mibia's communal land have perceived wildlife as threatening. It com-petes with livestock for grazing and water, may prey on livestock, and many species routinely damage crops (Weaver and Skyer 2003:7). This perception was strengthened under apartheid when ownership and management of wildlife were in the hands of the colonial administra-tion, undermining a role of the inhabitants of the homelands as custo-dians of wildlife. The resulting heavy poaching, in combination with droughts, resulted in critically low wildlife populations (id.:8). The act partly decentralises wildlife management by giving traditional commu-nities incentives to become involved. This is done by giving commu-nities who organise themselves in a conservancy ownership rights to game, which they can communally exploit by setting up tourism ven-tures (mainly in the form of safari camps and trophy hunting). These, in turn, also provide employment. The government closely monitors wildlife populations in the conservancies, and hunting is subject to a permit system.

Conservancies have been heralded as a success story of community-based natural resource management. Studies show recovery of wildlife populations (e.g. Weaver and Skyer 2003) and revenues (amounting to USD 1.3 million for all of Namibia in 2003) being used to supplement conservancy members' incomes, as well as to invest in education and healthcare (see Fuller 2006 and Weaver and Skyer 2003). With these successes the number of applications for the establishment of conser-vancies has risen sharply. The year 1998 saw the creation of the first conservancy; in 2003 there were 29 registered conservancies, covering a quarter of the total communal area landmass, and housing some 150,000 inhabitants. It is clear, however, that the successes are limited to a number of flagship conservancies, each of them major tourist at-tractions. The majority do not offer prospects of producing revenues that would significantly increase incomes (Sullivan 2002:167).

The continued interest in establishing conservancies has been ex-plained by pointing to the fact that communities, living in the post-in-dependence context of uncertain customary tenure, primarily concep-tualise this institution not as a means to manage wildlife, but as a way to strengthen traditional land claims (id.:165). Given that procedures for registering a conservancy require that its physical boundaries and membership be defined, they are understood as a tool to keep outsiders out. This is so, even though the rights conferred relate to wildlife and tourism, and therefore do not directly affect the rights of non-commu-nity members to grazing and water (Fuller 2006:15). As follows from the discussion in the previous sub-section, these properties of conser-vancies can be expected to be of additional importance to communities whose leaders have not been recognised under the Traditional Authorities Act.

It is submitted that conservancies could play a key role in addressing the problem of encroachments on communal land. Its primary function would be in the intra-community context, where it could provide a basis for the reconstruction of a common property regime that regulates rangeland access (according to Jones and Mosimane (2000:81), examples already exist). Despite challenges, conservancy committees have been shown to be reasonably representative of their community. They include younger people and women, tend to cooperate with, but remain independent from, local traditional leaders, and are perceived to distribute revenues fairly (Jones and Mosimane 2000; their composition and functioning is criticised, however, in Sullivan 2002). Where oversight by traditional authorities is insufficient, the establishment of a conservancy could, therefore, provide an inclusive platform to discuss and coordinate the diverging interests that different members of the community may have when it comes to rangeland access. Without suggesting that this would lead to ideal outcomes, it can be expected that the result would be more sustainable than what is achieved in places where conditions currently border on open access. Combined with the prohibitions of fencing and unauthorised use contained in the Communal Land Reform Act, better intra-community management could also work to reduce migrations to the communal land of neighbouring communities.

Conclusion

This text has shown that there are serious problems with tenure insecurity in Namibia that need to be addressed. Insecurity threatens the livelihoods and willingness to invest of some of the most disadvantaged segments of Namibian society.

We have seen that in many instances this insecurity is the result of the actions of the government itself. This is the case with forced relocations in communal and urban areas, and where the government sponsors the development of infrastructure or other projects without consulting the communities that are directly affected. A clear policy that sets out the limits to the rights that the state and its organs may exercise as ultimate owner of communal and undivided urban lands would be a relatively simple and cheap way to attenuate this insecurity. It was argued that in the urban context, such an approach might be more effective than the legalisation programme foreseen in the Flexible Land Tenure Bill. Such a policy should be based on the principles of consultation of those affected and compensation in conformity with market prices. And where traditional land is concerned, the state should include the cultural value of the land in the evaluation of whether individual or group rights should succumb to the interests of the general public. While such a policy would limit the government's freedom to steer development, it would increase the capacity of communities and individual Namibians to improve their situation.

We have seen further that there are problems with access to range land and illegal fencing in the communal lands. These problems are caused by a combination of apartheid policies that have undercut traditional authority powers and increased mobility and investment in communal areas since independence. The framework for managing rangeland access drawn up in the Communal Land Reform Act (of 2002) depends on the attribution of considerable discretionary powers to traditional authorities. It was suggested that where sufficient checks and balances on chiefly powers are lacking, the establishment of a conservancy, as foreseen in the Nature Conservation Amendment Act (of 1996), would offer a better guarantee of equal and sustainable use of rangelands, as it could be adapted to form an inclusive platform to discuss and coordinate the diverging interests that different members of the community may have when it comes to management of the commonage.

Notes

1   PhD student at the Center for Law and Economics, University of Amsterdam. Correspondence at: Roetersstraat 11, 1018 WB Amsterdam, The Netherlands. E-mail: Lankhorst@uva.nl. This research was neither supervised nor sponsored by the ACLE; all responsibility for views and errors is mine exclusively.
2   Given that these problems are diverse in nature, it is useful to explain how the terms 'land tenure' and 'tenure security' are used in this text. Land tenure regimes can take many different forms ranging from individual ownership of a defined portion of land to systems regulating various forms of overlapping use that different members of a community may make of jointly owned land. Consequently, insecurity about tenure may relate to the ability to continue to reside on a plot, but also to the ability of a community to keep outsiders at bay, or the ability of community members to gain adequate and equal access to the commonage. We will see that whether tenure is formally recognised by the state or is merely of a factual nature (but with a local claim to legitimacy) can have an influence on the level of security that is experienced.
3   No good data on the effects of AALS on production or other relevant parameters exist. Many entertain serious doubts, however, as to the economic effect for the beneficiaries of this scheme. It is indicative, for example, that 37 per cent of AALS farmers default on their loans, and that in 2005 a temporary moratorium on loans was declared (LAC 2005a:32). In addition, Chiari (Chiari 2004:34) reports that the Agribank, the institution administering the scheme on behalf of the government, considers only 50 to 60 per cent of the farms that are purchased through AALS as commercially viable. A contributing factor to the condition of the sector as a whole is that, as

Sherbourne (2004) points out, demand for farms amongst the new elite is driven to
a significant extent by the perceived effect on social status. Profitable exploitation will
often be a secondary concern.

4   To calculate this share, the data provided by Fuller on the amount of land involved in
    the purchase of farms were combined with the number of 36,000 hectares of total
    commercial farmland (Werner 2003:3).

5   Tapia Garcia's figures in this regard are based on unpublished information from the
    Ministry of Lands Resettlement and Rehabilitation.

6   Yields can be increased by investing in fertilisers and irrigation. Alternatively, and
    more relevant to a larger portion of Namibia, raising livestock may offer the prospect
    of better returns than planting crops. Cattle, however, is more expensive to buy than
    seeds. In both cases the construction and maintenance of waterholes and boreholes
    will be essential, as is the case for many forms of traditional and subsistence farm-
    ing.

7   Cf. the overview in UNDP (UNDP 2004b:186). PPP stands for purchasing power
    parity.

8   Namibia has one of the highest levels of income inequality in the world. Equality in
    income distribution is commonly measured by means of the Gini coefficient, which
    is a measure of statistical dispersion. A high coefficient indicates a high level of in-
    equality. Namibia has the highest Gini coefficient (0.7) in the global overview pre-
    sented in UNDP (2004b:190), which reflects 1993 data. Republic of Namibia
    (2006b:40) reports a 2003/2004 Gini coefficient of 0.6.

9   This is partly off-set, however, by more limited access to medical services, and ARVs
    in particular.

10 Although common in many developing countries, this process of urbanisation has
    specific features in Namibia (see Frayne and Pendleton 2002: 2). During the apart-
    heid period, much of Namibia's non-white population was barred from residing per-
    manently and owning property in productive centres (mostly towns) and remained
    confined to homelands governed by traditional authorities. Following independence
    from South Africa in 1990, these restrictions on internal migration were removed.

11 There are, of course, vast differences of approach and definitions between our tenta-
    tive survey (of only one informal settlement) and the government's statistical re-
    search. It is submitted, however, that the differences are sufficiently large to assume
    that aggregate figures for urban centres hide considerable differences within the ur-
    ban context.

12 As will be explained, this is not to say that other ethnic groupings are not affected.

13 It should be pointed out that the San are not a homogenous group. Suzman (2002:
    3) identifies seventeen San dialects occurring within five distinct San languages.

14 As is the case with the San, they are not a homogenous group. According to Harring
    (2004:63) there are fourteen distinct groups.

15 Homelands were also created for native communities whose traditional territories fell
    outside the Police Zone, see Figure 7.1. Members of these communities were there-
    fore not resettled on a scale comparable to the relocation of the Herero, Nama, and
    Damara.

16 The extensive historiography on migrant labour in Africa generally emphasises its
    negative social and economic impact on rural society. Kreike's (2004) study of the si-
    tuation in Owamboland provides an interesting addition to this literature, by showing
    how wages were invested in the rural economy.

17 Christensen, Werner, and Højgaard 1999:1. The remainder is state-owned land that
    includes national parks and diamond mining areas.

18 The registration of individual forms of customary land rights and the monitoring by
    land boards of traditional authorities form an interesting topic for study. Given that

the Act has been implemented very recently, however, and that registration has started on only a small scale (see Fuller 2006:15), little can as yet be said about the merits of this approach in the Namibian context. It is worth pointing out also that, although it may be assumed to be intended to prevent abuse of powers by traditional authorities, the precise problem that is addressed with registration is not spelled out in the literature with anything near the same amount of detail as seen in the discussions regarding encroachment of commonage, San land rights, etc.

19 For a broader discussion on this topic, see e.g. World Bank 2003d.

20 This is illustrated by the discussions below of the situation of the San and of plans to construct a dam at the Epupa Falls that threaten culturally important sites of the Himba tribe.

21 This may partly be explained by the fact the Himba form part of the powerful Herero people.

22 The situation of the Basters of Rehoboth – which lies in the former police zone and falls under the freehold regime – regarding the resettlement of members of other tribes, mainly Owambo, on their traditional lands (see Harring 2004 and Suzman 2002) is comparable, also.

23 This is more elaborately discussed in Lankhorst and Veldman, this volume.

24 Lengthy and costly procedures for sub-dividing municipal land and high prices on the commercial land market are the main reasons that have been advanced to explain this failure (Christensen, Werner, and Højgaard 1999:9).

25 The bill was originally prepared in 1997 and 1998; a final, fourth, version was issued in 2004.

26 A higher degree of certainty would be likely to lead to some increase in the plot prices charged on the informal market. Lankhorst and Veldman (this volume) quote selling prices established on the current informal market.

27 See Christensen (2004:7). Should they do so anyway, they would not receive compensation if, at a later stage, it turns out they have to move in order to allow for the construction of roads or service provision.

28 See the discussion below for more details on conservancies.

29 It is important to consider what rules of customary law may be invoked. Although the process escalated after independence, fencing of communal land started decades earlier under apartheid (Twyman et al. 2001:12). It is not unthinkable, therefore, that the powerful men who occupy such terrains will be successful in arguing that it is a sufficiently well established practice to be accepted as part of custom.

30 The history of conservancies in Namibia goes back further than 1996, however. See Fuller 2006:8).

8 Regulating or deregulating informal land tenure? A Namibian case study on the prospects of improving tenure security under the Flexible Land Tenure Bill

Marco Lankhorst[1] and Muriël Veldman[2]

Introduction

This contribution aims to highlight some elements of the decision-making process that policy-makers (and their donors) should follow when deciding, in a given situation, whether to legalise extra-legal urban land tenure. Our analysis focusses on an innovative form of legalisation developed in Namibia, the Flexible Land Tenure Bill, and is informed and illustrated by results of surveys conducted in the Namibian town of Otjiwarongo. Nonetheless, the implications of the argument we make reach beyond the Namibian context. The main point we stress is that it is crucial for policy-makers to consider the benefits that extra-legal tenure systems may offer, as extra-legal settlers may effectively defeat law reform if their interests are compromised.

The literature on land tenure legalisation in general, as well as the case studies on rural settings contained in this volume, suggest that the stronger the difference between the concepts of tenure underlying customary law and the formal (i.e. statal) law that supersedes it, the more problematic the results of legalisation will be. Such disparity may, for example, lead to a distribution of rights under the formal system that is considered inequitable by at least a portion of those affected. As a consequence of such problems related to legitimacy, possible benefits of legalisation – in terms of increased security, access to credit, and more efficient production – may fail to materialise or be cancelled out. In addition, it has been pointed out that the executive branch in most developing countries cannot manage the complex process of legalisation or ensure subsequent upkeep of the land tenure system, because of the capacity and resources required. These are the primary considerations that have compelled Platteau (1996) and others to argue that, at least in the rural African context, legalisation by means of titling is not an efficient policy.

In the urban setting, however, the prospects for land tenure legalisation would seem to be better. In these often young and fast-growing settlements, where people come to search for work and opportunities, influences of traditional customary law can be expected to be less pronounced. And indeed some empirical studies point to positive results of legalisation, in terms of improved security, increased investments, and other factors (for example Field 2006 and Galiani and Schargrodsky 2004).

These prospects are further improved by the work of scholars and policy-makers who seek to design systems of legalisation that reduce the complexity and costs of registration procedures. Namibia's Flexible Land Tenure Bill, which for some years now has been waiting to be passed into law, is a primary example of such efforts. As can be learned from Christensen, Werner and Højgaard (1999) and LAC (2005b), the bill aims to make legal tenure[3] accessible to the poor. For this purpose it introduces two new types of tenure titles. Registration of these titles is decentralised, and the procedures are considerably simplified as compared with the registration of freehold titles. A second major characteristic of the bill, which also works to lower costs, is that it allows those who seek to acquire title to share the costs thereof amongst each other, as members of a group. Botswana, with its Certificates of Rights (see e.g. Kalabamu 2000), and Tanzania, where a system has been created based on what is known as the Comprehensive Land Property Register (see e.g. Wanjohi 2007), provide other examples of simplified, low-cost titling systems.

Namibian urban centres are particularly suited, therefore, to study an issue that has only recently come into focus in the literature. The fact that customary influences can be expected to be less pronounced does not mean that slum dwellers live in a legal vacuum. Their tenure relations will generally be regulated by extra-legal practices of a local nature. A number of authors, including Durrand-Lasserve (2006) and Rakodi and Leduka (2005), doubtful of the benefits of large-scale legalisation, suggest that better results can be obtained by strengthening these practices.

The objective of this contribution is to expose these lines of thought to each other. It seeks to answer the question of whether a reduction of the monetary costs of legalisation as foreseen in the Flexible Land Tenure Bill has the potential to annul the validity of the claim that the best policy for urban areas is to bolster existing extra-legal practices. It is argued that it is insufficient to focus on the cost side of the equation. The benefits that extra-legality may offer to settlers should also be taken into consideration. In addition, we stress the need to examine the precise nature of the tenure insecurity that settlers experience in a given situation, so as to be able to assess the capacity of legalisation to provide an effective remedy. It is crucial to adopt the perspective of the settlers in this way, as we show that they may effectively defeat tenure reform if their interests are compromised. The implication for policy-makers is that the choice between low-cost legalisation and extra-legality has to be made on a case-by-case basis. Application of this framework to the situation we found in Otjiwarongo suggests that, under current conditions, the start of a flexible titling scheme is unlikely to produce satisfying results.

The rest of this work proceeds as follows. We first present the conceptual framework that underpins our approach. Then we report on relevant socio-economic indicators for Namibia, and Otjiwarongo in particular. This is a first step in charting the preferences of the extra-legal settlers as to the prospects of tenure reform. In the following section we bring the problem of tenure security into focus by presenting the results of a series of interviews with residents and local authority officials. Then we discuss the features of the Namibian Flexible Land Tenure Bill. We combine all this information by comparing the costs and benefits that existing and legalised tenure arrangements would offer residents, in order to determine the effect on their incentives. A final section concludes, and an appendix provides insight into the method of our case study.

Conceptual framework

The debate on tenure security draws contributions from economics, sociology, anthropology, and law. This section provides a detailed discussion of various concepts that are relevant to the debate on tenure security, in order to provide a background against which the analysis in the following sections should be appreciated. Notably, it tells us that the potential of the existing situation in extra-legal settlements should not be under-estimated.

Our research, essentially, deals with situations of factual legal pluralism, whereas legal practitioners commonly work with a normative concept of the law that designates the state as the ultimate source of the law.[4] Such a view holds that custom, which originates elsewhere, may also regulate behaviour, but only in as much as it is sanctioned by formal state law (formal pluralism of laws). The situation in Otjiwarongo, which guides our analysis, compels us to choose a different framework for analysis that looks at law as a social phenomenon. Whereas formal Namibian law certainly pretends to regulate behaviour in the extra-legal settlements of this town, in practice, as we will see, it has a limited impact on the lives of the residents. This does not mean that, from a factual point of view, they live in a legal vacuum. Residents tend to adhere to a set of local practices that is not sanctioned by formal law, but may indirectly be influenced by it.

This relative independence of local arrangements has important implications that are sometimes ignored. As Rakodi and Leduka (2005:8)
note, much research on urban tenure in Africa concentrates on the failure to extend the scope of formal laws and regulation to the dealings
of the poorest in society. Such an approach tends to foster a view of extra-legal settlers as playing a passive role and highlights the benefits
that their 'legal exclusion' forces them to forego. Thinking in terms of
the semi-independence of the rules that govern behaviour in these settlements, however, instructs us to recognise the agency of the residents
themselves. Rather than a detrimental effect, legal exclusion may be
thought of as a rational choice by the members of disadvantaged communities. This agency is crucial in any process that aims to improve
tenure security. It manifests itself in two ways. In the first place, these
communities are capable of producing law, that is, they generate rules
that guide behaviour within the settlements, and that present an alternative to formal law. Second, although disadvantaged in many ways,
the members of these communities have the means to oppose the force
of formal law. We first consider the nature of the law generated in urban extra-legal settlements, and then move on to discuss the means
and motives of their residents to resist being brought under the pur-
view of formal law. This opens up important insights into the possible
effects of (flexible) titling.

Durand-Lasserve (2006) uses the term 'neo-customary practices' to
describe the extra-legal arrangements that are generated by communities in slum settlements. This term reveals important characteristics
of the phenomenon that we study. On the one hand, it acknowledges
that extra-legal settlers may model their behaviour according to the customary rules that governed their dealings in their place of origin. This
is highly relevant in the context of rapid urbanisation in Africa,
although, as we will see, our research produced insufficient evidence to
support such a thesis. On the other hand, the term clearly expresses
that there may be other influences on these practices. These can take
the form of spontaneously emerging arrangements or emulations of
parts of formal law that are advantageous to extra-legal settlers, a process that has been dubbed 'inter-legality' by Hoekema (2003).

Before we address the crucial issue of the motives that extra-legal settlers might have to resist legal reform, it is appropriate to discuss the
means they can rely on to do so, as this shows their cooperation to be
indispensable to the success of legalisation. Leduka (2000) and Rakodi
and Leduka (2005) group the means of resistance under the heading
of 'societal non-compliance'. In a formal regulatory environment where
resources and capacity are scarce (think of under-staffed registries),
large-scale, unorganised non-compliance can offer relatively powerless
communities a strong tool to oppose unfavourable legal reforms. Lega-

lisation of tenure provides ample scope for such behaviour, as it critically depends on the internalisation of the new rules by the population.
With other types of legal reforms, sanctions such as fines or imprisonment and public enforcement may deter non-compliance. These instruments tend to be absent in the field of property law. Compliance, then,
is largely dependent on processes that are internal to the local population. The threat of nullity of the extra-legal transaction can be expected
to have only a marginal effect, as it depends on private enforcement in
an environment where there are generally high barriers to court.

Compliance with formal or informal (that is, customary or neo-customary) law can be said to be motivated by one of two factors. Either
the persons involved in a transaction may feel that they ought to act according to one of these systems, or, if this influence is not so strong,
they may choose the option that serves their interests best. A lack of legitimacy – that is, a poor fit with local traditions and senses of fairness
– has been advanced to explain the failure of formal property laws and
registries to take hold in rural areas (see e.g. Platteau 1996:55). In the
younger urban settlements, where people tend to flock in search of a
better life, the second explanation may be at least as powerful. This
would seem to be the case particularly in Otjiwarongo, where we found
little indication of strong influences of rural origin on tenure arrangements.

The implication is that the success of instituting a formal property
regime (that is not publicly enforced) depends on how well it serves
the interests of the tenure holders involved. They may choose extra-legality over the rules and procedures of formal law if this better accom-
modates their economic and other objectives. When evaluating the de-
sirability of legalisation in certain circumstances, it is therefore crucial
that the associated costs and benefits be brought into focus. A review
of the literature on legalisation of land tenure will tell us which types
of costs and benefits should be included in this process of evaluation.

Early contributions by members of the Property Rights School
stressed the costs of extra-legality and the benefits of formality.[5] In this
view, (neo-)customary regimes offer landholders a lower level of tenure
security than legalised property systems. This is argued to lead to less
investment in the land, to limit access to credit, and to lower the value
of transactions. Much later work (see Platteau 1996) points to the costs
of legalisation. There is a serious risk that differences in the concepts
of property that underlie customary and formal law will lead to a distribution of rights that is considered inequitable, at least by a portion of
those affected. The resulting problems of legitimacy will weigh down
the benefits of legalisation. In addition, registering land is a very expensive process, and the subsequent proper functioning of the system
is dependent on considerable administrative capacity and resources.

Namibia's Flexible Land Tenure Bill aims to change the balance of these costs and benefits by lowering the costs of the legalisation process, as well as its maintenance.

As is illustrated by the schematic overview below, if we want to know whether titling offers the prospect of improving conditions for extra-legal settlers, it is insufficient to look at the costs of extra-legality and the costs and benefits of formality. The benefits of the pre-existing situation must also be taken into account. Neo-customary practices evolve spontaneously or by borrowing from formal or customary law. We should not close our eyes, therefore, to the possibility that custom in these settlements may already offer some of the benefits that are sought by means of titling. If indeed they do, this reduces the likelihood that residents will choose to participate in such a scheme and urges us to consider whether bolstering these practices is not a better way to improve tenure conditions in these settlements.

Socio-economic indicators

This conceptual framework suggests that the outcome of the trade-off between flexible titling and the accommodation of extra-legal practices is determined by the cost implications of either alternative, the economic opportunities that they offer the settlers, and desirable or undesirable social consequences. The full trade-off itself, as it applies to Otjiwarongo, is made below. The present section complements the survey of socio-economic indicators at the national level presented in Lank-

Table 8.1   *Costs and benefits of legalisation vs. extra-legality*

	Legalisation	Extra-legality
Benefits	Old property rights advocates and De Soto c.s.: a) Enhances tenure security b) Provides access to credit c) Spurs the development of an efficient land market	Literature on the potential of (neo-) customary practices: a) Flexibility / adaptability b) Legitimacy c) Lower transaction costs?
Costs	Literature reviewed in Platteau (1996): a) Expensive administrative process b) Expensive up-keep of the system c) Introduction of new transaction costs for settlers (fees) d) Potentially large social costs (exclusion / unfair distribution)	Mirror image of the benefits of legalisation: a) Low level of tenure security b) No possibility to pledge the property c) High transaction costs?

horst (this volume) by looking at local conditions. This is an important first step in charting the likely preferences of Otjiwarongo's extra-legal settlers as regards tenure regimes.[6] This type of data allows us to start developing our thoughts about how they might value the opportunities offered by either regime (formal or informal), and it helps to gauge how the settlers might balance these against possible costs, such as the threat of relocation as well as surveying and registration costs.

The town of Otjiwarongo is situated in the northern half of the country, along the Trans-Caprivi highway, which constitutes an important artery for the transport of goods between Angola and other countries to the north and east on the one hand and Namibia's port in Walvis Bay and South Africa on the other. Much of the local economy depends on this traffic, as is evidenced by a surprising number of petrol stations. The town also serves as a focal point for the commercial farms of the region. As the administrative capital of the surrounding Otjozondjupa region, Otjiwarongo houses a considerable number of state, regional, and local government offices.

The 2001 national census counted a total of 22,614 inhabitants for the town of Otjiwarongo (Republic of Namibia 2001a). Local officials and NGOs, however, currently work with an estimation of 28,000.[7] In light of our findings as to the size of the extra-legal settlements reported below, we hold this to be a more realistic figure. This makes it a medium-sized town in the Namibian context (compare Fjeldstad et al. 2005:8). In addition, the Otjozondjupa region reflects many of the patterns witnessed at the national level. Per capita income (compare Republic of Namibia 2006b:36), the level of unemployment (compare Republic of Namibia 2001a), and household size (compare Republic of Namibia 2006b:9) are relatively close to national averages. Although no detailed recent data are available, it can be deduced from Republic of Namibia (2006a:4) and UNAIDS (2006:18) that Otjozondjupa has neither a very high nor a very low HIV prevalence rate, compared with other regions.

According to local accounts, Otjiwarongo's oldest extra-legal settlement emerged during the apartheid area, possibly during the 1970s or early 1980s.[8] Its name, Tsaraxa Aibes (we ended up not being laughed at so much anymore by pronouncing it as TsaraGAIbes) appropriately means 'dusty place' in the local Damara language. The members of that tribe were the first to settle here. Although there are no records of the size of the settlement during the apartheid period, the removal of the pass laws following independence from South Africa in 1990 is said to have spurred considerable growth of this and other new, extra-legal settlements around Otjiwarongo. A 1993 municipal census counted some 5,400 squatters. A municipal survey conducted in 1998 resulted in an estimated population of 10,500. The rough estimate that follows from our own research results in a 2006 population of about 15,000. This number includes the inhabitants of a second, neighbouring settlement called DRC (Democratic Republic of Congo), on account of it being even further away from the town centre than Tsaraxa Aibes (approximately seven km). Apart from Damaras, who are concentrated in the older parts of Tsaraxa Aibes, the settlements nowadays host substantial numbers of migrants from the north, including Owambos, Kavangos, and Caprivians. Our summary investigations of this matter suggest that the settlements are growing at a fast pace, on the order of five per cent per year, and that migration accounts for the larger part of the increases.

As can be expected, the socio-economic indicators for Tsaraxa Aibes and DRC compare unfavourably with those for the Otjozondjupa region and Namibia. It should be stated at the outset, however, that a high degree of accuracy should not be attached to any of the data we present, including our own.[9] A 1997 survey commissioned by the municipality showed that approximately 27 per cent of the households had at least one permanently employed member, while approximately 69 per cent of the households earned less than N$ 200 (roughly USD 40), and 97 per cent earned less than N$ 1,000 (roughly USD 250) a month. Another study commissioned in 2004 found a median household income of N$ 424, but it appears that the sample that was used to compute this number was rather small (40 interviews). Our own data, drawn from interviews with members of 105 households, suggests a 2006 median household income of N$ 606 (average N$ 777), and median household size of 5.7 (average 5.6). We found that 38 per cent of households had at least one permanently employed member, and a further nineteen per cent could rely on a pension or disability grant as a stable (but, at N$ 300/370, often insufficient) source of income. In almost all other households there was at least one self-employed member, i.e. someone with a regularly practised, income-generating occupation.[10] The employment rate among residents between sixteen and 59 years of age totals thirteen per cent, whereas a further twenty per cent are self-employed.

Not surprisingly, then, housing conditions are rather poor in Tsaraxa Aibes and DRC, despite continuing efforts by the municipality. Housing consists mainly of self-constructed shacks (primarily using corrugated iron, wood, and clay bricks). All dwellings lack drinking water connections, water being provided through municipal pumps that work on the basis of a pre-paid card system. Electricity is provided in some areas closer to town, but household coverage is far from complete, because of a sizable instalment fee. A sewerage system is absent, and most households rely on self-made latrines or the bush. A number of high masts provide street lighting. The municipality collects refuse at designated points. Schools and clinics, along with other public services, are absent. There are some shops, most of which sell only beer and soft drinks. It is against this background that the analysis in the following sections should be seen. We first focus on tenure security.

Tenure security

In this section we look at tenure conditions as currently encountered in Otjiwarongo's extra-legal settlements. This is important as it brings the problem to be solved by means of legalisation (flexible titling) into focus. Broadly defined, tenure security refers to the extent to which the holder of a parcel of land feels assured (both in the short and longer term) of his ability to access his land, to manage and use it, and to effectively exclude others. Otjiwarongo's extra-legal settlers do not encounter problems falling under all these aspects of tenure security. We focus on the ability to exclude others from accessing one's property.[11]

Tenure security must be distinguished from its effects. If an insufficient level of security is experienced, this will affect the holder's incentives to make investments. This can be very consequential, for instance if it keeps settlers from improving unhygienic conditions. In addition, uncertainty may have a bearing on the holder's dealings with third parties. It may weigh down the price that potential buyers would be willing to pay for the possession, and – supposing that the necessary legal machinery is in place – it can make banks reluctant to accept the property as collateral to a loan. This, in turn, may affect investments in other goods, such as a business or education (this is, essentially, De Soto's (2000) argument).

The existence of tenure insecurity and the question of its effects are, of course, factual issues that cannot be gleaned from law books. In this section we present the results of a series of interviews held in Tsaraxa Aibes and DRC that focussed on indicators for insecurity and the willingness to make investments. These show that actions by the local authority, specifically large-scale relocations of extra-legal settlers in the past, are the main cause for uncertainty experienced by Otjiwarongo's extra-legal settlers. To interpret these actions by the municipality, it is useful to begin describing the formal legal situation in these settlements.[12] After that, the issue of relocations as a source of tenure insecurity is discussed in detail.

The regulation of land tenure around Namibia's urban centres has undergone considerable change since independence. The land on which Tsaraxa Aibes originally emerged, like all unregistered terrains around urban centres, resorted to homeland authorities and was governed by communal law. In 1992, with the passing of the Local Authorities Act, all unregistered lands falling within municipal boundaries were transferred from the traditional authorities to the newly estab-lished local authorities. In the process the status of these terrains chan-ged. Henceforth, it was intended that they would be subdivided, ser-viced, and sold to the public with freehold title (see Juma and Christen-sen 2001; LAC 2005b:34). In formal terms, under this new regime the traditional occupiers of such terrains, including the settlers in Tsaraxa Aibes, saw their customary claims converted into tenancy (see Fjeldstad et al. 2005:16).

The second major change was the designation of Tsaraxa Aibes, and later DRC, as 'reception areas'. The large stream of internal migrants referred to above is channelled to these areas, where the newly arrived enjoy a *de facto* permit to occupy a plot (see LAC 2005b:22). Over the years the municipality has taken both a proactive and a reactive stance with respect to occupation. A number of times a street layout was made in advance, and plots were measured and pegged. On other occa-sions, however, parts of the settlement had to be 'regularised' ex post. Such settlers coming from the countryside are also considered to be tenants of the municipality. Again, however, tenancy is an intermediate state, as settlement in such areas is considered to be of a temporary nature. The objective is to resettle the inhabitants in permanent hous-ing elsewhere, ideally with a freehold title.[13]

There are several reasons why the emphasis has generally been on future resettlement rather than on legalisation of the existing area. One is a provision in the National Housing Development Act prescrib-ing that newly developed plots have a minimum size of 300 square metres, whilst the majority of the plots in Tsaraxa Aibes and DRC are smaller than that. Another is that in the current layout of the settle-ment, there is no room for public services to be provided (schools, clinics, police station, etc.) or for open spaces. Other more practical concerns include the fact that installing drinking water and sewerage grids is considerably more expensive in an inhabited settlement.

In terms of the settlers' rights and obligations, from a formal per-spective, the following can be said. The inhabitants of Tsaraxa Aibes and DRC are required to register with the municipality and pay rent for the use of a plot. Currently, the amount to be paid stands at N$ 42 per plot. The tenants are not entitled to transfer their rights to family members or others without prior permission of the town council. They can be evicted if the council decides to use the land for other purposes. In such an event, only the residents owning permanent structures or traditional homesteads (including houses built with sun-dried mud-brick) are entitled to compensation. Those who live in iron shacks are not eligible for compensation.[14] It should be noted, however, that Otjiwarongo's municipal regulations prohibit the erection of permanent structures in the area.

This discussion of the formal legal situation forms the background of our investigation of the tenure insecurity experienced by the inhabitants of Tsaraxa Aibes and DRC. We focus, first, on insecurity in the relation between plot holders and the municipality, caused by the threat of future relocation without compensation. At the end of this section, there is a brief discussion also of indicators of insecurity caused by third-party encroachment.

Relocations of extra-legal settlers have occurred with some frequency. In most cases, according to municipal officials and documents, this involved relocations from unrecognised settlements (i.e. outside the official reception areas, Tsaraxa Aibes and DRC) or from dangerous areas. At the turn of the century, for instance, several hundred families were moved out of the Single Quarters. This is the name used to refer to the hostel where during apartheid male black labourers, brought in from the homelands, would stay. After independence many of them sent for their families, and in a few years the place grew to be extremely crowded, and hygienic conditions were eventually considered untenable. The years 2004 and 2005 saw the resettlement of a further 250 families from an unrecognised extra-legal settlement known as Okamuti. In addition, over the past ten years the municipality has rather constantly moved settlers out of flooding areas, as well as other areas closer to town than Tsaraxa Aibes. At the end of 2006, there were an estimated 500 to 600 of such 'illegal settlers' (approximately 100 households) who were gradually being relocated. As far as we were able to witness, settlers tended to acquiesce, albeit unhappily, and there was no use of force or police assistance. To test whether these resettlements have an effect on tenure security in Tsaraxa Aibes and DRC, we conducted 36 in-depth interviews. Details about the method employed are given below, in the appendix.

In terms of uncertainty, we found the following. When asked about their personal history and the places where they had lived, seven respondents indicated having been asked to relocate by the municipality. All households but one were aware of relocations having occurred. Except for households who were themselves moved out of flood zones (two in number), people had little more than a vague notion, if any, of the reasons for relocations. Some speculated that the lands may have had to be freed up to make room for industry, whilst others suggested that extra-legal settlements were not wanted in areas close to wealthier residential districts. The members of thirteen households stated that they thought it possible that they might themselves have to relocate at some point in the future, and a further five indicated that they seriously considered this possibility. Only one of these five households had been relocated before. The members of the other six households that had already been relocated did not consider it possible that they would be relocated again, pointing either to (1) promises by the municipality or the central government that on account of having been relocated, or of being old, they had permission to stay on their plot permanently, or (2) the installation of an electricity network which constituted too large an investment by the municipality to abandon.

To see whether these experiences may also inhibit investments, we examined the effect on the willingness to make improvements to housing. The image that came out of our investigation was mixed. We followed a two-pronged approach by focussing on the desire and capacity to make improvements. Regarding the former, we asked respondents to rank their preferences as to the possible uses for their savings.[15] A sizable minority did not include improvements to their dwelling in their list of preferences. Asked for their reasons, some settlers told us that they did not intend to stay in Otjiwarongo for long enough and were planning either to move back to the countryside or to one of the larger cities in the south. This would appear to correspond to the findings of Tvedten and Pomuti (1995:14). The threat of relocation therefore cannot be said to directly affect the investments in housing of this group. It could be that uncertainty plays a role in their reasons for planning to move away, but we did not examine this question.

A lack of funds constitutes a major constraint on making improvements. About 68 per cent of the 105 households that were interviewed regarding their financial situation were unable to generate savings. The remainder is made up mostly of households with a stable source of income exceeding N\$ 899 per month and households that depend on a relatively high, variable income (e.g. contractors and taxi drivers). At least part of the savings of the latter group, however, are intended to cushion low-income periods. Nonetheless, the lack of savings is not an insurmountable obstacle in terms of making improvements, as mud and clay bricks, for example, are generally self-made and require no financial investment. Knowledge of how to make them appears to be fairly widespread. Of those households that indicated being able to make improvements and interested in improving their dwelling, two identified the threat of relocation as the main reason not to do so, and a further three mentioned it as one of the reasons for not upgrading. A much larger group of eleven respondents, however, already lived in a brick house, had recently made improvements, or had started to collect the necessary materials to do so. Four of them indicated that there was a risk involved in doing so.

To summarise, our interviews provide reasons to believe that, at least for a considerable portion of the residents of Tsaraxa Aibes and DRC, the possibility that future relocations might affect them constitutes a source of uncertainty about the continuation of their tenure. There appear to be gradations in the levels of uncertainty experienced, however, and as a consequence the effects on the behaviour of the settlers are not uniform. To bring this matter into focus, we identified those among our group of respondents who were both interested in and able to make improvements. Some experienced levels of uncertainty preventing them from making improvements to their dwelling. Others – who form a majority together with those who entertained no fears of being ousted from their plot – were willing to take a calculated risk.

To complete our analysis, we also looked for signs of uncertainty caused by factors other than the actions of the municipality. This produced no results. Given that almost all of the plots in Tsaraxa Aibes and DRC are pegged by the municipality and are fenced accordingly by the settlers, there are generally no disputes over borders. The only evidence we found of such disputes was in a case where heirs had subdivided a plot along contended lines. We also asked settlers what would happen if they were to leave their property unguarded for a period of a month, for example to visit family or work on a farm. All indicated that they would never do so and would ask a family member to watch over their house. Asked what would happen if they would leave it unguarded instead, the risk of theft was generally pointed out. None of our 36 respondents suggested that the house might then be occupied by others. Our data cannot be relied upon to confirm this, but quite probably this is explained by the fact that the settlers generally register with the municipality as tenants. This issue is discussed in more detail below. First, we turn to examine flexible tenure.

Flexible tenure

The Flexible Land Tenure Bill drafted by the Ministry of Lands and Resettlement and Rehabilitation is aimed at providing Namibia's urban poor access to secure forms of tenure that will enhance their economic opportunities (see section 2 of the 4th draft of the bill). The primary aim of the bill, therefore, is to improve the situation in which extra-legal settlers currently live. The innovation that is presented by the bill, as compared to earlier attempts at legalisation made all over the developing world, is that it addresses two problems related to legalisation itself (i.e. two problems falling in the 'costs of legalisation' box, at the bottom left, in).

The first of these problems involves constraints faced by the authorities charged with tenure regulation. Procedures for the development of new land under freehold title are very complicated in Namibia (Christensen, Werner, and Højgaard 1999:9). Limited capacity and resources

in the executive branch, therefore, constitute a serious obstacle to legalisation (compare with the problems discussed by Platteau 1996:47).
Second, the bill acknowledges that large parts of the population face
serious financial constraints. The costs of the formal procedures involved in the subdivision and registration of town lands under freehold
title, as they are paid by the acquirers, can therefore be expected to
further restrict the output of this channel of land delivery.

The bill seeks to provide a solution to these problems by (1) simplify-
ing and thus reducing the costs of the registration procedure, and (2)
allowing those who seek to acquire title to share the costs thereof
amongst each other, as members of a group. These simplifications depend, respectively, on the creation of local registries, complementary to
the deeds office in Windhoek, and on the institution of two new forms
of statutory tenure, parallel to the freehold system. The system introduced by the bill is designed as follows. Groups of settlers may acquire
a large tract of land under freehold title, as co-owners, following normal procedures. Local registries will issue certificates to individual
members of the group, attesting to their right to a defined (landhold title) or undefined (starter title) portion of this land. These forms of tenure can be upgraded according to the needs and financial capabilities
of the holders.

The 'starter title' (section 2) is the simplest of the two forms of tenure. It allows for perpetual occupation of a plot as part of a group-man-
aged block. To prevent speculation, the bill determines that no person
can hold more than one starter title. Transfer (both to heirs and third
parties) of a starter title is possible, and though it is required, the validity of a transaction is not undermined by the failure to register it.
When registering mutations, a fee is incurred. Plots held with a starter
title can also be leased out. Both the ability to transfer starter titles and
to enter into lease contracts can be made subject to consent, a right of
first refusal, or other conditions provided for in the group constitution
that regulates the interactions between the co-owners. In this regard
the bill indicates that the Minister will issue a model constitution for
starter title associations, which may contain compulsory provisions
(section 16(1)g).

A starter title can be upgraded and turned into a landhold title (section 9), which confers a tenure right that approaches freehold ownership more closely. It includes the right to transfer, mortgage, and lease
the plot, with the validity of the former two transactions being subject
to a registration requirement. The relevant authority is given broad
powers to impose conditions on plots forming part of landhold
schemes (section 12(6)), which includes the prohibition of transfer of
plots without its permission or within a specified period of time. A
land hold title can in turn be transformed into a freehold title.

As suggested, in both cases the block is registered as a single entity in freehold ownership at the Deeds Office in Windhoek. There the names of the owners gathered in the group are listed, but the boundaries separating individual plots within the block are not indicated. They are recorded in purposefully created and locally administered Land Rights Offices (section 4). Starter and land hold titles differ in that only in the latter case are individual household sites defined and indicated on a cadastral map (section 6), which is kept in this office. This system allows individual households to make considerable savings on the costs of acquiring a title. The pilot projects that were started during the preparation phase of the bill, for instance, allowed these costs to be shouldered jointly by 110 (Oshakati), 127 (Oshakati), and 207 (Rundu) households. Additional cost savings are made possible by lowering the professional requirements of the officials involved in registration. The Land Rights Offices are to be staffed mainly by paraprofessionals. Neither a conveyancer nor a legal practitioner is required to prepare starter or land hold title documents.

Two further features of the bill are of relevance to the analysis of the prospects of flexible titling in Otjiwarongo's settlements. First, the procedure for initiating a starter or land hold title scheme (sections 11-13) leaves the regional or local authority a considerable margin of discretion in deciding whether such a scheme should be engaged in, and whether and in what form to impose conditions on it. Second, the bill is somewhat vague as to the charges that local authorities may impose on settlers. It states that the relevant authority may require those involved to pay an amount which must be used for the purpose of covering the whole or part of the costs that will be incurred in the establishment of the scheme (section 11(3)). It is unclear whether the combination of these provisions may mean that participants in flexible titling schemes will be charged for the value of the land that is transferred, in addition to what is needed to compensate local authorities for surveying and registration costs.[16] For the purpose of the analysis of the incentives that flexible titling produces for extra-legal settlers, we will work under the assumption that is more true to the spirit of the bill, which is that the last of these provisions prohibits charging participants for anything more than these fees.

The prospects for flexible titling in Tsaraxa Aibes and DRC

The conceptual framework for our analysis that was drawn up above suggests that the success of legalisation critically depends on the cooperation of the extra-legal settlers, and therefore leads us to focus on the decision-making process that they may follow to choose between compliance and extra-legality. We saw that in doing so, it is essential to consider the costs and benefits of both flexible titling and extra-legality, instead of concentrating on the benefits of titling and the drawbacks of extra-legality. In subsequent sections we set out to fill in some of the blanks on our outline of this decision-making process. We charted the socio-economic conditions in the extra-legal settlements to produce a first indication of their inhabitants' preferences and priorities; the drawbacks of extra-legality were highlighted by showing that there are signs of tenure insecurity in Tsaraxa Aibes and DRC; and we examined the Flexible Land Tenure Bill, which aims to improve security and increase economic opportunities, while circumventing a number of problems traditionally associated with legalisation. In this section we begin by focussing on the part of the puzzle that is still missing: the advantages of extra-legality. We then return to the Flexible Land Tenure Bill, to examine whether the advantages it aspires to offer can be expected to materialise. This makes it possible to draw all the threads together and weigh the costs and benefits of flexible titling from the perspective of the extra-legal settlers.

An analysis of the currently available opportunities for the inhabitants of Tsaraxa Aibes and DRC must start from the premise that their formal position as tenants need not fully correspond to the factual state of affairs. From a formal legal perspective, a right of tenancy involves certain constraints. It offers less freedom, for instance, to dispose of the good than does ownership (however it may be conceptualised). If the municipality, as the owner, does not actively impose the constraints of tenancy on the settlers, then they may behave according to other patterns. As was suggested when discussing the concept of neo-customary practices, in doing so they may follow customary traditions, emulate aspects of formal law on tenure, or engage in spontaneously emerging practices. It is not unlikely, therefore, that the settlers effectively enjoy freedoms that under formal law would be associated with freehold ownership rather than tenancy.

We used the 36 in-depth interviews to gain a rough idea of these matters. It is important to emphasise that the questions we asked had a limited scope. Our investigations on this matter were geared towards charting the economic opportunities and constraints present in the current situation, so that they could be compared to the prospects offered by legal reform. Although it would certainly have considerably enriched our analysis, we did not thoroughly examine the nature (conventions or merely convenient modes of conduct) or the origins (customary or other) of the extra-legal practices we encountered, nor did we place these in a broader context of social inter-action. We conducted a limited and more abstract inquiry focussed on the ability to transact, and on indications of transaction costs. More specifically, in designing our survey we looked at the elements that distinguish tenancy and the various forms of tenure, including those introduced by the Flexible Land Tenure Bill. This led us to ask respondents primarily about their ability to transfer their land, to give it in use, and to use it as collateral. In addition, we looked for indications of customary influences on tenure arrangements that might require us to reconfigure our initial findings. Further details about our approach are given in the appendix.

To report our findings on existing arrangements in Tsaraxa Aibes and DRC, it is useful to distinguish the relation between plot holders and the municipality from the dealings of plot holders with others. The first of these, the relation to the municipality as perceived by the extra-legal settlers, is not easily characterised. The wording that respondents used to describe this relation is of considerable importance here. They generally chose the English word 'owner' or its Afrikaans equivalent *'eigenaar'* over 'rent' or *'huur'*.[7] Remarkably, this was different in some cases with plot holders who had been relocated. Moreover, there were indications that the settlers were at least to some extent familiar with the concept of rent. The use of a whole or part of a plot in return for monthly or weekly payment was found to be quite common in certain areas of Tsaraxa Aibes and DRC, and the words 'rent' or *'huur'* appeared to be used in this regard. The fact that plot holders register with the municipality appeared to us to contribute substantially to the difference settlers perceive between (1) the plot holder's relation with the municipality and (2) an ordinary tenant's relation with the plot holder. Given, however, that the precise connotations that our respondents had in choosing this wording were not examined, not too much value should be attached to these findings. All respondents, including those who had referred to themselves as owners, recognised that the municipality could charge them for their use of the plot, for which the term 'rent' or *'huur'* was generally used. And except for a small number that claimed to have somehow been given explicit guarantees (which includes six of the seven households in our sample that were relocated once), respondents also indicated that the municipality was in a position to ask them to relocate, if necessary, whereas such relocations were generally acknowledged to be unthinkable in the centre of town.

What we learned about rent payment further indicates that the relation to the municipality as construed by the settlers is best characterised as *sui generis*, or hybrid, rather than falling into one of the defined categories of formal law. The municipality takes a decidedly passive role when it comes to enforcing the debt. It fully depends on the inhabitants coming to the municipality offices (in the township of Orwetoweni, not in the extra-legal settlements) to recharge their water credits. A mail delivery system being absent, no bills or warnings are sent, and no house calls are made. Although a serious backlog in rent payments may cause municipality officials to issue warnings, the up-grading of water credits is generally not refused because a basic need is concerned. A strategy that we were told of more than once involved combining the purchase of water credit with a relatively small payment of rent. In addition, a refusal to upgrade water credits can, in practice, be circumvented by the settlers, with the help of neighbours. Tellingly also, evictions never occur because of non-payment. The municipality's accounts bear out these facts, with payment rates being below 25 per cent. This is in fact part of a broader phenomenon, prevalent also in South Africa, that has endured since apartheid, when collective non-payment of rents and service charges was used as a form of resistance (see Louw 2003).

When looking at the relation between plot holders and other extra-le-gal settlers, widespread deviations from the ordinary position of a te-nant were found that are more easily characterised. Although the mu-nicipality technically forbids the 'selling' of plots by residents, such transfers in return for payment appear to occur with some frequency. A total of thirteen respondents indicated that they had been party to or were aware of such a transaction, five of whom indicated that these transfers occurred often. Average selling prices could be quoted by ten respondents, which ranged between N\$ 150 and N\$ 500 for an empty plot (depending *inter alia* on the location), and N\$ 700 to N\$ 2000 for a plot with dwelling (in which regard building materials and the avail-ability of electricity in the area were reported to be important). The mu-nicipality's registry plays an important part in these transfers, as it was generally recognised to be in the interest of the buyer to change the name in the municipality's books. Despite its prohibition of sales, the municipality tends to cooperate with such requests, made jointly by the old and new occupant. According to local officials, who are well aware of the situation, this is because the municipality does not oppose the consensual substitution of one tenant for another, when no payments are involved, and the distinction, for them, is hard to make. For the same reason, the municipality does not place obstacles in the way of children assuming the rights of their parents to a plot, when they have passed away.[18]

The municipality does not have a policy on sub-renting by plot holders. It happens very frequently that a registered plot holder allows others – adult children, family, or friends – to use his plot, in which case the user is generally seen as being responsible for paying the rent to the municipality. Many plot holders also accommodate a second household on their land, with which they share the responsibility for the rent to be paid to the municipality. Yet another arrangement that is not uncommon is that a family member or friend lives in and adminis-ters the plot holder's shop (a *'cuka'* stall or *shabeen*; the plot holder re-

siding elsewhere). The majority of these arrangements are better classified as use rights rather than as renting. More closely approaching this
category is the situation we twice encountered in which the head of a
second household is asked to pay for the food of school-going children
of absent plot holder/parents. In some instances, however, more typical
features of sub-letting are clearly present. A total of six respondents reported being aware of prices charged for the use of a whole or part of a
plot, which were in the range of N$ 50 to N$ 100 per month.[19] This
suggests that the land is used to generate some income, rather than to
merely share costs. The accounts we heard suggest that migrants from
Angola and Zimbabwe who face difficulties in registering a plot in
their name constitute a considerable part of the group that rents/sub-
rents from plot holders.

Tenure arrangements being at least partially independent of formal
law, it is possible that customary laws exert some influence in Tsaraxa
Aibes and DRC, particularly since our investigations show that there is
considerable in-migration from rural areas (see above). No in-depth
studies of traditional tenure in Namibia and its development in the
post-apartheid period appear to exist.[20] It can be gleaned from reports
such as LAC (2005b:28) and UN Habitat (2005:65), however, that the
various systems of custom in Namibia regulate tenure in a way that
shares certain basic characteristics with customary arrangements encountered throughout southern Africa. Traditional leaders exercise control rights to land. They tend to grant access to land to individual men
or male members of a family. Women, therefore, do not generally acquire use rights. In rural areas they will nonetheless often be the principle users of the land. This led us to focus on two points in examining
whether customary law has influenced tenure arrangements in Tsaraxa
Aibes and DRC in a way that could affect our analysis. We studied the
role of traditional leaders, and we looked at the rate of female plot holdership.

These investigations did not lead to the conclusion that traditional
customs had a significant impact on the tenure arrangements described above. Both municipality officials and residents confirmed that
a number of chiefs live in the extra-legal settlements. These traditional
leaders are not without status. They were reportedly consulted for advice, they are generally members of representative ward committees
which aim to communicate the needs of the inhabitants to the municipality, and they are sometimes asked by the latter to inform those who
have settled in so-called 'illegal areas' that they have to relocate. Traditional leaders have no direct role in controlling access to land, however.
Our respondents indicated that they are not involved in sales, renting,
or use agreements, nor do they have a say in allotting new or empty
plots. A number of our respondents suggested that the role of tradi-

tional leaders and the method of distributing land would be different in their rural place of origin. Our study of the rate of female plot holdership pointed in the same direction. A municipal report on Tsaraxa Aibes, DRC, and Okamuti (from where settlers were later transferred to DRC) showed that slightly more than half (52 per cent) of the registered plot holders were women, which is confirmed by our own investigations. In 57 of the 105 interviews we conducted regarding socio-economic conditions, the person registered with the municipality was reported to be a woman.

At this point we are able to draw some interim conclusions. We saw that the tenure arrangements that prevail in Tsaraxa Aibes and DRC do not correspond to the formal legal framework. In the first place, this underscores the need identified above to see whether flexible titling provides settlers with incentives to join in a scheme and to continue to respect its regulations. Without such incentives, it can reasonably be expected that a starter or landhold title will be as meaningful to them as their current position of tenant. Our investigation also points out that plots are sold and sub-rented with some frequency. The absence of third-party-encroachment problems, which is related to the existence of a registry and the fact that plots are pegged and fenced, suggests that current arrangements enable such transactions in a way that would appear to fairly effectively shield buyers from competing claims. Therefore, the provisions in the Flexible Land Tenure Bill that enable holders of a starter or landhold title to engage in these transactions constitute neither an advantage nor a drawback. In fact, if we include in the analysis (1) the fees incurred in registering transactions involving starter or landhold titles (section 16(1)a) and (2) the various limitations on the freedom to engage in such transactions that the bill makes possible (section 6(4)c jo. 16(1)g, and 12(6)c), then we see that extra-legality may even constitute the more attractive alternative.

The ability to sell a plot, or to rent it out, is not the only potential advantage that the Flexible Land Tenure Bill is intended to offer to titleholders. The central objectives of the bill are to provide secure forms of tenure and to facilitate access to credit by allowing the owners of a landhold title to use their property as collateral. These opportunities may tilt the balance in favour of law reform. Because tenure security has strong implications for access to credit, we first address this issue.

We saw that the level of tenure security is determined by the ability to exclude others from accessing one's property. In principle, threats to the interests of the extra-legal settlers may come from all sides, but the results of our investigations reported above indicate that in Tsaraxa Aibes and DRC evictions by the municipality are the main cause for concern. In the past the municipality has moved large numbers of people out of over-crowded areas, and it continues to relocate persons who settle outside the designated reception areas. Future relocations appear to be made necessary by laws and regulations that prescribe minimum standards for newly proclaimed plots in terms of size and service provision. Given that the majority of plots in Tsaraxa Aibes and DRC are reported to be smaller than 300 square metres and that it is considerably cheaper to install services in uninhabited areas, eventual legalisation will likely take place in another location. The municipality's consequent refusal to signal to settlers that they may occupy their plot permanently appears to keep the fears aroused by the earlier relocations alive.

Starting a flexible titling scheme is not the solution to these problems of uncertainty, however. To begin with, individual settlers will continue to face these problems once they become starter title holders (Christensen 2004:7). They will be advised on the starter title certificate that they should not erect permanent structures before their rights have been upgraded, or before a layout for the area has been approved by the local authority. Should they do so anyway, they would not receive compensation if, at a later stage, it turns out they have to move in order to allow for the construction of roads or service provision. And, although this matter is still unsettled, it is to be expected that, for this very reason, no landhold titles will be issued in the absence of an approved layout. Titling would have to be combined with the design of a layout for the area, therefore, to remove the need for further relocations and reduce uncertainty. But the same result could be achieved by (1) designing a layout, or requesting the central government for dispensation from the problematic layout requirements, while postponing titling, or (2) by dropping the prospect of titling altogether. Put differently, the same results can be achieved under extra-legality.

Nor, it would seem, does flexible titling offer material benefits over extra-legality when it comes to opening access to credit. Extra-legality does not accommodate property-reinforced loans. But it is unlikely that landhold titles will, in practice, be used as collateral. In the first place, it is unclear whether such a title provides banks with sufficient security to extend a loan, as Christensen et al.'s account confirms (Christensen, Werner, and Højgaard 1999:66). One can easily imagine that restrictive conditions imposed by the municipality on the ability to transfer the property would make lenders reluctant. Foreclosure has proven to be very difficult to effectuate in other sub-Saharan countries (Platteau 1996:60). In addition, the history of circumnavigating the requirements of formal law in these areas may make them distrustful of the information contained in registries (see again Platteau 1996:60, for an overview of work showing similar results). Perhaps more importantly, with low levels of income and low values for the properties pledged, even if security issues do not arise, the loans that could be extended

are likely to remain small. This is not to say that they might not be valued by the debtor. It raises the possibility, discussed by Platteau
(1996:62), that they are considered commercially unattractive by
banks. In any case, it is unlikely that the majority of the population (73
per cent) that cannot rely on a stable source of income will be considered credit-worthy. Micro-financing programmes and saving groups, of
which there are quite a few active in Namibia (see e.g. LAC 2005b:13),
may offer settlers better prospects. In this regard it is worth emphasising also, in terms of the demand for credit, that residents themselves
may be unwilling to incur land-secured debts if they perceive the risk
of losing their property to be high (Platteau 1996:62).

In summary, it can be said that it is doubtful whether the Flexible
Land Tenure Bill could achieve its objectives in Otjiwarongo's extra-legal settlements. Low-cost titling would not, in itself, reduce existing
tenure insecurity. Neither does it offer material benefits in terms of
opening up access to credit to significant portions of the population.
And lastly, extra-legality appears to give the settlers more economic
freedom than the legal regime introduced by the bill.

Conclusions and policy implications

This contribution has sought to evaluate the prospects of the Flexible
Land Tenure Bill in the Namibian context, and, on a more general level, to tie together two strands of the literature on tenure security.

Our findings made in Otjiwarongo suggest that the eventual passing
of the bill should not be followed by a centralised and nationwide implementation policy that calls for the setting up of flexible titling
schemes regardless of local circumstances. Rather, a careful selection
of zones should be made where conditions for implementation are
more favourable than in Otjiwarongo. Our work suggests that in other
circumstances better results can be achieved – both in the short and
the intermediate term – by bolstering existing extra-legal practices (for
example by (1) requesting the central government for an exemption
from the 300 square metres rule and allowing permanent structures,
and (2) micro-managing the remaining layout problems by making use
of empty plots and, where needed, offering compensation).

The second objective of our work has been to tie together two
strands of the literature on tenure security. The history of debate on
this matter shows a continued widening of the scholarly perspective.
Early thought focussed on the perceived inefficiencies of communal
land tenure and on the superior protection offered by Western-style
property law. Later contributions, in reaction to failed titling projects,
expanded the analysis to include the social and financial costs of titling,

while some pointed also to the benefits offered by indigenous systems. This has led a number of authors to argue that legalisation is, on balance and in the current African context, not likely to be an efficient policy. These scholars suggest that bolstering existing (neo-)customary arrangements is a more promising way of improving tenure security. Others have worked to design a system of formal property rights that has the potential to significantly reduce the costs of titling in monetary terms. Such an instrument may therefore alter the balance in a way that makes legalisation feasible.

We have tried to address the question of how to decide between low-cost titling and strengthening neo-customary practices. We have argued that in determining whether to legalise tenure, it is not enough to take only the drawbacks of extra-legality and the costs and benefits of titling into account. We have underscored the need to include a fourth element in the analysis: the possibility that living in extra-legality offers advantages. Apart from obvious restrictions, extra-legality may offer settlers freedoms that are unattainable under formal tenure laws. It is crucial that policymakers analyse the perspective of the settlers in this way because their co-operation is indispensable to the success of legalisation. If there is limited capacity in the legal and regulatory system, settlers may correct perceived imbalances in their new legal status by non-compliance and continued extra-legality.

Appendix

This appendix sets out the research method that was followed in conducting the case study of the tenure situation in Otjiwarongo's extra-legal settlements. Before discussing the details of our approach, however, it is useful to point out that our data were gathered against the background of a request by the local authority to examine the prospects of titling in the extra-legal settlements. The Flexible Land Tenure Bill not having been passed into law yet, the request was to study the feasibility legalisation by issuing freehold titles. Specifically, we were asked to chart the residents' ability to pay for legalisation at the specified monthly amounts that related to different levels of services to be provided. The request had come to us via the intermediary of a local authority in the Netherlands that has a twinning relationship with the municipality of Otjiwarongo. The query presented in the present article was not, as such, commissioned by the municipality.

The research we conducted in Tsaraxa Aibes and DRC consisted of two components. We examined (1) the relevant socio-economic indicators (results were used to draft a report for the municipality), and we made (2) a study of the tenure situation. The latter study primarily con-

sisted of 36 in-depth interviews with residents. All 36 households interviewed regarding issues of tenure were also asked about their socio-
economic situation. After completing these 36 interviews, a further 69
households were selected and interviewed regarding only socio-economic indicators, bringing the total number of respondents on these
matters to 105. The majority of these additional interviews (60) was
conducted by local authority officials, who had previously been involved
in designing and improving this part of the research, but had not taken
part in the initial 36 interviews.

Before starting the first round of interviews, a total of 45 plots to be
visited was selected by means of a map of Tsaraxa Aibes and DRC, to
ensure that data would be retrieved at evenly distributed points. In
cases where there was nobody present at the selected plot or the residents were unable or unwilling to co-operate, an adjacent plot was
tried. Thirty-six of these interviews produced useful results. We were
assisted by two local interpreters, one who could translate into Damara
and Afrikaans, and another speaking Oshiwambo and Oshiherero. At
the suggestion of our interpreters and local officials, most interviews
were held in the late afternoon and early evening, when many of the
residents who worked would have returned home.

The interviews that we ourselves conducted were introduced by explaining our relationship to the municipality, as researchers from the
Netherlands, frequently by means of a drawing in the sand. It was explained that the first part of the interview (on socio-economic indicators) would be used to advise the municipality, whereas the second part
was for our own interest. In view of the delicacy of the issues involved
with tenure security, it was emphasised that neither their name nor
their plot number would be communicated to the municipality and
that none of our work would result in anything that could be traced
back to an individual or a plot. The first part of the interview was conducted using a purposefully created form, filled in by the passive inter-
viewer. The second part was open-structured, allowing respondents to
steer the conversation. Our input in these interviews had originally
been prepared by means of discussions with a number of key informants, both local authority officials and well-informed members of the
community. These interviews are not counted as part of the 36. In the
phase when the actual interviews were conducted, particularly in the
beginning, it frequently happened that later interviews produced new
insights. A number of earlier respondents were therefore revisited to
ensure that the results would remain comparable. After completion of
the interviews, forms were used to facilitate comparison and aggrega-
tion. Where feasible we sought to confirm our results by interviewing
local authority officials on the same matters, particularly those in fre-

quent contact with the population. It was, sadly, impossible to feed the results of our work in general back into the community.

Notes

1   PhD student at the Center for Law and Economics, University of Amsterdam. Please address correspondence to marcolankhorst@gmail.com. This research was neither supervised nor sponsored by the ACLE; all responsibility for views and errors is ours exclusively.

2   Ministry of Housing and Environmental Affairs, The Hague. This research was not sponsored by the Ministry. All responsibility for views and errors is ours exclusively.

3   In the sense of rights to land recognised, defined, and protected by the state.

4   See Merry 1988 on the distinction between factual and formal legal pluralism.

5   See Platteau 1996 for references. He groups these contributions under the heading of the 'Evolutionary Theory of Land Rights'.

6   Not incidentally, the factors that will be looked at are important elements in the UN-DP's Human Development Index.

7   See e.g. www.amicaall.org/publications/action/actionotji.pdf.

8   Possibly the settlement is of later date, as Fjeldstad et al. (2005:5) suggest that south of the Red Cordon Fence, where Otjiwarongo lies, extra-legal settlements emerged from 1988 onwards.

9   We gathered information regarding 588 persons, belonging to a total of 105 households (mostly by interviewing one, two, or three household members). This implies that, at a 95 per cent confidence level, our statements regarding socio-economic conditions at the household level come with a close to ten per cent error margin. Therefore, the results we report should be taken to be indicative only. For further details on the surveys we conducted, see the appendix.

10   A wide range of possible occupations can be thought of here, such as collecting and selling firewood, selling kapanna or vetkoekies, exploiting a shabeen or cuka stall, gardening, and driving a taxi.

11   Note that the term 'property' is used here in a broad sense to include land holding that might legally be qualified differently than full ownership, such as for example a lease.

12   This risks creating some confusion, however. The discussion in this section shows that there is a specific legal regime that governs the situation in these settlements (by way of their designation as so-called Reception Areas) and that the municipality has broad powers to request settlers to move. This may raise the question of why we refer to Tsaraxa Aibes and DRC as 'extra-legal' settlements. Our reasons for doing so are explained in detail below.

13   Thus far, however, no resettlement in this sense appears to have taken place in Otjiwarongo. In the past decade and a half, the municipality has made a considerable number of plots available in the area between the former township of Orwetoweni and the extra-legal settlements (probably between 200 and 300). Our survey of this area, in which 25 households were asked whether they themselves, or any of their neighbours that they knew of, had lived in Tsaraxa Aibes or DRC before moving there, suggested that the majority of residents either came from the former township or from outside of Otjiwarongo. In all likelihood, this is explained by the fact that most of the government and private programmes that provide loans with which the land can be purchased and a house can be constructed require evidence of a reliable source of income. Christensen *et al.* (1999:9) suggests that low-income groups

throughout Namibia have not been able to secure a title to developed land. They point to prices on the commercial land market (of the order of USD 12 per square metre), which are far out of reach for the large majority of inhabitants of extra-legal settlements. All of this underscores the importance of focusing on the cost side of legalisation, as the Flexible Land Tenure Bill discussed below does, if the residents of extra-legal settlements are to benefit. In this regard, see also the text accompanying footnote 175.

14 See Fjeldstad et al. (2005:16).

15 Both those who had previously indicated being able to make savings at least every now and then and those who were unable to do so were asked this question, the latter under the fiction that they would have a modest amount of savings to dispose of.

16 It should be taken into consideration that the Namibian system for financing local government provides municipalities with very few sources of income, and most face severe problems in balancing their budget. Except for Windhoek, Walvis Bay, and Swakopmund, a surcharge on the water distributed amongst their citizens constitutes the primary source of potential income for municipalities. (Until recently, electricity distribution to end users afforded municipalities another very important source of income. Changes in the system have left them without a direct say in that matter, however.) It is well known, however, that mainly for political reasons, water is in many cases distributed below cost (Fjeldstad et al. 2005:12). Not surprisingly, then, municipalities look at the town lands in their possession as an alternative source of potential income.

17 Our interpreters generally employed Afrikaans terminology also when speaking one of the native languages.

18 This too sets tenure relations in Tsaraxa Aibes and DRC apart from general conceptions of tenancy, as the latter arrangement normally ends when the tenant passes away.

19 We were able to follow up on four of these accounts.

20 Considerable work exists on the regulation of customary law by statute. In this regard, see e.g. LAC 2003 and LAC 1999. No detailed studies of individual customary regimes could be found, however.

9   Land reform in Senegal: l'Histoire se répète?[1]

Gerti Hesseling

Introduction

As a former French colony, Senegal inherited a French legal culture which differs from other postcolonial legal systems in Africa, such as those deriving from British legal culture. One of the major characteristics of the Senegalese legal system is a policy of legal codes, in which Senegal was a champion among the new African states (Le Roy 1985:254). It was the first former French colony to reform the colonial land legislation, and in 1964 the Law on the National Domain was adopted and was considered innovative, since it aimed at harmonising formal law and customary land rights (Lavigne Delville 1999:8):

> While retaining the principle of national property owned by the state (all non-registered land), in rural areas, the law distinguishes between 'pioneer areas' which remain under state control and *terroir* areas where land management is the responsibility of the rural municipalities (decentralised administrative bodies set up in 1972). The existence of local usage rights is recognised in the latter areas, but the land may be taken over by the state for development projects or allocated by the rural councils to whoever can 'develop/use its productivity'. In a way, such allocation mirrors – on a local scale and with fewer legal guarantees – the registration procedure, by which land may be allocated to individuals without taking existing rights into account (although, in practice, the rural councils rarely make allocations without the agreement of customary holders).

According to Touré and Seck (2005:12): 'This legislation removed the customary land rights of lineage groups and families in rural areas, stipulating that "all lands not classified as public property, which are not registered and whose ownership has not been recorded in the Mortgage Registry, are by right national lands." However, occupants of public lands who had "made continuous productive use" of the land at the time that the law came into force, were allowed to apply for it to be registered. This productive use had to be certified by an administrative decision, which the interested party had to apply for within six months of the publication of the enforcement order for the law.'

With regard to the organisational set-up of the land law, there has been a considerable delay. The rural councils were mentioned in the 1964 law but were only created from 1972 onwards with the adoption of the *Loi relative aux Communautés rurales*. The 1964 and 1972 laws are the twin pillars of national land law in Senegal. For a long time they were considered highly innovative and flexible compilations of laws and implementing decrees that provided for a legal framework for local communities to plan and implement community-based natural resource management activities including land management. As Schoonmaker Freudenberger (1992:2) states: 'The legislation is unique in West Africa for it sets in place "co-management" arrangements that are now so prevalent in current programs found across the Sahel.'

Hence, the Senegalese land tenure system introduced in 1964 was highly praised for its innovative character. An important question is how this land law regime, in place for more than four decades, worked in practice locally. To what extent did the members of the rural councils incorporate – explicitly or implicitly – local rules and local customs and institutions when they used their power to implement the official regulations with regard to land administration and conflict resolution? In the end, the question is of the extent to which the interaction between the state law and the local tenure institutions and norms has been able to provide secure land rights for smallholders and the poor, given the rapid developments in Senegalese society.

In this study we shall first briefly sketch the evolution of the Senegalese land tenure system before the reform in 1964. In the second part we will analyse the land reform of 1964, including the institutional set-up and its adaptations over the years. We will then look at some structural impediments of the land legislation and what these have meant for the Senegalese family farmers. The fourth part will be devoted to recent attempts to modernise the land law system in Senegal, and in the conclusion we will try to evaluate the positive and negative aspects of the current system and point out why – despite its innovative character – it still fails to provide secure rights to land for smallholders and the poor. The liberal regime, put in place since the election of President Abdoulaye Wade in 2000, seems to prioritise commercial farming and agro-business, and consequently to focus more on property rights at the expense of family farming. *L'histoire se répète?*

The evolution of the Senegalese land tenure system up to 1964[2]

The evolution of the Senegalese land tenure system, as nearly every-where else in Africa, can be divided into three phases: pre-colonial times, colonial rule, and post-independence times. Knowledge about the first phase of pre-colonial times is largely based on oral history, and one has to make do with research findings that are inferred from the nature of the pre-colonial social organisation. Senegal was a plural so-ciety divided into various fiefs that basically corresponded to the main ethnic groups. The major attributes of property rights – absolute dispo-sition, exclusivity, and perpetuity – were vested in the person of the king. The African conception of land prevailed. This means that the land had been given to mankind by the gods in order to assure the sur-vival of the species, and served therefore as a sacred space. Over this land, which should be preserved in its integrity and should be dedi-cated to its use by the group, individuals held no absolute rights. The kings generally were the sole 'owners' of the land, and their subjects were no more than precarious possessors.[3]

During the second phase – colonial times – the French lawmaker sought to establish a land law regime according to their conceptions. For the French and the assimilated natives, the new regime sought to introduce a type of tenure security comparable to that of, and deriving from, France. The tenure policy of the colonial authorities swayed be-tween two tendencies: 'On the one hand it proposed to preserve the tra-ditional system and to uphold customary rights but on the other hand it sought to transform them according to western conceptions of prop-erty, which would encourage investors' (Verdier 1971:78). The Civil Code that was introduced by decree in French-speaking West Africa on 5 November 1830 was declared to apply to all cases that involved a Frenchman or an assimilated native, and this naturally implied that the colonial lawmaker decided that the French property regime would apply to all legal and economic transactions of immovable goods if a Frenchman or an assimilated native was involved. The system of 'regis-tration' according to the Civil Code would be applied. The outcome was the creation of the first Senegalese land law regime, known as the Civil Code regime. This regime, also known as the mortgage regime, was aligned to the dispositions of the French legislation of 23 March 1855,[4] which enumerated the legal acts that had to be drawn up and de-termined the rights that could be derived from them. Because of its complex nature, but above all because it was not adapted to the local si-tuation, this legal regime failed. It was complex because it related the identification of rights to the holder of the title and not to the land as such. And it was not adapted because it totally ignored customary ten-ure and customary land rights.

In the face of this failure, between 1900 and 1906 the colonial law-maker introduced a regime of registration in the *Livre Foncier* in a gen-eral way, which applied to all lands. This regime established irrevocable and incontestable property rights. In the particular case of Senegal, this registration regime was introduced by the Decree of 20 July 1900,[5] but its dispositions were never really applied, mainly because registration remained voluntary,[6] a situation that lasted until 1906. The effective introduction of registration in French-speaking West Africa started with the issuing of the Decree of 24 July 1906,[7] subsequently modified by the Decree of 26 July 1932, concerning the reorganisation of the landed property regime in French-speaking West Africa.[8] Generally speaking, the registration regime was wholly unsuccessful where customary lands and rights were concerned, as they remained outside the newly established regime. Verdier (1971:78) argues that the holders of cus-tomary lands did not see the advantages of recurring to the lengthy and costly registration procedure.

The lawmaker then developed another approach which aimed for the consolidation of customary rights by introducing the possibility that customary right holders could have their rights confirmed. This was the objective of the Decree of 8 October 1925,[9] which sought to raise awareness among the African population regarding the patrimo-nial value of their lands and thus to ease the transition to a Civil Code property regime. This decree was as unsuccessful as its predecessors. The main reason was that it regulated the public confirmation of hold-ings only in function of personal rights and completely disregarded col-lective customary rights, although such collective rights were by far the most important rights in African social organisation. That is why, with-out abandoning the institution of the land book, the lawmaker inter-vened once again in 1955 and reformed the regime by making it apply to all forms of tenure, whether individual or collective. This was regu-lated by decrees issued on 20 May 1955 and on 10 July 1956.[10] These texts once again sought to clarify the customary land tenure regime and to promote the transformation of traditional rights into full prop-erty rights. The innovation was that now a distinction was made be-tween individual customary rights that 'involve the right of disposition and evident and permanent possession of the land' and other custom-ary rights that did not involve such definitive possession. This last ef-fort also ended in failure. However, the laws of 1906, 1955, and in par-ticular the law of 1932 still define the legal structure of registered land-ownership in Senegal (Golan 1990:10).

The principal reason for these failures of the colonial administration is that they collided with the natives' conceptions of land rights. As they had possessed their land in an uncontested way since time imme-morial, they could only perceive the efforts of the colonial administra-

tion to 'consolidate' their rights as useless and dangerous – useless because their rights were uncontested and recognised by the customary
authorities, and dangerous because complying with the requirements
of colonial law implied an implicit recognition of the 'colonial fact'.[11]

Thus, when independence came, the new states of French Equatorial
and West Africa inherited an extremely confused situation where land
rights were concerned. The newly independent states, which sought to
promote their countries' agrarian and more general economic development, therefore had to undertake reforms in order to achieve a more
or less uniform system of land rights. And they all tried to.

Actually, it was well before independence that the reform process in
Senegal got under way. A Committee for Economic Studies had been
formed in 1958[12] and was mandated to undertake 'the daunting and
difficult task to study the problems posed by the development of the
Senegalese economy.'[13] The Committee presented its report on 29 February 1959. In the second volume, dedicated to the rural world, the
Committee insisted on the need to 're-found the land tenure regime'.[14]
An inter-ministerial study group for reform of the land tenure system
was created in August 1959. Its first task was to present an overview of
the state of the tenure regimes inherited from pre-colonial and colonial
times, and its second task was to advise on guidelines for a new policy.
The study group proceeded to evaluate the land titles that had been registered following the procedures laid down in the 1932 Decree, the
rights that had been confirmed and inscribed in the Land Books according the 1955 Decree, as well as those issued according to the Civil
Code regime by the self-governing 'four communes'.[15] The conclusions
of the study group pointed to the difficulties arising from the coexistence of different property regimes, caused in particular by the absence
of registered titles for so-called 'civil code' properties.[16] It also noted
the frequency with which registered terrains were not put to productive
use (*mise en valeur*), in contravention of the 1932 Decree, and finally it
affirmed that a constitutional guarantee of acquired rights was needed.
A first draft of the land reform was rejected by the constitutional court
for being contrary to the constitution (it did not recognise common
property guaranteed by article 12 of the constitution). But in 1963 the
constitution was revised, and the stipulation 'individual and common
property is guaranteed by constitution' was replaced by 'property rights
are guaranteed'. On 17 June 1964, the president of the republic proclaimed the new law, and on 11 July 1964, it was published in the *Journal Officiel*, known as *Loi no. 64-46 relative au Domaine National*.

The 1964 Land Law has to be placed in the ideological context of the
Senegalese authorities at that time, which they called Senegalese socialism, to be distinguished from scientific socialism, and which was
based on 'negro-African' values. This kind of socialism sought to es-

cape from the political and ideological struggles between the two super-
powers by developing a political perspective through a synthesis between the positive elements of European socialism and African values.
Senegalese socialism was, above all, to be communitarian. In the words
of the then president, Léopold Sédar Senghor (1960:24): 'African society privileges the group over the individual and the community of
persons over their autonomy. It is a communitarian society'. And he
concluded that a 'realistic African socialism must be communitarian,
not only by erecting itself upon national structures but inasmuch by
stimulating intermediary groups and bodies to adopt a spirit of full participation in socialist society'.[17]

Without doubt, this wish to introduce communitarian values into development was at the root of the organisation of the rural world into
rural communities that were to support endogenous development. This
strongly influenced the general rules regarding the distribution and administration of lands as laid down in the 1964 Land Law. The issuing
of this law raised great expectations of development and progress. But
did this law and the related institutional changes also result in more
tenure security for the average Senegalese farmer?

The legal framework of the Senegalese land tenure regime

An overview of the land tenure regime in Senegal shows that there are
three broad categories. The first category is the state domain, which is
subdivided into a private and a public domain and regulated by Law
76-66 of 2 July 1976.[18] The public and private state domains are constituted by all the rights to movable and immovable goods that belong
to the state. This concerns only a relatively small part of the national
territory. The second category is the private domain, which is regulated
by the Decree of 26 July 1932 concerning the reorganisation of the
landed property regime in French West Africa.[19] Landed property is
guaranteed through the registration and publication of all real rights to
a tract of land in the *Livre Foncier* (Land Book). In practice, only a small
percentage of land (about two per cent) was officially registered, and registration mainly occurred in the urban centres, and even there only in
a partial way. The third category is the national domain, which is regulated by the National Domain Law of 1964, which is, in fact, a very
short document containing only seventeen articles. The last article
states that the conditions of implementation have to be drawn up in separate decrees.[20] According to article 1 of this law, the national domain
consists of 'all the lands that do not pertain to the public domain, lands
that are not registered or of which the property has not been inscribed
in the register of mortgages at the date at which the present law takes

effect. The national domain thus contains all non-registered lands. Also are excluded all the lands that, at this date, are in the process of being registered in the name of a person other than the state'.

At the time the law was adopted, three per cent of the territory was controlled exclusively by the state (state domain), a negligible but very important area as it borders commercially coveted lands along the sea fronts, rivers and lakes (Schoonmaker Freudenberger 1992:4). About two per cent consisted of private land owned by individuals (titles registered prior to 1964 or in the delay granted by the law). Consequently, the national domain covered over 95 per cent of the national territory. The majority of the farmers derived their land rights from the national domain regime. For that reason we will mainly focus on the national domain regime.

The national domain lands do not constitute a homogeneous whole because article 4 of National Domain Law divides them into four categories according to their vocation: urban zones, classified zones, *zones de terroirs* and pioneer zones. Classified zones are forest areas and protected areas such as national parks. The pioneer zones actually were not clearly identified and constitute a rather negatively defined residual category comprising the lands that do not fall into the other categories. This was done intentionally. The underlying idea was to create temporary land reserves that then could be re-classified and included into the categories of village lands or urban zones. This zoning exercise reflected a preoccupation with the rationalisation and orderly exploitation of the national space. The reform mainly organised the *zones de terroirs* or rural zones, the most important area spatially and economically (including at that time 58 per cent of the national territory). It concerns lands which are regularly used for family farming, pastoral activities or rural housing.

The legal framework with regard to the national domain is guided by the following principles:
- farmers have free access to the land[21]
- they have no private ownership, only non-transferable use rights
- the management of the land is in the hands of elected local councils under the tutorship of the administration (the *préfet* or the *sous-préfet*)
- the conditions for allocation or withdrawal of land by the councils are (1) the productive use of the land, and (2) beneficiaries have to be resident in the rural community[22]
- rural councils have the right to settle land conflicts, but if they fail to resolve the conflict, it goes to the formal court system.

These principles will be elaborated below. The national domain is an original legal construct intended to displace the problem of landownership toward one of simple possession. National domain lands are not the object of individual property but only of use rights. Indeed, the user of the land, even though unable to claim exclusive rights to the land, and even if his situation is defined by law or results from an administrative decision, can be assured of a certain stability on the condition that he puts the parcel he is assigned to into productive use (*mise en valeur*). Apart from the case of public utility, the land cannot be re-allocated unless the absence of productive use can be established. The legal regime of the national domain thus features the inalienability and non-transmissibility of the lands it comprises, among other characteristics, as well as their use free of charge. According to judicial decisions, the death of the person who was allocated the land entails the rightful extinction of his use rights.[23] The fact that these lands are allocated free of charge means that conditions of access gain relative importance. In practice, this rule of non-transmission is often breached. In case of death, the Rural Council rarely meets to re-allocate the land considering the capacity of the inheritors to exploit it. If it intervenes, it is simply to regularise the procedure. That further reinforces the feelings of ownership. But the practices of inheritance also demonstrate the resilience of local customs. Rural councils sometimes continue to build on customary practices and feel legitimised in doing so by the law.

The rules for allocation and re-allocation of national domain land have always been subject to two general principles. In the first place, the idea that underlies legislation regarding the national domain is that land should be made available to the members of the rural communities. According to article 8 of the National Domain Law, 'lands in the village land zone will be allocated to those members of the rural communities who can assure their productive use and will exploit them under supervision of the state and according to the law and regulations....' There was no intention to dispossess effective occupants and users to the benefit of the state but rather to deny any rights to those who do not personally till the land and to abolish the payment of land rent. By turning residence in the village into the criterion for land allocation, the authorities did not seek simply to ensure that farmers with land rights belong to a community but rather to maintain the peasant population in the countryside. The second principle has to do with the development objectives pursued by the law. In Senegal land has a fundamental economic value, and in order to achieve optimal productivity and profitability, land is only allocated to an individual on the condition of productive use (*mise en valeur*). Productive use is the key condition for access to land and for continued occupation.

According to the 1964 law the rural zones should be administered under the authority of the state by new councils, named *conseils ruraux*. The creation of these councils suffered quite some delay. They were only created from 1972 onwards with the adoption of the *Loi relative aux communautés rurales*.[24] This law sets up the institutional structure of the rural communities and defines the attributes of the members of the rural councils. A rural community consists of a certain number of villages with common interests and is capable of finding resources necessary for their development. The number of villages may vary from eight to more than 50, and the survey area also varies from about 50 to more than 300 km. Rural councils are structures democratically elected to five-year terms. Depending on the population, a council has from eighteen to 32 members. The members of the council elect one member as their president. From 1972 onwards, there was a phased introduction of the rural councils in the different regions (the last 'first' elections of rural councils were held only in 1985). At present, Senegal has 530 rural communities.[25]

The rural councils have sizable powers with regard to land tenure within their community. It is the council that allocates use rights to a farmer on the condition that the plot is exploited by himself with the help of his family in an economically productive fashion (*mise en valeur*). But the council also has the power to withdraw land: if the farmer ceases to use the plot himself, if the productive use of the plot is considered insufficient, or for reasons of general interest. It is the council which determines what is meant by 'productive use', since nowhere in the law is the concept of *mise en valeur* defined explicitly. Finally, the rural council has the right to resolve land disputes. The exercise of all these powers is subject to the authorisation of administrative authorities. This is called the system of *tutelle* (administrative oversight), inherited from the French. This means that the *sous-préfet* or *préfet* may in fact veto any of the council's decisions. In practice, however, *sous-préfets* and *préfets* rarely use these powers, so in the majority of cases the rural councils are left free to make decisions and have no fear of correction by higher officials.[26]

In 1996 a new administrative reform was adopted, which has to be seen in the context of the general trend in Africa towards decentralisation. The *Code des Collectivités Locales* modified the election and the powers of the rural councils.[27] According to the 1972 law one-third of the councillors was appointed, but since 1996 all members of the rural councils have been elected. At the same time one of the most important powers of the rural councils, the management of village land, was considerably reduced. Indeed, if land that previously belonged to the pioneer zone is reverted to the village land zone (*zone de terroir*), the state will continue to manage those areas that have been the object of special interventions. Thus, certain areas in the village land zone will be directly managed by the state. The reform also allows the state to hand over land that municipalities need to expand, and then proceed

directly with developments destined for urban housing (Faye 2008:9).
On the other hand, the *communautés rurales* have been officially recognised by the constitution, which specifies in article 90 the three levels
of local government in the republic: the region, the commune, and the
rural community.

The legal framework of land reform (1964) and administrative reforms (1972 and 1996) could be considered the twin pillars of the land
reform initiated in 1964. To some extent they introduced a new design
for tenure security. Instead of a gerontocratic structure, the legislation
introduced a democratic structure with elected councils. These councils
have the power to apply the principles of the National Domain to a certain degree, while taking into account local conditions and local practices. In theory, the members of the council may be sanctioned in case
of mismanagement, in the sense that voters have the possibility to not
re-elect them at the end of their five-year mandate. Although farmers
have no property rights, they have free use rights, and they are allowed
to continue the cultivation of their plots as long as they cultivate them
themselves or with the help of their family, and fulfil the condition of
mise en valeur. Their use rights are limited, however, by the fact that
they are neither transferable nor automatically transferred to their
heirs. Indeed, rights are allocated on a strictly personal basis. In case
of the death of a farmer, his heirs have to expressly request that the
use rights of the deceased be transferred to them.

In the following section we will confront the official rules pertaining
to the national domain as laid down in the land and administrative reforms with the reality on the ground: to what extent did the rural councils succeed in developing a new design for tenure security? How did
they use their legal power to develop tailored local rules in order to find
a balance between local, traditional, community-based tenure regimes
into the modern statutory land law? Or did councillors, as well politicians and bureaucrats, abuse the room for manoeuvring for their own
benefit and ultimately diminish the security of land rights for smallholders and the poor?

Structural weaknesses in the law

Although there have been numerous changes in the administrative
sphere, the legal tenure system introduced in 1964 has remained largely unchanged. More than 40 years later, we have to conclude that the
rural councils are still struggling with the implementation of the National Domain Law and that the interpretation of the law by the rural
councils shows notable variations depending on the local circumstances. Particular regional and local differences have to be taken into

account when assessing the implementation of the tenure legislation. The tenure situation along the Senegalese river valley is for instance quite different from that of the peanut production region or the Casamance. In addition, over the years, the political, economic, and social contexts in Senegal have been subjected to considerable changes. Consequently, within this multitude of practices, we make no claim to be exhaustive.

Nevertheless, and in spite of all the words of praise with regard to the innovative character of land reform, the literature on the land tenure situation in Senegal notes serious shortcomings. The most serious flaw in the legal framework is the failure to clarify exactly what was meant by productive use as well as by public utility and general interest. In addition, the rural councils were from the beginning ill-equipped to execute their duties properly. Finally, the composition of the rural councils has amply served to handicap an unbiased implementation of the law, including in the case of conflict resolution. We will illustrate these problems with some examples.

Right from the beginning, criticism was directed at the absence of a clear definition of what exactly constitutes productive use (*mise en valeur*), one of the central notions in the national domain law. The concept is fluid. Despite the importance of the notion of productive use, the law only enunciates this principle without specifying its content in legal terms. Article 10 of Decree no. 72-1288 empowers the prefect to fix the minimal conditions for productive use as well as the surface of parcels considered to be profitable. Such conditions have never been specified. Consequently, local communities developed a large variety of local rules with regard to what should be considered productive use of the land. This makes it understandable that the few interventions of the judiciary are mostly related to the question of productive use. In its verdict on the case El Hadji Massamba Sall, the Supreme Court argued that in the absence of a statutory definition, a rural council cannot motivate its decision of re-allocation with a simple reference to insufficient use 'without specifying in what way this reproach applies to the present user' (Supreme Court of Senegal, 25 March 1981. RIPAS 1982:424 *ff*). In theory, the absence of a definition may be deliberate, since the national domain law was conceived to be a general tenure system, leaving it to the rural councils to work out the practical details at the local level. But research shows that in general rural councils do little to verify the ability of applicants to make productive use of their land (Touré and Seck 2005). The criterion has hardly been useful in developing land tenure rules rooted in local customs and traditions and has often resulted in *ad hoc* and unpredictable decisions.

Up till now, in villages without pressure on cultivable land, village elders maintain that they have no knowledge of the land reform and the conditions for allocation or withdrawal of land. In 2008 in the rural community of Sadio – where as a consequence of the *exode rural* much land remains uncultivated – a village chief said to our researcher Fatimata Diallo: 'Mon père a créé ce village. Il y a construit le puit, les autres nous ont rejoint, donc les terres nous ont toujours appartenu et nous appartiennent encore. Nous cédons les terres à qui veut s'installer' (Diallo 2008). For the last six years no case of withdrawal of land for unproductive use has been noted in the rural community of Sadio. For most farmers in this community, the condition of productive use is not yet considered as an immediate threat, and they still feel their land rights protected.

In other cases the failure to define the concept of *mise en valeur* resulted in an abuse of the intent of the law. As Schoonmaker Freudenberger (1990:9-10) noted in a report for the World Bank:

> Powerful Mouride brotherhood has considered *mise en valeur* the act of clearing vast acreages and putting the land into peanut production. This has created serious conflicts between Mouride farmers and pastoralists. The history of disputes between pastoralists and Wolof cultivators is one dominated by the expansion of peanut cultivation into the territory long used by Fulbe pastoralists. Peanut cultivation has been viewed by the state as a more profitable form of land use than that of pastoralism and forest protection. (...) This position holds sway due to the considerable power of the Mouride sect.

Indeed, pastoralism is not considered 'making good use of land', and the power of marabouts to control large tracts of land in undeniable (Golan 1990:16). A striking and disingenuous example of the power of Islamic leaders, going back to 1991, is the destruction of 45,000 hectare of gazetted forest of Mbegué and the allocation of this area to the khalif of the Mouride brotherhood for the cultivation of peanuts. As a consequence, 6,000 herdsmen and 100,000 animals lost the pastureland and watering places they had used for centuries.[28] More recently, in 2007, 9,000 hectares belonging to the gazetted forests of Pout and Thiès have been allocated to marabouts from the Mouride and Tidjani sects by the national government without consulting the rural councils concerned.[29]

Another example of problems arising from the absence of a clear definition of productive use comes from the Senegal River Valley, a zone of high economic potential. Up to the early 1970s, state-financed irrigation of the Senegal River Valley was concentrated almost exclusively in the Delta area and on large-scale schemes for the cultivation of export crops, especially sugar cane and rice. With the introduction of the land reform, a large part of the valley was considered a *zone pionnier* managed by the parastatal SAED (*Société d'Aménagement et Exploitation des Terres du Delta*). The large-scale schemes were a complete failure. After the severe droughts in the 1970s, the SAED set up village-level irrigation perimeters (*Périmètres irrigués villageois*, PIVs). The drought also prompted the construction of two dams: the antisaline intrusion Diama dam near the mouth of the Senegal River (completed in 1985) and the Manantali dam in the southwestern region of Mali (completed in 1988). One of the objectives of the dams was to enable irrigation year-round (double cropping) of rice fields on both sides of the river. In 1986 reforms in agriculture policy resulted in the disengagement of the SAED from land allocation and the transfer of control over large amounts of land to the rural communities. A decree converted substantial parts of the *zone pionnier* in the region to *zone de terroir* and hence under the control of the rural councils.[30] In the course of the 1980s, the farmers on the village irrigation perimeters (PIVs) organised themselves in *Groupements d'Intérêt Economiques* (economic interest groups), which had access to credit for investments in the schemes. Those groups collectively received land allocated by the rural councils. This means that individual farmers only have rights derived from a GIE. In the event of a poor harvest and inability to re-pay debts, their use rights may be suspended by the GEI and given to someone else. The tenure status of plot holders within an irrigation scheme is thus ambiguous from a legal point of view. They have to maintain good relations within the group and especially with the GIE leaders. Farmers with a high social status are sometimes able to keep their plots for years, while others have to change plots frequently (Cotula and Toulmin 2004:50; Lavigne Delville et al. 2002:38, 79). Obviously, the criterion of productive use is no longer applied by the rural councils but interpreted by the GIEs as the ability to re-pay debts. The rural councils sometimes played a dubious role, as is shown by the following quotation (Bélières et al. 2002:12):

> From 1988 onwards, 'big farmers' and people of importance in the rural world wanting to increase their land holdings, together with newcomers and city-based investors seeking to engage in what was thought to be a 'profitable' activity of rice-growing, took part in a major land grab. Rural councils (*conseils ruraux*) did nothing to prevent this phenomenon and granted large areas of land to the applicants, in some cases over and above what was really available.

The insecurity resulting from the ambiguous concept of productive use drove possessors of land in the rural areas (traditional landholders, borrowers of land, beneficiaries of re-allocation, as well as illegal buyers) to demonstrate that their plots are fully exploited, even though some of the techniques used were ecological harmful.

A second problem is the definitional ambiguity of the notions of 'public utility' and 'general interest'. In the case of public utility, the state can take land for projects defined as such, and in the case of general interest, the rural council has the competence to re-allocate plots if required by the general interest of the community. According to the law allocated lands that are part of the national domain but that are required for operations declared for public utility will be registered in the name of the state.[31] About this notion all we find is an enumeration of cases in which public utility may be evoked, such as public health, interior security, zoning plans and urbanisation projects, and the development of management schemes.[32] This absence of definition and clear framing of the notion of public utility may be problematic, because we have to do with an instrument allowing for rapid and low-cost state intervention, and the state may be tempted to broaden its interpretation of the notion. It thus introduces an element of insecurity into local communities. Rural populations are rightly fearful that the state will expropriate traditionally held lands for the public interest. An early and striking example occurring in 1976 is the case of the villagers of Thiago contesting in vain the confiscation of their plots in the national domain by the local powerful sugar refinery with the approval of the state authorities (Niang 2004:22). Villagers can appeal the taking of land for *projets d'intérêt general*. However, the transaction costs are very high. First, the plaintiff must contest the decision by appealing to the various administrative authorities ranging from the *sous-préfet* to the governor. Failing these appeals, the case must be taken by the plaintiff directly to the Supreme Court. The transaction costs for the individual citizen appealing the taking of lands is naturally very high (see also Schoonmaker Freudenberger 1990:10).

Re-allocation by the rural council in the name of general interest is foreseen in the national domain law and was later specified in a decree.[33] Article 11 of this decree states that general interest means that 'the land is dedicated to a different use, particularly the passage of cattle or hydraulic works'. Those affected by re-allocation of their lands will receive an equivalent plot of land in compensation, but the law is silent about any compensation for improvements on the land, though that might be an indication of productive use. An aggrieved farmer has to appeal to the governor and in the second instance to the constitutional court (art. 15 Law 64-46 and art. 18 Decree 573; see also Niang 2004:14). For poor illiterate farmers without a profound knowledge of the law, this constitutes a quite impassable obstacle.

A recent example of expropriation by the state is the decision to liberate eleven plots in the rural community of Yène with the purpose of building a technical development centre, popularly called *le stade de FIFA*, since it concerns a project in collaboration with the Senegalese federation of football. The area of nearly nine hectares has been demarcated without previously consulting the rural council. It was only after the demarcation of the area that the president of the rural council was involved. Subsequently, the president organised a meeting with the villagers concerned and transmitted the council's agreement in principle to execute the project. The president of the rural council insisted that the question of compensation for the villagers concerned had to be settled before the start of execution. This happened in 2005 and 2006. However, interviews in the summer of 2008 with the villagers concerned revealed that although they never agreed to the withdrawal of their plots, the construction of the centre was finished, but they had not yet received any compensation, despite firm promises from the state. The compensation was estimated at fourteen million FCFA (Diallo 2008). According to Faye (2008:9) this action by the state seems to be in line with the 1996 administrative reform, which states that powers of national lands can be transferred to the state when it instigates a project on national land. The state can do so after simply consulting the regional council and the rural community or communities concerned and after informing them of the decision.

A third flaw in the legal framework is the absence of any form of registration or rural cadastre. According to the 1972 law, land allocations, transfers of land from one farmer to another, and the dispossession of land must be approved by a quorum of the rural council. These surveyed and demarcated transfers are to be written down in a land register, a *livret foncier*. These provisions were never implemented. The allocation of land and other decisions in the field of land tenure arrangements adopted by rural councils are in general only mentioned in the minutes of the rural councils. Although rural councillors sometimes mention such a public register, concrete examples of accessible, local *livrets fonciers* are not known. It would therefore not be surprising if they actually don't exist. Blundo (1996) argues with good reason that this seems quite consistent with the clientelist, factionalist way land is managed by elected members of the rural councils.[34] However, rural councils occasionally do deliver certificates of land allocation, especially in areas where land has monetary value, as is the case in the river valley. The importance of such a certificate is illustrated by Cotula and Toulmin (2004:49) describing the following land dispute in the village of Moudéry: 'A piece of land had been lent out by the head of the Sylla family to the Sow family for ten years. In 2003 the Sylla family reclaimed its land. The Sow family refused to surrender the land and brought the matter to court, arguing that the land belonged to the *domaine national* and that therefore the rights of users (*mise en valeur*) should be protected. The court, however, ordered that the land be surrendered to the Sylla family, as they could produce a certificate of land allocation by the rural council, while the Sow family did not possess any documentation.' Over time, the writing down of land transactions has become an expanding practice in rural areas. But the fact that tenure decisions taken by the rural councils are not systematically documented in a *livret foncier* as required by law has seriously hampered the development of new local tenure rules adapted to local customs and in line with the national land regime, which was the main objective of the National Domain Law in 1964.

Apart from these legal and conceptual problems, the rural councils are also confronted with other obstacles to implementing the land law legislation properly. When the rural councils were progressively introduced in the different regions of Senegal, the newly elected councillors – who were mostly illiterate – only received cursory training in the intricacies of the legislative corpus, the procedures to be followed, and their competences. And although this has improved slightly over the course of time, the level of educational qualifications and skill of the councillors is still quite low. In some cases nowadays, more and more educated people are elected to rural councils. The rural councils of Sadio and Yène, for example, have a former secondary school teacher (Sadio) and a geographer working at the University of Dakar (Yène) as president.

Another impediment to proper functioning is financial in nature. In theory, as a decentralised organism, rural councils enjoy budgetary autonomy, but the required resources have not been transferred by the state. The financial resources at the disposition of the rural councils are generally very small. They have no capacity to create, eliminate, or modify local taxes. Anyway, in areas where a land market is absent, it is difficult to asses the value of land and, hence, the level at which land-based taxes might be imposed. But as Toulmin & Quan (2000b:239) rightly state: local councillors are also 'caught in a bind, being reluctant to press their electors for tax payments, while equally wanting resources to build social infrastructures and carry out development projects'. This budgetary anaemia has impeded the implementation of the law with the direct consequence that the procedures foreseen are widely disregarded.

Probably the most serious problem is the highly politicised character of the rural councils. From the start, the composition of the councils reflected the national political situation. Councillors were predominantly members of the party in power under the presidents Senghor and Diouf, the *Parti Socialiste*. Consequently, members of the opposition parties run the risk of unfair treatment when applying for land allocation or when land disputes are brought to the council. From 2000 onwards, when Abdoulaye Diouf from the major opposition party, the *Parti Démocratique Sénégalais* (PDS), was elected president, the situation has been just the opposite: most councillors are now supporters of the PDS. The political and social constellation in rural communities has resulted in frequent practices of political patronage. Control over land and its allocation empowers and legitimates local authorities by providing them with control over a very important asset for allocation. The temptation of using land allocation as a means of rewarding friends and allies is therefore real (Blundo 1996; Toulmin and Quan 2000b:104, 240). Although the National Domain Law was meant to mark an important step forward in promoting democracy in the rural areas, and rural councils are indeed elected according to modern democratic standards, they do not always function democratically in everyday practice. Rural populations often have a reason to show mistrust in state institutions, including rural councils.

Although democratically elected, the composition of the rural councils is not a sample selection of the population. This is particularly true with regard to the representation of women: at present only 10.9 per cent of the councillors are women. In 2007, hundreds of women from all political parties and civil society took the initiative to encourage an equal number of men and women on the electoral rolls by proposing the gender equality law. The proposition was denounced by the powerful Islamic leaders, who claimed that 'gender parity is not yet possible in Senegal'. The gender equality law was ultimately annulled by the constitutional council. The ongoing under-representation of women in the rural councils is one of the reasons why the tenure security of women improves only very slowly. And yet, the law on the national domain was based on equal participation by all members of society in development programmes and an equitable distribution of generated income. This objective was repeated in 1972, when the rural communities that were to implement these reforms were established. However, the objectives of equality and equity are not specified with regard to women's land rights, and this neutrality does not mainstream gender, which is demonstrated by many empirical studies (Muthoni Wanyeki 2003). As is the case in most African countries, women's access to land has traditionally depended on their husband's family. Very often local traditions continue to apply, thereby preventing women from inheriting or owning land. Religion and ethnicity strongly influence women's land rights. For instance, under Serer and Diola customary law, women do own land, whereas in Wolof tradition a woman, whether married, divorced or widowed, cannot own land. According to Islam, women have the right to inherit land but always on the principle of fewer shares for women than for men. There is, however, a wide-spread belief that women cannot inherit land under Islamic law.[35] In practice, individual applications for land by women have little chance of being satisfied by rural councils. Rural councils continue to apply the unequal and inequitable principles of local customs and (perceived) Islamic law, a missed opportunity to create new and more modern local land rules embedded in statutory law. The way out for women is to create a women's association or a GIE and to apply for collective use rights. Such attempts have been increasingly successful (Hesseling and Ba 1994; Monimart 1993; Schoonmaker Freudenberger 1992:60; Von Benda-Beckmann et al. 1997).

Finally, the rural councils have been granted the power to resolve land conflicts. A wide variety of land-related conflicts have always existed in rural Senegal. Disputes occur between 'primary' and 'secondary' right holders (such as borrowers or sharecroppers), between herders and farmers, between residents and non-residents, inter-generational conflicts, about the boundaries between villages, and so on. Since the adoption of the *Loi relative aux communautés rurales* in 1972, the rural council is officially the most important local institution to settle land disputes. According to the law, the council-at-large may handle a conflict, but the president of the council may also delegate a commission of council members.

Especially in the beginning, councillors were ill-equipped for and knew very little about conflict management. The largely illiterate council members lacked the knowledge and ability to properly apply the subtleties of the land and administrative reforms. Consequently, villagers continue to bring their disputes before local, traditional authorities, such as the village chiefs, councils of elders and imams, but they also turn to the administration (*sous-préfets* and *préfets*). Due to lengthy and costly procedures, dispute resolution by the formal court system remains the exception. What emerges from the plurality of authorities involved in conflict resolution is an amalgamation of local and legal land norms, administrative pragmatism, and often illegal or extra-legal practices (Schoonmaker Freudenberger 1992:57-58). For poor illiterate farmers it is not always easy to find their way in all these competing and sometimes overlapping institutions. In general, and especially in areas without land scarcity, tenure conflicts have been more or less successfully settled, though mainly by village chiefs, councils of elders, imams and the like. Apparently, this works out quite well in small communities where everybody knows each other. At the same time, local social inequalities will persist. The way the administration (*sous-préfet*, *préfets*, and *gendarmerie*) resolves rural disputes is to our knowledge not documented, but farmers try to avoid bringing their conflicts to these officials. Rural councils certainly also play their role in local conflict resolution practices, although not as the most important institution for farmers. They have been able to resolve disputes and arrive at some type of negotiated arrangements without too much bureaucracy, as long as local tensions about land do not lead to violent confrontations. As said before, the absence of recorded decisions is a serious impediment to evaluating the extent to which they have been able to create new sets of local rules regarding access to and re-distribution of land. Under the current situation with increasing land pressure and a changing composition of the rural councils (more politicised and more educated members having better relationships with the rich and powerful), their role becomes more contested.

In sum, the weaknesses in the land reform enhanced the inability and sometimes unwillingness of the rural councils to develop tailored and transparent local rules. Their policy is indeed often unpredictable and subject to (political) machinations. In these cases, the fact that the possibilities for the rural councils to execute their duties properly are not optimal is pleaded as a poor excuse by the councillors for their failure to find a balance between local, traditional-based tenure regimes and the legal tenure system.

Evolving land tenure arrangements

In areas where rural land does not yet have great market value and where unexploited land is still available, the great majority of farmers inherited their plots, and 'traditional' tenure systems continue to function largely as in the past. Indeed, although according to the land reform heirs have to address an application to the rural council for the transfer of the deceased's use rights, this rarely happens. In general, they take over these rights with the silent consent of the rural council. But as population pressure on land increases, technologies change, and agriculture becomes more commercialised, local land arrangements are evolving elsewhere at high speed. This is particularly the case with land sales and loans and pawns of land.

Throughout most of rural Senegal, but particularly among the Serer and the Diola, the tradition of loans of land is still alive, and these loans are frequently contracted for an indeterminate period of time extending beyond several generations. Since the National Domain Law only contains very broad principles and does not specify a legal term after which a plot cultivated by the same user can be claimed by that farmer, this term has been generally interpreted as farming for at least two consecutive years, which actually bans such long-term loans. And indeed, in practice loans became a 'two-year usufruct' right (Galvan 2004:134 and note 10 on page 255). Lavigne Delville et al. (2002:51) re-

fer to short-term loans in the important groundnut production region
of Senegal among the Serer:

> (L)and is managed by farm households, lineage chiefs retaining
> the power to reallocate plots in the event of demographic imbal-
> ance, for instance when a migrant returns. The effect of land
> loans is to reduce disparities at farm level between available land
> and the farm labour force, but the extent of these loans varies
> from village to village and year to year. All categories of farmers,
> including compound heads, resort to borrowing. There is no
> rental or payment of other than symbolic fees whereas, in other
> Sereer areas such as Mbayar, rentals emerged in the 1930s. The
> duration of the loan, formerly two to three years (corresponding
> to a crop cycle), is now almost always one year, in order to pre-
> vent the beneficiary of the loan from using modern legislation
> as a pretext to refuse to return the plot. Ties between lenders
> and borrowers vary (kinship, arrangements between neighbours,
> friendship, belonging to the same religious brotherhood, etc.)
> (See also Guigou, Pontié, and Lericollais 1998).

Galvan (2004) investigated in depth the practice of land pawning
among the Serer before and after the introduction of the land reform.
He gives an example of a long-term oral pawn contract. On the day of
the funeral of his grandfather, Djignah Diouf paid the pawn amount to
the grandson of the tiller of the field, Niokhor Sène, and claimed back
his field. Diouf and his family approached the 'customary authorities'
who agreed that the family had the right to take back the field since he
had paid back the pawn amount. Sène went to the rural council, 'which
ruled without much hesitation in his favour'. Ultimately, however, Sène
voluntarily renounced the rural council's decision and gave back the
field to Diouf arguing that he did not want to disrupt the relationship
between the two families (Galvan 2004:164-165).[36]

In the southern region Casamance, among the Diola, borrowing and
pawning land has always been a frequent system to level out inequality
in land ownership. In the 1970s, in some villages about a quarter of
the rice fields were borrowed land (Sypkens Smit 1976). This system
has sometimes resulted in violent conflicts, but in general, thanks to
its flexibility, Diola families always disposed of enough land to make a
living. The flexibility of the system was greatly reduced after the adoption of the land reform and the introduction of rural councils in the
Casamance (Hesseling 1983; Van der Klei 1979, 1989:130-131). The perceived invasion of 'Northerners' – as the Diola of the Casamance call
the inhabitants living north of the river Gambia – is considered one of
the main reasons for the outbreak of a separation war, which started in

the 1980s and ended officially in 2004. After the severe droughts in the 1970s and 1980s in the northern part of the country, many Wolof and Toucouleur migrated to the Casamance and obtained large tracts of land for agriculture and horticulture. For example, in less than two years, 1980 and 1981, about 2,000 parcels of land in the neighbourhood of Ziguinchor were re-allocated exclusively to 'foreigners'. The rural councils, which were elected in the Casamance for the first time in 1979, were accused of arriving at their decisions based on party politics so that claims that had appeared justified in the eyes of the local population were not honoured (De Jong 2005).

Where loans of land were once common, they are now becoming increasingly rare or are limited to one or two years. In the latter case, the once oral contracts are often replaced by written contracts. Anyway, people only lend land to someone they trust, such as friends and relatives (Cotula and Toulmin 2004; Crousse, Mathieu, and Seck 1991; Schoonmaker Freudenberger 1992; Touré and Seck 2005). In the case of conflicts occurring over loans of land, the rural council generally grants the borrowed plot, if cultivated for more than two years, to the borrower. If the land owner appeals to 'traditional' authorities, their decision is quite often overruled. If the rural council accepts this, which happens for all kinds of social-cultural and political reasons, it is knowingly acting in contravention of the spirit of the National Domain Law.

Although the law expressly forbids the selling of land in the national domain, an active land market occurs in areas where new dynamics of land tenure are triggered by the process of urbanisation.[37] This is for instance the case in the Niayes region. The coastal Niayes is a unique ecological zone stretching from Dakar to Saint-Louis with rich soils particularly favourable for horticulture. The area is characterised by high population density as the result of natural growth and increased migration flows. Especially near Dakar, purchasing land has long been a common phenomenon. Buyers purchase land directly from village chiefs and the traditional 'owners' of the land. Many of them are so-called 'Sunday farmers': civil servants and merchants living in the capital and producing mangos and citrus fruit as a supplementary income. Since such transactions are illegal, it is hard to evaluate the actual number of sales. In areas such as the Niayes, numerous conflicts have arisen as local people oppose the intrusion of 'outsiders'.

The rural community of Yène provides another example of selling land to outsiders. Yène is a gathering of nine villages located on the Atlantic Ocean coast at a distance of about 50 kilometres from the capital Dakar. Part of the rural community belongs to the national domain and another part to public domain (*domaine public maritime*). Because of the proximity of Dakar and its location by the sea, Yène is becoming very touristy as well as becoming a residential zone. Village heads, local

notables, and also councillors are selling plots to rich town-dwellers for
high prices.[38] Knowing that sales are illegal, they insist that they are
just selling the expenses made by them on the plot. The beneficiary receives a *acte de cession* often signed by the president of the rural council
(who declared by the way that he feels obliged to do so since the owners are influential local notables and the buyers are often important politicians or famous people, but above all very rich). This document is
said to provide a *droit d'occupation*. In an interview with the son of one
of the village chiefs who sold all the family plots, he said:

> Partout ici il y a des problèmes avec le domaine national, mais
> l'Etat n'intervient pas. Les habitants sont protégés des ventes
> sauf si un ministre ou un commerçant veut ton terrain et que tu
> es pauvre. En ce cas tu veux bien vendre ton terrain. C'est ce
> que notre père a fait. Tous ses fils se sont alors réunis parce
> qu'ils considèrent que ces terrains font partie de la propriété de
> la famille. Mais tant que le vieux est là, nous ne pouvons rien
> faire. Donc il vend tout ce qu'il peut vendre. Nous ne savons
> même pas ce qu'il a fait avec tout cet argent. Mais après sa mort
> on va protester.[39]

Yène is one of the numerous areas in modern Senegal where the value
of land is increasing rapidly, giving rise to illegal land transactions with
the silent or open complicity of rural councillors. Sellers and buyers
both have to face insecurity. However, it sometimes happens that rural
councils and farmer organisations try to get involved in land use negotiations when urban expansion on farmland occurs. A telling experience in the 1990s took place in the rural community of Fandène on
the outskirts of Thiès, a rapidly growing town only 70 km from Dakar.[40] Together with the rural council and organisations in which rural
and urban representatives were represented, and with the legal support
from an NGO, a number of strategies have been designed to achieve
greater security of land tenure for the inhabitants of the rural community. First of all, general data were collected about the history of land
use development in the community as well as the land tenure status of
the inhabitants. Subsequently, it was recommended that farmers may
apply to the municipal authorities of Thiès to parcel out rural plots on
the outskirts of the town, either as a collective or as an individual and
to enter into a process of registration. A second option was to negotiate
cultivation contracts within the gazetted forest with the Water and Forestry Service. This interesting experience was made possible by the in-
filtration of the rural council by leaders of popular organisations to prevent it being taken over by politicians. Unfortunately, the process has

been hampered by bureaucratisation and obstructed by government representatives and politicians despite the initial good intentions.[41]

Towards a new land reform

The general discontent with the land and administrative reforms resulted in an animated debate on the future developments of the Senegalese land tenure regime. When in 2000 Abdou Diouf, the successor of Léopold Sédar Senghor – the initiator of the 64 land reform – was defeated in the presidential election, Senegalese socialism was no longer the ideology of the regime. The *Parti socialiste,* in power since independence, was forced to go into opposition and is no longer represented in the National Assembly since the elections in 2007. The new president Abdoulaye Wade and his party, the *Parti Démocratique Sénégalaise* (PDS), take a clearly neo-liberal stance. With regard to the rural sector, the new authorities are convinced that smallholder farmers use archaic and unproductive farming methods. Abdoulaye Wade decided to modernise agriculture and developed the OMEGA plan. This plan sees family farming as starved of capital, deprived of access to technological innovation, and trapped in a spiral of low productivity and falling incomes (Tan and Guèye 2005:46). The process of formulating a new agrarian policy resulted in 2004 in a draft framework agricultural law (*Loi d'orientation agricole*), including a reform of the legislation on land tenure. For the first time ever, the government decided to discuss its proposals with stakeholder representatives organised in the national co-ordinating committee for farmers (*Comité National de Coordination et de Concertation des Ruraux*, CNRS). The CNRS set up decentralised discussions and a national workshop, resulting in a long list of amendments, and succeeded in resisting some elements of the draft (Faye 2008). Ultimately, a new framework law on agro-sylvo-pastoral development (*Loi d'orientation agro-sylvo-pastoral*) was adopted in May 2004, taking into account most of the concerns of the CNRS (Niang and Dieng 2004:6; Tan and Guèye 2005:3; Touré and Seck 2005:43). Nevertheless, the new law was criticised by Sylla (2004):

> The law juxtaposes two visions of agriculture: family-run farms on the one hand, and industrial and commercial farming on the other. (...) Reading between the lines and judging by the preamble to the bill, it seems that family-run farming is seen as obsolete and agri-business is to be prioritised. (...) The framework law does have the merit of recognising pastoral activity as a valid mode of productive land use – filling the gap in the legislation.

(...) The most sensitive issue in this law, land reform, has been postponed until some future date.

If we look at the framework law itself, the following dispositions are relevant. In article 22, paragraph 1, the new law stipulates that 'the definition of a land tenure policy and a reform of the law on the national domain will be indispensable for the agrarian, forestry and pastoral development and for the modernisation of the agrarian sector'. The same article specifies in paragraph 2 that 'Land tenure policy will be oriented by the following guidelines: the protection of the exploitation rights of rural actors and the tenure rights of rural communities, a limited alienability of land in order to permit the mobility that favours the creation of more viable farm units, the transmissibility of land to successors in order to encourage durable investment in family farms, and the use of land as collateral for obtaining credit'. Paragraph 3 further spells out that 'land tenure reform aims at tenure security for agrarian endeavours for persons and rural communities, the promotion of private investment in agriculture, the provision of sufficient financial resources as well as competent personnel to the state and to local collectivities for efficacious, equitable and sustainable management of natural resources and the lifting of land tenure constraints on agrarian, rural, urban and industrial development'. These proposals perfectly fit the analysis we have developed in the foregoing, but they only boil down to wishful thinking. The land tenure reform that was to be carried through in 2006 according to article 23 has as yet not seen the light and will not see the light within the two years after its promulgation, as foreseen by law. Indeed, the national commission to reform the land law was only established by the Presidency in 2006, and farmer organisations form a small minority in this commission. Faye (2008:10) is probably right when he argues that 'there is no doubt that those in favour of privatising land at rural people's expense will return to the attack'.

The debate must go on![42]

To some extent, Senegal was far ahead of other former French colonies in Africa in 1964, when it adopted the National Domain Law and thereafter progressively introduced administrative reforms for its implementation. At first glance, it could be argued that Senegal's road to a new tenure regime constituted an interesting 'third way', harmonising formal law and customary land rights, which according to current thinking on tenure security should be the appropriate solution for rural Africa (Lavigne Delville 2000:97). And indeed, the national domain system has its virtues without doubt.

In the first place, the land and administrative reforms mark an important step forward in promoting democracy in the rural areas. Rural land is administered by the rural communities through a deliberative organ, the rural council and its president, both elected by universal vote. Those rural councils have the power to implement the land reform in a flexible way, taking into account local circumstances and beliefs. Second, with this law the peasantry was freed from the payment of fees and, at the same time, submitted to an objective situation which conferred rights and guarantees as a counterpart to obligations, essentially consisting in making productive use of the land. The rights and guarantees vary from one zone to another. Third, the decision taken in 1964 to keep the peasants who effectively exploit the land in place already reveals the desire to assure their stability following the principle that this stability of users of the national domain depends on their own effort. As long as productive use is made of the land, the allocation is for an undetermined period of time. Accordingly, in 1964 the idea of individual and collective security of tenure, following the reasoning about productive use was retained. Stability was to be assured as long as individuals and groups complied with the criteria of productive use. The national domain regime submits the ancient customary lands to a uniform, modern, and secular law. The 1964 lawmaker gave the state, the master of agrarian as well as of general economic development, the means of action to achieve its goals. The objective of the lawmaker was to restore the African dimension of tenure. There was no intention to de-possess effective occupiers to the benefit of the state, but to deny any rights to those who do not personally till the land and to abolish land rents. The inhabitants of village lands, the members of the collectivity present on the land, were to be given priority in its use. Land, as an object of labour, was to be put at the disposition of those who effectively till it. The peasantry was to be attached to the village land in order to encourage endogenous development. At the same time, lands in the national domain are considered a collective asset that has to be preserved for the common good. The repartition of the national domain into several zones, as well as the possibilities to withdraw parts from village land for the cause of public or general interest, is meant to serve sustainable development. On paper, as long as the pressure on land is not too high, the land and administrative reforms seem to provide a relative stability for smallholder farmers. They have use rights as long as they continue to exploit their plots, and those rights may be transferred through inheritance under the condition that the rural council receives an official request from the inheritors of the deceased and are convinced that they will continue to cultivate the plot. This stability should also be assured by the formal interdiction to sell lands of the national domain.

However, as has been shown above, there is a gap between this ideal picture and reality, and the very least we may conclude is that the Senegalese tenure reform has had mixed effects on security of tenure for smallholder farmers. In the more remote areas they continue to apply their local (customary but continuously evolving) land rules, even when inconsistent with the legislation. In areas where land is increasingly gaining monetary value, the official law is violated more and more, in particular with regard to the prohibition of land sales, and land-grabbing by elites has become a general phenomenon.

The land and administrative reforms introduced from 1964 onwards were in our opinion rightly praised for their originality and flexibility, and their attempts towards an approach which is democratic and consistent with local socio-cultural values. But quite shortly after the introduction of the land reform, and especially after the election of the first rural councils, a flow of studies were published to highlight the many malfunctions and unintended effects of the reform. As has been shown before, we also noticed that the land tenure system provides evidence of many institutional flaws creating confusion and fostering tenure insecurity. Over time, political and religious leaders obtained a strong hold over the decisions by the rural councils. Although councils sometimes arrived at occasional compromises trying to incorporate local tenure rules and customs into statutory law, they failed for a variety of reasons to create a transparent and predictable set of new land tenure rules. But it seems too easy to blame only the rural councillors. As Cernea (1994:189) rightly states: 'The local level derives strength not just from its "localness" and self containment, but from the extent to which the supralocal levels stand behind it.' Ultimately, we have to conclude that the reforms seem to be unsatisfactorily suited to address the galloping urbanisation of Senegal and to face the requirements of a modern agricultural development, both in terms of family farming and agri-business.

The debate on the future of Senegal's land tenure system is still incomplete, especially since the land reform announced in 2004, in the law on agro-sylvo-pastoral development, has been postponed. Unlike the situation in the years after independence, the farmers are now better organised, and their views are sometimes taken into account by the national authorities. They will try to strongly defend their rights against the tendency of the neo-liberal government to prioritise commercial farming and agri-business at the expense of their own tenure security. The future will tell us whether Senegal is again ahead of other African countries by being capable of facing the challenges and dilemmas involved in land policy and law-making. Will Senegal find a new 'third way' in land tenure and be able to combine the requirements of modern agricultural development with a human-centred approach to land rights? Or will Senegal just follow the tendency to privatise land laws in accordance with the call by Hernando de Soto?

Notes

1   I am grateful to Abdoulaye Dièye and Fatimata Diallo for their valuable contribution to the research, and to Willem Assies for his translation into English of the first draft of this article.
2   See Dièye 2004.
3   Not all ethnicities had the same hierarchical tenure structure. The Serer and Diola are considered to have different systems. See Pélissier 1996.
4   Bulletin d'Administration du Sénégal, 1855, p. 257.
5   Décret du 20 juillet 1900 relatif au régime de la propriété foncière au Sénégal et dépendances, BOC, 1900, p. 112.
6   Registration was obligatory in only two cases: on the one hand in the case of alienation or concession of domain land and, on the other, if an immovable good until then held according native custom for the first time was the object of a contract drawn up according to French legal rules.
7   Décret du 24 juillet 1906 portant organisation du régime de la propriété dans les colonies et territoires relevant du gouvernement général de l'AOF, BOC, 1906, p. 681.
8   J.O., AOF 29-04/1933, p. 426.
9   Décret du 8 octobre 1925 instituant un mode de constatation des droits fonciers des indigènes en AOF, BOC., p. 1647.
10 Décret No. 55-580 du 20 mai 1955 portant réorganisation foncière et domaniale en A. O.F. et en A.E.F., J.O. A.O.F. 1956, p. 1806; Décret No. 56-704 du 10 juillet 1956 fixant les conditions d'application du décret No. 55-580 du 20 mai 1955 portant réorganisation foncière et domaniale en A.O.F. et en A.E.F., J.O.R.F., 18 juillet 1956.
11 Obviously land has never been possessed in an uncontested way. Since land tenure is related to social relationships, there have always been many land conflicts.
12 Since the establishment of a general legal framework (loi-cadre), the colony of Senegal enjoyed certain autonomy in managing local affairs.
13 Cited from presentation of the summary report by the president of the Study Group, Mr. Karim Gaye to the president of the Council Mr. Mamadou. Archives Nationales Sénégalaises (A.N.S.), p. 1, 174, 1 à 16 Tome II: Introduction.
14 Rapport du comité d'études économiques, Tome II: Rapport de la commission du secteur rural.
15 Decentralisation in Senegal goes back to colonial times. In 1872 the communes of Saint-Louis and Gorée were created, followed by Rufisque and Dakar in 1880 and 1887. Together they are known as the self-governing 'four communes'.
16 In 1960 it was estimated that some 20,000 written property titles existed.
17 In this respect Galvan (2004:224) talks about 'one grand national narrative of nostalgia'.
18 JORS (Journal Official de la République du Sénégal) of 20 September 1976.
19 JORF (Journal Officiel de la République française) of 29 April 1933.
20 Loi no. 64-46 du 17 juin 1964 relative au domaine national.
21 Laws and regulations make no explicit reference to gender.
22 These conditions have become less rigid with the adoption in 1972 of a decree defining them (Décret no. 72-1288 du 27 Octobre 1972 relatif aux conditions d'affection et de désaffection des terres du domaine national comprises dans les communautés rurales).

23 See Madior WADE and other verdicts (CS du Sénégal, 24 mars 1982 – Madior WADE. RIPAS no. 4, avril-juin 1982).
24 Loi no 72-25 du 19 avril relative aux communautés rurales, JORS du 13 mai 1972, p. 755 e.s.
25 Over time, the number of rural communities has increased. For instance, in 2002 Senegal comprised 320 rural communities, in February 2008 324 and since August 2008 340 (Décret 202-166 du 21 février 2002 fixant le ressort territorial et le chef-lieu des régions et départements; Projet de loi du 1er février 2008 modifiant le découpage administratif du Sénégal). According to the local press, the government once again created a considerable number of new rural communities in January 2009 (Sud Quotidien January 19, 2009).
26 However, in some cases the local officials actually used their power to disapprove a decision of a rural council. See Ribot 1999.
27 All laws and decrees concerning the decentralisation reform are collected in République du Sénégal 2003.
28 Schoonmaker Freudenberger 1991.
29 http://nettali.net/spip.php?article3053, consulted 11-5-2007.
30 Decree no. 87-720 of 4 June 1987.
31 Article 29 of Decree no. 64-573 of 30 July 1964.
32 Article 2 of Law no. 76-67 of 2 July 1976 regarding expropriation on ground of public utility.
33 Law no. 64-46, article 15 and Decree no. 72-1288, articles 11,12, and 14.
34 See also Lavigne Delville 2003:102.
35 See Diop Tine and Sy (2003) for a comparison between Wolof, Serer and Peul.
36 For recent research about Serer farmers, see Galvan 2007.
37 According to Faye (2008:12) 'in Senegal 50 per cent of the population have been living in urban areas since 2005'.
38 In recent years leaflets are distributed in rich residential quarters in Dakar in which houses and plots situated at the coast are offered.
39 Interview by Gerti Hesseling made in May 2007. For other examples in Yène including sales of land pertaining to the public domain, see also Diallo 2008.
40 Information is extracted from Tall and Tine 2002.
41 Recently, the government launched two mega-projects, the construction of a new international airport and the creation of a special economic zone, both involving national domain land. From 2007 onwards, IED Afrique (Innovations Environnement et Développement en Afrique) is involved in an externally funded programme of legal empowerment for the benefit of the farmers concerned by the projects. See Kane 2008:83-91.
42 Subtitle in the article of Sylla (2004:19).

Tenure security in the periphery of Ziguinchor: The impact of politics and social relations

Gerti Hesseling and John Eichelsheim

Introduction

Until 1964, land use in Senegal was dealt with by the different ethnic groups and their respective land tenure systems. In 1964, Senegal introduced a new land law, the National Domain Law or *Loi relative au Domaine National*. Senegal was the first former French colony in Africa to adopt a land reform. Although this law aimed mainly at rural development, it also contained regulations regarding urban land tenure. Indeed, the 1964 law divides the national domain in four categories, one of them being the urban zones. The law was considered innovative since it did not try to unify the various colonial and customary land tenure systems in Senegal but recognised the existence of local use rights and left it to local institutions to work out the practical details at the local level (Golan 1990:20-21). To stimulate more private investment in cities, the government enlarged the possibilities for a citizen to acquire land as private property. Until now, this option has scarcely been used in cities with enough space to expand and to absorb, virtually without effort, the great rush of new urbanites. Rather, urbanites and urban migrants looking for a plot or a house followed unwritten rules and customs as they knew them from their village, and accommodated these rules, when necessary, to the urban context.

For years, the national and local governments paid little attention to the legal and policy aspects of urban land tenure and housing, and cities developed without any significant intervention on the part of the government. However, from the 1970s onwards the government has promulgated specific legislation on urban land and has started urban development plans including allotment (*lotissement*) and re-allocation programmes. This also happened in Ziguinchor, the capital of the southern region of Senegal, the Casamance. This is the most fertile region of Senegal, but as a result of one of the strangest legacies of the colonial era – the creation of the tiny country of Gambia situated like an enclave within Senegal – the Casamance is practically cut off from the rest of Senegal. In the 1980s a rebellious movement, the *Mouvement des Forces Démocratiques de la Casamance* (MFDC), demanded separation from Senegal, and the conflict quickly degenerated into a full-blown civil war with many casualties on both sides. In spite of many attempts to arrive at a peace pact (the last pact reached was in December 2004), fighting continues to flare up. Although this drawn-out conflict has a complicated background, it is now generally accepted that one of the origins of the conflict lies in land disputes, which began to arise during the implementation of a re-allocation programme in Ziguinchor.[1]

In this chapter we analyse the effects of the re-allocation programme on the life of the inhabitants of Ziguinchor. In the first part, we will give some details about the law relating to urban land, and we will introduce Ziguinchor and the re-allocation programme undertaken in this city. The next part is dedicated to the organisation of the Diola society – the dominant ethnic group in the Casamance – and the transition of the tutorial *adjiati* system from rural to urban settings. We will describe how both the urban environment and the re-allocation programme transform and politicise the position of the *adjiati* and the relationship with his followers. We will then analyse the effects of the re-allocation programme on urban people's tenure security and on the individualisation of urban land rights. We will conclude that in the peripheral areas where the re-allocation programmes have taken place, hardly anybody has obtained a legally valid title. Despite this lack of formal recognition of their land rights, most people regard their tenure as quite secure. This can to a certain extent be explained by their erroneous belief that their 'tickets' or other *petits papiers* provide them with a legally secure title, but also by their *de facto* secure tenure resulting from the acts and attitude of the municipal government. At the same time, they realise that protection of rights based on a clientelistic system is always to a certain extent insecure and vulnerable. The data derive from research undertaken since the 1980s (Eichelsheim 1990; Hesseling 1983, 1986, 1992). The research area was most recently visited in 2007.

Law relating to urban land

In Senegal, specific legislation on urban land, housing, and town planning dates from the 1970s. This is not to say that before the 1970s the urban areas were in a legal vacuum. They were certainly not, but the applicable legal arrangements were mainly of colonial origin and rarely referred to the town planning aspects of fast growing cities. The Senegalese urban land legislation is found mainly in three texts: the *Loi relative au Domaine National* (National Domain Law), the *Code de l'Urbanisme* (Urbanisation Code), and an order relating to requests for building permits in urban zones (*Arrêté relatif aux demandes d'autorisation de construire dans les zones urbaines sur des terrains faisant partie du domaine national).*

The National Domain Law was adopted by the Senegalese legislature in 1964. In the law, 'national domain' (*domaine national*) is defined in a negative sense, namely as all land that is not registered in the land books, i.e. land that is not 'state property' (*domaine de l'Etat*) and for which no private title exists. With this act, all land which was held under customary law passed into the control of the state. The state does not consider itself to be the owner but merely the custodian of this land; individuals only have non-transferable 'use rights'. This means that, among other things, the land may not be sold; only the buildings and other investments (wells, orchards, and other such improvements) are transferable. The national domain is subdivided into four categories, the first of which is designated urban zones (*zones urbaines*). This covers municipal territory that has been established by law. The other three categories are agricultural zones (*zones des terroirs*), classified zones (*zones classées*), and pioneer zones (*zones pionnières*).[2] Land within the national domain can be converted to state property.[3] This is frequently the case in the periphery of rapidly growing cities in Senegal. The state then instigates a process for the expropriation of the land for the general good; the land is thereafter registered in the name of the state (thus falling within the category of state property). All existing rights to the land are thereby abrogated. Damages are only possible insofar as buildings are concerned, but not when the land has been built on illegally.[4]

For the individual occupant the distinction is important, since his rights to the land differ. The allocation of land pertaining to the national domain to any individual can never be considered to include property rights. The occupant only has 'use rights', which are not clearly defined by the law. Inhabitants living on state property need to have a settlement permit or a long lease. A permit is a precarious title which authorises the holder to settle on a plot for a determined period. Since these permits can be withdrawn without compensation after three months' notice, it hardly offers any better security to the holder than the 'use rights'. Long lease is an agreement between the state and the leaseholder under which the latter pays rent to the state in return for the legal right to occupy a plot within the state property for a period of between eighteen and 50 years. Although it offers much better security to the holder, the long lease is hardly ever applied in a city like Ziguinchor because of the required obligations for the leaseholder.[5]

The national domain of Senegal accounts for more than 95 per cent of the national territory. Another three per cent of the national territory consists of state property, leaving two per cent of the land in the hands of individuals who had acquired private title to their land holdings prior to 1964.

In the same year that the National Domain Law was passed (1964), a *Code de l'Urbanisme* also came into being. In article 1, the aim of the urbanisation policy is put into words:

> The urbanisation policy in Senegal has as its aim the integration of the progressive and provisional arrangements of settlements in a general policy of economic development and social progress. It is leading, notably through its rational utilisation of land, to the creation of a framework for a propitious life for all of the population, and to a harmonious development on physical, economic, cultural and social level.[6]

In pursuance of this policy, town plans were to be drawn up, including plot layouts for the reallocation of rights in land in residential areas. The Code also decrees that whoever wants to build a house in a town has to be in possession of both a permit to settle as well as a building permit. An order (arrêté) of 1970 regulates how one should go about getting a building permit for a piece of land in the national domain.[7] A permit to settle is only granted after the building plans have been approved. It is non-transferable and lapses if construction has not commenced within two years after the initial granting of the permit.

Finally, in 1996 a number of laws and decrees were adopted that aimed at more decentralisation, transferring competencies from the state to local institutions such as regions, city councils and rural councils (République du Sénégal 2003). According to these regulations, allocation programmes and the distribution of residential plots are no longer the responsibility of the state but of the municipal council.

Ziguinchor

In Senegal, as in most African countries, an extremely rapid urbanisation process has taken place. Senegal is one of the most urbanised countries in sub-Saharan Africa: 46 per cent of the Senegalese people now live in cities. Although the capital Dakar attracts 55 per cent of the urban population, intermediary cities like Ziguinchor have also grown considerably. At the turn of the last century, the population of Ziguinchor was about 1,000, in 1960 it had risen to 30,000 inhabitants, and by 2004 the population was approximately 170,000.[8] The annual increase of more than five per cent can be attributed half to natural processes and half to the influx of immigrants from the surrounding villages and from other parts of Senegal. With this rapid growth in the city's population has come an increasing demand for building plots. A great area of agricultural land has been converted to residential uses. The city of Ziguinchor is still characterised by housing plots of some 400 square metres, broad roads with trees on both sides, and single-story houses. It is therefore not surprising that land nowadays has become rather scarce in the periphery of the city. Between the 1960s and 1980s, Ziguinchor expanded outside its central districts with little or no involvement from the local authorities. Because of the constant growth of the population and the comparatively low supply of legalised buildings by local authorities, people looking for housing plots have been driven to the periphery of the town.

Until 1964 land use in Senegal was dealt with by the different ethnic groups and their respective land tenure systems. Thus, the land of the ever-expanding city of Ziguinchor belonged to the inhabitants of the surrounding Diola villages. The Diola form the largest ethnic group in the region and an important ethnic group in the municipality of Ziguinchor.[9] Because the local government paid little attention to the way in which the town expanded, a great variety of so-called 'spontaneous' settlements developed in the periphery of the town. With permission from Diola landlords, one could easily acquire a plot of land. As we will show later, however, this 'anarchic' expansion took place in a thoroughly organised manner.

In 1964, the National Domain Law divided all land into three categories. These categories can easily be distinguished in the situation of land tenure in the municipality of Ziguinchor.

1. Land owned privately *(titres privés)*, concentrated mainly in the centre of the city.
2. Land which is state property: the greater part of urbanised space in Ziguinchor was registered in the name of the state.
3. Land which pertains to the national domain: all land that is not registered as private or state property. This affects mainly the western part of Ziguinchor, the less urbanised area of the city.

In the 1970s, the local authorities decided to reorganise the land situation in Ziguinchor to end the proliferation of unregulated 'anarchic' town development and replace it with sound town-planning regulation, marking residential areas as well as reserving space for roads, drainage systems, waterways, and other public facilities. This was intended to enhance the living quality and 'favour an active social life' (République du Sénégal 1980, 1991). The local authorities targeted both older districts of Ziguinchor, which are state property, and newer, 'spontaneously' developing residential areas on national domain land. The reallocation programmes were to be done on the basis of new plot layouts. A plot layout is a plan showing the parcelling out or the subdivi-

sion of the land into individual plots as well as the position of the access roads and footpaths. The procedure was relatively simple. In principle, every family head who was able to prove that he lived with his family in the district was eligible for a plot of about 400 m. To subdivide
the land according to the plot layout, however, approximately 60 per
cent of the existing houses had to be demolished. Not surprisingly,
quite a lot of the re-allocations developed into disputes, of which relatively few were brought to court (Hesseling 1990/91).

After the area was surveyed, a Plot Allocation Board was supposed to
supply each family head with a piece of paper ('ticket') with the number of the plot and his name. Most ticket-holders think that such a paper confers ownership of the land to them, but nothing could be
farther from the truth. They additionally have to go through a long and
fairly costly procedure to obtain permission to settle (*permis d'occuper*)
and, should they wish to build a brick house, a building permit (*autorisation de construire*) as well. Especially in the peripheral areas of the
town, very few of such ticket-holders have ever started these procedures.

As said previously, in Ziguinchor re-allocation programmes were executed both in areas where the land is state property and in areas where
the land falls under the category of national domain land. Due to the
different rights that can be obtained in these two categories of land,
the allocation programmes have a different effect on the respective
landowners, especially with regard to the possibility of requiring private
title. When a plot is located on state property and the beneficiary has a
building permit, he can ask for a lease (*bail emphytéotique*). The cadastre first prepares an official report of the value of the investments
made, and after a long process the lease can be transformed into a private title. But if the plot is part of the national domain, the state cannot
give out such a lease. The National Domain Law provides for a conversion of urban (re-allocated) national domain land into state property,
but to date no land in Ziguinchor that belonged to the national domain
and was the subject of the re-allocation programmes of the 1970s and
1980s has been converted into state property. This has only been done
in the case of some new and recent re-allocation programmes. Nevertheless, anybody can deposit an application for a lease, whether his/her
plot is on national domain land or on state property, and the regional
Domain Department will even register this application, although they
will not send it to Dakar for validation. The regional Domain Department nowadays even encourages citizens to ask for a lease on national
domain land, as they hope that a massive demand for leases will incite
the government to convert large parts of national domain land into
state property. This conversion would subsequently open the opportunity to obtain a lease and ultimately a private title. Despite this encour-

agement, not many people apply for a lease on national domain land. They do not see the use of paying the registration fees and the first year of the lease rent only to wait until the land on which their plot lies is converted into state property.

It should be mentioned that no data are available with regard to the number of people involved in a re-allocation programme who have succeeded in obtaining a private title following a lease. Registration figures show that land titles have only sporadically been registered in the last few decades. Until recently, there were considerably fewer than 3,000 land titles (*titres fonciers*) in the whole of the Ziguinchor region, an area of more than 7000 square kilometres and approximately 450,000 inhabitants. Most of these titles were registered prior to the introduction of the National Domain Law in 1964 or in the delay granted by this law. In 2006 the Domain Department registered only 190 new *titres fonciers*, mostly in the new urban district of Ziguinchor, Goumel. Here, at the end of the 1990s, a large area of rice fields on the outer confines of the town was divided into residential lots and converted from national domain into state property.

In sum, for people inhabiting a plot which belongs to the national domain, it is legally impossible to obtain a lease and subsequently a land title in order to have absolute tenure security in the form of private property. This requires a conversion of the land to state property, which has only taken place in a few areas that have recently undergone re-allocation programmes. In those areas, some land titles have been registered. It seems, however, that even in areas that have been state property for a much longer period, few land titles have been registered. This might imply that a simple conversion of land without a clear interest and commitment of the government to stimulate privatisation cannot be expected to have much impact.

Diola land tenure: The *adjiati* relationship in rural and urban settings

In order to understand the frame of reference for an urban migrant settling on Diola land in Ziguinchor, we must know how the land tenure system operates in a Diola village. The Diola have a long tradition of sedentary agriculture activities, mainly consisting of rice production. The best rice fields are those bordering the Casamance River and its tributaries, threatened by the salt water of the tidal Casamance River. These low fields, which have a high value because they are fairly scarce, require a lot of manpower to maintain the dikes. The hydraulic system is controlled by a small group of village elders, and this form of rice cultivation is centuries old. The fact that many generations invested their labour in the maintenance of these fields gives an extra dimension to their value. The Diola are more strongly attached to their land than groups practising shifting agriculture.

As is the case in many African countries, this also explains the existence of the following feature in the social organisation of Diola society, based on the control over land: a sharp distinction between the indigenous population and strangers (both from inside and outside the ethnic group). Over the years, each Diola village has witnessed both immigration and emigration flows. Those who control the land also control certain aspects of these migration movements and especially the location pattern of newcomers. These newcomers are in every way inferior to indigenes when it comes to settling religious and political matters. In Diola society the complex network of relations between indigenes and migrants is called the *adjiati* relationship. In these local patterns of interaction, the elders of the lineages control the newcomer's access to land by acting as host (*adjiati*).

The *adjiati* is a host who gives shelter and food to a newcomer in his own house. The guest or stranger (*adjaoura*) finds in the house of his *adjiati* his first shelter and access to the society he wants to become a member of; his first necessities of life are cared for. He has a solid basis from which he can explore the environment (social as well) and search for the possibilities for a new home. Then the *adjiati* provides his guest with the opportunities to settle: he gives him a plot of land to build his own house or otherwise puts him in contact with another elder who is prepared to cede land: the *adjiati* becomes landlord or 'middle man'. It is important that the *adjiati* establishes all new relations for the *adjaoura*. In exchange for shelter, mediation and access to land, the *adjaoura* has to acknowledge the social superiority of his *adjiati*. He has to treat him as some sort of father.

The so-called 'spontaneous' expansions of Ziguinchor originated mostly in the way described above. These districts have their own dynamics in patterns of organisation, in which control over land plays a crucial role (see also Eichelsheim 1986). The inhabitants of these 'spontaneous' districts consider their plot of land, on which they build their home, as a safe place, despite the fact that these places of settlement are not legalised or recognised as such by the national authorities or those of the municipality. The feeling of security of its inhabitants derives from the *adjiati* relationship. They feel protected by their *adjiati*, to whom they have fulfilled their obligations, or still do.

After the adoption of the National Domain Law, all land subject to customary law formally became national domain land and thus passed into the control of the state. This happened also in the areas of extension in the rapidly expanding city of Ziguinchor, where Diola landlords from surrounding villages lost their control over the land to the state.

At first, this new legislation did not have much effect on access to and regulation of land, but in the 1970s the municipal authorities decided to legalise and upgrade the 'spontaneous' settlements and started the re-allocation programme, in which they discarded the existing local rules. The case of Abdoulaye Diedhiou, discussed below, shows that those rules are nevertheless highly resilient. Even today, people gain access to land through *koudjiati* (plural of *adjiati*) without state interference. It also indicates the changes the *adjiati* relationship undergoes when transplanted into an urban setting, where law and politics of the state converge with the Diola system of norms and political leadership.

The case of Abdoulaye Diedhiou: From *adjaoura* to *adjiati*

Abdoulaye Diedhiou is a Diola from the village of Diatock, where he was born in 1939. In 1966, he wanted to settle in Ziguinchor, and in the 'spontaneous' area called Soucoupapaye he found a co-villager who was prepared to shelter him and thus become his *adjiati*. For his subsistence during the first years, Abdoulaye cultivated some rice fields in the nearby village of Niaguis. At home, in Soucoupapaye, he became more and more active in the then ruling political party, the *Parti Socialiste* (PS), and his star was rising in the hierarchy of this party. When, in the 1970s the municipality started the re-allocation programme in Soucoupapaye, Abdoulaye's *adjiati* received five official residential plots, marked parcels of land with a cadastre number. From him, Abdoulaye received two of the plots. But since he also wanted a plot for his two sons, he was one short. To resolve this problem, he decided to sell one of the plots he just received and to lease the other one. With that money, he bought a much bigger parcel in a not yet legalised district in the periphery of the town, Lyndiane.

There he met Sidy Sidibé, a high-ranking official in the Municipal Council. As the son of the landlord of Lyndiane, Sidibé occupied a large parcel of three hectares belonging to his patrilineage. Anticipating the re-allocation programme in Lyndiane, he decided to subdivide his parcel into smaller plots and to sell them. As a civil servant he knew that it was prohibited to sell his land, because it was located within the national domain. To avoid direct involvement in the sale, he therefore asked Abdoulaye Diedhiou to look for people interested in buying a plot and to handle the transactions. For his work he could keep one of the plots.

Abdoulaye Diedhiou grasped this opportunity with both hands. He had no problem in finding potential buyers amongst his friends and relatives. They trusted him because he had close relations in town via his political friends. He sold all the sites to relatives, friends, villagers, and co-inhabitants from Soucoupapaye in no time. After a while, people even started coming to him asking if he had plots to sell or if he knew somebody selling plots of land.

These transactions passed so smoothly that other landlords asked him to sell land for them. The agricultural value of these fields had decreased because they had been fallow for some years due to a lack of rainfall in the past few years and because fewer members of the patrilineage were prepared or able to cultivate the fields. And, after all, in the rhetoric of Diola social organisation, the elders of the patrilineages were considered to keep control over the fields, despite the fact they were 'sold' for money. This money was seen solely as compensation for the usufruct of the fields. In short, there were many reasons to 'lend' a small part of the land to strangers who wanted to pay for it. The landlords left all the work to Abdoulaye Diedhiou: he divided the land into plots, sought for buyers and established contacts between the buyers and the landlord. As compensation, he always received a piece of the land.

Gradually, Abdoulaye Diedhiou obtained a monopoly of all land transactions in the area. Buyers considered his good contacts with the outer world (read: prominent political figures who played an important role in the municipality) as a guarantee for their high investments in – officially illegal – transactions. In addition, he came to be considered the *adjiati* of all newcomers and the highest traditional authority to whom they could turn in case of problems or disputes.

Money was not the only requirement for gaining access to a building site in the new district of the city. Abdoulaye's monopoly allowed him to sell the plots of land selectively. Many of his transactions appear to be based on relations of trust or rather on relations of kinship (putative), because that is what the *adjiati* relationships were based on.

Abdoulaye Diedhiou profited greatly from his role as an intermediary. By selectively giving access to land, he could surround himself with people who would follow him in his political activities. This enabled him to determine the voting results in the new district of Lyndiane-Golomoute. As a result, he became good friends with executives of the largest political party. The party leaders nominated him district chief, which gave him considerable financial advantages. Furthermore, at the recommendation of party leaders, he took control over the dispensary in the district, and he built a coranic school on one of the plots given to him as a reward for his mediation. In short, he became a person to be reckoned with in the district.

The case of Abdoulaye Diedhiou shows how urban immigrants first seek provisional shelter, from which they investigate the possibilities to obtain a permanent and strong foothold in the city. The last stage is building a family house, which in turn will serve to provide shelter for young people from the surrounding villages who are attracted to the town by schooling and job opportunities. Thus, members of a family and villagers who already live in the city become more and more important as providers of first shelter in the urban environment. An immigrant (*adjaoura*) will always maintain contacts with the *adjiati* who opens the way to the city for him, even after he has obtained his own plot of land. This example demonstrates that the *adjiati* relationship continues to function in the urban context. Abdoulaye Diedhiou, who started being Demba's *adjaoura*, became the *adjiati* for many inhabitants in the new district of Lyndiane-Golomoute.

The *adjiati-adjaoura* relationship is not only about land. The *adjiati* also seeks other means to create personal bonds with his *adjaoura*. In urban areas, these are found in his contacts with the 'outside world': with local government officials and political party leaders and in his connections on a regional and national level. This implies a politicisation of the *adjiati-adjaoura* relationship. In Ziguinchor, the provision of first shelter and access to land, as the most important elements in the *adjiati-adjaoura* relationship, are thus gradually substituted by a smooth introduction into the urban environment. The wider one's network of valuable contacts in the city, the more one is respected and the more one will be chosen by urban immigrants as *adjiati*. In return, the *adjaoura* contributes to the prestige of their *adjiati*.[10]

This new feature in the role of the *adjiati* in the urban context is not opposed to the traditional order. It is recognisable and acceptable for members of the traditional society as an expansion of the *adjiati*'s function, which was already, in the organisational structure of the village, the highest political authority controlling the contacts with the outer world. Problems arise, however, when the *adjiati*, out of necessity or by choice, identifies himself too much with the outer world and neglects his obligations towards his *koudjaoura* (plural of *adjaoura*). Such a conflict of interest can for instance arise during the implementation of a re-allocation programme. In the next section we will show how the new involvement of the municipal authorities in urban land planning can alter the position of *adjiati* and the relationship with their *koudjaoura*.

Municipal involvement and its effect on customary land tenure systems

In order to gain some control over the promiscuous growth of the city, municipal authorities have drawn up town plans for the city of Ziguinchor since 1969. On paper, the 'spontaneous' residential areas were restructured into small building lots for housing and spaces for roads and public use, all according to a strict grid pattern. The intention was to upgrade these 'spontaneous' settlements in several stages.

First, the individual building lots, the proposed streets and the position of public places were laid out with little concrete markers in accordance with the plan. After that, the inhabitants had one year to adapt their environment to the new division, which meant that all houses standing on the newly traced roads or public places had to be demolished by the inhabitants themselves. The Lot Allocation Board supplied each family head in the district with a written note ('ticket') stating the name of the head of the household and the number of the building lot allotted to him. Within one year, the whole reshuffle of the district should have been completed. In reality, many disputes originated from the allocations made by the Lot Allocation Board, and many people refused to demolish their houses (Hesseling 1990/91).

It appeared that local politicians from the ruling PS had a considerable say on this board (Eichelsheim 1986:53). The subdivision of the 'spontaneous' settlement areas, whereby the municipality gave the then illegal inhabitants an official building lot, appeared to be a welcome new source of capital for these politicians. The population density in these residential areas subject to subdivision was low, and many building lots were not distributed after the subdivision. Assigning fewer or sometimes even no building lots to political opponents could even increase the number of 'spare' building lots. These spare lots were then given to members of the same faction within the party or sold to other interested people. Members of the military elite who were born in Casamance, members of the higher bureaucracy from the north, and natives of Casamance who worked in Dakar or France were particularly interested in the spare official building sites. In 1983, the prices paid for these building lots rose to one million F CFA (€ 1524) or even more.

It will be clear that the results of this form of subdivision – heavily influenced by politicians and political considerations – clashed with the existent organisational structure of the district, based on customary land tenure systems. Before the subdivision, as we have seen earlier, the *adjiati* gave the usufruct of land to his *adjaoura*, and with that, according to the old Diola organisational patterns, he automatically agreed to protect his *adjaoura* as though he were his own son. The selling of land to people from outside the *koudjaoura* group was at the expense of members of that group. The needs of all members of the *koudjaoura* group had to be satisfied first before 'outsiders' could gain access to land. In addition, members were defined in a very inclusive way: sons, daughters, and all other members of kin had priority over outsiders.

Within this perspective, the position of *adjiati* becomes untenable when the roles of *adjiati* and politician meet in the same person. A politician wants to surround himself with as many followers as possible, even from the outside, whereas the *adjiati* relationship is mostly focussed on a fairly small inner circle. As described before, the politicisation of the *adjiati* relationship is not surprising: dependent followers surround the *adjiati* as he provides the usufruct of land and other favours. According to ancient traditions, he is their political authority. However, when he wishes to partake in regional and even national political processes and power struggles, his role of local political leader expands to a broader horizon. He then must answer to purely political demands, even when they may hurt his inner circle.

When, in the eyes of his *adjaoura*, the *adjiati* does not fulfil the expectations related to his role, he will lose his authority. With great effect: the *adjaoura* feels betrayed and will turn against him and his political associates. High emotions usually accompany these tensions. In Ziguinchor this resulted in a lot of land law conflicts, in which 'outsiders' – immigrants and civil servants from other parts of Senegal – played a prominent role. General aversions arose against everybody and everything not originating from the Casamance, generating large protest manifestations and violence, and ultimately even the involvement of the national army.

The accumulation of protests and violence forced the Governor, in his function as the highest representative of the government, to look for an alternative and generally accepted arbitration commission. The Diola association *Karambenór* (work together) was useful. On the one hand, its leaders were strongly related to government, as many had been civil servants in colonial times. On the other hand, since they propagandised the old values of Diola society, the members of *Karambenór* were in general well respected in the districts of Ziguinchor. Thus, the Governor nominated members of *Karambenór* to an arbitration commission, which had to evaluate all lot allocations and, if possible, resolve disputes.[11] This meant that a board of 'wise men' joined the existing administrative arbitration commission, *la Commission des Litiges*, which consisted largely of civil servants. This resulted in a new approach: members of the commission went into the districts to evaluate disputes on the spot. This was a time-consuming approach that in effect prevented the civil servants from fully cooperating, and in time they left the work completely to the members of the *Karambenór*.

Between 15 February 1982 and 5 July 1983, members of this arbitration commission evaluated 5,171 lot allocations, of which they put 1,558 cases of conflict on record. By means of on-the-spot clarification of decisions made by the Lot Allocation Board, they were able to resolve 826 disputes. Through discussion and deliberation and by examining each case thoroughly, they were able to reconcile another 696 conflicts. After this success, the Governor decided to formalise this form of approach, and on 8 July 1983 a new commission was set up: *la Grand*

Commission Administrative.[12] This commission was divided into a technical board, consisting of representatives of the Governor and the municipality and all the departments involved, and a board of 'wise men',
consisting of district heads and dignitaries and members of *Karambenór*. In this form, the preparatory work on the spot by the board of
'wise men' was given the legitimacy it needed by the technical board.

The commission succeeded in evoking the old atmosphere from the
villages: long palavers under a big tree where everybody could have his
say. In the end an elder made a proposal, mostly a compromise, which
in general was accepted unanimously. Furthermore, the commission
took into account the old claims on land and the investments made by
individuals. It is also important to notice that, in the eyes of all involved, the state was not publicly represented. The representative of the
Municipal Council in the commission acted as a dignitary and not as
an official. The elders of Karambenór solved the land disputes as the
elders in the village. The working of the commission illustrates the discrepancy between the law and its perception by the citizens.

Effects of allocation programmes

The re-allocation programmes of the 1970s and 1980s have been the
subject of research (Eichelsheim 1990; Hesseling 1992). It is striking
that some peripheral districts in Ziguinchor in which the division of
plots was heavily restructured during a re-allocation programme in the
1980s remained in some other aspects almost unchanged even twenty
years after the implementation of the re-allocation programme. For instance in the area of Sougoupapaye, revisited in 2006 and 2007, there
has been hardly any improvement of the roads and the services in the
area, and some of the salient conflicts are still unresolved or in the process of being solved. In the sections below we will look at two anticipated consequences of re-allocation programmes, the enhancement of
tenure security and the individualisation of land tenure, and analyse
the extent to which they have materialised.

Tenure security

The large majority of the people involved in re-allocation programmes
in Ziguinchor has not gone through the process of registering their
use right permits as a first step to obtaining a lease or a *titre privé* on
their urban plot. These people expressed that they felt secure enough
in the current situation. Their feeling was based on the acts and attitude of the municipal authorities and was reinforced by the possession
of the small paper ('ticket') delivered at the time by the re-allocation

commission, which shows their name and the plot number, or of other formal or informal documentary material.[13] Some of them even made investments to improve their houses. And people are continuing to look for residential plots in the area. A schoolteacher in Soucoupapaye expressed his feeling of security as follows:

> Somebody who wants to buy a building lot in town quickly bumps into a broker residing around the Cadastre Department. They will propose several locations and will accompany you to take a look. When you are interested, they present you to the owner and discussions on the price will be held. If you agree with the owner on a price, you will then discuss with the broker on what price will be the official price mentioned on the mutation papers on which you have to pay a 15 per cent tax to the Domain Department. He will then also fix his percentage on the deal, but assures you that he will take care of everything and that his interference will be very beneficial for you. You then have to fill in a pile of bureaucratic papers with many seals and present witnesses. You pay small fees for seals and paperwork for each of which you receive receipts. It all looks very official and reassuring. If at the end they give you the sealed note that the building lot is on your name, you really think you are proprietor of the land. It has cost you some money, but you now are officially landowner! Moreover, look around you. When there is a problem, for instance when your building lot is on land designated for a school or mosque, the Municipal Council will give you another building lot and will even give you some money for your investments. So why worry? You can have confidence in the transaction. This was confirmed by Insa Manga of the Urbanism Department who told me: 'When you have a building permission, you have right to compensation.'

Another inhabitant of Ziguinchor, Lansana Sambou, states that he feels secure of his tenure because his uncle succeeded in changing the name of the 'ticket' in his favour. Lansana Sambou's father, Doudou Sambou, got the famous 'ticket' from the Lot Allocation Board in 1978, a small piece of paper with the number of the building lot and his name. Doudou Sambou died in 2000, but before passing away, he said to his elder son that the lot would be his. His elder sister would be married soon and thus would have no need for it. Nothing much happened after his father's death until an uncle, working in the national agricultural research centre, advised him to change the name on the 'ticket'. Why and how was not so clear to Lansana, so he left it all to his uncle who did all that was necessary. It was the uncle who went to

the tribunal and filled in the heritage papers to obtain a death certificate, a heritage certificate, a wedding certificate, and a birth certificate.
He also went to Cadastre to pay the 20,000 Francs (€ 30.49) fee for
the four concrete markers which were used in 1978 to demarcate the
building lot. Lansana only paid the € 30.49 and received a new 'ticket'
with his name on it.

His father had not built the house with durable materials but erected
the four rooms of dried mud, as most people do in this area. According
to Lansana, because the construction was not concrete, he did not need
permission from the Municipal Council. In his opinion, the situation
is okay as it is, although he would prefer that the municipality did
something with these mud roads that become violent torrents in the
rainy season. The municipality must know all these problems, as the
district head lives only 150 metres away, just near a canyon some three
metres deep:

> The municipality does nothing and what can we do? Poor people
> like us do not frequent official instances. We prefer to stay away
> from all that. Land ownership is very complicated, demands
> much paperwork and a lot of money. Furthermore, it is very
> hierarchically structured, where only the very rich can obtain full
> possession and become richer. We only want a home, a family
> house to live in. We do not need that entire fracas. My name is
> actually mentioned on the ticket, given in 1978, on top of the
> number of this building lot. What do I want more? I keep it in a
> metal box under my bed.

Another inhabitant of Soucoupapaye, Sidy Soly, never paid anything,
and yet he claims that the Lot Allocation Board not only gave him the
famous 'ticket' but also an official paper which explicitly mentioned
that his plot was his forever.

The above examples show that people feel to a large extent secure in
their tenure. This feeling is partly based on a false assumption that
their tenure is legally secure, but also on what they see happening in
practice. The municipal authorities only seldom interfere with their
houses and plots. And when they do demolish structures on a plot situated in an area designed for public infrastructure such as a school or a
health centre, people with a 'ticket' almost always receive another plot
in substitution.

Ignorance about the official land legislation is indeed widespread.
Even the district head of Soucoupapaye admits that he knows very little
of procedures leading to an official legalisation of the plots after the re-
allocation programme in the 1970s in his district. When inhabitants of
his district ask his advice, he can only tell them to meet the different

departments involved in the procedure, such as Cadastre, Topography, and the Tax Department. He tells us that in his opinion there is a great distinction between official land tenure legislation and the daily routine. The perception of land tenure security is, he says, mostly based on clientelism: many local people know somebody in the Lot Allocation Board who is willing to distribute a lot number with a personal name attached to it, the 'ticket'. And since members of this board are highly placed people, you can trust them. Problems only occur when these people lose their position and are no longer able to protect you. But, he continues: 'Why bother? You can have permission for this and permission for that. You can have many papers with official seals and have paid a lot of money for all those seals and permissions, but you know as we all do: if the government wants to take your land, it will take your land. Things can slow down if your protection is bullet proof, but in the end you will lose your land.' Despite a general feeling of tenure security, most people are realistic enough to realise that such threats are inherent to a personalised, clientelistic system.

Individualisation of land tenure

Although most people continue to live on the urban plots with their family members, and most of these family members feel quite secure when 'their family' has a 'ticket', in reality the 'ticket' grants the plot to one person only. This orientation of urban land tenure towards a more individual land tenure system causes many small family tragedies, as will be shown by the case of the Sagna plot. Safietou Sagna was married to Yaya Dieme who died in 1991. They lived in the Dieme family house in Soucoupapaye.[14] After the death of her husband, Safietou Sagna was not ready to accept her traditional transfer to the brother of her husband. She asked her father, then living in the village of Diatock, if he would allow her to live in her brother's house in Ziguinchor. This brother, Mamadou Sagna, had bought some land in the Lyndiane district in the year 1968. This piece of land was bought from a Serer farmer, whose daughter still lives on another piece of the land. Mamadou built a house with dried mud and allowed his brother Ousmane to live there, while he went to work in Dakar. When the authorities decided to re-allocate the area in which Mamadou's plot was situated, he gave a copy of his ID to a third brother, Ahmet, and asked him to make sure that the plot was allocated to him, Mamadou. But Ahmet put his own name on the 'ticket'.

Safietou's father and Mamadou allowed her to build a house on the corner of the building lot. As soon as the mud-dried rooms were ready, Safietou left the house of her deceased husband and started living in Lyndiane in 1992. The building lot was a microscopic labyrinth of minuscule alleys between mud-dried rooms where doors open and close, creating a buzzing atmosphere. This microscopic labyrinth is a small Diatock (the native village of the family) in an urban setting and creates a feeling of security with regard to the plot considered as family land. Finally, Mamadou retired and took the opportunity to visit Lyndiane. He asked his brother Ahmet to come to Ziguinchor to change the name on the 'ticket', but Ahmet refused. All this time, Safietou assumed that the building lot was family land and did not know that in fact Ahmet's name was on the 'ticket'.

A lot of time passed, and eventually Ahmet Sagna died. Mamadou Sagna was enjoying his retirement and still living in Dakar. It was only in 2006 that Safietou checked with the Cadastre Department about the building lot registration and discovered that it was in the name of her deceased brother Ahmet. What was she to do then? For the first time Safietou began to be anxious about her future. The four children of Ahmet Sagna continued to live on the family lot in the house of their uncle Ousmane. The building lot became more and more crowded, which from time to time created tensions between Safietou and her nephews and nieces. And although for the moment they did not want to take any initiative and force the situation, Safietou realised now that they – as the rightful heirs of their father – could at any time decide to claim the building lot and she would be compelled to leave her house. And she had no money to move. When she went to the municipal services for advice, she discovered how wrong her perception of the building lot as family land had been. The 'ticket' had a first name and a family name, and thus concerned only one person, in her case her deceased brother Ahmet. In Safietou's opinion the building lot should have gone to her eldest brother, Mamadou, who had promised that he would take care that the lot remained family land and that she could stay in her house. But the municipal services also told her that the procedures to change the name of the 'ticket' and subsequently obtain the property of the building lot and the houses in the name of Mamadou are long, complex and costly, and require the cooperation of Ahmet's children. After consultation with her brother Mamadou, she decided 'to keep silent' for the time being and not to take any action.

The case of the Sagna plot is representative of what is happening in many popular districts of Ziguinchor. It displays that the issuance of personalised 'tickets' leads to an individualisation of land that often used to be considered as family property. Many family members of 'ticket' holders feel secure in their tenure, either because they are unaware of this change or because they trust the 'ticket' holder to take care of his family. When the family situation changes, or personal relations come under strain, family members can be confronted with the insecurity of their tenure and come off worse. The urban land legislation aiming at private property of land and houses thus enhances the tenure security of some, but also endangers that of others. It increases the vulnerability of people who lack understanding of the legislation.[15]

Some concluding remarks

We have seen that in the Senegalese town of Ziguinchor, re-allocation programmes have been undertaken since the 1970s. These programmes did not replace the earlier land tenure situation based on Diola customary law, as they were naively envisaged to do. They rather created a new, hybrid system that combined a continued importance of the Diola *adjiati-adjaoura* relationship with a role for new actors involved in municipal town planning. In this new urban constellation, the position of the *koudjiati* became more and more politicised. This expansion of his role was acceptable for the members of the traditional society as long as the political ambitions of the *adjiati* did not result in him neglecting his obligations towards his *koudjaora* in favour of the interests of his other, 'immigrant', followers. When the *adjiati* starts to answer to political demands that hurt his inner circle, he loses his authority, and his *koudjaora* turn against him and his political associates. In Ziguinchor, this resulted in high tensions between locals and 'outsiders' and even in violent clashes.

The case of Ziguinchor clearly brings to the fore the well-known truth that land tenure and property rights are institutions in which people's access to, use of, and control over land are highly dependent on social relations. When these are transformed and reconstructed over the course of time and in a different environment, land tenure is readjusted accordingly (cf. Juul and Lund 2002). This chapter has posed the question of the effect of this changing constellation on people's tenure security. We have seen that people in the study area feel to a large extent secure in their tenure. Although most of them do not have a legally sound title to their land, many erroneously believe that their 'tickets' or other documentary material does provide a formal title. Very few really know their way in the legal labyrinth, and not every man in the street can visit a department director for correct information. But also those who know, from a legal point of view, that they may lose land and home with a stroke of a pencil do not really worry. Practice proves them right. The occasions are rare that houses are torn down without state compensation. For the people it is enough to know that they will receive compensation for the investments they made in case the government decides to upgrade the area in which their plot is located and their houses have to be torn down. Even when their rights to land are not legally secure, people trust the current state of laissez-faire to continue, and expect to be protected by political strong men, through their relationship with their *adjiati*, or with people involved in the municipal land planning system, such as members of the Lot Allocation Board. As long as this protection stands, they believe they are quite secure in their tenure vis-à-vis the government.

A different issue that has also been discussed in this chapter is the effect of the individualisation of family land due to the issuance of personalised 'tickets'. The case of the Sagan plots clearly highlights that the enhancement of tenure security of some people usually coincides with the erosion of that of others. The vulnerability of people who lack knowledge of urban legislation and who are dependent on family relations can be significantly increased by the drive for individualisation of tenure. When discussing the effects of re-allocation programmes on tenure security, one should thus always ask the question, whose tenure security?

Notes

1   For an extensive analysis of the conflict, see De Jong 2005. See also Evans 2000; Foucher 2003; Lo 2006.
2   The agricultural zone corresponds generally to the land exploited by farmers or herders; the classified zone consists mainly of the forest domain, and the pioneer zone consists of previously undeveloped and unoccupied land destined for development according to the plans of the state. See Caverivière and Débène 1998:81-82; Elbow and Rochegude 1989:14.
3   For a detailed discussion of the distinction between national domain and state property, see Caverivière and Débène 1998:85-88; Elbow and Rochegude 1989: notes 35 and 43.
4   The details of the expropriation procedure are governed by a separate expropriation law: Law no. 76-67 of 2 July 1976, which abrogated and replaced Law no. 66-01 of 18 January 1966, relating to expropriation in the cause of public utility and other land transactions for public utility.
5   Law no. 76-66 of 2 July 1976 establishing the *Domaine de l'Etat*.
6   The Urbanisation Code was abrogated and replaced by Law no. 66-49; see also Decree no. 66-1076 supporting the Urbanisation Code (Statutory Section); Decree no. 72-1297 modifying Decree no. 66-1076; Law no. 79-78 abrogating and replacing article 12 of the Urbanisation Code; Decree no. 81-803bis abrogating and replacing section II of the first title of the Urbanisation Code.
7   Order no. 6288 of 26 May 1970 relating to requests for building permits in urban zones which pertain to national domain. See also Gadiaga 1984.
8   For an overview of the historical development of Ziguinchor, see Bruneau 1979; Trincaz 1984.
9   For more information on the organisation of Diola society, see Pélissier 1996; Thomas 1959, 1968; with regard to the traditional law of the Diola, see Ki-Zerbo 1997.
10 Hesseling (1991) describes the various strategies employed by people who wish to become urbanites. See also Turner 1968, whose ideas have for a long time influenced urban developments in developing countries.
11 Decision No. 0434/GC du 16/02/1982.

12 Arrêté no. 6o/GC/AA.

13 For a critical discussion concerning tenure formalisation and the importance of *petits papiers* for the poor, see Durand-Lasserve 1986; Durand-Lasserve and Royston 2002; Durand-Lasserve and Selod 2007.

14 The importance of the family house in Africa has been documented e.g. by Le Bris et al. 1987. See also Monnier and Droz 2004.

15 Despite the fact that the people in Ziguinchor are relatively well educated (the region of the Casamance has the highest rate of primary education in Senegal), lack of knowledge of the ins and outs of urban legislation is ubiquitous. This is illustrated by the Sagna case. The Sagna family is a modern, well-educated family. Two daughters have their baccalaureate, one of them currently works as a teacher, the other has entered university. All family members carry mobiles, and the youngest children regularly visit the internet café. Despite their education and modern lifestyle, most of them are not well informed with regard to urban legislation.

11 Land tenure in Bolivia: From colonial times to post-neoliberalism

Willem Assies[1]

Introduction

Since the turn of the century, Bolivia has been the scene of social and political upheaval. The early months of the year 2000 saw the rise of protests against the privatisation of the municipal water supply company in the city of Cochabamba and, more broadly, against new legislation on water. According to its protagonists, the 'Water War' resulted in the first victory of the popular movement after fifteen years of neoliberalism as the privatisation was reversed and the water legislation substantially modified. In subsequent years popular protests of various sorts continued while the 2002 presidential elections, in which Evo Morales of the *Movimiento al Socialismo* (MAS, Movement towards Socialism) came in second with 20.9 per cent of the vote,[2] indicated that dissatisfaction with the established political parties and their support for the neoliberal model was growing. In October 2003 president Gonzalo Sánchez de Lozada was forced to resign after a massive wave of protests against the intended sale of natural gas to the United States through Chile – Bolivia's arch-enemy since the Pacific War (1879-1880) when it annexed Bolivia's coastal provinces. Vice-president Carlos Mesa stepped in but was also forced to resign in June 2005. In December of that year presidential elections yielded a landslide victory for Evo Morales who garnered 54 per cent of the vote in a country where, since its return to democracy in 1982, presidents had been elected with at best nearly 34 per cent of the vote (Assies 2004; Assies and Salman 2003; Crabtree 2005; Kohl and Farthing 2006).

With the election of Evo Morales, Bolivia became an exponent of the 'Left Turn' in Latin America.[3] At the same time this reflects the increased significance of the 'ethnic factor' in some Latin American polities (Van Cott 2005; Yashar 2005). It is this combination that explains why in late November 2006 the new government succeeded in passing a substantial modification of the Agrarian Reform Law – which had been adopted ten years earlier – through Congress, aiming for a more radical and swifter application, particularly in favour of the country's indigenous peoples. Similarly, the new government aims for a reorientation of urban policies in the context of a new conception of development which it describes as aspiring to 'live well'. This makes the country an interesting case, as it illustrates the search for a new development paradigm for a pluriethnic and multicultural country.[4]

In adopting a historical perspective, this chapter will provide insights into the ways in which land tenure regimes are forged in the service of ideas about progress, development, and nation-building. Some forms of tenure will be privileged over others since they are expected to contribute to such objectives, which are often stated grandiloquently. How things work out on the ground is another matter, as what is promoted 'from above' may be contested 'from below'. What is defined as legal or illegal and what remains in the limbo of extra-legality – not against the law but not recognised by law either – can be shown to be an outcome of such local struggles and their articulation into broader societal projects.

In taking this tack, the chapter furthermore sheds light on the legal concepts of the social and social-economic function of property and how these concepts underpinned the post-1952 agrarian reform process and were later preserved and re-interpreted in the subsequent agrarian legislation of 1996 and 2006. It will be shown how, in different socio-political contexts, such concepts provide the basis or justification for more or less radical redistributive policies and how these policies are contested by large landowners, who regard them as a source of legal insecurity and eventually may resort to 'white guards' to secure their 'rights'.

This chapter will primarily focus on the evolution of rural land tenure and then briefly turn to the question of urban land tenure and housing.

Colonial times

When in the early 1530s the Spaniards first ventured into what nowadays is Bolivia, they entered a region that had been incorporated into the Quecha-speaking Inca empire some 80 years earlier. The Aymara polities had been subdued, and the Inca system of religion and tribute had been introduced without bringing about profound socio-economic changes. The two cultures already shared important traits and forms of social organisation, such as the *ayllu*. This was an endogamous social unit consisting of various kinship groups organised according to a dualist pattern of complementary 'halves', each of which collectively possessed a specific, though often discontinuous, territory. The *ayllu* was the basic unit of the agro-pastoral societies occupying various ecological levels. In the lower and warmer areas maize and vegetables could be produced, often on irrigated land permanently possessed by the family who worked it. On higher levels potatoes and cold-resistant grains could be cultivated in an intricate system of community-regulated field and crop rotation that would allow for soil regeneration and risk spreading[5], while the still higher altitudes would be dedicated to pastoral use. The *ayllu* could be grouped into larger units or polities that in pre-colonial times spanned areas from the western coast, through the central Andean highlands, to the eastern mountain slopes descending towards the Amazonian savanna and forests.

The Spanish conquest and the emergence of the silver-mining economy, centred in Potosí, brought important changes to the Andes region. The gradual formation of large estates or *haciendas* to cater for the mines, and the *reducciones* policy that sought to concentrate the indigenous population in compact settlements, in tandem with population decline due to epidemics, resulted in a fragmentation of indigenous productive and political units. It did not entail the disappearance of the *ayllu* as minor *ayllus* were allowed to retain control over land in return for labour services and tribute in a relationship that Platt (1982) has characterised as a 'pact of reciprocity', albeit the power relations were obviously asymmetrical.[6] A series of local uprisings culminated in the massive revolts of the early 1780s under the leadership of Túpac Katari and Túpac Amaru in the La Paz and Cuzco regions, respectively (Andrien 2001; Walker 1999).

The hot eastern lowlands remained on the fringe of the colonial economy. This was the realm of a variety of indigenous societies, practising itinerant slash-and-burn agriculture in combination with hunting, fishing and gathering. In terms of culture, language, socio-political organisation, and patterns of land and forest use – adapted to the ecological conditions of the region – they were quite different from the Aymara and Quechua, who were more sedentary agro-pastoralists. By the end of the seventeenth century, the Jesuit Order had established some missions in the Santa Cruz region, and after their expulsion in 1767, *mestizo* farmers and ranchers took control in the savanna areas and set the population to work in cattle ranching. The remoter Amazonian forest areas to the north became regions of refuge for people practising itinerant lifestyles, while in the Chaco region the Guaraní Chiriguano fiercely resisted any incursions into their territories until they were defeated in a bloody expedition in 1892.

What we should retain from this very brief overview of colonial times is the incipient emergence of a pattern of regional differentiation[7] regarding land tenure and social organisation, which was a function of the pre-colonial organisation and subsequent colonial exploitation of the indigenous population. Such patterns set the stage for present-day regional divisions as well as different forms of indigenous-peasant organisation.

Republican Bolivia up to the 1930s

Independence, which came in 1825, brought little change to the situation of the indigenous population. Liberator Simón Bolivar, who became president of the newly created republic for a few months, introduced liberal legislation that abolished tribute and declared the lands
of the indigenous communities private property (Aylwin 2002:31; Hernáiz and Pacheco 2000:24). The objective was to create a class of yeoman farmers who would sustain the republic and contribute to the
wealth of the nation. This legislation, however, never took effect. The
Bolivian state soon found that it could not do without tribute and in
1826 reintroduced a *contribución indigenal*. The 'reciprocity pact',
whereby the *ayllus* retained control over land in return for various
kinds of tribute, was perpetuated for the time being (Klein 2003:105),
and the *ayllu*, though it had undergone changes throughout the colonial era,[8] maintained itself as the extant form of political, socio-economic, and cultural organisation, with permanently tense relations
with the Bolivian state and dominant classes. The indigenous-peasant
community was what has been called 'a mini-state in conflict' (Carter
and Albó 1988).

It was only by the 1860s, when silver mining recuperated and tin
mining and other endeavours gained importance, that state depen-
dence on the tribute tax declined and liberal views on land tenure re-
emerged, and an all-out attack on corporate landholding was launched
(Klein 2003:136). In 1866 it was decreed that within 60 days indigenous communities should assert their title and pay a fee of 25 to 100 *pe-
sos*, otherwise their lands would be sold through public auction. In
1874 a *Ley de Exvinculación de Tierras* promoted individual titling of *comuneros* and sought to substitute the *contribución indigenal* with a general property tax. Once the Pacific War (1879-1880) was over, implementation of such legislation accelerated and resulted in a massive expropriation of community lands in the highland and valley regions. In
many cases indigenous communities were incorporated into expanding
haciendas and became 'captive communities' – particularly in the highlands of La Paz – while in northern Potosí smallholders and medium-
size farms encroached upon *ayllu* lands (Rivera Cusicanqui and Thoa
1992:45). According to Thiesenhusen (1995:53), in 1846 over 63 per
cent of the indigenous population lived in freeholding communities,
while by the end of the century the figure was 27 per cent.[9] The number of *haciendas* increased from about 300 to 4,000 during the last
four decades of the nineteenth century (cf. Cárdenas 1988:510).[10] This
expropriation process triggered a cycle of revolts that continued
throughout the first three decades of the twentieth century (Cárdenas

1988; Hylton 2003; Rivera Cusicanqui 2003; Rivera Cusicanqui and Thoa 1992; Ticona Alejo and Albó Corrons 1997).

While during the last decades of the nineteenth century the highlands and valleys were the scene of *hacienda* expansion and resistance by the Aymara and Quechua peasantry, the eastern lowlands were marked by the rise of an extractive economy. Initially, the extraction of forest products, particularly cinchona bark (for quinine), brought new incursions into the forest areas, then from the late nineteenth century onward, the northern Bolivian Amazon region was affected by the rubber boom, which lasted until 1913. The new trade gave rise to the creation of *barracas* (rubber estates) and labour relations based on debt peonage. In the savanna regions further to the south, cattle raising expanded to supply the rubber estates, pushing the indigenous population towards more marginal areas or incorporating them into the ranches under conditions of virtual slavery.

The Chaco war, the 1952 revolution and the agrarian reform

The Chaco war with Paraguay (1932-1935) represented a turning point in Bolivian history. The most important effect of this bloody conflict was that it provided the opportunity for indigenous troops to mix with *mestizo* recruits and to meet people from different parts of the country and share the 'democracy of the trenches' (Rivera Cusicanqui 2003:93) that yielded the so-called Chaco generation. The experience radically changed the Bolivian political climate, as the land question, the Indian question, labour issues, the country's dependency on private mines and its domination by a small oligarchy of tin barons and large landowners became themes of national debate. The war experience gave rise to the emergence of a radical revolutionary political movement as well as a powerful and radical labour movement. The late 1930s saw a turbulent succession of military and elected governments. Nationalist measures, such as the nationalisation of Standard Oil (1937), were introduced as well as social legislation. A reform of the Constitution in 1938 introduced the concept of the social function of property[11] and provided some protection for community lands.

In this context new political parties emerged, most importantly the *Movimiento Nacionalista Revolucionaria* (MNR)[12], as well as a radical miners' trade union that later would become the backbone of the *Central Obrera Boliviana* (COB, Bolivian Workers' Central). In April 1952 the MNR managed to seize power and initiated a period of nationalist reformism. The 1952 revolution brought four basic transformations: universal franchise for all Bolivians, nationalisation of the holdings of the three tin barons, agrarian reform in 1953, and education reform in 1955, which introduced free, obligatory, and universal education.

In its 1942 party programme the MNR had demanded 'a scientifically based study of the indigenous agrarian problem with the aim of incorporating the millions of peasants that until now have been marginalised from it into national life and to achieve an adequate organisation of the agrarian economy in order to obtain maximal output'.[13] This neatly captures the attitude of the party, which aimed at assimilation of the indigenous population into the nation through *mestizaje*, and at modernisation understood largely in productivist terms. The term 'Indio' was banned from official discourse, and the rural population would be consistently addressed as *campesinos* (peasants), that is in terms of class, while downplaying ethnic or cultural features. Education was to be another pillar for the 'redemption' of the Indian.

Due to internal divisions, with a left-wing pushing for redistributive reform and right-wing landholders doing the opposite (Albó 2007:84), the new MNR government did not act quickly when it came to agrarian reform. The countryside had remained largely aloof from the April revolution, but the revolution opened the way for a breakdown of the system of rural domination, which forced the MNR government to move to control the situation. Direct action against *haciendas*, rural power relations, and trade monopolies became widespread after the 1952 revolution and forced the decreeing of an agrarian reform in August 1953. In the following years massive mobilisation by *sindicatos* (peasant unions) and *comunidades*, which acted through armed militias, broke up the *hacienda* system in the highlands and the valleys (Cárdenas 1988; Gotkowitz 2003; Rivera Cusicanqui 2003; Thiesenhusen 1995:51-68).

The nature and outcomes of the 1953 Agrarian Reform

The 1953 Agrarian Reform Decree (Ministerio de Asuntos Campesinos 1953)[14] articulated three basic principles. First, land should go to the tiller; second, ownership of land should also fulfill a social function; and third, the ownership of all natural resources was vested in the nation itself. The first principle aimed to make an end to relations of servitude but did not exclude wage labour. The other two principles implied a recognition of private ownership on the condition that it performed a useful function for the national community. If this was not the case, the land would revert to the state, which then would redistribute it.

The legislation sought to formally recognise and regularise various forms of tenure:
- The *solar campesino*, or peasant housing plot, too small to meet the subsistence necessities of a family and conceived as a supplement to land endowment to the *colono* (tenant) or agricultural worker.

- Small property, worked personally by the peasant and his (or her) family in such a way that it could rationally satisfy their needs, without excluding the eventual hiring of labour for specific tasks.
- Middle-sized properties, larger than small properties but not meeting the characteristics of a capitalist enterprise. It could be worked with the help of salaried workers and/or using mechanised and technical inputs in such a way that the bulk of production is destined for the market.
- Property of the indigenous communities, which was recognised according to established law[15] and was inalienable. This was the so-called *pro-indiviso* (undivided) mode of recognition. A later decree specified the modes of recognition, but as Hernáiz and Pacheco (Hernáiz and Pacheco 2000:104-106) indicate, this modality of tenure was not prioritised by the MNR government.[16]
- Cooperative agrarian property, which could be constituted in various ways.
- Agricultural enterprises, *characteris*ed by large-scale capital investment, relying on wage labour and employing modern technical/mechanised inputs (where feasible in view of topographical factors).

Some of these categories were subdivided further, and a special regime was introduced for the rubber-tapping and Brazil nut-producing areas, which were dominated by *barracas,* and for the envisioned colonisation areas (Hernáiz and Pacheco 2000:121-130) in the 'underpopulated' and non-integrated eastern lowland regions.[17] The legislation also foresaw a complex system of ceilings to the size of properties, according to local circumstances and classifications regarding carrying capacity. Extensions exceeding these ceilings or those exploited under feudal arrangements or technically deficient conditions – and therefore failing to comply with their social function – would revert to the state for redistribution or would be distributed to those who effectively worked the land. Community land appropriated after 1 January 1900 was to be returned to the original community as inalienable communal private property of the whole community, while individually held plots within communities were recognised as the private property of the family. This, again, was the *pro-indiviso* mode of recognition in which collective and individual titling could, at least in theory, be combined.

This classification of legally recognised forms of land tenure reflects the ideas on development and nation-building of the 1952 revolutionaries. However, in their study of the agrarian question in Latin America, Alain de Janvry et al (2001:203) classifies the Bolivian reform as a transition from pre-capitalism (or semi-feudalism) to a Junker road (as opposed to a farmer road) of development of capitalism in agriculture.[18] This is because most landowners were able to retain part or all of their holdings, and only a few were classified as *latifundios* who suffered partial or total expropriation. The remainder were classified as medium properties, according to lax criteria that allowed for rather large extensions, while the distribution of *hacienda* lands to *colonos* mostly involved the plots they worked before the reform. Their obligations to the landlord ceased, but their productive resources were not increased (De Janvry 1981:208-209; see also Albó 2007:86). This *characteris*ation of the Bolivian reform holds, as far as it goes. It suggests that the revolution only partly achieved its manifest redistributive objectives and therefore remained truncated.

De Janvry (1981) frames his discussion in terms of roads to capitalism and does not comment on the fact that the revolution and the land reform did not take account of the multi-ethnic composition of the Bolivian population or of the persistence of indigenous forms of organisation such as the *ayllu*. As noted, the term 'Indio' was banned from official discourse, the multicultural composition of the 'nation' was thus declared a non-issue, and the forms of local organisation regarding rights to land and land use were not taken into account. While the reform brought a break-up of the *hacienda* system in the valleys and part of the highlands, the promised restitution of lands to the communities hardly got off the ground. Rivera Cusicanqui and Thoa (1992:46, 61-63) qualify the reform as 'liberal and individualist' and underline its failure to take indigenous forms of organisation into account where land tenure arrangements and where community and supra-community organisation are concerned. Nonetheless, despite legislation, communities largely persisted in their adherence to the *pro-indiviso* principle of collective title and the distribution of lands according to customary rules of inheritance, transfer, and land management.

To implement the reform, two state agencies were created: a *Servicio Nacional de Reforma Agraria* (SNRA) was created in 1953 and an *Instituto Nacional de Colonisación* (INC) in 1966. The pace of the reform, however, was very much set by post-revolutionary developments, emerging policy orientations, and elite power struggles. The first years were characterised by peasant and community mobilisation in the western part of the country, but by the 1970s attention had shifted to the eastern lowlands. Under the military government of Hugo Banzer Suárez (1971-1978), large swaths of the lowlands, particularly in Santa Cruz, were transferred to large landowners supposedly dedicated to commercial sugar and rice production, cattle raising and, from the mid-1970s onward, soy production (Lavaud 1991:173-180; PNUD 2004; Thiesenhusen 1995:51-68). Further fraudulent land allocations took place under the narco-dictatorships – the military governments that were strongly involved in cocaine production and trade – of the late 1970s and early 1980s (Solón 1995).

Meanwhile, the *Instituto Nacional de Colonisación* (INC) promoted some 'directed colonisation projects', principally in the tropical Chapare and Chimoré regions of Cochabamba, the hot *yunga* valleys of northern La Paz, and in an area north of Santa Cruz (Yapacaní, San Julian). However, 'spontaneous colonisation' became prevalent, with peasants from the highlands migrating to the lowlands on their own account (Lavaud 1991:178-179). At the same time, the INC came to play a role in land distribution, parallel to the SNRA. Both institutions became marred by corruption, and land distribution and titling turned into total chaos. When, in 1992, the two institutions were finally audited by the state, it was estimated that between 30 and 60 percent of the national territory was affected by overlapping titles, and that in some cases as many as seven titles might overlap. Up to 60 per cent of the owners had questionable property rights due to overlap, irregular procedures, and other factors (MACPIO 2001:51-53; see also World Bank 1995). Given this situation of institutional chaos and corruption, when it came to tenure security, the fact of having a title was most often of limited relevance. It was often the local community, organised in various ways – as *ayllus* or as peasant unions, as will be discussed below – that would grant security on the condition of fulfilling obligations to the community (see, for example, Pacheco and Valda 2003:121-153).[19]

After some thirty years of land reform, the chaotic and corrupted implementation resulted in a renewed polarisation of land distribution. The 1984 agrarian census, which was only partial, suggested that 86.6 per cent of the holdings it covered amounted to only 3.7 per cent of the land (see World Bank 1995). This is the result of the post-reform fragmentation of landholding in the Andes region and the concentration of landholding in the lowlands, where large 'modern' enterprises arose, surrounded by a scattering of smallholders (Urioste and Pacheco 2000).

A further aspect of the reform process that deserves attention is the way in which it affected forms of peasant-indigenous organisation. The 1953 agrarian reform Decree recognised the peasant community and accorded it legal personality, and also recognised the *sindicatos* (peasant unions), but it failed to consider the persistence of the *ayllu* in particular regions, such as northern Potosí.[20] According to the law, through their legal representatives the communities could represent the interests of their members and should promote the well-being of the population in the areas of education, housing, health, production techniques, and economic and social relations, as well as promoting forms of cooperativism. The law further specified that these communities were independent, that no associations of communities could be established, and that they could not become part of centrals, federations, confederations, or other public entities. The peasant community differed from the peasant unions, the law said, in that it did not pursue goals of class struggle against sectors or elements foreign to the community, and because it could not become part of provincial, departmental, or national organisms. The law recognised the *sindicatos* as a means both to defend the rights of their members and to preserve those rights once gained. *Sindicatos* would intervene in the implementation of agrarian reform, and they could be independent or affiliate themselves with central organisms. This provided the framework for the top-down promotion of peasant unions and their centralisation in the *Confederación Nacional de Trabajadores Campesinos de Bolivia* (CNTCB).

The union structure soon became a patronage machinery through which the rural population became tied to the MNR-dominated state (Rivera Cusicanqui 2003). Under the Barrientos dictatorships and governments (1964-1969), this relationship between the state and the CNTCB would be formalised in the *Pacto Militar Campesino*, and on various occasions the peasantry would be mobilised to confront radicalised miners and workers. It is not the place here to delve deeply into the vagaries of the state-peasantry (indigenous) association, but we should note that this association was undermined by the attempt of the Barrientos government to introduce a new rural property tax and came definitely to an end with the heavy-handed repression of peasant protests against the economic policies of the Banzer regime in 1974. Under such circumstances the peasantry made various efforts to break away from military tutelage. The most important development was the rise of *katarismo* within the CNTCB, a process that involved the recuperation of Indian identity and a rejection of the designation as 'peasantry', though the organisation in unions was accepted.[21] The unraveling of the *Pacto Militar Campesino* brought a realignment with the workers' movement in opposition to the military regimes, and in 1979 the CNTCB was transformed into the *Confederación Sindical Única de Trabajadores Campesinos de Bolivia* (CSUTCB) (Albó 1991; Cárdenas 1988; Rivera Cusicanqui 2003; Ticona Alejo 2000; Yashar 2005:154-181).

It should be noted here that the spread of peasant unionism resulted in a regionally differentiated pattern of local organisation. In areas where the *hacienda* system had predominated, such as the Cochabamba valleys and the highlands north of La Paz, the *sindicato* became the predominant form of community organisation. In other areas, however, such as northern Potosí, the *ayllu* persisted despite attempts to impose the more 'modern' form of peasant unions, while in still other areas peasant unions and more traditional forms of organisation virtually merged (Ticona Alejo, Rojas Ortuste, and Albó Corrons 1995; Yashar 2005:160-161). In other words, the legal distinction between peasant union and community, and its disregard of the *ayllu*, were rather artificial.

Tenure security 40 years later

Such aspects have to be taken into account if we want to assess the degree of tenure security in different regions of the country and for different categories of landholders on the eve of the reform of agrarian legislation in the mid-1990s. A further issue that arises from the foregoing discussion is that perhaps we should distinguish more clearly between tenure security and security of access.

Let me start with the second point. Tenure security is often viewed in terms of the secure right of an individual or a family to a certain plot of land. The modes of community-level regulation in the Andes and in eastern lowland Bolivia call such a concept into question. Assignment of plots in a context of crop rotation in the highlands has historically relied on collective decision-making. Rights to some plots might resemble full ownership in the sense that while their duration was assured, transfers would be regulated by community rules and would be limited to intra-community transfers. In other cases collective rules and decisions about assignments of rights to plots or access to the commons would play a more determining role. Although the right to a determined plot might not be secure, the access to land and resources might be quite certain for stakeholders in the community who comply with their obligations to the community, whether organised according to the *ayllu* pattern, the peasant union mode, or some hybrid organisational form that combines Andean cultural patterns with the peasant union mode of organisation. Stakeholdership thus is the ultimate criterion for tenure security or security of access.[22] While it is often assumed that tenure security is the precondition for investment and therefore for 'development', this suggests an inverse logic: investment in a community effort is a precondition for tenure security. Something similar could be said about the complex constellation of local rights in the oriental lowlands where cultivation rights may not coincide with hunting or gathering rights.

This is related to the first issue. As noted, the indigenous-peasant community can be viewed as a 'mini-state in conflict'. The Bolivian state was and still is notorious for its precarious presence, at best, in most of its territory. It hardly corresponds to the Weberian imagery of a monopoly of violence within a certain territory, and still less to the idea of 'legitimate violence'. Until the 1952 revolution, control of the rural population was mostly delegated to private local powerholders, occasionally backed up by the army. With the break-up of the *hacienda* system in the highlands and valleys, the *ayllu* and peasant union mode of organisation gained importance in regulating local tenure arrangements, while the state remained something rather remote and secondary. As to the eastern lowlands, state agencies promoted colonisation by highland peasants and increasingly favoured the creation of large landholdings for a small but powerful local elite.

If we then seek to assess tenure security/insecurity for different categories of landholders in different regions, we can say that in the highlands and valleys, tenure became relatively secure in the wake of the 1952 revolution. Although a process of titling got under way, it was carried out in a haphazard fashion and became increasingly chaotic. What really mattered were arrangements on the ground among stakeholders, organised according to patterns rooted in Andean culture and agricultural systems, and with varying degrees of influence on the part of the peasant unionism promoted after the 1952 revolution. Conflicts over land, which can be taken as an indicator of tenure insecurity, were not absent in this region, but in the wake of the 1953 reform and in the context of subsequent policies, agrarian conflict definitely 'migrated' to the eastern lowlands.

In the highlands and valleys, intra-community conflict came to be related to inheritance issues and would most often be resolved at the community level through the intervention of the peasant union or *ayllu* authorities. Inter-community conflicts might go back to the early republican period and its drawing of administrative borders. Such conflicts involve more than tenure security, since they relate to local jurisdiction and territoriality.[23] As we will see, such issues became increasingly prominent in the course of the 1990s and represent one of the questions to be faced by the current government. They involve the issue of imagining and actually construing a plurinational state.

In the highlands and valleys, security of tenure is not the main issue. The more important issue became the fragmentation of landholding among the *nietos de la reforma agraria* – the grandchildren of the agrarian reform – (Urioste, Barragán, and Colque 2007) and the abandonment of the highlands and valleys (Urioste 2003) in the post-1952 agrarian policies that opened up the Bolivian market for USA dumping and increasingly privileged the eastern lowland agro-industrial sector.

After the 1953 reform, agrarian policies became increasingly geared to promoting the occupation of the lowlands through colonisation by peasants from the highlands and the sponsoring of large-scale agro-industries, cattle raising, and timber exploitation. The lowland indigenous peoples came under increasing pressure from this expanding frontier and by the 1970s began to organise to defend themselves from such encroachments.

Multiculturalism and the reform of the reform

In 1982 Bolivia returned to civilian rule, and after a first attempt to re-
suscitate the national revolutionary economic model, which ended in a
deep economic crisis, under the Paz Estenssoro government (1985-
1989) a harsh structural adjustment policy was introduced that became
known as the 'first generation reforms'.

Meanwhile, as the grip of *katarismo* within the CSUTCB weakened
and traditional left-wing currents – now incorporating some elements
of *indigenista* discourse – became hegemonic (García Linera, León, and
Monje 2004:118), new developments were taking place in the eastern
lowlands. With the help of anthropologists, the indigenous peoples of
the region had begun to organise to defend their interests. A *Confederación de Pueblos Indígenas del Oriente Boliviana* (CIDOB) had been created in 1982, and over the following years a series of other local organisations emerged under this umbrella organisation (Diez Astete 1998;
García Linera, León, and Monje 2004). In August 1990 some 300 indigenous inhabitants from the lowlands initiated a March for Territory
and Dignity from the town of Trinidad to La Paz, where 800 marchers
arrived after about a month. They protested the incursion of logging
companies and cattle ranchers on what they considered their territories. As one of the leaders of the march recalls:

> We the indigenous made the paths to our fields and along these
> same paths came the *carayanas*, that is, the White people. As
> they were knowledgeable in documents and papers, they began
> to consolidate the land, because they themselves were the autho-
> rities. 'Ok, this mine. Here is my title. What do you have? Noth-
> ing, Eh?' they would say. So we went further into the bush. We
> established our villages. But the White people came, so again we
> went further in, and again and again, until there came a time
> when there was nowhere else to go. When a wild animal is
> wounded, cornered and has nowhere to escape to, the only thing
> left for it is to attack (Méndez Vedia 2007:72).

The march was a spectacular event that suddenly dispelled the 'invisi-
bility' of the lowland indigenous population and drew attention to their
plight. The moral impact of the march prompted President Jaime Paz
Zamora (1989-1993) to immediately issue several decrees recognising
four indigenous territories. He also created a commission that was to
prepare legislation regarding the indigenous peoples of the *Oriente* and
the Amazon. During the years that followed, more decrees were issued,
bringing the number of territories recognised in this way up to nine.[24]
In 1991, Bolivia ratified ILO Convention 169 on Indigenous and Tribal

Peoples in Independent Countries (Terceros Cuéllar 2004), and during the Paz Zamora government a project for constitutional reform was prepared, which was to include the recognition of the 'pluri-multi' composition of the population.

Multi-culturalist reforms under neoliberalism

That reform package was further elaborated under the Gonzalo 'Goni' Sánchez de Lozada government (1993-1997)[25] and ratified in early 1995. A new article 1 recognised the multi-ethnic and pluri-cultural nature of the Bolivian population, and article 171 recognises, respects and protects the social, cultural and economic rights of the indigenous peoples. It specifically mentioned their rights to *Tierras Comunitarias de Origen* (originary community lands) and recognised the legal personality of indigenous and peasant communities and *sindicatos,* as well as the judicial function of the natural authorities of the indigenous and peasant communities as a form of alternative conflict resolution. Bolivia thus entered the era of multi-culturalism. Vigorously pursuing the neoliberal macro-economic course that had been set out in 1985, the Sánchez de Lozada government introduced a series of 'second generation' reforms, including 'capitalisation' (privatisation linked to a controversial reform of the pension system) of the major public enterprises. Other reforms included elements of multi-culturalism, such as the Popular Participation Law (1994), a decentralisation measure that created over 300 new municipalities, an education reform (1994) which introduced bilingual education, and new agrarian and forestry legislation (1996), among others.

Reform of the agrarian legislation was prompted by the 1992 '*Bolibras*' scandal.[26] This had exposed CNRA-INC corruption and resulted in the 'intervention' of the institutions in order to conduct a juridical audit. The initially foreseen intervention period of three months proved far too short to make sense of the chaos, and in the end the suspension of activities of the institutions lasted until 1996. Meanwhile, new agrarian legislation was initiated with the support of the World Bank (1995).[27] In 1994 the Sánchez de Lozada government presented an initial proposal, called 'INTI' (*Ley del Instituto Nacional de Tierras*), which was conceived as an instrument for institutional ordering without touching upon tenure issues, which were to be dealt with in a future new land law. The general orientation was one of market enablement and market-assisted reform. In response, peasant and indigenous organisations presented a hastily drafted counterproposal, the 'INKA' law (*Ley del Instituto Nacional Kollasuyo-Andino-Amazónico*).

By early 1995 a commission was created to formulate new legislation, consisting of government, business sector and indigenous and peasant representatives (Terceros Cuéllar 2004:38). Complex negotiations began in which, on various occasions, 'consensus' was reached and then undone by unilateral interventions by the executive. Such interventions prompted the indigenous and peasant organisations to call for a March for Land and Territory, Political Rights and Development in August 1996. New negotiations revealed the fragility of the alliance between the lowland indigenous organisation CIDOB, which had gained some important concessions regarding territorial rights, and the CSUTCB and CSCB (*Confederación Sindical de Colonizadores de Bolivia*), respectively representing the highland 'peasant-workers' and the 'colonisers' from the highlands who had established themselves in the eastern lowlands. These last two organisations withdrew from the negotiation process and accused the CIDOB of treason. On the other hand, commercial enterprises – in particular those of the Santa Cruz region – also vehemently opposed the proposed legislation because it did not fully open up the market in land and contained stipulations about the social-economic function of land instead of recognising absolute ownership rights. The new law was nonetheless approved in parliament, and on 18 October 1996 vice-president Víctor Hugo Cárdenas promulgated the *Ley del Servicio Nacional de Reforma Agraria* (*Ley No. 1715*) commonly known as *Ley INRA* (*Instituto Nacional de Reforma Agraria*) (CIDOB 1996; García Linera, León, and Monje 2004; Hernáiz and Pacheco 2000; Loayza Caero 2000; Salvatierra G. 1996; Terceros Cuéllar 2004).

As a result of this process, the new law is a 'hybrid', which only partly liberalises the land market. It is therefore classified as a special case by Deere and León (2000) because it is not an all-out market-oriented reform, as was the case in many other Latin American countries, but retains elements of social justice (see also Urioste and Pacheco 2000). The INRA law distinguishes between properties that conform to a 'social function' and those that have to comply with a 'social-economic' function. In the first category we find the lands that should contribute to the well-being and economic development of their owners, according to the carrying capacity of the land. Lands in this category are not subject to land tax. They are:

- The *solar campesino* or residential plot, which may not be divided or mortgaged but can be sold under certain conditions.
- Small properties that provide the owner and family with a livelihood and thus ensure their economic survival. These holdings, too, cannot be divided or mortgaged but may be sold under certain conditions.
- Communal properties, which are collectively titled to the corporate unit for subsistence purposes. They cannot be sold, mortgaged or divided.

- *Tierras comunitarias de origen* are the habitat of indigenous or originary peoples and communities, where they live according to their
  own forms of economic, social and cultural organisation.[28]

Lands that should comply with a social-economic function should be
dedicated to agrarian production, forestry, research, eco-tourism or biodiversity protection. In this category we find:
- Medium-size agrarian properties, which can be sold and mortgaged
  and are subject to land tax.
- Commercial agri-business enterprises, which can be sold and mortgaged, and also have to pay land tax.

Land tax was intended to stimulate market-led redistribution of rural
property. However, the taxation rate was established in direct relation
to the value of the land as declared by the owner and therefore became
ineffective as an incentive for market-led redistribution.[29]

Land redistribution could also occur through two other mechanisms:
reversion and expropriation. Reversion – without indemnification – to
the state could occur as a result of 'abandonment' of the land. Payment
of the land tax, however, was considered proof that the land was not
abandoned. Expropriation – with an indemnification according to the
self-declared tax value – could occur if the socio-economic function was
not fulfilled or related to public utility goals. Reverted land would become part of the stock of the *tierras fiscales* (public lands), which were
preferably to be redistributed in favour of peasant and indigenous communities (not individuals) by way of endowment (*dotación*), at no cost.
Peasant and indigenous organisations could thus demand land from
the state, when and where it was available. The other mechanism foreseen was the grant (*adjudicación*) at the market rate, through public
auction.

The process was to be accompanied by a clarification (*saneamiento*)
of land rights to be concluded ten years after the introduction of the
law. This could take three modalities: first, on request of the interested
party (*saneamiento simple*, SAN SIM); second, *ex office*, as a result of cadastral survey (*saneamiento integrado al catastro legal*, CAT SAN); and
third, in the *tierras comunitarias de origen* (TCO SAN) where the rights
of third parties were to be clarified.

The INRA law was the outcome of negotiations among a series of interest groups. Those who gained the most, theoretically at least, were
the indigenous peoples of the lowlands. They saw the territories recognised by Supreme Decrees between 1990 and 1992 confirmed as
TCOs, which would be provisionally titled pending clarification of the
rights of third parties. The law also admitted sixteen new demands for
TCOs in the lowlands and opened the way for further demands. How-

ever, it provided little solace for the highland indigenous peasantry, as it largely implied a confirmation of the status quo of fragmented land-holding that had resulted from the 1953 reform. And for those who migrated to the lowlands, the promise of reversion and redistribution of lands that did not fulfill a social-economic function remained unfulfilled.

Although INRA was required by law to complete the process of title clarification within a ten-year period, this activity has been exceedingly slow and frustrating in many cases. Regulating legislation was issued in July 1997 and was strongly criticised for its highly technical language, the demanding conditions to enter the clarification procedure, the complex and bureaucratic nature of the procedure itself, and the room it left for discretionary decisions (Terceros 2004:77, 95). By May 2005, of a total of some 107 million hectares subject to the clarification process, nearly 15 million (fourteen per cent) had effectively been clarified, 37.5 million hectares (35 per cent) were being processed, while for 54.8 million hectares (51 per cent) the process had not yet begun (INRA 2005; see also BID 2005:3 and Kay and Urioste 2007).[30]

Progress in accomplishing this task has depended heavily on multilateral and international cooperation. The Inter-American Development Bank and the World Bank have supported title clarification projects in the Departments of Santa Cruz and La Paz and part of the Beni Department, areas regarded as crucial for export agriculture (see BID 2005:11). The Danish government has strongly supported the titling of TCOs; the Dutch were involved in setting up a cadastral survey in the Department of Chuquisaca,[31] while the International Fund for Agricultural Development supported the clarification and titling of areas where conservation objectives and indigenous claims overlap. For its part, the European Union supported 'alternative development' in the Chapare region, while USAID sponsored land titling lands in that same region (BID 2005:9; Farthing and Kohl 2005).

A number of difficulties with the titling process have been identified by the Inter-American Development Bank (BID 2005). To begin with, it objects that only part of the clarified area has also been inscribed in the property register (cadastre), which it attributes to bureaucratic procedure and to problems with payment for the land received. According to the BID, Supreme Decree 27145 of August 2003 may help to overcome these problems. This ordinance extended the term of payment for adjudicated lands from one to ten years.[32] The decree also made it possible to convert small properties, which have to comply with a social function, into medium-size property, which has to comply with a social-economic function and can be mortgaged (BID 2005:3-5).[33]

In the second place, the BID (2005:8) claims that the World Bank-supported project for clarification of titles in the Santa Cruz and La

Paz Departments has not only contributed to clarification covering some 1.9 million hectares, but also has identified 500,000 hectares of public lands for redistribution. INRA (2005), however, only mentions 45,606 hectares for distribution in the whole country, and in negotiations between highland peasant-indigenous organisations and a ministerial delegation in September 2000, during the Banzer administration (1997-2002), the 3.8 million hectares available for distribution was a figure plucked from the sky by the minister (Defensor del Pueblo 2003). This suggests that realistic numbers are hard to obtain and subject to quite a bit of political manipulation. It also suggests that redistribution is severely limited as a result of pressures by the large landholders who circumvent the INRA law by fictitious subdivisions, or by moving herds from one place to another – 'cattle tourism' – to convince inspectors that the land is fully used.[34]

In the third place, the BID signals that where TCOs are concerned, at the national level 5.9 million hectares have been clarified and titled, while 12.5 million hectares are being processed. These figures fall far short of the total of 32 million hectares demanded as TCO. Here we may observe a number of things. First, that the process of TCO delimitation and titling is rather complex, costly and bureaucratic and that, despite international backing, it has proceeded slowly. Second, the process involves clarification and settling rights acquired by third parties (terceros). This means that the numbers of hectares clarified under the SAN TCO model do not simply refer to areas clarified to the benefit of indigenous peoples, but include also the lands claimed by others. Romero Bonifaz (2001:221) suggests that this may amount to nearly 60 per cent of the area clarified under the SAN TCO model. Ever since the proclamation of the INRA law, not only its own deficiencies but, above all, the lack of political will to implement it without bias in favour of the landholding elites of the eastern lowlands have generated frustration and conflict (Assies 2003; Villanueva I. Arturo D. 2004; see also Pacheco, this volume).

Forest and subsoil resources fall under different legislation. Forestry concessions, which were reconfirmed under the 1996 Forestry Law on the argument that they preceded the Agrarian Law, overlap with TCOs.[35] For the TCOs this constitutes a grave problem that has led to criticism by the ILO. Similarly, mining concessions, oil exploitation and transportation affect the TCO (Martínez 2000). Such problems, among other things, prompted indigenous people and peasants from the lowlands to undertake their 'Third March' for Lands, Territories and Natural Resources in June-July, 2000. Ensuing negotiations resulted in a modification of the procedure for TCO regularisation and a special regime for the former rubber-producing and now Brazil nut-producing northeastern Amazon region. Nonetheless, in one of its manifestations of bad faith, the Bolivian government signed an agreement in September 2001 with the commercial interests in the Santa Cruz region that went completely against what had previously been agreed with the indigenous-peasant sectors (Assies 2003; Villanueva I. Arturo D. 2004).

Two other issues deserve brief discussion. In the first place, when the INRA law was finally promulgated, the CSUTCB condemned it and has sought to modify it substantially or to replace it with a law of its own making. In contrast to this stance, by the late 1990s new movements consolidated in the highlands and sought to use the INRA law to their benefit. Particularly in Oruro and Potosí, a movement for the 'reconstitution' of the *ayllu* emerged from the mid-1980s onward, and by 1997 this process culminated in the formation of the *Consejo de Ayllus y Markas del Qullasuyu* (Council of *Ayllus* and Markas of Qullasuyu, CONAMAQ) (Choque and Mamani 2003; García Linera, León, and Monje 2004:324-348). This competitor takes the CSUTCB to task for being *sindicalista* and propagating a 'peasant-worker' identity while at the same time criticising the confrontational style of the CSUTCB (Choque and Mamani 2003:167; García Linera, León, and Monje 2004:336). CONAMAQ's affinities lie more with the lowland CIDOB and its often more pragmatic way of negotiating with government delegations, sometimes verging on cooptation.[36] The point to make here is that CONAMAQ and similar organisational efforts that stress 'traditionality,' cultural revalorisation, *ayllu*-based development, etc.,[37] created the climate for TCO demands in the highlands (Rada Vélez 2003).

Initially, it was often thought that the TCO model would only apply to lowland conditions and the particular practices of shifting agriculture of that region's indigenous peoples. A first TCO demand in the highlands was filed by the Uru of the Popoo lake area.[38] In 1999 this demand was followed by a demand for 2.5 million hectares by the Quechua communities in the Northern Lipez province of Potosí, who argued that the INRA law 'not only applies to the ethnic groups of the Oriente or Bolivian Amazon but also to the indigenous peoples of the occident of our country, given the principle of generality of the law' (Merz and Calizaya 1999:61). By mid-2003 the number of TCO demands in the highlands had risen to 103, claiming nearly 12 million hectares. According to Rada Vélez (2003), 62 of these demands can be classified as micro-demands that do not exceed 15,000 hectares and therefore will not allow for real territorial management. The meso-demands (up to 500,000 hectares) number 36 and refer to community and inter-community spatialities with limited possibilities for territorial management, while five macro-demands refer to extensions over 500,000 hectares that would allow for a partial reconstitution of histor-

ical territories, resource management, and some margin for indigenous autonomy.[39]

We have seen that the 1953 agrarian reform law left open the possibility of combining collective communal title with individual titling, according to the *pro-indiviso* principle. This combination was ruled out by
the 1996 INRA law that forced an either/or option. This has been
questioned by Pacheco and Valda (2003) and Urioste (2003), who highlight the complex local combinations between private family property
and community property and argue in favour of juridical formulas of a
'mixed' nature.[40] In contrast to this proposal, which would allow for
more market-based land allocation albeit according to community regulations, Rada Vélez (2003) argues that the INRA law allows for the conversion of collectively or individually titled lands into TCO and that this
can be the basis for a voluntary regrouping of properties that over-
comes the extreme fragmentation that has occurred in many cases.
This avoids an individual titling of lands that, in view of their extension, will not provide possibilities for productive development. Instead,
he advocates forms of community production as a more viable way
ahead.[41] Additionally, he argues that the proposal of 'mixed' titling mis-
understands the territorial character of the TCO, which implies that
they are more than just a form of tenure.

That brings us to a second point, the governability of the TCOs and
their place in indigenous strategising. In this respect, it should be
noted that the INRA law is strictly about property. The term *tierras comunitarias de origen* was invented precisely to avoid any clear reference
to territories, because it was thought that recognition of a domain – implying recognition of political authorities and jurisdiction – might lead
to a fragmentation or 'balkanisation' of the country (Vadillo 1997:343).
This contrasts with the case of Colombia, for example. In that country
the *resguardos* are recognised as collective property and at the same
time, at least theoretically, became political-administrative units on a
par with municipalities. The interesting thing here is to note that the
Bolivian Popular Participation Law of 1994, which was concerned with
administrative decentralisation, did involve a certain recognition of indigenous authorities and allowed for the creation of indigenous municipal districts under an indigenous *subalcalde*. It is becoming increasingly clear that in various cases, indigenous groups have devised a dual
strategy. On the one hand, they stake their claims for TCO with the
agrarian authorities, and on the other, they pressure the municipalities
in which they find themselves to create an indigenous municipal district that coincides with the TCO. It is a dual strategy of territorialisa-
tion. The next step then would be to part company with the original
municipality and become a municipality in its own right. While such

efforts were part of silent strategising, by the mid-2000s they were pro-
pelled to the forefront of the national political agenda.[42]

Searching for new ways after neoliberalism

The election of Evo Morales, Bolivia's first indigenous president who
took office in January 2006, has brought a change in the country's political climate, and among other things, the new government seeks to
address some of the issues discussed here. During the election campaign the *Movimiento al Socialismo* (MAS) proposed a *Pacto por la Tierra* (Pact for Land), and in late November 2006 it pushed an agrarian
reform bill (*Ley de Reconducción de la Reforma Agraria*) through Congress.[43] It does not replace, but substantially modifies, the 1996 INRA
law and aims to speed up and broaden redistribution of land in favour
of indigenous and peasant communities (Urioste, Barragán, and Colque 2007:201-202). The intention is to redistribute some 20 million
hectares in favour of this sector, and according to government sources
some 2 million hectares have already been identified as public lands
that can be granted to indigenous and peasant communities.

One controversial aspect of the new law is that the social-economic
function of land is further specified and that it will be verified through
on-site inspection every two years. While peasant and indigenous organisations demanded verification every six months, the opposition demanded a five-year period on the argument that if it were otherwise,
banks would not be willing to supply the credit needed by farmers and
agri-business. Lands that do not fulfill their social-economic function
will revert to the state, which can then grant them to indigenous communities as collective property or adjudicate them through public auction. In fact, this is not really different from the 1996 legislation and
the preference it established for granting land to indigenous and peasant communities; however, in June 2006 the Morales government issued a supreme decree that established that reverted land would only
be granted to indigenous and peasant communities as collective property. The opposition advocated the possibility of individual grants. A
further controversy revolved around expropriation for public utility or
necessity with a compensation that takes market value into account.
The new legislation stipulates that the needs for ethnic reproduction
can be a cause for expropriation, and the government intends to apply
this, for example, to cases in which indigenous people live under conditions of virtual slavery. The opposition wanted to limit the potential
scope of this principle by specifying that it would apply only to four indigenous peoples. Another issue was that according to the new legislation, decisions on agrarian rights by the director of the INRA can only
be appealed at the National Agrarian Tribunal in Bolivia's capital Sucre.

According to the opposition, this reflects an undue centralisation of agrarian justice.

This question of centralisation and decentralisation of agrarian justice is related to another controversial issue that will have to be addressed by the Constituent Assembly that started to meet in August 2006, namely that of 'autonomy'. Over the past few years the movement for autonomy at the department level has developed, led by the Santa Cruz Civic Committee, where agri-business interests are prominently present. The type of autonomy they pursue would, it is suspected, tighten the grip of local elites on local government and on agrarian justice to the detriment of the poor and the indigenous sectors. This has triggered a lively debate in which a spate of counterproposals has been forwarded. These include ideas about indigenous autonomies at various scales and levels, for example to address the governability problems of TCO discussed above. The outcome of the process is difficult to foresee, but it suggests a profound administrative and institutional redesign of the Bolivian state in which the chances of it becoming 'plurinational and intercultural, with autonomies' (Albó and Barrios Suvelza 2006) cannot be discounted.

An urbanising country

As noted in the introduction to this chapter, urbanisation in Bolivia accelerated after the 1952 revolution and was further boosted by the structural adjustment measures since the mid-1980s. In 1950 the country had about 2.7 million inhabitants, of whom 708,568 (26 per cent) lived in urban areas, while by 2001 it had 8.2 million inhabitants, of whom 5,165,882 (62 per cent) lived in urban areas, defined as areas with more than 2,000 inhabitants.[44] Due to the development policies after 1952, Bolivia's urban system became structured around what is called a 'central axis' consisting of the agglomerations around the cities of Santa Cruz, Cochabamba, and La Paz-El Alto.[45] The metropolitan regions of these cities account for 67 of the 156 cities in the country and concentrate 45 per cent of the urban population (Guardia B. 2004; Ministerio de Desarrollo Económico 2005b).

The process of rapid urban expansion has been disorderly and without the necessary investment in public services. It is characterised by irregular urbanisations and plots that have not been legalised, though in contrast with other Latin American countries, most urban housing plots have been acquired through purchase and sale contracts rather than through illegal invasion. In such processes *loteadores* (urban developers) play a key role. They purchase tracts of rural land and subdivide it into housing plots which then are sold through a system of installments. These are private transactions that do not involve legal titles to the land, often because such lands are situated in a legal limbo as they are classified as rural, though their incorporation into urban areas is tolerated.

According to estimates, about 50 per cent of Bolivian households live in dwellings[46] they own as a result of a sale and purchase transaction (Guardia B. 2004:168; Szalachman R. 1999). Especially for the lower income sectors, the plots they can purchase often lack proper documentation or title and fail to comply with urban regulations, and additionally the conditions of access and services are insufficient. There are other forms of access to housing including the *cedida*, a tenure situation in which a dwelling is temporarily lent, which is not at all uncommon (Beijaard 1995). Beijaard even found that, at least in La Paz, it occurs more frequently than renting. The *cedida* modality often involves kinship relations. On the other hand, the weak development of a formal rental market is often attributed to the post-revolutionary legislation regulating this form of tenure, which makes eviction very difficult and sets the maximum rent to be paid at ten per cent of the cadastral value of the property (IADB 2003; ILD n.d.).

For our purposes the regulations and forms of registry of urban real estate are of particular interest. In 1887 a *Ley de Inscripción de Derechos Reales* (Law on the Registry of Real Rights[47]) was enacted and remained operative until its modification and actualisation in 2004. According to this law, in each of the nine department capitals, a central office was to be established where mutations in rights to real estate could be inscribed on a voluntary basis in order to validate them and to protect them from claims by third parties. These offices are part of the judiciary, and they operate separately from the cadastre, which should be managed by the municipalities. When the registry of real rights was initiated, it was based on so-called *folios personales*, where the names of the persons involved in property transfers were manually recorded in 'books', without much further information on the property itself, such as its location, size, etc. The system was therefore quite unreliable.

Efforts at modernisation were undertaken in the late 1980s with the introduction of computerised index cards, and in 2001 further efforts were undertaken with the introduction of the *folio real*, which is related to the property rather than to the person claiming rights to it (ILD n.d.). It was only in late 2004, however, that the 1887 legislation was modified and updated, and clear stipulations about the way in which titles to real estate could be registered were introduced, specifying its location, size, borders, etc. The objective was to create an integrated system for the registration of real rights to real estate in both urban and rural areas. As we have already seen, the clarification of property rights in rural areas has proceeded extremely slowly. For urban areas a new

initiative was taken from the late 1990s onward, with the support of
the Inter-American Development Bank.

This registration system operates independently of the cadastres that
are to be managed by the municipalities, though some efforts at integration seem to have been made. One needs to keep in mind, however,
that until the introduction of the Popular Participation Law of 1994,
municipal administrations functioned only precariously in the nine departmental capitals and in about ten larger cities. With the Popular Participation Law the 314 provincial sections, administrative units that until then only existed on paper, were transformed into municipalities
and assigned various responsibilities. They would also receive twenty
per cent of the national tax income, to be distributed according to population size. Little progress seems to have been made, however, where
municipal cadastres are concerned, and where they exist, they seem
mostly to be in rather poor shape.

The creation of a legal framework for new initiatives regarding urban
land and the legalisation of irregular settlements was started in 1998
in an attempt to restructure the national housing policy.[48] In June of
that year, the Banzer government signed a loan contract with the Inter-
American Development Bank with the objective of supporting the implementation of a National Housing Policy. One component of this
programme was the regularisation of urban property rights. In May
2002 a Law for the Regularisation of Urban Property Rights was enacted, which was slightly modified in 2004. Implementation guidelines were issued by the end of that year charging the Vice Ministry for
Urban Development and Housing with the execution of the Program
of Support for Housing (PROVIVIENDA). The Vice Ministry was to
sign Agreements of Shared Responsibility with the municipal governments of La Paz, El Alto, Santa Cruz, Cochabamba and Sucre in order
to carry out pilot projects of regulation of urban property rights. These
projects were to be the beginning of a rapid and massive conversion of
informal into formal properties.

The law seeks to promote titling and inscription in the Registry of
Real Rights of all urban real estate, whether inscribed or not in the
Registry on 31 December 2000, and it introduces extraordinary, temporary procedures for the regularisation of municipal properties inhabited by occupants before 31 December 1998. In the first case settlements or urbanisations will be selected for regularisation. If there are
conflicts with third parties, the Ministry of Housing and Basic Services
will initiate an adverse possession procedure that should result in a
swift resolution in favour of the occupants of the terrain.[49] A further
possibility is that the municipal government seeks to mediate between
the occupants and the third party. If this fails, it can proceed to expropriation on the grounds of public utility and necessity, provided the oc-

cupants have agreed to pay for the land at a price established by the municipality and have deposited that sum in a bank account in favour of the municipality. The municipality pays for the land according to cadastral value. In the second case, exceptionally, municipalities are authorised to sell terrains they own to the occupants if they have been present at least since 31 December 1998. Green areas and areas zoned for other collective uses may not be sold. The remaining terrains will be sold at cadastral value, and the occupants can receive a mortgage credit of up to 95 per cent of that value.

According to the Ministry of Economic Development, 61,557 terrains had been processed by the pilot programme by May 2005 and were awaiting approval by the respective municipalities (Ministerio de Desarrollo Económico 2005a). However, while the Ministry of Economic Development presented the pilot project as successful, the *Instituto Libertad y Democracia* (ILD n.d.) signaled various difficulties, of a technical nature but also related to politicisation of the programme, for which reason it was suspended in El Alto. According to this evaluation, 'the most important programme for regularisation of urban land in Bolivia had limited reach and could not fulfill its objectives, despite its adequate design and the institutional reforms it introduced'. Although its design was inspired by the ILD-sponsored experience in Peru, there were also some differences that, according to the ILD, accounted for the failures. One problem identified is that the PROVIVIENDA programme did not concentrate competencies and functions but rather acted as a coordinator, leaving decisions to municipal governments and their political priorities. According to the ILD another problem is that the Registry of Real Rights was not reformed and modernised, in contrast to the Peruvian case where a simplified registry process was set up.

The current government of Evo Morales has established some guidelines for a housing policy based on the principle that access to housing is a human right. It seeks to recuperate the role of the state and has announced the objective of creating a million homes in five years to benefit the low-income sectors. It also seeks to establish a land bank in 50 priority municipalities and the assignation of public lands for urbanisation projects as well the implementation of cadastral systems in some 60 municipalities, both to facilitate urban planning, management, and territorial ordering, and to enhance the legal security of property rights. Such policies should also contribute to development, or 'living well', in cities where individual exclusion as it now exists is to be replaced by intercultural integration. However, these guidelines have only begun to be implemented so far.

By way of conclusion

In this chapter I have sought to provide an overview of the development of land tenure systems in Bolivia, taking account of their regionally differentiated nature. This overview shows the pull and push between indigenous land tenure systems and state regulation and the
way this transpires in designs for land tenure legalisation which, in
turn, are oriented by political circumstance and development policies
or models pursued. Designs for land tenure legalisation in Bolivia have
ranged from attempts at replacement of indigenous tenure systems to
what Hoekema (2006) has called forms of incorporation or recognition. Replacement to the detriment of indigenous landholding, for example, was the state strategy that emerged in the latter part of the
nineteenth century, imbued with liberalism and racist ideologies. It allowed for land-grabbing and an expansion of the *hacienda*. Certain
forms of incorporation were present in the post-1952 policies. The reforms introduced after 1993, in the context of neoliberal structural readjustment, moved in the direction of the recognition type, which is
clearly linked to the 'rhetorical constitutional recognition of multiculturalism' (Van Cott 2000a).

The 1953 agrarian reform sought to bring an end to feudal relations
and introduced the notion of the social function of landownership.
Although it referred to the indigenous community and stipulated that
community lands were inalienable, the reform privileged individual
tenure and formally sought to promote modernisation. Overall economic policies, however, resulted in a virtual 'abandonment' (Urioste
2003) of the indigenous peasantry of the highland and valleys . Meanwhile, in the eastern lowlands a sector of large landholdings was consolidated. As a consequence of indigenous-peasant mobilisation, the
1996 legislation maintained the notion of the social function of landed
property, which came to cover the *solar campesino*, small properties,
communal properties, and the *tierras comunitarias de origen* (TCO),
while medium-sized properties and agrarian enterprises were to fulfill
a social-economic function and could be sold and mortgaged. Although
the legislation included some mechanisms for redistribution, these
have hardly been effective, and particularly in the eastern lowlands conflicts have increased in recent years.

The 1996 agrarian reform legislation addressed the territorial claims
of the lowland indigenous peoples, albeit in a limited way. And its implementation has been an extremely slow and frustrating process. It
brought little solace for the highland indigenous peasantry. Their
plight is only partly a result of tenure systems and is due much more
to general agrarian and macro-economic policies. Some have argued
that promoting a land market might be helpful in bringing a redistri-

bution toward more efficient producers, but others have argued that *saneamiento interno*, negotiated regrouping of access to resources within communities that hold collective title, may probably be more effective (Kay 2005; Rada Vélez 2003; Zoomers 1998).

The 1996 legislation addressed indigenous territorial claims in a limited way in the sense that it understood the *tierras comunitarias de origen* as 'lands' rather than spaces for social and cultural reproduction and self-governance. It thus stopped short of what Hoekema (2006) would call recognition. We noted that recently, indigenous communities - 'mini-states' as Carter and Albó (1988) called them, referring to the Aymara communities in particular - have pursued a dual strategy in staking territorial claims through agrarian legislation and seeking further recognition of their local organisational structures through the Popular Participation Law, which would then result in the formation of indigenous municipalities and bring territory and self-governance together; land being not just an asset but also a space for social and cultural reproduction (see also Urioste, Barragán, and Colque 2007). The albeit sometimes reluctant occupation of spaces opened up by neoliberal multiculturalism, as Hale (2002, 2004) has called it, and the frustration with the limits of such multi-culturalism and with neoliberal policies in general, can help us understand much of what has been going in Bolivia in recent years. At present, and in the years to come, the country is likely to be a fascinating laboratory for the development of post-neoliberal alternatives, including issues of land tenure, land management, and territoriality in a diverse society.

Notes

1   This chapter is partly based on an article previously published in *The Journal of Peasant Studies*, Vol. 33, No. 4, pp. 569-611 and has greatly benefited from the editing process for this journal. A first draft of the article was presented at the Conference 'Land, Poverty, Social Justice and Public Action,' organised by the Institute of Social Studies (ISS) and the Inter-Church Organisation for Development and Cooperation (ICCO), 12-14 January 2006, at The Hague, in the Netherlands.

2   Gonzalo Sánchez de Lozada of the *Movimiento Nacionalista Revolucionaro* (MNR, Nationalist Revolutionary Movement), who had been the architect of the neoliberal structural adjustment policies in 1985 and had been president between 1993 and 1997, when he presided over a series of 'second generation' neoliberal reforms, garnered 22.5 per cent of the vote and eventually won the presidency.

3   The rise of the 'New Left' is reflected, to a greater or lesser degree, in the electoral processes in Argentina, Bolivia, Brazil, Chile, Ecuador, Nicaragua, Uruguay, and Venezuela.

4   It is commonly assumed that indigenous people constitute the majority of the Bolivian population. According to Bolivia's 2001 census, the country counted nearly 8.3 million inhabitants of which 62 per cent (of those over fifteen years old) declared themselves to belong to some indigenous people, principally the Quechuas (31 per

cent) and the Aymaras (25 per cent) of the Andean highlands and the colonisation
areas in the eastern lowlands, while the remaining six per cent accounts for some 30
different indigenous peoples in the eastern Amazonian lowlands (Instituto Nacional
de Estadística 2003). For a recent, in-depth study of ethnic identification in Bolivia,
see Molina and Albó (2006).

5   By planting various small fields with the same crop the risks deriving from weather
circumstances (frost, rainfall, etc.) would be diminished. If in one field the crop
failed, in another it might at least yield something. A classic, and still authoritative,
account is the one by Murra (1980). As Goodale and Sky (2000:4) put it, 'the internal organization of *ayllus* can best be conceptualised as a set of 'Chinese boxes,' with
each territorial and kinship unit part of an ever larger set of ethnic units, which cul-
minate in one grand unit ...'. They further comment on *ayllu* land tenure that '[A]
way to envision how this works is to imagine a large quilt, covered with many different patches'.

6   This arrangement provided the basis for a system of indirect rule and the division of
the colonies into a *república de españoles* and a *república de indios*.

7   Three large regions are often distinguished in present-day Bolivia. The highlands (*altiplano*) roughly correspond to the present day Departments of Potosí and Oruro and
part of La Paz. The valleys (*valles*) correspond to parts of the Departments of Cochabamba, Chuquisaca and Tarija. The lowlands (*tieras bajas*) include the *oriente* region
(the Department of Santa Cruz), the Chaco (parts of Santa Cruz, Chuquisaca and Tarija), and the Amazon, which covers the Departments of Pando and Beni as well as
the northern parts of the La Paz and Cochabamba Departments (cf. Terceros Cuéllar
2004:23).

8   The hereditary principle was gradually replaced by an elective system, and the *ayllu*
came to incorporate a civil-religious *cargo* system and became more 'territorialised'.

9   According to Lavaud (1991:173) the number of communities (freeholding) declined
from 11,000 in 1847 to 3,779 by 1950. Community freehold here in the sense that
the 'reciprocity pact' and, where applicable, colonial titles to community lands were
respected.

10 *Haciendas* would be worked under the *colonato* system according to which workers received a small plot to work on their own in return for a number of days of work on
the *hacienda* lands, as well as a series of other obligations. The system tended to be
more rigid in the highlands than in the more mercantilised valley regions.

11 Ideas about the social function of property can be traced back to late nineteenth-century Catholic social doctrine and early twentieth-century West European social consti-
tutionalism. Private property is respected on the condition that it contributes to the
well-being of the population. The issue then becomes the definition of this contribution and its measurement.

12 The other two important emerging parties were the Trotskyist *Partido Obrero Revolucionario* (POR) and the Stalinist *Partido de la Izquierda Revolucionario* (PIR).

13 'Movimiento Nacionalista Revolucionario: Sus bases y principios de acción inmediata,' reproduced in Arze Cuadros (Arze Cuadros 2002:605-643).

14 On the drafting of the decree, see Arze Cuadros (2002:160-161).

15 That is, communities that had managed to have their lands recognised under the late
nineteenth-century legislation.

16 The *pro-indiviso* mode worked through a system of double titling in which the community was titled but heads of households also received a certificate of their share in
the community lands.

17 Although redistributive land reform was on the agenda, Latin American governments
also promoted the occupation (colonisation) of the Amazon region in order to avert
redistribution and for geopolitical reasons. Redistributive reforms were therefore ac-

companied by state-sponsored colonisation projects and 'marches to the East' (Peru, Bolivia) or to the West (Brazil). The promise was to give 'land without people to people without land', without taking into account that such lands were often used by indigenous peoples and, therefore, were not 'without people'. State-directed colonisation schemes often failed to live up to their stated aims, but 'spontaneous' colonisation without state support came to play an important role.

18   Following Lenin's classic 1899 study of the development of capitalism in Russia (Lenin 1979).

19   Although a presidential decree of 1955 stipulated that lands not worked for a period of three years would automatically revert to the community, which then could redistribute them, this decree had little effect. Tenure security rather depends on 'internal pacts' within the local community (Urioste, Barragán, and Colque 2007:216).

20   The *selvícolas* (woodland or jungle dwellers) of the tropical and sub-tropical lowlands were set apart since they were considered to be in a 'savage state and have a primitive organisation' and were to be protected by the state.The Summer Institute of Linguistics and the New Tribes Mission came to Bolivia to bring them into 'civilised life'.

21   Often a distinction is made between *katarismo* and *indianismo*. Whereas *katarismo* emphasizes both class and ethnic identity, looking at reality 'with two eyes', *indianismo* solely stresses ethnic identity.

22   More recently, this has given rise to a debate about the rights of residents, people who most of the time live in a city or temprorily migrate to engage in rural wage labour as part of their livelihood strategy but also retain their rights in the community by complying with local obligations. Although they retain rights to community lands, the modes of land use may change, for example by giving priority to cattle raising instead of agriculture.

23   An instance of this kind of longstanding boundary dispute is the 'war' – in contrast to ritual battles – between the Layme, the Qaqachaca and the Jukumani *ayllus* on the border between the Departments of Oruro and Potosí. In 2000 this dispute escalated into extreme interethnic violence, claiming some 50 lives. It is far beyond the scope of this essay to discuss this episode or similar disputes and their resolution through the intervention of state agencies, international development agencies and NGOs.

24   The decrees are reproduced in República de Bolivia 1996.

25   Taking account of opinion surveys, Sánchez de Lozada invited a moderate Katarista leader, Víctor Hugo Cárdenas, to join him in the race for the presidency, and Cárdenas became Bolivia's first indigenous vice-president (Albó 1994; Van Cott 2000a).

26   Education Minister Hedím Céspedes and his Brazilian associates had obtained 100,000 hectares irregularly.

27   It should be stressed, however, that the push for reform of agrarian legislation also had other antecedents. In 1983-1984 the CSUTCB had elaborated a Fundamental Agrarian Law which was presented to President Siles Zuazo in 1984 'wrapped in ritual Aymara textiles' (Albó 1991:316), in line with *katarismo* uses. Albó highlights that this proposal was not simply about redistribution of lands but contained an outline for a new vision of the state. It centred on the community, the originary right to lands and resources, the recognition of authorities and jurisdiction, among other things. It also proposed the creation of a *Corporación Agropecuaria Campesina* (CORACA), which would be involved in marketing produce and procuring inputs and would be managed autonomously by the peasant-indigenous organisations (the proposal is reproduced in Urioste, Barragán, and Colque 2007:251-269). The initiative actually gained some ground and received support from Dutch development cooperation, among others, but it soon floundered due to 'administrative problems and over-dimensioning' (Albó 1991:333).

28 The definition used in the law is clearly inspired on ILO Convention 169. The TCO
    mode was basically geared to respond to the demands of the indigenous peoples of
    the eastern lowlands and to legalise large extensions of land including various com-
    munities.

29 By 2000, in the context of an 'economic reactivation' program launched by the Ban-
    zer government (1997-2002), the land tax was reduced to insignificance.

30 For earlier critical overviews of the process, see Romero Bonifaz (2001, 2003). Funda-
    ción Tierra (2004:30) comments that 'Saneamiento has been carried out as if agrarian
    reform has already ended and all that remains to be done is the legal formalisation
    of property rights'.

31 For a critical evaluation, see Hernáiz et al. 2001.

32 This caused alarm among indigenous-peasant organisations because the extension of
    the term of payment would further undermine the reversion mechanism that should
    make land available for distribution through endowment, at no cost.

33 This was only one move in an ongoing 'war of positions' and overt and covert pres-
    sures of indigenous-peasant organisations, on the one hand, and would-be entrepre-
    neurs, on the other (Villanueva I. Arturo D. 2004).

34 By the mid-1990s a *Movimiento Sin Tierra* (Landless Movement, MST), similar to its
    Brazilian counterpart, emerged in Tarija and then expanded to Santa Cruz and other
    lowland departments (García Linera, León, and Monje 2004). Through the occupa-
    tion of unused or underused lands, or properties that do not comply with their so-
    cial-economic function, the movement seeks to force a genuine redistribution and to
    fend off evictions based on dubious title or simple encroachment by large land-
    owners. Agrarian conflict has definitely migrated to the eastern lowlands and is in-
    tensifying there with landowners organising 'white guards'. In November 2001 six
    landless peasants were killed, as well as one attacker, in what is known as the 'Panan-
    ti massacre'. Crabtree (2005:61) characterises the situation as a 'political time bomb'.

35 According to law the TCO would have exclusive rights to the forest resources within
    their perimeter. The government, however, argued that forestry concessions granted
    before full legalisation of the TCO constituted 'acquired rights'.

36 Much of the history still has to be written. The CIDOB itself is subject to splits and
    realignments, as is CONAMAQ (García Linera, León, and Monje 2004).

37 This goes in tandem with a formalisation and codification of organisational struc-
    tures and regulations as, for example, in the *Estatuto de la Organización Originaria de
    Ayllus de Curawara Marrka, Provincia Sajama, Primera Sección – Depearamento Oruro,
    1999* (typos in the original) and its corresponding *Reglamento Interno*.

38 The Uru are considered the most ancient surviving people of the Andes region, living
    around the Popoo lake in Bolivia and the Titicaca lake in present-day Peru. The story
    goes that the Incas considered them so poor that they only required them to fill a
    reed with fleas as tribute to the empire.

39 In 82 of the cases, the demand is for endowment, and in the remaining 21 cases, the
    demand is to convert lands titled to the community under the 1953 legislation into
    TCO.

40 Our studies on Mexico suggest a similar pattern: while people may be interested in
    certification of individual or family rights, they do not relinquish community regula-
    tions and hesitate about or reject the individualisation, titling and registration pro-
    grammes promoted by government agencies.

41 The debate over more market-based and individualised resource allocation versus
    communal management is ongoing and, on the one hand, will have to take account
    of the often extremely complex forms of community- and inter-community-based re-
    source management and allocation under difficult climatic and soil conditions while,
    on the other hand, it should take account of the changing situation that has been

characterised in terms of a 'new rurality', highlighting the complex combinations of rural, urban and long-distance migration livelihood strategies that are affecting modes of land use and tenure (Giarracca 2001; Kay 2005; Urioste, Barragán, and Colque 2007).

42 For a recent contribution to the debate over the complex interrelationship between indigenous land tenure and territoriality in a context of social and economic change see Urioste, Barragán and Colque 2007.

43 The law was approved in the Chamber of Deputies, where MAS is in the majority, on 15 November, but sessions of the Senate were boycotted by the opposition until two *suplentes* (alternate senators) from the opposition and one senator made it possible to adopt the law. Outside Congress, indigenous and peasant organisations and agri-business interests mobilised in favour and in opposition to the reform proposal, respectively. At the time a list of large landholders circulated, which documented how politically well-connected families had acquired huge extensions of land under previous governments (for a detailed account see Fundación Tierra 2007).

44 Note that this implies that the rural population is still growing in absolute terms.

45 In 1988 the city of El Alto became independent from La Paz.

46 The term *vivienda* includes independent houses, separate room(s) inside a larger building or on a plot shared with other dwellings, apartments that consist of a number of rooms in a larger building or on the same plot as other dwellings but that, in contrast to the category of separate room(s), have private service connections, and, finally, improvised dwellings.

47 Real rights refer to the *ius ad rem* of ancient Roman law, which establishes the rights of a subject to an object of economic value and guarantees protection against claims by third parties. Real rights not only refer to private ownership but include rental, usufruct and other sorts of rights, provided that they are duly registered.

48 Since the mid-1920s, something like housing policies have existed in Bolivia under various modalities without, however, coming near to really addressing, let alone solving, the problem of the housing deficit. By 1998 it was decided to extinguish the *Fondo Nacional de Vivienda Social* (National Fund for Social Housing, FONVIS), which had been created in 1992. Like most of the earlier initiatives, it was riddled with corruption and had achieved very little. In 1998 a market-oriented National Program to Subsidise Housing was launched, but this also seems to have been hardly effective.

49 Depending on the documentation the occupants can produce, they must have peacefully occupied the terrain for five or ten years. The adverse possession procedure does not apply to public lands and cannot be invoked in cases of secondary or derived real rights, such as renting, usufruct, guardianship, etc.

12 Problems undermining the titling and tenure security of common-property lands: The case of indigenous people of Bolivia's lowlands

Diego Pacheco

Introduction

The recognition of indigenous jurisdictions has occurred in several countries of Latin America in the last decade as a process closely linked to the reforms of the state, not only as a result of indigenous people's protests and mobilisations (Assies 1999) but also in relation to the last wave of the twentieth-century decentralisation policies (Pacheco 2007). According to Van de Sandt (2003:125), one of the most notable features of the Latin American new constitutional frameworks is that for the first time in history they have come to acknowledge the multi-cultural and pluri-ethnic character of Latin American societies and states, incorporating or reformulating the recognition and protection of indigenous people's rights.

It is now widely understood that property rights refer to an overlapping bundle of rights and that there are multiple sources of property rights, such as: the state, customary law, religious law, project law, and local laws that provide the bases for claiming property rights (Meinzen-Dick and Pradhan 2002; Nkonya and Meinzen-Dick 2005). This scenario has also been called a polycentric legal system (Lund 1998), which suggests that legal and property relations do not evolve in a linear fashion from the customary to the formal in a sort of legal centralism but that they can coexist in a given context (Manji 2006a).

Bolivia is a country marked by legal pluralism where individuals as holders of rights and duties, and as members of different social networks, are subject to various legal orders (Prill-Brett 1994). In fact, Bolivia has initiated the implementation of the 1995 constitutional mandate of recognising legal pluralism and certain territorial rights guaranteed by the state (Van Cott 2000b) in order to ensure collective tenure security for indigenous peoples. In Bolivia as in other Latin American countries – such as Colombia and Panama – new legal arrangements for indigenous territorial autonomy have emerged, implying that indigenous peoples are allowed to govern themselves, within a certain territory and to a specific extent, according to their own cultural patterns, social institutions, and legal systems (Assies and Hoekema 1994). And it has been understood that in order to realise the foregoing postulates, indigenous peoples must have a clear delimitation of their common-property areas or territorial jurisdictions.

It is nowadays recognised that individualisation, titling, and registration (ITR) programmes often do not deliver the security they promise and are difficult to implement. As a result of the critique of such programmes, the World Bank Policy Research Report (2003d) takes a more flexible approach to communal titling. This report, drawn up by Klaus Deininger, argues that at lower levels of development, communal titling may be more cost-effective and may deliver a rather acceptable degree of tenure security.[1] However, the Bolivian experience shows that the formalisation of indigenous[2] rights to common-property areas is a lengthy and complicated process ridden with uncertainty. In Bolivia, the land regularisation process has not only been permanently delayed but has also been hindered and distorted by the three powers of the state: executive, judicial, and legislative (CEJIS 2001). This chapter analyses the broad set of hurdles in the process of titling common-property areas that obstructs the fulfilment of the promise of giving legal land tenure security to indigenous people. Taking the institutional analysis literature (e.g. Ostrom 2005) as a point of departure, I highlight the three main problems we encounter in the regularisation of common-property areas, namely problems of a contextual, motivational, or informational nature.

In order to analyse the extent to which these problems are manifested in the context of Bolivia's lowlands, I discuss two demands for regularisation of common-property lands or *originary* community lands (*Tierras Comunitarias de Origen* or TCO) made by the indigenous people of Guarayos and by the Chiquitanos-Monte Verde, both located in the Department of Santa Cruz. It is important to notice that after roughly twelve years of initiating the processes of land regularisation, only half of the Guarayos TCO has been titled, while the process in the Chiquitano TCO was formally concluded in 2006, and they received a legal title in July 2007.

In this chapter I shall first compare the already titled part of the Guarayos TCO with the area that has not yet been titled and analyse the extent to which contextual factors are creating problems in the titling process and how this impacts indigenous people's tenure security. Second, by comparing the cases of the titling process carried out in the Guarayos and Chiquitanos TCO, I seek to assess the influence of motivational and informational factors in the land regularisation process and how they impact tenure security.

I shall show that the rural context is highly dynamic, with a variety of actors making their moves in order to influence the regularisation programme. Indeed, although these programmes were being carried out, encroachment on forest land in the *de facto* possession of indigenous peoples increased. The programmes themselves seem to provide incentives for state officials and indigenous persons to become involved in corrupt practices and free-riding. Asymmetric power relations and lack of local control mechanisms contribute to this dynamic. I further discuss how the problem of the Samaritan dilemma contributes to delays in the process of land regularisation and maximises the impact of the inefficiencies in the land regularisation process.

This chapter is divided into six sections, including this introduction. The second section discusses the tenure situation of the indigenous people of Bolivia's lowlands as well as the main antecedents of the TCO land regularisation procedure. The third section introduces the theoretical framework developed in order to give a more comprehensive understanding of the problems that are likely to affect land regularisation procedures and tenure insecurity. In the fourth section I discuss some aspects of the research carried out in the two TCO selected for this study, namely the difficulties in achieving tenure security through the titling process and the problems created by the titling process itself. The fifth section is dedicated to a discussion of the main findings in light of the theoretical framework adopted for this study. And in the final section I summarise the main conclusions.

Background

Historically, the population of Bolivia's lowlands[3] consisted of indigenous groups who formed extended families and lived in domestic units that developed highly mobile lifestyles adapted to their tropical forest habitat. They combined shifting cultivation of small fields with hunting, fishing, and gathering. But particularly since the end of the nineteenth century, their access to forest lands has come under pressure as their areas of forest use were not recognised, and they were not legally empowered to defend them. Indeed, as soon as the new, independent Republic of Bolivia was constituted in 1825, the national government began a formal process of confiscation of indigenous people's forestlands by declaring them to be part of the national domain, since these areas were considered 'empty' and, even if they were inhabited, it was thought that these populations did not deserve the same citizens' rights as other Bolivians (Fawcett 1910).

In the course of the nineteenth century, indigenous people's forestlands were drastically reduced, and they were often forced to retreat to ever more remote and impenetrable refuges. In the twentieth century they faced an aggressive entry of forest concessionaries in a selective

search for valuable tree species. In the 1970s, with the help of anthropologists, a process of indigenous organisation got under way, bringing
together traditionally rival groups, in order to defend the areas needed
for their socio-cultural reproduction or indeed for sheer survival. In
1990 this organisation process enabled them to undertake a historical
March for Territory and Dignity from the city of Trinidad to La Paz, the
seat of government, located in the highlands at an altitude of nearly
4,000 metres. It is argued that for most Bolivian people, indigenous
groups did not exist until they presented their land claims for common-property regularisation.[4] With this march the indigenous peoples
of the lowlands successfully pressured the government of Jaime Pas
Zamora (1989-1993) to recognise eight territories they had been able to
control despite all the encroachments and invasions.[5]

At that time, there were two types of forestlands accessed and used
by indigenous people through customary law: (1) consolidated lands
where the main settlements of the community were located and which
were mainly devoted to shifting agriculture and small-scale livestock
raising, and (2) open-access forest areas for hunting and gathering forest products. These two types of areas were held by indigenous people
under *de facto* customary–property rights. In some cases these forestland areas did not form a single unit but were usually scattered around
the demarcated and fenced land of the large estates that had encroached upon the areas traditionally used by the indigenous population.

Customary law contains long-standing principles accepted by all
community members, which are adjusted to suit specific village situations and which are applied flexibly. Individuals are responsible for enforcing the rules within the community boundaries. Such rules usually
reflect the following principles: (1) community members are entitled to
use land but are not allowed to sell or mortgage forestlands; (2) all
community members, regardless of gender and age, have equal access
to the forest resources. Communities respect the right of 'first come-
first served' in claiming land and forest products and the right of 'who
works will benefit' in utilising common resources. In some indigenous
communities, however, the land was individually divided, corresponding roughly to 50 ha per person;[6] (3) precious and/or scarce forest products (e.g. game) are usually shared within the community, in that de-
limited areas are designed for hunting, and there are hunting regulations according to dry or wet seasons; (4) the village community as a
whole – and not only the local leader – has the right to make decisions
regarding the management of natural resources. This includes the decision to entrust individuals and/or groups with certain parts of the
land, e.g. agricultural fields; (5) outsiders, who ask for forest or land re-

sources, are usually granted access to the resource if they promise to live according to the indigenous groups' principles.[7]

Regarding organisational arrangements, there are three major decision-making levels: (1) the community assembly, the major decision-making body; (2) an elected committee of leaders whose composition and responsibilities may vary from one locality to another but which usually intervenes in the resolution of local disputes; and (3) a local leader who is the visible head of the community. All authorities are elected and removed freely according to their performance in carrying out their duties. Communities belonging to the same indigenous group are organised in an indigenous 'subcentral' — a democratically elected body in charge of managing both internal and external affairs of the indigenous group as a whole.

Indigenous groups of Bolivia's lowlands have obtained legal titles since the mid-twentieth century in three ways: (1) titles acquired through claims of lands by Catholic and Protestant churches for the indirect benefit of indigenous people; (2) titles granted by the state as common-property areas only at the level of small communities and in very specific areas of the country; and (3) titles granted in 1996 to indigenous groups who participated in the first indigenous march for territory and dignity – eight in total – using Supreme Decrees, though the total surface of the territory had to be validated through the new forest-land regularisation process in a period of ten months (Hernáiz and Pacheco 2000).[8]

As noted earlier, the Bolivian legal framework has never favoured indigenous peoples. The demand for legal titling of indigenous territories since the beginning of the 1990s showed that the biggest threat to tenure security of indigenous people was the progressive encroachment of agricultural estates, timber entrepreneurs, livestock ranchers, and small-scale farming migrants from the highlands on their forestland areas, significantly reducing the areas they occupied *de facto*.[9] The threat to tenure security consisted in the impediment to continue exercising withdrawal rights in their open forest areas. Because of Bolivia's particular historical process, tenure security for indigenous people is very closely related, on one hand, to getting legal forestland tenure and, on the other, to collectively defending the achieved legal property rights.[10]

In the year 1996 a new agrarian law was approved in Bolivia — known as the INRA[11] law. The goals behind this new legal design were to achieve a more efficient and transparent land administration system, to clarify the land tenure situation, to identify public land suitable for the settlement of small-scale farmers, and to promote a more sustainable use of Bolivia's land resources (World Bank 2006). The new law established new types of land property rights and a special common-property regime for indigenous people: the *Originary* Community Lands or TCO. Although indigenous leaders were demanding the titling of indigenous territories, the new law designated the common-property areas as TCO to make explicit the difference between this type of property and the conventional understanding of indigenous territories, which includes jurisdiction and ownership rights regarding renewable natural resources. Indigenous groups thus can gain formal collective proprietary rights over forestlands that they have occupied *de facto*. All of the community's members have withdrawal rights – the right to make use of the forestland – but no alienation rights that would allow them to sell or lease their forestland. The process of TCO land regularisation is in practice a metre by metre battle between indigenous and other rural actors that due to different circumstances are living within or claiming rights within the areas demarcated as TCO demands.

The INRA law also adjusted the state organisation for land administration and judicial conflict resolution by developing a new organisational framework for land administration and dispute resolution. The National Institute of Agrarian Reform or INRA was established to undertake the land titling procedure, and a National Agrarian Tribunal or TAN was created to resolve land disputes. Additionally, the Land Superintendence was established to oversee sustainable land management. In order to delimit rural land property rights, a process of land regularisation was launched, including all regions and rural actors, indigenous populations among them. The regulatory framework for land titling is very complicated and expensive, though for indigenous people a specific procedure has been elaborated: the TCO land regularisation process or SAN-TCO. According to the 1996 law, the clarification of land rights was to be executed in a ten-year period (through 2006), but since progress over the past ten years has been very modest, the period has recently been extended for an additional seven years (to 2013).

During the process of land regularisation for the indigenous peoples, the assessment of the rights of individual landholders – the so-called 'third parties' – is linked to the fulfilment of the Socio-Economic Function (FES). This means that state officials should verify that the claimant is effectively working the area claimed. In practice, this implies a very strong emphasis on the development of agricultural production and cattle-raising activities because it has been more difficult to verify the FES regarding forestry and biodiverse uses of forestland.

An indigenous group can obtain formal proprietary rights to the traditional forestlands that they have occupied *de facto* by filing a legal TCO titling claim with the central government. After the reception of the claim, two reports have to be elaborated by agencies of the Bolivian government: (1) a report of the spatial and economic needs of the indigenous people, which determines the amount of forestland that should be titled in favour of the indigenous groups according to its socio-economic needs, and (2) a certification of indigenous origin, which determines whether the claimant is indeed an indigenous group. Subsequently, land regularisation fieldwork is undertaken, consisting of the demarcation of the TCO frontiers and the verification of the FES for individual landholdings within the area demanded as TCO. In some cases this demarcation and verification are outsourced to private companies because INRA lacks the technical and administrative capacities to carry out the regularisation process, but such outsourcing rarely occurs in the SAN-TCO process. Table 12.1 highlights the principal steps in the SAN-TCO land regularisation procedure.

Table 12.1   *Steps of the land regularisation process*

Step	Entity in charge	Description
Formulation of the land claim	Indigenous people	Indigenous people formulate the forestland claim.
Presentation of the land claim	Indigenous people	Indigenous people present the claim to the Bolivian government.
Admission of the land claim	National Director of INRA	The INRA admit the land claim in order to initiate the land regularisation process.
Certification of indigenous identity	State entity in charge of indigenous people topics	The Bolivian government certifies if the claimers are considered indigenous people.
Geo reference	INRA national	The physical delimitation of the TCO boundaries is carried out.
Determinative resolution of the land regularisation process	INRA national	The INRA formally initiates the process of TCO land regularisation.
Report of indigenous spatial needs	State entity in charge of indigenous people topics	The Bolivian government establishes how much forestland is required by the indigenous people to satisfy their subsistence needs.
Public campaign	INRA departmental	Local people are informed about the land regularisation process.
Demarcation fieldwork	INRA departmental or land regularisation enterprises	The delimitation of the TCO limits and of the parcels of individual owners within the TCO is developed.
Technical and juridical evaluation	INRA departmental or land regularisation enterprises	The evaluation of the legal documentation of the parcels of individual owners is carried out.
Determination of land price for parcels subject to adjudication	Agrarian superintendence	The land price for land adjudication to individual possessors of land within the TCO is determined.
Publication of results	INRA departmental or land regularisation enterprises	The results of the land regularisation process are presented to the local people.

Step	Entity in charge	Description
Mistakes or omissions retrieval (to request)	INRA departmental	The re-evaluation of some specific observed mistakes is undertaken.
Final resolution of the process	INRA national	Resolution determining that the land regularisation process has been concluded.
Notification of final resolutions	INRA departmental	The results of the land regularisation process are notified to the landholders.
Resistance to TAN resolutions	Persons considered affected by the process	Individual and collective owners if they want can appeal the results of the land regularisation process.
Resolutions of endowment and titling	INRA national	Resolutions for granting land rights to indigenous people and individual parcels' owners are carried out.
Payment of adjudication land prices and land regularisation fees	Buyers of land	Individual land owners who possess land legally are required to pay for the land acquired.
Titling	President of the Republic	Titles are signed up.
Resolution declaring land regularised area	INRA national	The final resolution indicating that the area has been declared titled is undertaken.

TAN = National Agrarian Tribunal; INRA = National Institute of Agrarian Reform

In order to avoid conflicts between indigenous people and individual private landholders within the TCO area, the law determines that the latter should be titled only if they hold legal papers and fulfil the FES. Thus, the process of land regularisation in a TCO implies the revision of the legal documentation supporting the possession of the land and the verification of the FES of such landholders in tandem with the TCO demarcation. According to the Agrarian Law indigenous peoples should be compensated with the same amount of forestlands as that titled to landholders settled within the TCO area. Therefore, the TCO land regularisation process is aimed at identifying, on the one hand, which actors living within the demanded TCO area are considered legal landowners, and on the other, expelling those who settled illegally and demarcating the frontiers of the forestland belonging to each TCO.

In theory, indigenous people who have obtained legal title to a TCO should be protected from the biggest threats to tenure security that have emerged in Bolivia's lowlands in the last few decades. Nevertheless, the forestland regularisation process has been slow and bureaucratic, and the achievements are below the indigenous peoples' expectations. At present, from among 52 TCO claims only 30 have been titled (partly), representing only five million ha out of the twenty million ha demanded as TCO. This is because the land regularisation is excessively bureaucratic, procedures are complex, and agreements among rural actors are difficult to reach. Also, the regulations of the INRA law were modified three times, and there have been problems in achieving rural actors' consensus with respect to the assessment of the FES and the verification of individual landholders' property records (Betancur 2003).

The problems likely to undermine land regularisation processes and tenure security

The legal recognition of common-property areas

Formalising land tenure systems has been one of the most persistent policies regarding rural development in the last few years, particularly favouring individual private landholding because there was a widespread belief that individual, secure, and transferable property rights to land promotes investment, resource conservation, and efficiency (Heltberg 2002).

Although the common-property literature has pointed out that legalising customary tenure has major benefits for local people, only recently has there been a shift in the international donor community towards an understanding of the positive results of titling common-property areas (World Bank 2003d), making it easier for some developing world countries to move to legalisation of customary tenure. Common property refers to resources under communal ownership where access rules are defined through community membership (Heltberg 2002). This shift is related to the growing recognition of the benefits that can be derived from transferring control over natural resources from central governments to local bodies (Katon, Anna Knox, and Dick 2001). It is understood that communal ownership may give sufficient security of tenure since rules are enforced by legitimate local authorities and enjoy widespread acceptance. Also, it is argued that traditional rights tend to be even more secure when official land codes give legal recognition to communal systems or at least do not undermine them (Heltberg 2002).

The question is, however, how traditional common-property rights can be recognised at the level of the group. The answer is mainly related to the procedures that the process of customary tenure legalisation aiming at providing for a 'group right' should follow in practice. Fitzpatrick (2005) argues that there is no unique best practice model for legally recognising customary tenure but that a typological framework for developing legal responses to customary tenure can be developed that takes account of the nature and causes of tenure insecurity. According to this author, there are four possible models, of which three are relevant for the case at hand: (1) the minimalist approach in which customary tenure is recognised without a great deal of intervention in the groups' internal or external affairs; (2) the agency method in which the state seeks to identify the agents and to transform the institutions that recognise and manage customary land relations; and (3) the method in which interventions allow customary groups to incorporate and establish written constitutions for the governance of their own affairs.

The literature on legalisation of customary tenure usually assumes that this is a straightforward process, meaning that once central governments have made the decision to legalise indigenous forestland tenure, for example, there are no additional variables that can significantly hinder such a process. In fact, there is little literature analysing the problems of land tenure regularisation, and it is often assumed that land titling projects can improve tenure security almost automatically, though there is some evidence to the contrary in practice.

Heltberg (2002) mentions that there are costs, difficulties, and distortions associated with the titling process that mostly benefit the wealthy and better educated people, leading to unfair outcomes, conflicts, and inefficiencies. There is some empirical evidence collected in Honduras, Bolivia, and Mexico showing that individual land titling projects have triggered new conflicts, not only because there may be various subjects with superposed agrarian rights or because of inheritance problems but also because of the incapacity of bureaucracies and the mistaken assumptions about social organisations' property rights (De Ita 2003; Hernáiz et al. 2001; Jansen and Roquas 1998). Studies of processes of demarcating and titling common-property forestlands in Latin America do not describe the conflicts regarding land regularisation but are rather focused on understanding their history and the forces that come together and underlie the conflict (Offen 2003). There are, however, some studies that touch upon the conflicts in scenarios of common-property titling. For instance, in Colombia conflicts are related to the lack of political will of the national land agency's officials in charge, resulting in a substantive delay in the titling schedule and in a lack of coordination between those officials and indigenous communities' organisations (Ng'weno 2000). It has also been observed in other countries, such as Vietnam, that legalising customary land for community groups – in accordance with customary law – may achieve a high level of acceptance by community groups but can create conflicts with wider public-goods objectives related to land allocation and may not help to clarify land tenure in situations in which there are overlapping and contested claims to the same land (World Bank 2004a).

The difficulties for titling customary tenure

Titling a given forestland area as common property is not an isolated process. It is embedded in a situation characterised by political, social, economic, and biophysical issues, which I denote as contextual factors. As mentioned previously, in Latin America there has been a strong political shift towards the recognition and titling of community forestland on the basis of customary tenure. However, in each of the countries where such titling processes take place, they are shaped by distinctive characteristics.

The most important contextual factor is related to the different rural actors' interests regarding land use, which in tropical areas is the clash between agricultural uses and forestry uses, which is also a manifestation of the clashes between individual landholders and community landholders. Forestry systems based on customary tenure are prevalent in many tropical forest areas inhabited by indigenous populations. To date, at least a quarter of the world's forests (246 million ha) are possessed by indigenous community groups in common-property arrangements, which means that their access to forest resources has more than doubled in the last fifteen years, and can be expected to do the same in the next fifteen years (White and Martin 2002). However, vast forest expanses are still being converted to agricultural purposes, a land use decision that is contingent upon its costs against the expected income from agricultural or forestry-related activities. In fact, according to the FAO, deforestation in tropical areas occurred at a rate of 7.3 million hectares per year between 2000 and 2005 (FAO 2005).

There are also distinctive socio-economic stakeholders, and it has been observed that generally indigenous people are the poorest among the poor. As a result of the distinctive interplay among socio-economic interests regarding tropical forestlands, stakeholders are able to develop mechanisms to pressure governments to establish legal and administrative frameworks for implementing and enforcing titling procedures that benefit their own interests. If legal procedures are to be more responsive to local people's needs, complicated mechanisms may have to be designed to develop the land titling task. Several Latin American countries have been characterised by the presence of dichotomised land tenure structures and the conflicting interests between forestland-holders. The powerful are likely to create barriers to access to forest-lands for the less powerful. In such situations state law most often tends to favour the interests of the medium- and large-scale land-holders.

In order to have a more comprehensive understanding of these contextual issues and their impacts on local people, I used the Institutional Analysis and Development (IAD) theoretical framework outlined in

Figure 12.1 below. The IAD is a multiplex conceptual map showing contextual variables, an action arena, and patterns of local actors' interactions and outcomes (Ostrom 2005), which helps to explain the interaction of complex variables in specific action situations.

Figure 12.1   *The institutional analysis and development framework*

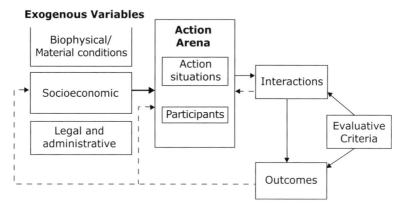

Source: Ostrom 2005.

According to this conceptual map, the titling process of community forestlands is influenced by some contextual variables such as the biophysical characteristics, socioeconomic structure, and legal-administrative systems. My empirical analysis assesses this scenario by looking at the extent to which contextual variables influence different outcomes regarding the land tenure security of indigenous people claiming community forestlands.

Local land owners tend to filter, modify, adapt and sometimes even ignore the formal *de jure* rules, interpreting the meaning of the land reforms and transforming the rules in form into rules in use. Also, the way in which local forest users respond to government policies and to the particular bundles of rights available to them depends on other factors, such as the presence of valuable land and forest products, market opportunities, and social networks connecting local users to market actors and government agencies, among others. Therefore, formal rules are reframed at the local level depending on power relations among actors, information and knowledge capabilities, and existence or lack of control mechanisms. I have identified the most important variables that are at play when talking about action situations in Table 12.2.

Contextual factors are in constant interplay with local actors' interactions in the creation of specific action situations. In the titling process there can be at least four action situations that result from the interac-

Table 12.2 *Problems likely to undermine the common-properties' titling process*

Contextual problems

C1	*Biophysical:* Distinctive biophysical features of the TCO areas.
C2	*Socio-economic:* Contested interest of rural actors' groups regarding forestlands involved in the process of land regularisation and titling.
C3	*Legal system:* Legal and administrative problems related to the titling procedures.

Motivational problems

M1	*Free-riding:* Not contributing to a joint effort, as the contributors benefits from what others contribute.
M2	*Rent-seeking:* Rents are returns on activities that cannot be competed away in an open competitive process. There is a possibility of tied aid opening opportunities for rent-seeking since the recipient country must purchase goods and services from the donor country.
M3	*The Samaritan dilemma:* The Samaritan (donor) is confronted with choosing between helping and not helping. If the Samaritan extends help and the recipient exerts great effort, the Samaritan will be benefited substantially as will the recipient — but from the recipient's perspective, they could be even better of if low effort was expanded.
M4	*Asymmetric power relationships:* In many situations, individuals face other actors with greater command over key resources. Frequently, power is distributed in a highly skewed fashion, and actors are embedded in the context of a pre-existing distribution of economic and political power.
M5	*Corruption:* Individuals who are allocated enforcement powers may hold up formal action unless illegal rewards are made available to them.

Informational problems

I1	*Trust-monitoring:* The bigger the community and/or the larger the relevant terrain, the more important the development of explicit rules and monitoring mechanisms.
I2	*Principal-agent situations:* Much of productive life is organised in hierarchies in which individuals in decision-making situations are arrayed in a series of superior-subordinate positions. All hierarchies involve delegated authority to agents who may have their own separate goals.
I3	*Adverse selection:* This occurs when individuals know their own characteristics — have private information — but others do not share this private information. This usually occurs when the selection of beneficiaries or future employee is a non-random process that tends to select for the least-productive individuals.

Note: Based on Ostrom et al. 2001

tions between: (1) the donors and the government; (2) the government and state officials in charge of carrying out the titling on the ground; (3) the direct beneficiaries and other rural interest groups or landholders; and (4) the government and both local and rural interest groups. In this context, donors are represented by the international cooperation that provides the funding for carrying out the titling process. The national and departmental governmental levels represent the entities and leading persons in charge of enforcing the state law's regulations for the titling process. State officials are the technicians who do the fieldwork necessary for demarcating and verifying the legality of claims to forestland. The beneficiaries are local communities that will benefit from the titling process. Finally, the interest groups are the landholders who are in permanent interplay with the TCO beneficiaries or indigenous people as simply neighbours or as competitors in the use and exploitation of forestlands.

My empirical analysis assesses these action situations by looking at the extent to which there are problems resulting from local actors' interactions hindering the titling process of indigenous common-property areas. These are problems of dysfunction that stand in the way of achieving joint benefits. In the institutional analysis literature they are typified as motivational and informational problems (Ostrom et al. 2001). The first category stems from people's inadequate motivation to contribute to the production of joint benefits even when participants have complete information. The second category is related to problems of missing information or asymmetric information about the actions being taken by actors or about the characteristics of these actors, exacerbating, in turn, the motivational problems (*id.*)

The empirical enquiry

In the foregoing I discussed the common belief that legalising common-property forests is a straightforward process leading automatically to tenure security. My empirical research is aimed at analysing: (1) the factors helping or hindering the titling of common-property areas of indigenous people of Bolivia's lowlands and then impeding their enjoyment of tenure security as a result of the titling process; and (2) the extent to which new problems have arisen as a result of the land titling process, making it difficult for indigenous people to achieve tenure security.

In order to explore these two issues, I have selected two TCOs, each belonging to a particular indigenous group, taking into account that the TCOs selected should favour a comparison of the two scenarios that I have described in terms of contextual, motivational, and informational problems. I have taken the Guarayos and Chiquitanos-Monte Verde TCOs as the case study sites, both located in the Department of Santa Cruz as shown in Map 12.1. For my PhD dissertation I carried out fieldwork in this region and have a detailed knowledge of the ongoing land titling processes there. My case study methods are qualitative, and my findings are based on a review of secondary information and a few extensive visits to some of the communities located in each of the TCOs where I carried out interviews with the principal leaders of the indigenous settlements in 2005. Additional interviews were carried out in early 2007 to update previous information.

According to Betancur (2003), the Monte Verde TCO is a symbol of the indigenous struggles in Bolivia not only because of the technical, political, and juridical irregularities that have been committed in the land regularisation process in this TCO, but also because of the indigenous mobilisations for titling its common-property areas. The titling

Map 12.1 *Location of case study areas*

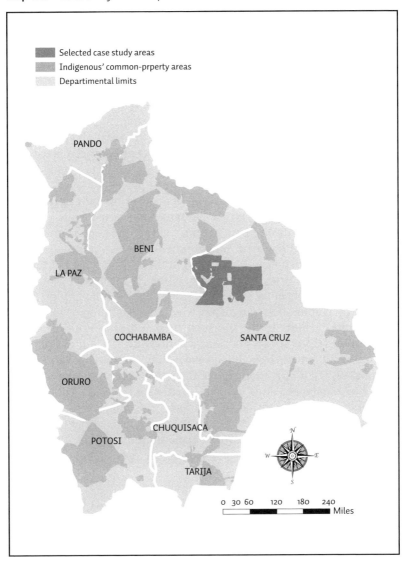

of this TCO was demanded almost a decade ago. The land claim was presented by the Chiquitanos' indigenous organisation in 1996 in the context of mobilisations and negotiations over the new Agrarian Law (Tamburini and Betancur 2003). The regularisation process took a decade, and only in 2007 did the Chiquitanos receive their TCO title.

The Guarayos TCO is another emblematic case. While it faced the same problems as the Chiquitanos-Monte Verde TCO, it is in addition an example of disunity among the indigenous inhabitants themselves and its repercussions on the titling process.[12] In 1997 the *Instituto Nacional de Reforma Agraria* (INRA) geo-referenced the area demanded by the Guaraya indigenous people. This resulted in the 'immobilisation' of an area of 2,205,537 ha on 11 July 1997, which means that for the time being the status quo should be maintained. In order to carry out the process of clarification and titling, the immobilised area was then divided into six polygons to facilitate the legalisation process by giving priority to the less populous and therefore less conflicted areas. The INRA thus eschewed addressing land conflicts among different actors in the region, and this approach meant that the areas claimed for the TCO but located in the vicinity of the agrarian frontier remained in a legal limbo. As a result, informal transfers and conflicts among different actors increased. Through this piecemeal process of legalisation by polygons, a little over half of the area demanded by the Guarayos has been titled since their demand was presented in August 1996.

The two peoples involved are among the first indigenous groups for whom the land regularisation programme has been initiated. The Chiquitano is an indigenous group located in the dry-forest area of the Department of Santa Cruz. It was not traditionally a cohesive group, but rather the result of the coexistence of a variety of ethnic groups differentiated by cultures and languages who developed a somewhat common cultural identity in the course of time and as a result of outside interventions (Díez Astete and Murillo 1998). In the mid-seventeenth century Jesuit priests brought forest-dwelling groups together in several missions. With the expulsion of the Jesuits a century later, some of them had their forestlands despoiled and were forced to work in livestock and on agricultural ranches. In the 1990s a few were able to obtain a legal title to their lands. By the 1980s the Chiquitano people had become involved in the process of organisation among the lowland indigenous peoples, and by the mid-1990s the new organisations filed demands for various territories with the Bolivian authorities, totalling some 1.4 million hectares. The regularisation process was only initiated in 1999, however. In the case of the Monte Verde TCO roughly 1 million hectares were claimed for some hundred different indigenous communities with a total of about 10,000 inhabitants. However, after a lengthy and conflictive regularisation process, the INRA finally issued a titling resolution, and the Monte Verde TCO received its final title in early July 2007 under the government of Evo Morales.

The Guarayos indigenous group is located in the north of the Department of Santa Cruz. Like other indigenous groups, the Guarayos used to move freely around in the forests until they were contacted, grouped, and settled first by Jesuit priests and later by Franciscans at the beginning of the 1880s. The mission era lasted from the 1840s to the 1940s, during which the Guarayos became involved in agriculture and cattle raising. By the mid-twentieth century a process of secularisation of the missions began, and pressure on Guarayo forest lands increased as a result of settling by migrants from the Andes region, expansion of livestock and agricultural ranches, and the activities of timber companies. Beginning in the 1960s Guarayos were able to legalise some forestland, but most of it remained untitled. In 1996, during the mobilisations around the adoption of the INRA law, they demanded that 2.2 million ha of their forestlands be designated as TCO, and by now titles have been issued to approximately 1.5 million hectares.

The influence of contextual variables on the TCO land regularisation process can most clearly be seen in the case of the Guarayos TCO because it allows us to compare areas that have been titled with areas that have not yet been titled, helping us to understand how contextual factors affect tenure security in these areas. Whereas the northern part of the Guarayos TCO is suitable for the development of forestry activities and further removed from the agrarian frontier, the biophysical characteristics of the southern part make it attractive for expansion of the agrarian frontier by middle- and large-scale entrepreneurs, and this has stood in the way of the titling process. Soybean producers have moved into the southern part of the forestlands claimed by the Guarayos, and the economic stakes in this area are higher, resulting in greater administrative and technical problems in the delimitation and recognition of property rights.

With respect to the legal framework, we can note that an important hurdle in the titling process in general is the complex regularisation procedure, not only for individual landholdings but also for common-property areas (see Table 12.1). In addition, the INRA does not comply with the norms, regulations, schedules, or plans for title regularisation, and uses technical and legal subterfuges to delay the titling process.[13]

When we look at how the interaction among local actors affects tenure security in the Guarayos and the Chiquitano TCO, we can see some variations between the two cases. Whereas the Chiquitanos have demanded that the whole area they claim should be titled at the same time, which implies that all the problems regarding the titling process should be solved before finishing it, the Guarayos have undertaken the contrary strategy of pursuing the titling process by parts,[14] so some parts of the TCO have already been titled while others have not. We thus have two broad scenarios in the titling of indigenous peoples' traditional common property areas and the way in which the titling process may affect tenure security among indigenous people.

Discussion of findings

Following the analytical framework presented before, in this section I discuss my findings in relation to contextual, motivational, and informational factors and their effects on the titling process and the achievement of tenure security.

Contextual problems

The contrast between the northern and southern part of the Guarayos TCO lends itself most clearly to an assessment of contextual factors. As noted, due to its biophysical characteristics the southern part is under strong pressure from medium- and large-scale landowners dedicated to soybean production. A variety of actors are competing for access to these lands, each of them holding a specific perspective on land use. In this context, deforestation rates in the area increased between 1991 and 2001, and deforestation has further accelerated between 2001 and 2004 (MDS 2005). The start of the titling process seems to have triggered a more rapid expansion of agricultural entrepreneurs into the southern forestland areas of the Guarayos TCO because they see it as a last chance to claim ownership rights in those areas which in their view were 'open access areas' despite their *de facto* use and occupation by indigenous people. The pending implementation of the 1996 agrarian legislation prompted illegal practices – or rules in use – among some local actors. According to the law – the formal rules – new land occupations after 1996 are illegal, but the law has been disobeyed. One of the most common practices has been the clearing of large swaths of forest land because deforestation was presented as proof of long-term productive use and compliance with the social-economic function requirement in a context where control mechanisms to verify the productive history of plots are weak or absent. As a result, in the course of the regularisation process, plots deforested after 1996 have not been considered illegal.

Because of the stakes involved, the regularisation process in this area is highly contested. On the one hand, indigenous people have constantly denounced the ways in which INRA has favoured individual landholders and uncritically accepted their phoney claims. Such denunciations, however, have turned out eventually to work against the indigenous, because the suspensions of the demarcation process provided an opportunity for the individual landholders to encroach on new forest lands and to invent new arguments to uphold their claims. Tenure insecurity among the indigenous is reflected in their loss of open forest areas and even in the invasion of agricultural lands of the consolidated areas. The issuing of a legal title to the southern part of the TCO would be one element in achieving a degree of tenure security at least more or less equivalent to that which they enjoyed before the regularisation process started.

Motivational problems

While contextual factors in combination with differential power relations have led to a slowing down and derailing of the regularisation process, as illustrated by the case of the Guarayos TCO, motivational and informational problems have also played their part. A look at the different strategies pursued in the Guarayos and the Chiquitano-Monte Verde cases provides further insights.

(i) Free-riding

The people of the Monte Verde TCO have chosen to demand the titling of the whole territory at once. This strengthened their territorial identity and ensured collective action in defence of their territory because it curbed the possibilities for free-riding. A main shortcoming of this strategy is that it is time-consuming, and they only received their title in July 2007. In the Guarayos TCO, the option for titling in parts made it possible for community leaders to free-ride the joint effort of TCO consolidation. This strategy allowed individuals to pursue personal benefits instead of dedicating themselves to the collective goal. Among the most common practices is the selling – on 'behalf' of the community – of pieces of TCO forestland to individual non-indigenous landholders and the sale of possession certificates to help them to consolidate their property rights in the course of the regularisation process.

In this situation indigenous people barely act as a cohesive group capable of collective action to influence the regularisation process, as there are groups and individuals who pursue their own interests and look at the land regularisation process only as an opportunity to make a profit on the common asset, the forestlands. This is supported by the fact that before starting the regularisation process, the TCO claimed it was not clearly viewed as a unified territorial entity but rather as a congregation of small communities, each with a small given territory. Currently, we observe that these micro-territories are in a process of inclusion into major territories as a result of the strengthening of supra-communal TCO-wide organisation,[15] though there is still a long way to go.

(ii) The Samaritan dilemma

Something that can be characterised as the Samaritan dilemma has often arisen in the context of the TCO land-titling process in Bolivia. Since the INRA does not view funding and technical help from international cooperation as a temporary measure, major inefficiencies occur in the land regularisation process. Governmental expectations of bail-out in case of financial trouble weaken incentives to economise and improve efficiency, and in fact breed inefficiency. The titling process in Guarayos and Chiquitania was financed by the Danish DANIDA, which repeatedly extended the INRA budget even though the institute did not reach the agreed targets.

This has created inefficiencies on the side of the INRA authorities who were sure that the donor would always supply new financial resources in order to finish the task, despite these inefficiencies and delays. Samaritans are furthermore faced with the puzzling problem that their dominant strategy is always to extend help, since in doing so they are better off, no matter what the recipient does. The issue is that once the recipient understands that this is the best strategy for the Samaritan, the recipient's best response is to expend a low level of effort (Ostrom et al. 2001). The relationship between INRA and DANIDA is a case in point. The situation resulted in help being extended with low targets being achieved.

(iii) Asymmetric power relationships

In Bolivia, individuals have different shares of economic and political power: indigenous people suffer higher rates of poverty, while the non-indigenous population has consistently enjoyed better living conditions. As a result, indigenous people have little to no capacity to exert influence over the state agencies and judicial courts because they lack economic assets and, until recently perhaps, political influence. Power asymmetries certainly also affect issues of tenure security. Medium- and large-scale landowners claiming forestland in *de facto* possession of indigenous peoples have developed strong networks for exerting pressure and for defending their group interests, which are strongly related to the economic power they hold. For instance, an attorney linked to the Agricultural and Livestock Association of Bolivia's Lowlands (*Camara Agropecuaria del Oriente* or CAO), an organisation of medium- and large-scale landowners, was the first director of the INRA and the first president of the National Agrarian Tribunal TAN. Also, the second National Director of the INRA (1999-2003) was a person closely related to the CAO. There are plenty of examples of the asymmetric power relationships in the land regularisation process, and I will discuss some of the most important ones.

First, significant increases of individual landholdings as well as claims to them were observed after the claims of the Guarayos and Chiquitanos had been formally accepted by the INRA. Administrative and judicial irregularities that benefit such land-grabbers have been documented, and arguably the INRA has contributed to conflicts surrounding the regularisation process since despite the agrarian legislation and its regulations, during its fieldwork it measured parcels that did not show any landholders' effective possession. Second, in 1997 authorities of the Forestry Superintendence developed resolutions to recognise ownership rights for forest concessionaries overlapping the Chiquitano-Monte Verde TCO jurisdiction (Tamburini and Betancur 2003), which were in turn ratified by INRA's authorities.[16] Third, the INRA responded to the pressure of individual landholders – so-called 'third parties' – within the Guarayos and Chiquitano-Monte Verde TCOs by paralysing the land regularisation process and promoting meetings of conciliation with illegal land possessors, bypassing the legal and technical norms that should guide the process (Tamburini and Betancur 2003). Fourth, despite being clearly in irregular, not to say illegal, possession of plots, some private landholders affected by the regularisation process have repeatedly sought recourse to the National Agrarian Tribunal (TAN) and have thus managed to delay the titling process.

In 2001 the National Agrarian Tribunal ordered a review of the Chiquitano-Monte Verde regularisation process from the initial stages of juridical and technical evaluation – a step that had been concluded the previous year after spending more than USD 1 million (Betancur 2003; CEJIS 2001). The TAN also opened the way for legalising fake titles, cancelling a regulation of the INRA law that declared inexistent the titles obtained through fraudulent and irregular procedures (Tamburini and Betancur 2003).

Finally, after seven years of work, the INRA presented the results of its efforts. According to this report, of the 159 individual claimants in the Chiquitano Monte Verde-TCO, 93 should be awarded a surface area of roughly 136,000 ha while the other 66 claimants to a surface area of 360,000 ha should be expelled. Some of them filed another injunction with the TAN, largely based on phony documentation and on the INRA's mistaken procedures in the past (Tamburini and Betancur 2003), which once more delayed the titling process. The Chiquitano-Monte Verde TCO thus became a showcase of the systemic bias of the INRA and TAN in favour of private 'third parties' affected by indigenous common-property claims.

In the Chiquitano-Monte Verde TCO, violence occurred when some non-indigenous forest exploiters who were declared illegal continued deforesting for agricultural activities. In reaction, Chiquitano communities installed control posts to defend their territory, which met with violent reactions from these land traders.[17] When the indigenous people denounced the presence of paramilitary persons in the TCO, penal processes were initiated against Chiquitano leaders (Betancur 2003; CEJIS 2001). Death threats against the president of the Chiquitano organisation were also common (Perez 1996).

Under the government of Evo Morales, who assumed office in early 2006, a difficult process seeking to achieve more balanced power relations has been undertaken by the Vice-Ministry of Lands through its investigations of cases of illegal land-grabbing, which are quite common in Bolivia. The penal processes initiated in early 2007 on the basis of technical-legal enquiries into the status of the Laguna Corazón and the Yasminka estates, both situated in the Guarayos TCO and both acquired unlawfully, merits special attention. In the first case the Vice-Ministry identified the crimes of material and ideological deceit, the use of falsified documentation, perversion of the course of justice, and undue influence on appointments. In the second case a similar series of criminal actions was exposed. The two estates belong to the family of Branco Marincovick who currently is the President of the Santa Cruz Civic Committee, known for its strong links to the land-grabbing elites of the region.[18]

(iv) Corruption

It is very difficult to prove corruption in the real world, but there is anecdotal evidence that corruption has been an issue throughout the land regularisation process and has implicated most of the actors involved. The most evident cases of corruption relate to the verification of the social-economic function. For instance, the 'loan of cows' or 'cattle tourism' among livestock estates is a common practice, so that the borrowers could show that they were effectively engaged in cattle-raising. This practice has been denounced by indigenous community leaders on several occasions, particularly in the context of the Chiquitano-Monte Verde TCO regularisation process (Tamburini and Betancur 2003).

Corruption allowed non-indigenous actors to enter the forestlands claimed for the TCO and to obtain titles in fraudulent ways. One can also suppose that bribing was a common practice and that it involved some indigenous community leaders and state officials, though this is very difficult to prove.[19] Indigenous leaders used to sell possession permits in the forestlands of the Guarayos TCO, authorising individual landowners to develop productive activities in the lands belonging to the indigenous people. In addition, INRA officials have condoned the illegal agreements between corrupt indigenous leaders and illegal intruders using the legal figure of the conciliations, which aim to reach an agreement between competing landholders. For instance, one of the Guarayos TCO communities originally claimed an extension of 2,000 ha but at the end of the titling process will only receive 200 ha because of corruption at all levels.[20] An important aspect favouring the indigenous people's corruption is the development of co-optation mechanisms by the government through the carrying out of development programmes financed by the international cooperation (CEJIS 2001), which result in weakening of the indigenous organisations.[21] Corruption is furthermore favoured by the fact that most of the time local people do not know about their leaders' activities, since leaders typically did not keep community members informed.

The COPNAG (Central Originaria de Pueblos Nativos Guarayos) is the organisation that represents the Guarayo, but it is divided into two factions. One group consists of former leaders and their followers, and the other of leaders who were not in leading positions at the time the illegal land transfers occurred. On the basis of various accusations, an emergency assembly was held in October 2004 and adopted a resolution in which it publicly denounced various ex-leaders as the intellectual and material authors of irregular land transfers within the TCO. In January 2006 an extraordinary assembly of the COPNAG created a Disciplinary Tribunal, composed of representatives of the community-level organisations, to further investigate the case and come up with a report within six months.

On the basis of a preliminary report, another extraordinary assembly was held in March 2006. On that occasion it was decided to impose moral sanctions (expulsion from the COPNAG, repudiation) and to initiate legal actions against the ex-leaders involved in trafficking land. At the same time the possible participation of people occupying leadership positions at that time was denounced, and they were asked to prove their innocence within 90 days. A consultative assembly was then planned that would have the power to dismiss those involved in land transfers from leadership positions. This decision was ratified by the Disciplinary Tribunal and by the community level organisations but not by the COPNAG leadership.

Another assembly was convened by the community-level organisations – which according to the COPNAG statutes are authorised to call such an assembly – and was held on 27 and 28 October, 2006. It elected a new COPNAG leadership, with Elida Urapuca as President. This new leadership, however, is unrecognised by the former leaders and by local institutions, though it is supported by the umbrella organisation CIDOB and by most of the community-level organisations. The other COPNAG faction organised its own extraordinary general assembly in February 2007 and elected a new directory, which is recognised by some local institutions but garners scant support among the community-level organisations and is not recognised by the CIDOB.

According to the final report by the Disciplinary Tribunal, the irregular transfers in the Guarayos TCO involved 482,000 hectares and a sum of USD 1.2 million. The report denounces the involvement of both former and present COPNAG leaders and asks INRA to return all lands that have been irregularly transferred to the TCO. These conflicts, which derive from the organisational debility of the Guarayos and the strong pressures of an informal land market that resulted in the corruption of many leaders, have stood in the way of the recuperation of the Guarayo territory and have facilitated the occupation of parts of the area originally claimed as TCO by other regional actors.

Informational problems

(i) Trust-monitoring

Indigenous people have identified monitoring as an essential factor in successful titling of their common-property areas. This is because the asymmetric information makes indigenous people more vulnerable in the land regularisation procedure. Indigenous organisations cannot expect favourable results from the regularisation process if they limit their interventions to the legal procedures signalled by the formal law (CEJIS 2001).

The SAN-TCO involves practices that indigenous people are not familiar with such as the use of GPS and a technical juridical jargon that regularly plays against their interests. Therefore, indigenous people need to develop relationships of trust with the technicians and to build capabilities to monitor the set of actors involved in the regularisation process. In practice, however, it has been very difficult to develop trust relationships or to effectively monitor the entities in charge of the SAN-TCO.

Ostrom et al. (2001) argue that the bigger the community and/or the larger the relevant terrain, the more important the development of explicit rules for enforcing monitoring mechanisms. This argument may explain why it has been more difficult in the Guarayos TCO to develop an explicit monitoring mechanism than in the Chiquitana-Monte Verde TCO,[22] since it comprises a larger territory and more heterogeneous communities composed of local people and small-scale farmers that have migrated from the highlands. In Monte Verde there were fewer problems since they are a more cohesive indigenous group and are more able to closely monitor the process developed by the INRA's teams.[23]

(ii) Principal-agent situations

In hierarchical organisations, individuals are arrayed in a series of superior-subordinate positions, the former being the principal and the latter the agents who only enjoy delegated authority and are supposed to comply with the orders given by the principal (Miller 1992). In hierarchies, information is a scarce commodity, and there is a permanent tension between the individual self-interest and group efficiency (Ostrom et al. 2001). The INRA, as the entity in charge of the regularisation programme, suffers the same problems affecting any hierarchy. However, in the land regularisation procedure there is an additional puzzle, which is how to control subordinates who have the expertise that the principals lack. This is even more relevant since in the land regularisation process most intervening professionals are attorneys and surveyors, and large gaps of knowledge exist among them and their principals, which become progressively wider as one ascends the hierarchy. This gives the local agents the option to free-ride on the targets of the INRA and to advance their own individual interests. It has been signalled that the acts and decisions of local public officials have been almost unrelated to legal mandates when they affected the interest of powerful local people (CEJIS 2001).

The Guarayos TCO leaders argue that the technicians in charge of the clarification process have developed their own rules, which they have imposed on the local population, but that their superiors who are supposed to monitor the clarification process were unaware of this.[24]

(iii) Adverse selection

Adverse selection usually occurs when beneficiaries are selected in a non-random process that tends to select the least-appropriate individuals (Ostrom et al. 2001). In the situation of common-property titling, in which all indigenous groups inhabiting a certain area are selected for the titling process, there is the problem that TCO claims started before indigenous groups had a cohesive demand for common-property and strong organisations for monitoring the process, controlling free-riding, and deterring corruption. The Guarayos TCO was most affected by such problems.

Tenure security in the Guarayos and Monte Verde TCOs can be evaluated according to the criterion of the permanent impediment to exercise withdrawal rights in open forest areas that were in *de facto* possession of indigenous peoples and the encroachment on the consolidated forestland areas.[25] This is because indigenous people systematically lost lands where they gathered forest products, hunted and pastured, as well as those areas they cultivated.[26] From the foregoing discussion of the contextual, motivational, and informational problems, some conclusions regarding tenure security among the indigenous people can be drawn.

First, the TCO land-titling processes have had contradictory impacts on tenure security in indigenous people's territories. Combinations of biophysical and socioeconomic factors have played against indigenous communities as they attracted medium and large entrepreneurs who developed illegal strategies for accessing the indigenous people's forestland and created tenure insecurity that had not existed, or at least was less acute, before the regularisation process began. The cure in this case has been worse than the illness. Second, motivational problems in combination with ill-conceived indigenous people's strategies, such as titling the TCO by parts, has undermined their capacity for collective action. When the TCO eventually is titled, the organisations will remain weak, and this will stand in the way of comprehensive natural resource management. On the other hand, a correct titling strategy has served to curb internal motivational problems, though motivational problems on the side of state officials have been difficult to control. Informational factors may attenuate the impacts of motivational problems or exacerbate them. In the Chiquitano-Monte Verde TCO, informational problems might successfully be handled, while in the Guarayos TCO the lack of capabilities to manage informational problems has increased the impact of the motivational problems and has thus contributed to tenure insecurity.

In general, I conclude from my interviews that communities have suffered a decrease of tenure security in the areas they possessed *de facto* as a result of the titling process, at least until the TCO titles are granted to them. The titling process triggered attempts at last minute land-grabbing by 'third parties'. The final issuing of TCO titles will establish *de jure* ownership, but as with any title, the security this suggests will depend on the capacity to enforce legal title and have it respected. Cases from Brazil, Colombia, and other Latin American countries show that even demarcation and legal titling of indigenous lands and territories does not bring real security if the political will or the state capacity to prevent encroachment by third parties is absent and the indigenous organisation is no match for third parties.

Conclusions

Bolivia's legislation was made under the expectation that people would sit still until the state law satisfactorily resolved forestland ownership problems through the probing of each actor's rights to a given piece of forestland. This expectation was unrealistic. As could be anticipated, the parties involved have proved to be dynamic and able to change state laws into rules-in-use adapted to their own interests. Contextual, motivational, and informational factors, with a different significance for the different actors, have played an important role in the process and its outcomes.

Regarding contextual factors, I found that indigenous people located in areas well-endowed with natural resources have more incentives to follow their own self-interest, which erodes the tenure security of the community as a whole. Conversely, indigenous people with less incentive to resign the common good may gain some local power as a result of the regularisation process. However, regardless of the strength of incentives to pursue the common good, indigenous peoples face the problem of controlling the implementation bureaucracy, which delays and distorts the titling process. As we have seen, the INRA bureaucracy, until at least 2003, was directed by persons with a history of serving large landowner organisations, and at lower levels the influence of local power groups was far from negligible. And NGOs, such as the Santa Cruz-based *Centro de Estudios Jurídicos e Investigación Social* (CEJIS), which trains indigenous leaders and provides legal assistance, have on various occasions been the target of violent attacks.

In the cases studied here, indigenous people's tenure security in areas that were considered to be in their *de facto* possession decreased since the SAN-TCO triggered the occupation of these areas by intruders. The significant increase in the number of non-indigenous individual landowners within the TCO after the regularisation process started can largely be explained by three of the above-mentioned factors, namely asymmetric power relationships, trust-monitoring, and principal-agent situations. There are also cases of tenure insecurity caused by the indigenous people themselves, through land transactions between indigenous people's leaders and illegal intruders which are then ratified by the INRA. Here corruption and adverse selection are significant factors. It is also important to note that small-scale farmers who migrated from the highlands and were invited to occupy an indigenous territory in order to justify the FES have created tenure insecurity in some communities because of the factor of free-riding. Even the motivational problem described as the Samaritan dilemma, which might be considered almost neutral, may have important implications for tenure insecurity, since inefficiencies on the side of the government create the conditions for other actors to act illegally. Therefore, regarding contextual, motivational, and informational problems, I found that overall they lead to tenure insecurity and make the titling of TCOs difficult.

There were also some problems that were controlled and solved in practice. The most important instrument to demand respect for the legal rights of indigenous people involved social mobilisations, either at the local or national level. In the last fifteen years we have seen three important indigenous people's marches from the lowlands to La Paz in order to pressure the Bolivian government to recognise indigenous people's territorial rights.

Where actions to obtain some balance in the asymmetric power relations are concerned, it is important to mention the support of NGOs for indigenous people, particularly in the defence of their land rights as well as by providing information and facilitating access to the agrarian state agencies, and by developing training programmes for indigenous leaders. The capacity of the indigenous organisations to make recommendations and suggestions has benefited from the technical support of persons and organisations facilitating the formulation of viable and pertinent proposals (CEJIS 2001). Furthermore, the positive attitude of the international community regarding indigenous topics, which were at the centre of the agendas of Bolivia's cooperation agencies in past few decades, has been influential. Finally, on this international level the development of juridical norms such as ILO Convention 169 is worth mentioning.

Notes

1 Such collective titling can occur at various scales or levels. In Bolivia a peasant community (understood as a settlement) may apply for a collective title. In the case that concerns us here, we are dealing with the territorial claims of indigenous peoples, and such territories may encompass various communities/settlements.
2 In this article we will use the term indigenous to refer to the indigenous peoples in the tropical eastern lowlands of Bolivia. In terms of international law the much larger Quechua and Aymara populations of the highlands would also be considered indigenous, but Aymara organisations in particular have insisted that they should be considered *originary*, emphasising that they were there before the arrival of the Spanish and before the later creation of an independent Bolivian state in 1825.
3 Bolivia's lowlands comprise most of the departments of Santa Cruz, Beni and Pando.
4 Interview, Carlos Leigue, Vice-president Management Committee of Monte Verde TCO, Concepción, 13 February 2007.
5 In the following years Bolivia ratified ILO Convention 169 in 1991, reformed its Constitution in 1994/95 and, with the enactment of new agrarian legislation, created the legal figure of *Tierras Comunitarias de Origen* (Originary Community Lands, TCO) as a form to legalise collective tenure of indigenous peoples. The 1996 agrarian legislation opened the way for new demands for the recognition, legalisation and collective titling of indigenous territories. See Assies, this volume.
6 Interview, Filemón Mamani, vice-president of the Central of Yotaú Community. 18 February 2007.
7 Interview, Manuel Peña, Concepción, 12 February 2007, president of the CCIC (Central of Indigenous Communities of Concepción), Francisco Mangary, member of the Cabildo of Monte Verde Community, 14 February 2007, and Tomás Candia, leader of the OICH (Chiquitano Indigenous Community), Concepción, 13 February 2007.

8   The INRA law's regulation converted the period of TCO land regularisation in more than 700 days (20 months) at least (CEJIS 2001).

9   Interview, Manuel Peña, Concepción, 12 February 2007, president of the CCIC (Central of Indigenous Communities of Concepción); Angel Yubanore, responsible for land and territory of COPNAG (Confederation of the Guarayo People), 17 February 2007; Filemón Mamani, vice-president of the Central of Yotaú Community, 18 February 2007.

10   Interview, Carlos Leigue, vice-president of Management Committee of Monte Verde TCO, Concepción, 13 February 2007.

11   The law created the National Agrarian Reform Institute, which replaced the agrarian reform institutions that had been created in the context of the 1953 agrarian reform.

12   Since the Guarayos and Monte Verde TCO claims were presented before the approval of the INRA law, they should have been titled within a period of ten months after enactment of the law (1996).

13   Some of the main issues were the approval of the manuals for the evaluation of the social-economic function of land, the procedures for the notification of interested parties, and the calculation of the surface to be included in the TCO (Betancur 2003). CEJIS (2001) notes that the norms and regulations developed by the INRA often contradict the stated objectives of the agrarian legislation. The verification of the social economic function of land is biased in favour of large landowners, studies for the assessment of the spatial needs of indigenous peoples are used to reduce the surface of their territorial claims in favour of entrepreneurial groups and forest concessions, and the National Agrarian Tribunal tends to give more support to entrepreneurial claims than to indigenous people.

14   This was a strategy pushed by the government in order to present results to the international cooperation financing the titling process and in order to reduce the pressure of the indigenous organisations over areas requested by interested third parties (Betancur 2003).

15   Interview, Filemón Mamani, vice-president of the Central of Yotaú Community, 18 February 2007.

16   In 1997 the Forestry Superintendence granted forest concession rights to non-indigenous people in an extension of 120,000 ha of native forests (Betancur 2003).

17   Interview, Daniel Leigue, Forestry Committee Santa Monica, 14 February 2007.

18   Viceministerio de Tierras, *Informe de Gestión 2007*.

19   Interview, Carlos Leigue, vice-president of the Management Committee of Monte Verde TCO, Concepción, 13 February 2007; Filemón Mamani, vice-president of the Central of Yotaú Community, 18 February 2007.

20   Interview, Filemón Mamani, vice-president of the Central of Yotaú Community, 18 February 2007.

21   An example is the hiring of the principal community leaders in order to develop studies of spatial needs and projects related to territorial management.

22   Interview, Filemón Mamani, vice-president of the Central of Yotaú Community, 18 February 2007.

23   Interview, Manuel Peña, Concepción, 12 February 2007. President of the CCIC (Central of Indigenous Communities of Concepción).

24   Interview, Angel Yubanore, Responsible for Land and Territory COPNAG, 18 February 2007.

25   Interview, Carlos Leigue, vice-president of the Management Committee of Monte Verde TCO, Concepción, 13 February 2007.

26   Interview, Lorenzo Pasabare, Counterpart of the CCIC (Central of Indigenous Communities of the Chiquitania) in CEJIS (Center for Juridical Studies and Social Research), Concepción, 15 February 2007.

13 Land tenure and tenure regimes in Mexico: An overview

Willem Assies and Emilio Duhau[1]

Introduction

In 1992 Mexico reformed its famous revolutionary article 27 of the Constitution, which had paved the way for redistributive agrarian reform and the creation of a 'social property sector' consisting of *ejidos* and agrarian communities, where members would hold land in usufruct. The 1992 reform ended the redistributive reform process and according to its proponents sought to enhance tenure security through certification. The reform opened the way for privatisation of lands in the social property sector under the expectation that this would dynamise the agrarian sector. With this reform and a new Agrarian Law that was enacted soon thereafter, Mexico joined the wave of Latin American land law reforms that had been pioneered by Chile in 1974 and that sought to undo the collective property sector that had been generated under previous agrarian reforms in favour of individual private landholdings (Deere and León 2000).

This chapter provides an overview of the evolution of land tenure and tenure regimes in Mexico. It first discusses the colonial roots of the agrarian structure and the nineteenth-century liberal land policies which resulted in the concentration of landholding in the hands of a tiny elite and thus created the conditions for peasant participation in the Mexican Revolution and the subsequent agrarian reform which created a social property sector. It then shows how by the 1930s the reform sector consolidated in the context of an emerging import-substituting development model in which the agrarian sector was increasingly relegated to a subordinate role to provide cheap staple crops, cheap labour, and cheap inputs. State regulation became an increasingly important feature of this model. By the mid-1960s, however, the agrarian sector began to show signs of stagnation, which gradually deepened into crisis. The 1992 reform of the Constitution and agrarian legislation was part and parcel of the structural adjustment policies adopted from the early 1980s onward and took place in a context of state withdrawal and trade liberalisation. It was expected that by making the privatisation of lands in the social property sector possible, and bringing them under a civil law regime instead of under agrarian law, a dynamic land market would develop, and new investment would be attracted. We shall see, however, that although certification of family holdings progressed fairly rapidly and may have helped to consolidate property rights and to sort out some boundary conflicts, the step to full private property under civil law occurred only in a very limited number of cases. The outcomes of the reform show that land policy and tenure regime reforms should be viewed in the broader context of agricultural and rural development and macro and trade policies. Land policy and tenure regime reform are insufficient by themselves, as Baranyi, Deere and Morales (2004:37) put it, to promote sustainable rural development and reduce poverty if a level playing field is not created for the survival of Latin American family farms and domestic-oriented agriculture.

From colonial times to the revolution

When the Spanish arrived in 1519, the population of what nowadays is Mexico was some 20 million, divided over about 120 different ethnic groups. By the end of the sixteenth century only some 2 million remained. Upon their arrival the colonisers initially introduced the *encomienda*, which meant that a certain number of natives were given into the custody of the conquering soldiers who should take care of their evangelisation in return for tribute in labour and in kind. The abuses to which this system gave rise, as well as the rapid population decline caused by wars, famines, and new contagious diseases, led to measures by the Crown and the introduction of the New Laws of the Indies (1542) that were intended to regulate and ultimately eliminate the *encomienda*. The state now assumed control over the native labour force through the *repartimiento* system, whereby Indians were forced to work for the Spaniards on a rotational basis for a fixed wage. Second, the state sought to resettle the remaining population through a policy of *reducciones* or *congregaciones* by which they were to be concentrated in *pueblos de indios*. Such villages were to be granted an *ejido*[2] where the Indians could hold their livestock. Other forms of possession, also introduced for the *criollos* (people of Spanish descent born in Latin America) and *mestizos* (people of mixed descent) were the *tierras de repartimiento* or family plots in usufruct, which could be lost if one left the village or did not cultivate the land for three consecutive years, and the *propios* or village lands that could be rented out to cover the costs of local administration. During the three centuries of colonial rule, the Spanish Crown distributed thousands of titles and *escrituras* (deeds) that laid the legal groundwork for the present-day agrarian communities. The evolving legal framework for colonial rule, with its complex system of administration of two 'commonwealths', a *república de espa-ñoles* and a *república de indios*, was consolidated in the Laws of the In-dies (1681), an assortment of more or less significant decrees and laws that formally institutionalised a Spanish version of 'indirect rule' that viewed the Indians as a 'separate nation' under the tutelage of the Spanish colonial state. However, despite these protective intentions, the communal property of the natives was subject to various forms of appropriation by the colonisers, whether through *mercedes* (royal land grants) or the confirmation of *de facto* occupation through *composi-ciones*, sales, or outright usurpation. This process was reinforced with the rise of the mining economy and the northward advance of the colo-nial frontier leading to the consolidation of the *hacienda*, the large es-tates practising various forms of labour control, ranging from wage la-bour to forms of leasing and sharecropping. The rise and consolidation of *haciendas* were closely associated with a boom in stock-raising in the sixteenth century when newly imported cattle and sheep rapidly multi-plied in their new environment and brought about an unprecedented and calamitous ecological transformation. By the end of the century, the herds began to die off as pastures were eaten more quickly than they could regenerate (Simon 1997). It is estimated that by the end of the seventeenth century, over half of the arable and grazing (*agostadero*) land in New Spain was in the hands of the colonisers who, in contrast to the natives, acquired full ownership of those lands (Secretaría de la Reforma Agraria 1998:21).

Although the leaders of the independence struggle (1810-1821) sought to do away with the *haciendas,* in fact no significant change in the agrarian structure was achieved. The newly dominant classes made attempts to attract Europeans to colonise the vast northern region of the republic, menaced by US expansionism,[3] but due to the political in-stability that reigned up to the late 1860s, no significant contingents of colonisers arrived. Meanwhile, as the anti-clerical liberals gained power after the expulsion of dictator Santa Ana (1855), concern grew over the vast areas of land that in the course of time had come into the posses-sion of the Church, which occasionally might lease them but most of-ten did not; it was said that these lands were in *mano muerta* (dead hands), which impeded the progress of the country.[4] In 1856, during the government of Benito Juárez – of Zapotec descent – Minister Mi-guel Lerdo de Tejada therefore promoted the *Ley de Desamortización de Bienes de Corporaciones Civiles y Eclesiásticas*, also known as the Lerdo Law, which sought to grant lands held by civil or religious corporations to those who leased them. This was one of the causes for the civil war that broke out in 1857. In 1857 the Lerdo law was incorporated into a new Constitution (art. 27). Whereas the original law had exempted *eji-do* lands (the village commons) from the *desamortización* (the lifting of inalienability), the new Constitution dropped this exemption so *ejido* lands could now also be 'denounced' and bought by private parties that claimed to have rented them. Despite some opposition that argued for a redistribution to the benefit of those with insufficient lands, including the native population, the liberal sentiment won the day, which viewed indigenous forms of communal tenure as an impediment to progress and modernity. Even if the intention of the Lerdo law may have been to create a sector of freeholding yeoman farmers, this objective was not achieved, and instead, as a result of a process of land-grabbing, the *latifundios* (large holdings) ended up being consolidated.[5]

Further concentration of lands took place under the long authoritarian rule of General Porfirio Díaz, the *Porfiriato* (1877-1910). This was a period of political stability at gunpoint, agro-export-driven economic growth, consolidation of the *hacienda* system, incipient industrialisation, and railway line construction. During this period the *Decreto sobre Colonización y Compañías Deslindadoras* (Decree on Colonisation and Demarcation Companies) of 1883 and the *Ley sobre Ocupación y Enajenación de Terrenos Baldíos* (Law on the Occupation and Alienation of Barren Lands) of 1894 shaped land policies. The two measures sought to identify lands presumably without owner in order to incorporate them through demarcation and sale to private parties. Some 50 companies were given concessions to carry out the demarcation process, for which they were to receive one-third of the surface demarcated. Between 1883 and 1910 they demarcated 59 millions of hectares and received 20 millions of hectares, or over ten per cent of the national territory, in compensation. The remaining 40 million hectares became public lands that subsequently were mostly acquired by large landowners, mining enterprises, and railway companies. Whereas the demarcation companies mostly worked in the relatively unpopulated north of the country and on the Pacific coast, the allocation of supposedly 'barren' lands mostly occurred in the more populous central states of the country, for which the social repercussions were much more incisive and created the breeding ground for revolutionary turmoil. Although demarcation and allocation formally required that the lands were 'barren', few communities or smallholders could present a title or *esritura* to support their claims, and most therefore lost their lands in the process.

The liberal policies of the republican governments, which were taken to their ultimate consequences during the *Porfiriato*, thus resulted in a huge concentration of landholding, with 87 per cent of the land occupied by rural holdings in the hands of 0.2 per cent of the landowners. The concentration of landholding and the (semi-)proletarisation of rural labour during the republican period, which brutally increased during the *Porfiriato*, was to fuel the first 'peasant war of the twentieth century' (Wolf 1973).[6]

Table 13.1 *Landed and landless rural population in Mexico on the eve of the revolution*

Rural population	Number	Percentage	Surface x 1,000 hectares	Percentage
With land				
Hacendados	8,431	0.2	113,800	86.9
Rancheros	48,633	1.3	9,700	7.4
Smallholders	109,378	3.0	1,399	1.1
Comuneros	150,000	4.2	6,069	4.6
Subtotal	**316,442**	**8.7**	**130,968**	**100.0**
Without land				
Administrators	4,561	0.1		
Leasehold (*arrendatarios*)	312,314	9.0		
Sharecroppers	1,536,685	42.6		
Indentured labourers	1,425,115	39.6		
Subtotal	**3,278,675**	**91.3**		
TOTAL	**3,595,117**	**100.0**		

Source: Secretaria de Reforma Agraria 1998:35

Revolution and agrarian reform

What in 1910 began as essentially a middle-class revolt against the re-election bid of dictator Porfirio Díaz soon turned into a generalised civil war. Warfare lasted for seven years and claimed about one and a half million lives. In 1911, in the central state of Morelos, indigenous peasant communities that had lost their lands to expanding sugar-cane-growing *haciendas* rose under the leadership of Emiliano Zapata to fight for 'Land and Liberty'. They drafted the famous Plan de Ayala which called for the immediate return of lost lands to the communities and the distribution of part of the *hacienda* lands among landless peasants and began to effectively implement the programme in their areas of influence (Womack Jr. 1970).[7] In the northern state of Chihuahua, Francisco 'Pancho' Villa emerged as a military leader and issued an expropriation decree in 1913, followed by an agrarian law, intended to apply nationwide, in 1915. This law reflected the circumstances in the north where freeholding ranchers had come under pressure from large cattle ranch expansion, but where the economy was also more diversified, and miners, industrial workers, middle-class members, etc., played an important role. Villa's proposal did not aim for a revival of traditional communal structures. Instead, large estates were confiscated and came under state control to finance warfare, while a rather

limited redistribution of lands to individual farmers took place to promote economic development and social well-being. A third major faction, the Constitutionalists, was led by Venustiano Carranza and had
its base in the states of Sonora, Coahuila, and Nuevo León where agrarian problems were less acute. It was under pressure from his more radical supporters that Carranza issued a decree on the return of lost village and community lands in early 1915. The decree declared nil all
alienation of lands, waters and forest lands carried out in contravention
of the 1856 Lerdo Law, which exempted *ejido* lands from the *desamortización* process, as well as concessions and demarcations to the detriment of villages and communities that had been practised after 1876
(Katz 1996; Secretaria de Reforma Agraria 1998:39-46).

These proposals provided the groundwork for the new article 27 of
the 1917 Constitution (Thiesenhusen 1995:34-35). This article stipulated
that all lands and waters originally belong to the nation, which can
transmit them to private parties as private property under certain conditions. Large estates would be divided up, and villages, *rancherías*
(small farmers' settlements), and communities lacking sufficient lands
and water had the right to be given such lands, which should be taken
from adjacent properties while respecting smallholdings. A ceiling for
private properties was to be established. Church-sponsored institutions
were barred from owning land not specifically related to their function.
Co-ownerships, *rancherías*, villages, congregations, tribes, and other *corporaciones de población* that in fact or by law preserved their communal
state were to be able to use their common properties. Carranza's 1915
decree on the return of lost village lands was reconfirmed and elevated
to the constitutional level. In the case of the breaking up of large estates, compensation was foreseen, but it would be based on tax rather
than market value and paid in five per cent bonds over twenty years.[8]

Article 27 established the legal framework for an agrarian reform
based on the principle that land belongs to the tiller. It created a 'social
property sector' which was to consist of *ejidos* and *comunidades agrarias*
(agrarian communities). The *ejidos* would be created as a result of petitions by *hacienda* workers who would then be collectively allocated part
or all of the *hacienda* land. *Comunidades agrarias* would result from the
recognition and/or restitution of lands taken from peasant communities or other corporate groups. Lands in the 'social property sector'
could not be sold or transferred. The main difference between the two
components of the 'social property sector' resided in the fact that requirements for *ejido* internal organisation – consisting of a General Assembly and elected governing boards – were stricter. Because the *comunidades agarias* were hardly ever promoted by the post-revolutionary
governments, many indigenous communities were organised according to the *ejido* scheme, while a large proportion of the *comunidades*

was not inhabited by indigenes (Secretaria de Reforma Agraria 1998:108-110).[9]

As we shall see, the pace of reform implementation would be set by considerations of political expedience while the modality of redistribution and tenure – the tenure regime – would depend on ideology and the overall development policy pursued. Effective large-scale redistribution only got under way during the government of Lázaro Cárdenas (1934-1940) and then would slow down and pick up under subsequent governments, pursuing various development models, until in 1991 President Carlos Salinas de Gortari announced his initiative for a substantial reform of article 27, which formally brought the process of redistributive reform to an end.

1920-1934: Post-revolution reconstruction and retrenchment

After the last turmoil of the revolutionary period Alvaro Obregón became president and was succeeded by Plutarco Elías Calles, who remained the strongman behind subsequent presidencies.[10] Despite revolutionary rhetoric the changes that took place in this period were rather modest and perhaps most significant in the areas of education and culture, as reflected in the famous murals, the rise of *indigenismo*,[11] and secular education. Under Obregón, land distribution hardly progressed, while under the Calles presidency it was stepped up, but only rather unproductive land was distributed, and no serious effort was made to provide the beneficiaries with resources to work the land. Both Obregón and Calles regarded the *ejido* as a transitional arrangement that should usher in the creation of small private farms.

Reforms, including the land reform, met with the firm resistance of the Church, among others, which promoted the *cristero* rebellion (1926-1927) in central and western Mexico. To counter such opposition and to unite the 'revolutionary family' – the political leaders and local *caudillos* (political-military strongmen) who dominated the country since 1920 – Calles organised the National Revolutionary Party (PNR) in 1929 that under different names would rule the country until December 2000.[12]

1934-1940: The Cárdenas years

Under Lázaro Cárdenas, who managed to escape from Calles's control by sending him into exile, reformist policies received a new impetus, and, for better or for worse, the revolution was transformed into permanent structures. Labour, organised in a new *Confederación de Trabajadores Mexicanos* (CTM, Mexican Workers Confederation), the peasantry, organised in a *Confederación Nacional Campesina* (CNC, National

Peasant Confederation), the military, and a popular sector that included the middle class and public employees were turned into the main pillars of the revolutionary party, renamed the *Partido de la Revolución Mexicana* (PRM, Party of the Mexican Revolution) in 1938. This new coalition and the organisations that underpinned it provided support for industrial relations reforms, land reform, the promotion of national industry, and the nationalisation of oil companies. Over the years, these organisations became increasingly dependent on and controlled by the government party in symbiosis with the state apparatus. The corporatist structures of the Mexican pyramid of domination – based on the organisation of society according to functional groups – came into being.

Land distribution was strongly stepped up during the Cárdenas government for various reasons. The agro-export model that had come into being from the mid-nineteenth century onwards suffered from the 1929 Wall Street crash and subsequent depression. Like other Latin American countries, in the wake of the crash Mexico adopted a model of import-substituting industrialisation, but in the Mexican case this was accompanied by a strong emphasis on rural development (Gollás 2003:229). The crisis also prompted the expulsion of a million Mexicans from the United States. Rural unrest erupted in the states of San Luis Potosí and Veracruz (Martínez Saldaña 1991; Thiesenhusen 1995:36-37). Rather than considering the *ejido* a transitional arrangement that would soon be dissolved to give way to smallholder private property, it now came to be considered a permanent institution that would help in the modernisation of the countryside and support a new development model adopted in the wake of the 1929 crash. The *ejido* was propagated as genuinely Mexican and 'neither socialist nor capitalist'. In the *ejidos*, land would be held communally, and each of the members would be entitled to use a parcel. Political control and a certain measure of representation were achieved by interweaving the affairs of the *comisariados ejidales* (*ejido* executive boards) with various state institutions and through the CNC structure in an intricate hierarchical network of institutions (see also Bizberg and Meyer 2003 :202). The *ejido* was not only a form of organisation of production but also a mechanism of political control and peasant representation. Credit from government agencies was to be channelled through the CNC, and CNC members would be favoured in the process of land distribution. In return, they were expected to be loyal clients and vote for the ruling party.

During the Cárdenas government more than 20 million hectares were redistributed – twice as much as in the preceding nineteen years – benefiting nearly 800,000 peasants, while between 1917 and 1934 about 950,000 peasants had benefited from redistribution. By 1940 22.5 per cent of the agricultural land and 47.4 per cent of arable land was in the hands of the *ejidos*. The share in irrigated land rose from thirteen per cent in 1930 to 57.4 per cent ten years later, and the share of rain-fed land rose from 14.2 per cent to 46.5 per cent. At the same time, under pressure of the reform drive, private owners subdivided their lands in order to avoid expropriation. If 481,000 owners controlled 123 million hectares (255 hectares on average) in 1930, 1,122,000 owned 100 million hectares (89 hectares on average) in 1940 (Secretaria de Reforma Agraria 1998:59). Although this suggests deconcentration of land ownership, in many cases the subdivision was only a formal one, the land going to family members or *prestanombres* (people 'lending' their name).

1940-1992: From the 'Mexican Miracle' to neo-liberalism

The Cárdenas period was one of reformism and modest improvement of the condition of the masses, with policies favouring the rural sector. The following period[13] saw a reversal of policy trends and a greater emphasis on industrial development, which became known as stabilising development. Meanwhile, the hold of the state over national politics and social organisations became more rigid, and the corporatist party machinery was perfected. In 1946 the PRM was renamed *Partido Revolucionario Institucional* (PRI), now with the peasant, worker, and popular sectors as its three pillars.[14]

While industrial production rapidly increased and Mexico became known as a miracle of economic growth, under the Camacho, Alemán, and Cortinez presidencies (1940-1958) land distribution was sharply reduced, and policies were geared to the promotion of large-scale private agriculture, for instance by the construction of massive irrigation projects concentrated in northern and northwestern Mexico.[15] As a result of such investments and a policy of unaffectability that halted further expropriations, the concentration of land ownership grew, and a new, modernised, private commercial sector emerged. The *ejido* sector and smallholdings increasingly came to serve as a pool of cheap labour for commercial agriculture and urban areas, as well as a supplier of low-unit-cost foodstuffs. Productivity was boosted by the initial impact of green revolution technology. By the late 1950s land distribution policies made a return in response to large-scale peasant unrest and land invasions in the northern states led by the leftist independent *Unión General de Obreros y Campesinos de México* (UGOCM, General Union of Workers and Peasants of Mexico) (Bizberg 2003a).

By the 1960s, the Mexican miracle was losing steam, and political and social unrest mounted. The student protest of 1968 and its savage repression are often viewed as a turning point marking the rise of opposition forces. The early 1970s saw the emergence of radical rural movements involved in land invasions and of guerrilla activity in various parts of the country. To counter such trends, a new period of reformist policies started during the first years of the Luis Echevarría presidency (1970-1976) in an effort to shore up the damaged image of the Mexican political system. This included some degree of political liberalisation and efforts to improve the conditions of the urban and rural populations, which included a brief renewal of land redistribution (Bizberg 2003b; De Grammont 1996b:25).[16] After 1973, however, a gradual policy reversal took place, a trend that was to be continued under the José López Portillo presidency (1976-1982). One of the issues that plagued the Mexican economy, framed after the import-substitution model, was the increasing balance of payment deficits resulting from capital goods imports, as well as growing imports of basic foodstuffs to make up for the poor performance of the agrarian sector in this respect. In response, Mexico devalued its peso in 1976.

Meanwhile, a New Federal Agrarian Law had been passed in 1971, which was meant to speed up the handling of demands for land, while it tightened state control over the social property sector. During subsequent years various investment plans targeting rural areas were launched. By the mid-1970s the Mexican economy seemed to be saved by the discovery of vast oil and gas deposits on the east coast. The 'petrolisation' of the economy was translated into ambitious plans for integrated national development, and in 1980 a *Sistema Alimentario Mexicano* (SAM, Mexican Food System) was launched to regain food self-sufficiency[17] mainly through support for the surplus-producing peasantry (Fox 1993). The non-surplus-producing peasantry, or nearly 80 per cent of total producers, were ignored. And, while designed to emphasise rain-fed peasant production, SAM became a generalised grain production policy. At the same time, the regulation of crop prices, coupled with rising inflation and budget cuts after 1981, meant that the benefits for the peasantry were rather limited. Illegal renting out of *ejido* land to commercial farms increased along with proletarianisation, landlessness, and migration.

By 1982 world oil prices plummeted, triggering the Mexican crisis followed by IMF-prescribed austerity policies and a dramatic break with the economic model that had emerged since the 1930s.[18] This meant severe cut-backs in public spending, while staple crop prices remained low and production costs increased, resulting in an agrarian crisis that above all affected the 'social property sector' and triggered widespread loan default among *ejidatarios*.

During the period reviewed here, Mexico underwent a profound transformation promoted by the industrialisation policies and an economic growth averaging six per cent per year during the 'miracle' years between 1940 and the late 1970s. Meanwhile, whereas in the 1940s some twenty per cent out of a population of nearly 20 million lived in urban areas, by the mid-1990s 73 per cent of a total population of nearly 90 million lived in urban areas.

Rural Mexico on the eve of the 1992 'reform of the reform'

By the 1980s the agrarian reform process, which began with the Mexican revolution and went on until 1992 when redistribution officially came to a halt, had resulted in the creation of some 28,000 *ejidos* and the recognition of some 2,300 *comunidades*, which together made up the social property sector. They comprised a little over half of the Mexican farmland and some 3.5 million *beneficiados* (beneficiaries), about a third of the agrarian workers (Jones 1996; Mackinlay and Juan de la Fuente 1996; Robles Berlanga 2003; Thiesenhusen 1995:29-49). The typical or average *ejido* possessed some 2000 hectares, of which two-thirds were used collectively, and the rest was used individually as the parcels of 74 *ejidatarios* and nine *posesionarios* (possessors, who are not official members of the *ejido*). These people would live in the urban nucleus of the *ejido* together with 29 *avecindados* (neighbours, who live in the urban nucleus but do not possess *ejido* land and are not members). The average *ejidatario* would possess 9.2 hectares in two parcels and have access to 28 hectares of the commons. Distribution was unequal, however, and a little over half of all *ejidatarios* with rights to a parcel possessed less than five hectares. Non-agricultural activities accounted for about half of their income (Mohar Ponce n.d.:31-32; Robles Berlanga 2003).

As a land tenure institution, *ejidos* and *communidades* were regulated by law as corporations (though very different from business corporations). Tenure rights had three distinctive features: they could not be transferred to third parties, they could not expire, and they could not be seized through an injunction. These three features implied that *ejidal* and agrarian community tenure were constituted as a non-marketable kind of use rights and that the exercise of rights was, at least formally, subject to federal government surveillance through its agrarian branch. In practice, much would depend on local power relations and shifts therein.

The main features of the *ejidal* corporate organisation were as follows until 1992. First, when it came to productive organisation, the *ejidos* and agrarian communities could opt for collective exploitation of the land according to agrarian law, though in practice the great majority chose to subdivide the arable land into individually held and cultivated parcels. Second, the land was owned by a legal subject (the agrarian corporation) which was different from the individual peasants (*ejidatario* or *comunero*) who constituted the group.

Also, the corporate organisation of the *ejido* meant that there were several internal authorities with specific functions: the *asamblea* (assembly), which was the highest authority of the *ejido* and was made up of all the members of the *ejidal* community; the *comisariado ejidal* (*ejido* executive board), a body of three people elected by the assembly from amongst its members; and the *comité de vigilancia* (oversight committee) that supervised the *comisariado* administration. Until the 1992 reforms, the *comisariado ejidal* enjoyed ample discretionary powers, both *de jure* and *de facto*. These powers were important when land was located near an expanding city, since not all the *ejidatarios* had the same opportunity to decide if land was to be urbanised, and not all of them obtained the same benefits from the sale of land (illegal or otherwise). Usually, those who benefited the most were those in control of the *comisariado ejidal* and the *comité de vigilancia*. Very often the members of these two organs belonged to the families of the old chieftains and of the eminent members of the town.

On the other hand, the *ejido* system represented the most significant legal expression of the relationship between the peasantry and the state in post-revolutionary Mexico. Unlike other developing countries, where rural communities' land rights can often be traced back to pre-colonial arrangements, *ejido tenure* was the result of a redefinition of the position of the peasantry within the political system during the decades that followed the Revolution. Through this form of land tenure, peasants were assigned a specific position as subjects-of-law and, consequently, gained a new status in the political system. Indeed, one of the bases for the legitimacy of the post-revolutionary Mexican state was generated through these agrarian institutions. The support that successive federal administrations received from the so-called 'peasant sector' was organised through the *ejidos* and *comunidades*. In other words, they were both a product and a supporting element of the Mexican political system. Thus, it is possible to understand the paternalism which prevailed in the relationship between the agrarian communities and the government. Agrarian institutions have functioned as if peasant organisations owed their existence as subjects-of-law to the government. Their rights to land were constituted from the top, as an act of the state, and their disappearance also depended until 1992 on a unilateral act on the part of the government authorities in the name of public interest.

The features of *ejido* tenure rights, together with its corporate organisation, played a double role in the history of the agrarian reform. On the one hand, they gave the agrarian communities effective protection against losing their lands, a loss that could derive from the operation of market forces. This, together with the maximum size established for agrarian private property, prevented a monopoly of land in the hands of a reduced number of landowners, as was the case before the Revolution. In this sense, restrictions imposed by agrarian law on *ejido* and communal land tenure allowed for the permanence of agrarian communities as such. Legislation was rather restrictive in the sense that transactions of individual parcels (rentals and sales) were prohibited, the commons could not be divided, membership of the *ejido* was controlled by the Agrarian Reform Bureaucracy - which tended to discourage incorporation of new members in order to avoid fragmentation into small plots - and *ejido* parcels and rights could only be bequeathed to a single descendant or the spouse. *Ejidatarios* would formally lose their rights if they did not work their land for a year. These restrictions, on the other hand, also meant that the communities did not have the right to decide on the future of their land, for example in the context of urban expansion.[19] In practice, such detailed legal stipulations resulted in all sorts of extra-legal or 'illegal' arrangements according to local power relations, in which the agrarian bureaucracy was but a player that most often had to negotiate its presence rather than enforce elaborate and detailed legislation (Nuijten 1998). From the point of view of the technocrats who would promote the 1992 reform, the legislation in itself and the ways in which it was circumvented formed a source of tenure insecurity. Furthermore, although *ejidos* and agrarian communities effectively were communities of sorts, we should not infer that they were always harmonious communities or that disputes over land, resources, and power were absent, a consideration which points to another possible source of insecurity.

Alongside the 'social property sector' a private sector existed, which by the 1990s consisted of about one and a half million production units, half of the number of production units in the 'social property sector'. Of those in the private sector no more than 15,000 possessed large businesses, concentrating nearly half of the value of rural production, and 150,000 held small private operations. The rest were smallholders mainly producing for subsistence and engaging in further 'complementary' activities (Bartra 2004:23; Robles Berlanga 2003; see also Otero 2004).

It should be noted that some 4 million agricultural workers had no land of their own (Arroyo Sepúlveda 2001) and that part of the land distributed, especially after the Cárdenas reform drive, was less suitable for agriculture, while institutional support for the 'social property sector' decreased. Many rural families therefore supplemented their income with other economic activities, which included, notably, long-distance migration to the US.

Reform of the reform: 'Liberty and Justice' replaces 'Land and Liberty'

It was against the backdrop of the NAFTA negotiations in November 1991 that President Carlos Salinas de Gortari announced his initiative to reform article 27 of the Constitution. 'Liberty and Justice for the Countryside' was what he promised because, as Stephen (2002:67) notes, 'ending the government's obligation to redistribute land made the slogan "Tierra y Libertad" obsolete.' 'Liberty' now meant to strengthen individual property rights over the *ejidatario*'s parcel and therefore to deconstruct collective decision-making, in line with neoliberal thinking and echoing some of the nineteenth-century liberal land reform attempts.

While NAFTA negotiations played a role, the reform proposal was also inspired by World Bank recommendations (Heath 1990) which suggested titling of *ejido* lands irrespective of parcel size, simplification and clarification of restrictions for private farmers on holding size and land use, ending restrictions on renting and sharecropping by *ejidatarios*, allowing *ejidatarios* to sell their land to other members of the *ejido* (but not to outsiders), improving management of communal lands, extending credit to individual *ejidatarios* on the basis of credit worthiness, ceasing to have the whole *ejido* bear the burden of loan default, and providing credit wholly in cash so that *ejidatarios* could decide what inputs to buy and what crops to plant. These were aspects of what broadly was defined as tenure insecurity, which was to be addressed by a reform of article 27 and agrarian law. Furthermore, any efforts at redistribution – another source of insecurity – would be cancelled.

To sustain his reform proposal, President Salinas argued that: (1) there was no more land to redistribute and that now the task would be to improve productivity; (2) federal agrarian tribunals should be created to substitute the administrative-jurisdictional procedures to resolve tenure issues within and between *ejidos* and/or communities; (3) in order to capitalise the countryside, security was needed and that while ceilings on rural property would remain in force, associations with *sociedades mercantiles* (mercantile societies) should be made possible, among other things to achieve economies of scale; (4) individual small properties would be protected and that, given that redistribution would be ended, they would no longer need certificates of unaffectability; (5) new forms of association among different forms of tenure, through shareholding, should be stimulated in order to achieve economies of scale, while at the same time *ejido* and community tenure would be constitutionally protected, along with the territorial integrity of indigenous peoples[20], and that housing plots would be the exclusive property of their inhabitants (Secretaria de Reforma Agraria 1998:76-79).[21]

The initiative came as a shock, since it had been preceded by unilateral economic liberalisation that apparently was to pave the way for NAFTA. Agricultural trade had been liberalised in 1990, subsidies had been cut or sharply reduced, guarantee prices for all crops but maize and beans had been eliminated, crop insurance had been abolished, and development bank credits had been retargeted to serve only peasant growers whose operations were deemed profitable, while commercial growers had to borrow from commercial banks (Gates 1993). Meanwhile, encouraged by Salinas, the official CNC and UNORCA had formed a *Consejo Agrario Permanente* (CAP, Permanent Agrarian Council),[22] which initially denounced the initiative as a 'counter-reform'. Through a policy of heavy pressure and manipulation, the government managed to gain some reluctant support from the 'officialist' organisations, leading to deep divisions within these organisations, while the autonomous organisations were sidelined in the process. The outcome was that all organisations were put on the defensive and the reform was pushed through, resulting in the debilitation and splintering of the rural movements that had seemed to be so strong in previous years (Bizberg 2003b; Foley 1995; Secretaria de Reforma Agraria 1998).

The reform of article 27 was approved by early January 1992, and implementing legislation followed in February 1992. The main provisions of the new legislation can be summarised as follows (based on Cornelius and Myhre 1998):[23]

1. The government's constitutional obligation to distribute land is ended.
2. Private landowners can make capital investments on their land without risking expropriation, since improvement will not lead to a reclassification of the land.
3. Land rights disputes between *ejidatarios*, and between *ejidos* and/or private holders, are to be settled by a decentralised system of presidentially appointed Agrarian Tribunals.[24]
4. Ejidatarios can obtain individual certificates of their land rights if their *ejido* agrees to participate in the *Programa de Certificación de Derechos Ejidales y Titulación de Solares* (PROCEDE, Program for the Certification of *Ejido* Land Rights and the Titling of Urban House Plots[25]). Participation in the programme requires an initial meeting by the *ejido* assembly, attended by half of the members plus one. If this cannot be carried through, a second meeting can be called for which no quorum is established. The decision to participate in the certification programme may or may not lead to a future decision to privatise or disband the *ejido*. Privatisation means that the certificates under agrarian law are turned into ownership titles (*dominio pleno*) under civil law. This can occur in two ways: (1) full privatisation and therefore disbanding of the *ejido*; or (2) partial privatisation

whereby the *ejido* assembly allows members who wish to do so to apply for *dominio pleno*. It is also possible for agrarian communities to convert into *ejidos* (and vice versa) and then to convert to the *dominio pleno* regime.

5. *Ejidatarios* who have had the boundaries of their parcels certified have the right to legally sell, rent, sharecrop or mortgage their land, but the decision to sell *ejido* lands to outsiders must be approved by a two-thirds vote of the *ejido* general assembly, witnessed by a government representative. A quorum of 75 per cent of the *ejido* members is required for a vote to privatise, but the necessary quorum drops to 50 per cent if a second or third meeting is needed. If the legal quorum is present, it takes two-thirds of the vote to permit privatisation of land within the *ejido*. The common lands can similarly be sold off for commercial development.

6. *Ejidatarios* are no longer required to work the land personally in order to retain it, which means, for example, that migrants can leave their parcels under a sharecropping arrangement or can have it cultivated by others from inside or outside the *ejido*, without running the risk of losing their land rights.

7. To prevent excessive concentration of privatised *ejido* land, legal limits on maximum property size will continue to be enforced. The individual limit for agricultural land is 100 hectares. For grazing land the limit is set at the land needed for 500 large animals, and forest property cannot exceed 800 hectares. Corporate entities are limited to 2,500 hectares per company, and mercantile societies are required to have at least 25 individual members. Joint *ejido*-private firm production associations may not own more than their total membership would be permitted to acquire as individual landowners.

8. *Ejidatarios* who opt not to sell or rent their land can enter into joint ventures with outside investors or form associations among themselves to maximise economies of scale. They can also sign long-term production contracts with outsiders.

9. The *ejido* sector is open to foreign direct investment, but foreign investors may not own more than 49 per cent of the land owned by the enterprise.

The reform generated both expectations and apprehension. According to its proponents, it merely legalised the ongoing extra-legal practices in the *ejidos* (such as the sale and rental of lands), freed the *ejidatarios* from the dead hand of state 'paternalism', and would help to overcome the crisis in the sector through increased tenure security, an inflow of capital, increased productivity, and the promotion of entrepreneurial forms of organisation.[26] Critics foresaw a reconcentration of landholding and pointed to loopholes in the new legislation that would allow this (Cornelius and Myhre 1998:3-4; Foley 1995:65n; Gledhill 1997). They also pointed to the conjunction of the reform with trade liberalisation in the NAFTA context and the dismantling of state support for the 'social property sector'. Under such conditions they foresaw a massive new wave of migration to the cities.[27]

By late 1992 the PROCEDE certification programme got under way, initially aiming for certification of the social property sector's area in two years while critics predicted widespread rejection of the programme. As De Ita (2006) notes '[A]fter ten years of operation neither has occurred. The arable land area of Mexico has still not been entirely certified, yet there was also no massive rejection of PROCEDE.' And an official government report, which provides an overview of the 1992-2005 period and announces that PROCEDE will be phased out in August 2006, elliptically states that:

> [T]he critique by some peasant organisations that affirm that PROCEDE privatises *ejido* lands has turned out to be unfounded.
> Through the adoption of *dominio pleno* or the bringing in of common use lands into mercantile societies, only 1,466,000 hectares, representing 1.4 per cent of the lands in the 'social property sector', have been converted to private property. At the same time, 1,276 new *ejidos* have been created, amplifying the 'social property sector' by 387,000 hectares.[28] In sum, only one per cent of 'social property sector' land has been privatised. Some 60 per cent of those *desincorporadas* lands[29] have been needed for the growth of cities, for which their *desincorporación* was necessary (Secretaría de la Reforma Agraria 2006, our translation).

This is a rather curious statement in that it turns vice into virtue and actually admits that some main objectives of the 1992 reforms – promoting private property and associations with the private sector in order to capitalise the *ejidos* – have not been achieved. In conjunction with De Ita's (2006) comments, this suggests that *ejidos* and – at a later stage – agrarian communities have 'voluntarily'[30] joined the certification programme without, however, scrambling for privatisation, with the exception of some areas of incorporation of *ejido* lands into urban expansion schemes. Galeana (2004) argues that if individuals seek to obtain full ownership titles, this is related to opportunities to sell their land for urbanisation rather than to ask for credit. In some cases the acceptance of certification may have been a way to settle internal disputes.

Practising 'Liberty and Justice'

According to the *Registro Agrario Nacional* (2005), of the 29,942 agrarian
nuclei (27,664 *ejidos* and 2,278 *comunidades*), 28,709 (96 per cent) had
'voluntarily' adhered to the PROCEDE programme. A total of 26,031
agrarian nuclei (87 per cent of the national total) had been regularised
through the dispatching of 8,421,108 certificates and titles: 4,649,590
parcel certificates, 1,738,247 common use certificates – which grant
access to a percentage of common use lands – and 2,033,271 house plot
titles. The programme thus certified or titled some 76.2 million hectares
and benefited some 3,843,798 people. Of those 76.2 million hectares,
23,009,640 were certified as parcels, 52,951,034 were certified for common use,[31] and 300,335 hectares were titled, presumably as housing
plots, as the new 1992 law prescribes.

By the end of March 2005, the PROCEDE programme had measured 85,562,262 hectares out of the 103,515,321 hectares belonging to
the 'social property sector', that is, 83 per cent. Progress in coverage,
however, was uneven across the states of the Federation. Generally, coverage in the northern states was greater than in the south. The advance
in the northern states may be related to less severe demographic pressure on *ejido* lands and an already existing clearer definition of land
tenure rights, due to the agricultural potential of the lands (Zepeda
2000). The southern states, in contrast, were characterised by a higher
number of smaller *ejidos*, higher demographic pressure, and more difficult access due to their rugged geography. In the state of Oaxaca, 62
per cent of the land was held by agrarian communities, which were
also mostly indigenous.

The PROCEDE programme advanced by tackling the least problematic areas first. By 2003 it was reported that 4,735 (15.5 per cent) of
the then existing 30,513 agrarian nuclei (*ejidos* and *comunidades*) had
problems. A quarter of these problem cases had rejected the PROCEDE
programme, twenty per cent were involved in disputes over limits, and
ten per cent suffered internal conflicts (cf. De Ita 2006). The agrarian
nuclei that accepted the programme possibly took it as an opportunity
to update membership lists[32] and to sort out and consolidate tenure.

What then about the expected benefits of the 1992 constitutional reform and the new agrarian legislation? Zepeda (2000:271), paraphras-
ing Galileï's '*Eppur si muove*' ('Nonetheless, it moves'), argues that despite the reform 'nonetheless...it does not move'. As already noted, contrary to what some expected, in only a few cases was *dominio pleno*
opted for, and no vibrant land sales market has come into being except
for peri-urban areas. Sometimes this has been attributed to the fact
that private property unlike 'social property is subject to taxes' (Brown
2004; cf. De Ita 2006). However, there are many indications that sug-

gest other reasons for this lack of interest in privatisation. For most of the 'social property sector', land is much more than a simple commodity. Often its 'conquest' has been the result of a long struggle, and losing it would mean becoming a simple day labourer (Zepeda 2000:272). Moreover, most of the 'social property sector' serves as a refuge economy geared to subsistence production that is complemented by other activities (De Janvry, Gustavo Gordillo, and Sadouleth 1997:203-204; World Bank 1998:11). As Gledhill (1997) argues, only fifteen per cent of the *ejidatarios* could be viewed as commercially viable producers on the eve of the 'second agrarian reform', and they, along with the stratum of relatively prosperous private small farmers, suffered the devastating effects Mexico's structural adjustment shock treatment. His research between 1991 and 1994 identified a clear pattern of 'richer peasants reducing their rental of land and switching to production of lower value crops' (see also Gledhill 1995), which points to a process of 'agricultural involution'.

This brings us to the question of land rental markets. It is often asserted that enhanced tenure security – perhaps less a result of changes in the legal framework than of implementation of PROCEDE (Deininger et al. 2001) – has contributed to a vitalisation of rental markets,[33] though comparison with the pre-1992 situation is quite difficult. After all, the reforms were justified with the argument that renting was a 'widespread' though illegal practice. The consequences of such enhanced rental market activity are not clear, however. According to De Janvry et al. (1997:201-202), those *ejidatarios* with smaller plots and greater involvement in off-farm activities and migration are the ones who rent out their land without losing their tenure rights in the *ejido*. The operational area of small *ejido* farms thus decreases as a result of land rental and migration, and, according to the authors, this abandonment of small farms can be expected to accelerate. This is a symptom of what they call the 'severe crisis of the *ejido* sector', a crisis that announced itself in the mid-1960s and that only deepened under structural adjustment in the 1980s and free-trade measures in the 1990s. In contrast, Deininger et al. (2001), who are rather optimistic about the Mexican reform, assert that in 'non-certified *ejidos* it is the large farmers who rent in land and the small farmers who rent out while the opposite is true in certified *ejidos*'. They suggest, invoking the 'inverse size-productivity relationship,'[34] that 'in non-certified *ejidos*, the rental market tends to contribute to land concentration instead of redistribution towards smaller producers' and that in this situation 'rental markets might actually decrease efficiency', whereas in 'certified *ejidos* the exact opposite is true'. Several other documents, however, also suggest that small producers generally enter the rental market from the supply side and then engage in other activities.[35] The inconsistencies in the argument presented by Deininger et al. (2001), which also filtered into the World Bank (2003d:120-121) Policy Research Report, have been pinpointed by Baranyi, Deere and Morales (2004:34). The World Bank's own research (Olinto, Klaus Deininger, and Davis 2000:6) shows that small farmers were more prone to rent out their land, while larger farmers would rent in. Other studies (Concheiro Bórquez and Quintana 2003; Lewis 2002) also suggest processes of land concentration and do not support the 'win-win' scenario of increased land access for the poor and renting out of land by the rich as presented by the World Bank.

As to credit, access to which was expected to increase as land could be used as collateral, De Janvry et al. (1997) argue that the 1992 reform took place in the context of an 'institutional vacuum'. During the 1980s many public institutions were privatised, scaled down, or liquidated. Access to credit, but also to insurance, markets, modern inputs, and technical assistance had been severely reduced, and hardly any alternative institutions had emerged to cater for the *ejido* sector. They note that the number of *ejidatarios* with access to credit increased due to the *crédito a la palabra* (credit without collateral) programme that was launched in the context of the National Solidarity Program (PRONASOL) on the eve of the 1994 elections. It is one of what have been called 'neopopulist solutions to neoliberal problems' (cf. Knight 1996:4). While the number of people receiving credit temporarily increased, the total amount of credit to which the *ejido* sector had access decreased, and access to credit decreased again – from 30 per cent of *ejido* households in 1994 to twenty per cent in 1997 – once the elections were won,[36] and the programme was phased out (World Bank 1998:16) and replaced with focused programmes aimed at human capital formation,[37] such as PROGRESA under the Zedillo administration (1994-2000) and OPORTUNIDADES under the Fox government (2000-2006).

The 'institutional vacuum' together with the 'profitability crisis', which was due to trade liberalisation, inefficient marketing channels, 'adjustment noise' after the 1995 peso crisis, and the world market price decline (World Bank 1998:9-10), resulted in a sort of technological involution (De Janvry, Gustavo Gordillo, and Sadouleth 1997; Zepeda 2000:286), which also affected the private sector, 'better off' stratum of peasants and farmers. Manual labour replaced machines, local seeds took the place of 'improved' seeds, fertilizer use dropped – trends that had been present before 1992 and that were not reversed by the reform of the legal framework, as propaganda had it. Market liberalisation for agrarian products initiated in 1982 took place in a context of overproduction of basic grains in the USA and Europe and a ferocious struggle for markets to get rid of the 'surplus'. The low-priced exports by the USA of maize and beans provoked a crisis among the Mexican producers, which only grew more profound after the ratification of NAFTA. Between 1985 and 1990 the principal products of rain-fed agriculture, which is the realm of the small and medium-sized producers, fell by 0.60 per cent per year, and between 1990 and 1994 they fell by 4.35 per cent per year. Between 1990 and 1994 rain-fed maize production fell by 4.64 per cent annually and that of beans by 2.63 per cent. At the same time, a process took place known as the 'privatisation of maize', that is, an increase in production on irrigated land by agrarian enterprises in the north of the country (Rubio 1999:43-44), effecting a brutal decline in income for the smaller producers in the south.

The crisis of small and medium Mexican agriculture only deepened after the NAFTA treaty became operative on January 1, 1994. It was a treaty between unequal partners. Production costs were higher in Mexico, while USA agriculture was strongly subsidised, and the average size of exploitations was much larger. During the negotiations Mexico accepted a generous duty-free import quota and an above-quota tariff for maize and beans that it never enforced (World Bank 1998:9). Mexican imports of grains and oil-seeds increased from 8.8 million tons in 1993 to about 20 million tons in 2002. Before NAFTA, at most 2.5 million tons of maize were imported per year, but by 2001 6 million tons were imported. Unemployment and poverty in rural Mexico increased, and according to official data, 70 per cent of the rural population was poor (cf. Gómez Cruz and Rindermann 2003; Quintana and Víctor 2003).

Farmers had already started to mobilise when the NAFTA plans became public, demanding exemptions for various products, such as maize, beans, and dairy products. In response, in 1993, the government launched the PROCAMPO programme. This was a subsidy that was to compensate for income losses and assist the adjustment to the removal of price guarantees and market supports. It covered maize, beans, wheat, cotton, soybeans, sorghum, rice, barley, and safflower. It was paid per hectare, and payments were expected to be constant for ten years and then to be phased out in the subsequent five years, though in real terms payments actually declined by five per cent per year.[38] It was another instance of 'neopopulist solutions to neoliberal problems' as the income subsidy was sufficient to keep peasants and farmers growing their crops, but insufficient to help them make the transition to other commercial crops, also given the virtual absence of technical assistance and the subsistence logic of much of the peasant sector.

Protests increased over the course of the 1990s with the emergence of the *El Barzón* movement, led by farmers affected by the scissors movement of increasingly rigid credit conditions and falling prices, which drove them into bankruptcy (see De Grammont 1996a). The pace of protest was set by the lifting of nearly all import restrictions on agricultural products under NAFTA by 2003 and the issuing of the USA Farm Bill in May 2002. By 2002 mobilisations converged in the movement *El Campo no Aguanta Más* (The Countryside Endures no More), which in early 2003 forced the Vicente Fox government to sign a National Accord for the Countryside, an accord that was considered minimal or insufficient by many farmer and peasant organisations (Bartra 2004). They had demanded a renegotiation of the NAFTA agriculture chapter, a revision of article 27 of the Constitution, and the recognition of indigenous peoples' rights. These were not included in the rather lengthy and confused document – counting 282 paragraphs – that was eventually ratified during a lacklustre ceremony.

One of the points of the agreement was to revise agrarian legislation, which by March 2005 resulted in the presentation of an initiative for a new Federal Agrarian Law in the Chamber of Deputies. Since then, however, the legislative process has stalled and was to be taken up by the newly elected Congress after the July 2006 elections.

Low-income illegal settlements and tenure regularisation on peri-urban *ejido* lands[39]

Besides the agrarian and peasant questions addressed through the agrarian reform and the land distribution process, *ejidos* and communities whose lands were situated on the outskirts of fast-growing urban centres would, sooner or later, face a situation in which those lands could be assigned for urban uses such as public utilities, urban development projects, or housing. And, in fact, *ejido* lands have been and still are absorbed for all kinds of urban uses. But up to 1992, only in the case of low-income housing could the process of *ejido* land development be controlled illegally by *ejidatarios* themselves. The incentives for the subdivision of land come from the obvious fact that it offers *ejidatarios* the opportunity to make more money than with agricultural production. Besides, in many cases, it concerns lands of minimal or no agricultural productivity. But it is clear that the urbanisation of *ejido* lands is almost inevitable, to an extent, when they are located on the fringes of rapidly expanding cities. So far, subdividing land and selling plots to low-income urban dwellers has for *ejidatarios* been the main way to keep control over land development initiatives and to obtain good earnings with minimum investments.

The development of low-income settlements on *ejido* lands can be divided into two main periods. The first period runs from the mid-1940s to the beginning of the 1970s, and the second from the creation of the

Commission for the Regularisation of Land Tenure (*Comisión para la Regularización de la Tenencia de la Tierra*, CORETT) in 1973-1974 to the mid-1990s. This can be regarded as a transition period during which *ejidatarios* and irregular land developments on *ejido* lands adjusted their practices and adapted to the new legal framework.

During the first period, agrarian communities resorted to the 'urban area device' in order to legitimise the sale of plots. Originally designed to house peasants on their land, this legal figure was used as a loophole to create housing settlements in peri-urban areas. Up to the present day agrarian legislation allows for a tract of the *ejidos'* land to be set aside for the *ejido's* village or 'urban area' (*zona de urbanización ejidal*) where besides *ejidatarios'* houses, *avecindados* may be admitted and sold a plot. *Avecindados*, which literally means neighbours, are defined as those who are not *ejidatarios* but who are willing to live in the *ejido* village and to devote themselves to an activity which is 'useful to the community' (artisans, shopkeepers, etc.).

Despite the legal prohibition to designate 'urban areas' for reasons other than to meet the communities' needs, between 1950 and 1970 the creation of such areas was systematically used by *ejidos* in the periphery of Mexico City as a mechanism to establish low-income settlements on *ejido* lands. According to Ann Varley, 91 per cent of the *ejidos* around Mexico City had at least started the procedures leading to the constitution of an urban area by 1970. The fact that people who settled as *avecindados* outnumbered the *ejidatarios* by up to six times shows that the legal notion of the urban zone was used to legitimate the subdivision of land in order to develop low-income settlements (Varley 1985).

Given that the generalised resort to this device provoked numerous conflicts opposing settlers and *ejidatarios*, *ejidatarios* and their internal authorities, and local authorities and settlers, increasing pressure began to be felt by the federal authorities involved, and the artifice of the 'urban area' lost its legitimating power. Besides, by then, the issue of 'irregular settlements', concerning *ejidal* as well as private and public lands, had become a central dimension of the 'human settlements' national agenda (Duhau 1998), which included the development of several procedures and programmes for the 'regularisation' of those settlements. To regularise irregular settlements established on *ejido* lands, in the early 1970s a federal commission was created, the CORETT. With the CORETT, what would turn out to be a long-lasting regularisation process was institutionalised. The effect was that it stabilised the expectations of the social actors involved and, in that way, indirectly contributed to the reproduction of a rather ordered, albeit irregular, market in *ejidal* land. The scope of CORETT action can be appreciated if we consider that during the period 1974-2000, at a national level, it regularised land tenure for urban uses over a surface area of roughly 136,000 hectares, and issued more than 2,191,000 property titles for housing plots.[40]

Thus, during several decades, *ejidatarios* have been irregularly subdividing and selling their lands, mostly to low-income dwellers; sometimes on a small scale, as when an *ejidatario* subdivides and sells plots in an individually owned parcel, sometimes on a massive scale, as when *ejidatarios* collectively decide to urbanise lands owned in the same way. Particularly in these latter cases, the sale of plots becomes a real planned subdivision: the layout of the streets and the size of the plots are standardised, a range of prices per square meter is established according to the location of the plots, and usually the plot is paid for in instalments.

How to explain the tolerance of agrarian and urban authorities towards agrarian communities that illegally urbanise their lands? It can be summarily explained by considering several factors regarding the question of low-income housing in Mexico, and the socio-political rationale that for decades has driven the relationships between agrarian communities and the state. First, despite the public social housing programmes institutionalised since the 1970s, there have been huge numbers of families that do not have access to those programmes and cannot afford any of the housing alternatives existing on the formal housing market (Duhau 1998). By selling cheap, unserviced plots to these families, *ejidatarios* have performed a valuable service for the state, since this alleviates social conflicts around housing issues arising from unfulfilled housing needs. There is a basic cultural element here: *ejidatarios* are not seen by low-income households as 'speculators'. Although by urbanising their lands they do get an important share of the urban revenue without investing almost anything, usually they are seen as ordinary peasants. Within the cultural heritage of the agrarian reform, *ejidatarios* are not accorded any public responsibility, including that of paying taxes over their lands, since they have traditionally played a passive role as victims rather than beneficiaries of agrarian policies. Second, within the organisation of the *Partido Revolucionario Institucional* (PRI, Institutional Revolutionary Party), which was the national ruling party for seven decades until 2000, peasant organisations had the function of providing social support for campaigns and elections; support that would have been difficult to obtain if public authorities prosecuted them for selling *ejido* lands. Third, the public authorities in charge of the agrarian reform, once they had fulfilled the obligation to distribute available lands, had very little to offer to improve the revenues and the economic condition of *ejidatarios*, mostly operating as subsistence farmers. Should agrarian authorities devote themselves to law enforcement, their main activity would have been that of prosecuting *ejidatarios* in suburban areas for selling their lands. Arguably, tolerance towards this informal land market has functioned as a compensation for the implicitly admitted social and economic failure of the agrarian reform. Finally, the fact that there are enough buyers to support the informal *ejidal* land market, and that the process of irregular urbanisation of those lands has usually taken place without causing significant conflicts, also contributed to the institutionalisation of the *ejidal* land tenure regularisation programmes in charge of the CORETT since 1973.

Regarding the features of this programme and the question of tenure rights that it involves, the following must be emphasised. First, although the legal rule according to which *ejido* land sales were null and void formally applied until 1992, this was in fact offset by the certainty that, given the presence and stability of CORETT, regularisation of land tenure would eventually take place. Second, regularisation of land tenure in irregularly urbanised *ejido* lands is a form of state intervention that requires minimal assignment of budgetary resources, since the CORETT is supposed to be self-financing and to fund its operational costs from the charges levied on beneficiaries (Azuela 1994). This means that low-income settlers on *ejido* lands pay twice for acquiring a plot. First, they pay for the 'purchase' of a plot (legally invalid), and when the regularisation procedure takes place, they pay a sum for the associated costs, including a compensation payment for the concerned *ejidatarios* whose lands are 'expropriated' for reasons of public interest, that is, the regularisation of a low-income settlement. Third, although the CORETT's regularisation actions, as such, cost the state very little, they have major social and political implications (although some of these are subject to debate; Iracheta 1989; Legorreta 1994; Varley 1989). Fourth, over the last three decades, tenure regularisation concerning *ejidal* lands but also other forms of land rights has been a core urban policy consistently applied by the Mexican government, particularly in Mexico City and its metropolitan area (Duhau 1998). As a result, the informal land market has become a preferred way for low-income households to gain access to housing. Given the continuous expansion of illegal settlements, though recently the pace has slowed down, regularisation has become a routine form of state intervention in the field of low-income housing, particularly in Mexico City. There can be no doubt that it delivers a loud and clear message about the government's attitude to informal development to all actors involved in the process.

With the 1992 changes in the *ejidal* land tenure regime, *ejidal* land – particularly when located in a peri-urban area – becomes susceptible to being incorporated into the formal real estate market. Nevertheless, according to information collected by the Procuraduria Agraria, this has happened only in a few cases. Between 1992 and 2003, at a national level, only 25 *ejidos* have contributed lands to businesses societies, and less than half of the cases imply the constitution of a real estate business oriented to urban subdivisions and housing projects (Procuraduría Agraria 2004b). Why do *ejidatarios* persist in informally selling land even though they now have the possibility of engaging in formal real estate businesses?

In spite of the current possibility of converting *ejidal* land to a full private property regime and selling it legally to outsiders, the tenure rights concerned must first be certified by the PROCEDE programme, and after that specific procedures must be followed in order to convert them from the *ejidal* tenure regime into freehold. Additionally, once these requirements are satisfied, the subdivision and conversion of *ejidal* land to urban uses are always subject to procedures laid down in planning regulations. By 2003, the first step had been taken by 82.4 per cent of 30,077 agrarian nuclei, that is, 24,792 *ejidos* and communities, almost three-quarters out of them located in the northern Mexican federal states. Of the certified agrarian nuclei, only 1,595, accounting for 0.7 per cent of the surface of the 'social property sector', have been converted to a full private property regime. At the same time, always according to the Office of the Agrarian Attorney, 6,194 agrarian nuclei show irregular settlement developments (Procuraduría Agraria 2004b), almost four times the number of privatised ones. Therefore, it is clear that subdividing and selling land irregularly continues to be extensively practised.

Apparently, for *ejidatarios* a powerful reason for not taking the second step and becoming freehold proprietors is to avoid paying land taxes as well as municipal fees like those for the provision of potable water and, in a more general way, to avoid becoming liable private proprietors. But we also have to take account of the fact that being an *ejidatario* or *comunero* usually signifies not only being the owner of a piece of land, but a member of a landed corporation recognised and acting as a local power. This condition would disappear once the corporation was dissolved or many individually owned parcels were segregated from the *ejido*.

Last, but not least, irregularly subdividing and urbanising their lands, instead of becoming partners of a real estate society, keeps *ejidatarios* in control of the process and the resulting profits, while having to invest almost no cash resources. By contrast, entering into a partnership with a private developer would imply that it is the latter who would contribute the financial resources needed to carry out the formal real estate development, and who would surely try to take control of the business. Additionally, what private developers usually want from *ejidatarios* is to buy their land, mainly under advantageous conditions, rather than to enter into a partnership with them.[41]

By way of conclusion

In this chapter we present an overview of the evolution of land tenure and tenure regimes in Mexico in the context of changing power relations and accumulation regimes. From the colonial economy, a *hacienda* system emerged that consolidated under the liberal legislation of the second half of the nineteenth century in the context of an increasingly agro-export-oriented economy. By the early twentieth century this had resulted in an extremely skewed distribution of landholding which contributed to making the Mexican revolution the first 'peasant war of the twentieth century' (Wolf 1973). Initially, however, the revolution did not substantially change the agro-export orientation of the Mexican economy, nor did it bring about a substantial redistribution of land. Despite the Zapatista inspiration of constitutional article 27, the post-revolutionary regimes regarded the *ejido* as a transitory form of tenure and privileged private ownership.

A new development model of import-substituting industrialisation emerged in the early 1930s. Initially, and in contrast to most other Latin American countries, the agrarian sector was assigned a privileged role in this new model and received extensive government support. Land redistribution peaked under the Cárdenas government, which consolidated the *ejido* as a form of tenure and experimented with collective *ejidos*. In the 1940s, policy emphasis shifted away from the agrarian sector, which was now assigned the role of providing cheap food for an increasingly urbanising and industrialising country. The 'social property sector' became subject to increasing state regulation, and an intricate system of price regulation and subsidies emerged. At the same time, policies tended to favour the development of the private sector and the production of high-value exportables. This gave rise to a dual agrarian structure and a deepening regional differentiation between 'the north' and an impoverished 'south', where additionally most of Mexico's indigenous peoples can be found. The 'social property sector' increasingly became a reservoir of cheap labour and subsistence-oriented production on gradually fragmenting parcels (*minifundia*). The 1982 Mexican crisis brought an end to the 1970s' brief flurry of development policies oriented toward the 'social property sector', and free trade policies contributed to a deepening crisis of this sector.

It was in this context that the 1992 reform initiative was taken. On the one hand, one of its stated aims was to reduce state intervention and regulation, and on the other hand, it was to promote a market in land by opening the way to privatisation of lands in the 'social property sector' so that land would be allocated to the most efficient user. An extensive 'voluntary' programme for certification of lands in the sector was launched. This, however, did not result in massive privatisation, as some had expected, nor in the emergence of a vibrant land market. Land rentals increased, but it is not clear if this was really related to certification (World Bank 1998:26), and it should also be noted that most of the transactions remain informal. It is also doubtful whether this rental market really benefits the poor (Baranyi, Deere, and Morales 2004:34; Concheiro Bórquez and Quintana 2003). Quite probably, the effects are regionally differentiated and depend on the quality of the land, which is low in most cases. At the same time, land is much more than a commodity, and membership in an *ejido* or agrarian community may bring benefits and securities that account for the persistence of this form of organisation.

The 1992 reform failed in its intention to dynamise the agrarian sector, in a context of economic liberalisation and implementation of the NAFTA agreement, as is reflected in the continuing crisis of the 'social property sector' and in the protest movements led by private sector farmers. The reform took place in the context of an institutional vacuum, created by the dismantling of state agencies and services in previous years, and a profitability crisis of most of Mexico's agriculture resulting from trade liberalisation. It therefore did not bring about the expected 'agrarian transformation' (Secretaría de la Reforma Agraria 1998) because, as Zepeda (2000:275) puts it, 'the peasantry does not live by legal security alone'. The 'development' path pursued by Mexican governments since 1982 may have benefited a small group of export-oriented private enterprises and some large agro-industrial conglomerates, such as the *tortilla* industry, which benefited from the liberalisation of importations of basic inputs – often heavily subsidised in their countries of origin.[42] In such a context, tinkering with the land tenure regime and promoting privatisation and freehold as the ultimate forms of tenure security cannot be expected to be the 'silver bullet' that will dynamise Mexican agriculture.

One of the reasons put forward to justify the 1992 reform was that the prohibition on the sale of social property sector land in fact created an illegal land market. However, we have argued that, although such a market certainly existed, the newly opened possibility to enter the legal market seems to be hardly attractive for the peasantry in the social property sector, which is reflected in the fact that the option to convert to freehold was made only in a very few cases. Even under conditions of mounting market pressure, as in peri-urban areas, informal transactions apparently continue to be the rule rather than the exception.

Notes

1   Parts of this chapter were earlier published in the *Journal of Agrarian Change*, Vol. 8, No. 1, January 2008 under the title "Land Tenure and Tenure Regimes in Mexico: An Overview." We thank the Journal editors and anonymous reviewers for their comments.

2   At the time the term *ejido* referred to the village commons. After the revolution the term came to be used to designate a self-governing tenure institution created in the context of the agrarian reform.

3   In 1847 the US invaded Mexico and annexed Texas.

4   The church may have controlled nearly half of the land (Skidmore and Smith 1997:228).

5   During the French intervention (1864-1867), Emperor Maximilian von Habsburg refused to return lands to the Church but sought some sort of an alliance with the peasant and indigenous population by returning their communal lands and seeking some sort of agrarian reform, though given the political circumstances and the fact that many of the supporters of the emperor had reaped benefits from the *desamortización* process, the attempts at agrarian reform remained without effect.

6   The second half of the nineteenth century had already seen a series of revolts throughout the country (Wolf 1973).

7   Under the post-revolutionary regimes these lands would be individualised.

8   The original article 27 is reproduced in Silva (1959:250-255).

9   For an overview of indigenous landholding and tenure, see Robles 2000.

10 Obregón was elected in 1920, to be followed by Calles in 1924. After some constitutional engineering, including the extension of the term of office to six years, Obregón was re-elected in 1928 but was assassinated three weeks later. During the following six years three presidents held office, but the real power behind them was Calles, the *jefe máximo*.

11 *Indigenismo* began as an intellectual current that in the Mexican case became the inspiration for official state policy in relation to the indigenous population.

12 In 1938, during the Cárdenas government, the party was renamed the Party of the Mexican Revolution (PRM), and in 1946 it became the Institutional Revolutionary Party (PRI). The re-namings were accompanied by reorganisations of the representation of corporate interest groups and the reduction of the formal presence of the armed forces.

13 The 1940-1970 period covers the presidencies of Avila Camaco (1940-1946), Miguel Alemán Valdés (1946-1952), Adolfo Ruiz Cortines (1952-1958), Adolfo López Mateos (1958-1964) and Gustavo Díaz Ordaz (1964-1970).

14 The popular sector included the middle class and public employees.

15 At the same time rural-urban migration rapidly increased as well as labour migrations to the US.

16 The policy shifted away from redistribution and meant that expectations of groups whose principal demand was still centred on land could no longer be channelled through the official organisations. Independent *agrarista* organisations formed the Coordinadora Nacional Plan de Ayala (CNPA) (Bizberg 2003b:207). On the other hand, the 1970s saw the rise of independent *productivista* organisations that sought to gain control over the productive and commercialisation process and by the early 1980s would form the *Unión Nacional de Organizaciones Regionales Campesinas* (UNORCA), which was more adept at pragmatic negotiating with the government. The private sector created an independent organisation in the 1980s, the *Consejo Nacional Agropecuario* (CNA), which was officially recognised in 1984 in the context of govern-

mental attempts to repair relations with the sector, after the break during the Eche-varía government.

17 Grain imports had risen from 1.4 per cent of national consumption in 1970 to 36 per cent in 1979 (Fox 1993:69).

18 In 1986 Mexico entered the General Agreement on Tariffs and Trade (GATT), and a few years later negotiations over inclusion in the North American Free Trade Agreement began.

19 The way to legally incorporate *ejido* land into this process was not through the peasants' will, until the 1992 reforms, but through an expropriation procedure that had to be ratified by the President of the Republic, if *ejido* and community land was concerned. The issue is further addressed in Duhau, this volume.

20 The proposal for a reform of article 27 virtually coincided with another reform that was to recognise indigenous peoples' rights, after Mexico had ratified the 1989 ILO Convention 169 concerning Indigenous and Tribal Peoples in Independent Countries in 1990, being the first Latin American country to do so. The 1992 constitutional reform was rather limited (Hindley 1996), however, and debate resurged with the Zapatista uprising in January 1994, leading to a renewed reform effort in 2001, the results of which were also quite unsatisfactory for the indigenous movements. With its indigenous population of over 10 million, or about eleven per cent of the total population, Mexico counts the largest indigenous population in Latin America in absolute terms (Ramirez 2006).

21 Within government circles a certain division existed between *campesinistas*, as for example Gustavo Gordillo (1992), with Maoist antecedents, and 'modernising technocrats'. Whereas the former argued that the *ejido* still had a role to play, the latter were in favour of its dissolution (Cornelius and Myhre 1998).

22 The *agrarista* CNPA refused to join the Council.

23 Full texts of article 27 and implementing legislation can be found in Procuraduría Agraria 1998.

24 The new legislation created new institutions: the agrarian tribunals with jurisdiction to settle disputes, which before had been an attribution of the president; the *Procuraduría Agraria* or Agrarian Ombudsman; a deconcentrated National Agrarian Registry; and the *Secretaria de la Reforma Agraria* (Ministry of Agrarian Reform), charged with the coordination of agrarian policies and the general ordering of property.

25 That is, house plots in the *núcleo urbano* (urban core or housing area) of the *ejido*.

26 A report by Soloago (2003) summarised the expected benefits as follows: 'First, they would encourage investment in *ejido* land, as farmers gained greater land security and therefore a higher expected value of future income and investments in the land. Second, the reforms would increase the supply of credit, as farmers could now use their land as collateral for a loan. Third, the ability to engage in rental and sale transactions would promote a more efficient allocation of land among agricultural producers, as land would be passed from less to more productive farmers.'

27 Often a World Bank study is cited, according to which trade liberalisation would cause an additional 400,000 people to migrate over a ten-year period, on top of the 1.1 million who would have migrated anyway. Although this would depress urban wages that would be offset by lower food prices and thus contribute to Mexico's comparative advantages (Foley 1995; Young 1995).

28 This reflected the *rezago agrario* (agrarian backlog) of demands for land that had been pending for years. No new demands were admitted, but in the state of Chiapas the government saw itself forced to continue redistribution in the wake of the 1994 Zapatista rebellion.

29 Lands moved out of the 'social property sector'.

30 As De Ita (2006) notes, joining the program was rather induced. Governmental institutions illegally required PROCEDE certification for access to other programmes that were meant to ease the pain of trade liberalisation and structural adjustment (see also Appendini 1996:4).

31 'The fact that the common use category is twice as large in surface as the parcel category is quite notable. On the one hand this reflects, over time, the decreasing quality of lands allocated to the "social property sector" in the course of the reform process, and on the other hand it reflects the turn to cattle raising among above average smallholders whose off-farm activities allow them to "accumulate capital" in the form of livestock.'

32 Paradoxically, the PROCEDE program included the incorporation of *avecindados* and *posesionarios*, which contributes to further fragmentation of landholding (Concheiro Bórquez and Quintana 2003).

33 The World Bank (1998:26) wonders whether PROCEDE has contributed to the development of rental markets. Although the rate of land transactions is higher among people with titles than among people without, increases in the rate of transactions between 1994 and 1997 were the same in both groups. The perceived 'PROCEDE effect,' of a higher rate of transactions among people with title, may have to do more with the program's 'selection bias' because it first targeted the most accessible and well connected *ejidos*.

34 This is an old argument for redistributive reform, but a distinction should be made between land and labour productivity. Land may be more productive in small-scale operations due to more intensive and unremunerated, but marginally less productive, labour.

35 The World Bank (1998:28) also points to the persistent informality of transactions (although they may be recorded in writing) and notes that (1) this may render the PROCEDE cadastre obsolete in a few years and (2) this may indicate that new institutions have not yet sufficiently penetrated the *ejido* sector or that it is not considered important to formalise transactions. See also Robles 2003.

36 This time more or less 'clean' in contrast to the 1988 elections that had brought Salinas de Gortari to power.

37 Perhaps the 'neo-corporativism' of Salinas's 'social liberalism' fell in line with the 'social capital' vogue to be replaced by the more individualistic PROGRESA and OPORTUNIDADES approaches, which emphasise 'human capital'.

38 For a comment see Cord and Wodon 2001.

39 Concerning the antecedents and main traits of irregular/illegal urbanisation of *ejidal* lands, we mainly base ourselves on Azuela 1989 and Duhau 1998.

40 See Comisión para la regularización de la Tenencia de la Tierra – CORETT (2001). www.corett.gob.mx/Avances, 08-07-2001.

41 This issue is further discussed in Duhau, this volume.

42 The adherence of the Bush administration to bio-fuel programmes exposed the disadvantages of this bet and the precariousness of Mexican food security and sovereignty. As production for strongly subsidised bio-fuel programmes became more profitable than exporting low-quality maize to Mexico, the price of *tortillas* in that country skyrocketed and triggered a veritable *tortilla crisis*. The deliberately debilitated local producers catering for the domestic market are not in a condition to expand production rapidly.

14 A case study on the implementation and outcomes of the 1992 reforms on the Mexican agrarian property institutions: An *ejido* in the frontier of the urbanisation process

Emilio Duhau

Introduction

This study focusses on an *ejido* – a property institution created by the Mexican agrarian reform, which we will discuss in more detail below – in a peri-urban setting. The *ejido* Santiago Teyahualco is located on the periphery of Mexico City's Metropolitan Zone (ZMCM).[1] Though its lands are currently mainly assigned to agrarian uses, they are surrounded by land dedicated to urban uses and activities (manufacturing, commerce, housing projects, irregular settlements). Therefore, we are dealing with an *ejido* whose location makes it reasonable to assume that in the medium/long term its lands will be converted to urban uses. Our focus on an *ejido* in a peri-urban context means that this study can tell us little about the issue of property rights in truly agrarian contexts in Mexico, but it allows us to see how the new agrarian legislation enacted in 1992 defines and guarantees *ejidal* property rights as well as the degree to which it allows for the accommodation of local property arrangements, in a context that offers many incentives and opportunities for land rent-seeking. Since the *ejidal* and communal agrarian property institutions in Mexico were created by state law, the aim of this study is to analyse the impact of legal changes concerning agrarian property rights and property rights regularisation rather than to analyse a process of legalisation of extra-legal forms of land tenure.

This chapter is divided into two main parts. The first part provides a brief description of Mexican agrarian property institutions; the main changes they suffered as a result of the legal reforms introduced in 1992; the general impact of these reforms and the main results of the programme for *ejidal* property regularisation that accompanied them; and the general evolution of conflicts over agrarian property after those reforms. The second part is dedicated to the case of the *ejido* Santiago Teyahualco. It begins with a description of the *ejido* and its local context; discusses the observed effects of the 1992 reform on certainty con-

cerning property rights; the evolution of land uses and land rent appropriation strategies, linking them to the new rules defined by the Agrarian Act; observed conflicts over the exercise of property rights; the rationale behind the *ejidatarios'* refusal to adopt freehold tenure; and some
issues associated with the *ejidatarios'* juridical culture.

The description of the Santiago Teyahualco *ejido* and the analysis of
its evolution in terms of property rights and land uses are based on various sources: direct field observation and data collection; open interviews with *ejidatarios*, members of the *Comisariado Ejidal* and the Vigi-
lance Committee, the visitor of the Agrarian Attorney's Office (*Procuraduría Agraria*) assigned to the *ejido*; and a number of documents
concerning the *ejido*'s creation, functioning, and governance, as well as
the Tultepec Municipality Urban Development Plan which is currently
in force.

A short overview of the recent evolution of Mexican agrarian property institutions and rights in Mexico

Ejidos *and* comunidades

In a technical-juridical sense, *ejidos* and *comunidades agrarias* (agrarian
communities) are agrarian property institutions regulated by the Agrarian Law involving collective as well as individual property rights. They
were created in the context of the agrarian reform and the process of
land redistribution, which was one of the main outcomes of the Mexican Revolution (1910-1917). The exercise of *ejidal* or communal property rights implies the mediation of a collective entity or corporation
consisting of the group of duly recognised and registered *ejidatarios* or
comuneros in each agrarian nucleus (i.e. each *ejido* or *comunidad*).

In all, more than 101 million hectares, or 55.4 per cent of the national territory, are held in Mexico by *ejidos* and *comunidades* (Procuraduría Agraria 2004d:20). While two-thirds of lands granted to *ejidos*
and *comunidades* were (and still are) held collectively, individuals in
most *ejidos* and many *comunidades* have had long-term use rights to
particular parcels that they cultivate independently.

The main difference between *ejidos* and *comunidades* has to do with
the origins of property rights. While *ejidos* (by far the most important
of the two) are the result of land grants assigned by the state to groups
of landless peasants, *comunidades* hold their lands as a result of the state's recognition or restitution of pre-existing property rights concerning
specific lands. Together these two property institutions created in the
course of the agrarian reform process make up what in Mexico is
known as the 'social property sector', where, as we shall see, property
rights are subject to specific rules.[2] Given that our case study concerns

an *ejido* and that it would take too much space to explain other legal differences between *ejidos* and *comunidades*, from now on I shall only refer to the former.

Lands comprising *ejidos* are classified into three types: human settlement lands, common use lands, and parcelled lands. Human settlement lands are those allocated to the *ejidal* village. Common use lands may be used by all the *ejido*'s members and are regulated through collective decisions. Parcelled lands are the plots of lands that were assigned to each *ejidatario* for him/her to use and exploit individually until the 1992 reform, and that after that reform are recognised as pertaining to each *ejidatario* as a proprietor who receives a certificate through the *ejidal* property regularisation programme.

Ejidos do not need to consist of these three elements, and many *ejidos* are made up of either common use lands and the area allotted to the *ejidal* village only, or the latter and parcelled lands only. In the case of *ejidos* whose lands are classified as forest or rainforest, subdivision is not allowed. As we shall see, the *ejido* of Santiago Teyahualco, our case study, has no common use lands. Currently, two-thirds of all *ejidal* lands in Mexico are common use lands, and only 31 per cent is parcelled out. The common use lands are usually non-irrigated and non-arable (Procuraduría Agraria 2004a).

As local communities, *ejidos* are composed of all the people inhabiting the *ejidal* village. But as self-governed and legally recognised corporations, they have always exclusively constituted (and still do) the group of recognised and registered *ejidatarios*. This means that although they also have specific rights acknowledged by law, individuals recognised as *ejido* settlers (*avecindados* – who live in the *ejido* village but have no rights to *ejido* lands) and de facto possessors of parcelled land (*posesionarios* – whose temporary use rights to land not currently in use by an *ejido* member may be recognised by the *ejido* assembly) do not take part in the *ejido*'s binding collective decisions (Brown 2004:12). The 'supreme organ of the *ejido* is the assembly where all *ejidatarios* participate' (*Ley Agraria*). Besides the assembly as a self-governing body, *ejidos* have an administrative body (*Comisariado Ejidal*) constituted by three *ejidatarios*, elected by the assembly through secret ballot, and a surveillance body (*Comité de Vigilancia*) constituted by another three, similarly elected *ejidatarios*.

Prior to the 1992 constitutional reform and according to the former *Ley de Reforma Agraria*, collective property rights over *ejidal* lands as well as individual agrarian rights (see box) over *ejidal* common use and parcelled lands were non-transferable and were inalienable (other than through inheritance) and could not be leased or mortgaged (Brown 2004:24).[3] These restrictions were originally intended to protect peasants from being despoiled of their lands as well as to preserve the so-

cial character of *ejidal* lands and to avoid the reconstitution of *latifundia*. This also explains why, although the Mexican agrarian reform allowed private property alongside the social property sector, in agrarian legislation it was contemplated only under the form of *pequeña propiedad* (small property). Small agrarian proprietors can currently own 100 to 300 hectares of irrigated land, depending on the crop it will be used to farm, or the equivalent in several types of rain-fed land. All in all, including urban areas, private property – which basically falls under the civil law regime – accounts for 38 per cent of the national territory, compared to 55.4 per cent in the social property sector ruled basically by agrarian law.

The *Ley de Reforma Agraria* in force up to 1991, defined the *ejidal* corporation as the proprietor of the lands granted to it (*Ley de Reforma Agraria*: art. 51 A), while it called agrarian rights the rights held by each *ejidatario* over common use lands or over the parcel or parcels granted to him or her (*id.* art. 69). In other words, the agrarian law defined the *ejidal* land as a collective property of the *ejidal* corporation, but the rights held by each *ejidatario* over parcelled or common use land as use rights.

Despite the aforementioned legal rules of non-marketability of *ejidal* and communal lands, five main types of irregular/illegal moves around *ejidal* collective property rights and individual agrarian rights were common:

1) The informal leasing of individually held parcels (Quintana, Concheiro Bórquez, and Pérez Avilés 1998);
2) The sale of a parcel, usually to another *ejidatario* or resident of the same *ejido* (Quintana, Concheiro Bórquez, and Pérez Avilés 1998:8).
3) The illegal subdivision of *ejidal* common use or parcelled lands, mostly to sell building plots for low-cost housing in *ejidos* and *comunidades* whose lands, due to their proximity to urban agglomerations, were susceptible to being transformed to urban uses (Duhau 1998:Ch. 4).
4) The allotment or cession of arable parcels to individuals other than those having the right of inheritance of agrarian rights;
5) The de facto holding of agrarian rights by inheritance from the original holder without due registration in the National Agrarian Register;
6) The subdivision of a parcel among multiple successors of an *ejidatario* (Brown 2004:24).

In sum, prior to the 1992 reforms, there was an informal (illegal) *ejidal* land market as well as a set of informal practices concerning the cession of land rights to *ejidatarios'* inheritors or other people pertaining to *ejido* communities. According to some authors the 'illegal market transactions were estimated at around 50 per cent of the best *ejido* and communal land' (Martínez et al. 1990, cited in Quintana, Concheiro Bórquez, and Pérez Avilés 1998:8).

Within the legal framework defined by the former *Ley de Reforma Agraria*, there were three main kinds of tenure insecurity. The first concerned disputes over land possession and boundary limits between *ejidos* and between *ejidos* and *comunidades* or private proprietors, as well as intra-*ejido* disputes for similar reasons. The second concerned the de facto creation, through illegal selling and informal allotments and cessions of land, of a class of landholders who did not have formally recognised agrarian rights and therefore were in a precarious tenure condition.[4] The third source of land tenure insecurity came from the legal provision stating that the agrarian rights held by an *ejidatario* could be withdrawn for different reasons, among them: in the event that he/she does not cultivate his/her parcel personally or with his/her family during the course of two or more years, or if the *ejido* has adopted the regime of collective exploitation, he/she does not execute the tasks assigned during the same amount of time; or when the parcel is given a forbidden use (*Ley de Reforma Agraria*: art. 85). Thus, the *ejidatarios* who did not cultivate their parcels or gave them a forbidden use (such as leasing them) could be denounced by other *ejido* members – usually with the interest of obtaining the agrarian rights at stake for themselves. This kind of dispute made land possession uncertain and was a permanent source of internal conflict (Zepeda 1999:15-16).

Main changes in agrarian property institutions and rights after the reforms enacted in 1992

In 1992, article 27 of the Mexican Constitution, which originally formed the basis for agrarian reform, was modified. This brought land redistribution formally to a close and opened the way for new agrarian legislation, which was introduced soon after the reform of the Constitution to replace the 1971 *Ley Federal de Reforma Agraria*. The explicit purposes were: (1) to give peasants and agrarian actors in general certainty about their land property rights; (2) to liberate peasants from state tutelage; (3) to allow the social property sector, that is, *ejidal* and communal lands, to benefit from private investments; and (4) to make agrarian property rights marketable (cf. Tellez 1994).

In order to accomplish these ends, the new *Ley Agraria* included a number of provisions implying a deep transformation of the *ejido* as a property institution, which can be summarised as follows. First, *ejidal* property rights were redefined to make them resemble private property, or ownership rights. On the one hand, *ejidal* parcelled lands are currently allowed to be leased out to or sharecropped by anyone and may be transferred or sold to another *ejidatario* pertaining to the same *ejido* or to an *ejido* settler, and the right to use them can be given as a guarantee for bank loans.[5] On the other hand, common use lands can be contributed as an investment in business enterprises, and the individually held parcels can be converted to *dominio pleno*, that is, freehold under civil law. It is important to emphasise that the former group of new property rights can be exercised by each *ejidatario* without asking permission from the Assembly or any external authority, but that in order to make the two latter possibilities effective, the authorisation by a qualified majority of the Assembly members is required.

Second, while they did exist before the legal reforms of 1992, nominally the *ejidal* corporate bodies were the same as they are now, and provisions currently enforced substantially empowered the assembly and, therefore, *ejidatarios* at large, by attributing to this body some outstanding capabilities. Among them, recognition and regularisation of individually held parcels and of *ejidal* village plots; decisions on the allocation of common use land to a business corporation; and authorisation of the adoption of the freehold regime over parcelled lands. Additionally, the new agrarian legislation curtailed the attributions held by the *comisariados ejidales*, reducing them to the application and registration of Assembly decisions, and the administration of *ejidal* goods and facilities.

A third group of remarkable changes introduced by the new agrarian law concerns the role played by government officials and bureaucrats in the working and governance of *ejidos*, and in the exercise of *ejidal* property rights. Before the reforms, *ejidal* property relations and rights were widely mediated by a federal agrarian bureaucracy exerting a strong tutelage on *ejidos'* internal life and decisions. In addition, there was no independent judiciary in charge of mediating agrarian property disputes and protecting agrarian property rights. Now there are agrarian courts that are autonomous from the government and its agrarian branch. And an Agrarian Attorney Office (*Procuraduría Agraria*) has since been created as an advisory and dispute-mediating agency, which although it can attest to the accomplishment of the formalities required for those *ejidal* Assemblies, where matters like the association with a business corporation or the adoption of the freehold regime are decided, it cannot take any binding measure or decision concerning the internal life of *ejidos* and the exercise of *ejidal* property rights.

Fourth, in order to allow the new contents of *ejidal* property rights to be exercised, in 1993 the federal government launched the *Ejidal*

Rights and *Ejidal* Villages Plots Certification Program (PROCEDE), aimed at regulating collective and individual *ejidal* property rights by mapping and measuring collectively held lands, individually held parcels and *ejidal* village plots, and extending the corresponding certificates of rights.

Nevertheless, despite the stated objective of giving certitude about property rights, the current agrarian act shows several loopholes and establishes some regulations that may be subject to different interpretations. Among the former is the issue of the *posesionarios* (*de facto* holders) of parcels. In fact, in order to regularise all existing land tenure conditions, the Agrarian Act creates the *posesionario* tenure status by giving the assembly the capability of recognising *posesionarios*, but it states nothing concerning the rights they have, other than those of receiving the tenure certificate and using the plot of land whose possession was recognised by the assembly (see box).

REGLAMENTO DE LA LEY AGRARIA - CHAPTER III

About the regularisation of *de facto* landholders (*posesionarios*)
Article 36. The Assembly may regularise the land possession of *de facto* landholders (*posesionarios*), (...)

Article 37. The *de facto* landholders (*posesionarios*) recognised by the Assembly will have the rights of use over the parcels concerned, except in those cases in which the Assembly decides to grant them additional rights over other lands or goods pertaining to the *ejido*.
(...)
Article 40. If the Assembly, when regularising land possession by *de facto* landholders, does not define their rights in the corresponding minutes, it will be assumed that they only acquire the rights of using their parcel (...)

As to the property rights on subdivided lands, the currently enforced *Ley Agraria* makes four main provisions. First, *ejidatarios* can freely designate their inheritor by registering a succession order list with the National Agrarian Register (see box). If an *ejidatario* does not register that list, his/her property rights will be assigned in the first place to his wife/her husband or to his male/her female partner, and successively to one of his/her children, to one ascending relative, or any other people economically dependent on him/her.

> The combined result of the 1992 reforms and [the] certification pro-
> cess has been to convert what was once thought of a household re-
> source into the individual property of the *ejidatario* (...). Other family
> members have few legal rights over the *ejidal* land rights (...) ... if
> the *ejidatario* decides to sell the land (...) his family cannot stop him
> or her. His family only has the right of first refusal to purchase the
> land themselves from the *ejidatario* if they want to keep the land.
> Furthermore, the *ejidatario* now also has the right to select the in-
> heritor of his or her choice, whereas under previous law the *ejidatar-
> io* had to transmit his or her rights to a member of his or her im-
> mediate family (Brown 2004:16).

Second, *ejidatarios* can utilise their individually owned parcels directly
or concede its use or usufruct to any other *ejidatario* or third party under any legal arrangement (renting, sharecropping, etc.) without asking
permission of the assembly or any other internal or external authority.
Third, *ejidatarios* can hand over or sell their property rights over individual parcels to another *ejidatario* belonging to the same agrarian nucleus, or to an *ejido* settler (*avecindado*). Fourth, once the *Ejidal* Assembly has authorised the adoption of freehold tenure (civil law property
regime - *dominio pleno*) over subdivided lands, the *ejidatarios* interested
in doing so can adopt it for their individually owned parcels by asking
the National Agrarian Register to remove it from its registers and issue
the corresponding property title which then can be inscribed in the
Public Register of Property. To be approved, the assembly's authorisation for adopting freehold requires the favourable ballot of a two-thirds
majority of members assisting at a meeting called for that purpose.
The law stipulates that a quorum of two-thirds of the *ejido* members is
required in the first calling, or in the second calling a quorum of one-
half plus one (*Ley Agraria* 1992). As we shall see, it is mostly around
these provisions that conflicts, controversies, and irregularities regarding the exercise of property rights over individual parcels arise in the
ejido Santiago Teyahualco.

General evolution of agrarian institutions, ejidal *property regularisation, and
agrarian land property conflicts after the 1992 reform*

The Agrarian Attorney Office, as well as Agrarian Courts and the programme for the certification of agrarian property rights (PROCEDE),
were put into operation with remarkable celerity and efficacy. This
clearly reflects the priority the federal government accorded the implementation of the new agrarian legislation, which it expected to tackle
ongoing agrarian conflicts and to attract private investment – foreign

capital included – to the Mexican countryside. The latter has not occurred thus far, but the performance of the new agrarian public bodies
and some statistical figures they have released give us an overview of
the main results and induced effects of the implementation of the
1992 agrarian legislation reform.

PROCEDE not only progressed quickly during its first years of operation but brought into focus – given its mission of measuring, counting,
etc. – an accurate image of the *ejido*'s reality that was not previously
available. According to data released by the *Procuraduría Agraria*, up to
December 2003, of a total of 30,077 agrarian 'nuclei' (*ejidos* and *comunidades*), 24,792 had been already certified (83.1 per cent), among them
23,543 *ejidos*. That corresponds to 68.8 million hectares and roughly 3.2
million agrarian rights holders (Procuraduría Agraria 2004b:8).

But what about the commodification of *ejidal* lands? As noted, the
new agrarian legislation provides two main ways for putting them on
the private property market. The first consists of contributing common
use lands to a business endeavour, be it about agrarian production or,
depending on the location of the *ejido*, about real estate projects (tourism, housing, leisure). The second way involves the adoption of freehold tenure on parcelled lands. As to the former, up to December 2003
the paltry number of 25 certified *ejidos* had contributed a total of 13,078
hectares of common use lands to business enterprises (*id*.:22-23).

Concerning the second path, again by December 2003, 1,595 agrarian nuclei (5.6 per cent) had adopted freehold tenure on parcelled
lands, involving a total surface of 732,625 hectares, that is 0.7 per cent
of the area held by agrarian nuclei (*id*.:10). Yet, what is still more remarkable is that the adoption of the freehold regime had been until
then virtually non-existent in rural localities (i.e. those having up to
2,500 inhabitants), and only 2.8 per cent of the cases corresponded to
ejidos and *comunidades* located in localities with 2,500 to 15,000 inhabitants (*id*.:16). This means that 97 per cent of the freehold adoption
cases were linked to urban and peri-urban settings in the vicinity of agglomerations with more than 15,000 inhabitants and that rural *ejidos*
had been virtually untouched by the theoretically expected privatisation
fever. To be more accurate, it seems evident that *ejidatarios* are only
prone to and interested in being private owners if they have opportunities of capturing differential land rents arising from the conversion
of their lands from agrarian to urban uses.

Conflicts around ejidal *property and the role of agrarian courts*

When the 1992 reforms were enacted, a great number of agrarian conflicts and disputes were ongoing. The Agrarian Mixed Committees (*Co-
misiones Agrarias Mixtas*) – the non-judiciary bodies in charge of deal-

ing with them – passed them on to the newly created Agrarian Courts. But, as could be expected, thousands of other conflicts and disputes came to light once these courts as well as the Agrarian Attorney Office began to operate.

The Agrarian Attorney Office (AAO) was created to advise *ejidal* bodies and *ejidatarios* in matters concerning the due use and interpretation of *ejidal* property rights and to mediate property rights disputes. Therefore, it is a body which is expected to deal with such disputes as far as possible by way of voluntary accords before they are brought to the courts. It is for that reason that the statistics compiled by the AAO on the disputes that it sought to resolve between 1992 and 2003 give a reasonably accurate picture of their territorial distribution, main causes, and actors.

As we can see in Table 14.1, up to December 2003, almost 670,000 agrarian disputes were attended by the AAO. Individual property rights were the main cause of conflict, accounting for 66.3 per cent of the cases. Upon seeing these figures, it might be thought that the provisions of the new agrarian legislation have induced a great number of land conflicts. But one should not overlook that one of the main virtues of the new agrarian rules and public bodies is precisely that they have allowed the conflicts and disputes that plagued the Mexican countryside to be channelled through them in peaceful ways.

As to the Agrarian Courts, they are composed of a higher agrarian court (*Tribunal Superior Agrario*) and 49 ordinary courts (*Tribunales Unitarios Agrarios*), which up to May 2005 had altogether received more than 345,000 cases, of which a quarter have been resolved by means of voluntary agreements (Tribunal Superior Agrario 2005). If anything, the growing credibility of this previously non-existent agrarian judiciary can be derived from the fact that the number of claims it received has been rapidly growing from one year to the next since 1992. Thus, while during its first six years of functioning it received around 109,000 claims (Zepeda 1999:15), in the following eight years it received more than twice that number.

In contrast to the rest of the national judiciary, agrarian courts have operated from the beginning by way of oral procedures, which has gi-

Table 14.1 *Controversies concerning individual property rights posed before the agrarian attorney office national figures (%) 1992-2003*

Posession of a parcel	33.1
Inheritance of ejidal rights	33.2
Ejidal villages' plots	11.6
Parcels' boundaries	7.9
Other	15.8

Source: Procuraduría Agraria, 2004

ven people access to them by merely showing up. In spite of that, when an ordinary court's judgment is appealed, the resolution of a case may take up to two years (Zepeda 1999).

The case study: The *ejido* of Santiago Teyahualco

The setting

Situated in the municipality of Tultepec, which currently forms part of Mexico City's Metropolitan Zone, the *ejido* of Santiago Teyahualco was constituted in 1930 on 462 hectares of land expropriated from the Cartagena estate and granted to landless peasants from the village of Santiago Teyahualco (Comisión Nacional Agraria 1930), who had petitioned the government to be benefited with a land endowment since 1925 (Comisión Local Agraria del Estado de México 1928). It is worth taking into account that until 1992, the Agrarian Reform Act allowed landless peasants to ask the federal government for land endowments and the state was obliged to satisfy their land applications, taking lands that were eligible for expropriation.

The *ejido* of Santiago Teyahualco has no common use lands. It consists of the *ejidal* village called *Colonia 10 de Junio*, *ejidal* roads, irrigation utilities, some public facilities such as a primary and a secondary school, and 207 individual parcels. Most of these parcels have an area of roughly 2.3 hectares, although there are smaller ones.

The composition of the soil makes Teyahualco's lands suitable for the cultivation of grains and fodder, and traditionally the parcels have been used to cultivate maize and a kind of fodder called *alfalfa*, as well as for raising dairy cattle. Because irrigation water nowadays is contaminated by domiciliary and industrial waste, *ejidatarios* are not allowed to produce maize for human consumption. Common local opinion holds that the raising of dairy cattle and dairy production have been decreasing for the last two decades because of the urbanisation of surrounding areas, the growing circulation of vehicles on the *ejido's* roads, and the limited scope of the local market. Therefore, at present, only around twenty *ejidatarios* continue raising dairy cattle. Nevertheless, a dairy products cooperative is in operation, in which roughly ten *ejidatarios* participate. All in all, the income that most *ejidatarios* obtain from the exploitation of their parcels is not sufficient to make a living, and most of them hold jobs or engage in petty entrepreneurial activities outside the *ejido*, making those who live exclusively on their parcels' production a minority.

As we can observe on the satellite image, Santiago Teyahualco is at present almost completely surrounded by land dedicated to urban uses and activities: housing projects and irregular settlements to the south and west, and manufacturing plants, workshops, and warehouses to the east and south. Given Teyahualco's peri-urban setting, *ejidatarios* are currently facing many incentives to give up agrarian activities and either allocate their parcels to other kinds of endeavours, or simply sell them to outsiders. Viable alternative uses are manufacturing plants, warehouses, production services, low-cost formal housing projects, and irregular settlements. There already exist several, rather small, informal settlements as well as a limited number of workshops and warehouses. As to formal housing projects, large housing developers usually seek to acquire large tracts of land at once, a condition hardly attainable in Teyahualco, given that, as we shall see, there are many Tuyehualco's *ejidatarios* that are not willing to sell their parcels.

In any case, according to the municipal urban development plan approved in 2003, the likely evolution of land uses in Santiago Teyahualco would imply 'an irregular process of land sales and a disorderly mix of industrials, services, housing and agrarian land uses'. Remarkably, the plan itself allocates almost all Teyahualco's lands to two main uses: light, middle, and small-sized industries in the northern portion and a metropolitan services centre in the southern one, but includes neither housing developments nor agrarian uses (Gobierno del Estado de México 2003). It is clear that the state and municipal governments are convinced that given the current pollution of the water used for cultivation and the growing urbanisation of the municipality, the lands of Teyahualco should to be used for manufacturing industries and services.

Threats to certainty about property rights

Ejidatarios as such, that is, those people whose property status has been confirmed in the PROCEDE certification process, and those who have been recognised by the *Ejidal* Assembly as *ejido* settlers (*avecindados*), whose rights over definite parcels have been recognised by the Assembly and have been registered in the National Agrarian Register, can be said to enjoy irreversible property rights. In contrast to the former Agrarian Reform Act, which stated several actions conducive to the loss of agrarian rights, among them the desertion of the *ejido* or the assigned parcel for more than two years, the 1992 Agrarian Act has made *ejidal* individual property rights irreversible, save in cases of their voluntary transfer or expropriation for reasons of public benefit.

What could be observed to this regard in Teyahualco is that if, for instance, an *ejidatario* irregularly subdivides a parcel and sells plots for housing construction, he/she may be prosecuted under the charge of 'clandestine subdivision' and eventually might be jailed, but that would not affect his/her *ejidal* property rights. This clearly contrasts with the situation under the former legal framework when, because of an *Ejidal*

Assembly's request made before the agrarian authorities in 1991 (Se-cretaría de la Reforma Agraria 1991), 31 *ejidatarios* were dispossessed of their parcels for having deserted them for more than two years (Tribunal Unitario Agrario Décimo Distrito 1993).[6]

Therefore, it can be said that under the present conditions, for recognised *ejidatarios* and *posesionarios*, the threats to their status as agrarian proprietors do not arise from the legal framework itself but from the contextual factor of the ongoing urbanisation process in combination with the shaky economic situation experienced by many of them. The urbanisation process implies that arable parcels are losing their appeal against potentially more profitable urban land uses. The shaky economic conditions many *ejidatarios* are suffering mean that they may be prone to accept disadvantageous land deals.

Land uses evolution and current strategies of Teyahualco's ejidatarios

In cases of *ejidos* such as Teyahualco which, given their peri-urban location, are facing circumstances that are at odds with their continuity as agrarian endeavours and which do not have common use lands, it seems that the rules of the game as defined by current agrarian legislation also impede the adoption of collective strategies regarding land

Figure 14.1   Ejido *Santiago Teyahualco – Satellite image*

Source: Google Earth

uses and property rights. As each *ejidatario* or *posesionario* can give any
use to their parcel(s), unless it is forbidden by local regulations, or just
sell them without concern for the opinion or support of the other *ejidatarios*, we can expect that a plethora of individual strategies will
emerge. In Teyahualco we observed the following.

Between 1994 and 2005, roughly following legal provisions, eighteen *ejidatarios* sold the rights over their parcels. Of these eighteen,
three sold rights over two parcels. Some of the buyers were other Teyahualco's *ejidatarios*, but others were outsiders. In these latter cases, the
sellers promoted the recognition of the buyer by the *Ejidal* Assembly as
ejido settler (*avecindado*) as a way of legitimising the transaction. It
seems that in these cases of sale to outsiders, the sellers benefited
more because the prices they obtained were related to future uses contemplated in the municipal zoning plan: uses like warehouses, workshops, and industrial plants. The buyers expect that turning the land to
such uses will be possible in view of the zoning provisions in the present Municipal Development Plan, which will be implemented once
the *Ejidal* Assembly approves the adoption of *dominio pleno*.

A small number of *ejidatarios* have subdivided their parcels and sold
the plots for housing construction. This is a rather risky alternative,
since it is illegal.[7] And it is much less profitable than selling a whole
parcel; which is either legal or can be made legal by taking advantage
of certain legislation loopholes, as is the case when *ejidatarios* promote
the recognition of an outside buyer as *avecindado*. If anything, it is
clear that in Teyahualco, irregularly subdividing a parcel for selling
housing plots is not well regarded. The most active, informed, and economically stable Teyahualco's *ejidatarios*, generally the younger generation, deplore that senior *ejidatarios* pressed by personal or family needs
have sold their lands at prices they consider derisory.

Some *ejidatarios* are renting out their parcels in order to have them
cultivated at the same time that they engage in other economic activities, sometimes linked to fodder production. A number of them
(around ten) take part in a dairy products cooperative. Some *ejidatarios*
within this group rent out their parcels to have them cultivated and obtain some income, while the future of Teyahualco's lands is defined.
Among them are those who, being foreign to the *ejido* and having legally acquired one or more parcels, expect to profit from the uses intended by the municipal zoning plan, which they expect will be possible once freehold is adopted.

A fifth group is composed of *ejidatarios* who seek to obtain better incomes from their parcel than they might obtain through maize or fodder production, or from dairy cattle raising. They have opted to rent
out fractions of their parcels or to apply them to non-agrarian uses
themselves: mostly warehouses, metallurgical workshops, and soccer

fields. The soccer fields, of which there are around twenty, are rented during the weekends and allow their owners to obtain, by local standards, pretty good incomes (of the order of a monthly amount of USD 800 each). In any case, these are uses that, although irregularly introduced, do not involve an offence and benefit from the blind eye of local authorities.

Finally, there are a number of *ejidatarios*, mostly senior ones, who continue cultivating their parcels themselves and are fixated on the *ejido* as a local community and as an agrarian endeavour. All in all, in spite of the non-agrarian uses already introduced for Teyahualco's lands, according to estimations of several rather knowledgeable key informants, roughly 80 per cent of the parcels are still cultivated. And indeed, if we examine the satellite image minutely, this estimate does not seem to be too far off the mark.

Conflicts and disputes about property rights and ejido functioning

As might be expected from the statistics on agrarian conflicts released by the AAO, in Teyahualco disputes concerning individual property rights are also the most numerous. In the words of the lawyer acting as AAO's visitor in Teyahualco, there are two main reasons why this type of conflict arises. First, there is the issue of inheritance of property rights, which most often arises when an *ejidatario* did not register a succession order list, or when the validity of the registered list is challenged by one of the potential beneficiaries. In such cases the appeal is usually based on assumptions about the absence of the due conditions for the 'real' expression of the will of the deceased (insanity, severe illness). It seems that this type of conflict is not very different from those arising commonly in Mexico (and almost everywhere) around inheritance rights. We should, however, note a specificity of *ejidal* property rights that probably explains why many of Teyahualco's *ejidatarios* avoid expressing their will through a succession order list. According to the agrarian law, an *ejidal* parcel can only be inherited by one person. We can suppose then that *ejidatarios* do not deposit their succession order list to avoid family conflicts while they are alive.[8]

A second cause of conflict involves parcel boundaries. Although at the moment of implementation of the PROCEDE certification all these boundaries were measured by the National Institute of Statistics, Geography and Informatics (INEGI) and approved *unanimously*, in many cases there were well-known differences between the customarily accepted boundaries and those formalised in the *ejido* map issued by INEGI. Therefore, it seems that in order to have their rights formalised and regularised as soon as possible and to avoid delaying PROCEDE's completion, some *ejidatarios* accepted a measurement of boundaries

that did not reflect realities on the ground and was therefore not satisfactory in the long run.

According to the aforementioned informant as well as interviewed
ejidatarios, another kind of conflict frequently observed in Teyahualco
concerns the occupation of one or more fractions of a parcel by relatives of a deceased *ejidatario* whose eviction is requested by the parcel
inheritor. This kind of situation occurs when an *ejidatario* wishes to
hand on 'a tract of land' to all his/her nearest relatives, without taking
into account the legal nullity of the intended distribution. In such a
way, many poorly informed *ejidatarios*, instead of contributing to their
relatives' welfare, sow the seeds of bitter disputes that, at least in Teyahualco, are usually only settled in an Agrarian Court.

The issue of the adoption of a freehold regime

Teyahualco is an *ejido* whose regularisation by PROCEDE was accomplished early, dating from 1994 (Ejido de Santiago Teyahualco 1994),
and during the twelve years that have elapsed since then, the *Ejidal* Assembly has been called many times with the specific aim of voting to
authorise the adoption of the private property regime. But so far the *ejidatarios* promoting this change have not been able to obtain the two-
thirds majority required. Though it was not possible to find out when
the last attempt took place, according to the ballot results of an Assembly conducted in February 2002, where 109 of the total of 193 *ejidatarios* were present, 67 voted for and 42 against the authorisation of *dominio pleno* (Ejido de Santiago Teyahualco 2002). Such ballot results
show not only that there is still a significant minority opposed to *dominio pleno*, but that there is also a considerable number of Teyahualco's *ejidatarios* who either remain indifferent concerning the future of
the *ejido* or, more probably, did not go to the meeting in order to obstruct the formation of the required quorum. Although the adoption of
the *dominio pleno* on the parcelled lands of an *ejido* does not necessarily
imply its dissolution, in the case of Teyahualco that would be the most
probable outcome, given both its peri-urban location and the fact that
it has no common use lands.

Some senior *ejidatarios* expressed the opinion that for them adopting
the *dominio pleno* would imply losing many things, among them a way
of life. This is an idea that they do not verbalise as such, but express by
invoking specific burdens like having to pay property taxes and drinkable water fees, which as *ejidatarios* they do not currently pay. According to a lawyer who acts as an informal advisor to the present president
of the *Comisariado Ejidal*, there are other specific circumstances that explain why a number of *ejidatarios* are against the adoption of the freehold regime. There is an apparently shared belief that due to a long-

standing boundary dispute between the Tultepec municipality and the neighbouring municipality of Tultitlán, in case of the *ejido*'s dissolution, its lands would be reclaimed as part of Tultitlán's territory, registered in its cadastre as private property and taxed according to the higher land values applied in this municipality.

Meanwhile, some of *Teyahualco's* apparently well informed *ejidatarios* believe that because of the imminent construction of a highway that will cross through the *ejido*, many parcels will be expropriated. They assume that the affected *ejidatarios* would obtain a much better cash compensation if they adopted freehold tenure over their parcels. Therefore, the dominant point of view among the younger and better informed *ejidatarios* is that the authorisation of freehold by the assembly is not only desirable but its adoption constitutes an increasingly pressing issue.

Nevertheless, we have so far no evidence supporting the supposition that freehold tenure will be authorised by the assembly in the near future. If not for other reasons, because many *ejidatarios* fear that they will be unable to cope with the charges and duties that they believe would arise from having the status of private proprietor. Therefore, they will probably continue abstaining or voting against it. But we also have to consider what land means to those who, as is surely the case among the older *ejidatarios* of Teyahualco, assume themselves to be *peasants* who got their land because they fought for it. As Quintana et al. write, 'For the Mexican peasantry, land transactions are determined by the conception they have of land as a multifaceted space used for production and as a place to live. For them, land also means territory, the foundation of their history and their social identity (...) Land, more than merchandise of factor of production, is a strong referent of identity. It represents the recognition of social authority, and it is a patrimony, a place of residence, a source of status, and a foundation of the local and regional structure' (Quintana, Concheiro Bórquez, and Pérez Avilés 1998:5 and 7).

Abiding by, interpreting and using the law

Something that attracts the attention of outside observers concerned with local juridical cultures the first time they arrive in Santiago Teyahualco and talk to *ejidatarios* about the *ejido*'s affairs and problems is their usually poorly informed notions about agrarian legislation as well as municipal competencies. We observed two main types of confusion in this respect.

The first has to do with the scope of the agrarian law, the *ejido*'s autonomy, and the local authorities' competencies. The *ejidatarios*, including the best informed among them, do not seem to be clear about the difference between the effects of the adoption of freehold tenure and land use changes. They tend to think that adopting freehold over a parcel is equivalent to the authorisation to introduce any land use. We even heard a very active *ejidatario* talking about the municipal zoning provisions – which he is opposed to – as follows: 'the *ejido* is above the municipal power'. Here we have to take into account that *ejidos* functioned during many decades as agrarian bodies that generally also managed local utilities and public facilities and were used to dealing more frequently with federal and state agrarian bureaucracies than with municipal powers. Additionally, *ejidos* were perceived – and still are to a large extent – not only as collective property institutions but as local powers.

Thus, having experienced the *ejido* as a local power until very recently, largely autonomous from the municipality, it is not surprising that Teyahualco's *ejidatarios* are still prone to ignore municipal competencies as well as being unaware of the role of municipal authorities and urban legislation and ordinances in the regulation of land use in areas that, as is the case of Santiago Teyahualco, are subject to the urbanisation process.

The second type of confusion concerns the contents of the agrarian law at large and the meanings of private property, as well as the duties that being a private landowner entails. In general, in this regard the less educated *ejidatarios* exhibit many misunderstandings or simply gross ignorance (see box).

Conversation between a senior female *ejidatario* and a research assistant:

Q: Mrs. B, what is your opinion about *dominio pleno?*
A: I think it is desirable.
Q: Why do you think it is desirable?
A: I don't know, really.

But the more informed and educated *ejidatarios* also seem not to be free of some confusion. We can mention for instance the member of the *comisariado ejidal* who counselled a hydraulic engineer – who worked with the *ejido* regarding irrigation facilities – about the regularisation procedures concerning a housing plot he had irregularly acquired in another *ejido*. When explaining to the engineer what he had to do, he expressed a number of misunderstandings about the issue. Among others, he confounded the capabilities given by the law to the *ejidal* assembly to regularise and recognise the land tenure of *posesionarios* and *ejidal* village settlers with the procedures that have to be followed to regularise irregular settlements on common use or parcelled *ejidal* lands. We also heard another member of the same body saying to an *ejidatario* that 'according to the current agrarian act, the issue of the succession order list is not nowadays as it was before, and that now an *ejidatario* must mention on the list one and only one successor'. If those who are in charge of administering the *ejido*'s affairs, to whom most *ejidatarios* usually resort to deal with the *ejido*'s day-to-day affairs, transmit to their fellows these kinds of false ideas and misinformation, it is not difficult to understand why a good number of *ejidatarios* are lost when it comes to the current meanings and scope of the *ejido* and the *ejidal* property rights.

It is probably these generalised confusions and misunderstandings, therefore, as well as some tricky issues posed by the agrarian act that explain why even though wishing to comply with the law, many *ejidatarios* fail to do so and also fail to profit from the optimal strategies potentially within their reach of their now enhanced individual property rights. Instead, they frequently settle for deals over their lands that reduce these possibilities. At the same time, precisely because of their lack of adequate information, many *ejidatarios* seem susceptible to manipulation by their better informed colleagues. However, what Teyahualco's case shows is that the 1992 agrarian property reforms have clearly empowered *ejidatarios* at large vis-à-vis government bureaucracies and local leaders.

In addition, Teyahualco's case shows that regarding the interpretation and enforcement of the law, *ejidatarios* currently enjoy access to a couple of bodies they widely trust, namely the Agrarian Attorney Office and Agrarian Courts. They trust the former probably because it is a body without the capacity to make decisions, but which is dedicated to helping and advising *ejidatarios* in dealing with their collective as well as their individual land/property affairs. Teyahualco's *ejidatarios* usually resort to the assigned AAO's Visitor, whom many of them refer to as 'our delegate', mostly when facing a conflict over their rights or when they wish to file a complaint or request.

Notwithstanding, Teyahualco's *ejidatarios*, as seems to be the case with *ejidatarios* all around the country, are bringing their cases increasingly before Agrarian Courts. Sometimes, according to the aforementioned AAO's Visitor, *ejidatarios* do this by ignoring her and resorting directly to the courts and hiring a trial lawyer to represent them.

Final remarks

So far, it is apparent that the current agrarian legislation, while considerably enhancing the *ejidatarios*'s security and protection regarding their property rights, has made it rather difficult for them to define and adopt collective strategies to their benefit by exercising those rights when facing contextual factors that are at odds with the continuity of agrarian activities. In fact, those senior Teyahualco's *ejidatarios* who are against the adoption of freehold tenure probably fear that this would imply the erasing of the *ejido*'s basis as a collective endeavour and a local community, and most likely they are right.

A closer examination of the property rights provisions contained in the current agrarian act shows us that beyond being inspired by a will of liberating *ejidatarios* from government tutelage and promoting the commoditisation of *ejido* lands, these provisions are flawed by some ambiguities and loopholes. Among them are those concerning *de facto* landholders (*posesionarios*) and the supposed restrictions concerning to whom an *ejidatario* can turn over his/her rights to a parcel. These latter, as we have observed in Teyahualco, can be easily bypassed, and probably for the better.

Finally, one thing that has to be emphasised regarding the main outcomes of the 1992 Mexican agrarian property reforms is the convenience of distinguishing between land property rights security and protection, and the freehold tenure regime itself. This is a distinction that individualistic property theories seem to fail to take into account. While it is evident that Mexican peasants have seized the advantages offered by the agrarian rights certification process and the possibilities opened to them by the enhancement of their property rights, generally without much reticence, the great majority of the *ejidos* have so far not opted for freehold tenure. This refusal is expressed through the reluctance of many Teyahualco's *ejidatarios* to become private owners, despite their lands being currently situated on the frontier of the urbanisation process.

Notes

1   Here I call the Metropolitan Zone of Mexico City the conurbation composed by both the Federal District (Mexico's capital) whose urban area is called 'Mexico City' and is subdivided into sixteen administrative partitions (*Delegaciones*) and 28 municipalities pertaining to the neighboring State of Mexico. Until the year 2000, the urban area of this conurbation spread over roughly 140,000 hectares. Officially, however, the ZMCM comprised the Federal District plus 59 municipalities, many of which did not yet form part of the conurbation.

2   In this essay I broadly follow the working definition of property and ownership stated by De Janvry et al. (2001:2): '(W)e start here from the proposition that property over a resource is composed of a multiplicity of rights that include access, the appropriation of resources or products, provision of management, exclusion of others, and alienation by selling or leasing (...).These different rights over a particular land parcel may be held by different actors (....). It is only ownership that conveys the accumula-

tion of all these rights.' I will use the terms 'private property' and 'freehold' as translations of the Spanish term *dominio pleno* to refer to this type of ownership.

3   Additionally, then as now, *ejido* parcels could not be legally subdivided (including upon inheritance) in order to avoid fragmentation into economically unviable holdings, a prohibition that often was flouted, which was tolerated by the agrarian authorities.

4   These de facto landholders were recognised, under the label of *posesionarios*, by the *Ley Agraria* enacted in 1992, and their rights over the parcels they keep can currently be regularised by *Ejidal* Assemblies or, when faced with the Assembly denial, claimed before an Agrarian Court. The number of *ejidal* landholders not having their land use rights formally recognised *prior* to 1992 can be inferred from the fact that, among 3.2 million people whose agrarian land rights were certified up to 2003 by the *PROCEDE*, thirteen per cent or about 422,000 *ejidal* landholders obtained a certificate of land use rights as *posesionarios* (Procuraduría Agraria 2004c:7).

5   Nevertheless, banks do not currently accept *ejidal* parcels as a loan collateral (World Bank 1997).

6   The request to withdraw the agrarian rights of these 31 *ejidatarios* was made in 1991, that is, *before* the new *Ley Agraria* was in force. Therefore, the subsequent legal process was conducted and concluded in accordance with the principle of no retroactivity of legal rules, following the provisions of the former *Ley de Reforma Agraria*.

15 Land reform and tenure security in China: History and current challenges

Li Ping, Roy Prosterman, Ye Jianping, Wu Jian, Benjamin van Rooij

Introduction

Land reform has been central in the Chinese Communist Party's (CCP) rule of China. First, it played a major role in the CCP's original claim to power in the 1930s and 1940s, as it was through massive land redistributions that the many poor land tenants and landless farmers came to recognise the CCP as representing their interests. Land reform was also a method for a new social stratification, urging the poorest to revolt (*fanshen*) against the existing ruling elite, an essential move in the CCP's grab for power and part of their communist revolution (Hinton 1972). Once power was firmly in the hands of the CCP, land reform again played a major role in experiments with collectivisation in the 1950s and 1960s, when large people's communes were formed, introducing collective ownership and management of the land. Since the late 1970s, land reform has continued to be an important element of the CCP's policy to stay in power. Following the challenge to legitimacy that came with Mao Zedong's death and the shock the Cultural Revolution (1966-1976) caused in Chinese society, the CCP sought new legitimacy in providing stability and economic prosperity (Zheng 1997). The reform policies that were initiated to develop such prosperity consisted of another land tenure restructuring. Based on local experiments, a national policy to give farmers household use rights to plots of land was initiated and later adopted in legislation.

This country study of land reform in China will discuss the historical development of land tenure regimes under CCP rule. It will trace the historical roots that gave rise to the last decade of land tenure reform, during which existing experiments and policy-based land tenure arrangements were legalised in national legislation with the introduction of the 1998 Land Management Law and the 2002 Rural Land Contract Law. The study will further look at the extent to which the new laws have been implemented and what this has meant for tenure security. Finally, it will analyse what the major challenges are at this moment and what role the new Property Law, introduced in 2007, can play in solving existing problems.

As the concept of land tenure security is central in this chapter, we should define and examine the concept of land tenure security before starting the historical overview of land reform in China. Land tenure security can generally be defined as existing when an individual perceives that he or she has rights to a piece of land on a continuous basis, free from imposition or interference from outside sources, as well as the ability to reap the benefits of labour and capital invested in the land, whether in use or upon transfer to another holder (Place, Roth, and Hazell 1994:19). However, rather than defining land tenure security as something that either exists or does not exist, it is more accurate to think of it as a continuum that can be measured by three criteria: breadth, duration, and assurance. Breadth is a measurement of the quantity and quality of the land rights held and may include the rights to possess land, to grow or harvest crops of one's own choice, to pass the land on to heirs, to sell land or to lease it to others, to pledge land rights as security for credit, to prevent trespass, to protect against state expropriation, among many other rights (Knetsch 1993). Land tenure rights are not a single entitlement in any land system but are multiple and varied and can be analogised to a 'bundle' of sticks. Breadth measures the quantity and quality of the sticks that make up the bundle. Duration measures the length of time for which these rights are valid (Place, Roth, and Hazell 1994:20). Typically, the same duration applies to every stick in the bundle of rights, but this is not necessarily so. In general, as duration lengthens, tenure security improves. However, duration need not be perpetual to create an adequate incentive framework for land investments and improvements. Assurance, the third criterion, is a measurement of the certainty of the breadth and duration of the rights that are held. If an individual is said to possess land rights of a specific breadth and duration but cannot exert, enforce, or protect those rights, they have no assurance. A land 'right' that cannot be exerted or enforced is not a right at all.

This chapter is based on several sources. First, it uses the existing body of written primary and secondary sources about land tenure arrangements in China. In addition, it uses nationwide survey data collected over the last ten years by the Rural Development Institute and Renmin University (Prosterman, Schwarzwalder, and Jianping 2000; Schwarzwalder et al. 2002; Zhu et al. 2006). The quotations in the text used to illustrate larger historical events have been drawn from a case study on the history of land reforms carried out in Rendikou Village in Puyang County in Henan province.

Pre-1949 land reforms by the communists

It is worth reviewing the early history of Chinese Communist land-reform measures, because some of the issues faced and approaches taken remain live and debated reform options in China today.

Ever since its founding, the CCP has been keenly aware of the problem of landlessness that Chinese farmers faced and has constantly placed land reform as one of its top priorities in its fight with the Nationalists for control over China.[1] Soon after it established its first administrative region in northern Jiangxi Province in the early 1920s, the CCP promulgated its first land law, setting up the basic framework of communist land reforms: confiscation of land from landlords and distribution of the confiscated land among peasants with little or no land (Jinggangshan Land Law, December 1928). There are five salient features in this law. First, the land confiscated is owned by the administrative region government (*id.*, at art. 1) and its use rights are allocated to peasant households. Second, while the land is mainly allocated to peasants for individual farming (*id.*, at art. 1(i)), the law allows allocation to peasants for joint farming (*id.*, at art. 1(ii)) and to administrative region government farms (*id.*, at art. 1(iii)). Third, the term of peasants' right to farm the land owned by the administrative region is unspecified. Fourth, sale of the confiscated land is prohibited (*id.*, at art. 2). Fifth, land is allocated on an egalitarian basis, and men and women have equal right to allocated land (*id.*, at art. 4(i)). With the expansion of the communist-controlled area, the Land Law of the Soviet Republic of China[2] was adopted in 1931. Unlike the earlier communist land law, the new Land Law did not explicitly attest that land is owned by the government; instead, it emphasised that the confiscated land be 'distributed among poor and middle peasants' (Land Law of the Soviet Republic of China, art. 1) and 'all temple land and other public land shall be granted to peasants without condition'. The lawmakers intended to give peasants full ownership (*id.*, at art. 6).[3] Second, this Land Law was simply silent on the allocation of confiscated land to peasants for joint farming or allocation of such land to government farms. Third, it allowed lease and sale of land among peasants, but landlords were still prohibited from purchasing land back, and rich peasants were prohibited from engaging in land speculation (presumably, purchase with intent of resale) (*id.*, at art. 12).

The most important communist land law before the founding of the People's Republic of China in 1949 was the Platform of Chinese Land Law adopted at the CPC national land conference on 13 September 1947. For the first time, the Chinese Communists declared the explicit principle that China would adopt 'a land system of land to tillers' (Platform of Chinese Land Law, art. 1). In order to fulfil this principle, the

Platform further provides that except for large forests, irrigation projects, large mining sites, large and contiguous tracts of grassland and wasteland, and lakes, all land confiscated from landlords and the land traditionally owned by communities shall be distributed among all rural residents and owned by individuals (*id.*, at art. 6). All rural residents, regardless of age and gender, are entitled to the same share of land (*id.*). It requires that land ownership certificates be issued to all landowners (*id.*, at art. 11). It also provides that landowners 'have the right to freely manage and sell the land, and lease the land under certain circumstances'(*id.*). Local communist governments promulgated specific rules for implementing the Platform. For example, the Northeast Administrative Commission adopted an implementing rule for the Northeast Liberated Region requiring that a region-wide uniform land ownership certificate be designed by the commission and issued to all landowners by governments at county level (Supplemental Measures for Implementing the Land Law Platform in the Northeast Liberated Region, art. 11). In its implementing rule, the Shanxi-Hebei-Shandong-Henan Border Region government made a distinction between arable land and the land used for fish farming, fruit production and bamboo growing and let peasants decide whether to distribute these categories of non-arable land for private ownership (Shanxi-Hebei-Shandong-Henan Border Government Supplemental Measures for Implementing the Land Law Platform, art 7).

Land reforms in the 1950s

While the CCP had made a start experimenting in land reform and distributing land from landlords to poor and landless peasants in all areas under their control, widespread redistribution did not start until it gained power and founded the People's Republic in 1949. At that time, land distribution was still highly unequal. As shown in Table 15.1, less than ten per cent of the population (elites such as landlords and rich peasants) owned nearly 52 per cent of the arable land and more than 57 per cent of the population (consisting of middle/poor peasants and farm labourers) owned only 14.9 per cent of the land.

On 28 June 1950, the Chinese communist government promulgated the first land reform law that was applicable to all parts of China (except for Taiwan, which was then governed by the Nationalists who had fled the mainland after their defeat in China's civil war). The Land Reform Law of the PRC embodied the major provisions of the Platform on land allocation and land ownership. The law provided that China adopts a 'peasant land ownership system' (Land Reform Law of PRC 1950, art. 1). The land confiscated from landlords, except for that

Table 15.1 *Rural land distribution before 1950 land reform in mainland China*

Class	Household %	Population %	Land %	Land/household (mu)[1]	Land/person (mu)
Landlord	3.79	4.75	38.26	144.11	26.32
Rich peasants	3.08	4.66	13.66	63.24	9.59
Middle peasant	29.20	33.13	30.94	15.12	3.05
Poor peasants and labourers	57.44	52.37	14.28	3.55	0.89
Other	6.49	5.09	2.86	6.27	1.83

Source: Du (1996)

[1] Mu (亩) is a common measurement unit of land in China. 1 hectare equals 15 mu.

owned by the state in accordance with this law,[4] was to be allocated to poor peasants 'fairly, rationally and uniformly for them to own' (*id.*, at art. 10). The law also stated that all landowners are allowed to freely manage, sell and lease their land (*id.*, at, art. 30).[5] To provide evidence of land ownership, the law required that a land ownership certificate be issued by the people's government to landowners (*id.*, at, art. 30). The Land Reform Law also authorised the regional people's government[6] to promulgate implementing rules, taking into consideration local circumstances (*id.*, at art. 39). The measures of one of the regional people's governments, the Mid-Southern Military and Administrative Committee, on implementing the Land Reform Law approved by the State Council and promulgated by the Committee in 1950 are worthy of note. Among the substantive provisions on the rights of landowners which these measures contain, are that land may be inherited by the owner's spouse, children and other direct relatives upon the owner's death (Measures of the Mid-Southern Military and Administrative Committee on Implementing the Land Reform Law, art. 9(vii)) and may be mortgaged, sold and leased without restriction for most landowners (*id.*, at art. 9(ix)).[7] The measures also emphasized the need to respect women's land ownership rights (*id.*, at, art. 9(viii)). They explicitly allowed women to have full rights to the land they owned free from others' interference upon marriage, divorce and remarriage (*id.*).

Although the Land Reform Law required issuance of land ownership certificates to all landowners, it did not spell out any formalities concerning the certificates. However, under the Mid-Southern Region's implementing rule, each landowner was given an option either to have his or her own certificate or to have a single certificate covering all land in the household (*id.*, at art. 9(xi)). It further required that all names of individual owners in the household be listed on the certificate if a household certificate is to be issued (*id.*).

In a separate measure, the land in the suburban areas previously owned by landlords was confiscated and placed under state ownership

(Regulation of Suburban Land Reform 1950, art. 9). Use rights to such state-owned land were to be allocated to peasants who had little or no land 'fairly, rationally and uniformly' (*id*). To secure peasants' use rights to such land, state-owned land use rights certificates were to be issued to peasant land users (*id.*, at art. 17). However, the land users could not lease, sell or leave state-owned land idle (Land Reform Law of PRC 1950, art. 27). The land-reform programme distributed 46.7 million hectares of land to about 300 million peasants, thus covering about one-half of China's total arable land and more than 60 per cent of the total rural population (CIRD:31-32). The 'land to the tiller' programme proved a noteworthy success in increasing agricultural productivity: annual grain production went up from 113.2 million tons in 1949 to 166.8 million tons in 1953, and further to 192.7 million tons in 1956. This 70 per cent increase in grain production was accompanied by an increase of 85 per cent in total farm income during the same period (*id.*, at 32; Gensheng 2001:3-4).

Interviews with elderly farmers in Henan Province, recounting their experiences with the 1950s land reform, demonstrate the extent to which these reforms were appreciated by poorer farmers. One farmer recalls: 'Peasants were extremely happy about land distribution. No one would be against additional land, right? More land means more security to our livelihood. We the ordinary people finally had more land to cultivate. We vouched to put all our efforts in the land.' Meanwhile another farmer illustrates the amount of courage it took to participate in the reforms: 'We were in high spirits during the land distribution process. But some of us were quite scared that powerful landlords might take the land back or take revenge on us, so some of us secretly returned the land distributed to us to the landlords so as to avoid possible conflict. We were a vulnerable group after all and could not really stand up to rich and powerful landlords. You never know when this group of rich people would "rise up" again or how long the Party's power would last.'

Collectivisation of Chinese agriculture

Despite the positive experiences with land distribution and the improved agricultural output, private ownership and individual farming on rural land did not remain the policy for long. Soon after the completion of these rural land reforms, the Chinese government introduced the concept of collective farming following the example of the Soviet Union. In 1955, the Central Committee of the Chinese Communist Party issued the Decision on Agricultural Cooperation, formally launching the movement to collectivisation. Collectivisation through legislative measures began in 1956 when the National People's Congress' Standing Committee passed 'The Charter of Agricultural Production Cooperatives'.[8] Although the charter did not legally change private ownership, it established the creation of public ownership of rural land as a goal for collectivisation.[9] According to the charter, all land owned by members of the cooperative 'must be submitted to the cooperative for uniform use' (Charter of Rural Production Cooperatives, art. 17). Each member was allowed to keep no more than five per cent of the village's average landholdings per capita as private plots (*id.*) Contributors of land were entitled to some compensation for their land contribution, but such land compensation was not to be more than compensation for labour contribution (*id.*, at art. 18).

Such cooperatives were soon converted into collectives. Accordingly, the nominal private ownership of farmland under the cooperative system was transformed into formal collective ownership only three months later when the Third Plenary Session of the National People's Congress passed 'the Charter of Advanced Agricultural Production Cooperatives' in June of 1956. The Charter explicitly stated that collective members 'must transform privately owned land, draft animals, and large farm equipment and other major production means into collective ownership' (The Charter of Advanced Agricultural Production Cooperatives 1956, art. 13.). Private plots were absorbed into collective ownership; individual households, however, were allowed to keep ownership of the residential land (*id.*, at art. 16).

Despite problems with farm management and production incentives, the collectivisation campaign proceeded rapidly. By the end of 1958, the agricultural collectives were abruptly merged into Rural Peoples' Communes. Approximately 90 per cent of the rural population became commune members within half a year. From an ownership aspect, the fundamental characteristic of the commune was the abolition of the last vestiges of private property. The commune took sole ownership of all property, except for foundation plots which was later announced as collectively owned in 1962. Participating in production activities governed by the collective authorities on the collective's land and with the collective's equipment and inputs was the only means of personal earnings for the commune members. Under this system, none of the farmers had an individual stake in the land; they worked together on the land. The communes effectively severed farmers from their land.

The collectivisation campaign proved to be a huge disaster to China's agriculture and Chinese people. Grain production declined substantially for three years in a row starting in 1959, leading to perhaps the planet's worst famine of the twentieth century.[10] Having realised the grave consequences of the commune system that had completely strangled farmers' incentives for farming, a mild reform in an attempt to reduce the size of the collective was conducted in early 1960s. The Central Committee passed Revised Regulations on Rural People's Commune (commonly called the Sixty-Article Regulation) in 1962. The regulation attests that the production team, the lowest of the three-level collective ownership, would be the 'basic accounting unit' (The Central Committee of CPC Revised Regulations on Rural People's Commune [hereinafter Sixty-Article Regulation], art. 2) 'for at least 30 years' (*id.*, at art. 20). All land within the sphere of the production team is owned by the team (*id.*, at art. 21). The team may designate five to seven per cent of the team's land as 'private plots' and allocate that land for 'member households to use for long term without change' (*id.*, at art. 40). It also allows the team collective to allocate 'appropriate amount of firewood mountain as 'private mountain' for member households 'to operate ... for a long term without change' (*id.*). With respect to members' houses, the regulation notably declares that 'members' houses are owned by members in perpetuity' (*id.*, at art. 45). The significance of the Sixty-Article regulation is that it stopped the course heading for escalation of the scale of the collective entity through administrative mergers and reinstated the level of the collective closest to farmers, namely, the production team, as the basic accounting unit responsible for all operational activities within its geographical boundaries. With respect to property rights, the regulation established the rule that collective ownership of land is exercised at the production team level; use rights to some of such team-owned land may be allocated to collective members as 'private plots' for individual household farming. The regulation functioned as the basic framework regulating collective farming and land ownership till the decollectivisation campaign in the late 1970s and early 1980s.

However, recovery from disasters brought by the giant people's communes was a slow process, and further complicated by the society-wide 'Cultural Revolution' which began in the mid-1960s: social instability was ubiquitous in every walk of life, even the most remote areas were not spared; political struggle rather than economic production became the national as well as personal goal, while grain production decreased. During the 1970s, about one-third of the rural population did not have a stable food supply (Zhang, Li, and Shao 2006).

Interviews with elderly villagers looking back at the collective farming system and the communes portray the disappointment some farmers felt when their newly acquired land was incorporated in the commune. One farmer stated: 'People felt discouraged and dismayed. They had thought they could own the land and the good life was just an inch away. Some began to resent Communist rule, but no one dared to say it openly.' Other villagers talked about the economic inefficiency of the commune system; one of them stated: 'We reported to work every day but scamping was the rule rather than the exception. Long ago before the sun began to set, every worker had already begun to pack their things and got ready for leaving.' Other interviews illustrate the political atmosphere that existed in villages and the amount of insecurity this caused: 'The propaganda was widespread. Loudspeakers located in several corners of the village propagated the positive side of collectivisation. We were told that we were moving toward communist society. It depicted a very rosy picture of our future, but we did not really know what was going on. A better educated villager told me that a political movement was going on. When I probed further, he could not clearly tell me what sort of political movement that was.' The disaster the commune experiment led to has left a deep impression on the elderly villagers interviewed in Henan. One villager recounts: 'The previous years of collective agriculture and three years of natural disasters from 1959 to 1961 caused severe famine. All the villagers had to eat bran which was used to feed pigs. We suffered from oedema. My two children were too weak to go to school, and they lay in bed for almost 1 year. If such conditions kept persisting, we had two choices: die or revolt.'

Decollectivisation under the Household Responsibility System

After ten years of the Cultural Revolution and more than twenty years of collective farming, China's rural economy came to the edge of collapsing prior to the tenure reform beginning in the late 1970s. Indeed, 1977 per capita grain production was lower than that of 1956 (Carter and Zhong 1988:5; Lardy 1986:91). The sluggish performance in the farm sector was accompanied by extremely slow growth in peasant incomes. In 1978, the average annual rural income was 133 yuan per capita, and more than 250 million rural people suffered semi-starvation (Statistics Bureau n.d.).

When the new leadership began to clean up the huge mess of collective farming after Mao's death in 1976, the most imperative issue was to decide whether to abandon collective ownership of land and, if so, what rural land system to adopt.

Although private ownership of land was deeply rooted in Chinese history and the Chinese communists had strenuously pushed forward a 'land to the tiller' programme before and immediately after they took power, more than twenty years of collective farming promoted and insisted on by paramount leader Mao Zedong between the mid-1950s and mid-1970s had left a political legacy of public ownership. The new leadership was clearly aware that any tenure reform would be derailed if it crossed the threshold from public to private ownership.

With the death of Mao Zedong, the new reform-minded leadership headed by Deng Xiaoping began to explore the way to bring rural China out of poverty and famine in the late 1970s. At the same time, a group of poor farmers in Anhui Province, driven by the need for survival, invented a land-contracting system in which collectively owned land was contracted to participating farmers for private farming who, in return, were committed to meeting collective demands for quota grain, taxes and fees based on the quantity of the land allocated to each participating farm household. This land contracting system would later become known as the household responsibility system (HRS).

The same occurred in other villages in China, as the Chinese people were disappointed with collective farming which for many had been disastrous. As one villager from Henan recounts: 'We were sick and tired of so-called "communist goals". We did not want a utopia. We simply wanted a good material life. We wanted to have a say in our own land and production, not to be told what to do by some bureaucratic cadres.' It was in this period that experiments with HRS also started in Henan. Another villager states: 'The village head and the cadre of the production team were distant relatives of many of the villagers. They could not bear to see us suffer. They clandestinely divided the land among the villagers and let them manage the land. But cadres only attempted such a move after Fengyang County and several places in our provinces experimented with HRS and were unpunished by higher authority. Our neighbouring villages soon followed suit. HRS became a very pervasive practice in no time.'

This new form of private farming aroused a fierce debate among policymakers (Xiang 2001). The key issue in the debate was whether this new model represented a negation of Mao, with its design to replace collective ownership of land with private ownership. The pragmatic faction of the new leadership argued that the new model of farming was merely an experimental way of organising farm production aiming at motivating farmers, instead of changing rural land ownership. Thus, a mechanism was created, with a feature of separation of use rights to land from ownership of land in which the collective entity would continue to hold ownership but use rights to land would be allocated to members of the collective for individual farming. This approach of emphasising decollectivisation of farming practice apparently worked because most decision-makers realised the damage that had been brought to China's agriculture by collective farming. A compromise was reached among decision-makers about introducing a new land system, later called the HRS, throughout the country.

By 1983, virtually all arable land had been allocated to individual households, usually on a per capita (though sometimes on a per worker) basis, and more than twenty years of collective farming had finally come to an end.[11] This land-contracting system immediately demon-strated its huge advance over collective farming and received strong support from central leaders.

The land reforms made during this period correlate with positive devel-opments in productivity, income and income distribution. Grain pro-duction increased by 8.6 percent per year during the first years of HRS, in 1980-1984 (SBS 1980, 1984). These productivity increases had a dramatic impact on farmer incomes and consumption patterns, both in absolute and relative terms. Between 1979 and 1984, average net income for rural residents increased by eleven per cent annually, compared to an average annual increase of 8.7 per cent for urban resi-dents, narrowing the income gap between urban and rural residents from 3.03:1 to 2.49:1 (SBS n.d.). The gap in consumption between ur-ban and rural residents also narrowed during this period, from a ratio of 2.8:1 to 2.3:1 (Xinhua News Agency 2003).

Further improvements to the HRS

The first move that China took in improving the HRS was to lengthen the duration of farmers' individual land rights and expand the breadth of such land rights. The initial land rights that farmers received under HRS were uncertain, usually for a term of one to three years, subject to local decisions (Runsheng 2003:38). At the end of each term, collec-tive cadres conducted a land readjustment within the village in re-sponse to demographic changes occurring during that term to ensure absolutely egalitarian possession of land rights among all members of the village.[12] The breadth of farmer's rights had been restricted in sev-eral ways. A compulsory production plan was in force to the extent that farmers were required to produce and sell to the state a certain amount of grain at a price much lower than market price. Nor were farmers al-lowed to transfer their land rights.

To address these tenure insecurity issues, the Chinese central gov-ernment decided to standardise allocation of land rights for private farming. The first step was to lengthen the duration of farmers' land rights under HRS. In 1984, the Central Committee issued an impor-tant Document No. 1. In order to reverse local practices of contracting land to farmers for very short periods, the document required farmers' land rights be prolonged to fifteen years nationwide. In addition, the document formally sanctioned an emerging rural land rights market by allowing transfers of such rights.[13]

However, the document did not make any rules on how to assure implementation of the extended term or facilitate transfer of land rights. Studies done by RDI and other organisations showed that the new fifteen-year rights were still subject to a mechanism of a 'small re-adjustment' every year and a 'big readjustment' every three to five years, which effectively cut farmers' land rights to a term ending at the next readjustment (Kung and Liu 1996). The uncertain duration of rights to a specific landholding greatly limited the scope for any rural land rights market, leaving room only for short-term transfers. The grain quota remained in place, and farmers were required to set aside at least part of their contracted land for growing grain, which represented a limitation on farming autonomy.

Capitalising on the pervasive existence of unregulated land readjustment practices, local governments and cadres of collectives in some rural areas started to introduce mechanisms that presented even more serious threats to farmers' tenure security in the late 1980s and through the 1990s. Typical among them were the so-called 'two-field system',[14] 'scale farming'[15] and 'recontracting' farmers' land to non-village bosses.[16] Although these mechanisms took different forms, they shared a similar feature: taking back farmers' contracted land through compulsory land readjustment. Because these schemes facilitated rent-seeking by local officials and collective cadres, they rapidly spread throughout large areas of the country. Central government responses to these new threats to farmers' land tenure security are discussed below.

The duration of farmers' land use rights was addressed again nearly ten years after the 1984 issuance of Document No. 1, when the central government decided in November 1993 to extend the term of use rights to collectively owned arable land for another 30 years upon the expiration of the fifteen year rights nominally mandated in 1984.[17] Although the 1993 Document No. 11 stated that '[i]n order to avoid frequent changes in contracted land and prevent land from being further fragmented, no readjustment in response to population changes should be promoted within the contract period',[18] it did not provide any guidelines on how to implement this policy.

It was not until four years later – when farmers' fifteen year land rights (though still generally nominal and nonexistent in practice) were about to expire in most villages in China – that the Chinese government for the first time put forward a series of specific policy measures to restrict the land readjustment practice that had been conducted as a norm in most rural villages since the adoption of HRS. The measures were contained in Document No. 16, issued in mid-1997.[19] These policy measures include explicit prohibition of village-wide big readjustments, serious restrictions on small readjustment, prohibition of introducing the two-field system in villages so far unaffected by such practices, and banning the practice of taking back farmers' contracted land for 'scale farming.' These new policy measures were widely interpreted as mandatory policy guidelines for implementation of a second round of contracting.

As compared with the new land system that was about to emerge under Document No. 16, China's rural land tenure system during the first round of contracting (1983-1998) bore the following characteristics. First, virtually all rural households had access to some arable land. Rural landlessness was virtually non-existent. This is a major accomplishment. Broad, virtually universal access to land has provided important household nutritional and income security throughout rural China (Burgess 2001) and creates a solid foundation for rapid and broadbased rural growth.[20] Second, landholdings were distributed among households in a substantially egalitarian fashion, usually based on one equal land 'share' per household member. While land per capita differences among regions resulted in inter-regional discrepancies, differences within villages and localities were remarkably small. Third, the land system rules and practices were not uniform throughout the country. Collective ownership of land and allocation of specific parcels to individual households have been essentially universal throughout China since 1983. However, the duration of those rights, the specificity with which the use rights are defined, the prevalence and type of administrative land readjustments undertaken, and other important qualitative aspects of the land use rights varied considerably among regions and among localities within regions. Finally, most villages have attempted to balance two competing objectives in establishing and implementing land system practices: continuing equal per capita access to land for welfare or subsistence purposes and stable, secure land use rights for productivity purposes. To this was added the desire of local cadres to make individual profit through continued meddling in land allocations. As discussed above, in most Chinese villages the resultant of these various pressures was a practice of periodically readjusting household land rights to reflect demographic changes in the village and the individual household. The frequency and extent of those readjustments were not uniform, however, among those villages.

Legalisation of the existing practices and policies

Thus, the HRS system was developed first informally through local experiments and was subsequently formalised in the 1984, 1993 and 1997 policy directives. It was not until the adoption of the 1998 Land Management Law (LML) that the original experiments and policies obtained a firm legal basis, legalising 30-year land use rights. This law was adopted by the Standing Committee of the National People's Congress on August 28, 1998. The second round of land contracting, which was to start in 1999, some fifteen years after the first round of HRS contracting had started under the 1984 policy document, was thus to be done on a legal basis.

The 1998 LML attempted to address three major shortcomings related to rural land tenure security in China under the original HRS policy: the short or uncertain duration of the use term, the lack of written land use contracts, and the practice of frequent land readjustments. Concerning the duration of use term, the law states that 'collectively owned land shall be contracted to the members of the collective economic entity for... 30 years'(Land Management Law, art. 14). On documentation of land rights, article 14 further required that 'the contract issuing party and the contracting party execute a contract stipulating the rights and obligations of the two parties' and that 'farmers‛ land contracting rights shall be protected by law'. Equally important, article 14 embodied into law the land readjustment provisions of Document No. 16. It ruled out village-wide big readjustment while allowing small readjustment only to be conducted among 'isolated households' upon 'consent by two-thirds of villagers or villager representatives and approval by township government and county government agencies in charge of agriculture'.

However, the 1998 LML devoted only one article to the actual procedures and content of the rural household contract between the collective owner and the household land user, leaving much unclear, and failed to deal with a vast range of issues with respect to the farmers‛ 30-year rights. Thus, after more than three years of further drafting and deliberation, the Standing Committee of China‛s National People's Congress adopted the Rural Land Contracting Law (RLCL) – the first modern Chinese law to deal exclusively with the issue of rural land tenure – on 29 August 2002. The law came into effect on 1 March 2003. The RLCL sets forth a series of rules addressing a very broad range of tenure issues. The legal framework governing land readjustments under the RLCL is composed of three basic rules. First, article 27 sets up the general principle of prohibiting all kinds of readjustment during the 30-year term with only a narrow exception for 'a natural disaster that seriously damaged the contracted land and other special circumstances' under which a small land readjustment may be conducted. Second, in order to further restrict these narrowly permitted small readjustments under special circumstances, the RLCL reiterates the important procedural requirements that the consent of two-thirds of the villager assembly or two-thirds of villager representatives as well as approval by the township government and the county agricultural administrative body must be obtained prior to the commencement of such a readjustment. Third, the law validates those contracts (where already issued under the 1993 and 1997 policy documents or the 1998 LML) that contain a complete prohibition of land readjustment. In the mean-time, it also explicitly invalidates any provisions of land contracts that violate the mandatory legal rules with respect to land readjustment (Rural Land Contracting Law, art. 55).

Regarding the breadth of farmers' 30-year rights, the law stipulates that farmers' land rights include 'rights to use, profit from, and trans-fer land rights, and the right of autonomy over production operations and disposition of products' and 'the right to receive the corresponding compensation' for the land taken by the state or collective for non-agricultural purposes (*id.*, at art. 16).

On the right to carry out land transactions, the RLCL further states that farmers' land rights 'may be transferred [to other village house-holds], leased [to non-village households], exchanged, assigned, or transacted by other means in accordance with law'(*id.*, at art. 32). The LML, however, strictly forbids using collectively owned arable land for construction or other non-agricultural purposes (Land Management Law, art. 41 and 63),[21] thus limiting transfer of land-use rights only for agricultural purposes.[22] In order to safeguard farmers' interests in land from being violated by local officials through various kinds of compulsory land transactions, the RLCL emphasizes the principle of 'equal consultation, voluntariness and with compensation' (Rural Land Con-tracting Law, art. 33), establishes farmers as 'the party to any transactions of' rural land use rights (*id.*, at art. 34), and explicitly prohibits lo-cal officials to 'intercept or reduce' the proceeds from such land trans-actions (*id.*, at art. 35).

It is important to note that prior legislation, although permitting transactions of rural land use rights, had not provided any guidance with respect to the scope of this right and the procedures to exercise this right,[23] and the RLCL filled this legal vacuum. For example, the RLCL requires that transactions of rural land rights be proven with a 'signed contract' and that such transaction contracts should contain ele-ments like 'the name and address of each of the parties; name, loca-tion, area and quality class of the land to be transferred; the transfer period and the starting and ending dates of the transfer contract,... transfer fees and the payment methods'. To prove farmers' land rights, the RLCL requires that written contracts be issued to farmer house-holds (*id.*, at art. 21). In addition, the RLCL mirrors legal requirements for documenting urban land use rights by requiring that county gov-ernments issue land rights certificates to farmers to affirm such rights (*id.*, at art. 23). Such requirements are extremely important to protect farmers' land rights because these written land documents provide powerful evidence in any dispute resolution[24] process and offer deter-rence against possible violations.

The RLCL also contained improved provisions on the 'assurance' aspect of tenure security. Unlike the dispute resolution provisions in the 1998 Land Management Law and Administrative Review Law, which require exhaustion of administrative reviews before a complaint can be filed with the People's Court (Land Management Law, art. 16; Administrative Review Law 1999, art. 30), the RLCL explicitly gives farmers a choice between consultation, mediation, arbitration and suing in the People's Court (art. 51 and 52). Because cadres of collectives and local government officials are themselves often parties to land disputes, requiring administrative review would make little sense. Enabling aggrieved farmers to seek judicial redress directly could substantially improve farmers' ability to resolve such disputes satisfactorily.

Notably, the RLCL contains a series of well-articulated remedial and penalty provisions with respect to the protection of farmers' land rights. It establishes very clear and strong rules prohibiting violations of farmers' land use rights by local officials, including illegal land readjustments, taking back the farmer-contracted land and re-contracting it to others, and forcing farmers to plant crops against their will. Civil penalties, including monetary damages and restitution, and equitable remedies to forestall or reverse the illegal action now apply to any such violations (*id.,* at art. 54).

Implementation of LML and RLCL and current land tenure security challenges

Studies conducted since the introduction of the 1998 LML and the 2003 RLCL portray a mixed picture of both success and failure in the implementation of these laws. The most important sources currently available for understanding the implementation of land law in China are the nationwide surveys conducted by Prosterman, Schwarzwalder, and Jianping (2000), Schwarzwalder et al. (2002), and Zhu et al. (2006).

Such empirical research demonstrates that since the introduction of the 1998 LML, some progress has been made. First, since 1998 many farmers (78.9 per cent) have become aware of their 30-year land use rights, a necessary condition for implementation (Zhu et al. 2006:791). Second, the 2005 survey found that 82.6 per cent of the villagers reported that their villages had started to implement the new laws and had carried out a second round of contracting of 30-year land use rights (Zhu et al. 2006:792). As a result, 63.2 per cent of the farmers have received some form of documentation attesting to their thirty year land use rights (either contract or land certificate) (Zhu et al. 2006:789). And where, prior to the 1998 LML, land readjustments had been common, a 2002 survey found that 82.1 per cent of the farmers interviewed reported that their village had not conducted a land re-adjustment since the completion of the second round of contracting, which had started in 1999, even though it should be noted that only three years had passed at the time (Schwarzwalder et al. 2002:169).

The data from the last survey also point to implementation challenges. Farmers' awareness is mostly limited to an understanding of the broader outlines of the laws, while they lack knowledge of important details about their rights (Zhu et al. 2006). And even though many villages have started to implement the laws and two-thirds of the farmers now have some form of documentation of their rights, only 10.4 per cent of the farmers possessed a document – either contract or certificate – that met all the requirements of the RLCL (Zhu et al. 2006:789). Furthermore, although earlier surveys signalled a decline in land readjustments (Schwarzwalder et al. 2002), the latest survey, when compared to earlier surveys, found a continued and increasing incidence of prohibited land readjustments (Zhu et al. 2006:794).

Perhaps most alarming, and not part of earlier surveys, is the increase in farmers losing their land use rights through compulsory land acquisitions initiated by local governments or village leadership, without receiving satisfactory compensation. Since 1998, such land takings occurred in 26.8 per cent of the villages where farmers were surveyed, and the data about when such takings occurred show a steep increase since 2000. In addition, 65.5 per cent of the farmers whose land had been taken said they were dissatisfied with the compensation received. In a third of the cases, no compensation was paid even though it was promised, and only 21.8 per cent of the farmers were consulted about the amount of compensation to be paid, even though a compensation minimum and consultation about compensation are provided for in the law (Zhu et al. 2006:782-783). Although the current LML explicitly prohibits the embezzlement and misappropriation of such compensation (Land Management Law, art. 49 (ii)), embezzlement practices are not uncommon.[25] Making matters worse is the fact that farmers who have lost their land without proper compensation have only rarely used their improved remedies under the RLCL. Only 7.8 per cent of them demanded a hearing on compensation, 4.7 per cent filed a grievance with the government about compensation, and 0.9 per cent filed a lawsuit in court to demand more compensation (Zhu et al. 2006:783). Feeling that there is nowhere to turn, many farmers have rallied in protest. In 2005, according to figures reported by the Ministry of Public Security, there were 87,000 protests and other 'mass incidents' related to land loss (Erie 2007).

Based on these data, it becomes clear that even though China has legalised its existing land tenure policies and has increased the duration and breadth of land use rights, aspects of the laws are not well implemented, threatening the assurance element of land tenure security, and so threatening land tenure security itself.

The 2007 Property Law: What good will it do for tenure security?

In 2007, after more than a decade of deliberation, China adopted the Property Law. [26] The law is heralded by some as a major watershed in China's development and seen as a major step towards better protection of land rights.[27] The Chinese press, for example, reported that the law may help Chinese farmers to safeguard their rights when faced with land expropriations (Xinhua News Agency 2007). It is said to do so through specific provisions on land expropriation and the law's rules on compensating farmers for land lost (Xinhua News Agency 2007; Beck and Guo 2007). The Washington Post quoted a Chinese dissident stating: 'This is the first law in our country for property protection. The public can at least cite a specific law when their property rights are violated' (Fan 2007).

Although the functional role of the Property Law should not be exaggerated, it is important to note the significant improvements on farmers' land rights under the Property Law. First, the Property Law clarifies a longstanding ambiguity concerning the nature of farmers' land rights by defining such rights as usufructuary property rights. From a legal perspective, property rights are stronger and enjoy better and enhanced protection than obligatory rights created by contracts. This article enhances the breath of land tenure security of farmers' rural land use rights. Second, article 126 provides that when the present 30-year term expires, 'the holder of land contracting and operation rights may continue contracting the land in accordance with relevant laws'. This is the first time that Chinese law has clarified the uncertainties with respect to farmers' present 30-year land rights when they expire. Through this renewability clause, the law may create a de facto perpetual land right for farmers because the central government and legislative intent clearly favour long-term security for farmers' land rights. Thus, the law enhances the breadth of farmers' land tenure. Third, with respect to compensation for land takings, article 42 of the property Law reiterates the requirement to pay for loss of land, resettlement subsidy and loss of standing crops and fixtures under the LML, and further requires the government to 'make arrangement for social security costs, secure the livelihoods of the disposed farmers and protect lawful interests of the dispossessed farmers'. The added measures and principles are certainly an improvement on existing compensation laws. Fourth, article 132 explicitly provides for the first time that the holder of rural land rights, when such rights are taken through state expropriations, are entitled to the compensation package as provided under article 42, including compensation for loss of land, the largest component of the compensation package as prescribed under the LML (Wang 2007:289). As we know, existing laws require that the compensation for loss of land be owned and retained by the collective owner (Regulations for Implementing the PRC Land Management Law, art. 26). The new Property Law clearly strikes down the exclusive right of the collective owner to the compensation for loss of land. Fifth, article 132 also requires the compensation to be paid to the holder of use rights to the land taken by the state while it is silent on the eligibility of unaffected villagers whose contracted land is not taken. This may at least arguably be interpreted as avoiding an egalitarian distribution of the compensation among all villagers followed by a village-wide land readjustment that will substantially reduce tenure security for all villagers. Sixth, article 99 explicitly allows partition of common property under either of two situations: substantial cause for partition or loss of the basis for holding the property at issue as common property. Article 105 makes such rules applicable to usufructuary rights including rural land rights. These stipulations open a door for rural women to partition their land shares from household landholdings when they move out of the household as a result of marriage and divorce. This is a big improvement on existing laws governing rural women's land rights that are silent on the partitionability. Seventh, article 59 defines collective landownership as 'owned collectively by all members of the collective',[28] filling a definitional vacuum with respect to who should own collective land. From a legal perspective, this definition at least characterises rural land as jointly and indivisibly owned by all members of the community rather than by a group of 'social elite' (e.g. villager committee or collective cadres) as conventionally perceived.

However, the Property Law fails to further improve farmers' tenure security in several aspects. First and most notably, it maintains the existing prohibition of mortgage of rural land rights (Property Law, art. 184). The fourth draft of the Property Law contained a provision permitting rural land use rights to be mortgaged for loans under certain conditions, but it was unfortunately removed when the law was finally adopted based on unjustified grounds. Second, article 245 provides that when a plaintiff seeks the remedy of restitution on the ground of wrongful possession, the claim must be filed within one year of when the wrong possession starts. Compared to international practice, a one-year limitation seems rather short for a claim based on property rights. This may also facilitate unlawful possession of farmers' land rights through illegal re-contracting or scale farmings. Third, it fails to define the 'needs for public interests' under which the state may expropriate rural land as widely expected during the debate on drafting of the Property Law. Given the current problems related to land expropriations, this is an important omission. It is hoped that future amendments to the LML will provide more clarity on the circumstances under which expropriation is allowed.

Further clarification should be made, either through judicial interpretation or legislative explanation, on the provisions that at least seemingly heighten tenure security for farmers. Two examples are offered. First, article 42 requires the government to make arrangements for social security costs for the dispossessed farmers. However, the wording of the provision is not entirely clear regarding whether the social security costs are a supplemental compensation or merely a replacement of all or part of the three traditional categories under LML. Given the fact that China will establish a minimum livelihood social security safety net for all farmers, there should be no reason for the local government to use all or part of the dispossession compensation to finance the social security benefits that all farmers are supposed to have. It appears that a certain type of authoritative interpretation is imperatively needed. Otherwise, the local government may take advantage of this legal vacuum to reduce their financial obligations to restore the dispossessed farmers' livelihoods. Second, article 132 appears to specify that the holder of rural land rights, when the land is taken, is entitled to the compensation package as provided under article 42. Previous laws did not specify who is entitled to the compensation package when part of the village's land is taken. This often results in egalitarian distribution of compensation among all villagers followed by a big land readjustment. However, under article 59, allocation of compensation for loss of land is decided by members of the collective, giving rise to a possibility that such land compensation will be allocated among all villagers followed by a land readjustment. It appears necessary to have an authoritative interpretation based on the spirit of article 132 that only farmers whose contracted land is lost to state expropriation are entitled to such compensation.

Conclusion

Over the years, China has executed several rounds of massive land reforms, completely changing existing practices several times over. Results have been mixed, some ending in a huge disaster, such as the horrible famine during collectivisation, while others have had more positive results, improving agricultural production and leading to greater tenure security for farmers.

China's many land reforms from the 1920s until the 1970s are exemplary of two extremes: private landownership-oriented land reforms before or soon after the Communists took power, and socialist land reforms when its powerbase was consolidated. Post-Mao land rights reforms are somewhat special, as unlike the 'shock approach' of other transitional post-socialist systems, an evolutionary approach was adopted, including immediate legalisation and privatisation.[29] China sought a balance between adhering to socialist ideology and a market-based economic system that would foster economic growth and increased agricultural production. This led to a series of changes, introduced in an incremental fashion, slowly moving land tenure towards more privatised and legally recognised forms.

Although different and sometimes opposite in content, the various land reforms share some common methods of operation. Most importantly, periods of experimentation, with the use of ad hoc, policy-based rules and small-scale arrangements, are followed by large top-down reform movements, during which relatively uniform rules are applied to widely different contexts.[30] Such experimentation has led to creative solutions to existing dilemmas. For instance, with this experimentation approach, the HRS system was developed at a time that this was necessary but not yet universally politically acceptable.

However, the top-down reform method has undermined the realisation of changes introduced for enhancing tenure security. First, some of the original experiments based on experiences in some areas may not be successful in other areas, causing considerable difficulties or even outright disaster, as happened during collectivisation. Second, and perhaps more important for the current land tenure issues, is that the top-down manner of policy formation combined with the post-Mao fragmentation of power has severely challenged implementation. In China's currently fragmented power structures, local governments, often cooperating with local land developers, have a large amount of local autonomy and have been able to thwart the implementation of Beijing's policies and laws they deemed unfavourable.[31] In addition, reaching the Chinese masses from Beijing continues to be a major challenge, strongly affecting the possibility of creating sufficient awareness to initiate grassroots invocation of the norms introduced.

Options for improvement include changes in existing legislation. First, China's current land laws include vague rules about the circumstances under which land can be expropriated, leaving a large amount of discretion to local governments known for pursuing their own interests over those of farmers. Second, the LML provides insufficient compensation, especially when compared to the market values of the land taken. Third, the prohibition of mortgages on land use rights, as regulated even in the latest Property Law (Property Law, art. 184) which strongly affects the breadth of current land tenure arrangements, could be abandoned. This prohibition was installed to protect arable land and avoid reckless mortgages leading to foreclosure, although such protection could be achieved through an effective zoning system and improved banking practice. It is questionable, however, whether such legislative changes will be politically acceptable at the moment. Some of the suggested changes, such as the possibility of mortgaging land use rights to arable land, were parts of earlier drafts of the Property Law but were explicitly changed to appease anti-reform elements within the Chinese national polity.

While these and possibly many other legislative changes may enhance land tenure security on paper, they will be useless if not successfully implemented. As demonstrated above, even the existing legislation is not well implemented, as farmers lack awareness of their rights, land certificates and contracts have not been properly issued, prohibited land reallocations continue, and land is expropriated without following proper procedures or paying due compensation. The weak implementation of law, combined with limited access of farmers to redress mechanisms, strongly undermines the assurance element of tenure security in China, even though the legalisation of the HRS has led to better duration and breadth.

It seems that the improvement of assurance requires action directed at the land bureaus enforcing the law, at courts and other adjudicative bodies able to deal with land conflict cases, and at farmers and social organisations representing them to build their capacity to invoke the law.[32] Underlying many of the implementation issues is a question of power distribution. Methods have to be found to successfully limit the current power and autonomy of local governments cooperating with local land developers and to enhance the power of farmers. It seems that such a shift in power requires special empowerment measures such as allowing farmers to organise themselves, enhancing their access to justice institutions and intermediaries necessary to represent their rights there, and giving greater freedom to the media to report on ongoing injustices. While some of these suggestions may seem sensitive in the current polity, they may help to prevent further widespread social unrest, which itself could ultimately undermine the central authority.

Notes

1   In these cases the illegality has to do with the State of Mexico Penal Code, which typifies non-authorised land subdivisions in order to sell building plots as a criminal offence.
2   The subdivision of *ejido* parcels is prohibited by agrarian law to avoid fragmentation into economically unviable units.
3   The great majority of non-landowning Chinese agricultural families were tenant farmers rather than landless labourers.

4   The Soviet Republic of China, also known as the Jiangxi Soviet existed from 1931 to
     1934, as an independent government established by the Communist leaders Mao Ze-
     dong and Zhu De in Jiangxi province in southeastern China.

5   The lawmakers' intention to grant to peasants full ownership is more visible when
     comparing the language of land allocation in article 6 and the language of article 8
     concerning allocation of the confiscated farming tools and draft animals. Article 8
     specified that the confiscated tools and draft animals should be 'allocated to poor and
     middle peasants for use in cultivating land', and the users should pay a user fee.

6   Several categories of land are listed as state-owned under the Land Reform Law: large
     tracts of forestland, the land on which large irrigation facilities are erected, large
     tracts of wasteland, large tracts of salt-producing land, mines, rivers, lakes, harbours.
     The large and contiguous tracts of land for growing bamboo, fruits, tea and mulber-
     ries which were previously owned by landlords were also converted to state owned
     land. See Land Reform Law of PRC 1950, article 18 and 19.

7   Unlike the Platform, which allows land lease only under 'certain circumstances', the
     Land Reform Law does not contain such a restriction.

8   A region was composed of several provinces. Regional people's government was abol-
     ished in the mid-1960s when the Cultural Revolution began.

9   The landowners who were previous landlords but currently did not engage in agricul-
     tural production were prohibited from possessing such rights to transfer for 'a cer-
     tain period' after the land allocation. See *Ibid.*

10   Standing Committee of the National People's Congress, the Decision on 'the Charter
     of Rural Production Cooperatives', *People's Daily*, Mar. 18, 1956.

11   Charter of Rural Production Cooperatives, article 1, in which it states, '(c)ollectives
     shall uniformly use its members' land, draft animals and agricultural production
     tools, and gradually realize the goal of public ownership of these production means'.
     See also Decision of the Sixth Plenary Session 1955. The decision defined agricultural
     cooperatives as a form of semi-socialist organisation in the transition to full public
     ownership of rural land.

12   Fifteen to 30 million incremental deaths occurred, as agricultural production plum-
     meted. See Peng 1987:639; Weigeln-Schwidrizik 2003.

13   *Ibid.*, at 172. See also Qinghe 1992.

14   As household and village population numbers change, land readjustment is designed
     to ensure absolute equality of per capita (or sometimes per worker) landholdings in a
     given community. Not all land readjustments are of the same magnitude. 'Big' or
     comprehensive readjustments involve an overall change in the landholdings of all
     farm households in the village. In a big readjustment, all farmland in the village is
     given back to the collective entity and reallocated among village households so that
     each household receives entirely new land. A 'small' or partial readjustment consists
     of adding to or taking from a household's existing landholdings when that house-
     hold's size changes. Under small readjustments, households that neither add nor
     lose members will continue to farm the same landholding. Such readjustment for po-
     pulation change is not found in any of the world's highly developed agricultures but
     can be found in a few customary tenure regimes. There are also historical examples
     in a few other societies; and it appears to be contemplated, though with a far longer
     duration of 49 years and 'readjustment' in the fiftieth, in the Old Testament refer-
     ence to reallocation in the 'year of the Jubilee' (Leviticus 25:23).

15   Central Committee of CPC's Notice on Rural Work in 1984 (Document No. 1 of
     1984), issued Jan. 1, 1984.

16   The two-field system breaks with the typical pattern of distributing all farmland on a
     per capita basis. Instead, cultivated land is divided into two categories: 'consumption
     land' and 'responsibility land'. Consumption land is divided in each village on a per

capita basis to meet each household's basic needs. The remaining land is contracted to farm households as responsibility land through a variety of methods which in many cases results in a non-egalitarian land distribution. On top of the regular grain quota farmers pay for the use of consumption land, an additional contracting fee is typically charged for responsibility land. For an analysis of the two-field system and its implementation in China, see Prosterman, Hanstad, and Ping 1994.

17 Scale farming involves the consolidation of small, labour-intensive farms into larger, mechanised farms. Scale farming can be accomplished through a variety of approaches, but typically involves the contracting of large areas of arable land to a few farmers or the operation of large-scale farms by the collective land owner. Recollectivisation of farmland was the ultimate goal of at least some experiments with scale farming in the early 1990s. For a discussion of scale farming and its relevance to China, see Prosterman, Hanstad, and Ping 1998.

18 Compulsory re-contracting means that cadres of the collective, usually in cooperation with township officials, take farmers' land back and re-contract it out to non-villagers or corporations including foreign corporations, without consulting farmers and with no or little compensation to the farmers whose land is affected. The motivation behind re-contracting is rent-seeking by cadres of the collective, who cannot legally impose contracting fees on the land allocated among village households but can impose such fees on the third-party contractor through the process of re-contracting. For a typical case of re-contracting as it still occurs in present-day China, see the Licun case discussed in Van Rooij, this volume. See also Van Rooij 2006b: ch. 9.

19 The Central Committee of CPC and the State Council's Policy Measures on the Current Agricultural and Rural Development, Nov. 5, 1993 (Document No. 11 of 1993). See also the more general 'Decision of the CCP Central Committee on Some Issues Concerning the Establishment of a Socialist Market Economic Structure', adopted by the 14th Central Committee of the CCP at its third plenary session on 14th November 1993, article 31 available in LEXIS (database on-line), News Library, BBCSWB File (18 Nov. 1993).

20 Document No. 11, sec. 1.

21 Notice Concerning Further Stabilizing and Protecting the Rural Land Contracting Relationship (1997) No. 16, issued by the Central Committee on August 27, 1997 (hereinafter Document No. 16).

22 Empirical studies show that – at the country level – broad-based access to land is associated with higher rates of economic growth (Deininger and Olinto 2000: 3-4, 9).

23 Making exceptions for the construction of collectively owned enterprises, rural housing (although not more than one per household, art 62) and other buildings with public facilities to be used by the collective.

24 Construction on collectively owned arable land is only allowed after a procedure in which the collective land ownership is converted to state ownership, following which the land use purpose can be converted, if certain procedures are followed, including compensating farmers for land use rights lost. See LML, article 43-49.

25 The 1998 LML had simply repeated the general principle that 'land use rights may be transferred in accordance with law' (art. 2).

26 In recent discussions, Chinese officials stated that the Peoples' Court will refuse to consider any farmer's complaint about the non-payment of compensation in takings of land for non-agricultural purposes if the farmer cannot produce one of these documents showing that the farmer holds rights to the land in question.

27 For examples see Van Rooij, this volume.

28 This property law provides general rules applicable to all kinds of civil law relationships that arise from the ownership and use of property. (Property Law art. 2 (i)) The law defines two forms of property: movable and real property. (Property Law art. 2

(ii)) Property rights include both full ownership rights, as well as more limited rights including usufructuary rights and security property rights such as mortgage and the right of pledge. (Property Law art. 2 (iii) Finally, the law distinguishes a tripartite differentiation of state, collective and private property rights. And even though the law stipulates that such ownership rights, and actually all property rights, are protected (Property Law art. 4) in the 2004 Constitution (art. 16 of the 1982 Constitution after amendment in 2004), the law also states that it maintains a basic socialist economic system with public property playing a dominant role and diverse forms of ownership developing side by side (Property Law art. 3) (Editorial 2007).

29 See for examples of positive accounts of the new law Beck and Guo 2007 and Wang 2007. For more skeptical views see Beck and Guo 2007, Erie 2007 and Wang 2007.

30 See also Wang 2007:129 which clearly states that 'rural collective economy entity, or villager committee, or villager group is not the owner of collective property'.

31 Compare with Taylor who distinguishes between the shock approach and the evolutionary-institutionalist models concerning legal reforms in Central and Eastern Europe (Taylor 2007:84). She follows Roland 2000:328.

32 We mainly discussed this for the development of the HRS into the LML and RLCL, but it also applies to the development of land redistribution from the small-scale, communist-controlled regions in the 1930s and 1940s to the large-scale land redistribution in the 1950s. The massive switch towards collectivisation and ultimately to people's communes was also one that started with local experimentation, at the time in Henan province in which 27 cooperatives were formed into one immense commune of 9,369 households. See Luo 2003:19; Spence 1990:578-579.

33 For more detail, see Van Rooij, this volume.

34 For more detail, see Van Rooij, this volume.

16 Land loss and conflict in China: Illustrated by cases from Yunnan province

Benjamin van Rooij[1]

Introduction

In the 1980s China introduced the Household Responsibility System (HRS), a policy which gave China's rural households a fifteen-year use right to a plot of land (Yang 2003). Under the HRS, such a use right was allocated to households, while China's rural land remained collectively owned, in most cases, by the village collective (VC). Since 1998 the revised Land Management Law (LML) legalised and length-ened the HRS policy into a legally recognised, 30-year land use right (LML § 14.1), which is to be established through a land use contract (LML § 14.1), including the right of transfer (LML § 2.2). In 2003, the Rural Land Contract Law (RLCL) provided further detail as to the rights and duties concerning the household land use rights, especially con-cerning the content of land use contracts(RLCL § 21) and the transfer of the use rights through exchange, lease, or assignment (RLCL § 32-43). In addition, the 2003 RLCL provided farmers with extensive legal remedies against infringements of their rights, establishing very clear and strong rules prohibiting violations of farmers' land use rights by local officials. Violations are punishable through civil liability, adminis-trative sanctions, and even criminal penalties (RLCL § 54-61). In addi-tion, the 2003 RLCL has broadened access to justice possibilities for aggrieved farmers by allowing direct appeals to court (RLCL § 51).[2] Thus, on paper at least, it seems that the 1998 and the 2003 laws have strengthened household tenure security.

Empirical research has demonstrated that although full implementa-tion is still an ideal, progress has been made in the realisation of the law's norms (Prosterman, Schwarzwalder, and Jianping 2000; Schwarzwalder et al. 2002). Such research found that already by 2000, and even more in 2002, most farmers were aware of their 30-year land use rights, and in most villages the implementation of the 30-year land use right system had begun. It also demonstrated that a growing num-ber of farmers (app. 45 per cent in 2002, and 63 per cent in 2005) have received some form of documentation attesting to their 30-year land use right (Schwarzwalder et al. 2002:168; Zhu et al. 2006:788). Progress has also been made in relation to land readjustments. These are practices of redistribution of collective land use rights within the collective, which had been common prior to the 1998 LML and which, since the 2003 RLCL, have been largely banned in order to enhance tenure security. A 2002 survey found that 82.1 per cent of the farmers interviewed reported that their village had not conducted a land read-justment aside from those necessary for distributing the 30-year land use rights in the first place (Schwarzwalder et al. 2002:169).[3]

Despite the stronger formal recognition of farmer's land use rights and the progress made in the implementation of the new laws, land tenure security remains weak in China. The largest threat has been a sharp rise over the last decade of cases in which farmers lost their land use rights and received little to no compensation (Zhu et al. 2006:782-783). This has led to an increase in land disputes and protests initiated by farmers resisting the taking of their land and demanding more compensation (Erie 2007). China's land loss conflicts pose a puzzle: How is it possible that land loss conflicts continue despite the progress made in the lawmaking and implementation of the LML and RLCL? In order to analyse this question, knowledge about what causes such conflicts is necessary; in addition, it is important to find out to what extent the existing problems are related to the efforts made at enhancing land tenure security as adopted in the LML and the RLCL. The analysis of China's land loss conflicts will enhance our understanding of current bottlenecks in rural land tenure security in China and future directions for land reform.

The present chapter seeks to understand which factors explain China's land conflicts. It makes a critical assessment of the current litera-ture by combining existing primary and secondary sources with data gathered during a year of fieldwork in Yunnan province. During this fieldwork, several cases of land conflicts in peri-urban villages near Yunnan's capital Kunming were studied in detail.[4] Findings from this fieldwork are used to illustrate and critically analyse data from second-ary and primary sources about such regulation in China.

In addition, the present chapter will conclude with observations about what the ongoing land loss disputes mean for rural land tenure security in China.[5] For this analysis, the chapter distinguishes land ten-ure security in terms of its breadth, duration, and assurance.[6] Follow-ing Ostrom, the breadth of the land use rights can be evaluated by checking which bundles of rights farmers have, including: access, with-drawal, management, exclusion, and alienation (Ostrom 1999:339). Duration covers the time limitations of land tenure rights. Assurance, following Place, Roth, and Hazell (1994), is made up of 'the assurance in exerting rights and the costs of enforcing these rights which should not be inhibiting'.

This chapter first discusses four land loss cases from Yunnan province and then briefly outlines current land loss conflicts in China. After this, using Yunnan and other cases, the chapter continues to analyse the causes of the land loss conflicts. It first looks at the relationship between the land loss conflicts and the existing land legislation. In addition, it analyses the incentives for land development that have caused such conflicts. Finally, it analyses the existing systems of checks and balances in place to control land acquisition and protect farmers from losing their land, both those systems initiated by farmers themselves and those organised through state institutions. In the conclusion, the chapter discusses what China's land loss conflicts mean for the country's land tenure security.

Four land loss cases from peri-urban Kunming

Data derived through fieldwork in Yunnan province provide illustrations of how land acquisition conflicts occur in real-life situations in one particular area of China. This section discusses four such cases.

'We are going to lynch him,' shout the angry Xiaocun[7] farmers some twenty kilometres south of Kunming, the capital of Yunnan province, as they turn towards the Village Committee (VC)[8] headquarters to find their village president. These Chinese peasants feel cheated as they have discovered that each of them has lost 10,000 RMB (about USD 1000) in compensation for their arable land loss. The farmers have lost their land due to forced state expropriation to build a highway to the provincial capital Kunming. They do not suspect, rather, they think they know for certain that their own village leadership has somehow taken their money. As the mob prepares for violence, the scared village chairman, the democratically elected leader of the village, tries to explain that it was not him but the bureaucratically appointed superior township leadership that took the money. The village leader speaks to no avail, as the angry farmers still beat him up badly. Afterwards, the shaken village president resigns, and the county police are called in to patrol the village for more than a month to prevent further unrest.[9]

A couple of years earlier, in Jiacun village, just ten kilometres north of Xiaocun, farmers also rallied against their local VC over land. The first conflict involved the construction of a Buddhist temple. When an energetic young monk convinced the village leadership to support his plans for the restoration of the Jiahuasi village temple, a large plot of land (60 Mu[10]) in sub-village one was assigned for construction. Because of the sensitivity of religious construction, the Buddhists were careful not to upset any of the local stakeholders and offered an extremely generous compensation for the farmers' arable land loss,

200,000 RMB/Mu, more than twice the usual amount paid in this
area (80,000 RMB/Mu) and well above the statutory minimum of
18,000 RMB/Mu (six times the average annual agricultural output of
the three proceeding years, which cannot have been higher than the
3000 RMB a year that farmers make on Jiacun's prime land) (LML §
47.2). Furthermore, the owners of two houses located on the former
temple premises which were to be demolished for the construction demanded 600,000 RMB in compensation. Monk Li expressed his frustration to me during one of our conversations: 'Their houses cost no
more than 80,000 RMB to rebuild. They know we are powerless to refuse their demands, so they just ask what they like.' This case was
settled, and the temple paid 300,000 RMB. The temple further helped
pay for a new road from the highway to the temple that crosses Liujia's
most important industrial area. Cynically enough, the Buddhists' generous compensation did not prevent village unrest directed at the new
temple. In the months that followed, villagers believed that the temple
had taken more land than it had compensated for and organised protests against the temple and their own VC leadership. The protests
came to a boiling point during the 2001 democratic VC elections, in
which a majority of the farmers tried to nominate a mentally disabled
villager as their village leader to show their dissatisfaction about these
land practices.[11]

The elections did not end the land protest in Jiacun village. In 2002,
when a new school was to be built on a 23 Mu plot of land in sub-village three, villagers rallied once more. They protested against the
amount of compensation they had been offered for their land use
rights over the land on which the school was to be built. The VC had
offered to pay them 100,000 RMB per Mu. The amount offered was
generous by local standards and well within the above-mentioned legal
minimum compensation for land taken by the state of about 18,000
RMB. The villagers in sub-village three were dissatisfied with this
amount because they thought it was unfair that other farmers in sub-
village one had received 200,000 RMB per Mu from the Buddhist temple construction project. At first, when the VC refused to pay more
than they had offered, the angry farmers turned to higher levels of government. They wrote petitions (shangfang), and the government sent
teams to Liujia to investigate the situation. Their petitions were in vain
as all higher-level government teams ruled in favour of the VC's school
project and found that the compensation was in order. At this time, the
VC decided to start construction, and the land was cleared and prepared for building the school. The villagers of sub-village three did not
give up. First, they tried to sabotage the project itself by cutting down
the power-lines at the building site. When this did not help stop the
project, they turned on the VC itself.[12] One day, angry villagers sur-

rounded the VC headquarters and blocked the gate so that no one could leave or enter. They even locked the only entrance to the building to force their demands on the village's democratically elected leadership. This act of physical protest forced the VC to negotiate with the villagers. It was clear from the start that their demands could not be fully met because it would set a precedent for high compensation precluding other construction projects in the village. Elected village head Mr. Yang was able to forge a compromise under which the farmers would get 100,000 RMB per Mu land and retain small plots of land on the outside of the school premises on which they could build shops.

In Licun Village – located some 50 kilometres southwest of Jiacun – local leadership converted arable land to construction land. The leadership believed that 2004 was the right time to begin doing so, because the new highway would soon create a fast connection with Kunming, which would certainly bring development and thus enterprises in need of construction land to the area. To start using this land for construction, the VC leadership leased several plots of arable land from farmers, who had the land use rights. The farmers received 500 RMB per year per Mu for wet land and 300 RMB per year per Mu for dry land, a total of 12,000 or 7,200 for the remaining 24 years of usage rights that the farmers still had.[13] The VC then took this land and leased it to enterprises to construct premises on, for lump sums ranging from 80,000 to 90,000 per Mu. According to the VC leadership the enterprises would receive land contracts for *changqi* (long term), which actually meant indefinitely. 'We did this because the law does not allow transfer of ownership, but we actually wanted to sell the land itself to the firms,' Licun Village's CCP secretary explained one day. He knew that what they did was in violation of the Land Management Act (LML § 43.1 and § 63.1). 'If we had gone by the book we would never have been able to sell the land of the villages, all the costs of compensation and procedural fees to the land bureau would have raised the price per Mu to about 170,000 RMB per Mu, and there is no company willing to pay that.' Villagers in Licun felt cheated out of their land, as they have not received the satisfactory compensation for losing their land rights and furthermore suspect their leadership of keeping the profits made on this land deal. In total, after payment of compensation, the VC made over 1.5 million RMB.[14] Farmers have stated that they do not know how the 1.5 million is being used. They do not believe the VC's explanation that all of the money is being invested in village development for roads and electricity projects. The farmers think that the group of family and friends who have held power over Licun for decades used the money for their own personal benefit. They have no way of proving this and only voice their anger in the privacy of their homes. The men say they felt helpless as they could not refuse land requisitioning, nor could they protest. They say that complaining to the township government is of no use as they are old friends and even family of the VC. According to the unhappy farmers, there is nowhere they can go with their problems. Unlike Xiaocun's and Jiacun's active protesters, Licun's farmers seem to have accepted the situation as a fact of life. Not even the new election system gives them hope, as they say it is dominated by the same tight group of powerful Licun leaders who will be able to exclude anyone who threatens their dominion.

China's land loss conflicts: An overview

From these cases we see that farmers lose their land use rights in several manners and for several reasons, involving different actors. First, there are cases that involve land loss following expropriation. In some cases the state (at various levels of administration, depending on the case) expropriates arable land use rights for public interests, such as building roads or government premises. In these cases the state will order the expropriation but also pay for compensation. While land use rights holders have a legal right to compensation (RLCL § 16.2), the compensation is payable to the village committee (VC), the village elected body of self-government, which is not a part of the state.[15] The VC thus plays an intermediary role as it negotiates the amount of compensation payable and divides the compensation amongst rights holders.[16] Expropriation not only takes place for construction for public use, but also in cases where collectively owned arable land is to be used for commercial construction purposes, by private or semi-private parties, other than those for rural housing, collective enterprises, or village public utilities. In these cases the LML provides that such construction requires conversion of ownership from the collective to the state, and is thus also an expropriation (LML § 43). Following an approval procedure for the land use conversion from arable to construction, as well as the expropriation and thus the conversion of ownership from collective to state, the land developer leases or buys the land use right from the state. Meanwhile, the land developer has to pay compensation to the VC, which negotiates the amount, manages it, and divides it amongst rights holders.

In a second type of land loss case, farmers lose their arable land use rights without expropriation. Such cases include collective construction projects that are allowed on collectively owned arable land, including the construction of collectively owned enterprises and collective premises such as schools or VC buildings. In these cases land loss is largely a village affair, where the VC has to come up with measures to compensate those farmers who have lost their land. Rights holders are entitled to receive compensation for losing their land rights in this manner. However, the law provides little detail as to how much and how this is payable.[17] In another type of case, farmers lose their land rights because the VC illegally leases or transfers such land use rights for commercial construction to third-party land developers. As stated, such practices are in violation of the LML which stipulates that construction on collective land for non-collective uses is only possible after expropriation, while specifically forbidding the direct lease or transfer of land use rights to collective arable land for such non-collective construction purposes (LML § 43.1, 63.1). They occur because smaller, privately owned enterprises often do not have the resources to pay for these procedures, which require great lump sum payments at the start of the business venture, when there is little security about its profitability.[18] As these practices are illegal, China's land law does not provide provisions concerning compensation. In these cases, sometimes VCs have used the proceedings made from the land lease or transfer to pay compensation to households who have lost their land use rights, or in other cases to pay a dividend to all collective members.[19] In all these different situations, conflicts have occurred when farmers were unsatisfied with the amount of compensation they received after having lost land use rights.

Yunnan is no exception, as numerous farmers in China have lost their land without sufficient compensation (Cai 2003; Chen 2003:39; Guo 2001b; Xiao 2003:257-259). Many Chinese farmers have voiced their anger about land-grabbing through demonstrations. And this is only the tip of the iceberg, as many Chinese peasants do not even rally in protest when their land is taken away. The official number of demonstrations in 2005 was 85,000, involving over 3 million citizens, of which a significant part concerned land acquisitions. According to a recent study, 25 per cent of all farmers has been affected by land use rights losses, of which two-thirds have not been satisfied with the compensation (Zhu et al. 2006). The problem is widespread; one commentator notes that an 'economic war is going on at the local level in China today especially on the fringes of expanding urban areas' (Subrahmanyan 2004). Alarmingly, the conflicts are becoming increasingly violent, with strong clashes between farmers, police, and hired thugs. In the worst case so far, armed police in Shanwei village in Guangdong province were called in to control a mob of 10,000 people who were protesting against the construction of a wind power plant on their land without sufficient compensation. The mob had gathered on site in order to demand the release of three of their appointed negotiators who had been detained earlier. As the 1,000 armed police officers faced the protestors, things turned ugly. Following an exchange of tear gas canisters and bricks and home-made explosives, the police opened fire, shooting to kill. Their live ammunition wounded over 100 villagers and killed between three and twenty villagers, according to eyewitness accounts (Ang 2005). After the incident, police sealed off the village, and one villager stated to the press: 'The riot police are gathered outside our village. We've been surrounded. Most of the police are armed. We dare not go out of our home. We are not allowed to buy food outside our village. They asked nearby villages not to sell us goods. The government did not give us proper compensation for using our land to build development zones and plants. Now they have come to shoot us. I don't know what to say' (id.).

The central government knows that the land loss conflicts are a volcano waiting to erupt. In a speech made on December 29, 2005, Premier Wen Jiabo voiced his concern that farmland seizures were provoking widespread social unrest, stating: 'We absolutely can't commit an historic error over land problems.' He warned that despite strong efforts to end local officials' land grabs, farmers still often receive little compensation for land loss (Buckley 2006). Decreasing rural underdevelopment has become a major theme of central policy in the last few years, and in 2006 the National People's Congress launched a new nationwide policy of *xin nongcun* (new villages), a policy which aims to protect farmers' interests. For the Chinese Communist Party, a political organisation that owes its present dominion over the country to its supposed role as the champion of China's poor and landless peasants who were once dominated by local elites, the current resurgence of farmers feeling that they are being exploited by elites must be very frustrating.

Changing legislation is necessary but no panacea

If China's leaders are to find solutions for dealing with the current land loss conflicts and if China is to secure farmer's land tenure security, a deeper understanding of the causes behind the current land acquisition conflicts is necessary. A primary cause, often discussed in the literature, is China's current land legislation.

A primary legal problem responsible for the ongoing land loss is that China still has a socialist system in which the law prescribes that unless land is collectively owned, it is state owned. The socialist ownership system, combined with the rule that most construction should take place on state-owned land[20], has created a state monopoly on managing construction land. Ding has argued that such a monopoly has enabled local governments to abuse their powers and profit from the value gap between urban and rural land (Ding 2007:2). It should be noted that there are many land conflicts in which state institutions are not involved. In the cases studied in Yunnan, acquisition problems existed without state interference and were solely the result of collective institutions and the Village Committee (VC), the village self-elected body of government, which is not part of the state structure.

Ambiguous ownership rights are a second legal cause for concern. Ho has blamed the ambiguous ownership rights – that exist because the LML fails to clarify who exactly owns China's rural land[21] – for the continuing land ownership conflicts. Collectively owned land, which covers most of China's agricultural land, is operated and managed by the *cun jiti jingji zuzhi* (VC economic organisation) or by the *cunmin weiyuan* (the VC members) (LML § 10). The law adds that land that has been owned collectively so far by two or more collective organisations within the village shall be managed by such sub-village organisations, which in most areas are called *xiaozu* (small group) or *zirancun* (natural village) (*id.*). The law further provides that land which already belongs to the township (or town) shall be operated and managed by such a township (or town) (*id.*). Because of China's turbulent land history and the differing operations of the communes that preceded the present land rights system, there is a large degree of ambiguity about which collective unit used to own the land. This original ambiguity has been left intact by the LML. As a result, there have been many conflicts between natural villages, administrative villages, and township level leaders about who owns the land and, as a result, who can control procedures of land expropriation (Ho 2001, 2003). Ho argues that township governments especially have been able to use the ambiguity of the past to profit from village land that they should not be allowed to manage and acquire (Ho 2001). The argument is convincing and clearly present in the cases Ho studied concerning conflicts occurring before 2000. However, it is less clear whether the ambiguity of ownership is highly influential in the recent surge of land loss conflicts studied in this chapter, which largely concern the loss of land use rights. In the cases studied in Yunnan, vague ownership rights were not influential in the ongoing acquisition abuses, nor were they the basis of land loss conflicts in any of the recent cases reported in the Chinese media or in scholarly studies on such recent land loss conflicts as those studied here. Land loss conflicts involving township governments in the cases studied here concerned governments that embezzled villagers' compensation, as happened in Xiaocun village in Yunnan (Van Rooij 2006b: Ch. 9). In these cases, township officials were able to do so in their role as intermediary between the villagers and the district government, but not out of a legal claim based on ownership.[22]

The law's use of the vague term of '*gonggong liyi*' (public interests) as a prerequisite for land expropriations forms the third legal problem (LML § 2.4).[23] Current analysis holds that this vague term has made it easier for predatory local governments to expropriate farmers' land legally (Ding 2007:7; Subrahmanyan 2004). Therefore, as some scholars have advised, it is sensible to create a better definition of 'public interests', limiting the possibilities for legal land loss for non-public interest purposes.[24] However, such a change of legislation is unlikely to stop all or even a substantial part of the ongoing land loss conflicts at hand. In the land loss cases in Yunnan, governments and the VC leadership did not try to legitimise their actions with this term. In Licun village, outright illegal commercial construction for non-public purposes has been done on land leased from land use rights holders without any reference to the law's public interests (Van Rooij 2006b:Ch. 9). The VC leadership never did so, because their practice of renting the land to enterprises without first converting the land ownership to the state was in clear violation of the LML anyway (LML § 63). Clearly, Licun's leaders did not fear engaging in an illegal practice (Van Rooij 2006b:Ch. 9). And likewise, even when the state or local VCs acquired land for clearly public purposes such as building a road in Xiaocun, or a school or a temple in Jiacun village, villagers rallied in protest nonetheless (id. at Ch. 7). In those cases, the protest was not directed against the purpose of land use but against the compensation farmers were to receive.

The existing regulation on compensation for arable land loss is the fourth and most important legal concern discussed here.[25] Ever since the adoption of the LML[26] there has been criticism about the provisions for compensation of farmers' loss of land. First of all, there is a certain lack of clarity in the law concerning the scope of application of compensation rules and the exact procedure for distributing compensation from the village collective to households. On the one hand, the RLCL provides that households whose land use rights are expropriated (zhengyong) or occupied (zhanyong)[27] should receive compensation. On the other hand, the LML and its 1998 State Council Implementing Regulations provide rules about the procedure and approximate amounts of compensation payable. However, these rules seem only to apply to cases in which farmers lose their land use rights when the land is expropriated (zhengyong) (LML § 47). They do not stipulate whether these rules apply to cases where land is lost for construction for collective purposes. Another unclear point concerning compensation is that the 1998 Implementing Regulations provide that compensation belongs to the collective economy (1998 State Council LML Implementing Regulations, art. 26), without specifying exactly how it is to be distributed to farmers who have lost their land use rights. Both points of uncertainty undermine farmers' right to compensation, especially in cases in which their land is taken by VCs, or in which the VC refuses to transfer the compensation paid to the households that have lost their land. Perhaps the most cynical aspect of the current compensation norms is that they do not apply to illegal situations in which land has been taken for construction without going through the proper procedures, such as occurred in Licun and Jiacun.

The 2007 Property Law has not solved these issues and actually may have made matters worse. Article 132 states that in case of state expropriations, land use rights holders are entitled to compensation. Here the new law nearly repeats the RLCL, but with one important difference. The new law only provides for compensation in case of expropriation by the state (Property Law § 132 and 42),[28] and not as the RLCL does in case of construction, by the collective without such expropriation. It seems that on this issue further clarification is needed in all three laws. The best option would be to grant land use rights holders a right to compensation, providing clear standards as well as procedures for negotiations and payment, regardless of the manner in which their land has been taken, whether through expropriation or not, in a legal manner or in violation of the law.

Another problem concerns the legal procedure for compensation. At present, China's LML only provides that farmers are to be consulted about the land requisitioning and the compensation to be paid (LML § 48). Thus, farmers are not directly involved in bargaining about the compensation amount and have no formal legal instrument for stopping land acquisition when they do not agree with the amount of compensation offered. An important and logical change would be to grant farmers rights of negotiation about compensation prior to the land acquisition approval.[29] In local Beijing municipal regulations, farmers have gotten a stronger voice in the compensation negotiation process as the local rules require that a written agreement between the requisitioning unit and the rural collective economic institutions or village committees is required, governing the compensation amount and procedures (Subrahmanyan 2004). However, whether such changes in the law will affect current practice remains to be seen. Even the existing procedure is not well implemented, as recent research found that only twenty per cent of the farmers who are about to lose their land use rights have received the legally mandated prior notice about compensation (Zhu et al. 2006). This shows that even if negotiations become obligatory in the law, many land developers are still able to start construction without following the procedure, whether it is the duty to provide information at present or the duty to enter into negotiations in the future. In addition, our study of negotiations about compensation for collective construction on arable land in Jiacun village in Yunnan demonstrates that even if farmers are able to enter into negotiations with developers and the VC leadership they still rally in protest, sometimes just to get more compensation (Van Rooij 2006b:Ch. 7). Therefore, the issue of compensation is not so much one of procedure but predominantly one of the amount of compensation paid.

Most of the protests concern the amount of compensation.[30] Zhu et al.'s data demonstrate that 67 per cent of the farmers whose land has been expropriated is unsatisfied with the amount of compensation received (Zhu et al. 2006). Thus, it seems perfectly logical to blame the existing statutory minimum amounts for compensation, as most analysts have done. As previously stated, an initial problem is that when the law is followed to the letter, the current compensation minima only apply to land loss cases involving expropriation by the state, and not cases where farmers lose their land use rights for collective construction. In addition, China's statutory compensation minima for land acquisition are based on the idea that farmers should be compensated sufficiently to continue to provide for their livelihoods for a set amount of years in a fashion to which they have been accustomed.[31] Current compensation minima are therefore not based on the economic value of the land acquired, and the fairness of current compensation minima is questionable. First of all, the statutory minima at present may not always be enough to enable farmers to retain the same standard of living, as the law, for example, does not allow for raised costs of living, especially for farmers who, having lost their land and their main sources of income, have to leave rural areas and get by in much more expensive urban centres (Chan 2003:145). Second, the compensation minima are unfair as they do not relate to the value of the land once it is acquired for construction purposes (Chan 2003:33, 144; Fan et al. 2003).[32] It seems reasonable that farmers should be allowed to share in the immense wealth the land conversions bring. Guo's research from Yunnan has shown that many farmers there have rallied in protest against land expropriation cases, not so much because they disagreed with the overall amount of compensation but because they thought it unfair when compared to the amount of money that land developers were making (Guo 2001b). Such feelings of unfairness were also at stake in my own research in Jiacun village in Yunnan where farmers rallied in protest when a school was built, not because the compensation was insufficient to sustain their original income, which it was not, but because it was lower than what a temple construction project had paid their fellow villagers a year earlier (Van Rooij 2006b: Ch. 7).

The amount of compensation is thus a problem that needs to be addressed in the law. At present, there have been efforts, both in local legislation in Beijing as well as in national policy documents and legal interpretations, and supposedly in the new draft LML, to incorporate higher compensation minima which are not solely linked to output value. In a Beijing local initiative, for example, local rules offer a minimum compensation standard that is to be set 'based on the agricultural output value, land location, and compensation for resettlement, as well

as adjusted according to social and economic development' (Subrahmanyan 2004). A true change that would link compensation to land
market value seems to remain difficult to accomplish. First, there may
not be sufficient support to make such a change in the national legislation, and second, as long as the land market is not well developed, it
remains difficult to determine a fair price on which to base such compensation (Ding 2007).

It is doubtful, however, whether a change in legislation over the
amount of compensation will solve the existing land disputes. The problem remains that even the existing laws with their relatively low minimum standards for compensation are widely violated. Such cases include farmers who have received sub-minimum compensation, such as
those in Licun (Van Rooij 2006b:Ch. 9), and situations in which the
compensation, even if it may have been offered in compliance with the
law, has been embezzled by elites that have acted as intermediaries between the farmers and the land developers. Research in Shandong province found, for example, that in cases in which compensation is paid,
only 15-30 per cent ends up with the farmers, while the rest is kept by
the VC, and that there were even cases where farmers received nothing
(Zhao 2003). This also happened in Xiaocun village in Yunnan where
township officials embezzled part of the compensation offered by higher level governments to local farmers.

In sum, although the current land loss conflicts can be attributed to
the text of the law and a change in the law would lead to amelioration,
in many cases the problem is largely related to how the law functions
in practice. Therefore, land loss conflicts cannot be explained merely
through a legal analysis. Neither can all such land conflicts be solved
through changes in legislation. Land acquisition conflicts will continue,
unless other factors are taken into account. This chapter will continue,
therefore, by looking at the ways in which the law functions in practice
and the non-legal factors that have influenced the ongoing land disputes.

Understanding land loss: Incentives and pressures

Land loss conflicts first occur when local governments,[33] VCs, and/or
commercial land developers stand to benefit from land transactions. In
China, these benefits derive from the wide gap between the value of
land used for agricultural purposes, based on the agricultural output,
and land used for construction purposes based on the real estate market (Subrahmanyan 2004). In Licun village in Yunnan, for example,
the local VC was able to enrich themselves by leasing rural land use
rights for 12,000 RMB/mu and then leasing it out as construction land

for 80,000-90,000 RMB/mu. In Fujian province a local government paid 10,000 RMB/mu to farmers and then resold their land use rights to developers for a minimum of 200,000 RMB/mu, and in some cases even up to 750,000 RMB/mu. In another case Hangzhou farmers were paid 160,000 RMB/mu in compensation, while the land use rights were then sold for housing for 2 to 4 million RMB/mu (Ding 2007:4-6). The biggest value gap in China exists on the outskirts of cities, where the high-value urban construction land encroaches hungrily upon the adjacent rural plots, and it is exactly in these peri-urban areas where most land conflicts take place. World Bank land expert John Bruce compares going from urban to rural land in terms of its value to falling off a cliff (Subrahmanyan 2004). Bruce argues that the only so-lution to ongoing land loss conflicts is decreasing this incentive and de-creasing the value gap between rural and urban land (*id.*). One way of doing so would be by making the construction land value the basis for compensation of rural land lost. The value gap is central in any under-standing of conflicts related to land-grabbing. The gap explains why there is such a struggle for land.

An additional manner in which VCs and local governments, espe-cially township and sometimes district level governments, benefit from the land transactions comes from the money that can be made from il-legally diverting compensation funds. In Xiaocun, the township leader-ship embezzled part of the compensation that the district government had to pay local farmers (Van Rooij 2006b:Ch. 9; Zhao 2003). Ironi-cally, this could mean that if farmers are able to negotiate a higher compensation from land developers, local governments have a greater incentive for embezzling such funds and thus as a result for participat-ing in land acquisitions with more land conflicts.

The fact that local governments and VCs are increasingly pressed for funding exacerbates the incentive for profiting from land transactions created by the land value gap and the possibility to embezzle compen-sation. While Deng Xiaoping's post-1978 reforms led to decentralisa-tion and extra local tax revenue, they also increased local government expenses as the local tasks and the local bureaucracy increased. The 1993 Tax Reforms had a major impact, giving local governments more tasks without additional revenues. Consequently, local governments have faced increasing budgetary deficits (Ding 2007:5). Land leasing is an increasingly important form of local government revenue. Ding pro-vides the example of Hangzhou city (3 million inhabitants) where twenty per cent of the municipal city's budget was derived from land revenues. 'Revenues generated from land can account to 60 per cent of total fiscal incomes of local governments' (Ding 2007). For village le-vel authorities the situation is different, yet similar. VCs, the directly elected bodies of village self-government, are not part of the state bureaucracy and thus do not receive state funding related to taxes. As such, these local officials who often have to spend considerable time in village management must be paid from local income. In all of the Yun-nan villages studied here, such income was largely related to profits made on land deals. Thus, local leadership is directly paid through money made from land acquisitions. A related problem is that local governments have lately lost tax revenue opportunities. This happened when the central government first decreased and then later abolished rural taxes, in order to lighten peasants' burdens. In many commu-nities, especially purely rural ones where local governments cannot tax industry, local fees or other taxes have for a long time continued to be levied in spite of the central level reforms.[34] However, once these new reforms take root and local governments can no longer tax their farm-ers, they will be further pressed to make use of income related to the farmers' land. Ironically, this might mean that the tax measures adopted to protect farmers could actually cause them to lose their land.

An additional local government pressure that explains increasing land loss conflicts arises from a need to develop arable land because such governments have to demonstrate local economic growth. Eco-nomic growth, whether in the form of urbanisation or industrialisa-tion, requires land conversions for building roads, factories, or hous-ing. [35] Within China's system of governance, the centre exercises con-trol over local governments through a vertical management system. Under this system, local governments are evaluated based on certain performance indicators. If they do well, local government leaders can receive bonuses and promotions, and if they fail they may be fined.[36] In the evaluation system (*kaohe*), economic growth and social stability are always the two main yardsticks against which success or failure are measured (Edin 2003; Huang 1996).[37]

In sum, the land value gap, the lack of local state and VC revenues, and the pro-growth pressure and strategy can explain why land preda-tors, in these cases local governments or VC leaders, have engaged in land transactions as a result of which farmers have lost land use rights without satisfactory compensation. This cannot explain, though, how land predators have been able to grab land, often in clear violation of the law, without successful opposition by those aggrieved or by the state whose laws and policies are aimed to prevent and stop such abuses. In other words, why have the land predators not been stopped, especially now that both local farmers and the central state have made it clear that they want these practices to end? In the next two sections we will discuss possibilities for keeping land predators at bay, first by discussing the farmers' options for redressing these situations, and sec-ond by discussing the state's efforts at punishing land predators who have violated the law.

Empowerment: What can farmers do? Legal and factual remedies

Given the existing strong incentives and needs, only an effective system of checks and balances can stop ongoing land abuses in China.
Such a system can exist in one of two manners, and would ideally exist
in both. First it can exist in a bottom-up manner, making local governments and land developers accountable to citizens and grass-roots organisations. Second, it can exist in a top-down manner, when higher level
state institutions are able to control local governments and land developers in such a way that they refrain from unfair land appropriations.
This section will address the bottom-up system and look at the actions
land-grab victims can take when faced with an unfair land acquisition.
It will also discuss farmers' legal and extra-legal options for controlling
land loss without satisfactory compensation.

A first observation is that judicial options – initiating civil or administrative litigation against unlawful behaviour of land developers or local government – have not been used much or with much success. In
the cases from peri-urban Kunming, the case of Yunnan studied, as
well as in the cases from other parts of China discussed so far, farmers
who lost their land did not turn to the courts, but instead resorted to
extra-legal factual measures to address their grievances.[38] This observation is supported by nationwide data on legal address for land-takings
which demonstrated that only 0.9 per cent of the aggrieved farmers
filed a lawsuit for more compensation (Zhu et al. 2006). Clearly, going
to court has not been a preferred option for land-loss victims.

A lack of legal and rights awareness is seen as a primary reason why
few farmers have gone to court.[39] Especially in more remote areas, literacy is still low, making legal awareness even more problematic. In
addition, in many cases farmers are informed of their rights by local
governments and local leaders who may not always tell them the full
content of such rights. On the other hand, farmers are increasingly
well informed about their rights. First, the central state has initiated
nationwide legal education campaigns (pufa) in which special attention
has been paid to the 1998 Land Management Act and the 2003 Rural
Land Contract Law, giving local governments little opportunity to dis-
tort the flow of information. Research has also demonstrated that farmers have increased knowledge of their land rights and know about the
30-year land use right regulations and the fact that these cannot be violated at will (Schwarzwalder et al. 2002). Peri-urban Kunming villagers
illustrate this. When asked about their land and their land rights, local
farmers there proudly talk about the 30-year land rights policy. Even in
areas where the level of knowledge was traditionally not high, there are
village activists who have started to study land legislation and land policies and who have used their self-obtained knowledge to start protests.

In one Yunnan case, a district government initially forced a village to provide 100 mu of arable land for a landscape theme park. When this land was not duly compensated and another 100 mu was to be requisitioned, one of the local farmers went to the local city bookshop to get books about the existing land laws. Through self-study, he learned about their rights, which eventually led to extra-legal protest.[40]

So if farmers have an increasing legal awareness, why do they not turn to the courts for protection? An initial answer to this question may be that successful civil and administrative litigation requires hiring a lawyer to take up the case.[41] Without a lawyer to defend their case and prepare such defence in accordance with China's increasingly complex procedural rules, most undereducated peasants do not stand a chance in court. One problem is that lawyers in China are highly risk averse and do not like taking on sensitive cases (Michelson 2006). Lawyers are therefore not inclined to take cases against local governments, whether civil or administrative, especially if they concern volatile, highly politicised matters such as land acquisitions (Peerenboom 2002a). In addition, farmers are not ideal clients, as they have little money to pay for a well-prepared defence, and their cases do not have a high potential for winning to start with. As lawyers in China are struggling to make ends meet, they tend to refuse cases with a low fee potential (id.). Lawyers' lack of independence from local governments further exacerbates matters, as lawyers do not wish to upset this relationship. Lawyers' fees form another obstacle for farmers, who often barely made a living when they still had their land. In the peri-urban Kunming villages in Yunnan, which are not poor by local standards, villagers rarely go to court, as they state that getting a lawyer is just too expensive. Only in cases such as divorce, when there is no alternative, do they go to court. In some areas legal aid clinics, especially at universities, have been set-up to help aggrieved citizens get their rights defended. In one Hunan case, a team of Tsinghua University lawyers got involved when residents who had protested a forced eviction from their homes had been detained without grounds (Fu 2004). Beijing-based lawyers in particular have become increasingly active in helping victims of national scandals, probably because of the fame such cases bring them.[42]

In the Hunan case, lawyers did not initiate litigation but sought negotiations instead, while petitioning higher levels of government. This shows that even if land-loss victims find legal aid, going to court is not always the preferred option. The reason for this is that the chances of winning a case against a local government or against land developers with good local connections are slim. Courts are paid and partly managed by their local governments and have tended not to bite the hand that feeds them. In addition, the context of judicial corruption and personal favours (*guanxi*) further denies poor peasants success in the courtroom. One problem is that the courts, like lawyers, have refused to take on land cases, claiming not to have jurisdiction or that litigants do not have a right of standing (Phan 2005:634). However, even if litigants are able to get their case tried in court, research about administrative law practice has demonstrated that the government has a much higher chance of winning (Peerenboom 2002a; Pei 1997). In a large number of cases, the court never reached a verdict, and plaintiffs instead settled with local governments and repealed their suits. Pei has argued that this has become part of citizens' strategies of getting the most out of administrative litigation. Such a strategy developed because the plaintiff's chance of winning a case is slim, while local governments are afraid of losing a case,[43] even though this rarely happens. Citizens have thus initiated administrative litigation in order to boost their negotiation power, in which they can threaten to pursue the case through to a verdict, unless some of the grievances are addressed (Pei 1997). Even if citizens do win a case in court, whether administrative or civil, such a winning verdict does not necessarily mean that they get their land back or that they get compensation. Executing judgments has been notoriously difficult in China, especially against powerful local actors (Chen 2002; Clarke 1996; Peerenboom 2002b).

Given these formidable obstacles to judicial remedies, aggrieved farmers have turned to other options available to them. An important method has been to send a formal letter of petition complaining about the local abuses to a higher level of government or part of the higher level bureaucracy. Such petitioning is a Chinese legacy that has continued throughout the communist era until today (O'Brien and Li 1995). All of China's bureaucracies have specialised bureaus complete with service counters to receive citizens' petitions. In Kunming one can see long lines of complainants waiting to hand in their petition to officials they hope can help them.

For land-loss cases petitioning the higher-level government, the state land resource management bureau or the construction bureau has become popular. Petitioning has been used much more widely than formal litigation. In Beijing, for example, the total number of real estate-related cases in court in 2003 was 3,948, while the petitions about land-related abuses in the first half of 2004 to the Ministry of Construction alone already numbered 18,620 (Phan 2005:634). In the cases studied from peri-urban Kunming in Yunnan, none of the aggrieved farmers attempted to petition higher-level governments about the matter. This is not to say that such petitioning does not occur in Yunnan province. In Qincun, a village some 200 kilometres south of Kunming, villagers lost several 100 Mu of arable land to a landscape theme park development project without satisfactory compensation.

Dissatisfied, one of the local villagers bought some legal books and found that their rights had been violated. When a second batch of land was to be taken, he tried to petition municipal and provincial level governments to stop the local township and district authorities from taking the land without paying in full. The district authorities reacted by arresting this local champion of the people, whom local villagers had started calling their own 'Deng Xiaoping' and placing him under arrest. This shows that petitioning is not devoid of danger, nor does it guarantee a successful intervention in the local context.[44]

The Qincun petition-related arrest is not an uncommon phenomenon in China. In Shishan village, in Fujian province, Lin Zengxu, a local land petitioner, was arrested by a local police squad of twelve men as he napped one afternoon. The police gave Lin a severe beating and wanted to take him away to jail. However, family, neighbours and friends were able to fight off the police and rescue the man who had for years tried to stop illegal land-grabbing and get higher compensation for farmers losing their land. Lin later escaped to Beijing (Cody 2004). Also in Fujian province, in Qingkou Town, another leader of a peasant protest movement against illegal land seizures, who had filed a higher-level petition, Xiao Xiangjin, tried to escape the police when they came to lift him from his bed in the middle of the night. At first, he was able to flee, though later, when boarding a plane to Beijing to submit a petition to the central government, he was detained and questioned at Fuzhou airport. Upon his return in Fuzhou, he was arrested and sent to a 're-education through labour' (*laojiao*) camp 'for having entertained prostitutes four times in his home and office at Qingkou' (*id.*). Only the provincial level authorities would have been able to detain Xiao Xiangjin at Fuzhou airport, which shows how high up the local protectionism in these kind of cases can run. If even the provincial level authorities are involved in protecting and covering up local land abuses, farmers have nowhere to go other than Beijing. Recently, even there, many petitioners have been detained or sent straight back in a central level effort to control some of the land-related protests (Phan 2005).

Even if higher-level authorities are willing to receive a petition and support the grievance made, the petition's impact on the local situation has often proved to be limited. When superior authorities are called in to investigate local scandals, a temporary measure may be taken. However, once the higher authorities leave and in some cases the press attention for the case subsides, the local elites may return to old practices while punishing those who have betrayed them (Peerenboom 2006).[45] An extreme case of this involved Li Changping, at the time a township party secretary in Hubei province, who wrote a complaint letter to prime minister Zhu Rongji about how local governments, from the vil-

lage to the district, had been maltreating local peasants. Li's letter was
at first successful as Zhu Rongji send a personal investigative team to
Li's district, and the team made strong recommendations for changes
to be implemented locally. However, as time passed, and subsequent
central-level missions felt satisfied that a real change had been made,
local power holders were able to reassert their influence. This was best
evidenced by the fact that Li Changping felt threatened in Hubei Province and had to move elsewhere, losing his position and home (Li
2002a).

Since the late 1990s, China's peasants have also been able to use village elections to voice their dissatisfaction with land-takings and seek
amelioration by installing new leadership. The central government set
up a system of self-government at the rural grass-roots in 1987.[46] During the 1990s the officers in the self-government were increasingly
elected democratically, especially after the 1998 new Organic Law on
Village Committees introduced truly direct elections with more candidates than positions (id.). Such elections have sometimes been used by
farmers against land malpractices. As previously discussed, Jiacun village in Yunnan is an example where villagers tried to nominate a mentally disabled person to partake in the elections as their village leader.
Although their nomination finally failed because of the nominee's
mental handicap, the attempted nomination did send a clear signal to
the incumbent village leader to pay attention to the villagers' demands.
In Jiacun there is now a good working system of *fenhong* (literally divid-
ing the red) which allows all villagers to share in the land-related profits, providing farmers with a per capita income of 2,000 RMB a year,
which increases according to land revenue increases (Van Rooij 2006b:
Ch. 7). In Qincun village in Yunnan, farmers did successfully elect a
new leader when they found that their old leaders had not secured sufficient compensation from state land developers. Their new leader actively tried to get more compensation when a new batch of land was to
be taken and was even arrested when he filed a petition with a higher-
level government.[47] However, elections have not been a successful tool
to voice land-related concerns in all cases. As we saw in Licun village
in Yunnan, for example, farmers who lost their land without satisfactory compensation have not tried to use the elections. They state that
the local elite that has just taken their land also dominates the election
process, and farmers stand no way to win against the families who
have controlled the village for decades and have strong connections
with government officials at higher levels. Similarly, elections offer no
protection against land-takings by higher-level authorities as they are
not directly elected. In the Xiaocun village, where the township-level
government had embezzled compensation funds, remedy through election was not possible (Van Rooij 2006b:Ch. 9). Given the weak legal

and participatory options farmers have against land-takings, in many cases they either do nothing or rise in physical protest. Licun village in Yunnan is a good example of the first scenario: even though the local elites have robbed local farmers of their land without paying satisfactory compensation, and even though it was the elites and not the community who benefited from the money made in these transactions, farmers have done nothing. When interviewed, they express cynicism and helplessness. None of them believes that going to court, petitioning, or elections will change existing power relationships. So far, their dissatisfaction has been kept inside. In Licun no active protest has erupted (Van Rooij 2006b).

Meanwhile, in many other villages in Kunming and China, helpless villagers have initiated protests, sometimes of a violent nature. There have been different reasons for protesting and different methods of protest. Some protests are initiated by villagers when they find out about unfair land-takings. This happened in the cases observed in Xiaocun and Jiacun village in Yunnan. In other cases, violence erupts when villagers protest against the imprisonment of one of their petitioners, as happened in the Dongwei case in Guangdong. One method of protest involves surrounding the leadership headquarters so that no one can enter or leave the building. This happened, for example, in Jiacun village in Yunnan when villagers felt they had been unduly compensated for land lost for the construction of a Buddhist temple.[48] Another method is going to the city to demand attention for the matter. One such case occurred on August 20, 2004, in Beijing, when hundreds of farmers blocked the capital's traffic with their bicycles and rickshaws in a desperate effort to vent their frustration about a new development project for the city's new rich seizing their land (Cody 2004). In other cases, protesters block or sabotage the construction project that is to take place on their land. This happened, for example, in Jiacun village where villagers cut the power lines of a new school construction project they felt they had not been properly compensated for.

Protests have led to violence. Ang writes: 'The clashes have become increasingly violent, with injuries sustained on both sides and huge amounts of damage done to property as protesters vent their frustration in the face of indifferent or bullying authorities' (Ang 2005). Catherine Baber, deputy Asia director at Amnesty International states: 'The increasing number of such disputes over land use across rural China and the use of force to resolve them suggest an urgent need for the Chinese authorities to focus on developing effective channels for dispute resolution' (id.).

In conclusion, farmers have had weak weapons against land abuses. Judicial and other institutional options have not been able to protect them from land-takings. Farmers are left with no alternatives but acceptance or outright protest, sometimes even combined with violence. There are two important points to be made. First, from the cases studied in Kunming, activism seems to occur in places where farmers have sufficient autonomy from local leadership. In Jiacun and Qincun where farmers were most active, local income was to a large extent related to non-local sources, sources independent of the local leaders involved in the land abuses. In contrast, Licun villagers, who have not done anything against much clearer and worse land-takings, mainly depend on agriculture that is largely controlled by the local elites. A second observation is that most of the action against land-takings is of a disorganised or at least of a locally organised type. There has not been a national or even provincial or municipal organisation in which aggrieved farmers try to combine their weak positions into larger, stronger institutions to fight those who have taken their land. This is not surprising given China's current political context, in which local protest is condoned as long as it does not directly criticise the central government or become a larger organisation that can indirectly threaten the party's supremacy.

Street-level bureaucracy: The important role of state enforcement and its failure due to local protectionism

In order to deal with land-loss conflicts, the state has instituted a system of laws and regulations combined with an enforcement system to punish and stop violations of such norms. The state has established an institutional land management structure at all levels of administration from the centre in Beijing to the township level. Informally, the state bureaucracy even penetrates into China's 1 million villages and even larger number of sub-villages. There VC leaders are responsible for implementation of the land law, supposedly working under the supervision of the township-level governmental land bureau.

So far, most studies of land conflicts have paid scant attention to the role these state institutions have played in the land-loss conflicts. As detailed above, part of the problem may be that the norms themselves are insufficient to protect farmers; however, an equally important problem is that the existing norms are violated – and thus also future amended and improved norms. There is an enforcement problem, which is especially serious now that we know that farmers themselves have not been successful in securing their rights.

The enforcement is largely left to the State Land Resource Protection Bureaus (SLBs). The law provides for different sanctions for various violations related to the LML's norms for protecting farmers from unfair takings. The sanctions mainly cover the unprocedural taking of land, for which violators can be ordered to give back such land, to pay back illegal proceeds, to pay fines related to the illegal proceeds, and in extreme cases even be criminally prosecuted through the criminal justice system (LML § 73, 77, 76).

If the Chinese state wishes to squash illegal or unfair land-takings, why has it not been able to do so? The main problem is a lack in vertical reach. Here it is important to understand China's current grass-roots system of governance. In China's current system, local state institutions are to a large extent independent of control either by higher-level state organs or by local citizens. The lack of state vertical control over local-level bureaucracies results from the fragmentation of governmental power that originated in the post-1978 reform programme.[49] Cohen writes, 'contrary to American images of the PRC as a ruthlessly effective authoritarian regime whose writ runs from the Standing Committee of the Politburo in Beijing to the most remote hamlet, in many respects contemporary Chinese government resembles a series of feudal baronies more than a totalitarian dictatorship' (Cohen 2001).

As a result of the post-1978 *de facto* devolutionary governance set-up, local governments are largely autonomous of higher levels of administration. The Kunming Land Bureau is subordinate to the provincial SLB and the provincial government. In practice, of these two 'masters' the provincial government is the strongest, because it controls the bureau's budget and leadership appointments (see next sections).[50] Law enforcement is largely left to bureaus (SLBs) that reside under the lowest local governments at township and district levels. Such bureaus used to be paid and staffed by the local government. Thus, they are ill equipped to enforce the law against such local governments who are in many cases directly involved in illegal land practices. As a result, enforcement has been weak as local land bureaus protected the interests of the local elites, a practice called *'difang baohu zhuyi'* (local protectionism).

A second problem is that the enforcement bureaus lack the legal authority to act against some compensation violations. For cases in which compensation was not paid in compliance with legal standards, either because the amount of compensation offered and paid was below the legal standards or the amount of compensation promised was not paid in full, the land bureau has no clear enforcement authority. Only if compensation is embezzled can the embezzler be prosecuted and fined (LML § 79, Criminal Code § 271, 272, 382, 384, 342). In other cases, the bureau has no direct enforcement authority. In such cases, the Kunming SLB explained that they will try to negotiate a better compensation for the farmers with the land-grabbing actors. In order to exercise power in such negotiations, the land bureau in Kunming has used its authority over land use approval as leverage by denying approval until full compensation or more satisfactory compensation is paid.[51]

Apart from the local protectionism and the lack of legal enforcement authority, enforcement bureaus suffer from internal problems. The first problem is that they lack funding. Deficient funding has partly caused goal displacement, as enforcement bureaus have had to engage in entrepreneurialism in order to pay their staff. They do so through *shiye danwei*, semi-subordinate agencies who carry out consultancy and other commercial activities. The Kunming SLB's enforcement department has a staff of 22, of which only sixteen are paid through regular funds.[52] The other six must thus be paid through other means.[53] Because of the meagre funding, the Kunming SLB enforcement division lacks staff and cars to carry out their inspection work properly for such a large region. Second, the quality of the staff is problematic for enforcement. Land Bureaus have had problems in attracting the right kind of staff. In the post-Cultural Revolution 1980s and early 1990s, China, and especially peripheral provinces such as Yunnan, did not have a large number of university graduates at the Bachelor (*benke*), let alone the Master (*suoshi*) level. The predecessors of the SLBs were established during this period. Therefore, they had to start by employing staff with a lower level of education, with at most professional two-year degrees (*dazhuan*) or several years of working experience (cf. Li 2004:167; Tang et al. 1997:869). Recently, staff educational standards have been raised, especially for enforcement personnel: all new staff must have passed the civil servants exam, for which a Bachelor's degree is compulsory. Moreover, enforcement agents also need an enforcement permit, which requires extra training.[54] The Kunming SLB has recently been able to attract two new enforcement agents with a Master's degree. Third, weak personnel incentives and controls further explain China's ineffective enforcement performance regarding land-taking. The internal structure and management procedures in the land bureaus are insufficient to ensure job conformity of enforcement agents.[55] Consequently, bureaus risk their agents shirking their duties. Finally, land bureaus are largely centrally managed institutions in which the bureau's leadership has a final (direct or indirect) influence on almost all major personnel decisions (except for their own positions) (Van Rooij 2006b). This has strengthened local protectionism, because local governments, through their power over appointing the powerful bureau leadership, have a strong indirect influence on all bureau personnel decisions.

The central government has recognised the need to improve its performance and strengthen its action against illegal land-takings. This is no easy task as it faces formidable obstacles such as local protectionism, weak bureaus, and difficult enforcement procedures. As for other enforcement problems,[56] the state has organised political campaigns to enhance the enforcement of land law. The first campaigns were organised in 1997 and 1998, mainly attempting to stop further loss of arable land and to prepare for the introduction of the 1998 LML. In 2003 another campaign was organised to stop ongoing illegal and irregular land practices, especially to stop the further development of economic development zones, which were an important reason for farmers losing their land. Nationwide data reported just after the campaigns of late 2003 and early 2004 were optimistic. According to those reports, the campaign detected more than 170,000 illegal land-use cases, in 128,000 of which sanctions were issued (Editorial 2004b).[57] Furthermore, during the campaign, 732 governmental officials received internal disciplinary sanctions (*chufen*) for their involvement in these cases, and 134 individuals were prosecuted under criminal law. Similarly, national reports proudly announced that the campaign had been successful in curbing the illegal land used for so-called development zones. Of the 5,658 development zones that existed, 2,046 (over 35 per cent), were disbanded during the 2003 campaigns (Editorial 2003b). Furthermore, the Ministry of National Land Resources published nine model violation cases, five in November and four in December, which it had detected and severely punished, just as the campaign had planned (Editorial 2004a). These national data are not the full story, however. The validity of the data presented in the reports is doubtful, like that of any data in China.[58] An indication of this is found in our fieldwork. When we first started our research in Kunming in January 2004, the 2003 campaign had just ended. By that time, the 2003 campaign had not affected local villages such as Jiacun, Licun, and Xiaocun, as the national reports would lead us to believe. Some of the violations discussed above were still ongoing in early 2004, and the 2003 campaigns had not stopped them or even addressed them in any way. In one of the townships where research was carried out, Kouxiang Township, a development zone still existed in 2004. Even though the 2003 campaign aimed to curb all further development of such zones, especially by township governments, the Kouxiang government proudly explained their development zone work to me in May 2004.[59]

Apart from the campaigns, the central government also tried to address the many land-loss conflicts through a reform, recentralising the devolutionary land enforcement structures. In this reform, called the 'vertical management reform', the provincial level's control over land management and enforcement is to be strengthened (Ye 2004:6). The reform has just started, and from Kunming we know that there the lowest levels of land management administration, city district level bureaus, were converted into offices directly subordinate to the municipal level SLB, which will allocate their resources and appoint their person-

nel.[60] In Jiacun Township, the newly vertically reformed SLB Township
office is worried about its new inspection responsibility. As one of the
agents told me, 'In the past our work was easy, we just did what our
township government wanted, but now we have to inspect for the District SLB, and they do not want to consider our local conditions. We
fear that there will be conflicts between our new superiors and our local leaders'. The vertical management reform has not taken away the
conflict of interests and powers that lies at the heart of local protectionism so it seems. The question is whether the recentralised land bureaus will be strong enough to enforce the law against local elites such
as township-level governments and VC leaders.

Conclusion

If land tenure legalisation is seen as the process where possession (including use) and management (power to decide) of a tract of land is incorporated into the legal system, whereby the rights and obligations of
individuals and collective entities are defined, China's 1998 LML and
the 2003 RLCL are legalisation projects. Although the implementation
of both laws, in terms of awareness of the new rights, as well as the
signature of land contracts and the issuance of land certificates is remarkable, the sharp rise in land-loss conflicts warns that land tenure
security is still lacking, perhaps even more so than before. In China it
seems that land tenure legalisation has increased the breadth and the
duration of land use rights with the 1998 and 2003 laws, but it has
done so without increasing the assurance. The single largest threat to
farmers' security in exercising their new rights is the widespread and
often illegal taking of their land without satisfactory compensation.

   Land-loss conflicts continue in China for a number of reasons. They
occur first of all because the value gap between arable land and construction land makes land conversion and thus forced land acquisitions
highly profitable. Current legislation is to blame as it fails to provide
clarity on the circumstances under which land can be taken away from
farmers and on who originally owns such land. In addition, current
legislation fails to provide standards of compensation that are satisfactory and fails to give farmers sufficiently strong rights to negotiate for
compensation they deem sufficient. Legislative problems are further
exacerbated because of the weak checks and balances on local governments and VCs that engage in land acquisition practices; neither farmers themselves nor the state have been successful in guaranteeing that
land acquisition is done according to present legal standards. Given the
current weak checks and balances and the resultant weak implementation of law, it is doubtful whether changes in legislation alone are suffi-

cient to decrease current land-loss conflicts. It seems rather that legislative changes should be combined with measures that help to enhance implementation. Such measures should be a combination of improving state law enforcement action against violations of the law, and increasing possibilities for access to justice for aggrieved farmers.

Behind the weak checks and balances, and thus a major cause for the ongoing land-loss conflicts, are not so much legal or socio-legal problems, but rather political problems related to the existing power relations. At present, elites consisting of VC leaders, various local governments, and land developers have been able to co-opt many of the arrangements that have been introduced to protect weak and poor farmers. When sufficiently powerful, such elites have influenced the functioning of courts and lawyers; they have influenced the effectiveness of petitions and law enforcement; they have even undermined local VC elections meant to directly affect their power and the accountability of VC leadership. At its heart, the current land-loss crisis is thus one of power, involving weak farmers and strong elites. Future reforms should be directed at such power imbalances, and as with any institutional change adopted, the risk of elite co-optation should be considered.

Enhancing land tenure security in China therefore involves empowerment of the weak and poor. Such empowerment first involves enhancing their access to the legal system. Some scholars and practitioners working on general issues of access to justice in a context of development, including Anderson and the UNDP, look for broad access to justice solutions that involve reforms in the state sector, including changing current legislation to better represent the interests of the poor and weak, decreasing costs of litigation, stimulating the independence of the courts, and enhancing the capabilities for enforcing court judgements (Anderson 2003; UNDP 2004a). Given the extent of current power asymmetries in China, such methods may not be sufficient. Perhaps more radical empowerment options that go beyond improving access to justice[61] are necessary, reforms that would directly affect the power relations. Here Golub's work is important, which argues that apart from work on legislation and legal assistance, direct work on changing the power relations and thus empowering the poor is important (Golub 2000, 2006; Golub and McClymont 2000). He argues that to achieve this, the role of civil society is essential, while work should also focus on general development activities such as literacy training, strengthening community organisation, and legal awareness promotion. For the case of land-loss conflicts in China, one could think of several measures, including allowing farmers more freedom to organise themselves, allowing NGOs more freedom of operation in representing the interests of the disenfranchised, installing direct elections at higher levels of government, at least at the township[62] and probably also at the district level, and in general granting greater freedom of association, speech, and press. While there is no indication that at present the CCP is willing to introduce such reforms, the seriousness of current protest and social unrest related to land-loss cases may in time convince the CCP leadership to take such steps.

Notes

1   Van Vollenhoven Institute for Law Governance and Development, Faculty of Law, Leiden University, the Netherlands. B.vanrooij@law.leidenuniv.nl.
2   In contrast to LML § 16 and Administrative Review Law 1999 § 30.
3   By 2005, however, a survey found that land redistributions were on the rise again, and the percentage of villages without such redistributions had dropped to about 70 per cent (Zhu et al. 2006:794).
4   For the detailed methodology and case descriptions see Van Rooij 2006b: Ch.1, 7-10.
5   By tenure security following Bruce and Migot-Adholla, we mean 'the perceived right by the possessor of a land parcel to manage, and use the parcel, dispose of its produce and engage in transactions, including the temporary or permanent transfers without hindrance or interference from any person or corporate identity, on a continuous basis' (Bruce and Migot-Adholla 1994:3).
6   Here we follow Bruce and Migot-Adholla (1994:4) who distinguish the extent (robustness), duration and certainty (assurance).
7   The names of all Yunnan villages in which fieldwork was carried out have been changed in order to protect the identities of those interviewed.
8   The Village Committee is a self-elected body of village self-government. It forms a self-government of the village collective of which all villagers are members. Within villages there are sometimes also sub-villages or small groups which have their own directly elected bodies of self-government, the small group committee. The VCs and small groups are not part of the state structure but are controlled to a certain extent through party cells and the village party secretary of the Chinese Communist Party (CCP). The state levels of administration run from the centre (in Beijing) to the provincial, the municipal, the districts, and the township level. In this chapter local governments refer to all sub-national levels of governments, but in many cases especially the district and township governments.
9   This case is based on interviews with a Chinese scholar who has extensively worked in the village where these events took place. He has published about pre-1997 crime and punishment in this peri-urban village, see Zhu 2003. The case described here is further supported by our fieldwork in neighbouring villages in which the facts of the case were corroborated by local villagers and village leadership and through interviews with the Kunming land bureau, Department of Compensation officials.
10 One Mu is about 660 square metres.
11 Our findings here contrast with those of Pastor and Tan (2000:511) who argue that free elections can be a source of stability in the village. In Liujia and surrounding villages, elections have been highly contentious and have been used to vent dissatisfaction. Periods of election are quite unstable and unruly here. Ordinarily, protests consist of petition letters or physical action, but as we see here election can also be used to protest (cf. O'Brien and Li 1995). For an overview of how the village election sys-

tem was set up in the 1980s and 1990s, see O'Brien 1994. Another case of election as a form of protest is described in Liu 2000b.

12 O'Brien (1996:43) has noted that protest in China is a question of forum shopping at as many fora as possible.

13 This is much less than farmers get in Liujia village. Liujia farmers get about 5,000-10,000 per year per Mu.

14 This phenomenon of local governments or VCs making high profits on land deals has been widely reported. See for example Ding 2007; Phan 2005; Subrahmanyan 2004.

15 See LML § 49, as well as § 26 of the 1998 State Council LML Implementing Regulations. Since the 2007 Property Law this has changed, as it regulates that compensation be paid to the holder of land rights. See § 132 Property Law.

16 This division depends on the type of case. There is quite some legal ambiguity on this point. Until 2007, the law (RCLC art. 16.2) stipulated on the one hand that land use rights holders are entitled to compensation, while on the other hand the 1998 LML Implementing Regulations provided that the compensation paid belongs to the collective ownership of the village, without specifying how it is to be divided amongst rights holders. In practice, it seems that in some villages rights holders who have lost land are compensated directly for the amount of land lost. In other villages the compensation is paid equally to all collective members as an annual dividend following the collective profits. In such cases land reallocations may take place to compensate land rights lost by those rights holders directly affected by the land transfer.

17 See RLCL § 16 and the explanation about this article by the NPC-SC Legal Affairs Bureau (NPC SC Legal Affairs Office 2002: § 45). It seems logical that the same standards contained in the LML and the 2007 Property Law would apply.

18 Based on interviews with enterprises in Yunnan. See Van Rooij 2006b: Ch. 9.

19 Also in this case, even though it is illegal, the letter of the law provides farmers with the right to compensation (RLCL § 16). As said, the law here provides no detail about how much is payable and how it is to be paid.

20 Exceptions are construction projects for farmers' use or for village collective use, such as schools or housing. LML § 43.1

21 For a detailed analysis of this point see Ho 2001.

22 The new property law has not clarified the ownership issue. See Ping et al., this volume.

23 Farmers can also lose their land use rights to the collective if the collective needs farmland for *gonggong sheshi* (public facilities) or *gongyi shiye* (public utilities). LML § 65.

24 Such a change was not made in the 2007 Property Law. See Ping et al., this volume. A reason cited by Chinese scholars working for China's Ministry of National Land Resources is that a strict definition is not yet possible in China's current rapid developmental situation (Fan et al. 2003:33).

25 The LML provides for a standard of compensation six to ten times the annual average output value of the three proceeding years and a resettlement fee of four to six times average annual output. The law also provides absolute combined compensation maxima of no higher than fifteen times annual output or when approved by provincial authorities no higher than 30 times the annual output of the land compensated. The specific standards are determined at the provincial level. Both Village Committees and farmers are to be consulted in the requisition compensation. Compensation payment shall be made public, and the new act explicitly states that it is forbidden to embezzle or divert compensation funds (LML § 47, 48, 49).

26 Even during the LML amendment approval process, there was criticism. During the law-making process, commentators, including local governments, complained that

the proposed compensation was too low, that the procedure lacked transparency, that a hearing for farmers should be instituted, and that payment of compensation should be done in public. Finally, some thought that monetary compensation was not sufficient and farmers should be helped in finding new employment. In reaction, the NPC Legal Committee held that the amount of the compensation fee is a difficult issue and that circumstances vary from place to place. Therefore, the committee found that it is impossible to improve the draft to cover all points raised concerning compensation. The Committee did make suggestions for changing the draft to allow for more transparency by instituting a hearing, making payment of fees public, and a rule that local governments should do their best to help farmers who have lost their land to start enterprises. These suggestions made it into the final law (NPC Legal Committee 1998:316).

27 The word *zhanyong* (occupation) in this clause indicates the revocation of household land use rights by the village collective according to the legislative explanation issued with the RLCL (NPC SC Legal Affairs Office 2002:45).

28 It uses the word *zhengshou*, which literally means to levy or impose, but which according to the legislative interpretation of the law means that the state takes collective or private property (Wang 2007:87).

29 Again this has not been done in the new Property Law of 2007. See Ping et al., this volume.

30 Phan states that the process of expropriation has been a vital problem for farmers. We are not convinced by the support she provides for this conclusion. In our view, the process is often only mentioned in order to get better compensation. This opinion is based on the cases studied in Kunming, where as long as satisfactory compensation was pai,d nobody cared for the correct procedures, which were often not followed anyway (cf. Phan 2005).

31 For more detail, see note 419.

32 Ding notes, however, that compensation based on market value requires well-defined property rights and functioning real estate markets, both of which China at present lacks (Ding 2007:8).

33 Mostly district and township levels of governments. For an overview of different levels of state administration, see note 402.

34 Good examples can be found in Chen and Chun who have detailed how farmers in Anhui have attempted to protest against illegal tax practices, a situation in many ways similar to the land-grabbing discussed here (Chen and Chun 2004).

35 Because of China's legacy of a planned economy and the economic decentralisation since 1978 in which local governments got to own and invest in local enterprises, local governments have retained close ties with local industry and thus also benefit themselves from local economic development, which then forms an important revenue for China's poor local bureaucracies (Phan 2005; also quoting Zhang 2002).

36 For more detail see Chou 2005: 45-47.

37 For the link between this and weak enforcement see Liu 2000a: 1.

38 Of course there have been some instances where citizens have made use of courts. Examples can be found in Phan (2005: 633) who details urban acquisition cases from Liaoning in which neighbourhood organisations have made use of legal aid support to get their rights asserted.

39 For a good study of legal awareness in China from the 1990s, see Gao 2000. For a more recent study about urban awareness and litigiousness, see Michelson 2003.

40 Based on an interview with a local Yunnan researcher, April 2006. For similar examples of how local self-study has led to protest, see Chen and Chun 2004.

41 Having a lawyer as a representative is not compulsory in China's civil and administrative procedure. The law dictates that citizens have the right to be represented by one. Civil Procedure Code § 49, 58, Administrative Litigation Law § 29.

42 Good examples are the Sun Zhigang case where a team of Beijing lawyers was able to influence the State Council to revoke regulations on detaining citizens without proper papers and the Songhua pollution case where a team of Beijing lawyers tried to file a public interest litigation suit.

43 Due to the harm this causes their reputation as undisputed leaders, locally representing the CCP.

44 Based on interviews with local researchers in April 2006.

45 Peerenboom provides data from several provinces showing how rare effective responses to petitions are.

46 For an overview of this process see Liu 2000a; Manion 1996; O'Brien 1994; O'Brien and Li 2000; Shi 1999; Xu 1997.

47 Based on interviews with local researchers, April 2006.

48 It is interesting to note that this manner of protest was also used by Falungong members in 1999 when they surrounded the CCP headquarters, Zhongnanhai (Human Rights Watch 2002).

49 Lieberthal and Lampton have used the term 'fragmented authoritarianism' to describe this phenomenon (Lampton 1987; Lieberthal 1992, 1995; Lieberthal and Oksenberg 1988).

50 Most literature on environmental enforcement in China recognises these issues. See for example Jahiel 1997, 1998 (reprinted in 2000); Ma and Ortolano 2000; Sinkule and Ortolano 1995.

51 Interview with Kunming Land Bureau, 3 December 2004.

52 Based on an interview with enforcement staff of the Kunming SLB.

53 It is not clear how this is done as Kunming informants refused to explain at the time of interview.

54 Based on interviews with SLB enforcement and personnel staff, autumn 2004.

55 For an elaborate account of this problem, see Van Rooij 2006b: Ch. 13.

56 See, for example, the enforcement of pollution control regulation, Van Rooij 2006a.

57 For older reports see Editorial 2003a.

58 The problem of positive bottom-up reporting is well known in China. A lack of accountability and transparency makes it difficult for higher levels to get trustworthy information from subordinate departments.

59 For details, see Van Rooij 2006b: Ch. 14.

60 Based on an interview with the Kunming SLB, Personnel Department, 3 December 2004. This is also what the State Council Notice of 2004 orders SLBs to do (Council 2004).

61 Gready and Elsnor (2005) call the access to justice-based forms of empowerment the legal reflex.

62 There have been experiments with this already (Li 2002b).

17 Peri-urban land tenure legalisation: A tale of two districts[1]

Ye Jianping and Wu Jian

Introduction

In this study we will take a closer look at two peri-urban areas in China that illustrate land tenure insecurity and illegal tenure situations in such areas, and also look at subsequent state attempts to legalise illegal tenure and to take a pro-active stance in policy formulation that attempts to prevent the development of illegal tenure and achieve balanced rural-urban development. The first case is the Bao'an district in Shenzhen city, in which we focus on illegal land use by farmers and on the government's attempt to bring this phenomenon to an end by recognising and legalising illegal land use, as well as by construction. The second case is the Dongli District of the Tianjin municipality. It is the pilot site of a national project, called the Small Cities and Towns Project, which aims to prevent the development of new situations of illegal tenure and to achieve balanced urban-rural economic development, controlled urbanisation, the protection of tenure security, and the capitalisation of farmers' fixed assets.

Before delving into the details of these cases, we present a very brief review of the rural land tenure structure in China, the key processes leading to urbanisation, and the problems this brings. The interplay of these factors sets the stage for our discussion of the governmental efforts in the two case studies to legalise illegal land tenure and prevent the development of new illegal tenure situations.

Rural areas and the drive for urbanisation

Rural land tenure and rights

The preceding country study provides an overview of the evolution of land tenure in the People's Republic of China. It specifically shows the changes in the rural land tenure regime: when the Chinese Communist Party came to power in 1949, private ownership was soon replaced with collective ownership, which in turn subsequently gave way to the Household Responsibility System – a type of contracted land use right – and to further attempts to strengthen tenure security through the introduction of policies and laws, in particular the Rural Land Contracting Law (RLCL). Apart from cultivated land, another equally valuable asset held by farmers in China is their rural houses. According to law, farmers own their houses, but the land on which these houses are built, named the Rural Residential Land Site (RRLS), belongs to the collective. Figure 17.1 is a graphical representation of the dualist rural land system in China. By dualist we mean that land is owned by the collective as long as it is used by the collective – for agriculture, farmers' residences, or collective enterprises – but needs to be requisitioned by the government when the land is converted to other uses.

Urbanisation

China displays a huge income gap between the urban and rural populations. There is also a virtual absence of medical and education facilities in rural areas. This can partly be explained by unbalanced development polices that have favoured cities over rural areas. As a result, coastal cities and cities in the east have witnessed one of the most amazing economic growth phenomena in history. Recognising the plight of the rural poor, the agenda of the Communist Party now aims to let the rural population share in the fruits of economic growth. This is seen not only as a humane side of development but also as a key to ensuring social stability. The solution they envisage lies in increased urbanisation, which is one of the key measures that the government is currently advocating to improve the livelihoods of China's 800 million farmers.

In the last decades, rapid industrialisation and the flow of international capital into China have already brought about urbanisation. China's economic development since 1978 has been miraculous, with an annual GDP growth of over ten per cent and the urbanisation rate having increased from 17.9 per cent in 1978 to 41.7 per cent in 2004. In a period of 26 years the urban population has increased by 366 million, and it is forecast that in 2020 the urbanisation rate will reach 60 per cent, i.e. an urban population increase of a further 360 million. Currently, there are 660 cities in China with a total population of 520 million, while some 800 million people live in rural areas. Even if the current urbanisation rate remains stable, 20 million rural residents will be moving into the cities every year. In 2000, the Central Committee of the Communist Party and the State Council issued Opinions on Promoting the Healthy Development of Small Cities and Towns, which stated: 'The timing and condition are mature for expediting the process of urbanisation. To seize the opportunity, it is time to direct the healthy development of small towns. This should be an important task for current and future rural reform and development.'[2]

Figure 17.1   *Graphical representation of the Chinese rural land tenure system*

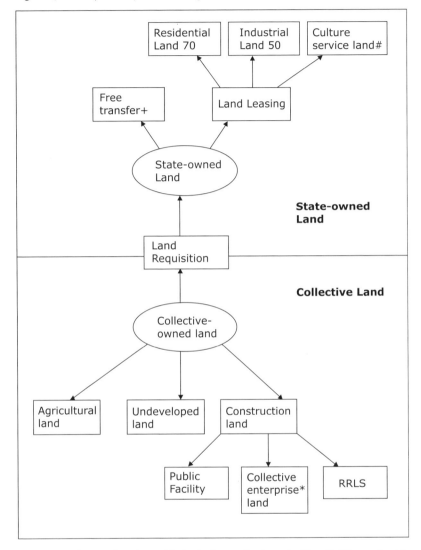

Notes: +: Land is transferred to public institutions, schools, and military facilities and public infrastructure free of charge.

*: Also commonly known as town and village enterprises.

#: culture and service land refers to land leased to culture and service industries.

However, urbanisation is a double-edged sword. Manufacturing-led urbanisation will inevitably bring about encroachment on agricultural land. Thus, choosing the right way for urbanisation to progress is of crucial importance. China is the most populous country in the world. Although food security and self-sufficiency have always been high on the political and economic agenda of the Communist Party, China's 0.11 ha of land per capita is less than half of the world's average of 0.23 ha (MLR 1999). According to the 11th National Five-Year Plan, by the end of 2010, the total arable land area should not fall below 18 billion mu[3] (Xinhua News Net 2007-4-12). Rapid urbanisation, industrialisation, population growth, and natural disasters are all culpable for arable land loss in China. A total cropland area of nearly 10 million ha was converted into built-up, forest/pastures, or horticultural lands, or was destroyed by disasters in the years between 1987 and 2000. And even after taking into account the land area added by land reclamation and rehabilitation of abandoned lands, the net loss of cropland area is still a stunning 4.5 million ha during that period (Tan 2005:187).

According to statistics from the Ministry of Land and Natural Resources (MLR), in 2006 the area of cultivated land that was used for construction purposes was 3.878 million mu (258,500 ha) (Xinhua News Net). The major part of this land is situated in peri-urban areas. These areas have experienced the most dynamic economic growth as a result of urban sprawl and industrialisation, which enhances the need for land to accommodate more people and on which to build factories. For instance, a frenzy of 'enclosure' spread quickly in many Chinese cities in the early 2000s. Local governments, at different administrative levels, were competing with one another to establish 'economic development zones' – designated industrial zones that attract both domestic and foreign investment with favourable policies, such as land leased below the market price. Although these zones sped up economic development, they also took up a substantial amount of good quality farmland in peri-urban areas. In addition, many of these zones set up by local governments were illegal, and consequently the land given to land users was also illegal. The central government was soon alarmed by the loss of farmland and called an immediate halt to these practices. By the end of 2006, the number of development zones was reduced from 6,877 to 1,568, and the total area designated for this purpose decreased accordingly from 38,600 km to 9,949 km.

Land requisition and rural conflicts

Between 1990 and 2002, 66.3 million farmers lost their agricultural land through requisitioning by the state. Naturally this brings about rural conflicts. It is thus not surprising that among the 130 cases of major rural conflicts since 2004, 87 are land related (Southern Weekend 2004-09-02). According to Guo, 'land expropriation has been one of the "externalities of development", primarily responsible for the proliferation of rural conflicts in China' (Guo 2001a). In order to prevent further violence, prime minister Wen Jiabao urged, 'We must protect the democratic rights and provide material benefits to rural citizens' (NY Times, 2006-1-20). It is worth mentioning here that the root of the resentment of, or resistance to, land expropriation is not just a reaction on the part of the farmers to protect themselves against infringements of their tenure security and rights. The roots of rural conflicts can also be attributed to the rise in rights consciousness among farmers as well as their increasing expectations and demands of compensation for requisitioned land. Two-thirds of the farmers affected by land-taking are not satisfied with the amount of compensation they receive (Zhu et al. 2006). The land's value multiplies many times after its conversion from farmland to construction land and as a result of public investment in infrastructure and facilities such as water and electricity. Therefore, farmers are usually unhappy with the compensation even if the amount is not low when compared to the land's agricultural productivity – which is the land valuation method used. However, the farmers want to share in the land price appreciation. This is a controversial issue among policy-makers and academics because there is no 'market' for rural land to provide a benchmark value. Farmland's value only materialises after it has been requisitioned and become state-owned and re-zoned for development. Unlike in a market economy, where the value of land is appraised from a third-party perspective by a professional company, in China no such company exists, and as a result the government gauges the value of rural land based on the agricultural productivity of the land (Zweig 2000:128).[4]

Farmers' resentment toward compensation packages is understandable, because for many of them, land is a life-long insurance. Losing farmland implies the possible loss of sustainable livelihood. Although the law stipulates that after land requisition farmers' standard of living should not decrease, it is sometimes difficult for farmers to retain the same standard of living due to the lack of training and work opportunities, without which the compensation package alone cannot sustain them for long.

Illegal land markets

After the conversion of collective farmland into state-owned construction land, land will be eligible for paid transfer on the land markets. Land users will get the land through bidding or auction and pay a land-transfer fee to the government. However, if a collective organisation, be it a village or township, illegally rents out collective land to urban land users without going through the ownership conversion process, the collective organisation can earn rent while the new land users pay a lower rent than for state-owned land. Thus, an incentive is present for both the land user and the collective to enter into illegal transactions. An eye-catching event frequently reported in the Chinese media in recent times illustrates this issue. House prices in major Chinese cities have increased by leaps and bounds during the last few years. Some peri-urban collectives in Beijing (and in other major cities such as Guangzhou) snatched the opportunity and began to build on collective-owned land. This is forbidden by law, as farmland can only be used for agricultural purposes, RRLS, or collective enterprises. For non-agricultural purposes, including construction use, land has to be requisitioned and become state-owned before it can be leased to land users for 40, 50, or 70 years, depending on the type of land use. Of the approximately 400 residential real-estate projects currently selling residential plots in Beijing, eighteen per cent percent, or 72 project sites, which cover a total area of about 7.2 million m, are found on collective land.[5] Houses built on collective land are much cheaper than those built on state-owned land since real-estate developers do not pay the government for the conversion of land from collective to state-owned. The Bureau of Land in Beijing has called a halt to the sale of such 'illegal houses', but it has not come up with a solution as to how to deal with those houses that have already been sold, especially given the fact that some of the transactions took place years before. This presents a dilemma for the government: on the one hand, if it accepts those residents living on collective land, collectives and house buyers will be encouraged to build and buy such houses; on the other hand, if it evicts the residents and demolishes the building, social unrest and conflict will be unavoidable.

In the following sections two attempts to deal with such situations are presented: the first is an example of ex-post legalisation, and the second illustrates government efforts to prevent the creation of new illegal land use and constructions through policy-making. They allow a closer look at government policy responses to the challenges posed by land use conversion and land tenure in peri-urban areas.

Case 1: Bao'an District, Shenzhen City

Setting the scene

In 1980, four cities, Shenzhen, Zhuhai, Shantou, and Xiamen were designated as 'special economic zones'. These cities served as 'experimental sites' for market-led economic reform and open-door policy. In fact, the first experiment with a market-based, 'paid' urban land use system took place in Shenzhen.[6] In less than three decades, Shenzhen has transformed itself from a small, tranquil fishing village into one of the most vibrant Chinese cities in terms of economic development and innovation. In 2005, its GDP exceeded 64 billion US dollars, and its GDP per capita was 8000 US dollars, the highest GDP in China. Shenzhen consists of six districts: Futian, Luohu, Nanshan, Yantian, Bao'an, and Longgang. In this study, our area of focus is Bao'an district which covers an area of 733 km. As urban land can hardly supply the land needed for economic development, land users are lured to peri-urban areas with collective agricultural land. Farmers or rural collectives welcome these land users, as they can reap higher gains from land rented out than from agricultural production.

In Bao'an city we find many 'illegal' land use practices. Not only is the use of rural land for construction purposes illegal (not having gone through the due conversion procedures from collective to state ownership), but the structures, both industrial and residential, built on such unconverted land are also considered illegal. The Bao'an government has sought to legalise illegal land use and illegal buildings. They have divided the illegal land use and buildings into three categories based on the date they came into existence: before March 5, 1999; between March 5, 1999 and October 31, 2003; and after October 31, 2003. For each category, they set the conditions for legalisation, and the longer the illegal land use and buildings date back, the less stringent the conditions are.

Social and economic factors behind illegal land use

The rapid pace of industrialisation and urbanisation in Shenzhen drives a gradual encroachment on the rural land on which farmers' livelihood has depended for generations. The requisition of rural land and its conversion into state-owned construction land make farmers feel threatened about their future livelihood. One interviewee told us: 'We feel that we need to take preemptive action to make money from land. If we don't do it, the land will eventually be converted to state-owned land. If we make enough money from renting out land now, we can save enough for social security the day we lose the land.'[7] Cashing in on land is regarded as a potential source of social security by farmers, which is needed because the compensation paid by the government is regarded as insufficient by the farmers.

The RLCL grants farmers 30 years land use rights for agricultural production. However, within this period, the government can requisition agricultural land in the name of 'public interest', which is not defined in the Land Management Law (LML). Faced with insecure tenure, it is only rational for farmers to engage in rent-seeking activities.

With the open-door policy, many enterprises – domestic, foreign and joint venture – flocked into Bao'an. This drove up the demand for sites for manufacturing plants, but the government's response to this demand was slow, and this created a breeding ground for illegal land use practices. In the economically developed areas, towns and villages are competing with one another to set up industrial zones to attract manufacturing. But the conversion process from collective land to state land is costly in terms of time and money. A higher land price implies a disadvantage in attracting investment. Consequently, many villages and towns do not follow the conversion process.

Manufacturers started to rent collective land without going through the time-consuming process of converting collective land to state land. Furthermore, the economic boom attracted a huge number of migrant workers to Bao'an. This group of people needs cheap, affordable, and temporary housing. A worker told the researcher that an average worker earns about 1000 yuan per month. After deducting 300 yuan for living expenses, they don't have much left for housing, as they need to save most of the remaining 700 yuan to send back home.[8] In response, farmers started to build temporary houses on their rural land to rent out. Houses fetch eight to ten yuan per m per month. Hence, farmers have strong incentives to build and rent out multi-storey buildings rather than farm the land. One landlord built a five-storey building with a floor area of 500 m on his own rural residential land site. He invested 260,000 yuan in the building (he owns the land, so this costs him nothing), and he charges his tenants eight to ten yuan/m per month which yields him a monthly income of about 4,000-5,000 yuan.[9] In sharp contrast, the annual agricultural income from 1 mu of land (666 m) is only around 2,000 yuan.

Law enforcement

The magnitude of the illegal land use problem is shown by the estimations in Table 17.1 and 17.2. A large number of illegal land use cases, however, are not detected, investigated, or demolished. This can be seen in Table 17.3 which shows the illegal floor surface area demolished in Bao'an District between 1994 and 2003. The area demolished is only a tiny fraction of the total area of illegal construction. Effective monitoring and prevention of illegal land use are seriously hampered by the lack of enforcement staff. The investigation team of the Land Bureau consists of only nineteen people, and they have to patrol an area of 700km. In addition, it is extremely difficult, if not impossible, to demolish buildings that are already in use. Resistance from building owners who have invested heavily and from tenants whose eviction will result in homelessness often forces law enforcers to back off. This leaves law enforcement to deal only with buildings that are still in the process of construction and owners who are less 'thorny' or 'troublesome'.[10]

Formalisation and recognition of illegal land use and constructions

The Shenzhen government has been issuing regulations and orders to prevent illegal land use since as early as 1982, but it is obvious that these regulations have not had much impact. It has become virtually

Table 17.1   *Illegal residential building and land area up to March 1, 2003*

Town	Number of reported cases	Estimated building surface area (m²)	Estimated land area (m²)
Xi Xiang	13,622	5,797,502	1,879,385
Fu Yong	9,516	5,091,242	1,604,244
Sha Jing	15,697	4,799,438	2,117,925
Song Gang	10,240	4,565,158	1,443,304
Gong Ming	11,583	4,892,129	1,338,208
Shi Yan	5,316	2,140,282	760,466
Long Hua	12,247	5,830,421	2,143,594
Guan Lan	7,013	2,852,763	903,951
Xin An	3,925	1,936,055	482,128
Guang Ming	746	22,0357	151,687
Total	89,905	38,125,347	12,824,892

Source: Shenzhen Bao'An District Office for Dealing with Illegal Residential and Production Operation Buildings

Table 17.2   *Illegal operation and production site building and land area up to March 1, 2003*

Town	Number of reported cases	Estimated building area (m²)	Estimated land area (m²)
Xi Xiang	871	3,154,428	2,088,450
Fu Yong	2090	8,378,301	2,403,384
Sha Jing	3289	13,120,309	6,071,696
Song Gang	4152	9,350,057	5,423,524
Gong Ming	5073	12,806,589	5,442,116
Shi Yan	1224	2,760,768	2,635,989
Long Hua	2043	5,542,725	3,198,624
Guan Lan	2224	4,854,437	9,595,574
Xin An	234	785,786	18,297
Guang Ming	82	351,283	606,026
Total	21,282	61,104,683	37,483,680

Source: Shenzhen Bao'An District Office for Dealing with Illegal Residential and Production Operation Buildings

Table 17.3 *Illegal floor surface area demolished from 1994 to 2003*

Year	Area dismantled (m²)	Fine (10,000 yuan)
1994	8,000	55
1995	46,000	360
1996	36,750	199
1997	1,300,000	350
1998	780,000	700
1999	860,000	-
2000	1,345,885	-
2001	936,500	2,086
2002	1,346,600	594
2003#	1,851,294	2,083

For the year 2003, the figure we have is for January to September.
Source: Wang, Shanhua. *Notice on Collective Land Management in Bao'an District* (official document)

impossible to demolish all the illegal buildings, due to their large number, fierce resistance from building owners, the lack of enforcement staff, and the government's inclination to maintain a 'harmonious socialist society'. In March 2002, the Shenzhen municipal government issued Implementing Regulations for Dealing with Illegal Constructions for Production and Operation Purposes in Shenzhen Special Economic Development Zone. In line with the spirit of the regulations of the municipal government, in September 2002, Bao'an district government issued two ordinances regarding the legalisation criteria and implementation procedures for illegal housing and for other types of construction (i.e. constructions for manufacturing and other operation purposes), respectively. These two ordinances manifest the will of the Bao'an government to solve illegal land use problems by legalising the illegal buildings. The Bao'an government decided to divide illegal land use and constructions into three categories in the hope of solving the problem of illegal land use and constructions once and for all:

1) Illegal land use and buildings dating back to March 5, 1999. Cases in this category are defined as 'historical legacy' and are all recognised as legal.

2) Illegal land use and structures created between March 5, 1999, and October 31, 2003. If the land falls within the perimeters of the urban zone designated in the urban planning document,[11] the land can be converted to state-owned construction land, provided that members of the collective who currently use the land pay the necessary fees for this change of tenure regime and land use type (i.e. the land conversion fee); the land use and the structures will then be recognised as legal. Land and buildings that fall outside the zone

designated for urban development are to be demolished, and members of the collective who currently use the land are to be fined.

3) Illegal land use and structures created after October 31, 2003. Land that falls within the urban zone can still be converted to state-owned land, but besides having to pay the routine conversion fees to the government, a fine will also be levied on the collective member. Buildings that fall outside of the zone are not only to be demolished unconditionally, but the collective member will also be fined more heavily than for illegal land use before October 31, 2003.

There are some conditions attached to the legalisation process. First, the 'illegal' land user must be a collective member. For instance, a piece of collective land 'rented' by an urban entrepreneur for building a factory cannot be legalised. In addition, the following categories of land cannot be formalised even if they predate March 5, 1999: land that occupies parts of a road, public square, greenbelt, high-tension electrical wire; land that is located in an area that seriously impedes urban development; land in a zone of basic farmland protection; land used for temporary construction structures. The purpose of these conditions is to remove any potential barriers to infrastructure and planning. Most of the land used illegally and the illegal structures qualify for legalisation, as they are occupied by members of the collective and fall outside of the conditions listed above.

For legalisation, land used illegally and land on which illegal structures are built needs to be surveyed (the fee is about five yuan for each m surveyed); then certificates of registration will be issued, which recognise the legality of the property. Interestingly, in the appendix of the certificate, it will be stamped 'in violation of the law'. A staff member in the certification office explained to us: 'The certificates that these owners get are legal and protected by law. But according to Shenzhen Special Economic Zone Real Estate Registration Ordinance, to be issued a certificate of registration, the registration receiver must submit a number of certificates which should have been issued by the relevant government departments covering each stage of building construction. These certificates, which include a building permit, construction permit, building completion certificate, etc., represent a formal and legal procedure for the realisation of a real estate project. Since the owners of illegal buildings do not have these certificates, they would not be issued the certificate of registration if the 'amnesty' had not been given by Bao'an district government. The 'in violation of the law' stamp does not in any way diminish the rights enjoyed by the newly legalised owners; it merely serves as a 'distinguishing indication' from ordinary legal owners'.[12]

Summary

In a time of rapid urbanisation and fast economic growth, farmers are prohibited from benefiting from the lucrative business of converting land from agricultural to nonagricultural uses owing to the dualist land tenure structure. However, rational action on the part of farmers and the ineffectiveness of the state regulatory apparatus inevitably give rise to illegal rent-seeking behaviour. As a result, farmers began to illegally construct buildings on their agricultural land or rural residential land site. Illegal land use and illegal buildings have become a permanent feature of the peri-urban landscape over a period of more than one decade, and it has become virtually impossible to demolish the buildings and re-convert the land to agriculture, as the administrative and social costs are too high. Left with no other feasible alternatives, the Bao'an government recognises illegal land use. But fearing that recognition without conditions would encourage further illegal behaviour, the government decided that only illegal land use and structures dating back to before March 1999 would be unconditionally legalised, while for two other categories conditions would be stricter and fines higher. In contrast to the Bao'an case, the next case we examine is an example of a pro-active strategy devised by the national government to formalise and stabilise rural land tenure so as to avoid the creation of illegal land use and constructions such as in Bao'an.

Case 2: Dongli District, Tianjin Municipality

Setting the scene

In 2007 the government initiated the 'Land Exchange Program' of the 'Small Cities and Towns Project'. This project aims to achieve a balance among urbanisation, the need for more construction land, farmers' tenure security, and their desire to capitalise on their land asset, which is a conundrum the government has to solve if it wants to pursue healthy economic growth and achieve social harmony. The second case study looks at the first national pilot project of the Land Exchange Program, whose policy formulation process has been finished, and which soon will be put into action.

The first pilot experiment of the Land Exchange Program will be carried out in the town of Huaming in the Dongli district of the municipality of Tianjin.[13] Huaming town is located between the Tianjin city centre and Tianjin Binhai New District – an industrial zone in Tianjin that was recently created by the State Council, which is to serve as the engine of economic growth for north China. Huaming covers an area of 150.6 km, which is about one-third of the area of Dongli district. Tianijin is also one of the most developed cities in China. Dongli is a sub-urban district, situated in the east of the city. It occupies an area of 477 km. The district has a total population of 300,400, of which 196,000 are registered as rural residents.[14]

Small Cities and Towns (SCT) project

The Small Cities and Towns (SCT) project refers to the development of new towns in rural areas. It is hoped that with SCT development, sec-ondary and tertiary industries will be installed. As a consequence, some rural population will be transferred out of agriculture, and farmers' liv-ing conditions (in terms of education, social security, lifestyle, etc.) will converge with that of their urban counterparts. Urbanisation is an in-evitable process in which various pull and push factors prompt impor-tant migration flows to the cities. Due to the meagre incomes from me-nial jobs in cities, low levels of education, and the dualist urban-rural household registration system, the vast majority of migrants is not really absorbed by the cities. They become what is popularly known as 'floating population' – an immense number of rural workers migrate to cities to work but cannot settle there on a permanent basis. The gov-ernment devised the SCT plan to promote the development of inter-mediary towns that are to act as a buffer zone preventing the inflow of large numbers of rural migrants to major cities and thereby averting the formation of urban slums and the consequent risk of social in-stability. At the same time, these small cities and towns are to become engines of growth to propel the industrialisation and modernisation of rural areas. In 2004 the Ministry of Construction with five other min-istries selected 1887 SCTs out of more than 20,000 as strategic devel-opment poles. A key element of the SCT project is the Land Exchange Program on which we will focus here.

The Land Exchange Program in a nutshell

We have seen in Figure 17.1 that land in China can be divided into two broad categories according to the way it may be used: land that may be used for agricultural purposes and land that may be used for construc-tion. Agricultural land belongs to the collectives, and only state-owned land can legally be used for construction purposes (art. 43 Land Man-agement Law).[15] The law allows for the conversion of agricultural land into construction land through a set of procedures. Agricultural land has to be first requisitioned by the state and become state-owned, then the state leases the land to new users. The most important transforma-tion that takes place during this process is the change in land owner-ship: collective-owned land becomes state-owned land. The land-use conversion process is tedious, however, and its duration and cost incite illegal land use. Commercial land users often opt for the faster and cheaper, although illegal, construction on collectively owned land, and there also exists a vibrant illegal residential housing rental market.

With the Land Exchange Program, the government devised a plan to address these problems and to avoid loss of farmland resulting from urban expansion. As there is no strict planning requirement such as plot ratio on rural houses, the extensive use of RRLS has been quite common.[16] The government plan is to move farmers out of their rural houses into high-rise buildings that allow for a much more intensive land use. By doing so, RRLS becomes state-owned. Although the construction of high-rise buildings will initially take up some agricultural land, this loss will be made up by reconverting part of RRLS into agricultural land. The remaining part of RRLS will remain state-owned and will be used for construction purposes. As a result, not only the total cultivated land area is maintained but also more construction land is released owing to the exchange between extensively used RRLS and intensive land-use houses. Figure 17.2 is a graphical representation of the exchange process.

As the Land Exchange Program requisitions and converts all land at once, it prevents commercial land users from circumventing the tedious land conversion process, and thus decreases the incidence of illegal land use. The project is furthermore expected to destroy a part of the illegal residential housing rental market, as it takes away RRLS. As mentioned, it is often the case that only RRLS are extensively used. Farmers' dwellings usually occupy only a portion of the RRLS. The remaining part of the RRLS is occupied by a courtyard. In many such courtyards, illegal houses have been built and rented to migrant workers. Some families also have more than one RRLS, which gives them the opportunity to rent houses out to migrants. Other people have left the rural areas but still keep their RRLS and rent it out for a profit. By transferring farmers to high-rise buildings and taking away their RRLS and rural houses, this illegal rental market is cut off.

Our concern here is the trajectory of property rights during this process. Figure 17.3 replicates Figure 17.2, but the exchange is now represented in terms of ownership rights: collectively owned agricultural land is requisitioned for the construction of high-rise buildings and becomes state-owned. The government then proposes to exchange apartments in these high-rise buildings for collectively owned RRLS and the farmers' private houses. Consequently, RRLS becomes state-owned. Part of that land is then reconverted to agricultural uses to keep the total area of cultivated land unchanged; this part of the land returns to the collective ownership. The remaining part of the land that is re-

Figure 17.2 *The exchange process*

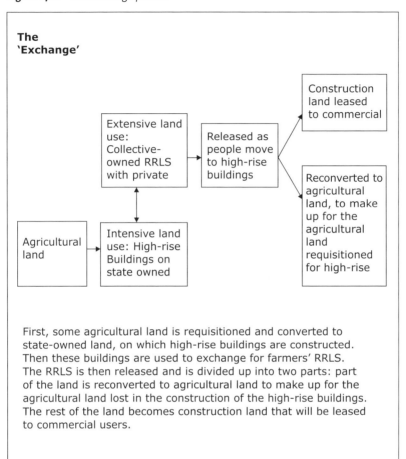

The 'Exchange'

Agricultural land → Intensive land use: High-rise Buildings on state owned → Extensive land use: Collective-owned RRLS with private → Released as people move to high-rise buildings → Construction land leased to commercial / Reconverted to agricultural land, to make up for the agricultural land requisitioned for high-rise

First, some agricultural land is requisitioned and converted to state-owned land, on which high-rise buildings are constructed. Then these buildings are used to exchange for farmers' RRLS. The RRLS is then released and is divided up into two parts: part of the land is reconverted to agricultural land to make up for the agricultural land lost in the construction of the high-rise buildings. The rest of the land becomes construction land that will be leased to commercial users.

leased through the exchange remains state-owned and is then leased by government to commercial users.

The method of exchange

There are three subjects of exchange: the villagers, the villagers' committees, and the government.[17] The objects of the exchange are the villager's rural residential land site and apartments in a newly urbanised area. There are in fact two exchange actions taking place more or less concurrently during this process. The first is between the villagers' committee and the government: the villagers' committee exchanges with the government the ownership of RRLS (and constructions on it) for ownership of the apartment units in high-rise buildings and use

Figure 17.3 *Transformation of ownership during the exchange process*

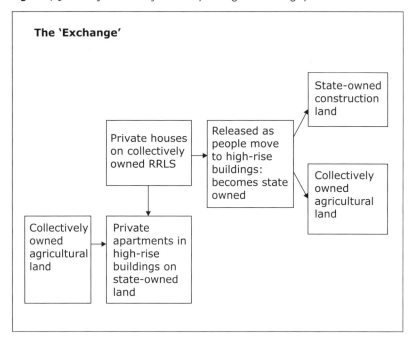

right of the land on which the new building is erected. The second exchange action is between villagers and the villagers' committee: villagers exchange with the committee the ownership of rural houses and
use right of RRLS for ownership of a new dwelling in a high-rise building. The need for this two-step procedure is due to the transformation
of ownership involved. The collective is considered as the representative of the farmers and their interests.[18] Although land belongs to the
collective, farmers have established use rights in the land. Therefore,
the collective needs to gain approval from/reach an agreement with the
farmers before proceeding to exchange it with the state.

When villagers give up their RRLS, they in fact give up two rights:
the use right of RRLS and the ownership of their rural houses. The
first step of the exchange process therefore consists of the government
paying compensation for these two rights. For RRLS compensation,
the RRLS area per capita is used as basis for calculating a compensation standard. Total RRLS area is divided by the number of people in
the village in order to obtain the RRLS area per capita. Accordingly,
each household will get a sum that corresponds to the compensation
price for RRLS per capita times the number of people in the household. For value appraisal of the rural houses, professional agencies will

be hired. Rural houses are of different types and quality: mud brick house, brick house, bungalow, storied building. The appraisal standard for each type has to be decided before any assessment takes place. Thus: compensation for each household = compensation for RRLS/capita x no. of persons in the household + house compensation

In the second step of the exchange process, village households can use the compensation money to buy apartments in the new high-rise buildings. Under the SCT exchange scheme it is planned that each household will be allocated 80m of new housing space in the high-rise building.[19] The price of 1 m of the new apartment is set at 2,300 yuan, which is its construction cost. Therefore, the cost of 80m is 184,000 yuan. Compensation received from selling RRLS and rural houses varies for each household due to the difference in number of persons in a household and the value of the house. In general, households receive around 300,000 yuan. Therefore, the compensation level is well above the cost of the new residence. An additional, hidden compensation component comes from the house price itself. The market price for 1 m of the same quality apartment in the vicinity of Huaming would cost about 3,500 yuan. By selling the houses at construction cost (2300 yuan/m), a rural household stands to gain 1200 yuan for each m.

Farmers only receive the compensation for their RRLS after their requisitioned rural houses have been torn down, and they have proven that they have an alternative legal shelter. The purpose of this prerequisite is twofold. First, it prevents farmers from selling their rural houses for immediate cash without securing a stable residence. Unsettled farmers might cause social instability and contribute to the growth of urban slums, as has happened in many developing countries. Second, the demolition of rural houses as a prerequisite is intended to avoid farmers refusing to move out once they have cashed their compensation.

Discourse and reality of exchange

(i) The purposes of exchange
The official purpose of the Land Exchange Program is to speed up and better manage the urbanisation process and the establishment of satellite towns in the periphery of cities.[20] A concurrent official goal is to ameliorate the houses and living conditions of rural residents and let them enjoy the spillover effects of the urbanisation process. Although both aspects are targeted in the Land Exchange Program, the programme in reality also seems to be highly geared towards getting more land for construction. For example, in Huaming town, RRLS takes up 7,794 mu of land, of which 3,475 mu is to be re-cultivated to make up for the agricultural land that will be used to construct new houses:

2,983 mu of land will be used to build urban houses that will accommodate the farmers who vacate their rural residence; the other 492 mu will be used for public facilities, including schools, museums, and the new administrative centres. Living in the SCT will thus allow residents to have access to better public facilities, education, medical care, and services that were previously the privilege of urban residents. The Land Exchange Program will also generate 4,319 mu surplus land. This land will be leased by the government to commercial users to develop a real-estate sector, industrial zones, and other commercial establishments. This land would otherwise not have been available, at least not legally, for construction to accommodate further economic growth and industrialisation. Huaming town is only a pilot programme; many more towns will probably follow its footsteps, providing the government with substantial amounts of land to set up economic development or industrial zones from which commercial users may rent land with easy access.

(ii) The principles of exchange

In theory, the project abides by the following principles: equality, voluntary participation, mutual benefit, and strict protection of cultivated land. 'Equality' means that the government, villager's committees, and villagers enjoy equal status in the Land Exchange Program. 'Voluntary participation' implies that villagers are not coerced by administrative orders to take part in the program. 'Mutual benefit' means that all parties involved in the exchange will benefit from it in a win-win situation. The 'strict protection of cultivated land' principle means that there should be no encroachment on cultivated land which is regarded as an important source of food security, and thus the livelihood of China's vast population.

In reality, the exchange is not a voluntary process, but it appears to be voluntary because it receives almost no resistance. The economic incentives given to farmers make them happy and willing to take part. Interviews conducted by the authors show that the farmers are generally happy with the exchange and that they are willing to participate for the following reasons: first, they believe that the Land Exchange Program will diminish their dependency on farmland, as it will enhance urbanisation and therefore increase opportunities to derive income from other sources such as jobs in village and township enterprises; second, most farmers look forward to the new lifestyle, since living in a high-rise building serves as a symbol of status. A few years ago when high-rise buildings existed only in the urban areas, only the rich could afford them; third, farmers are generally happy with the compensation level and below-market price of the new apartment unit.

Another pervasive trope in official documents on the Land Exchange Program is the 'democratic principle'. Words like 'respecting farmers' wishes' and 'democratic decision process' surface again and again in the speeches of officials. However, nowhere can there be found concrete procedures or examples of how the democratic process will be carried forward, and so it seems more rhetoric than reality. This does not imply that farmers are forced into entering the Land Exchange Program. Talking with farmers reveals that they do think the programme is beneficial to them in terms of better living conditions and more liquid assets. However, farmers' acquiescence to and support for the programme is quite different from the presumption that the programme is the result of a democratic process.

It is not surprising that the state puts such a strong emphasis on 'democracy'. The Communist Party has been reforming and trying to make its rule democratic, or to at least appear democratic. One of the most notable reforms is the election of grassroots leaders, i.e. village leaders. Land is one of the thorniest issues, and mishandling of it could severely undermine the Party's rule. Therefore, the 'democratic' rhetoric is as important as the actual policy itself.

An examination of policy papers regarding the Land Exchange Program reveals that 'bottom-up' initiatives are hardly mentioned. Instead, in the authors' opinion, the development of SCT is primarily a top-down initiative aimed at solving the urban-rural dualist structure and absorbing the vast rural population in an era of rapid economic growth. The exchange is just a strategic step in achieving the development of SCT.

Also with regard to the principle of mutual benefit, one should make a caveat. Though it is true that the market values of RRLS and houses are very low, as claimed in the official discourse, and farmers thus substantially gain from the Land Exchange Program, it has to be borne in mind that the low market value of rural residential land is solely due to the prohibition of its circulation by law. If the government were to allow the free transaction of rural houses, the price farmers would get for them would exceed the value that they are now being paid by the government by a large margin. Through the Land Exchange Program – despite the rhetoric of mutual benefit – the state is thus in fact capturing the rent that belongs to farmers.

(iii) The legality of exchange
The Land Exchange Program entails a significant transformation of property rights. First, collectively owned agricultural land is transformed into state-owned residential land. Second, collectively owned RRLS is exchanged for state-owned land and then partly leased to commercial users for construction and partly reconverted to collectively

owned agricultural land. But what are the legal foundations for these transformations? No laws refer to the Land Exchange Program. The only governmental document that lends somewhat partial support to the exchange is a policy directive entitled Opinions About Standardisation of the Combination of Increase in City and Town Construction Land and Decrease in Rural Construction Land in Experimental Sites, released in October 2005 by the Ministry of Land and Natural Resources. Acknowledging that the increase in construction land inevitably involves the expropriation of agricultural land, this directive recommends that current rural construction land (in our case RRLS) be cultivated to keep the total area of cultivated land unchanged. This policy document does not, however, provide an explicit foundation for the transformation of property rights involved.

Before the actual resettlement of farmers can take place, the government has to requisition agricultural land to build new houses. The legality of this requisition is questioned. According to the LML, agricultural land can be converted to construction land for public interest purposes through a requisitioning by the state. The LML does not, however, define what constitutes public interest. It is a vague, ambiguous, and ill-defined concept (Ding 2004). Can government-led requisition in the case of the Exchange Program be defined as public interest oriented? On the one hand, the requisition of agricultural land can be seen as public interest driven, since the agricultural land requisitioned was a prerequisite for the Land Exchange Program to start, and this programme can be seen as a public project. On the other hand, a public interest project should not be a profit-making activity. The Land Exchange Program will eventually be a profit-generating activity. Through the Land Exchange Program, the government will get additional land, which will be leased to commercial users. The Land Exchange Program thus calls for a re-examination and re-definition of 'public interest' in the realm of land requisition in future Chinese laws (op. cit.).

With regard to the second transformation, neither the LML nor any other law gives a legal foundation for the requisitioning of RRLS and rural houses to be converted into agricultural and construction land. The legality of this conversion is therefore also being questioned.

Effects of exchange

(i) The capitalisation of residential land

An additional effect of the Land Exchange Program is the capitalisation of rural residential land. We have seen that rural land belongs to the collective, and farmers are allocated personal use rights in RRLS for an unspecified period of time. Although farmers own their rural houses, they do not have full disposal rights: they can only transact the houses with fellow village members, and law prohibits the sale of land to non-collective members or the use of land for purposes other than their own residence. Houses are usually one of the most valuable assets that farmers hold, but it is essentially an illiquid asset. Limited liquidity consequently makes rural houses under-priced during circulation within the collective circle and dead capital outside that circle. Through the Land Exchange Program, rural houses will be exchanged for new apartments in small cities and towns, which are classified as 'commodity housing'. As the name implies, this type of housing is a market commodity which can be transacted on the housing market, and its price is more or less determined by market factors. Owners of this type of housing can transact freely – either by renting or by sale – in the real-estate property market. Thus, what farmers get after the exchange is an apartment unit built on state-owned land. Although farmers still only own the apartment and not the land, their property is much more valuable than rural houses because now they can rent, sell, or mortgage it. Moreover, the newly passed Property Law stipulates that the lease of the state-owned land on which commodity housing is built will be renewed automatically for another 70 years after the current land lease expires. Such a long period of leasehold of the land, combined with the right to transact the house, gives commodity housing owners more or less the equivalent right that is enjoyed by owners in a freehold system. In this manner, 'dead capital' – rural houses – is brought to life in the form of urban apartments with market value. As a liquid commodity, farmers can now enjoy the returns from their houses through sale, renting, and the appreciation in value. In addition, they could mortgage the apartment when in need of capital. As said above, it should be kept in mind that rural housing was only a 'dead' asset because the law prohibited its free circulation. Therefore, it is nothing but the state and the property rights arrangement it imposes that make rural houses illiquid.

(ii) Tenure security
In 1998, the policy to grant the 30-year use right of agricultural land policy was adopted in the new version of the LML. In August 2002, the Standing Committee of the National Peoples' Congress (NPC) adopted the ground-breaking Rural Land Contracting Law (RLCL), replacing the single article of the LML that had dealt with farmers' land-tenure rights with detailed stipulations regarding farmers' land rights and dispute resolution mechanisms. The far-reaching and monumental importance and significance of RLCL in recasting farmer's tenure rights were succinctly summarised by the Rural Development Institute immediately following its adoption by the NPC in August 2002: 'RLCL is the first modern Chinese law to deal exclusively with the issue of ru-

ral land tenure, and it represents a breakthrough for the land-tenure rights of China's 210 million farm families' (Rural Development Institute 2002).

In the Land Exchange Program, the farmers' contractual rights to agricultural land are not affected. Individual farmers' share of contracted land will not be affected since the total agricultural land area will remain unchanged upon the completion of the programme. From this perspective, tenure security of farmers' agricultural land is guaranteed. Nevertheless, the requisition of RRLS and rural houses may serve as an alarm bell for tenure security. If collective RRLS and personal houses can be requisitioned so easily, there is no reason to believe that agricultural land may not one day also be requisitioned for one reason or another, such as the possible future expansion of SCT. Lack of tenure security is dangerous, as it will not only discourage farmers from investing time, labour, and inputs in the land, but also gives them the motivation to carry out informal activities, such as building and renting out 'illegal houses' to maximise their economic returns from land. Celebrated jurist Wang Liming rightly calls attention to the necessity of turning contractual rights to agricultural land into real rights. He elaborates, 'If the contractual management right cannot be a real right, but only a right in contract, it can hardly become a long-term stable property right, and the contractors can hardly defend themselves against unlawful interference and damage' (Wang 2006:320).

Summary

With the Small Cities and Towns Project and the Land Exchange Program, the Chinese government has devised an innovative strategy to speed up the urbanisation process and solve the problems arising from land shortages and the urban-rural dualist tenure system. It is not the perfect strategy, as it is a top-down administrative measure without due participation from farmers who are largely excluded from sharing the economic benefits arising from the economic development taking place on the formerly collective peri-urban land. That being said, the innovation of this policy plan should also be acknowledged. It juggles considerably well the issues of urbanisation, industrialisation, farmers' welfare, and the attempt to dismantle institutional rigidities and barriers that have bred illegal land use.

Conclusion

The weakness of China's current land tenure system is increasingly being challenged and 'the original justifications for maintaining the system no longer appear to be as true as they were twenty years ago' (Lohmar 2006:99). The first case discussed in this chapter is at the forefront of land tenure issues. It is a manifestation of the current land tenure system being challenged through the recognition and formalisation of illegal land tenure. The second case demonstrates a general strategy toward economic development and urbanisation, of which rural land tenure issues are a major component. It displays a practical response to the challenges, with an innovative strategy to prevent the problems arising from the urban-dualist tenure system.

Although both interventions have a number of positive effects, these cases also clearly reveal the importance and complexity of land tenure issues in a fast-growing economy that lacks standardised and well-defined land tenure institutions. They bring to the fore, furthermore, that for a thorough overhaul of the land tenure system, the 'two-tiered' government-regulated collective land and market-based state-owned land tenure regimes need to converge to form a unified, market-based, agricultural and non-agricultural land market.

Notes

1   This paper is based on researchers' fieldwork trips in Shenzhen and Tianjin in 2004, 2006 and 2007. During these trips, the researchers carried out semi-structured indepth interviews with local farmers, government officials and local media reporters. The authors also collected necessary data from relevant district government departments. The names of interviewees are not mentioned in the paper to protect their privacy.
2   The titles of ordinances and sentences in official document sometimes are crafted in very bureaucratic language and tone. We attempt to translate word-by-word so as to keep it close to the original language.
3   1 ha = 15 mu.
4   According to article 47 of the Land Management Law (amended in 1998), compensation for requisitioned land has three components: compensation for land, resettlement compensation and compensation for land attachments and young crops. Compensation for land should be six to ten times the average annual output value of requisitioned land in the preceding three years; compensation for resettlement per person affected is set at four to six times the average annual output value of requisitioned land in the preceding three years. However, resettlement compensation per hectare of land should not exceed fifteen times the average annual output value of requisitioned land in the preceding three years. The total amount of land and resettlement compensation, subject to the approval of provincial authority, can be increased to no more than 30 times of average output value of prior three years in an attempt to maintain the living standard of affected farmers.
5   See statistical survey carried out by the well-known real estate agency, ZhongDa-HengJi (Xinjingbao newspaper 2007-06-26).
6   'Paid' land use system distinguishes this type of land use system from the pre-1982 land system in which all urban land was state-owned, and the government allocated it to users free of charge. In 1982, Shenzhen became the first city to implement the

paid land use system, i.e. land users pay an upfront amount of land use fees to the government in exchange for a land use right. During the term of leasehold, land users can rent, sell (use rights), and mortgage the land.

7 Interviewee 12.

8 Interviewee 9.

9 Interviewee 2.

10 Interview with one law enforcement officer.

11 This zone outlines the designated spheres of construction land and agricultural land in the city planning scheme. Agricultural land that falls within the sphere of construction can be converted to construction land if all the due processes of converting land from collective to state are carried out.

12 Interview with certification staff.

13 Five such projects are planned across three districts in Tianjin. The other four sites are Xiaozhan town in Jinnan District, Daliang town, Houpubang village and Nanbeixinzhuang village of Wuqing District.

14 Urban and rural household registration is a vestige of China's urban-rural dualist dichotomy. It is a feature that was used and to some extent still is used to separate the urban and rural population. Some provinces have begun to eliminate this divide by abolishing rural household registration. The complete abolition of such a system still has a long way to go in the foreseeable future. Different types of households enjoy different rights. For example, the current social security system only covers urban residents.

15 There is an exception to this article: rural collective-owned land can be used as construction land in the following cases: land used by rural town and village enterprises; the construction of houses for rural residents (RRLS); rural public facilities (see Figure 17.1).

16 Article 62 of Land Management Law stipulates: Each rural household is entitled to only one RRLS, and it surface area cannot exceed the standard stipulated by provincial, autonomous regional and municipal government. In Tianjin the area of RRLS is set at 167 m per household. But the actual occupied area can reach 200-300 m. The reasons for this extensive use of land are manifold: some families are allocated two RRLS through connection with village cadre; the lack of planning and monitoring mechanism also contributed to this wasteful use of land, etc.

17 There are generally three criteria to qualify a person as a member of the collective (commonly known as the villager): 1) his/her household registration is in the village; 2) she/he has a legal residence in the village; 3) she/he lives in the village. A villager needs to fulfil all the three criteria in order to be a member of the collective, while the first criterion is the most important one, as this has to do with the rural-urban dualist household registration system.

18 As elucidated earlier, the villagers' committee is not the 'collective' but is taken as the 'collective' by the state when dealing with collective matters.

19 In Huaming town the average number of persons per household is 3.2. Accordingly, each person would receive 25 m of living area.

20 Official goals, principles, and methods of the Exchange Program are obtained from government official documents such as project training manuals, minutes of conferences; speeches given by officials, and interviews with government officials. However, due to confidentiality of the documents and the requests of interviewees, the titles of documents and the names and positions of officials are omitted.

Government documents (in Chinese)

Tianjin Small Cities and Towns Experimental Site Training Class Materials Compilation, Dec. 2006.

Small Cities and Towns and New Countryside Planning and Construction Management Training Class Materials Compilation by Tianjin Commission of Economic Development and Reform, June 2006.

On the Exchange of Rural Residential Land Site for Houses by The Exchange Project Team, July 2007.

Report on the Implementation of 'the Exchange of Rural Residential Land Site for Houses' in Huaming Town to Promote the Construction of Small Cities and Towns by Dongli People's Government, Jan. 2007.

Understanding and Reflection during the Process of the Exchange of Rural Residential Land Site for Houses in Huaming Demonstration Small Cites and Towns. A Report by Fu Jinqiang, Director of the Bureau of Land Managements of Dongli District.

Using Scientific Development Perspective to Guide the Healthy Development of Small Cities and Towns Experimental Site, a speech made by Zhu Zhixin, Deputy Director of National Commission of Economic Development and Reform, during a working conference on the Construction and Development of Small Cities and Towns Experimental Site. July, 2004.

Opinions About Standardisation of The Combination of Increase in City and Town Construction Land and Decrease in Rural Construction Land in Experimental Sites by the Ministry of Land and Natural Resources.

Newspaper articles

Nanfang Zhoumo Newspaper. 'The Change of Focus of Protection of Farmers' Rights: From Tax and Fees Disputes to Land Rights Protection' (in Chinese) 2004-09-02.

New York Times. 'Chinese Premier Says Seizing Peasants' Land Provokes Unrest' 2006-1-20

Xinhua News. 'Ministry of Land and Natural Resources: The Area of Arable Land in Our Nation has Decreased to 1.827 billion mu', http://news.xinhuanet.com/politics/2007-04/12/content_5968006.htm. (in Chinese) 2007-4-12

Xinjingbao Newspaper. 'Beijing Calls a Halt to the Sale of Illegal 'Small Property Rights' Houses' (in Chinese) 2007-6-26

18   Land law in Indonesia

Herman Slaats, Erman Rajagukguk, Nurul Elmiyah,
Akhmad Safik

Introduction

Indonesia is the world's largest archipelago, consisting of five large islands (from west to east: Sumatra, Java, Kalimantan, Sulawesi, and Ir-
ian) and thousands of smaller islands. The distance from the most
northwestern top of Aceh on Sumatra to the eastern border with Papua
New Guinea is roughly 4,000 km (the distance between London and
Baghdad). Approximately 70 per cent of the Indonesian territory is officially qualified as 'forest land' over which no private property rights on
land can be registered. However, extensive areas have been, and still
are being, deforested by commercial large-scale logging, for small-scale
local agriculture, and for housing. For example, Palangkaraya, the capital city of Central Kalimantan, with a population of 160,000, is officially forest. The remaining 30 per cent of land is unevenly distributed:
'some 69 per cent of the land is owned by sixteen per cent of the population; and the average parcel size of a rural holding in the crowded island of Java is shrinking from what is already a non-viable 0.85 ha.'
(Heryani and Grant 2004:5).

Indonesia's population of over 200 million is made up of many distinct ethnic, linguistic and religious groups which display a great variety of cultural characteristics and historically developed local/regional
land rights and tenure arrangements, which still have relevance today
in spite of overarching nationwide legislation and land policies under
colonial rule and after independence.

Approximately 120 million people live on Java, the smallest of the
large islands, which makes this island of 132,000 km^2 one of the most
densely populated areas in the world (more than 900/km^2). The other
islands are underpopulated. The majority of the population lives in rural conditions and depends on small-scale farming, cattle breeding,
and horticulture for their livelihood. The availability of land and access
to land are indispensable for them. Particularly for Java with its high
population pressure, this presents acute problems.

This chapter first outlines the main developments and characteristics
of the colonial and post-colonial land rights regimes. It then introduces
the foundation of independent Indonesian land law – the Basic Agrar-

ian Law of 1960 – and discusses some of its most significant elements. These include: the notion of 'state land' and its various interpretations; customary land rights and tenure arrangements and their position in national law, policy, and practice; the effect of the 'social function' of land on individual rights; land reform, obstacles to land reform, its failure, and recent attempts at re-introduction; the registration of land rights, governmental projects to promote registration, and effects of registration. The next section identifies problems of decentralisation of the previously strongly centralised national land management authority. A few remarks on the relevance of Indonesian land law for non-agrarian interests will be made in the following section. The conclusion argues that the security the formal national legal system claims to provide does not guarantee substantive security on the ground. On the contrary: in spite of the formal recognition of traditional law (as defined by the state), rural traditional land rights and tenure arrangements, and their securities, usually lose out to claims based on national law. Instead of such a formal recognition based on a generalised and distorted definition of traditional law, genuine substantive recognition would imply that national law is tailored so as to accommodate the realities of traditional land rights and tenure arrangements and to facilitate their development, basically confirming/sanctioning the securities they provide.

Historical prelude

Officials of the privately owned Dutch East Indies Company (VOC: *Vereenigde Oost-Indische Compagnie*) set foot ashore the island of Java at the end of the sixteenth century. During the first few decades the interests of the VOC were purely commercial: the trade of tropical agrarian products for the market in Europe on the basis of equal relationships with their counterparts: indigenous chiefs (Javanese *radja's*, princes, etc., and later also persons in authority from other islands in the archipelago). The character of these relationships soon changed. The drive for expansion of economic interests and the necessity to protect assets against colonial competitors such as England, Spain, and Portugal allowed the VOC to assume state-like administrative/imperialistic power and to exercise sovereign rights. Gradually, a colonial practice developed that was geared toward the exploitation of resources and the transfer of profits to the European investors and entrepreneurs (planters). The VOC operated on the basis of indirect rule and of the principle of non-intervention. They superimposed their authority over the existing indigenous feudal structures, which were left intact and used as extensions of their administrative machinery. They refrained from intervening in indigenous organisations (unless their interests were at stake) and simply used the indigenous feudal system, in which it was common for local rulers to charge their subjects with levies *in natura*, to extract the desired products. Copying that system, the VOC charged the indigenous rulers. Conservatism, mismanagement and corruption led to the bankruptcy of the VOC at the end of the eighteenth century. Its debts and assets were taken over by the (then) Dutch Republic, and the Indonesian archipelago formally became a colony of the state. The Dutch ruled Indonesia until the beginning of the Second World War (with the exception of the British interregnum from 1811 till 1815). Colonial exploitation reached its summit under the Culture System of compulsory cultivation of products for the European market in the early nineteenth century. The Javanese farmers had to make one-fifth of their paddy fields available for the cultivation of prescribed crops which had to be concentrated on an area measuring the mathematical total of the individual one-fifth plots. This implied a reshuffle of land use/tenure which seriously affected the traditional land tenure and use patterns. Growing criticism against excessive exploitation, uncontrolled pursuit of profit, and the unrestrained exercise of power in the colony led to the abolition of the Culture System and eventually to a mitigated and more humane colonial policy. In 1870 the 'Agrarian Law' (*Agrarische Wet*) and the 'Agrarian Decree' (or 'Domain Statement': *Domeinverklaring*) were enacted, the impact of which still resonates today.

The purpose of these agrarian regulations was twofold: on the one hand, they intended to facilitate access for non-Indonesian investors and entrepreneurs to land for commercial enterprise, such as the establishment of plantations, whereas on the other hand, they guaranteed the protection of indigenous land rights. The Domain Statement ruled that all land to which no civil law ownership title could be proven was to be considered domain of the state.[1] Since customary rights were not civil law titles and could not be registered, this rule implied that indigenous land fell in the category of 'state domain'. In order to protect and safeguard indigenous rights, a differentiation was made between 'free domain' – land free of native rights which would be available for the state to issue long term lease concessions to (non-Indonesian) entrepreneurs – and so-called 'unfree domain' – land used by the native population, in which the State could not issue any rights. Debates ensued in the Dutch parliament as to the interpretation of the terms 'used by the indigenous population': did it include areas which were not apparently and not permanently in use, but which the indigenous communities considered to belong to their territory, such as fallow land and forest areas where they hunted and collected fire wood, building materials, and other forest products? Supporters of an extensive interpretation of 'free domain' had it that these areas were state domain and thus at the disposal of the government. Those who adhered to a restrictive interpretation supported the indigenous view that these lands belonged to the village territory. At the turn of the twentieth century, the 'Ethical Policy' of the colonial government embodied an explicit shift from colonial exploitation to moral responsibility for native welfare, and a focus on the preservation and protection of indigenous legal systems (*adat*). The Leiden *adat* law scholar Van Vollenhoven successfully thwarted governmental plans for the unification and codification of native law, arguing that this would rob indigenous law of its essential characteristics of flexibility and adaptability.

Dutch colonial rule effectively ended at the beginning of World War II with the Japanese invasion of Indonesia and the internment of the Dutch. The Japanese, pretending to assist 'their Asian brothers' in their endeavour to set themselves free from colonial oppression, allowed the nationalistic movement under the leadership of Sukarno to flourish. Indonesia unilaterally declared independence in 1945 after a colonisation of more than three centuries.[2] The impact of this historic event was more drastic in the political domain, where it constituted a radical break with the past, than it was in law as Dutch colonial law continued to be applied, as parts still are, in one way or another pending replacement by Indonesian legislation. The Dutch prisoners of war failed to notice the social and political developments that were taking place and the serious impact these would have; most of those who survived the Japanese camps dreamt of the good old times and the restoration of the old order. The Dutch eagerness after the war to restore colonial rule and re-assume possession of plantations and other properties resulted in two small-scale wars ('police actions') against the nationalistic rebels and the failure of the negotiations between the Dutch government and the young self-proclaimed Republic to establish peaceful relationships. Only in 1949 did the Dutch recognise the independence of Indonesia. In 1957 Indonesia expelled the last Dutch citizens and nationalised their possessions.

A nationalistic, anti-colonial élan marked the early years of Indonesia's independence. Resistance against the common enemy – the Dutch, trying to re-establish colonial rule/power – functioned as a catalyst in the creation of national unity.[3] The fight for independence and the forging of the idea of one nation were the policy themes of Indonesia's first president, Sukarno. The endeavour to forge a national unity out of the patchwork quilt of ethnicities, cultures, and languages, and cultivating the awareness among the population of being one Indonesian nation was not unsuccessful: within a few decades the Indonesian language (adapted from Malay) became the *lingua franca*, and the notion of being Indonesian settled among the population in general. In the domain of law and legal policy, the nationalistic ambitions aimed at the abolition of the dualistic colonial (civil) law that was felt to be discriminatory, and the creation of a new, genuine Indonesian law to replace it. Land law was one of the first domains to be tackled.

Sukarno's flirtation with communism and the disastrous effects of his nationalistic, even isolationistic policy on the nation's economy were the main reasons why he was made to step down. His successor, General Suharto, focused on economic restoration. Under his administration of almost 30 years, a remarkable economic development was achieved. Trade and industry flourished, foreign investment was attracted. Indonesia was one of the 'Asian Tigers' until its economy collapsed due to the financial crisis that afflicted many other Asian countries. Although this economic success improved the overall standard of living of the population, its benefits were very unevenly distributed. They mainly accumulated in the hands of a small group of elite: the president, his family, and the cronies around them, as well as captains of industry and the army. Relatively little trickled down, leading to a slight but undeniable rise in the standard of living of the population at large and the formation of a more prosperous middle class. The economic success, however, was achieved by virtue of increasing social and political repression, opportunistic policies, widespread corruption, and selective application, if not abuse, of the law. Features like these very much determined the way Suharto's 'New Order' administration dealt with land matters.

The Indonesian Basic Agrarian Law

Soon after the declaration of independence in 1945, a committee was established for the drafting of a new land law. It took another three committees and fifteen years altogether to arrive at the *Undang-undang Pokok Agraria* (Basic Agrarian Law: BAL). The BAL abolished the colonial regulations pertaining to land contained in the *Agrarische Wet* and *Domeinverklaring* of 1870 and the Civil Code.[4] It ended colonial dualism and the distinction between 'Western' land subject to civil law and 'indigenous' land subject to customary law, and substituted the colonial provisions with a set of unitary legal regulations ('principles of land law') inspired by customary law concepts, principles and institutions in 58 articles which were to reflect the genuine Indonesian characteristics and needs.

Some of the major underlying leading principles of BAL are: nationalism (non-Indonesians are excluded from land rights), socialism (all Indonesians shall have access to a minimum of land), and 'Indonesianism' (land law is based on traditional, customary law: *adat*). These characteristics are reflected in the provisions:

- that the Indonesian territory belongs to the Indonesian people as its national wealth (art. 1) and is controlled/managed by the state, representing the people (*tanah dikuasai oleh Negara*) (art. 2);
- that the law pertaining to land is traditional (*adat*) law (art. 5), but the communal rights – as far as actually existing – must be exercised in accordance with national interest and law (art. 3);
- that rights in land have a social function (art. 6), i.e. that the exercise of individual rights in land should not be detrimental to the society;
- that only Indonesian subjects – men and women alike – can have full property rights in land (*hak milik*; art. 9), implying the exclusion of non-Indonesians;
- that maximum and minimum size of land ownership will be determined to guarantee the welfare of the population (BAL art. 17 and Government Regulation in lieu of Law 56/1960);
- to guarantee legal security, land will be registered (art. 19)

Each of these provisions will be elaborated in the sections below; the rule that only Indonesians can have property rights will be discussed here. The BAL does not apply to land in areas officially qualified as forest: these are subject to the Forestry Law, the major implication of which is that no private property rights can be registered in forest areas. Whereas in many traditional land rights and tenure regimes relations to land are predominantly communal in nature (Tjondronegoro 2003:4), the rights defined in the BAL are strictly individual. Although the BAL refers to the notion of communal right (*hak ulayat*) (art. 3), it is lacking in the catalogue of land rights that can exist (art. 16).

The term *ulayat* is derived from the West Sumatran Minangkabau concept *tanah ulayat* that refers to 'area' (*wilayah* in Indonesian), viz. the area or territory that the inhabitants of a village consider as belonging to the community. It not only includes the built-up area of the village and the gardens and fields, but may also include fallow land and even forest.[5] It is the very area of 'unfree' domain, the size of which was the subject of intense debates during the colonial period. Under different names this type of 'communal land' also exists in other ethnic groups than the Minangkabau throughout Indonesia.[6] The concept of *ulayat* was transposed from the Minangkabau customary law level onto the national level as shorthand for all regionally/locally different forms of communal land rights.

Although the existence of *ulayat* rights are formally recognised in the BAL (art. 3), their substantive recognition has been a problem. As mentioned, communal rights are not included in the catalogue of rights in the BAL, and neither the BAL nor other laws give regulations for the documentation and registration of communal rights. Furthermore, the recognition in the BAL is conditional: implementation of *ulayat* rights, as far as they still exist, shall be in accordance with national and state interests and shall not be in variance with the law and other regulations. But even *ulayat* rights that meet these requirements do not have absolute validity. The Elucidation to the BAL (§ II(3)) explains that it is not justifiable to invoke *ulayat* rights if higher interests require use of the land; it also cannot be tolerated that a community repudiates – on the basis of its *ulayat* rights – the organised clearing of forest areas if that is needed, for example, for food supply or for transmigration. The interests of a local community are subordinate to national and state interests.

Under Suharto's centralised administration, it came to mean that village communities were denied the possibility to invoke their *ulayat* rights against concessions for large-scale commercial logging and other forms of exploitation of *ulayat* land which were issued under the pretence that these activities were of 'general interest'. The neglect of customary law and the tendency to restrict its scope of application were supported by legislation, such as the Law on Foreign Investment[7] that favoured foreign investment to the detriment of the rights and interests of local populations, and the Forestry Law that impeded the exercise of communal land rights in forest areas.

As most of the existent implementing regulations of the BAL fail to elaborate, and even contradict, the *adat* principles, the recognition of customary land rights and customary systems of tenure has become a critical element of contention (Heryani and Grant 2004:4). During Suharto's 'New Order' administration, many among the policy-makers and legislators preferred to cherish the opinion that *adat* law had completely faded away, or at least had changed to a degree that it could be assumed to have become irrelevant. Their conclusion was usually based on a comparison of the present-day rural land rights and tenure arrangements and practices with early (colonial) studies of customary law:[8] if today's conditions are found not to fit the old descriptions, they are not considered to be customary (*adat*). This approach denies one of the most essential characteristics of unwritten customary law – its flexibility and adaptability (Ter Haar 1939) – and wrongly attributes legal/normative significance to historical descriptions (Djojodigoeno and Tirtawinata 1940).

Review of the BAL, which has not been modified since its enactment in 1960, was difficult until recently because of a strong band of formalists who believe land law cannot be changed (Heryani and Grant 2004:4). Since the resignation of Suharto, these views are changing, and a re-orientation towards customary law is occurring.

'State land'

The colonial 'domain statement' was considered to have served the interests of colonial exploitation to the detriment of the Indonesian people. Independent Indonesia rejected the colonial notion of the state as
the proprietor of 'unused' land and redefined the position of the state
with regard to land rights in terms of the public law (Harsono
1997:219) 'right of the state to manage/control land' for the benefit of
the nation (BAL art. 2: *hak negara menguasai tanah*, for short: *taneh na-
gara* – state land). The Elucidation to the BAL explains that this right
of the state can be understood as a kind of 'communal right' (*ulayat*) at
the highest level, i.e. of the entire Indonesian people,[9] the scope of
which can be restricted by traditional communal rights, although these
may not be invoked to obstruct higher interests or hamper development.[10]

Suharto's 'New Order' administration applied a very restrictive interpretation of traditional communal rights which virtually ruled them
out of existence. The train of thought underlying this approach is the
assumption that the BAL transferred the authority to manage land matters from the traditional communities to the state as the national community. The 'community' (i.e. the state) can then give user rights on
land to individuals (Indonesian citizens) but retains the power to revoke or annul these rights if this is desirable in the interest of the
'community'. The traditional *hak ulayat* of the communities has been
absorbed by the *'hak ulayat'* of the Indonesian nation, hence there is
no longer a basis for maintaining traditional communal lands, and
therefore all lands can be individualised (Löffler 1996:48 note 127,
quoting the draft version of Evers 1995). In spite of the recognition of
traditional communal rights (*ulayat*) in the BAL (art. 3), the revision of
the 'state land' concept did not reinstate traditional communities' rights
over their original *ulayat* lands. The traditional *hak ulayat* was deemed
to have been superseded by a National *Hak Ulayat*, whereby the state/
government would henceforth fulfil the traditional role of village elders
and issue rights of use to Indonesian nationals (Evers 1995:7).

This approach materialised in the frequent expropriations – often
without consultation with the community and with or without adequate compensation – of communal land for 'general interest' or 'development' purposes. More often than not, these were no more than private interests of the president's family and the elite surrounding him,
disguised and represented as 'state interests', like the construction of
golf links. One of the initial reactions of the population after the fall of
Suharto in 1999 was, not surprisingly, the re-occupation of land plots
that they claimed were unjustifiably taken from them, which they immediately started ploughing and cultivating. In the meantime the gov-

ernmental approach towards the role and significance of *adat*, in particular of communal land rights (*ulayat*), changed also, as will be elaborated below.

Customary land rights and tenure arrangements

The BAL (art. 5) states that the agrarian law applicable to the earth,
water and air space *is adat* law (*hukum adat*: Indonesian customary
law).[11] The Elucidation to the BAL (III(1)) explains that this provision
should be understood to mean that the new land law is based on customary law. Either way it expresses the intention that the new land law
should be uniquely Indonesian, reflecting the cultural and normative
properties of the population. But in spite of the ideological intentions,
the relationship between customary law and the BAL (and other laws)
has been, and still is, very problematic and the subject of continuing
debates. This can be explained by three issues: the diversity and complexity of local/regional forms of customary law; the assumption that
customary institutions and processes can be mimicked at the national
level; and the extensive interpretation of legal restrictions on the applicability of customary law.

First of all there is not one single, uniform system of Indonesian
customary law: there is a great variety of very different regional and local forms which are the product of long historical developments and
which reflect the cultural properties of the different communities.
Communities may be territorially organised, and the social organisation of others may be based on kinship, either patrilineal, parental, or
matrilineal. Many customary communities are hierarchically organised,
others have an egalitarian stratification. In many communities official
religions (particularly Islam) may have influenced or even replaced customary (marriage and inheritance) arrangements; in others traditional
beliefs prevail. Factors like these account for the great regional and local variety of customary land rights and tenure regimes.

Notwithstanding these variations, at a more abstract level most customary land law and tenure regimes have some general characteristics
in common:

– village communities identify a certain area of unused land (fallow
  land, community forest, etc.) beyond the built-up and cultivated
  area as territory that is the communal right of the village community (*ulayat*).
– land rights are usually not strictly individual rights but are often
  embedded in the more inclusive rights/claims of a larger community (family, 'clan', village); the idea of private property is unheard
  of among some ethnic groups which practice communal farming
  (Tjondronegoro 2003:3). Individuals have access to land by virtue of

their belonging to the community. As such they are entitled to clear a plot of fallow land and begin cultivating it. First cultivation of 'vacant' land creates an individual bond which intensifies by continuous use. The community's relationship, however, never disappears completely: if, for example, the land is abandoned, the community's relationship is restored, and the land is available for cultivation by other community members (Ter Haar 1939). Through inheritance, individualised land becomes the common property of the less inclusive community of heirs ('re-communalisation') (Von Benda-Beckmann 1979:150 ff).

- in most customary law systems land is not merely a commodity, it is an element of a spiritual, metaphysical universe.
- they may not even have developed traditional provisions for selling and buying land. Land used to be abundant: whoever needed land could clear a plot in the community's *ulayat* area. Under today's increased pressure on land, the need for transfers becomes acute and is gradually becoming more accepted.
- within the small, traditional agrarian communities the villagers know who is using which land and why; one used to be relatively secure of one's position regarding land: the 'internal' security (community) was strong. The 'external' security, the security of rights in relation to community external actors (e.g. the state, banks, investors) is weak, however. These actors are not acquainted with customary law or prefer not to care about it, and they usually refer to the state's land rights systems, which often do not cover the specific properties of customary relations to land.
- customary law is usually unwritten and lacks a body of clearly formulated rules; it is flexible and adaptive. Of central significance, particularly in the more egalitarian stratified communities, are the traditional decision-making processes in which the norms and principles to be applied in concrete cases are created, maintained, adapted, or even distorted.

A second cause of the problematic relationship between customary law and the BAL is that the assumption underlying the BAL – customary law can be lifted up to the national level and be used as a blueprint for genuine Indonesian land law – is false. What in fact happens is that the legislator and legal experts create something new, inspired by their understanding of what customary law might be or should be. Besides this argument of principle, there is the observation that the understanding of customary law in administrative and policy-making circles is usually Java-centric.

Third, Suharto's New Order administration tended to make conditions for the recognition of customary law (BAL art. 5) more stringent and tried to deny its existence whenever possible. Customary law was downplayed as 'anachronistic and out of character in a modern market driven economy' (Heryani and Grant 2004). This was combined with the fact that the determination of whether or not customary law and customary law communities existed was not an empirical question but an administrative decision. The recognition of *adat* and its applicability were virtually reduced to zero. If *adat* rights could not be proven, the land was automatically looked upon as state land and amenable to 'national interests' to which more weight was attached than to *adat* rights (Löffler 1996:11).

The practice in the communities at the grassroots level, however, is usually more viscous than governments, policy-makers, and legislators might wish. Even after more than 40 years since the enactment of the Basic Agrarian Law in 1960, customary land rights and tenure arrangements are the primary normative framework in most rural agrarian communities, adapted over time by the population to their needs and circumstances. It cannot be denied that state-legislated rules have some impact, particularly when people get entangled in court cases, but in their minds people focus on the traditionally developed norms and principles rather than on the legal rules of the state of which they usually have little knowledge and understanding.

Realising that the traditional rights of customary law communities have frequently been neglected and violated in the past, the approach of the government towards customary law is changing. Under the post-Suharto democratisation and decentralisation movement, the government now endeavours to recognise and protect these rights. Notions like 'national interest', 'state interest', and 'higher interests of the society', which have been used for decades to override the exercise of customary law, are now being questioned. Law 39/1999 regarding Human Rights (art. 6) states that the differences and needs in customary law communities must be observed and protected by the law, the public, and the government, and that the cultural identity of customary law communities should be protected, including their rights to communal land. Furthermore, state institutions are beginning to pay attention to customary law more substantively by defining what 'customary law communities' are[12] and by recognising some rights of such communities, e.g. the right to collect forest products for daily needs or to improve their welfare, and the right to manage the forest according to customary law if it is not contradictory to any legal regulations.[13]

The Indonesian Constitution recognised customary law communities for the first time in 2000 in the statement that: 'The State shall recognise and respect customary law community units and their traditional rights insofar as they are still in existence and are in accordance with the development of the community and the principles of the Unitary State of the Republic of Indonesia, to be regulated in a Law'.[14] Law 32/2004 on Regional Administration reconfirms the obligation of the state to recognise and respect customary law communities and their traditional rights (art.. 2(9)). At the same time, however, its article 203 (3), which states that local traditional rights are applicable if laid down in a Regional Regulation, potentially restricts this recognition: if customary law communities and their traditional rights are not defined in a Regional Regulation, they do not have legal status. Their existence is at best recognised as social fact. This may lead to the marginalisation of not officially recognised customary communities, which tend to come out as losers if conflicts over communal land occur with the state or large enterprises.

Social function of land: Public interest vs. individual rights

The BAL (art. 6) states that all land rights have a social function, which in the Elucidation to the BAL (II(4)) is explained to mean that the use (or non-use) of land should not be in individual interests only; individual and public interests should be in balance in order to achieve the principal goals: prosperity, justice, and happiness for the entire people.[15]

The exercise of the individual land rights listed in the BAL (art. 16) is restricted accordingly. First, in order to avoid harming the public interest, excessive ownership and control of land are prohibited (art. 7). Possession of land in excess of a maximum to be prescribed in additional regulations will be expropriated against compensation for redistribution (art. 17). Second, land rights can be revoked in the public interest against proper compensation (art. 18). Two major problems deserve discussion here: the concept of 'public interest' and the question of proper compensation.

Although 'public interest' is the touchstone for the restriction of the exercise of individual rights, its meaning is not clear, as no definition is given in the BAL. Later regulations involving restrictions of individual rights are not very helpful either, as they contain no definition or define the concept in vague terms, leaving room for interpretation. What the BAL and these regulations have in common is the statement that the public interest includes national and state interests, and/or interest of the general public, and/or development.[16] The various regulations list a number of specific activities considered to be in the interest of development (such as public roads, public hospitals, public marketplaces), the number of which varies between seven and 21 in the consecutive regulations, in addition to which the President reserves the right to determine other forms of development activities if required for public interest.[17] One of the criteria for the determination of whether activities are in the public interest is their commercial or non-commercial character. Public interest activities were supposed to be non-commercial. If the private sector is engineering government projects that support the public interest, or that are part of public and social facilities construction, the procedure of expropriation in public interest can be used.[18] As previously mentioned, in the Suharto era 'public interest' came to be interpreted very broadly and arbitrarily. Under the umbrella of 'interest of the state' and (economic) 'development', many projects were carried out that could actually not be justified as being in the public interest. Many plots of land that were officially expropriated for national development purposes in fact mainly benefited the ruling elite.

The BAL (art. 18) only mentions that land acquisition for public interest necessitates proper compensation and delegates the formulation of detailed procedural provisions to later laws and regulations. The question of compensation includes at least three elements: determination of what is to be compensated, the form and the amount of compensation. The physical and/or non-physical loss caused by the expropriation of land, buildings, vegetation, and/or other objects associated with the land is what must be compensated. Compensation should provide a better socio-economic standard of living than before the land acquisition.[19] It is unclear whether and on what grounds compensation of immaterial loss/damage can be claimed.[20] Compensation may take the form of money, replacement land, resettlement, a combination of two or more of these forms, or other forms agreed upon by the parties concerned.[21] Resettlement of expropriated landowners has to be carried out in such a way that they will be able to continue their business or earn a livelihood as they did before.[22] A titleholder who does not want any of these options can be given compensation in the form of shares.[23] For the expropriation of communal land of a (village) community (*tanah ulayat*), the compensation may be in the form of a public facility development or other forms that will benefit the local community as a whole.[24]

The acquisition of land in the public interest must be done by way of amicable negotiation (*musyawarah*) over the form and amount of compensation between individual title holders (or representatives of groups of title holders) and the official body concerned.[25] A Land Acquisition Committee must verify the rights on the land involved and make proposals regarding the amount of compensation. The value has to be established objectively without disadvantaging either party, whereby the 'local market price' (the average price of sale and purchase transactions of land/buildings/vegetation in the neighbourhood over a certain period of time) can be used as a guideline for the determination of the value.[26] If no agreement on the form and amount of compensation can be reached between the government and the title-holding community members, the Land Acquisition Committee can set the amount of compensation.[27] Objections against the decision of the Land Acquisition Committee may be filed to the Regent/Mayor, the Governor, or the Minister of Home Affairs. If the problems cannot be solved, the last step will be a request to the President for revocation of the title on land and objects on the land, signed by the Minister concerned and the Minister of Justice and Human Rights.[28]

The multitude of the sometimes very detailed legal regulations proved not to be a guarantee against infringements of land rights by the government or government-supported private enterprises during the Suharto administration. The rules were manipulated or simply neglected and, as said above, under disguise of 'development' and 'public interest', many land expropriations occurred without proper consultation with landowners and with no or inadequate compensation. The repressive regime and corrupt judiciary made redress virtually impossible.

Almost immediately after Suharto stepped down, a wave swept through the country of spontaneous re-occupations of land plots that were claimed to have been taken by the government illegally or against inadequate compensation. The situation has significantly improved under successive post-Suharto administrations. Additional regulations have been enacted to redress the weaknesses in the legal system, and the rules are implemented more prudently, taking into account the needs of the population and their traditional institutions and procedures. Nevertheless, there are still many problems in practice. One of the major complaints today seems to be that the amount of compensation is almost always below the market price.

Land reforms

The implementation of provisions regarding maximum and minimum size of land ownership prescribed by the BAL (art. 17) and determined in Government Regulation in lieu of Law 56/1960 implied land reform. Land reform was most relevant – and needed – for Java, the most densely populated island of Indonesia, with a population of around 42 million in 1960 (318/km²) and of more than 120 million currently (909/ km²). Almost half of the farming households in Java (53.86 per cent) had their own paddy-fields (*sawah*), 12.4 per cent were tenants or sharecroppers on *sawah* owned by others, and 33.74 per cent of these households worked as agricultural labourers (Hardjosudarmo 1970:65-70).

Land use and ownership conditions in Java began to deteriorate after the Second World War, when the worsening economic conditions caused the value of land to increase, and inflation (ten to 25 per cent per month in 1962 (Soen 1968:61-62)) compelled many small farmers to sell land. A middle class, virtually non-existent before the war, emerged and began to invest in land. A trend developed towards the accumulation of increasingly greater land holdings in the hands of a small group of landowners. Economic pressure and fragmentation of land through inheritance increased the disparity between the large landholders and the small farmers. Statistics from 1957 show that 70 per cent of households in Java owned less than 0.5 hectare, 25 per cent between 0.5 and one hectare, three per cent between one and two hectares, 1.5 per cent between two and five hectares, and only 0.5 per cent had five hectares or more at their disposal.

Furthermore, conditions of sharecropping arrangements in customary law worsened. Those conditions used to be based on the principle of mutual aid. When the number of farmers who needed land became larger than the area of land available, the relationship gradually developed into one of supply and demand in which customary considerations of mutuality and justice played no role. It placed the sharecropper in a disadvantageous position: his share might be half of the harvest if he bore all production costs, but usually his share was not in balance with the energy and expenses he spent in cultivating the land (Hüsken 1979:148).

In his State Address on Independence Day 1959, President Sukarno announced a programme of land reform which he said would result in a more equitable distribution of income among citizens and create a social structure that would encourage a higher national production of rice.[29] Basically, the idea was to permit ownership of land only to those who actually tilled the soil. This would simultaneously obliterate sharecropping. The proposal met with opposition from various parties. Not surprisingly, Islamic groups, supported by prominent Muslims and Islamic schools (pesantren) who owned large tracts of land that might be affected by the proposed system, opposed the idea. They argued that shifting the ownership of land to the tiller was in variance with customary law in which proprietary rights to land are inalienable divine rights to be inherited by descendants. The Nationalist Party in turn opposed the proposal because many village officials, most of whom were party members or supporters, controlled vast areas of land 'in lieu of salary' (tanah bengkok) which they might lose under the new system. And finally, although the Indonesian Communist Party (PKI) propagandised the idea of giving land to the tiller, they basically advocated the complete abolition of private ownership rights and the establishment of a collective system. President Sukarno reiterated that the Indonesian land reform was not to be considered a communist land reform, that rights of individual ownership would be maintained, and that people still had permanent rights of ownership. In the end, a compromise was reached, consisting of the recognition of individual ownership of real property up to a set maximum, even if the landowner did not till the land himself, and the restriction of absentee land ownership.

These ideas are reflected in the BAL's provisions regarding maximum and minimum land ownership (artt. 7 and 17) and absentee ownership (artt. 10 and 24) that are the foundation of land reform legislation in Indonesia. They are formulated in very general terms and refer to later laws for detailed regulation of the subjects. The BAL (art. 7) prohibits ownership and control of land beyond certain limits. Land owned in excess of the limits to be determined in later laws will be taken by the government against compensation for distribution among those who need land (art. 17). The maximum and minimum limits were set in a Government Regulation in lieu of Law 56/1960. The maximum varied by region, depending on population density, between fifteen hectares of paddy-fields (*sawah*) or twenty hectares of dry land in underpopulated areas, and five hectares of *sawah* or six hectares of dry land in highly populated areas, such as Java. The minimum size of land holding was set at two hectares per household (art. 8). Failure to comply with the rules regarding transfer land owned in excess of the set maximum was able to evoke criminal sanction and lead to forfeiture of the right to compensation (art. 10).

BAL article 10 rules that those who hold a right to land have to work or use it themselves ('land-to-the-tiller principle'), and article 24 says that the use of land by others than the owner will be restricted. The latter provision was elaborated in Government Regulation 224/1961 (art. 3) that determined that those who own land outside the sub-district of residence or the adjacent sub-district shall transfer such land to an inhabitant of the district where the land is situated.[30] If one fails to comply with this provision, the land will be expropriated against compensation and redistributed by the government.

Rules regarding compensation of landowners for the expropriation of land owned in excess of the set maximum were determined in Government Regulation 224/1961. The compensation for the first five hectares of expropriated land was ten times the annual net production; for the second, third, and fourth plots of five hectares it was nine times; any further excess land would be compensated with seven times the annual net production.[31] Farmers who received expropriated land had to pay the government the equivalent of the compensation paid to former land owners, plus a ten per cent administration fee.[32] It soon became clear, however, that it would be impossible to implement the provisions regarding maximum land ownership and to redistribute land owned in excess.

(i) Obstacles to land reform

As early as 1961 Ladejinsky, the architect of land reform in Japan, reported several obstacles that hindered the smooth implementation of land reform in Indonesia. First of all, he found that the provision of redistribution of land held by absentee landowners, and land exceeding the maximum limit, could serve only a small number of farmers and would not be sufficient to provide the many landless households with land. Furthermore, the provision for minimum ownership was unrealistic because there was not enough land to guarantee that each household would receive the prescribed two hectares (Walinsky 1977:297).

Official records[33] prove him right. These indicate that between 1963 and 1969 some 7.75 per cent of approximately five million landless families received 0.43 hectare on average per household.[34] Due to the scarcity of available land, the policy of redistribution to all landless families was not further enforced. The rule of minimum ownership was adapted: farmers in densely populated areas who owned one hectare or more would not receive any additional land, whereas those who owned less than one hectare would receive additional land to increase their total to a maximum of one hectare. Farmers who did not themselves own land would be given a plot of 0.5 hectare.[35]

Ladejinsky pointed at other obstacles, such as the long process of obtaining the excess land (there were no less than fifteen institutions which had to approve applications), the selection of beneficiaries, and the question of compensation to the old owners. He criticised the composition of the village land committees involved in the redistribution of land and the selection of beneficiaries. Their membership was generally composed of the village heads and representatives of farmers organisations which almost always represented the interests of the large landowners (Mortimer 1972:18).[36] They often allowed for false reporting in the surveying of land. Landless peasants rarely had a voice in matters affecting them. Laadejinsky claimed that, in order to be effective, the committee members needed to be elected by all concerned, and in any case, landless peasants should make up the majority.[37] Even for well-meaning village land committees the categories of recipients were too numerous and their categorisation too complicated to administer. They faced too many choices; a situation that was further complicated by the fact that the land to be redistributed was, in most cases, only a very small amount (Walinsky 1977:343-347).

Large landowners disliked the compensation system because the difference between the compensation paid by the government and the market price was so great that expropriation was considered confiscation. A parcel appraised by the government might in the market realise seven to thirty times as much. In order to avoid expropriation, it became common practice among large landowners to fictitiously transfer land to other family members by means of pre-dated transfer of titles, so that officially they did not possess land beyond the maximum limit (Adicondro 1980:2-3). Transfers to relatives were not necessarily a violation of the law as long as those relatives had cultivated the land as tenants prior to the enactment of the law. But usually that was not the case, and many transfers of land plots were faked, with the intent of obscuring excess ownership and preventing expropriation.

To deal with the confusion and difficulties surrounding compensation, the government set up a land reform bond system in 1963:[38] compensation was to be given in the form of a ten per cent deposit to a savings account in the former landowner's name, and the remainder was in the form of government bonds to be paid over twelve years at three per cent interest per year.[39] Due to the extremely rapid inflation between 1963 and 1965[40] and economic decline, compensation given to former landowners thus amounted to a loss.

(ii) The fate of land reform

Between 1962 and 1965 land reform became the primary source of political conflict between Sukarno's Nationalists and the Islamic parties on the one hand, and the Communists on the other. Most of the landowners belonged either to the Indonesian Nationalist Party (PNI) or to the Islamic party Nahdlatul Ulama (NU). Landless peasants, in spite of their hard lives, mostly supported the parties or organisations of their employers, on whom they depended. They were hesitant to join the farmers' organisation of the Communist Party (Utrecht 1976:273-282). Some of the landowners, however, also supported the Communist Party, financially or otherwise, in exchange for which they enjoyed protection against the forced 'unilateral occupation' of land (aksi sepihak) by landless peasants at the instigation of the Communist Party. The communists, who found that land reform developed too slowly and was entirely manipulated, considered these 'unilateral actions' as just and legal means of seriously implementing the BAL (Aidit 1964:21-22, 89-90). These actions created an extremely tense situation in which the Communist Party confronted Islamic groups, the nationalists, and the army. The conflict over land reform was no longer between landowners and landless peasants – it was now a case of communist against anti-communists.

The political conflict culminated in the tragic attempted coup d'état in 1965 followed by a massive wave of violence that swept through the country in which large numbers of members and followers of communist organisations, suspected sympathisers, and many innocent people were murdered.[41] Land reform came to be stigmatised as a product of the communists. The implementation of land reform and the distribution of excess and absentee land came to a stop, and many former landowners reclaimed land plots that had been taken from them (Tjondronegoro 2003:12). In this troubled period of social and political turmoil, one's rights in land (and, for that matter, in other property) were far from secure.

Since the mid-1970s there have been several attempts to restart the realisation of land reform as required by the BAL and other regulations.[42] In 1982, for example, Land Reform Advisory Committees were established at the national and regional (provincial/district) levels[43] that should, among other things, make an inventory of lands with absentee owners and land exceeding maximum ownership for the purpose of redistribution.[44] In the years thereafter, instances of reallocation of land to landless families did indeed occur, but the total amount of reallocated land and the size of individual plots were relatively insignificant in relation to the actual needs. Besides, these allotments cannot be considered as instances of land reform redistribution, as the reallocated plots were mostly taken from former colonial 75-year leases and state-owned land. They did not originate from excess or absentee holdings.

Although these attempts demonstrate at least some degree of political will on the part of the government at the time to provide land to those in need, they also show that unless changes are made in the maximum and minimum limits of ownership and unless the prohibition of absentee landownership is enforced, these good intentions will not of themselves be sufficient to improve the lives of landless peasants in Java, whose numbers have greatly increased since 1960.

(iii) New land reform programme in the post-Suharto 'Reformation Era'

The situation remained virtually unchanged until September 2006, when the Indonesian government announced a new policy of gradual land reform to be implemented between 2007 and 2014 in order to improve the living standard of economically weak groups. A total of 8.15 million hectares of land is to be distributed, 6 million of which is destined for poor farmers who meet specific criteria. The size of the plot to be distributed to each family varies, depending on the needs of the families and the availability of land in the region[45]. The remaining 2.15 million hectares would be granted to small entrepreneurs under the Right of Exploitation (*Hak Guna Usaha*) or the Right to Use (*Hak Pakai*), which rights can be revoked by the state if the land is not used for productive purposes.

The plans for this land redistribution policy were thoroughly commented on and criticised. The Indonesian Legal Assistance Group (PBHI) criticised the government's intentions to allow the allocation of land to entrepreneurs. They were of the opinion that, in the framework of land reform, land should be distributed to tillers. They demanded

that the government give priority to the needs of farmers and customary communities and revoke all laws and regulations that do not favour
them.[46]

The Indonesian Farmers Union Federation (FSPI) in turn argued
that the BAL was inadequate to realise the envisaged reforms and that
a new law was required whose provisions follow the principles of the
BAL 1960.[47] They held the view that the structuring of land ownership
in the agricultural sector must begin from the implementation of the
land reform programme that includes ownership scale modification
and the division and fusion of farm operation units. They point to a
number of other conditions for success. First, the capacity of farmers
needs to be enhanced through educational programmes, subsidies, improvement of farming technology, fair distribution and trade systems,
and support to farmers' organisations and farmers' cooperatives. Second, an inventory of unresolved land conflicts should be drawn up in
preparation of their settlement, and a systemic, organised and comprehensive conflict settlement mechanism should be formulated. Third,
land rights that have been violated should be restored, taking into consideration the sense of justice of the people who have become victims.
Many of these critical arguments have come to play a role in the discourse about the restoration of the land rights situation in post-Suharto
Indonesia.

Registration of land rights

The BAL (art. 19) states that the government will register all land
throughout Indonesia 'in order to guarantee legal security'. This provision has, however, remained a dead letter for a long time; registration
advanced at a snail's pace. It was estimated in 1995, when Indonesia
engaged in a large World Bank-supported land registration project, that
only some seven to ten per cent of all land had been registered (Evers
1995:21; Walijatun and Grant 1996). Most of these registrations were
so-called 'sporadic' registrations, the expensive and time-consuming
standard procedure of registration of single plots of land at individual
request by Westerners during the colonial period and by urban elites
and companies after independence.

The agrarian population apparently felt no urge or was unable to
have their rights registered. They continued to manage their land
rights and tenure affairs under the traditional system they were familiar with, which defined the communal and individual relations to land.
Amongst themselves, community members were relatively secure of
their land rights, and traditional decision-making mechanisms were
available for dealing with doubts and disputes. The 'internal' security
of traditional land rights and tenure regimes is jeopardised, however,

when external parties (the state, companies, individuals) choose to lay hands on land in the community's territory. In the Suharto era this often happened without paying much attention to customary rights under the political justification of 'development'. Traditional systems provided no security against such external infringements.

Traditional/customary land rights cannot as such be registered. They have to be officially 'released' from the traditional context first through a 'Release of *Adat* Land Document' (*Surat Bukti Pelepasan Tanah Adat*) and converted into a legal right according to the BAL (Rieger et al. 2001:48)[48] that seemed more or less equivalent to the relationship in the traditional sphere. One of the major theoretical problems of this procedure is that BAL rights are strictly individual, whereas customary rights have communal characteristics. Even individual land rights and tenure relations are usually embedded in the rights of a larger group of relatives and co-villagers. These characteristics are lost in the conversion into BAL rights. The low registration numbers of 1995 show that the opportunity to transfer customary rights into BAL rights has not been widely taken up.

(i) Promotion of registration

The government undertook several attempts to accelerate the registration of land. In 1984 the 'National Agrarian Project' (*Proyek Nasional Agraria*: PRONA) was initiated. Farmers could apply for registration under the project, which used the relatively expensive method of 'sporadic' registration but would be cheaper for applicants than an individual registration at their own request because the government subsidised the project. It resulted in an increase of registrations, but not to the degree that was hoped for. One of the reasons for the disappointing results was probably the fact that apparently political considerations played a role in the selection and admission of applicants: supporters of Suharto's political party, Golkar, seemed to be favoured, antagonists ignored. Furthermore, potential applicants often refrained from applying because they did not trust the government and its projects, and did not believe that registration would benefit them.

A more effective measure was the Indonesian Land Administration Project (LAP) that was launched in 1995 with the assistance of the World Bank and the Australian government, modelled upon a similar project in Thailand (Onchan et al. 1990; Slaats 1999; World Bank 2003c). It aimed at the systematic registration of all land throughout Indonesia in 25 years. Unlike the normal procedure of 'sporadic' registration used in previous registration projects, LAP was based on 'systematic' registration, meaning that all inhabitants of a selected area would be approached one-by-one, door-to-door as it were, by registration officials in order to determine which rights they had on land, to mark its border, to enter the data in the central record, and to issue certificates. The system is much more accurate and efficient, and thus provides faster and cheaper registration, than previous projects.[49] Substantive subsidisation by the government enabled the families/individuals in the selected areas to have a land plot registered at an extremely low price of approximately USD 3 (the cost price would be around USD 26) (World Bank 2004b:44).[50]

Initially, the implementation of the systematic registration project was restricted to the densely populated Java, where customary land rights regimes were considered to be non-existent or of too little relevance to stand in the way of individualisation through titling and registration. Before registration could be started in the areas outside Java, research had to be carried out to answer the question of whether communal customary rights on land were still extant, and what that meant for registration. Although the research took place in only four different areas, among communities with very different cultural characteristics and land rights regimes, its results suggest that throughout Indonesia customary land regimes and communal rights on land still apply that are not easily reconcilable with individualisation through registration. The government was advised to acknowledge traditional communal rights and respect the communities' authority (Slaats 1997:12/1) and to refrain from registration of individual plots in rural areas.

Ministerial Regulation 5/1999 was the first that confirmed the existence of traditional *ulayat* rights and made some substantive provisions. Among other things it states that the authority to dispose of *ulayat* land, by allowing other parties (including the state) access to it, is in the hands of the traditional community concerned. In the years thereafter a process of revitalisation and reinvention of *adat* set in, which has been well received in government circles. Many district administrations are designing (or have issued) *adat* land law regulations. NGOs have joined the process and have significantly increased their activities in the field of defending and promoting (putative) *adat* land rights. Many land claims which had been suppressed under the 'New Order' regime have now resurfaced and are often justified/reinforced by reference to their *adat* status (Bakker 2005). The process, however, also creates room for political opportunism by rent-seekers and power-seekers to enlarge the scope of their authority or to obtain positions they never had under the customary system (Bakker forthcoming).

The set-up of the project and its implementation were well considered. On the basis of available information (maps, aerial photographs, population numbers, etc.), small workable areas were demarcated where the actual registration activities would be carried out by officers of the National Land Agency (*Badan Pertanahan Nasional*), who had been recruited in great numbers from all over Indonesia, and who had been trained for the job. These activities were divided into two types: adjudication and survey. An adjudication team would visit the inhabitants of the area, door-to-door, to establish whether they had land, where it was located, and what kind of rights they had. If no valid official documents of ownership were available, other written documents and oral testimony by the applicant and other witnesses (formal and informal local leaders, friends and neighbours) were allowed to prove claimed rights. If a claimed plot appeared to be state land, the National Land Agency would investigate the possibility of granting ownership rights on that plot to the applicant.[51] Applicants were requested to demarcate their land plots in the presence of the owners of neighbouring plots. In case of disputed borders (or other disputes) which could not be settled through mediation of the adjudication team, a plot would not be registered for the time being until the dispute was settled in court or otherwise. The results of the investigation of the adjudication team were posted at the local land office so that each could be checked. Objections could be submitted within 60 days. Then a survey team would enter the field to measure the surface and exact location and position of each demarcated plot. The data of all teams were collected at the office of the National Land Agency and entered into the land register, after which, usually with some ceremony, certificates stating the physical and legal properties of the land (and restrictions thereof) were handed out to the entitled individuals.

Generally, the LAP was better organised and more transparent than previous registration projects. Before registration was implemented in an area, information on costs, rights and obligations, and the process of registration was disseminated in public meetings with the population, in which the participation of women was encouraged. The interim results were published prominently in the village, and there was an opportunity to dispute the outcome of surveys. Certificates were usually issued as promised. Instances of additional informal payments, unusual delays in processing, exercise of administrative discretion, and fraudulent documentation did occur, but far less often than in other government-supported registration projects or under the system of sporadic registration.

Due to the Asian economic crisis, the budget for the LAP was severely reduced, implying that the implementation slowed down and was restricted to primarily urban areas. Yet at the end of 2003 the number of registered land plots was estimated to have risen to 27 per cent (approximately 23 million out of 85 million of land plots; BPN (National Land Agency) 2003).[52] In order to register the remaining plots within a relatively short period of time, the implementation process had to be adapted. For the acceleration of land registration, the government initiated the Land Management and Policy Development

Project, whose target was the registration of 2.5 million plots during the period of 2005-2009. In 2005, however, the project achieved only 75 per cent of the target (260,315 out of 315,000 plots; BPN (National Land Agency) 2006:1).

(ii) Effect of registration

Registration of land rights is supposed to provide legal security (BAL art. 19) and therefore enhance tenure security. After the registration data have been processed, the title holder receives a certificate for each of the registered land plots. The certificate is proof that a plot of land has been registered and that the physical and legal data therein correspond to the data in the measurement letter and the land book.[53] It does not, however, provide waterproof evidence of right, because registration is based on the 'negative registration system' in which the state does not guarantee the accuracy of the registered data. Thus, a party whose name is recorded as the title holder in the land book and on the certificate is still at a risk of being sued by other parties claiming to have a right to the land.[54] The objective is to strike a balance between the legal certainty of all parties who possess in good faith (with or without registration).

The security certificates are supposed to offer is furthermore jeopardised by the fact that not infrequently different people hold a certificate for the same plot of land, in other words: several certificates on the same plot of land are in circulation. Some of these are simple counterfeits, but often the certificates are official (drawn up by an authorised official) but fraudulent ('bought' through corruption). The phenomenon is so common that the Indonesians have a term for such certificates: *aspal* (*asli palsu*: original but false).

Besides providing security of title (as envisaged in the BAL art. 19), the registration of land rights was assumed to have positive economic effects. One of the underlying assumptions of LAP was that registered land (certificates) could be used as collateral for bank loans to be invested in agricultural activities. Under colonial and Indonesian law, customary land rights could not be registered and used as collateral for loans, and the opportunity to have these rights converted into BAL rights was rarely used. The farmer population used to turn to relatives, neighbours and semi-professional moneylenders for loans (usually very expensive). They had virtually no access to institutional moneylenders, as banks were not inclined to provide loans on unregistered land.

Law 4/1996 on Security Rights replaced the provisions of the colonial Civil Code on mortgage (*hypotheek*) on land and other immovable properties that had been in force until then. Under the new law, unregistered land (including customary land) could be used as collateral if simultaneously with the conferment of the security right, a request was made for registration of the land.[55] On the one hand, this can be considered a promising step ahead in the endeavour to speed up the registration of land. On the other hand, it remains to be seen whether this option will be frequently used given the costs of individual (sporadic) registration requests.

Land registration seems to have increased the number of bank loans to farmers with their land as collateral, also in rural areas,[56] although banks are hesitant to provide substantive loans in remote rural areas, as collateral land may be unsaleable or have too little liquidation value. On the other hand, it also happens that local branches of banks provide petty loans to farmers on the basis of an unofficial written promise that land (unregistered) will serve as security, or even without any security. These transactions are usually short-term and expensive (high interest rate) and based on trust and personal relationships. The institutional moneylender thus enters the domain of unofficial borrowing from relatives and other unofficial moneylenders whose services are still widely used in rural customary law areas.

Given the above discussion of Indonesian land law and its developments, the remaining sections focus on two additional issues: the reallocation of authority in land matters in the framework of post-Suharto decentralisation, and the question of the ability/inability of the BAL to accommodate non-agrarian, modern industrial, and commercial interests (investments in land).

Decentralisation and land management authority

The administration of non-forest land is in the hands of the National Land Agency (*Badan Pertanahan Nasional*).[57] This agency has the authority to issue rights on state land (right of exploitation: *hak guna usaha*), is charged with the implementation of registration projects, processes and records registration data (both from systematic and sporadic registrations), and issues land certificates. By virtue of its strictly centralised organisation and the repressive character of Suharto's New Order administration, the agency developed a powerful authoritarian position in land matters, accompanied by an intimidating display of power and rent-seeking (corruption).

Its position came under scrutiny after Suharto was forced to step down in 1998, and his successor set in motion a process of democratisation and decentralisation. In 1999, after more than 30 years of a strong, centralised government, the authority in a number of domains, including the administration of land, shifted from the centre to the lower, regional administrative levels: the district (*kabubaten*) and cities/municipalities.[58] The land sector is for obvious reasons (see above) one of the domains which is coloured by the tug-of-war between the central government, which tends to retain all authority over land matters, and regional governments who like to have their say in land affairs.

The original plan for the devolution of all land affairs to the regional level was modified: the National Land Agency was maintained as a central agency, but its role was limited to legislation, performance standards, uniform land registration procedures, training, and the provision of some services (Heryani and Grant 2004:11). Presidential Regulation 10/2006 on the National Land Agency, which ordered the establishment of branch offices of the agency at the various regional levels, provoked protest from regional government institutions.[59] They asserted that the regulation implicitly maintained the centralised structure of land administration and reduced regional autonomy, which is in contradiction with the principle of Law 32/2004 that land issues are fully under the authority of the regional government at the provincial, district, and city level. They found that autonomy in land affairs was vital for districts and cities to develop spatial layout strategies and allocate land, and requested the central government to immediately transfer the authority in land affairs to the autonomous regions.

The All-Indonesia Association of Provincial Governments went even further in its criticisms and proposed that the BAL be amended and be brought into agreement with the principle of decentralisation in order to be able to meet the demand for agrarian services necessitated by population growth, advancement of science and technology, spatial layout changes, and the securing of land rights, including communal and individual customary rights.

The influential non-governmental Agrarian Reform Consortium (*Konsorsium Pembaruan Agraria*), on the other hand, advocated that not all authority should be given to the region, but that there should be a balanced distribution of authority in land matters between the central and regional governments. Agrarian reform requires a national policy. If no attention is paid to agrarian reform and structural change within governmental organisation, discussions about the distribution of authority are a waste of energy. These disputes are ongoing, and the distribution of authority in land affairs between the central and regional government is still not clear today.

Land law and non-agrarian interests (investments)

We have seen above that many critics advocate adapting various aspects of the BAL. There are others who go even further and propose the withdrawal of the BAL and its replacement with a new land law that will answer the present-day requirements. They argue that the BAL primarily focuses on rural, agrarian relationships and interests, and that it is not geared to accommodate non-agrarian, modern, economic (industrial, commercial and investment) interests. They point at two obstacles in the BAL. One is the provision of article 9(1) and 21 that only Indonesian subjects and government-acknowledged corporate bodies can have property rights (*hak milik*) in land. It excludes not-recognised Indonesian corporate bodies, foreigners, and foreign corporations. This arrangement stems from the isolationist policy under Indonesia's first president, Sukarno, who opposed foreign investment and even withdrew Indonesia from the United Nations, the IMF, and the World Bank. For some time, foreign aid and foreign investments were refused, except from socialist countries, such as the Soviet Union and China. Sukarno was forced to abandon this policy of isolationism by then general Suharto who made him accept a law to allow and facilitate foreign investment.[60] Although foreigners and foreign companies still could not have full property rights (*hak milik*) in land, they were allowed the legal opportunity to obtain one of the more restricted rights (use rights, cultivation rights, rights of building). This, however, did not solve the second obstacle: the relatively short duration of these restricted land rights. The duration of 25 years (with the possibility of extension for another 25 years) for the Right to Cultivate (*Hak Guna Usaha*) and 30 years for the Right to Building (*Hak Guna Bangunan*) was insufficient for many entrepreneurs.

It was not until 1996 that an attempt was made to solve this problem by issuing a Government Regulation that extended the periods of validity to 95 years for the Right to Cultivate, 80 years for the Right to Building, and 70 years for the Right of Use (*Hak Pakai*). The Regulation, moreover, allowed applying for the extension or renewal of the right simultaneously with the initial granting request. This Government Regulation solved the problem only partly because it was not of the same status as a statute, and was not considered to provide sufficient legal certainty.

The final solution lies in the Foreign Investment Law[61] that Parliament accepted in March 2007. It formulates the provisions of Government Regulation in a law which brings them in line with the provisions in countries such as Malaysia, Singapore, Vietnam, and China, where the land rights for investors range between 75 and 90 years. It is hoped that this will attract the substantial domestic and foreign investments which are required to solve Indonesia's economic problems, in which an increase of economic growth to 6.3 per cent is needed to remedy an unemployment rate of more than ten per cent. [62]

Conclusion

Until the change in the colonial mentality under the 'Ethical Policy' of the early twentieth century, the welfare of the indigenous Indonesian population was not of major interest to the colonial government. A system of social, economic, and legal dualism facilitated the efficient and profitable exploitation of the country's natural wealth by the colonial government and foreign enterprises. The generated profits were exported to the homeland in Europe, while virtually no investments were made in the indigenous economy. World War II brought an end to Dutch colonial rule. The colonial economy had collapsed, and Indonesia found itself in the economic state of an underdeveloped agrarian nation, which it had always been.

Young independent Indonesia wanted to do away with the discriminatory dualistic colonial system and the laws that had served colonial interests. The Basic Agrarian Law of 1960 (BAL) abolished colonial regulations pertaining to land. The law formulated the basic principles of a new national land law that was to express the specific Indonesian cultural and normative characteristics and to serve the interests/aspirations of its people. This is expressed in, among other things, the BAL's reference to traditional law (adat) and traditional communal rights (ulayat), and in the redefined position of the state. The intention of the BAL to improve the economic position of the poor and landless peasants is reflected in the provisions regarding the redistribution of land owned in excess of the set maxima (land reform). Registration of land rights was to guarantee legal security.

That many of the goals set out in the BAL have not been achieved is partly due to the ambivalence and vagueness of the BAL itself. The reference to traditional law (adat) and communal (village) rights (ulayat) proved to be a legal formality that had no substantive consequences. The strictly individual land rights defined in the BAL lack the characteristics of communality inherent in traditional land tenure relationships, and thereby weaken the prevailing systems of internal securities of tradition-based land rights and tenure relationships in rural communities. Until recently, traditional rights have been virtually neglected, since they usually come off worse when confronted with claims based on BAL rights.

Land reform, unpopular amongst landowners in general, failed as it became associated with communism. It was doomed to fail in the overpopulated island of Java where there was too little land available to provide so many farmer families with the prescribed minimum. Registration of land rights, anticipated in the BAL to provide legal security, remained a dead letter for a long time. It apparently did not appeal to the masses, as the low number of registrations before the 1995 introduction of systematic registration programmes indicates. Some traditional communities recorded the boundaries of their village territory themselves to avoid the loss of village communal land as a consequence of official registration. Even today many countrymen do not see the benefit of title registration, and find their tradition-based internal security satisfactory.

Besides the flaws in the BAL itself, the proliferation of often inconsistent lower regulations and poor implementation – if not abusive government practice – contributed to the failure to realise the promises of the BAL. The 'New Order' regime of Indonesia's second president, Suharto, managed to improve the overall economic standard of the nation. A reasonably well-off middle class emerged. However, the benefits mainly accumulated among a small elite group around the president. The masses of peasants and the poor enjoyed little of the economic improvement. Corruption, collusion, and nepotism marked the 30 years of 'New Order' government. More often than not, the law seemed to be used as a recipe of how to evade the rule of law, rather than as the basis for implementation, in order to serve the interests of the political and economic elite in the guise of national or state interests. Many communities and individuals lost land through expropriation against no or inadequate compensation for purposes that cannot reasonably be justified as general interest. Traditional land rights were most vulnerable, but legal rights under the BAL were not exempt from infringement either. Social resistance was unthinkable under the repressive regime, whereas appeal to justice was useless because of corruption and the courts' legalistic attitude and lack of affinity with traditional law. Traditional landowners could be sure only of the insecurity of traditional land rights and tenure relationships against external claims. External interventions contributed to the erosion of traditional land rights and tenure securities.

The significance of registration, stepped up by the state-supported large-scale Indonesian Land Administration Project, is questionable. It may be beneficial in urban environments and for the small landowners in Java where land ownership has become individualised over time. In the rest of Indonesia, however, registration implies the transformation of tradition-based land rights and tenure relationships into individual BAL rights. Such transformations, in which the communalistic traits of traditional relationships are embezzled, uncontrollably affect the fabric of social relationships. The cancellation of the registration project in areas outside Java, triggered by the Asian economic crisis, may be a blessing in disguise. The land rights and tenure systems prevailing there remained untouched and were (temporarily) left to take their own course of development at their own speed.

The post-Suharto developments give rise to optimism. Processes of democratisation and decentralisation have set in, demanding a greater measure of bureaucratic transparency and governmental responsibility. The division of power between central and decentralised bodies is not yet balanced, but the lower level authorities are closer to the constituencies whose expectations they have to answer. They tend to pay more attention to local conditions and demands. Many regional/local governments have issued regulations that give some form of recognition to traditional land law that applies at the local level. Throughout the country land rights are claimed/reclaimed, rightly or wrongly, on the basis of traditional claims.

The contention that the BAL unified land law is a formal legal argument that disregards the reality of the great diversity of local/regional land rights and tenure arrangements that still exist on the ground despite 40 years of national legislation. Recognition of this diversity is the first step in a sound national land rights policy and the basis of adequate, effective legislation.

The conditions of overpopulated Java require different land rights provisions than other parts of the country. In Java, communalistic traits of traditional land rights have almost completely disappeared; land rights have become strongly individual. A shift from uneconomic/untenable husbandry on fragmented land plots to decentralised/dispersed labour-intensive industrialisation may be one of the means to alleviate/tackle the economic problems of overpopulated Java. It may help to stop and reverse the drift from the countryside to the city. The variety of land rights and tenure systems elsewhere in the country are to a greater or lesser degree still based on rules and practices that have been handed down from generation to generation. This traditional law is not merely a rigid relic of the past; it has continuously been adapted to arising changes and challenges. It has survived in spite of imposed national legal rules.

An adequate understanding and substantive recognition of these local arrangements seem to be prerequisite for attempts to bridge the gap between these arrangements and national law. Rather than top-down imposition of law, a facilitative government policy that leaves room for bottom-up incentives and takes account of the demographic and environmental diversity may lead to more realistic and effective legislation. Accepting the conditions prevailing in viable traditional communities and taking them into account in national law development policy might be more efficient and promising than neglecting them or ruling them out of existence. Thus, the traditional decision-making processes that are vital as the constituent source of norms in tradition-oriented communities should be taken seriously by the legislator as well as by external parties (e.g. enterprises) in their negotiations for land. Excessive traditional conditions, however, may require marginal intervention by national law. For the settlement of rural internal community disputes as well as external disputes about land, traditional dispute-handling institutions and processes should be incorporated in Indonesia's adjudicative hierarchy as the fourth and lowest level.

Systematic registration of land under the nationwide land administration project should refrain from registering individual plots in tradition-oriented communities and should be restricted to recording the outer boundaries of the village territory, including communal lands (*ulayat*), for protection against external infringements. Instead of centralised registration, land rights in tradition-oriented communities should be recorded by a simple local documentation system that can be easily accessed and controlled by title holders. The recorded data can form the basis for higher-level registration, if desirable, and for (semi)-institutional loans.

Facilitative policy also implies that people in communities that are moving away from traditional rule and developing individual land rights should be given the opportunity to subject themselves to the application of statutory law (BAL). Indonesian land law, finally, should provide for communal rights, both individual rights embedded in communal rights (e.g. of kin groups) and village communal rights (*ulayat*). Besides general cultural diversity, the diversification of land law would thus be a significant expression of Indonesia's national motto '*Bhinneka Tunggal Ika*' (unity in diversity).

Notes

1   *Staatsblad* 1870/118.
2   Java was colonised for more than 300 years. The history of the colonisation of the other islands is shorter; the last areas were brought under colonial rule not until early twentieth century.
3   A similar strategy was later applied in the confrontation with the Dutch over the transfer of New Guinea, and the confrontation with Malaysia over Borneo in the 1960s.
4   With exception of the rules of mortgage (*hypotheek*) which remained in force until the enactment of Law 4/1996 on Security Rights on Land and Objects connected to Land (*Undang-Undang Tentang Hak Tanggungan Atas Tanah Beserta Benda-Benda Yang Berkaitan Dengan Tanah*).
5   The Dutch scholar Van Vollenhoven (1918) coined the term '*beschikkingsrecht van de gemeenschap*' (the community's right of avail); cf. Holleman 1981:43,137. See also Rieger et al. 2001:48.
6   In most traditional systems relationships to land are not expressed in terms of 'rights' but in types or categories of land, e.g. Minagkabau: *tanah ulayat* (communal land); Karo Batak (North Sumatra): *taneh kuta* (village land).
7   Respectively, Law 1/1967 on foreign investment and Law 5/1967 on forestry.

8   In particular, the work of the Dutch scholar Van Vollenhoven (1918) and his Indonesian followers.
9   Elucidation to the BAL § II(1).
10   Elucidation to the BAL § II(3); Harsono 1997:85, 125-26.
11   Customary law as shorthand for normative arrangements (mostly unwritten, flexible and adaptive) that developed in rural communities (usually small-scale) through tradition from one generation to the next.
12   E.g. Regulation Minister of Agrarian Affairs/Head of the National Land Agency 5/1999; Forestry Law 41/1999 article 5 (2), 37 and 67.
13   Forestry Law 41/1999 article 67.
14   Article 18B paragraph (2) of the Second Amendment to the 1945 Constitution adopted in 2000.
15   Elucidation to the BAL II (4).
16   BAL, article 18; Presidential Instruction 9/1973 on the Implementation of Revocation of Rights on Land and Objects on Land, article 1 (1).
17   Presidential Instruction 9/1973, article 1 (3).
18   Minister of Home Affairs Regulation 2/1976 on the Use of Land Expropriation Proceedings for Government Interest for Land Expropriation by the Private Sector, article 1 (withdrawn).
19   Presidential Regulation 36/2005, article 1 (11).
20   Resistance against compensation for immaterial damages originates from the Dutch Civil Code that only allowed that sort of compensation for cases of death, grave injury and humiliation. In 1993 the Supreme Court set a precedent by granting a substantial compensation for immaterial damage suffered from the construction of the Kedung Ombo Reservoir in Central Java. On Judicial Review, however, the Supreme Court revoked its decision on formal grounds (damages had not been proven, and no appraisal basis had been given).
21   Presidential Decree 55/1993 article 13, and Presidential Regulation 36/2005 article 13 (1).
22   Presidential Instruction Number 9/1973, article 6 (2).
23   Presidential Regulation 36/2005, article 13 (2); the article does not specify which shares will be given as compensation.
24   Presidential Regulation 36/2005, article 14.
25   Presidential Decree 36/2005 article 8 and 9.
26   Presidential Instruction 9/1973 appendix article 5 (1), and Decree of the Minister of Finance 523/KMK.04/1998 on Determination of Classification and Amount of Tax Object Sale Value as an Imposition Basis for Land and Building Tax, article 1 (1) and (2).
27   Presidential Decree 36/2005 article 10.
28   Presidential Decree 36/2005 article 17 and 18.
29   Presidential Speech August 17, 1959. Jakarta, Departemen Penerangan 1960:53.
30   The rule does not apply to, for example, government officials and members of the armed forces in active service.
31   Government Regulation 224/1961, article 6. By comparison, the Taiwanese government bought land for two and one-half times the annual product, while in South Korea the price was three times the average annual product (Ravenholt 1981:51-52).
32   Government Regulation § 224/1961, article 15 (2, 3 and 5). Payment could be in cash, or in instalments at an interest of three per cent per year. In 1964, the interest rate increased to five per cent per year and the administration fee was lowered to six per cent (Peraturan Pemerintah (the Government Regulation) No. 41 of 1961, art. II).
33   Republik Indonesia Departemen Dalam Negeri, Direktorat Jenderal Agraria, Direktur Land Reform, Hasil Redistribusi Tanah Obyek Land Reform (Republic of Indonesia,

Department of Internal Affairs, Director General of Agrarian, Director Land Reform, the result of land distribution subject to land reform), Jakarta, 1986, pp. 60-65.

34 Ladejinsky predicted in 1963 that only six per cent of the four to five million landless families would benefit from the program (Walinsky 1977:342).

35 Government Regulation 224/1961 article 10.

36 See also Sadjarwo 1978:24 and Soetiknjo 1983:93-94.

37 In Japan, the committees at the village level were comprised of ten members: five representing landless peasants, two representing small landowners and three representing landowners with excess land. Each was chosen by their respective group (Hewes 1995:80).

38 Government Regulation in lieu of Statute 23/1963.

39 Government Regulation 224/1961 article 7 (1, 4 and 5) and Government Regulation 41/1964, art. IIa.

40 By the end of 1965, it had risen to 650 per cent.

41 There are no precise figures. However, hundreds of thousands of people were killed in 1965. See Mortimer (1972:65-66). There are two versions concerning the attempted *coup d'état* of 1965. The first version stated that the communist party PKI was not involved in this movement, but that the *coup d'état* resulted from internal conflict among the military (Anderson, McVey, and Bunnell 1971). The Indonesian government version stated that it was a response to attempts by the PKI to take over the government. See also Brackman 1969:111-112.

42 Such as Government Regulation in lieu of Law 56/1960, which concerned the maximum limitation of land ownership; Government Regulation 224/1961 pertaining to land distribution and compensation; and Government Regulation 41/1964 regarding the amendment of Government Regulation 224/1961.

43 Presidential Decision 55/1980 concerning the Organisation and Process of Land Reform Implementation.

44 Instruction of the Minister of Domestic Affairs 11/1982.

45 Tempo Interaktif, '*Pemerintah Bagikan 9 Juta Hektar Tanah*' (The Government Distributes 9 Million Hectares of Land) Thursday, September 28, 2006 19:54 WIB http://www.tempointeraktif.com/hg/ekbis/2006/ 09/28/brk.20060928-84977.id.html.

46 PBHI, '*Rencana Pemerintah menjalankan 'Reforme Agraria' di Indonesia*' (The Government Plan to Implement Agrarian Reform in Indonesia), http://www.pbhi.or.id/content.php?id=251&id tit=7, October 192006, 21:11:01.

47 FSPI, '*Pandangan dan Sikap FSPI tentang Program Pembaruan Agraria Nasional*' (FSPI Views and Position concerning the National Agrarian Amendment Program), on the site http://www.fspi.or.id/index.php? option=com content&task=view&id=366&Itemid=37, Wednesday November 29, 2006.

48 Cf. Löffler 1996:112 for the process of obtaining title to *adat* land.

49 In absolute numbers LAP was more expensive because of its pretentious dimensions.

50 The cost of standard sporadic registration on individual request may go up to USD 600 or more.

51 Government Regulation 24/1997.

52 Heryani and Grant (2004:2), however, report that the percentage of registered plots was ca. 24 per cent in 2004.

53 Government Regulation 24/1997 article 32.

54 The possibility for a party who is not the holder of a certificate to claim rights has been restricted to a period of five years following the issuance of the certificate. Elucidation to Government Regulation 24/1997, article 32.

55 Law 4/1996 article 10 (3).

56 No exact data available.

57 Forest land, officially some 70 per cent of Indonesia's territory, comes under the competence of the Ministry of Forestry.

58 Law 22/1999 on Regional Government, amended by Law 34/2004. The domains of Foreign Affairs, Defence and Security, Justice, Fiscal Law/Finances, and Religion remained under the authority of the central government.

59 Such as: the All-Indonesia Association of Provincial Governments (APPSI), the All-Indonesia City Governments Association (Apeksi), and the All-Indonesia City DPRD Association (ADEKSI).

60 Law 1/1967 on Foreign Investment.

61 Replacing Law 1/1967 on Foreign Investments and Law 5/1968 on Domestic Investments.

62 Kompas 16 March 2007: 'Indonesia Perlu Suntikan Investasi Rp. 989 Triliun' (Indonesia needs an investment injection of 989 trillion rupiah); Republika 16 March 2007: 'Pengganguran Naik 2.5 Juta Orang' (Unemployment increased to 2.5 million).

19 Land registration programmes for Indonesia's urban poor: Need, reach, and effect in the *kampongs* of Bandung

Gustaaf Reerink[1]

Introduction

The overall majority of Indonesia's urban poor reside in so-called *kampongs*, traditional low-income settlements. Three categories of land tenure are generally found in these settlements: formal, customary, and informal. Dwellers with formal tenure have a property title to their land on the basis of rights acknowledged by the 1960 Basic Agrarian Law (BAL), which remains the general framework for Indonesian land law.[2] At the same time, customary tenure is still common in *kampongs*, usually taking form in individual, inheritable *adat* ownership rights (so-called *hak milik adat*). The BAL acknowledges communal rights (so-called *hak ulayat*) – provided that certain requirements are met – but not *adat* ownership rights. Still, the latter type of rights arguably have a semi-formal status as they are acknowledged as legitimate claims for legalisation, as will be discussed below. *Adat* ownership rights continue to be applied in kampongs. Finally, a third category, informal land tenure, is found in *kampongs*. Informal tenure is usually the result of dwellers squatting land on which the state holds a direct state right of avail (state land) or, less often, on which others have established private rights. This category carries no legal status.

Both customary and informal tenure can be legalised. Customary tenure can be legalised through the legal conversion of 'old' colonial *adat* ownership rights, thus contributing to the BAL's aim of unification, whereas informal tenure can be legalised by granting 'new' rights over state land to its occupants.[3] Indonesian land law does not acknowledge the concept of adverse possession – acquisition of title by occupation of land for a certain period under certain conditions. Informal tenure, therefore, cannot be legalised on grounds of extended occupation of land on which others have established private rights. Such private rights may be forfeited, however, for instance through neglect of the land. In this case, land passes to the state, over which it can again grant 'new' rights (Harsono 2005).[4]

The legalisation of both customary and informal tenure requires the registration of land, which can be done sporadically – registration of one or several plots at the initiative of landholders – or systematically – registration of several plots in the same area at the initiative of the government. Systematic registration is usually done in the framework of large-scale land registration programmes. The first land registration programme dates back to 1981, and several have followed. In 1994 the Indonesian government started the World Bank and AusAid funded Land Administration Project (LAP). It takes a De Soto approach of providing land titles to poor landholders at low cost, as well as institutional reforms. The LAP and other programmes have resulted in the registration of millions of land parcels, particularly in cities.

While impressive in scale, little is known about the contribution of these programmes to their primary aim of enhancing legal security for the urban poor. To fill this knowledge gap, this chapter presents an analysis of the need, reach, and effect of systematic land registration in the Indonesian city. It particularly focuses on land registration programmes in *kampongs* – settlements that form the home of hundreds of thousands of low-income, customary or informal landholders – in Bandung, Indonesia's fourth-largest city and the capital of West Java. It is based on quantitative as well as qualitative research methods, including a survey, participant observation in *kampongs*, and interviews with officials.[5]

The chapter first assesses whether low-income *kampong* dwellers are actually able to do sporadic registration, thus evaluating the need for large-scale land registration programmes. This is followed by a discussion of systematic land registration in general, and the LAP in particular. It discusses the activities that have been carried out and studies the extent to which low-income *kampong* dwellers actually have a chance to participate in this project. Finally, and most importantly, the chapter assesses the extent to which registration of land through programmes such as the LAP contributes to the legal security of participants – by providing them with legally valid titles that allow them to reside on the land and which can stand the test of time – and also to their tenure security.

Integrative potential of sporadic registration

In practice, it has proven hard for landholders to register their land, which means that Indonesia's contemporary land administration forms the 'bell jar' De Soto is moving against. This is the result of several factors, including the stringent evidence requirements for the registration of customary rights, which do not reflect the complex land relations in urban *kampongs*; a lack of political will to register rights of informal landholders; maladministration and resulting barriers; and the negative perceptions of landholders regarding the registration process.

Even after the 1961 Government Regulation – with its stringent documentary evidence requirements for the registration of old rights – was replaced by the 1997 Government Regulation on Land Administration, evidence requirements still prove difficult for customary landholders to meet.[6] This is especially the case in cities such as Bandung. In urban areas, land is often purchased instead of inherited, and evidence for such transactions are usually private contracts (*surat zegel, perjanjian jual-beli*) or sales receipts (*kwitansi jual-beli*). These documents do not meet the evidence requirements for registration (The Smeru Research Team 2002). Documents that do meet evidence requirements, such as notary deeds of sale (*akte jual beli*), are generally far more expensive, so it is difficult or practically impossible for low-income dwellers to obtain them. Frequent purchases of land also make it hard for landholders to prove that the land they live on has been inhabited for at least twenty years (by themselves and possible previous landholders), which otherwise would allow them to register land on the basis of testimonial evidence.

In an interview with *Republika daily*, the Head of Bandung's Land Office argues that land mostly remains unregistered because people have no legal basis for occupying the land and thus cannot meet the evidence requirements to obtain a certificate.[7] The state could grant or transfer rights to dwellers who do not meet evidence requirements, but this statement already illustrates that there is no political will to do so. Initial registration of real rights granted by the state on state land (registration of 'new rights') only occurs on a limited scale in Bandung.[8] Instead, usage rights (*hak pakai*) or management rights (*hak pengelolaan*) are granted to public entities, which means that the state no longer has a direct right of avail (*tanah yang langsung dikuasai oleh negara*).[9] The municipality, for instance, claims 51 per cent of the city's land. It could transfer the rights to this land to dwellers upon request for a price decided upon by a municipal committee and agreed on by the mayor and the municipal council.[10] However, in practice this only occurs on a limited scale. This can be explained by the fact that the municipality leases out the land to an increasing number of residents, including informal landholders, thus generating significant revenues while at the same time keeping the land 'available' for future development projects.[11] Depending on the municipal spatial plan, land is leased out for one, five, or ten years.[12] Annulment of rights on neglected land and redistribution of such land (after the state has regained its direct right of avail) also seldom occur in Bandung, although a lot of squatted land qualifies as such.[13] Even if it were to occur, few *kampong* dwellers would probably be capable of registering their land, due to the costs involved.

High costs, complexity, and tardiness of the registration process form other obstacles to registration. These problems are to a large extent the result of weak performance and even maladministration of the state institutions involved. The NLA in particular has a bad reputation in this respect. It is generally considered one of Indonesia's worst-performing public bodies. Exercising authority over 300 district land offices, it 'has been characterised as over-centralised, secretive and unresponsive to landholders' and the land registration process itself 'is complex, paper-intensive and manual' (World Bank 2003a:45). Corruption forms another serious problem. The NLA 'has been used by prevailing political and bureaucratic establishment for personal and political gains' (World Bank 2003a:45). So it is common that landholders wishing to register their land have to pay bribes. These revenues are a welcome addition to the modest salaries of NLA officials. Not surprisingly, 'registration fees are excessive, among the highest in the world' (World Bank 2003a:45). Maladministration of the NLA also affects the accuracy of the land register, a matter that we will discuss below.

The previously discussed problems can be illustrated by the results of our survey among lower-income *kampong* dwellers in Bandung. We asked respondents who in the past ten years had obtained a land certificate through sporadic registration about the costs and duration of the procedure. On average, the respondents paid almost Rp. 1,600,000, which for most lower-income *kampong* dwellers in Bandung is more than a month's income.[14] The duration of the procedure varied between one and twelve months. However, on average it was relatively short at 3.18 months.[15]

Perhaps more importantly, landholders have negative perceptions regarding the costs, complexity, and duration of registration and will therefore not even try to obtain a certificate. We asked landholders with a converted colonial land right why they had not yet registered their land. Costs formed the foremost reason: 63.2 per cent of the respondents were of the opinion that land registration is costly, and 23.1 per cent of the respondents believed the procedure demands a lot of time and trouble, arguing that they did not know how to obtain a certificate, that the procedure is complex and takes a long time, or that they did not have the energy to get it done. Only 3.2 per cent of the respondents believed that a land certificate is useless. One of these respondents explained that he had not obtained a land certificate because he believed that the land evidence he held, in his case a colonial tax document, is more reliable.

We asked those respondents who believed that land registration was too costly to make an estimation of costs and whether they thought

Table 19.1   *Reasons cited by customary landholders for not having a land certificate*

Reason	Percentage
Land registration is costly	63.2
Land registration is cumbersome	23.1
Trying to obtain a land certificate	4.2
Impossible to obtain a land certificate	3.2
A land certificate is useless	3.2
Other reasons	3.2

Note: *n* = 95

these costs formed an official charge or involved bribes. On average, they estimated that the costs of land registration would be almost Rp. 2,000,000.[16] Notably, almost one-third of the respondents believed that these costs involve bribes.[17] Comparing these data with the actual costs spent by title holders who had obtained a land certificate in the past ten years, it seems that respondents were generally well informed, which allows them to make a rational decision as to whether to register their land.

The negative perceptions of Bandung's low-income *kampong* dwellers about the NLA form no exception, as a 2007 survey of the Anti-Corruption Committee shows. Among 3,611 respondents from Jakarta, Bogor, Depok, Tangerang, and Bekasi, the NLA was considered one of the two bodies (the other being the Department of Justice) with the least integrity among 30 national public bodies. In particular, the services related to land registration were qualified as very poor, namely surveying and certification.[18]

Considering the stringent evidence requirements for the registration of customary rights, which do not reflect the complex land relations (particularly in urban *kampongs*), the lack of political will to grant 'new' or transfer existing rights of public entities, high costs, complexity, and tardiness of the registration process caused by poor administrative performance, and the resulting negative perceptions of landholders regarding registration, it is clear that low-income *kampong* dwellers have difficulty in undertaking sporadic registration. Here we see that it is actually the legal system itself that generates 'extralegal' tenure. Systematic land registration programmes could be of help, provided they can take away the barriers occurring in cases of sporadic registration. The next paragraphs will take a closer look at these programmes, their reach, and their effect.

Land registration programmes in Bandung

As a response to the slow process of land registration, at a relatively
early stage Indonesia initiated large-scale registration programmes. In
1981 the Indonesian government initiated the National Agrarian Operation Project (*Proyek Operasi Nasional Agraria* or PRONA), a programme that aimed at increasing legal certainty and security to particularly economically weak landholders by mass registration and the resolution of land disputes.[19] In some regions Regional Agrarian
Operation Projects (*Proyek Operasi Daerah Agraria* or PRODA) were
launched, similar programmes that are financed by the regional governments. Around 1988 the government intensified land registration
efforts. The number of registered parcels grew at about 1 million per
year. However, since the total number of parcels continued to grow
even faster, the Indonesian government would never have been able to
catch up (World Bank 1994:3-4). Therefore, the need for a more ambitious approach was felt.

Renewed enthusiasm for the land registration approach, in which
De Soto played a catalytic role, also struck Indonesia. In 1994 the Indonesian government and the World Bank started the Land Administration Project (LAP), which as part of a broader policy approach acceler-
ates land registration through systematic as well as sporadic registration (World Bank 1994). In total, 1.2 million land parcels in regencies
and municipalities in Java would be registered systematically, benefiting about 4 million people, including about 100,000 families that were
estimated to be below the low-income line (World Bank 1994).[20] Another goal of the project was to improve the institutional framework
for land administration, which included a systematic review and draft
of land laws and regulations and the training of NLA staff. Finally, the
project was meant to support the government of Indonesia to develop
long-term land management policies through the organisation of semi-
nars and workshops (World Bank 1994). The total costs of the project
were budgeted at USD 140.1 million (World Bank 1994).[21] The successor of the LAP, the Land Management and Policy Development Project,
was initiated in 2004 and is scheduled to end in 2009.

The LAP was particularly beneficial for West Java. This province had
the lowest coverage of land registration in Java at the time the project
was initiated, namely thirteen per cent of all parcels (World Bank
1994). This was mainly caused by the large number of parcels, the rapid increase in the number of parcels due to economic and population
growth, and the large number of informally occupied parcels (World
Bank 1994).[22] For this and other reasons, 68 per cent of the planned
1.2 million certificates would be issued in two municipalities and four
regencies in West Java, including 101,500 ownership right (*hak milik*)

Table 19.2 *Output land administration project in Bandung Municipality*

Year	Number of municipal districts	Number of municipal sub-districts	Number of parcels
1996/1997	7	29	30,792
1997/1998	6	29	39,042
1998/1999	10	35	37,098
1999/2000	12	30	22,839
2000/2001	2	2	3,092
Total	37	125	132,863

Source: Internal document of the Bandung Municipality Land Office (titled *'Daftar: Rekapitulasi Pelaksanaan Proyek Administrasi Pertanahan di Kota Bandung Tahun* 1996/1997 S/D Tahun 2000/2001')

certificates in Bandung (World Bank 1994). Although all eligible parcels were expected to be registered under the project, this has not been the case in Bandung (World Bank 1994). Still, an impressive number of parcels has been registered, even more than planned, namely 132,863 parcels, as Table 19.2 shows.

By comparison, sporadic registration in Bandung in about that same period only led to a fraction of the number of parcels being registered under the LAP, namely 4,630 parcels, as Table 19.3 shows.[23]

The NLA estimates that currently about 600,000 land parcels in Bandung Municipality have been registered. Still 30 per cent or 5,019 hectares of all land remain unregistered, despite the fact that many occupants of this land meet the registration requirements.[24] Thus, even under current criteria, land registration programmes could still benefit many landholders in Bandung Municipality.

Under these circumstances it is laudable that the World Bank continues with land registration. The successor of the LAP, the Land Management and Policy Development Project, is now well under way. It is even more ambitious than LAP, with a stronger focus on land registra-

Table 19.3 *Output sporadic registration in Bandung Municipality*

Year	Registration of customary rights in number of parcels	Registration of new rights on state land in number of parcels	Total number of parcels
1998	2,071	517	2,588
1999	182	557	739
2000	84	478	562
2001	32	301	333
2002	62	346	408
Total	2,431	2,199	4,630

Source: Internal document of the Bandung Municipality Land Office (Titled: *'Laporan Bidang Pengukuran dan Pendaftaran Tanah'*)

tion and institutional development (World Bank 2004b). Its goal is to issue 2.5 million certificates in areas of high poverty and high economic potential through systematic registration (World Bank 2004b).

Aside from impressive results in numbers of registered parcels and relatively low costs and short duration of the registration procedures, the question remains whether LAP and other land registration programmes or any sporadic registration effort have reached low-income groups and contributed to their legal security. So far, at least three studies have been done about the LAP, to which the remainder of this chapter will also refer. The first was a World Bank commissioned evaluation by Hardjono, in collaboration with a number of local NGOs, which had a qualitative character, using methods like focus group discussions and in-depth interviews with members of communities, and was conducted in nine urban, peri-urban, and rural city quarters and villages, including a city quarter in Bandung (Hardjono 1999). The second study was also a World Bank commissioned evaluation, this time conducted by the Indonesian research institute Smeru, which was quantitative in nature, organising a comparative survey among LAP and non-LAP participants in various villages and city quarters in fourteen districts and cities, including a total of 110 respondents from two city quarters in Bandung (The Smeru Research Team 2002). The third study was a PhD research by Soehendera, who conducted qualitative research in a low-income *kampong* in Central Jakarta's Rawa City Quarter (Soehendera 2005). Specifically, Smeru evaluated the project positively in relation to the registration process itself, the economic and social impacts of the project, as well as wider socio-economic effects. The current research does not fully support these conclusions, as will be discussed in the following paragraphs.

Reach of land registration programmes

Smeru concluded with regard to the LAP that 'there has been a clear bias towards locations in which most households are not well off', and Hardjono stated that 'there was [...] at least a very conscious effort to ensure that the poor were not overlooked' (Hardjono 1999; The Smeru Research Team 2002). In the current research, however, the assessment of whether the LAP and similar programmes have reached low-income groups led to a mixed picture: some of the general obstacles hindering sporadic registration discussed earlier have been overcome, but not all.

Many low-income *kampongs* could not participate in the LAP because of the location selection criteria. Locations were selected where lower-income households formed the majority of households, no more than

30 per cent of land parcels were registered through sporadic registration or other land registration programmes, and rapid urbanisation was occurring. At the same time, locations where land registration was expected to be difficult were avoided. So locations were selected where many land transactions took place through Land Deed Officials (officials of the Sub-District Office or public notaries), where parcels without certificates were concentrated instead of widely dispersed, and where basic village maps were available and technical control points in the national projection system already existed. In some areas other requirements applied as well, such as the absence of major land disputes. Areas involving conflicts over state land, especially, were avoided (The Smeru Research Team 2002). However, these conditions often characterise the poorest *kampongs*, which means that registration programmes often do not target settlements where most members of the programmes' target group reside.

As far as the programme was initiated in low-income *kampongs*, stringent evidence requirements regarding the registration of customary rights and the lack of political will to grant new rights remained an obstacle for landholders and particularly, for reasons discussed above, for the poorest, when it came to registering their land through a programme like the LAP. Hardjono concludes that landholders who could not benefit from the LAP included those with inadequate proof of claims and occupants of state land (Hardjono 1999).[25] What she does not conclude, and we do, is that lack of evidence is connected to lack of financial means to obtain the right documents. Documents that meet evidence requirements are expensive, and particularly for customary landholders with low incomes, this may be a reason to have never obtained them. Informal landholders to whom new rights could be granted often squat land because they lack financial means.

Obstacles formed by costs, complexity, and tardiness of the registration process were in large part overcome by a land registration programme such as the LAP. We asked title holders who had obtained a land certificate through systematic registration in the past ten years (through LAP and other land registration programmes) about the costs of land registration and the duration of the procedure. On average, they spent Rp. 78,000, which is only five per cent of the costs spent by title holders who obtained their land certificate through sporadic registration.[26] Moreover, the average duration of the systematic registration procedure was shorter than sporadic registration, namely 2.2 months.[27]

Although these costs seem reasonable, they exceeded the official charge and still prevented low-income dwellers from registering their land through a programme like the LAP.[28] According to Hardjono, costs depended greatly on what participants needed from local officials

in terms of documentation and legalisation (Hardjono 1999). To re-
mind the reader, it is likely that particularly poor customary landholders – those for whom this also forms the biggest burden – had to
obtain new documents in order to meet evidence requirements. Soehendera argues that costs resulting from officials asking for bribes for
their services, as well as mediators having to be paid, prevented dwellers in *kampong* Rawa from participating in the programme. As a result
of past experiences, residents also had negative (cost-related) perceptions regarding the registration process, particularly in relation to the
NLA. Those who did participate depended on informal networks and
patron-client relationships to get their land registered through the programme (Soehendera 2005). In the location described by Hardjono
where landholders occupying state land could participate in the LAP,
they decided not to do so because of the tax that has to be paid upon
registration of new rights (Hardjono 1999:9, 40). Still, according to
the Smeru Research Team, 94.7 per cent of those who did participate
in the LAP said that the costs in terms of money, time, and effort were
small compared to the benefits of a land certificate (The Smeru Research Team 2002). Hardjono even argued that middle- and upper-in-
come groups would be willing to pay 'somewhat more' to get their land
registered through the LAP (Hardjono 1999:40-1).

Obstacles similar to the ones discussed above mean that in Bandung, too, land registration programmes like the LAP do not reach the
kampong dwellers with the lowest incomes. The average monthly income of titleholders who obtained their certificate through a systematic
registration programme is lower than those who obtained it through
sporadic registration, namely around Rp. 1,600,000 versus Rp.
1,800,000.[29] Yet their income is still much higher than that of customary or informal landholders residing in the same *kampongs,* which
is Rp. 1,400,000 and Rp. 1,280,000, respectively.[30] This difference of
income cannot be explained merely by the economic effects that registration is said to have.

Land registration and legal security

The last question that this chapter wishes to address is whether land
registration programmes have actually contributed to legal security for
kampong dwellers. Our research shows that this contribution remains
limited.

To be able to assess the effects of land registration programmes on
the legal security of customary and informal landholders, we first need
to consider their position before registration. Our research shows that
their tenure security is surprisingly strong, in the sense that they enjoy

a high degree of administrative recognition. First, most landholders, even informal landholders, have been living on the land for decades, which means that the state has for a long time condoned non-formal land tenure. Second, the state has improved the infrastructure in *kampongs* and provided *kampong* dwellers with basic services, such as water, electricity, and identity cards, which again demonstrates administrative recognition. Third, and this is the most important point in this context, most customary and even informal landholders hold state-issued, land-related documentation. Customary landholders obviously hold colonial tax assessment notices and other documentation issued – often recently – by the state that they could use for registration. Yet even informal landholders have such documentation, often consisting of multiple purpose letters (*surat serba guna*), clarification letters (*surat keterangan*), or declaration letters (*surat pernyataan*) stating that they reside on the land, usually issued by City Quarter Offices. The City Quarter Offices do not have the competence to provide such documentation, at least not under these circumstances.[31] However, an interviewed City Quarter Head explained that in practice they do. It is common for people to come to the offices and ask for such documentation.[32] Officials are reluctant to deny such a request, probably also because they can earn some pocket money with it.

To what extent then do titleholders enjoy higher legal security than informal or customary landholders? The difference is limited for at least three reasons. First, there is the fact that a significant proportion of Bandung's lower-income *kampong* dwellers with a land certificate may not undertake derivate registration of their land. We asked titleholders whether they would do so in case of future land transfers (see Table 19.4). Generally, only 73.7 per cent of titleholders who had obtained their land certificate through sporadic registration claimed they would undertake derivative registration. Even fewer of the titleholders who had obtained their land certificate through systematic registration would do so, namely 52.4 per cent. If we take these two groups together and include titleholders whose land has already been registered by earlier titleholders, the percentage of future derivative registration is 60.8 per cent. A significant percentage of 7.9 per cent, 26.2 per cent, and 16.5 per cent respectively, would let a buyer of the land decide whether to do derivative registration or not.

Hardjono, who also conducted research on this issue, argued that few titleholders perform derivative registration because they do not understand the importance of it, Sub-District and City Quarter Offices are willing to provide alternative land-related documentation, derivative registration involves substantial administrative costs and tax levies, and the procedure demands time and trouble (Hardjono 1999:38-40). The expenses for derivate registration, which likely also consist of bribes,

Table 19.4 *Estimation on derivative registration in case of future land transfers*

	Titleholders by sporadic registration [a]	Titleholders by systematic registration [b]	Titleholders total (including land registered by earlier titleholder) [c]
Derivative registration	73.7 %	52.4 %	60.8 %
Derivative registration if buyer wants to	7.9 %	26.2 %	16.5 %
No derivative registration	18.4 %	21.4 %	22.7 %

Note: [a] $n = 38$, [b] $n = 44$, [c] $n = 97$

particularly form an obstacle for titleholders who have obtained their land certificate through systematic registration. After all, on average, these titleholders have lower incomes than titleholders who have obtained their land certificates through sporadic registration.

The low percentage of titleholders performing derivative registration in case of future land transfers may not come as a surprise, but it is no less worrisome. It means that despite initial land registration, many titleholders will again lack proper documentation to prove that they have a right on the land in the future, which will affect their legal security. Worse, the low percentage of derivative registration also means that the register loses its accuracy. This affects not only titleholders who do not undertake derivative registration, but any titleholder. After all, general trust in the land register depends on its accuracy.

A second reason for the limited effect of current land registration programmes on legal security is the result of public law requirements regarding residential land. Residence is not legalised through land registration alone. Since 1929/1931 Bandung Municipality has a Building Code, which requires a building permit for any building activity.[33] Nowadays, various permits are needed to legally reside on land, namely a Land Use Permit (*Izin Peruntukan Penggunaan Tanah*), a Building Permit (*Izin Mendirikan Bangunan*), and a Building Use Permit (*Izin Penggunaan Bangunan*).[34]

It is a troublesome process to obtain these permits, both in terms of duration, costs, and administrative burden, with several municipal agencies involved. The regulations are not clear about the duration of application procedures, except for the Building Permit. If all requirements are fulfilled, the procedure for a Building Permit should take no longer than nineteen days.[35] The costs of obtaining the permits generally depend on the function, location, size of the plot and building, and costs of surveying and mapping.[36] These procedures are also often accompanied by substantial bribes, among other things because of the involvement of disreputable persons (*oknum*) and middlemen (*calo*), as well as deviations from prescribed procedures.[37] It is for this reason that not only the NLA but also municipal agencies are commonly referred to as the 'wet sector' (*sector basah*). Besides, it is not uncommon for the agencies to set additional non-financial requirements (Niessen 1999). The reputation of the agencies involved in issuing permits seems in part the result of the complexity of the procedures on the one hand and repressive powers of the agencies on the other hand. Based on fieldwork in Bandung in the mid-1990s, Niessen hence concludes that 'the process is notorious for its tardiness, expense, and unpredictability' (Niessen 1999). These factors form an obstacle for applying for a permit, particularly for low-income (and poorly educated) *kampong* dwellers, all the more because they have strong negative perceptions regarding these procedures.[38]

Zoning, sub-division, and building requirements to obtain permits as set out in the spatial planning and building regulations form another obstacle for *kampong* dwellers. For instance, many *kampongs* are located alongside a river or railway track. These locations are designated as protected areas, where no building is allowed.[39] Zoning provisions have been enacted, and the Mayor cannot temporarily allow residence in these areas. Furthermore, in most *kampongs* 80-90 per cent of the land is covered with buildings, which exceeds the allowable building rate.[40] Finally, an average *kampong* house does not meet building standards, including standards regarding facilities.[41] Therefore, many of the dwellers of these *kampongs*, including those who have obtained a land certificate through a land registration programme, will never be able to fully legalise their tenure.

Municipal building and spatial planning regulations set severe sanctions for not meeting permit requirements. The Mayor of Bandung Municipality can command closure, clearance or demolition of a building or prohibit its use.[42] Despite the threat of such severe sanctions, it may not come as a surprise that very few *kampong* dwellers have such permits.[43] We asked respondents from all tenure categories whether they have a Building Permit (see Table 19.5). The overall majority of respondents answered that they did not. The more formal the land tenure status, the higher was the percentage of landholders with a building permit. So more titleholders had a Building Permit than informal landholders. Yet, still 82.8 per cent of titleholders had no building permit. This percentage was slightly higher with landholders who had obtained their certificate through systematic registration, namely 84.1 per cent. Despite land registration the overall majority of titleholders thus did not meet the requirements to reside on the land.

We asked respondents from all tenure categories with no building permit why they had not obtained one (see Table 19.6). Most believed

Table 19.5 *Possession of building permit per land tenure category*

	Formal tenure			Customary tenure [d]	Informal tenure [e]
	Sporadic registration [a]	Systematic registration [b]	Total [c]		
Building permit	16.2 %	13.6 %	14.1 %	2.1 %	1.9 %
Equivalent of building permit	5.4 %	2.3 %	3.0 %	1.1 %	0.6 %
No building permit	78.4 %	84.1 %	82.8 %	96.8 %	97.5 %

Note: [a] $n = 37$, [b] $n = 44$, [c] $n = 99$, [d] $n = 94$, [e] $n = 161$

that there was no need for a building permit. A considerable share of these people were not even aware that they were under the obligation to obtain a permit. Others argued that no one in the neighbourhood had a permit, that their buildings were modest or located in an alley, that their buildings had been constructed years ago, or that they held other documentation allowing them to build on the land. The second most important reason for not having a permit was that they considered the permit procedure to demand a lot of time and trouble. Respondents argued that they did not know how to obtain a permit, that the procedure was complex, or that they did not have the energy to get it done. Relatively few respondents argued that they did not have a permit because of the procedure's costs. Depending on tenure status, more (informal status) or fewer (formal status) respondents argued that they did not have a building permit because they could not meet the permit requirements.

The municipality seems to be aware of the dimension and causes of the problem. An interviewed senior official of the Municipal Building Service estimated that about 35 or 40 per cent of all buildings in Bandung are constructed without a permit. Bandung's municipal govern-

Table 19.6 *Reasons cited for not having a building permit*

	Formal tenure			Customary tenure [d]	Informal tenure [e]
	Sporadic registration [a]	Systematic registration [b]	Total [c]		
No need of permit	50 %	61.5 %	59 %	60.4 %	48.4 %
Permit procedure is cumbersome	25 %	25.6 %	26.5 %	24.2 %	19.7 %
Permit procedure is costly	25 %	10.3 %	13.3 %	8.8 %	3.2 %
Do not meet requirements	-	2.6 %	1.9 %	6.6 %	28.7 %

Note: [a] $n = 28$, [b] $n = 39$, [c] $n = 83$, [d] $n = 91$, [e] $n = 157$

ment now tries to make people aware of their obligations. It is implementing an Integrated Legal Information (*Penyuluhan Hukum Terpadu* or *Lukumdu*) programme at the city quarter level, where applicable laws are being 'socialised'.[44] Apparently, the programme has had limited effect though.[45] Although the number of building permits that are being issued by the Municipal Building Service is on the increase, in the past few years it had issued only about 3,000 building permits per year, as Table 19.7 shows.

A third reason for the limited effect of current land registration programmes on legal security is related to the partial protection that the land administration system offers, which is again the result of a combination of major weaknesses in the legal framework and maladministration.

The BAL creates a negative registration system combined with elements of a positive system, which means that a land certificate is not conclusive, but only forms strong evidence regarding a land right. A third party can dispute the right of a titleholder during the five years after the certificate has been issued.[46] In order to protect right holders against such claims, the BAL recognises the concept of forfeiture of rights. So the land right of a former right holder may be forfeited if he has neglected the land for a certain period of time. This concept is also meant to serve as an alternative for the concept of adverse possession (Harsono 2005).

The legal framework thus has some weaknesses, but the main problems derive from maladministration. As previously discussed, the NLA has a notorious reputation as a result of incompetence – both from a technical and from an organisational perspective – and corruption.[47] It is common for NLA officials to issue more than one certificate for the same plot of land. Indonesians even have specific names for such certificates, such as *sertifikat ganda* (double certificate) or *sertifikat aspal* (original, but false certificate).[48] In 2003 a former Head of the Bandung Municipality Land Office was arrested for issuing a certificate to a third party to another person's land plot.[49] Aside from the failure of titleholders to carry out derivative registration of their land,

Table 19.7   *Number of building permits issued by the Municipal Building Service*

Year	Number of Permits
1998/1999	2,295
1999/2000	2,187
2000	2,830
2001	2,859
2002	3,195
2003	3,409

Source: Internal document from Bandung's Municipal Building Department

the issuing of double certificates further affects the reliability of the land register.

As part of the evaluation of LAP, the World Bank concluded that the institutional development component of the project 'was less than successful' (World Bank 2004b). It is therefore reasonable to expect that incompetence and corruption are not just problems of the past. Ironically, land registration programmes may increase these problems because the administration is not used to mass registration of land and will hence impose an excessive burden (Payne 2001).

It is not the land administration system alone that offers partial protection, but land law generally. Whether land forms state or private land, it always keeps a 'social function'.[50] This concept is said to be derived from *adat* law and means that individual rights must be balanced against the interests of the community (General Elucidation, chapter II, under 4) (Fitzpatrick 1999). The state right of avail is a useful tool to maintain the social function of land. The BAL creates several mechanisms for the state to annul land rights for the benefit of the community, such as mechanisms for land acquisition in the public interest, annulment of rights on neglected land (*tanah terlantar*), and land reform.[51] Rights on neglected land that can be annulled are real rights, including state management rights and legal claims to hold the land that have not yet become rights. Land is considered neglected if it is not used in accordance with its physical condition or with the form and goal of the right to which it is subject. This includes the use of land that is not in accordance with spatial planning regulations, particularly if land is subdivided without permission, and the failure to obtain a statutory land right.[52] This again shows how important it is for *kampong* dwellers to hold all of the required permits. However, they may be saved by the provision that land will not be classified as neglected land if the titleholder is in an economically weak position or because there is a conflict regarding the land.[53] Land reform includes annulment of land rights if a right holder has too much land or the land qualifies as absentee land. Such land can also be redistributed to vulnerable groups. Land reform, however, only applies to agricultural land.[54] In all cases, the law contains certain safeguards that should protect landholders. It falls outside the scope of this chapter to discuss this issue in more detail, but in view of past experiences, it is questionable whether the Indonesian state takes these safeguards under consideration.

Conclusion

This chapter has explained why it is so difficult for *kampong* dwellers, particularly the poorest, to register their land. Stringent evidence requirements, a lack of political will to grant new rights to informal landholders, high costs, complexity, and tardiness of the registration process as a result of poor administrative performance or even maladministration, along with related negative perceptions of *kampong* dwellers regarding the registration process, ensure that sporadic land registration only occurs on a limited scale. There is thus a great need for systematic registration through land registration programmes.

Since 1981 the Indonesian government has initiated several land registration programmes. These programmes have been able to overcome financial, bureaucratic, and time constraints and related negative perceptions regarding the registration process. Nonetheless, on the basis of income data, it appears that in Bandung, land registration programmes such as the LAP do not reach the *kampong* dwellers with the lowest incomes. This limited reach can be explained by the fact that the LAP is only implemented in locations where registration is relatively easy, which means that locations where many low-income dwellers reside are ignored. Besides, some of the same obstacles occurring in the case of sporadic land registration remain in force, namely the stringent evidence requirements for initial registration and a lack of political will to grant new rights to informal landholders.

Land registration programmes in Bandung not only have a limited reach, they also contribute little to legal security for *kampong* dwellers. Assessing the tenure security of customary and informal landholders, we can conclude that this is surprisingly strong, in the sense that they enjoy a high degree of administrative recognition. At the same time the legal security of title holders is limited for at least three reasons. First, most *kampong* dwellers predict that they will not perform derivate registration after a change in the legal status of the land. This can probably be explained by the significant administrative costs involved and – depending on the value/condition of the property – tax levies that come with derivative registration. This not only means that future titleholders will enjoy less legal security, but also that the register loses its accuracy, which affects any titleholder in Indonesia. Second, few titleholders have the permits they need to legally reside on their land. Besides a land certificate, people need spatial planning related permits, consisting of a land use permit, building permit, and building use permit. Again, the processes to obtain these permits are costly, complex, and tardy. However, most people fail to obtain these permits because they are not aware of the need to do so. Finally, the land administration system and even land law in general are dispossessory in nature, which is again the result of major weaknesses in the legal framework and maladministration.

The previously discussed findings teach us that land registration does not inherently lead to legal security for landholders. This is often overlooked in the tenure security debate, in which it is assumed that registration automatically generates legal security for participants and consequently enhances their tenure security. Whereas in the current case registration did not lead to legal security, there are clear indications that it did increase the participants' tenure security. Tenure security ultimately depends on the way state authorities and third parties actually value the possession or lack of land certificates and other documents required to reside on land, for instance in case of land acquisition, which is often influenced more by politics than by law. In addition, the registration of land may strengthen the landholders' perceptions of tenure security. It falls outside the scope of this chapter to discuss this in detail, but further data from the current research show that in Post-New Order Bandung, the actual tenure security (measured by interference from third parties) of low-income *kampong* dwellers holding land certificates (but often not fulfilling other legal requirements) as well as their perception of tenure security are stronger than among those who do not have such documents.[55] This for instance also means that the former invest more in their land and housing than the latter (Reerink Forthcoming).

The Land Management and Policy Development Project addresses some of the problems that have been identified in relation to systematic land registration. In the project appraisal the World Bank recognises the need of a land policy 'as an integral element of a broader policy dialogue rather than as a string of narrowly oriented technical interventions' (World Bank 2004b). It wishes among other things to increase the coherence and consistency of land administration and management-related laws and regulations, promote institutional development, and provide training and capacity building to all local governments (World Bank 2004b). Yet as long as the other problems mentioned in this chapter have not been addressed, even this programme will probably fall short of expectations.

Notes

1   G.O. Reerink is a PhD researcher at the Van Vollenhoven Institute for Law, Governance and Development, Faculty of Law, Leiden University. This research is part of a larger PhD study on Land Tenure Security for Indonesia's Urban Poor, which forms part of the Dutch Royal Academy of Sciences funded INDIRA project. INDIRA stands for Indonesia-Netherlands studies on Decentralisation of the Indonesian '*Rechtsstaat*', and its impact on '*Agraria*'. INDIRA is a joint research project undertaken

by Indonesian and Dutch universities. For further information, kindly refer to: www.
indira.leidenuniv.nl. I wish to extend my gratitude to the Treub Society for Research
in the Tropics, the Netherlands Organisation for Scientific Research, the Adat Law
Foundation and the Leiden University Fund, which gave financial support for my
fieldwork in Bandung, the Law Faculty of Parahyangan Catholic University for host-
ing me as a foreign researcher, and the students and alumni from Padjajaran University who assisted me in the research. Comments are most welcome and can be sent
to: g.o.reerink@law.leidenuniv.nl.

2   Law No. 5/1960.

3   Article 22(2), 31, 37, 41 Law No. 5/1960 in conjunction with Regulation of Department of Home Affairs No. 6/1972, Government Regulation No. 24/1997 and Regulation of the Department of Home Affairs No. 5/1973.

4   Government Regulation No. 36/1998 in conjunction with article 27, 34, and 40 BAL.

5   The survey was conducted in seven widely dispersed kampong city quarters (*Kelurahan*) among a total of 420 households, purposively consisting of respondents with a
land certificate (formal tenure), respondents without a land certificate but who did
have a customary claim on the land (customary tenure), and respondents who had
occupied the land (informal tenure). Aside from tenure status, the households were
selected randomly after consultation with the Head of the Neighborhood (*Kepala
RW*) and Head of the Housing Block (*Kepala RT*), who had given prior permission to
do the survey.

6   The replacement of the 1961 Government Regulation by the 1997 Government Regulation was part of the systematic review and drafting of land laws and regulations under the LAP.

7   'BPN: 30 Persen Lahan di Kota Bandung Belum Bersertifikat', *Republika*, 28 November 2005.

8   See Table 19.6 of this paper on the output of sporadic registration in Bandung Municipality.

9   Informal landholders hold priority rights to obtain new rights on much of this land,
but they appear to be unaware of this, and the state simply ignores it.

10   Article 3-7 Regional Regulation of Bandung Municipality No. 24/2001.

11   Still, an estimated fifteen per cent of the municipal land is used without a permit
(data derived from internal document of the Housing Service of Bandung Municipality; document on file with the author).

12   It can be questioned whether the municipal government is entitled to do this. The
BAL stipulates that the state cannot lease out land, since it is not the owner of the
land (Explanatory Memorandum art. 44 and 45 BAL). There is no reason to suggest
that this would be different for the municipal government. It is probably for this reason that it does not grant a lease right (*hak sewa*), but a so-called Land Use Permit
(*Ijin Pemakaian Tanah*), which is not to be confused with the Land Use Permit discussed below.

13   A good example of such land in Bandung is land on which the Indonesian Railway
Company has a management right. PT KAI manages a total of 269,900,000 ha in
the whole of Java. Only 1,140.75 ha or 0.42 per cent is leased out to people (interview
with senior manager of the Indonesian Railway Company, 19 January 2005). Most of
the land that has not been leased out is simply neglected, which explains why so
many people can squat it.

14   n=15.

15   n=38. In a comparative research as part of an evaluation of the Land Administration
Project (LAP) conducted by the Indonesian research institute Smeru, respondents
who had undertaken sporadic registration in Bandung stated that certificates cost be-

tween Rp. 2 and 3 million and took years to obtain (The Smeru Research Team 2002).

16 n=63. The actual estimated costs are on average Rp. 1,943,333.

17 n=64. The precise percentage of respondents believing that the estimated costs of land registration involved bribes was 31.3 per cent.

18 'Survey KPK: BPN dan Dephukham, Instansi Pemerintah dengan Pelayanan Terburuk', *Hukum Online*, 30 March 2008.

19 PRONA finds its legal basis in the Third Five-Year Plan (*Repelita III*), as elaborated by Decision of the Minister of Home Affairs No. 189/1981. Beside PRONA and PRODA, the Indonesian government also initiated a village-by-village registration program, which was based on GR No. 10/1961, the PP10 program.

20 Aside from this, the project supported sporadic registration in eight areas in Java and Sumatra (World Bank 1994).

21 To compare, in 2003 the Indonesian Government allocated Rp. 300 million or about USD 30,000 for the issuance of 2,600 land titles through PRONA. See '*Pemerintah Terbitkan Sertifikat Prona*', *Pikiran Rakyat*, 6 February 2003.

22 In Bandung, one of West Java's major cities, 60.18 per cent of all parcels had been registered (World Bank 1994).

23 Arguably, the output of sporadic registration may have decreased as a result of sporadic registration under LAP I.

24 'BPN: 30 Persen Lahan di Kota Bandung Belum Bersertifikat', *Republika*, 28 November 2005.

25 Hadjono does, however, refer to one case in Semarang, where squatters of state land managed by the Indonesian Railway Company (*PT Kereta Api Indonesia* or PT KAI) were granted new rights. She suspected that political motives influenced this decision, which was taken shortly before the 1997 General Elections (Hardjono 1999:17).

26 n=33. The costs mentioned in the current research are significantly higher than the average costs calculated by The Smeru Research Team, which calculated on the basis of 85 titleholders in the cities Bandung, Depok, South Jakarta, Semarang, Palembang and Medan that these costs were Rp. 40,978 (The Smeru Research Team 2002). These results suggest that either registration through the LAP is cheaper in other cities than Bandung, or that registration through other programmes than the LAP is more expensive.

27 n=44. The Smeru Research Team calculated a similar average duration of the LAP registration process (The Smeru Research Team 2002).

28 Under the LAP the costs in urban areas were Rp. 11,500, and since 1999/2000, registration was even free of charge. Landholders who receive a new right are also exempt from the requirement to pay Entry Money (art. 20 Law No. 20/2000 in conjunction with art. 1(a), under 1 and 3, and 2(a) and (c) Decision of the Minister of Finance No. 561/KMK.03/2004). They may have to pay the Fee for Acquisition of Rights to Land and Buildings. However, those with a low income can then request a tax reduction of as much as 76 per cent. The Smeru Research Team draws the same conclusion and notes that particularly the costs of documentation needed to meet evidence requirements were considerable (The Smeru Research Team 2002).

29 n=38; n=44.

30 n=95; n=160.

31 The competencies of the City Quarter Offices are formulated in Regional Regulation No. 8/2001; Decision of Mayor of Bandung No. 329/2001; Decision of Mayor of Bandung No. 335/2001.

32 Interview with City Quarter Head, 3 January 2005.

33 'Bouw en Woningverordening van de Stadsgemeente Bandung' (see: Niessen 1999). Only in 1999 was this bylaw replaced by Bylaw of Bandung Municipality No. 14/1998.

34 The Land Use Permit consists of a Planning Permit and a Planning Recommendation, which are both granted by the Municipal Town Planning Service (art. 2 Bandung Municipality Bylaw No. 4/2002). It forms an administrative requirement for the granting of a Building Permit (art. 3). The Permit also forms a requirement for the granting of a Permit for the Use of Municipal Land and/or Buildings (*Izin Pemakaian Tanah dan atau Bangunan* or IPTB) (art. 4(1)). The request for the Permit and Recommendation should come with additional documentation, including land documentation (art. 6). It will only be granted if the land use is in accordance with zoning provisions of the Municipal Spatial Plan, and the land is not subject to conflict (art. 7). The Land Use Permit is valid for one year and can be extended for another year. Within that term a request for a Building Permit should be submitted to the Municipal Building Service (art. 4(2)). A Building Permit is required for any building activity from the Municipal Building Service (*Dinas Bangunan*) (art. 4 Bylaw of the Bandung Municipality No. 14/1998). A permit request should again come with additional documentation, including proof of land ownership and, as was noted before, a Land Use Permit. It is not indicated whether proof of land ownership means a land title or can also include other documentation. The Building Permit will only be granted if the building plan meets zoning, sub-division, and building provisions as set out in the municipal building regulation itself and spatial planning regulations (the Municipal General Spatial Plan, Detailed Spatial Plan and the Technical Plan). The Mayor may temporally allow kampong dwellers to use land for residence until zoning provisions regarding that area have been enacted. A Building Use Permit should be obtained from the Municipal Building Service before a new building can be used (art. 28(2)). A request for such a permit will only be granted if the building fulfils the building requirements as determined in the Building Permit (art. 28(1), 39 and 40).

35 Article 18 Bandung Municipality Bylaw No. 14/1998.

36 See article 9-20 Bandung Municipality Bylaw No. 4/2002; Bandung Municipality Bylaw No. 24/1998.

37 This is also confirmed by a recent joint study of the Municipal Research and Development Office and a consultancy firm (Pemerintah Kota Bandung 2004a).

38 See also the research report mentioned in the previous footnote.

39 According to the Building Regulation, building is forbidden at less than four metres from a road and five metres, or in a densely built area, four metres from a canal (art. 351 juncto 346 and 348 of Bylaw No. 14/1998). From a river, residential buildings should be positioned at more than 10-30 metres, depending on its depth (art. 358 juncto 355 Bylaw No. 14/1998). According to Municipal Spatial Plan the distance should be at least three metres (Art. 70 juncto art. 36(3)). However, the Plan refers to regional regulations such as the Building Regulation. No building is allowed within ten metres of a railway track (Art. 36(3)). See also Pemerintah Kota Bandung 2004b.

40 The building rate should be no more than 80 per cent (art. 46 Bandung Municipality Bylaw No. 14/1998 juncto Table 5, Annex 1 Bandung Municipality Bylaw No. 2/2004). See also Pemerintah Kota Bandung 2004b.

41 For that matter, a recently enacted public order regulation determines fines of up to Rp 1,000,000 and/or administrative sanctions against those who do not maintain their buildings (art. 49) or do not have such facilities as sewerage (art. 49 (1 sub i and l) Bandung Municipality Bylaw No. 3/2005). The regulation does not form a direct threat in terms of tenure security, in the sense that dwellers cannot be evicted for that reason.

42 Article 31, 36, 256, 352 Bylaw No. 14/1998; 116 Bylaw No. 2/2004.

43 See also Niessen 1999.
44 Personal communication of a senior official of Bandung's Municipal Building Department, January 2005.
45 It may be for this reason that the Head of the Municipal Building Service Ubad Bachtiar in an interview with the daily *Pikiran Rakyat* speculated about a more repressive approach to increase the percentage of building owners meeting permit requirements. He suggested that a building permit should become a requirement for the provision of electricity (See 'Jadikan IMB Syarat Pasang Listrik', *Pikiran Rakyat*, 4 January 2005). The idea was never taken up though.
46 Article 32 GR No. 24/1997 (and Elucidation) in conjunction with article 19(2c), 23(2), 32(2) and 38(2) BAL.
47 See also Zevenbergen 2002:143-4 & 150-1.
48 See also Bedner 2001.
49 See: 'Mantan Kepala BPN Tangerang Ditahan, Diduga Selewengkan Dana Proyek Prona Swadaya', *Kompas*, 8 August 2001; 'Kasus Korupsi Pembuatan Sertifikat Prona Diusut', *Sinar Harapan*, 2 November 2001; 'Mantan Kepala BPN Kota Bandung Ditahan Polisi', *Kompas*, 15 January 2003. It is not clear whether the officials have been convicted.
50 Article 6 BAL.
51 On land acquisition in the public interest, see: article 18 BAL.
52 Article 3, 4, 8 GR No. 36/1998 in conjunction with article 27(a1), 34(e), and 40(e) BAL.
53 Article 11 GR No. 36/1998 in conjunction with article 27(a1), 34(e), and 40(e) BAL.
54 Article 7, 10, 17 BAL.
55 A distinction should be made between formal and customary landholders on the one hand and informal landholders on the other. Whereas the tenure security of formal and customary landholders is comparably high, informal landholders enjoy relatively little tenure security. This indicates that registration programmes could particularly benefit the latter.

20 The mystery of formalising informal land tenure in the forest frontier: The case of Langkawana, Lampung, Indonesia

Myrna A. Safitri

Introduction

Land tenure in Indonesia has inspired Hernando De Soto (2000:170-171) to restate the urgency of discovering local property arrangements for transforming informal property rights – he prefers to use the term extra-legal arrangements – into formal rights. Many have agreed with De Soto that legalisation of property rights is central in creating more security of tenure to land, and that this tenure security will induce higher investments, which in turn will lead to economic growth and poverty reduction (Dam 2006; Deininger 2003; Demsetz 1967).[1] However, it remains to be seen how such legalisations can be successfully carried out in areas that, like Indonesia, are characterised by a fragmented legal framework of land tenure; an imbalanced allocation of land to the state, private companies, and people; and tight competition for land rights amongst local people.

This chapter discusses the extent to which attempts to provide security of land tenure for people through legalisation can be supportive of either poverty alleviation or the transformation of land into capital in a particular village of Lampung Province, Sumatra, Indonesia. The village, named Langkawana, is inhabited by migrants from Java who have been struggling for decades to obtain more security of tenure over their land. The land is partly situated in an area designated as forest area that is controlled by the Ministry of Forestry (MoF). The remaining part is located outside the forest area and falls under the jurisdiction of the National Land Agency (NLA). In the latter area, some villagers have formally registered their land and acquired certificates of ownership; however, in the former area no land rights can be granted to them. The fact that all land within the forest areas is controlled by the MoF has been a primary obstacle to people having their rights to land individually registered. They can only obtain a community forestry license, a government's permit for temporarily using forestland. Unlike the right of ownership, the community forestry license is not able to provide people with full rights over the land. Interestingly, land markets in the forest areas are more active than in non-forest areas. In addition, the legalisation of land in forest areas, mostly used as agro-forest gardens, contributes significantly to reducing village poverty.

These issues raise a number of questions. What is the effect of formalisation of land tenure – either through land titling or through the granting of a community forestry license – on poverty alleviation and the enhancement of a land market? What factors determine the linkage between the formalisation of rights to land, tenure security, land transactions, and poverty? This chapter discusses these issues by elaborating the following points: (1) an overview of Indonesia's legislation regarding land tenure in forest and non-forest areas; (2) land use in forest and non-forest areas in Langkawana; (3) local norms and practices of land tenure; (4) legalisation of informal land tenure in forest and non-forest areas; and finally, (5) a comparative analysis concerning the impact of different paths of legalisation of land tenure in forest and non-forest areas on poverty reduction and land transactions.

Forest and non-forest areas in Indonesia's legislation

To understand land issues in Indonesia, one must consider the fact that land has been classified into two legal categories, namely forest areas (*kawasan hutan*) and non-forest areas. The forest areas cover all lands the government, in this case the MoF, has declared as 'forest areas', which may be forested or not. Indonesian forest areas cover 134 million hectares of land or approximately 60 per cent of the country's land (Ministry of Forestry 2008). The real forested land within the areas, however, is only 86 million hectares. The remaining areas consist of villages, agricultural land, roads, or plantations. The non-forest areas are located beyond the forest areas. Similar to the forest areas, the non-forest areas sometimes indicate land with natural forests as well as land used for settlement, agricultural purposes, and the like. The terms forest areas and non-forest areas illustrate how legal categories of land and forest are very often incompatible with ecological conditions. Political considerations and administrative decisions drive the MoF's decisions in establishing forest areas. Thus, the forest areas in Indonesia provide a good example of the phenomenon referred to as 'political forests' (Vandergeest and Peluso 2006:33) or as Scott (1998:4) puts it, the 'administrative ordering of nature'.

In Indonesia's legal system, all land and natural richness is administered under a single law, namely the Basic Agrarian Law (BAL-Law 5/1960). The BAL provides umbrella provisions, conveying basic principles and regulations in the field of land and natural resources (*'agraria'* is the BAL's term), whilst other detailed provisions can be found in other laws or regulations. An exception has been made for forests, which are regulated not by the BAL, but by the Forestry Law (Law 41/1999). This law distinguishes private and state forests. Private forests are those with private land rights, while forests growing on land without private land rights are designated as state forests. Forestry officials and operational regulations of Law 41/1999 act from the assumption that forest areas must be state forests. But since state forests by definition only occur on land without private land rights, the MoF's assumption of forest areas as state forests is an argument it has used to control all the land in those areas.

The MoF's control of forest areas has restrained people from obtaining private land rights in forest areas, and only in non-forest areas can such rights be acquired. These lands are administered directly by the NLA on the basis of the BAL. Based on article 16 (1) of the BAL, the NLA can issue land certificates to individual citizens, corporations, or other legal bodies with the right to own (*hak milik*), right to commercially cultivate (*hak guna usaha-HGU*), right to use buildings (*hak guna bangunan-HGB*), and right to use (*hak pakai*). Government institutions can be issued use rights for lands they use themselves, for instance where the government has built offices. When the government manages land on behalf of third parties, the government must be issued a management right (*hak pengelolaan*). The management right is not a private land right but is a kind of state control right that has been delegated to certain government institutions (Parlindungan 1989; Sumardjono 2008:197-215). All government institutions must thus have land certificates to manage certain lands. Interestingly, despite this requirement, the NLA does not issue any land right to the MoF. It is therefore not clear which land rights the MoF holds on the 60 per cent of the country's land that they manage. This makes Indonesian land tenure legally complicated.

Forest areas are divided into three functions: production, protection, and conservation. When the main function is to generate forest products, the area is considered production forest, whilst protection forest is forest area designed to protect life-supporting systems such as hydrology, flood prevention, erosion control, seawater intrusion prevention, and soil fertility maintenance. Conservation forest is forest area to be used primarily for preserving plant and animal diversity and its ecosystem (Law 41/1999, art.1 point 7,8,9). People have different degrees of access to forest resources depending on the applicable forest function. As conservation forests are mainly intended to preserve biodiversity and ecosystems, resource exploitations in these areas are highly restricted and even forbidden in certain parts. In protection forests, one can still utilise resources but to a limited degree. Production forests provide the greatest access to forest resources.

The MoF has the authority to determine the particular function of the forests. A 2004 Government Regulation concerning Forestry Planning (GR 44/2004) elaborates sets of criteria and procedures in designating those functions; however, very few of these have been followed. In several provinces, such as in Java and Sumatra, including Lampung, the MoF simply confirmed the forest functions as they were established by the Dutch colonial government. In other cases, as in Langkawana, the MoF did change the function of colonial forests, for instance by changing protected forest to conservation forest, yet without following the criteria and procedures mentioned above. Another way the MoF has sometimes designated forest functions is by simply declaring logging concession areas as production forests. In this way, and also by granting logging concessions in other areas than production forests, many logging concession areas have been issued without taking into account ecological as well as social considerations in the forests, two of the criteria mentioned in GR 44/2004.[2]

Although no private land right can be found in forest areas, people can still access the land and forest resources. Law 41/1999 provides several options for access rights to forest areas, including: *adat* forests, or forests used for customary-based communities, village forests, forests for specific purposes such as for conducting research and preserving cultural heritages, and community forests (*hutan kemasyarakatan*). The community forests allow people, either *adat* or non-*adat* communities, to manage parts of forest areas for a maximum period of 35 years. Nonetheless, the MoF does not allow the license to be used as a basis for acquiring private rights on forest areas, as state forests must be free from private ownership.

Langkawana in Lampung: Its historical and social landscape

Lampung, a province situated in the southeast of Sumatra Island, is the gateway for land transportation from Java to Sumatra. The area's economy is geared toward agriculture and plantation, and its products supply many big cities throughout Indonesia. The province is also known for exporting coffee. Lampung can be seen as a miniature Indonesia, as it is inhabited by a great diversity of ethnic groups: Lampungese, Javanese, Sundanese, and some Minangs. Such ethnic heterogeneity is a result of a long history of migration, particularly when in 1905 the Dutch colonial authorities began to move Javanese to Lampung to relieve Java of its high population density. Post-independence governments continued this policy, most notably under the New Order's massive transmigration programmes of the 1970s-1980s. During this time Lampung's population experienced rapid growth. From 1971-1980, for instance, population growth reached 5.77 per cent annually, higher than the national annual rate of 2.32 per cent (Safitri 1997).

Located in the west of Bandar Lampung, the capital of Lampung, is the conservation forest Wan Abdulrahman Grand Forest Park. Before being designated as a conservation forest by the MoF in 1992, it was a protection forest, namely Register 19 of Mount Betung forest, having been designated as a protection forest in 1941 by the Dutch colonial government. Currently, the park covers an area of approximately 22,000 hectares and is surrounded by a number of villages, including Langkawana.[3] Even though it is a forest village, Langkawana is not remotely situated. It is easily accessible from Bandar Lampung. Administratively, Langkawana is a village unit (kelurahan)[4] under the territory of Bandar Lampung Municipality. With a total area of 498 hectares, it is populated by 760 families, or 2,709 people.

Langkawana consists of two different areas, namely the west and the east. In the west, roughly 500 families reside within the forest borders, whilst in the east the remaining 200 families reside in another neighbourhood located closer to the city. In addition to the physical divide between the west and east, there exists a social boundary as well. Western Langkawana is the old settlement and the origin of Langkawana village. It was once a sub-village unit (lingkungan)[5] of Kelurahan Beringin Raya before the municipality government of Bandar Lampung changed it to an independent kelurahan in 2000. Nowadays, Langkawana covers three sub-village units within its administrative territory, i.e. Lingkungan I and II in the west, and Lingkungan III in the east. The inhabitants of Lingkungan I and II are most notably agro-forest farmers, whilst in Lingkungan III the residents are predominantly employed as civil servants, private employees, and entrepreneurs.

Western Langkawana is a pluralistic community with different ethnic groups. Lingkungan I is inhabited mostly by Javanese who live in Langkawana Bawah (Lowland Langkawana), whilst in Lingkungan II, the Sundanese dominate the area called Langkawana Atas (Upland Langkawana). Both ethnic groups have their own settlement history. The Javanese came to Langkawana in the 1940s as labourers of a Dutch rubber plantation operated on the border of Mount Betung. The company supplied its labourers with housing in a location now known as Langkawana Bawah. Each labourer was given a small house called a bedeng. Every day the Javanese followed the same route from their bedeng to the plantation without ever entering the forest. There are at least two reasons why they never entered the forest. First, from the 1920s to 1940s, the Dutch colonial forestry administration was applying forest delineation and enforcing forestry law, especially in Lampung. To avoid legal problems, the plantation administrators continuously warned their Javanese labourers to keep away from the forest.

Second, the Javanese labourers were more dependent on the plantation than on the forest for their livelihood, and so they had no interest in entering the forest. In the 1950s, however, the population in Langkawana *Bawah* increased, and the Javanese had to search for additional land for their housing. Consequently, they used the vacant land near the plantation to build new houses. Within a short time, the Javanese settlement expanded, and a hamlet called Dusun Langkawana was established.

The Sundanese came to Langkawana in the 1950s. They migrated from Banten, Western Java, to Lampung primarily due to poverty in their home villages. In the Mount Betung protection forest, the Sundanese found plenty of grass and vacant land, mistakenly thinking that the land was unowned. Prior to the arrival of the Sundanese, the Lampungese had utilised the land. These Lampungnese had formerly resided in an area called Sukadanaham, around ten to fifteen kilometres from Mount Betung, and had migrated into the forest to avoid the war in the early years of the Japanese occupation (1942-1943), or about a year after the Dutch designated Mount Betung as a protection forest. After Indonesian Independence in 1945, the Lampungese went back to their original village and left the land in the forest fallow and full of grass (*alang-alang, Imperata cylindrica*).

When the Sundanese first came to Mount Betung and found the land fallow, they built their small houses and planted food and perennial crops there, creating a small hamlet consisting of five or seven houses in the forest, called *umbulan*. The Sundanese pioneers obtained their land by clearing the fallow land. At that time, a family could have five to ten hectares of land depending on their ability to clear it. Soon after the Sundanese settled on this land in the forest, the Lampungese, one by one, came in and claimed the land for themselves. Considering their vulnerable position as new migrants, the Sundanese never challenged these claims but rather paid the Lampungese for their claims. Payment of compensation (*ganti rugi*) was the common term for indicating land sales between the Lampungese and the Sundanese. Compensation, however, did not guarantee the permanent transfer of land rights, because multiple claims were made by the Lampungese to the same plots. Consequently, the Sundanese paid for compensation several times to different Lampungese. Only after the Sundanese population increased did the claims of the Lampungese begin to wane and eventually stop.

The Sundanese were the first to make agro-forest gardens in the area. The Javanese followed their example and entered the forest in the middle of the 1950s and the 1960s. By this time, the plantation company where they had worked as labourers had collapsed and finally closed. For this reason, they were looking for an alternative source of income. Some of them went back to Java, while others remained in Lampung and entered and cleared primary forest in Mount Betung.

Gradually, population pressure on the forest increased, and the forest of Mount Betung began to be destroyed. Lampung Provincial Government carried out reforestation projects in the early 1980s, part of the grand policy of forest rehabilitation in Lampung. The Forest Services assumed that reforestation would be successful if the forests were freed from encroachments. Assisted by military forces, they relocated people living in the forest, including those living in the Sundanese hamlets. The Forest Services destroyed everyone's gardens and planted Indian rose wood (called *Sonokeling* in Bahasa Indonesia or *Dalbergia latifolia* in Latin), a kind of commercial timber tree on those gardens. In 1982, the Forest Services had relocated approximately 140 Sundanese families and sent them to a transmigration area in the north of Lampung. In 1986, the Forest Services would conduct the second phase of relocation for the remaining 30 Sundanese families. Yet, these families refused because they knew that this new home would be less than ideal and doubted it would provide them with a better life. The transmigration areas in North Lampung were well known for their unproductive land, and thus the Sundanese preferred not to be relocated to those areas but to live on the border of the forest. They bought the land near the forests from Javanese and Lampungese owners and then set up their new settlements on the land, now known as Langkawana *Atas*.

Land use in forest and non-forest area

As legislation has divided land into forest and non-forest areas, in Langkawana the villagers labelled forestland as *tanah kawasan* (land designated as forest area), sometimes also called *tanah kehutanan* (land owned by the forest services). For the non-forest area where the villagers built their houses, they use the term *tanah marga*.

Tanah marga is originally a Lampungese term used to indicate territorial sovereignty over both the villages as well as the land located between and around the villages. Prior to Dutch colonisation, *marga* served as a territorial and socio-political unit of the indigenous Lampungese. The Lampungese continued to call their land *tanah marga* (the *marga* land), though the Dutch abolished the political unit of *marga*. Then in the 1920s, the Dutch revitalised the territorial unit of *marga*, the main aim of which was to use the *marga* system as a mechanism for collecting revenues (Elmhirst 2001:298-299). After independence, the socio-political unit of *marga* was once again abolished. With Law 5/1979 on Village Government, Suharto's New Order regime unified all traditional governments and converted them to new administra-

tive units called *desa* or villages. In this process, *margas* were also transformed into villages. Even though *marga*, as a socio-political and administrative unit, has disappeared, the term '*marga* land' is still used,
even by the migrants. Migrants and indigenes, however, mean different
things by this term. The indigenous Lampungese perceive *marga* land
as their traditional territories covering both forest and non-forest land.
For the migrants, the term '*marga* land' refers to all non-state-owned
land, i.e. private lands located in non-forest areas.

Due to the fact that *marga* land lacks agricultural soil, villagers of
Langkawana use forest areas for their agro-forest gardens. Around 472
households in Western Langkawana have agro-forest gardens on almost 500 hectares of forest area. Survey results indicating the size of
land holdings in forest areas are displayed in Table 20.1.

Langkawana villagers are truly forest-dependent people, as they have
no agricultural land outside the forest. A simple survey of the household income of agro-forest farmers in Langkawana that I carried out in
2005, for example, illustrated that people believed their gardens,
planted with around 30 tree species, had contributed to at least 64 per
cent of their monthly income (see Table 20.2). The gardens produce
commercial commodities such as cocoa, coffee, and fruits. In addition,
Langkawana villagers use the forest for firewood, water supply, building materials, as well as herbal medicine. Their non-forestry income
comes from small-scale trades such as owning stalls and acting as
middlemen. Another source of income is to work temporarily as a

Table 20.1 *Forest land tenure in Langkawana, 2004*

Size of land	Number of households	Percentage
Less than 0.5 ha	177	37.39%
0.5 – 1 ha	144	30.59%
1 – 2 ha	88	18.70%
More than 2 ha	63	13.32%

Source: Data processed from Langkawana's Forest User Groups (FUGs), 2004

Table 20.2 *The household incomes of Langkawana agro-forest farmers, 2005*

Size of forest gardens (ha)	Forestry-based income (monthly)		Non-forestry income (monthly)	
	IDR	%	IDR	%
Less than 0.5	239,090	53%	213,800	47%
0.5 – 0.99	300,150	53%	267,630	47%
1 – 2	372,400	72%	143,790	28%
More than 2	685,450	77%	210,670	23%

Source: Field Survey, 2005
1 USD = app. IDR 10,000

hired motorcyclist (*pengojek*) to transport people from the village to the city.

Agro-forest gardens have contributed significantly to people's livelihood. Nevertheless, the farmers experienced many restrictions in using their gardens, because they did not possess formal land titles. As mentioned previously, forest areas fall under the jurisdiction of the Forestry Law, and thus no private land rights are recognised in these areas. While people cannot acquire individual property rights over their agricultural land, this is not the case for residential land located outside the forest areas or in *marga* land. This land is under the BAL's jurisdiction. According to the *Kelurahan* administration, 413 parcels, together comprising 169.8 hectares of non-forest land, have already been registered and titles provided to the owners. In this calculation, 34 per cent of non-forest or *marga* land in Langkawana has been registered. However, 157 hectares of the registered *marga* land is not owned by the Langkawana villagers but belongs to a private foundation with the right of commercial cultivation (*HGU* title). The 412 parcels of villagers that have been registered only comprise 12.8 hectares. Consequently, of all residential land owned by the villagers, only 3.8 per cent is registered (see Table 20.3).

Local norms and practices of land tenure and land transactions

As noted, Langkawana's land has been divided into either forest or non-forest (*marga*) land. The villagers have developed their own norms and practices of land tenure in both categories. Land, whether used for residential purposes or gardens, is generally regarded as individually owned. It can be acquired through land clearing, land sales, inheritance, or land exchange. Land-clearing practices took place in the early period of Langkawana's settlement. The Sundanese and Javanese cleared the formerly Lampungese gardens and sometimes primary forests, marked borders on the land, and converted the land to plots. Land ownership was obtained only after the cleared land had been cultivated for a certain period. In addition to land-clearing, one can acquire land through sales. Land sales occur both in forest and non-forest land. The first wave of land sales took place when the Lampungese reclaimed their fallow land that had been used by the Sundanese for their gardens or housing. As mentioned above, the Sundanese bought the land from the Lampungese claimants. The second wave of land sales occurred when the Sundanese were relocated, and many of them sold their land located in the forest to their neighbours or sometimes to people from the city before they left for the transmigration areas in North Lampung. Others who decided to stay looked elsewhere for their residential land. They became involved in land transactions with the Lampungese, who at that time owned most of the land in the forest frontier, now known as Langkawana village.

Inheritance has been used for transferring ownership from parents to children. What makes inheritance unique in Langkawana is that it takes place prior to the parent's death. Both Javanese and Sundanese use the principle of 'musyawarah' or consensus to divide the inheritable property. There is no fixed formula to bequeath property. The division results from negotiation among family members. Even though all Langkawana's villagers are Muslim, they do not use Islamic inheritance law, since when dealing with inheritance, customary law is dominant. There exists no significant difference in the inheritance systems of the Sundanese and Javanese. In principle, there is no discrimination among children – son or daughter – to inherit their parents' property. However, children can inherit property of varying quantity and quality, depending on their parents' wisdom and the condition of the property itself. The oldest children living in the same village as their parents, for example, may inherit more property or may have first priority in choosing their inherited property. In contrast, the younger children or children living in a different place may inherit a smaller share of the property or no land at all.

Frequently, inheritance is assumed to be a key factor of land frag- mentation in villages where land is limited. Land is continuously di- vided among children until only very small parcels of land remain. However, this is not the case in Langkawana. When people only own one or a few small parcels of land, the land will be bequeathed to only one or a few of the children, while the other children inherit no land. As such, it can also happen that siblings inherit parcels of differing size and quality. A young Javanese woman informed me that she had inherited only a small piece of land of poor quality from her father. The land was located far away from the village and situated on a hill. As a result, she needed more time and additional labour inputs to culti- vate the land. Consequently, she and her husband decided to disregard the land and work hard towards buying another piece of land. They purchased a parcel of land which was small but of better quality than her inherited land. In her opinion, the inheritance system is not always fair, since as the youngest child she was forced to accept less valuable land than her siblings. However, she also voiced the opinion that their father had made an honest attempt to divide the land fairly, yet unfor- tunately he could not do much since he had limited land to divide.

Land exchange is another modus of acquiring ownership. Land ex- change occurs when two parties agree to exchange their ownership rights to a parcel of land. The reasons for doing so vary between the parties. Usually, the exchange will occur if two interests are met. Pro-

vided that one party feels unable to make the land more productive because of the distant location from home or limited labour to cultivate
the land, he or she can try to persuade the other party to exchange the
land. There exists no written documentation of land exchange agreements, because all transactions are based on trust.

Various secondary rights can be derived from a parcel of land,
namely, sharecropping (*bagi hasil*), leasing (*sewa*), pledging (*gadai;
gade*), and cultivating another's land for free (*numpang tanam*). One
can find these secondary rights mostly in forest gardens. Sharecropping takes place when one utilises and cultivates another's land without paying a sum of money in advance, but rather shares the harvested
crops with the landowner. Sharecropping habitually works based on
verbal agreements between the landowner and the sharecropper, determining the duration of the land use as well as the size of the crop-shar-
ing. In practice, there is no difference between the Javanese and Sundanese with regard to sharecropping practices. Sharecropping agreements are typically valid for one year, after which period parties can
agree to renew it. The owner and the cultivator mostly share the crop
in an equal manner (people use the term of *maro* or *paroh lahan* for
this sharecropping system). Kano (1984:71) deduced that in the nineteenth century, sharecropping in Java was not the result of an imbalanced agrarian structure in which the functioning of the landlord system and the relationship among farmers were based on class. In contrast, sharecropping was mostly based on mutual assistance among
neighbours and relatives, in which landowners allowed sharecropping
because they lacked the labour to cultivate the land. In a similar vein,
Rajagukguk found that in the 1980s sharecropping had nothing to do
with the phenomenon of the landless farmer but was caused by other
factors, such as the availability of labour, the time required to cultivate
land, and the interest in having additional income (Rajagukguk
1988:228). Parallel findings can be seen in Langkawana. One reason
for Sundanese and Javanese landowners' involvement in sharecropping
is the lack of labour in their household to cultivate their own land. Another reason is the limited time people have for cultivation due to a
variety of reasons, including the distant location of gardens resulting
in the need to spend more time to reach the land. Meanwhile, sharecroppers are interested in cultivating others' land because they desire
some additional income. They often do not come from landless households, but are trying to increase their area of productive land with limited financial resources.

Another popular tenancy agreement is the land lease. This agreement allows the lessee to use the lessor's agricultural land on the advance payment of an amount of cash money. The lessee and the lessor
agree on the rate of rent freely. However, they do consider the size of

the land as well as the number and value of plants located on the land. The larger the piece of land and the greater the number and value of plants on the land, the higher the rental price will be. In terms of duration, people have different types of agreement. Some prefer to use monthly or yearly agreements, while others prefer to use the harvest season as the time limit of their agreement. Negotiation is an important factor here.

Pledging or *gadai* refers to the agreement in which one borrows money from another with land as the collateral. Subsequently, the lender has physical control of the land. He may cultivate, benefit, even sharecrop or pledge the land to someone else. Like sharecropping, *gadai* is one of the traditional land tenancy agreements in Javanese and Sundanese villages. The Indonesian law on the maximum size of agricultural land (Law 56/Prp/1960) remarks that land pledging is the main cause of the unjust agrarian structure in villages, and so the law intends to end land pledging. Article 7 of the law, for instance, mentions that anyone who controls another's land for seven years or more because of land pledging must return the land to the owner a month after he/she harvests any plants currently on the land, without asking for compensation from the landowner. Meanwhile, for pledging agreements of less than seven years, or pledging that occurs after the enactment of the law, a landowner can ask for the land any time after the harvest season ends, but he/she should pay compensation to the pledge right holder according to a certain formula of compensation.[6] In practice, the law has had little effect. Hardjono (1987:113) assumes that this can be explained by the fact that pledging is a well-established local institution that has operated for centuries in Java. It has flourished even in state-owned forestland near Langkawana village.

The last secondary right is *numpang tanam*: the right to cultivate another's land free of charge. This is also a traditional land tenure institution in Java. The right to use another's land (*hak menumpang*) can apply, in most villages in Java, to agricultural land as well as housing land. In Langkawana, land owners only grant *numpang tanam* on their agricultural land. People can have *hak menumpang* only on fallow and unused land (*tanah bongkor or belukar*) in which they can plant vegetables while clearing the land. They are not obliged to pay or share the crops with the landowner. However, sharing may still be practised to keep good relations or as a form of gratitude to the owner. Even though the *numpang tanam* seems to be based mostly on social considerations, it has economic implications as well. The *numpang tanam* demonstrates a mutual symbiosis between the owners of the land and the cultivators. The former uses the latter as free labourers to clear land and to act as keepers of their property. Once the land owners are ready to cultivate the land, they need no additional labour to clear the land. The activities of cultivators on the land also prevent illegal occupation of the land. For the cultivators, the benefit is clear: they have the opportunity to cultivate land other than their own. Not all cultivators are landless, and many of them have their own gardens. However, similar to the practice of sharecropping, sometimes the cultivators need more land for production because their own land is already completely planted. When this occurs, *numpang tanam* would be their best option.

What can be learned from the Langkawana's practices of land tenure? First, land tenure has had a private-individual character. Lands have clear borders and are generally regarded as owned by individual villagers. The Sundanese and Javanese migrants have transplanted the traditional norms and practices from their home areas to their new land in Langkawana, including to state-owned forest land used as agroforest plots. The state's and people's property arrangements thus overlap. Second, land transactions have occurred since the beginning of Langkawana history. Land transfers occur either permanently, as in the case of land sales, inheritance, or exchange, or temporarily, as in the case of pledging, leasing, and the like. This illustrates how land transactions have been integrated into informal property arrangements. Yet, an interesting question remains over the extent to which, as De Soto believes, the legalisation of such informal property rights is able to enhance land transactions. This question will be further discussed below, in the section on land transactions.

Legalising the extra-legal (1): Registration of residential land in non-forest area

The first land registration of residential land in Langkawana took place in the year 2000. A government-funded systematic land registration project, entitled PRONA, was implemented in the village. At that time, 212 land parcels, totalling 8.2 hectares, were registered, and the rights holders obtained certificates of their ownership rights. However, due to limited funds the PRONA registered only 1.6 per cent of the total people's land in Langkawana (see Table 20.3). Trusting that the certificate would provide legal certainty to their land, villagers were enthusiastic to register their residential land. Soon after the PRONA project finished, villagers who had not been able to register their land under PRONA indicated their interest in registering the land through sporadic registration with the Head of the Sub-Village Unit (*kepala lingkungan*). The *kepala lingkungan* then consulted with the *lurah*. It was the *lurah*, who is also a civil servant of the municipality government, who had a significant role in the land registration process. A few months after the PRONA, he lobbied some officials at the Land Office of Ban-

Table 20.3 *Registration of residential land in Langkawana*

Land rights	Parcels	Hectare	Percentage to total residential land
Ownership rights (PRONA)	212	8.2	2.4 %
Ownership rights (Non-PRONA)	200	4.6	1.4 %
Unregistered land	-	328.2	96.2 %

Source: Monografi Kelurahan Langkawana, 2003

dar Lampung Municipality (*Kantor Pertanahan Kota Bandar Lampung*) and encouraged them to carry out non-PRONA or sporadic[7] land registration in Langkawana. He was successful, and another 200 land parcels were then registered.

Of the group of villagers who registered their land, most expressed their satisfaction with non-PRONA land registration. The only problem was the additional cost. Officially, the cost of obtaining a land certificate was IDR 150,000 (USD 15); in reality, however, the villagers had to pay twice as much. The officials of the Municipal Land Office as well as the *lurah* argued that additional money, known as 'cigarette money' (*uang rokok*), was needed to cover the transportation and meal expenses of the officials. After sporadic registration of the 200 parcels was finished, the land officials, again through the *lurah*, offered to help other landowners to register the remaining land. However, they have not yet responded, and the cost of land registration continues to be their main obstacle. Some villagers, particularly those with a lower income, maintain that they dream of land certificates, but that they are unable to save at least IDR 300,000 (USD 30) to register their residential land. The result has been that only a small number of land parcels have been registered. As said above, 34 per cent of all village land is registered. But of this registered land, the larger part is land with an *HGU* title, which is owned by the Foundation of Racing Drivers. Land registered by villagers accounts for only 2.5 per cent of the total village land. In Langkawana, the registration of residential land neither increased the number of land transactions nor resulted in the more than 400 owners starting to use their registered residential property as formal or informal credit collateral. Although they did, to a certain extent, invest in their houses and their residential areas, this had much less impact on poverty reduction than the investments in forest gardens. These issues will be further discussed below.

Legalising the extra-legal (2): A community forestry license for agro-forest gardens

As mentioned above, since 1986, Wan Abdul Rahman Park has been cleared of people's plots and hamlets. The Sundanese have been re-moved either to the transmigration areas in North Lampung or to Langkawana village. Yet, this has not meant that agricultural activities have ceased to exist. The Sundanese and Javanese in Langkawana con-tinued their normal routines in the forest after the Forest Service and military forces left the forest, and they re-cultivated their destroyed gar-dens. The Forest Services conducted occasional forest inspections, and forest rangers threatened the villagers with repercussions if they con-tinued to farm. Nevertheless, the law was never enforced consistently, and villagers could protect their gardens by bribing the rangers with money, coffee, or fruits. Acting in accordance with the law, when they caught villagers in the actual cultivation of forest gardens, the rangers would seize their machetes. Nevertheless, the law was open to debate, and the rangers offered people the chance to 'negotiate the law', mean-ing to negotiate payment for the return of the machetes. Unbalanced power relations between the people and forest rangers have fed this sort of underground economic activity. The villagers must maintain good personal relations with the rangers or risk the destruction of their gardens. Just as Scott (1985) terms one weapon of the weak 'everyday forms of resistance', as they engage in unequal power relations, the Langkawana perform everyday forms of negotiation.

Besides inspections by forest rangers, cultivators also faced a con-stant threat from within – theft by other villagers. In an environment of full awareness of the fact that no one has a legal right to one's gar-den, the phrase *'thieves cannot blame each other'* has gained great cur-rency locally. Ensuing conflicts typically have been resolved through mediation by village officials. Also common is what Nader and Todd (1978:9) describe as the 'lumping it' strategy, in which claimants who knowingly decide that the gain is too low and cost too high prefer to ignore or avoid local conflicts. For Langkawana villagers, overt internal conflict has high social costs. Ignoring conflict best preserves social harmony, yet this is reached at the expense of tenure security over their gardens.

In mid-1998, a research team from Jakarta that was seeking a site for applied anthropological research arrived in Langkawana and chan-ged the villagers' lives. Along with a local university and NGO partners, the researchers adopted the role of community organisers (COs) with the aim of establishing Forest User Groups (FUGs). FUGs create and enforce group rules to manage the forest, resolve internal conflicts, and set up cooperation to protect the forests.

The existence of FUGs and group rules have decreased conflicts over the forest, including incidences of theft. The COs convinced the central and provincial governments that the villagers were serious about preserving their forest, and they were successful in encouraging the MoF to issue a community forestry license to Langkawana villagers. In November 1999, the MoF issued a temporary community forestry license to the Langkawana FUGs Association, allowing its members to use 492.75 hectares of forest land. Valid for five years, the license could be extended as long as the groups demonstrated good forest management.

The community forestry license, which is basically a legal right to manage, use, and benefit from state forest land, can be seen as a tool for providing land tenure security to people. Although it is unable to provide people with full security of tenure and private land rights such as they can acquire on their residential land, the community forestry license made people's forest gardens legally secure, albeit still in the shadow of the state's property. The Langkawana villagers realised that asking for land ownership of their forest gardens was something unachievable and believed that the community forestry license was the most realistic option and would protect their gardens.

In November 2004, the community forestry license in Langkawana expired. Lampung Forest Service officials opted not to extend the license because in 2001 the MoF had changed the community forestry legislation. The new legislation prohibited the issuance of community forestry licenses in conservation forests. The Forest Services instead offered people a one-year license to cultivate their gardens which was based on a Provincial Regulation enacted in 2000 (Perda 7/2000). The villagers refused to accept the situation and argued that they had demonstrated good forest management for five years and thus deserved an extension, as the government had promised earlier. Yet the Forest Services could do nothing, since the central government's policy had changed. So they convinced the villagers that the new one-year license would also provide them with tenure security over their land, as long as they agreed to be supervised by the Forest Services and paid a levy.

Provincial Regulation 7/2000 has been used to collect such levies on forest products, including on agro-forest products in Lampung. The decentralisation process implemented in 2001 inspired the Lampung provincial government to seek as much revenue as possible, which included revenue from the agro-forest farmers. After enacting the Provincial Regulation 7/2000, the forestry officials persuaded the agro-forest farmers in Langkawana to pay the new forestry levy. The community forestry license was not extended in 2004, but people continued paying the levies. Clearly, the levies became illegal. Nevertheless, both the officials and communities have their reasons to continue this transaction. For the officials, mobilising communities to pay the levy is important to boost their career prospects, as their performance is judged according to the amount of levy they collect. The villagers, in their turn, believe that the levies they pay provide a certain measure of tenure security over their agro-forest gardens.

Poverty alleviation, land registration and community forestry license

Land registration and community forestry license are two examples of legalising the informal land tenure in Langkawana. The two have had different paths of legalisation because forest land and non-forest land are two different legal categories. People can obtain individual ownership rights over their residential land located in non-forest areas. Meanwhile for their plots situated in forest areas, they can acquire a community forestry license. The degree of tenure security of the two options certainly varies; however, the more interesting question is how the implementation of these options influences poverty alleviation in Langkawana.

In Langkawana, the greatest contribution to the villagers household economy originates from their agro-forest gardens located in the forest areas, not from their residential lands. The latter only meet people's housing needs, whilst the former provide cash incomes. Thus, community forestry is a good point of departure for assessing the extent to which land legalisation affects poverty reduction in Langkawana. The community forestry license protected the agro-forest gardens from outside interference. This increased people's investment in the land. Prior to obtaining a community forestry license, the Langkawana villagers preferred to plant coffee, vegetables, and non-perennial crops such as bananas and beans; however, once they acquired a community forestry license they diversified and planted more perennial and cash-producing crops. Planting such perennial crops as cacao, durians, and rubber, the more popular plants in the agro-forest gardens, illustrates the farmers' growing investment of labour and time.

The agro-forest gardens comprise approximately 60 per cent of household incomes. People use their forest-based incomes to send their children to school, build brick houses to replace their bamboo houses, buy motorcycles, and the like. This indicates a change in the economy of the village. Table 20.4 shows some economic indicators in 1998 and in 2005, as stated by the people. It shows that people's quality of life has improved significantly during this period, which coincides with the higher tenure security of people's forest gardens.

Incomes from the agro-forest gardens represent a substantial contribution to the villagers' livelihood in Langkawana. In addition, the forest

Table 20.4 *Village economic indicators in Langkawana, 1998-2005*

Indicators	1998	2005
Stalls	19	26
Middlemen	9	14
Brick houses	90	130
Cars	4	6
Motorcycles	20	65
Toilets	25	130
Education:		
Drop out from elementary schools	65	33
Attendance elementary schools	800	821
Attendance junior high schools	552	534
Attendance senior high schools	420	463
Attendance university	2	6

Source: Field Survey and Field Notes, 2005

provides clean fresh water, construction materials, herbal medicines, and the like. All these products from the forests must be included when conducting poverty assessments in forest surrounding villages. Unfortunately, many poverty alleviation policies and programmes in Indonesia, although they are implemented in the forest frontier, largely neglect forest factors such as these (Wollenberg et al. 2004:3). Trapped into legal categories of forest and non-forest land, the policies and programmes follow the incorrect assumption that natural forests play no role in people's agricultural activities and livelihood strategies. As previously stated, Wan Abdulrahman Grand Forest Park offers many productive lands as well as sources of economically valuable products. This has made the forest a significant factor in poverty reduction in Langkawana. As a result, in Langkawana, the legalisation of forest gardens through a community forestry license had a greater impact on people's livelihood than the legalisation through registration of residential lands in non-forest areas. The Langkawana case thus shows that legalisation of informal land rights has a greater effect when it targets land that is highly productive than when it targets unproductive land

Therefore, it is important to assess the productivity of land. Such an assessment must consider economic and social values of land, which are derived from physical, social, economic and legal factors (Gwartney 2008). Physical attributes such as the location and fertility of land, for example, are important factors in determining the productivity of the land. Social attributes of the land include, for example, the amount of family labour that can be used to make the land more productive, and the social norms that enable or prohibit access to the land. Economic factors refer to the existing and prospective economic value of resources available on the land. Meanwhile, legal attributes of the land refer to the legal rights of people to the land and resources. All these attributes alter people's perceptions regarding the land.

If the possession of legalised productive land is a key factor in reducing poverty, the question follows that if the land has been distributed unfairly, how then can such productive land be provided to more people? Here another complexity emerges. When the majority of land has been allocated as state forests, and most agricultural land in non-forest areas belongs to private companies, where can the common people farm? The situation in Langkawana clearly illustrates this issue. Approximately 30 per cent of non-forest land is under the *HGU* title of a private foundation. In the entire province of Lampung, the number reaches 12.5 per cent. Due to city development, agricultural land has also been converted into private real estate. This shows how strong the competition for land is in non-forest areas. In such a situation, people with less economic power will be easily marginalised, as has happened to approximately 500 families in western Langkawana. Most of them cannot afford agricultural land outside forest areas, even though they know that such land will provide them with more legal security, as they are able to obtain full ownership rights to this land.

Thus, while Langkawana villagers have a strong desire to obtain more security in land tenure by purchasing agricultural land outside the forest, very few of them can transform their forestry-based assets to buy land in non-forest areas. The tight competition of the land market outside the forest has pushed them further into the forest. Thus, providing people with more secure land rights on forest land is a key to reducing poverty, as long as there is no land redistribution of non-forest areas. The legalisation of forest land and the redistribution of non-forest land are thus two complementary strategies to enhance the livelihoods of the Langkawana villagers.

Land transactions

A central argument of the advocates of legalisation is that the integration of extra-legal property into the formal legal system will enhance the market and increase the number of property transactions. It is generally thought that individual property rights will most strongly enhance the property market. In this section, we will discuss what makes land transactions occur, on what type of land they occur, and under what property arrangements.

The Langkawana villagers have engaged in land transactions ever since they came to Lampung. In the history of Langkawana, two big waves of land transactions occurred. The first wave consisted of the transactions between the Sundanese migrants and the Lampungese in the beginning of the Sundanese's settlement in Mount Betung (1940s-1950s). The second wave of land transactions occurred following the re-location projects which removed people from the forest in the 1980s. After the first relocation in 1982, for example, the Sundanese, who were forced to relocate to the transmigration areas in North Lampung, sold their housing land and plots either to their neighbours or to outsi-ders. Then, when the second relocation occurred in 1986, the remain-ing Sundanese who refused to be relocated to North Lampung pur-chased land in the forest frontier where they then built their houses. The manner in which those who were relocated acquired new land was highly dependent on their kinship networks and financial resources, as well as their personal preference of residence. Those having sufficient money to buy land could go anywhere and thus had more options in choosing their housing land. Most of them preferred to buy land situ-ated near their former homes or gardens in the forest. The *marga* land in Langkawana *Atas* was the best location to access their forest gardens. Meanwhile, those who lacked money were dependent upon their rela-tives to either live in their homes free of charge (*tumpangan*) or to ne-gotiate the purchase of their relatives' land at a lower price. Those who had no opportunities to acquire land in Langkawana went to another village, and some even returned to their home villages in Java.

After 1986, there have been occasional land transactions, in particu-lar of forest land. Interestingly, the number of land transactions de-clined after people obtained their community forestry license, which provided them with better tenure security. And not only did land sales decline, other forms of land transactions, such as land leases, also dropped significantly. This phenomenon, which will be accounted for later, is in contradiction to the common assumption that increasing tenure security will enhance the land market (Deininger 2003:115; Place, Roth, and Hazell 1994:17). Despite the declining number of land transactions in forest areas, land transactions as well as informal access to credit through pledging occurred more often in forest areas than in non-forest areas, although the latter is able to provide people with more legal security. This can be explained by looking through the eyes of Langkawana villagers. First, residential land is not seen as a marketable commodity, and most land sales therefore occur in plots located in for-est land. In the people's view, having no plots is less risky than having no land at all for housing. With no plots, they can still survive by rent-ing land or sharecropping with other villagers. There is no tradition of renting land for housing in Langkawana. Thus, people must have their own land for building their houses. This makes people eager to defend their ownership right on residential land. In addition, people strongly believe that selling their housing land characterizes them as losers be-cause of their inability to defend their primary safety net. Second, land transactions predominantly occur when people are unable to make their land more productive. Lack of labour inputs in people's household with which to cultivate the land or the remote location of land are two general reasons for transferring ownership or renting the land. How selective people are in selling their land can be seen, for instance, in a land transaction case below that involved a Langkawana villager and an outsider.

> A Langkawana villager, Karsaya, was trapped in a big debt. He did not have sufficient money to pay all his debt. Then, he decided to sell one of his parcels of land in the forest situated far away from his house in Langkawana. For him, the land was not so productive because of its distant location. He persuaded his brother-in law living in another village to buy the land. The brother in-law had no agricultural land both in the forest and in non-forest land. He was very interested in purchasing the land because it was situated near to his village. The transaction, finally, took place. Karsaya received IDR five millions for his 1.75 ha of uncultivated land. His brother-in law obtained a parcel of agricultural land to support his livelihood. For both parties, the transaction was a clear expression of mutual help among relatives.

Land transactions are driven by complex factors, and tenure security is only one of them. The situation in Langkawana has shown that enhanced tenure security will have no effect on land transactions when people regard their land primarily as a safety net, and will only sell it in situations of serious distress. The Sundanese and Javanese migrants in Langkawana prefer to keep as much land as possible in their hands rather than to sell it. Only in certain conditions where they fail to obtain alternatives for cash money do they sell their land. In the absence of state services, people sell, lease, or pledge their land due to their need for money for education and health costs, as well as for celebrating their children's wedding parties. They prefer to transact land with relatives and neighbours. In these transactions, economic concerns are not always the primary motive, since they are also attracted by the social mechanism of mutual help (*tolong-menolong*) with relatives and neighbours. As the motive for land transaction is often laden with social considerations of mutual help, the seller can frequently buy back the land. This makes land transactions with relatives or neighbours the preferred method.

Let us now try to explain why an increase in tenure security – through the community forestry license – led to a decline rather than an increase in land transactions in forest areas. When people consider a transfer of land, they prefer to part with lands that they are unable to make more productive and that are insecure in tenure. The Langkawana villagers reason that the more productive the land, the greater the profits they can expect, and the less willing they are to engage in a land transaction. While land productivity is dependent on labour supply and accessibility, expected profits are also based on people's perception of their security in cultivating the land. Tenure security and land profitability can be thought of as a two-sided coin. The less tenure security, the less one can count on profits from the land in the future, and the more people will be willing to transfer the land. Land transactions are a mechanism of transferring economic and legal risks to others. The other way around, higher tenure security creates incentives to make the land more productive, which in turn makes it less likely that people will transfer their land. This can explain why the number of land sales and land rents in Langkawana's agro-forest gardens declined following the community forestry license. The license provided people with more tenure security and made them feel safe to cultivate their land, which created less intention to sell the land.

Another explanation for the low number of land transactions lies in the existence of local norms that prohibit land transactions to outsiders. The Langkawana villagers set up their Forest User Groups prior to obtaining the community forestry license. The groups crafted local norms in relation to forest use, including the prohibition of transferring land to people who do not reside in the village. The norms have effectively prevented land transactions with outsiders.

Similar to what has happened with the land transactions, access to credit is not determined solely by legal security. Residential lands in Langkawana are never used as formal or informal credit collateral. People prefer to engage in pledging of their agro-forest plots rather than their residential lands. The fact that there is no bank or formal credit institution willing to provide them with credit is one factor. However, the leading factor is people's reluctance to use their housing land as collateral. The perception of housing land as their primary safety net has dissuaded them from doing so. Thus, they prefer to use their agro-forest plots in the forest areas as collateral. The only possible way to use forest land as collateral is through informal credit mechanisms, such as pledging to their relatives or neighbours.

Langkawana's experience has pointed out that the absence or limited availability of basic public services determines the land market. People see their land as a safety net and prefer to hang on to it as long as possible, only selling it in times of serious distress. In such a situation the enhancement of tenure security through the legalisation of land rights will not have much effect on the land market.[8]

Conclusions

The orthodox view of land law and land tenure holds a linear assumption of land tenure security, investment, poverty reduction, and marketisation. It is widely believed that the legalisation of informal land rights will increase the degree of land tenure security, which in turn will result in more land and labour investments, higher productivity, land capitalisation, and poverty alleviation. It is furthermore assumed that the highest level of tenure security can be acquired through the titling and registration of individual property rights in land. This is thus seen as the best legalisation process to enhance land markets and reduce poverty. This view has inspired legal and economic discourses, as well as foreign aid projects for legal and economic reform in less developed countries. Indonesia is one of the countries where this vision has informed land management.

In this chapter I have described two different legalisation processes in Langkawana, a village in the forest frontier of Lampung. The first involved the registration of individual property rights in residential non-forest land. Although this legalisation enhanced the legal status and the tenure security of the land, it did not lead to an increased use of the land as collateral for loans nor to a higher number of land transactions. Langkawana villagers do not consider their residential land as a marketable commodity, but as an asset that needs to be held onto at all costs. Legalisation of the villagers' residential land did not change this attitude.

The second legalisation process involved the granting of a community forestry license on forest land. Although this did not provide the villagers with individual titles, it did enhance their tenure security, i.e. the extent to which the villagers felt assured of their ability to access their land, to manage and use it, and to effectively exclude others.[9] As a result, people invested more time and labour in their forest gardens, diversified their crops, and planted more perennial and cash-producing crops. This led to a significant improvement of the people's quality of life. Interestingly, after the granting of the community forestry license, the number of market transactions decreased. Although this contradicts the abovementioned theory, it can logically be explained by the fact that villagers prefer not to sell secure and productive land. The greater the profits that can be expected from land, the less willing people are to transfer their land. The less tenure security, the less one can count on profits from the land in the future, and the more people will be willing to transfer the land. Higher tenure security, on the other hand, creates incentives to make the land more productive, which in turn makes it less likely that people will transfer their land. In Langkawana, the community forestry license provided people with more tenure security and made them feel safe to cultivate their land, which created less intention to sell the land.

The above case thus shows that legalisation of land rights does not always lead to marketisation and poverty reduction. As the case of Langkawana shows, the people's decision to take part in land transactions is determined by their perception of land and the contribution of land to their household economy. The legal status of land is merely one factor, but not the major one, in determining land transactions. In addition, registration of individual property rights in residential land in non-forest areas has had less impact on people's livelihood and their level of poverty than legalisation of forest gardens through a community forestry license. The relationship between legalisation of land tenure and poverty reduction will be determined not only by the kind of rights – individual or communal rights, ownership or use rights – granted to the people but also by the quality of lands on which these rights are granted. In other words, it will have a greater effect on poverty reduction to target lands that are highly productive than to target lands that are unproductive. However, in a country like Indonesia – where all forest land has been designated state land – the legalisation of productive forest land is nearly impossible. Programmes of land legalisation therefore need to be preceded by a land reform programme. Unfortunately, this has been neglected by the proponents of simplistic projects of land legalisation.

Notes

1   Broadly defined, tenure security refers to the extent to which a holder of a parcel of land feels assured (both in the short and longer term) of his ability to access his land, to manage and use it, and to effectively exclude others.
2   In 1987 the MoF recognized that of 50 million hectares of forest concessions, only 75 per cent were located in production forests. Others could be found in protection and conservation forests. Many of them were even located outside the forest areas, in this case on people's land (Safitri, Bangun, and Philippus 1999:4). This led the logging companies to become engaged in conflicts with local communities.
3   To protect the privacy of my informants, the village's name has been changed.
4   According to the elucidation of article 127 of Law 32/2004 on Regional Autonomy, kelurahan is a working area of a village chief (lurah). This area is located within a subdistrict (kecamatan) territory. A kelurahan differs from a village (desa) in terms of its degree of autonomy. The village is politically and economically more autonomous. The village head (kepala desa) is elected directly by the villagers. The village has its own assets and authority to manage them. In contrast, the kelurahan is led by a lurah who is an appointed civil servant and is responsible to the mayor or head of the district (bupati). For this reason, the kelurahan is defined as a working territory of a lurah rather than as an autonomous social, political, as well as economic unit of the people.

5   *Lingkungan* is part of *kelurahan* territory, headed by a *kepala lingkungan*. Unlike the *lurah*, the *kepala lingkungan* is not a civil servant. He/she is appointed by the *lurah* after considering the people's aspiration. People elect their *kepala lingkungan*, then nominate the elected person to the lurah. The *kepala lingkungan* is accountable to the *lurah*.

6   According to Law 56/Prp/1960, the formula is (7+1/2) – pledge duration × the loan.

7   Government Regulation 24/1997 on Land Registration divides the registration into two: systematic and sporadic registration. The systematic land registration is a government-led land registration project which is conducted in certain areas as determined by the National Land Agency. The sporadic registration refers to people-driven land administration.

8   Nevertheless, the fear of land transfers is the official explanation for the MoF's reluctance to grant land rights over forest areas to the people. They claim that they fear that land transfers will immediately follow the granting of land rights. Therefore, in all community forestry regulations, there has always been a clause of not allowing people to obtain land rights. Certainly, this reduces the degree of legal tenure security of the community forestry.

9   See footnote 594 for the definition of tenure security.

References

Abudulai, Sulemana. 1996. Perceptions of land rights, rural-urban land use dynamics and policy development. In *Managing Land Tenure and Resource Access in West Africa: Proceedings of a Regional Workshop held at Gorée, Sénégal, November 18-22, 1996*, edited by Ministère de la Coopération, Overseas Development Administration, L'Université de Saint Louis, GRET and IIED. London: IIED.

—. 2002. Land rights, land-use dynamics & policy in peri-urban Tamale, Ghana. In *The Dynamics of Resource Tenure in West Africa*, edited by C. Toulmin, P. Lavigne Delville and S. Traoré. London: IIED.

Adams, Martin, Sipho Sibanda, and Stephen Turner. 1999. Land tenure reform and rural livelihoods in Southern Africa. *Natural Resource Perspectives* 39.

Adicondro, G.Y. 1980. Bagaimana Mengelakkan Ketentuan Luas Tanah Maksimum - Studi Kasus Tanah Guntai di Desa Benkak, Kabupaten Benyuwangi, Jawa Timur. In *Hasil Loka Karya Hukum Tanah untuk Lembaga-Lembaga Pembina Swadaya Masyarakat Desa*.

Ahmed, M.M., S. Ehui, Berhanu Gebremedhin, S. Benin, and Amare Teklu. 2002. Evolution and Technical Efficiency of Land Tenure Systems in Ethiopia. Nairobi, Kenya: International Livestock Research Institute.

Aidit, D.N. 1964. *Kobarkan Semangat Banteng, Maju Terus, Pantang Mundur*. Djakarta: Jajasan Pembaruan.

Albó, Xavier. 1991. El retorno del indio. *Revista Andina* Año 9 (No. 2):299-366 (including the comments by various scholars).

—. 1994. And from Kataristas to MNRistas? The Surprising and Bold Alliance between Aymaras and Neoliberals in Bolivia. In *Indigenous Peoples and Democracy in Latin America*, edited by D. L. Van Cott. New York: St. Martin's Press.

—. 2007. Movimientos indígenas desde 1900 hasta la actualidad. In *Bolivia en Movimiento: Acción colectiva y poder politico*, edited by J. Espasandín López and P. Iglesias Turrión. Barcelona: Ediciones de Intervención Cultural/El Viejo Topo.

Albó, Xavier, and Franz X. Barrios Suvelza. 2006. Por una Bolivia plurinacional e intercultural con autonomies. La Paz: PNUD.

Alden Wily, Liz. 2003. Governance and land relations: a review of decentralization of land administration and management in Africa. London: International Institute for Environment and Development.

Alden Wily, Liz, and Daniel N.A. Hammond. 2001. Land Security and the Poor in Ghana. Is There a Way Forward?: DFID Ghana Rural livelihoods Program.

Amamoo, J.G. 1958. *The New Ghana: The birth of a new nation*. London: Pan Books.

Amankwah, H.A. 1989. *The Legal Regime of Land Use in West Africa: Ghana and Nigeria*. Tasmania: Pacific Law Press, Hobart.

Amanor, Kojo Sebastian. 1994. *The New Frontier: farmers' responses to land degradation*. London: Zed Press.

—. 1999. Global Restructuring and Land Rights in Ghana. In *Research Report No 108*. Uppsala: Nordiska Afrikainstitutet.

—. 2001. Land, Labour and the Family in Southern Ghana: a Critique of Land Policy under Neo-Liberalisation. Uppsala: Nordiska Afrikainstitutet.

—. 2005a. Equity in Forest Benefits Sharing and Poverty Alleviation. In *Equity in Forest Bene-fit Sharing: Stakeholders' views*, edited by K. S. Nketia, J. A. S. Ameyaw and B. Owusu Jr. Wageningen, Netherlands: Tropenbos International.

—. 2005b. Global and local land markets: the role of the customary. In *Land in Africa: Mar-ket asset or secure Livelihood? Proceedings and summary of conclusions from the Land in Afri-ca Conference held in London, November 8-9, 2004*, edited by J. Quan, S. F. Tan and C. Toulmin. London: IIED, NRI, Royal African Society.

Amanor, Kojo Sebastian, and M. K. Diderutuah. 2001. *Share contracts in the oil palm and ci-trus belt of Ghana, Land tenure and resource access in West Africa.* London: International Institute for Environment and Development.

Amanor, Kojo Sebastian, and O. Pabi. 2007. Space, Time, Rhetoric and Agricultural Change in the Transition Zone of Ghana. *Human Ecology* 35 (1):51-67.

Amhara National Regional State (ANRS). 1997. A Proclamation to Provide for the Establish-ment of Kebele Social Court of the Amhara National Region, edited by Zikre Hig: 24 June, Bahr Dar.

—. 2006. The Revised Amhara National Regional State Rural Land Administration and Use Proclamation, edited by Zikre Hig: May 29, Bahr Dar.

Andargachew Tiruneh. 1993. *The Ethiopian Revolution 1974-1987.* Cambridge: Cambridge University Press.

Anderson, B, R McVey, and F.P. Bunnell. 1971. *A Preliminary Analysis of October 1, 1965 Coup in Indonesia.* Ithaca NY: Cornell University.

Anderson, Michael R. 2003. Access to justice and legal process: making legal institutions re-sponsive to poor people in LDCs *IDS Working Paper* (178).

Andrien, Kenneth J. 2001. *Andean Worlds: Indigenous History, Culture, and Consciousness un-der Spanish Rule, 1532-1825.* Albuquerque: University of New Mexico Press.

Ang, Audra. 2006. *Chinese Village Surrounded After Shootings.* Associated Press, December 9 2005 [cited 20 February 2006]. Available from http://sfgate.com/cgi-bin/article.cgi?f=/n/a/2005/12/09/international/i092407S20.DTL.

Annor, K.P. 1985. Cultural and social identities in Africa: Chieftaincy and political change in Ghana. *Verfassung und Recht in Ubersee* 18:153-159.

Antwi, Adarkwah Yaw. 2006. Strengthening customary land administration: A DFID/World Bank sponsored project in Ghana. In *Promoting land administration and good governance, 5th FIG regional conference.* Accra.

Antwi, Adarkwah Yaw, and John Adams. 2003. Rent-seeking behaviour and its economic costs in urban land transactions in Accra, Ghana. *Urban Studies* 40 (10):2083-2098.

Appendini, Kirstens. 1996. Changing Agrarian Institutions: Interpreting the Contradictions. North York, Ontario: York University, CERLAC.

Arhin Birempong, K. 2001. *Transformations in Traditional Rule in Ghana (1951-1996)* Accra: Sedco.

Arroyo Sepúlveda, Ramiro. 2001. Los excluidos sociales del campo. *Estudios Agrarios*, 105-124.

Arze Cuadros, Eduardo. 2002. *Bolivia: El Programa del MNR y la Revolución Nacional; Del Movimiento de Reforma Universitaria al ocaso del modelo neoliberal (1928-2002).* La Paz: Plural.

Asante, S.K.B. 1969. Interests in land in the customary law of Ghana–a new appraisal. *Uni-versity of Ghana Law Journal* 6 (2):99-139.

—. 2003. African traditional systems and the growth of democracy and good governance. Pa-per read at Conference on African traditional leaders, August 3, 2003, at Kumasi.

Askale Teklu. 2005. Land Registration and Women's Land Rights in Amhara Region, Ethio-pia. London: IIED.

Assies, Willem. 1999. Multiethnicity, the state and the law. *Latin America Journal of Legal Pluralism* 49:145-158.

—. 2003. From Rubber Estate to Simple Commodity Production: Agrarian Struggles in the Northern Bolivian Amazon Region. In *Latin American Peasants*, edited by T. Brass. London, Portland OR: Frank Cass

—. 2004. Bolivia: A Gasified Democracy. *European Review of Latin American and Caribbean Studies* 76:25-45.

—. 2007. Legalising Land tenure for Development: A bibliography. Leiden: Van Vollenhoven Institute (CD-Rom available on demand).

Assies, Willem, and Ton Salman. 2003. Crisis in Bolivia: The Elections of 2002 and their Aftermath. London: University of London, Institute of Latin American Studies.

Assies, Willem, and André J. Hoekema. 1994. Indigenous Peoples' Experiences with Self-Government. Copenhagen: IWGIA, University of Amsterdam.

Aston, T.H., and C.H.E Philpin. 1985. *The Brenner Debate: Agrarian Class Structure and Economic Development in Pre-Industrial Europe*. Cambridge: Cambridge University Press.

Atwood, D.A. 1990. Land registration in Africa: The impact on agricultural production. *World Development* 18 (5):659-671.

Aylwin, José. 2002. El acceso de los indígenas a la tierra en los ordenamientos jurídicos de América Latina: un estudio de casos. Santiago de Chile: CEPAL.

Azuela, A. 1989. La ciudad, la propiedad privada y el derecho. México: El Colegio de México.

—. 1994. Corporativismol y privatización en la regularización de la tenencia de la tierra. In *Cambios Económicos y Periferia de las Grandes Ciudades. El caso de la ciudad de México*, edited by D. Hiernaux and F. Tomas. México: IFAL /UAM-X.

Bahru Zewde. 1991. *A History of Modern Ethiopia 1855-1974*. Addis Ababa: Addis Ababa University Press.

Bakker, L. 2005. Resource Claims between Tradition and Modernity: Masyarakat Adat Strategies in Mului (Kalimantan Timur). *Borneo Research Bulletin* 36:29-50.

—. forthcoming. Politics or tradition: Debating Hak Ulayat in Pasir. In *Reflections on the Heart of Borneo*, edited by G. Persoon and M. Osseweijer. Wageningen: Tropenbos International.

Baranyi, Stephen, Carmen Diana Deere, and Manuel Morales. 2004. Scoping Study on Land Policy Research in Latin America. Canada: The North-South Institute.

Bartra, Armando. 2004. Rebellious Cornfields: Towards Food and Labour Self-Sufficiency. In *Mexico in Transition: Neoliberal Globalism, the State and Civil Society*, edited by Gerardo Otero. Nova Scotia, London, New York: Fernwood Publishing, Zed Books.

Bassett, T.J. 1993. Introduction: The land question and agricultural transformation in sub-Saharan Africa. In *Land in African Agrarian Systems*, edited by T. J. Bassett and D. E. Crummey. Wisconsin: University of Wisconsin Press.

Beck, Lindsay, and Shipeng Guo. 2007. *China property law bolsters private rights*, 8 March 2007 [cited 7 June 2007]. Available from http://www.reuters.com/article/worldNews/idUSSP36543620070308.

Bedner, A.W. 2001. *Administrative Courts in Indonesia, A Socio-Legal Study*. Leiden / London: Kluwer International.

Beijaard, Frans. 1995. Rental and rent-free housing as coping mechanisms in La Paz, Bolivia. *Environment and Urbanization* 7 (2):167-181.

Bélières, J-F, P-M Bosc, G Faure, S Fournier, and B Losch. 2002. What Future for West Africa's Family Farms in a World Market Economy? London: IIED.

Benning, R.B. 1996. Land Ownership, Divestiture and Beneficiary Rights in Northern Ghana: Critical issues. In *Decentralisation, Land Tenure and Land Administration in the Northern Region of Ghana*. Konrad Adenauer Foundation, Accra: 20-40.

Berhanu Adenew, and Fayera Abdi. 2005. Land Registration in Amhara Region, Ethiopia. London: IIED.

Berry, Sara. 1993. *No Condition is Permanent. The Social Dynamics of Agrarian Change in Sub-Saharan Africa*. Madison: The University of Wisconsin Press.

—. 2002. The everyday politics of rent-seeking: land allocation on the outskirts of Kumase, Ghana. In *Negotiating Property in Africa*, edited by K. Juul and C. Lund. Portsmouth: Heinemann.

Betancur, AC. 2003. El Proceso para la Titulación de la TCO Monte Verde. Santa Cruz: SNV-CEJIS.

BID. 2005. Bolivia: Programa de saneamiento de tierras y catastro legal: Propuesta de préstamo, Banco Interamericano de Desarrollo.

Bierschenk, Th. 1993. The creation of a tradition. Fulani chiefs in Dahomey/Bénin from the late 19th century. *Paideuma* 39:217-244.

Bizberg, Ilán. 2003a. Auge y decadencia del corporativismo. In *Una historia contemporánea de México, Tomo I: transformaciones y permanencias*, edited by Ilan Bizberg and L. Meyer. Mexico: Oceano.

—. 2003b. Estado, organizaciones corporativas y democracia. In *México al inicio del siglo XXI: democracia, ciudadanía y desarrollo*, edited by Alberto Aziz Nassif. Mexico: CIESAS, Miguel Ángel Porrúa.

Bizberg, Ilán, and Lorenzo Meyer. 2003 *Una historia contemporánea de México, Tomo I: transformaciones y permanencias*. Mexico: Oceano.

Blundo, G. 1996. Gérer les conflits fonciers au Sénégal: Le rôle de l'administration locale dans le sud-est du bassin arachidier. In *Démocratie, Enjeux Fonciers et Pratiques Locales en Afrique: Conflits, gouvernance et turbulences en Afrique de l'Ouest et centrale*, edited by P. Mathieu, P.-J. Laurent and J.-C. Willame. Bruxelles / Paris: Institut Africaine-CEDAF / L'Harmattan.

Boafo-Arthur, Kwame. 2003. Chieftaincy in Ghana: challenges and prospects in the 21st Century. *African and Asian Studies* 2 (2):125-154.

Boni, Stefano. 2005. *Clearing the Ghanaian forest: theories and practices of acquisition, transfer and utilisation of farming titles in the Sefwi-Akan area* Legon: Institute of African Studies

Botchway, J. 1993. Implications of Farming and Household Strategies for the Organization of a Development Project. In *Cultivating Knowledge: Genetic diversity, farmer experimentation and crops research*, edited by W. De Boef, K. Amanor, K. Wellard and A. Bebbington. London: Intermediate Technology.

BPN (National Land Agency). 2003. Accelerated Land Registration Strategy, edited by BPN.

—. 2006. Land Management and Policy Development Project (LMPDP), Final Report, edited by BPN.

Brackman, A.C. 1969. *The Communist Collapse in Indonesia*. New York: Norton.

Brown, Jennifer. 2004. Ejidos and Comunidades in Oaxaca, Mexico: Impact of the 1992 Reforms. Seattle: Rural Development Institute.

Bruce, John W. 1993. Do Indigenous Tenure Systems Constrain Agricultural Development? In *Land in African Agrarian Systems*, edited by T. J. Basset and D. E. Crummey. Madison: University of Wisconsin Press.

Bruce, John W., A. Hoben, and Dessalegn Rahmato. 1994. After the Derg: An Assessment of Rural Land Tenure Issues in Ethiopia. Madison, Wisconsin: Land Tenure Center.

Bruce, John W., and Shem E. Migot-Adholla, eds. 1994. *Searching for Land Tenure Security in Africa*. Dubuque, Iowa: Kendall/Hunt.

Bruce, John W., Shem E. Migot-Adholla, and Joan Atherton. 1994. The findings and their policy implications: institutional adaptation or replacement? In *Searching for Land Tenure Security in Africa*, edited by J. W. Bruce and S. E. Migot-Adholla. Dubuque: Kendall/ Hunt Publishing Company.

Bruneau, J-C. 1979. *Ziguinchor en Casamance. Une ville moyenne du Sénégal*. Bordeaux: Centre d'Etudes de Géographie Tropicale.

Buckley, Chris. 2006. China Land Grabs fuelling unrest, says premier. *Reuters*, January 20.

Burgess, R. 2001. Land and Welfare: Theory and Evidence from China. London: London School of Economics.

Bush, Jennifer. 2002. Baseline Report. Household Food Economy Assessment, Boloso Sore Woreda, Wolayita Zone, SNNPR. Addis Ababa: Christian Aid and ICCO.

Busia, K.A. 1951. *The Position of the Chief in the Modern Political System of Ashanti: a Study of the Influence of Contemporary Social Changes on Ashanti Political Institutions*. London, New York, Toronto: Oxford University Press.

CACC. 2003. Ethiopian Agricultural Sample Enumeration, 2001/02 (1994 E.C). Results at Country Level, Part I. Addis Ababa: Central Agricultural Census Commission.

Cai, Yongshun. 2003. Collective Ownership or Cadres' Ownership? The Non-agricultural Use of Farmland in China. *China Quarterly* 175 (September):662-680.

Cárdenas, Víctor Hugo. 1988. La lucha de un pueblo. In *Raíces de América: El mundo Aymara*, edited by X. Albó. Madrid: Alianza Editorial.

Carney, Judith, and Michael Watts. 1990. Manufacturing dissent: work, gender and the politics of meaning in a peasant society. *Africa* 60 (2):207-241.

Carter, C., and Fu-Ning Zhong. 1988. China's Grain Production and Trades.

Carter, William, and Xavier Albó. 1988. La comunidad Aymara: un mini-estado en conflicto. In *Raíces de América: El mundo Aymara*, edited by X. Albó. Madrid: Alianza Editorial.

Caverivière, M., and M Débène. 1998. *Le Droit Foncier Sénégalais*. Paris: Berger-Levrault.

CEJIS. 2001. Tierras Comunitarias de Origen Saneamiento y Titulación: Guía para el Patrocinio Jurídico, Algunas Enseñanzas de la Experiencia. Santa Cruz: CEJIS (Centro de Estudios Jurídicos e Investigación Social).

Centre for Democracy and Development. 2000. The Ghana Governane and Corruption Survey. Evidence from Households, Enterprises and Public Officials.

Cernea, M.M. 1994. Environmental and social requirements for resource-based regional development. *Regional Development Dialogue* 15 (1):186-198.

Chan, Nelson. 2003. Land Acquisition Compensation in China, Problems & Answers. *International Real Estate Review* 6 (1):136-152.

Chen, Guikang, and Yao Chun. 2004. *Zhongguo Nongmin Diaocha (Research on Peasants in China)*. Beijing: Renmin Wenxue Chubanshe.

Chen, Jianfu. 2002. Mission Impossible: Judicial Efforts to Enforce Civil Judgments and Rulings in China. In *Implementation of Law in the People's Republic of China*, edited by J. Chen, Y. Li and J. M. Otto. The Hague: Kluwer Law International.

Chen, Xiaojun (et al.). 2003. *Nongcun Tudi Falüzhidu Yanjiu, Tianye Diaocha Jiedu (Research in the Village Land Legal System, an Analysis on the Basis of Fieldwork)*. Beijing: Zhongguo Zhengfa Daxue Chubanshe.

Chiari, G.P. 2004. Draft report: UNDP mission on rural livelihoods and poverty in Namibia. Windhoek: UNDP.

Choque, María Eugenia, and Carlos Mamani. 2003. Reconstitución del Ayllu y derechos de los pueblos indígenas: El movimiento indio en los Andes de Bolivia. In *Los Andes desde los Andes*, edited by E. Ticona. La Paz: Yachaywasi.

Chou, Bill K.P. 2005. Implementing the Reform of Performance Appraisal in China's Civil Service. *China Information* XIX (1):39-65.

Christensen, S.F. 2004. The flexible land tenure system - The Namibian solution bringing the extra-legal settlers under the register, Working Paper presented at the UN-Gigiri Expert group meeting on secure land tenure. In *New Legal Frameworks and Tools*. Nairobi, Kenya.

Christensen, S.F., W Werner, and P.D. Højgaard. 1999. Innovative land surveying and land registration in Namibia. London: Development Planning Unit, University College London.

CIDOB. 1996. La marcha indígena y el papel de CIDOB, un balance necesario. In *Artículo Primero*: CIDOB.

Clarke, D. 1996. The Execution of Civil Judgements in China. In *China's Legal Reforms*, edited by B. Lubman. Oxford: Clarendon Press.

Cody, Edward. 2004. China's Land Grabs Raise Specter of Popular Unrest, Peasants Resist Developers and Local Officials. *Washington Post Foreign Service*, October 5, A01.

Cohen, J. *Statement to U.S.-China Economic and Security Review Commission Hearing on China Trade/Sectoral and WTO Issues*, 14 June 2001 [cited]. Available from http://www.uscc. gov/textonly/transcriptstx/tescoh.htm.

Coldham, Simon. 1979. Land tenure reform in Kenya: the limits of law. *The Journal of Modern African Studies* 17 (4):615-627.

Comisión Local Agraria del Estado de México. 1928. Dictamen emitido en el expediente de dotación de ejidos, promovido por el poblado de SANTIAGO TEOYAHUALCO (sic), Opios. De Tultepec, Dto. De Cuautitlán, Toluca, 08/27/1928.

Comisión Nacional Agraria. 1930. Acta de posesión y deslinde de la dotación definitiva de ejidos dada al pueblo de Santiago Toyahualco (sic). municipio de Tultepec, ex - distrito de Cuatitlan, Estado de México, el día 15 quince de enero de 1930 mil novecientos treinta: CNA.

Concheiro Bórquez, Luciano, and Roberto Diego Quintana. 2003. Estructura y dinámica del Mercado de tierras ejidales en 10 ejidos de la República Mexicana. In *Políticas y regulaciones agrarias; Dinámicas de poder y juegos de actors en torno a la tenencia de la tierra,*, edited by É. Léonard, A. Quesnel and E. Velázquez. Mexico: CIESAS, Miguel Ángel Porrúa.

Consolidated Laws of Ethiopia. 1972. Edited by Faculty of Law Haile Selassie I University. Addis Ababa: Haile Selassie I University Press.

Corbett, A. 1999. Presentation on behalf of the Himba traditional leadership. Paper presented at the World Commission on Dams, Geneva.

Cord, Louise, and Quentin Wodon. 2001. Do Agricultural Programs in Mexico Alleviate Poverty? Evidence from the Ejido Sector. *Cuadernos de Economía* Year 38, no. 114:239-256.

Cornelius, Wayne A., and David Myhre. 1998. *The Transformation of Rural Mexico: Reforming the Ejido Sector*. San Diego: Center for U.S.-Mexican Studies, University of California.

Cotula, Lorenzo, and Camilla Toulmin. 2004. Till to Tiller: International migration, remittances and land rights in West Africa. London: IIED. Issue paper no. 132.

Cotula, Lorenzo, Camilla Toulmin, and Ced Hesse. 2004. Land Tenure and Administration in Africa: Lessons of Experience and Emerging Issues. London: IIED.

Cotula, Lorenzo, Camilla Toulmin, and Julian Quan. 2006. Better Land Access for the Rural Poor: Lessons from Experience and Challenges ahead. London: IIED, FAO.

Council, State. 2005. *Guowuyuan Guanyu Zuohao Shengji Yixia Guotuziyuan Guanli Tizhi Gaige Youguan Wenti de Tongzhi (State Council Notice on Solving Problems Related to the Management Reform of State Land Management Institutions Below the Provincial Level)*. Chinalawinfo.com 2004 (cited 20 September 2005 2005). Available from http://law/chinalawinfo.com/newlaw2002/slc/SLC.asp?Db=chl&Gid=53188.

Cousins, Ben. 2000. Tenure and Common Property Resources in Africa. In *Evolving Land Rights, Policy and Tenure in Africa*, edited by C. Toulmin and J. Quan. London: DFID/IIED/NRI.

—. 2002. Legislating negotiability: tenure reform in post-apartheid South Africa. In *Negotiating Property in Africa*, edited by K. Juul and C. Lund. Portsmouth: Heinemann.

Cox, J., C. Kerven, W. Werner, and R. Benke. 1998. *Privatisation of rangeland resources in Namibia: Enclosure in Eastern Oshikoto*. London: Overseas Development Institute.

Crabtree, John. 2005. Patterns of Protest: Politics and Social Movements in Bolivia. London: Latin America Bureau.

Crook, Richard C. 1986. Decolonization, the colonial state, and chieftaincy in the Gold Coast. *African Affairs* 85 (338):75-105.

Crousse, B, P Mathieu, and S. M Seck. 1991. *La Vallée du Fleuve Sénégal. Evaluations et perspectives d'une décennie d'aménagements*. Paris: Karthala.

Crummey, Donald. 2000. *Land and Society in the Christian Kingdom of Ethiopia*. Addis Ababa: Addis Ababa University Press.

CSO. 1967. Results of the National Sample Survey, First Round, edited by Central Statistical Office and Addis Ababa: August.

Dam, K.W. 2006. Land, Law and Economic Development. Chicago: John M. Olin Program in Law and Economics, University of Chicago.

Danaa, H.S. 1996. Interests in Land in Northern Ghana: A historical review of legal issues. In *Decentralisation, Land Tenure and Land Administration in the Northern Region of Ghana*: Report on a Seminar held at Bolgatanga 28-30 May, Konrad Adenauer Foundation, Accra: 44-52.

Daniels, C. 2004. Indigenous rights in Namibia. In *Indigenous people's rights in Southern Africa*, edited by R. Hitchcock and D. Vinding. Copenhagen: IWGIA.

Danquah, J.B. 1928. *Gold Coast: Akan Laws and Customs and the Akim Abuakwa Constitution.* London: Routledge.

De Grammont, Hubert Carton. 1996a. La organización gremial de los agricultures frente a los procesos de globalización en la agricultura. In *Neoliberalismo y organización social en el campo mexicano*, edited by Hubert Carton de Grammont. Mexico: Plaza y Valdés, UNAM.

—. 1996b. Neoliberalismo y organización social en el campo mexicano. Mexico: Plaza y Valdés, UNAM.

De Ita, Ana. 2003. Mexico: Impacts of demarcation and titling by PROCEDE on agrarian conflicts and land concentration. México, D.F.: Centro de Estudios para el Cambio en el Campo Mexicano y Red de Investigación Acción sobre la Tierra. Report no.

—. 2006. Land Concentration in Mexico after PROCEDE. In *Promised Land: International Agrarian Reform and Resistance*, edited by Peter Rosset, Raj Patel and M. Courville. Berkeley: Food First Books.

De Janvry, Alain. 1981. *The Agrarian Question and Reformism in Latin America*. Baltimore and London: The Johns Hopkins University Press.

De Janvry, Alain, Gustavo Gordillo, and Elisabeth Sadouleth. 1997. Mexico's Second Agrarian Reform: Household and Community Responses. San Diego: University of California, Center for US-Mexican Studies.

De Janvry, Alain, Jean-Philippe Platteau, Gustavo Gordillo, and Elisabeth Sadoulet. 2001. Access to Land and Land Policy Reforms. In *Access to Land, Rural Poverty and Public Action (UNU/WIDER studies in Development Economics)*, edited by A. De Janvry, Gustavo Gordillo, Jean-Philippe Platteau and Elisabeth Sadoulet. Oxford: Oxford University Press.

De Jong, F. 2005. Contested Casamance. *Canadian Journal of African Studies* 39 (2).

De Soto, H. 1989. *The Other Path: The economic answer to terrorism.* New York: Basic Books.

—. 2000. *The Mystery of Capital: Why capitalism triumphs in the west and fails everywhere else?* London: Black Swan.

Deere, Carmen Diana, and Magdalena León. 2000. Género, propiedad y empoderamiento: tierra, Estado y mercado en América Latina. Bogotá: TM Editores, Universidad Nacional – Facultad de Ciencias Humanas.

Defensor del Pueblo. 2003. Informe Especial: Los derechos a la propiedad y la tenencia de la tierra y el proceso de saneamiento. La Paz: Defensor del Pueblo (Programa de derechos humanos del campesinado y pueblos indígenas).

Deininger, Klaus. 2003. Land policies for growth and poverty reduction. A World Bank policy research report. Washington, Oxford: World Bank, Oxford University Press.

Deininger, Klaus, Daniel Ayalew Ali, Stein Holden, and J. Zevenbergen. 2007. Rural Land Certification in Ethiopia: Process, Initial Impact, and Implications for other African Countries. In *World Bank Working Paper, WPS 4218*. Washington, D.C.

Deininger, Klaus, Isabel Lavadenz, Fabricio Bresciani, and Manuel Diaz. 2001. Mexico's 'Second Agrarian Reform': Implementation and Impact. Washington D.C.: World Bank.

Deininger, Klaus W., and Pedro Olinto. 2000. Asset Distribution, Inequality, and Growth. World Bank Research Working Paper #2375. Washington: World Bank

Demsetz, H. 1967. Towards a theory of property rights. *The American Economic Review* 57 (2):347-359.

Dennis, P.C.W. 1957. A note on land revenue and local government in Ghana. *Journal of African Administration* 9 (2):84-88.

Dessalegn Rahmato. 1984. *Agrarian Reform in Ethiopia*. Uppsala: Scandinavian Institute of African Studies.

—. 1993. Land, Peasants and the Drive for Collectivization in Ethiopia. In *Land in African Agrarian Systems*, edited by T. Basset and D. Crummey. Madison: University of Wisconsin Press.

—. 1994. *Land Tenure and Land Policy in Ethiopia after the Derg*. Trondheim: University of Trondheim Press.

—. 1996. Land and Agrarian Unrest in Wollo, Northeast Ethiopia, Pre- and Post-Revolution: Institute of Development Research, Addis Ababa University.

—. 2004. Searching for Tenure Security? The Land System and New Policy Initiatives in Ethiopia. Addis Ababa: Forum for Social Studies.

—. 2006a. Land Registration as a Tool for Tenure Security? Brief Bibliographical Review, Paper prepared for the 2nd Mystery of Legal Failure Workshop. Leiden, 10-12 May 2006.

—. 2006b. Peasants and Agrarian Reforms: The Unfinished Quest for Secure Land Rights in Ethiopia. Unpublished paper, Addis Ababa,.

Dessalegn Rahmato, and Meheret Ayenew. 2004. Democratic Assistance in Post-Conflict Ethiopia. Impact and Limitations. In *FSS Monograph Series 3*. Addis Ababa: Forum for Social Studies.

—. 2006. Electoral Assistance and Democratic Transition in Ethiopia. In *Promoting Democracy in Postconflict Societies*, edited by J. de Zeeuw and K. Kumar. Boulder and London: Lynne Reinner Publishers.

Dessalegn Rahmato, and Taye Assefa. 2006. Land and the Challenge of Sustainable Development in Ethiopia. Conference Proceedings. Addis Ababa: Forum for Social Studies: 103-165.

DFID. 1999. Land Rights and Sustainable Development in Sub-Saharan Africa: Lessons and Ways Forward in Land Tenure Policy. Report of a Delegate Workshop on Land Tenure Policy in African Nations. Berkshire: DFID.

—. 2001. Further Knowledge of Livelihoods Affected by Urban Transition, Kumasi, Ghana. Natural Resources Systems Programme. Final Technical Report: DFID.

DFID/Toulmin, C., D. Brown, and R. Crook. 2004. *Project memorandum: Ghana Land Administration Project Institutional Reform & Development: Strengthening Customary Land Administration*.

Diallo, F. 2008. Etudes de Cas des Communautés Rurales de Yène et de Sadio. Saint Louis: Université Gaston Berger.

Dièye, A. 2004. Domanialité Nationale et Développement: l'Exemple du Sénégal, Université Cheikh Anta Diop, Dakar.

Diez Astete, Alvaro. 1998. Apoyo a los pueblos indígenas. In *report elaborated for API-DANIDA*.

Díez Astete, Álvaro, and David Murillo. 1998. Pueblos indígenas de tierras bajas. La Paz: MDSP / VAIPO / PNUD.

Ding, Chengri. 2007. Policy and Praxis of land acquisition in China. *Land Use Policy* 24 (1):1-13.

Diop Tine, N, and M Sy. 2003. Women and Land in Africa: A case study from Senegal. In *Women and Land in Africa. Culture, religion and realizing women's rights*, edited by L. Muthoni Wanyeki. London / New York / Cape Town: Zed Books / David Philip Publishers.

Djojodigoeno, M. M, and Tirtawinata. 1940. Het Adatprivaatrecht van Midden-Java. Batavia: Departement van Justitie.

Dowuona-Hammond, Christine. 2003. State Land Management Regime: Impact on land rights of women and the poor in Ghana. Accra GTZ Legal Pluralism and Gender Project.

Du, Runsheng. 1996. *Zhongguo tudi gaige [Land Reform in China]*. Beijing: Modern China Press.

Duhau, Emilio. 1998. Hábitat popular y política urbana. México: M. A. Porrúa.

Dumett, R.E. 1998. *El Dorado in West Africa: The gold mining frontier, African labour, and colonial capitalism in the Gold Coast, 1875-1900*. Athens, Ohio: Ohio University Press and Oxford: James Currey.

Durand-Lasserve, A. 1986. *L'Exclusion des Pauvres dans les Villes du Tiers-Monde*. Paris: L'Harmattan.

—. 2006. Informal settlements and the millennium development goals: Global policy debates on property ownership and security of tenure. *Global Urban Development* 2 (1):1-15.

Durand-Lasserve, A, and L Royston. 2002. *Holding their ground: secure land tenure for the urban poor in developing countries*. London: Earthscan.

Durand-Lasserve, A., and H. Selod. 2007. The Formalisation of urban land tenure in developing countries. Paper presented at the World Bank's 2007 Urban Research Symposium, May 14-16, Washington DC.

Edin, Maria. 2003. State Capacity and Local Agent Control in China: CCP Cadre Management from a Township Perspective. *China Quarterly*:35-52.

Editorial. 2005. *Guanyu Tudi Shichang Zixu Zhili Chengdun youguan Qingkuang de Tongzhi (Notice on the Circumstances of the Land Market System Control and Overhaul (Campaign))*, 4 December 2003a [cited 20 September 2005]. Available from http://www.land-china.com/query/content.ASP?Article_ID=475&TitleImage=subject.gif.

—. 2003b. Zhengdun Tudishichangzixu Feifa "Quandi" 738 Ren Bei Chanchu (Overhaul of the Land Market, 738 People have bEen Punished for Illegal Land Occupation). *Beijing Chenbao*, 12 February.

—. 2004a. 2003-Tudi Zhengdun Fengbao (2003-A Land Overhaul Storm). *Nanfang Zhoumo*, 8 January.

—. 2004b. Gedi Jiajin Chachu Tudi Weifa Anjian Chachu Lidu Jiada (Throughout China Land Violations are More Urgently Punished with Greater Force). *Renminrinbao Haiwaiban*, 25 March.

—. 2007. *China Passes New Law on Property*, 16 March 2007 [cited 7 June 2007]. Available from http://news.bbc.co.uk/2/hi/asia-pacific/6456959.stm.

Edusah, Sampson E, and David Simon. 2006. *Land use and land allocation in Kumasi peri-urban villages. CEDAR/IRNR Kumasi paper 9, DFID Project R7330*. Royal Holloway, University of London and University of Science and Technology, Kumasi 2001 [cited 6 April 2006]. Available from http://www.gg.rhul.ac.uk/kumasi/Project_Related_Papers/Cedar_IRNR/Paper_9/paper_9.html.

EEA. 2002. A Research Report on Land Tenure and Agricultural Development in Ethiopia. Addis Ababa: Ethiopian Economic Association.

Ege, Sveins. 1997. The Promised Land: The Amhara Land Redistribution of 1997. In *Working Papers on Ethiopian Development No. 12*. Trondheim Norwegian University of Science and Technology.

Eichelsheim, J.L. 1986. *Hoe Spontaan zijn 'Spontane Woonwijken'; De problematiek rond herverkaveling in Ziguinchor, Senegal {How spontaneous are 'spontaneous districts': Issues concerning re-allottment in Ziguinchor, Senegal}.*. Amsterdam: Free University.

—. 1990. The discrepancy between the local perception of tenure security and modern legalities: Private or popular land property in the city of Ziguinchor. *The Netherlands Review of Development Studies*, 3.

Ejido de Santiago Teyahualco. 1994. Acta de la Asamblea General de Ejidatarios, 05/21/1994.

—. 2002. Acta de la Asamblea General de Ejidatarios, 02/15/2002.

Elbow, K, and A Rochegude. 1989. *A Layman's Guide to the Forest Codes and Forest-related Land Laws of Niger, Mali and Senegal*. Madison: Land Tenure Center.

Elmhirst, R. 2001. Resource Struggles and the Politic of Place in North Lampung, Indonesia. *Singapore Journal of Tropical Geography* 22 (3):284-306.

Erie, Matthew. 2007. Land Grab Here and Real Estate Market There, Property Law Reform in the People's Republic of China. *Anthropology News* May:36.

Evans, M. 2000. Briefing Senegal: Wade and the Casamance dossier. *African Affairs* 99 (397):649-658.

Evers, P. 1995. Preliminary policy and legal questions about recognising traditional land rights in Indonesia. *Ekonesia: A Journal of Indonesian Human Ecology*:1-23.

Eyasu Elias. 2002. Farmers' Perception of Soil Fertility Change and Management. Addis Ababa: SOS-Sahel and Institute for Sustainable Development.

Fan, Maureen. 2007. China Looks To Protect Private Property. *Washington Post*, March 9, A16.

Fan, Mingcai, Ling Wang, Xiaoling Zhang, Gang Yan, Lihua Lu, and Yanping Liu. 2003. Tansuo Jiejue Zhengdi Wenti de Gaige Lu (An Exploration Towards Reforms Solving Land Acquisition Problems). *Jiangnan Luntan* 2003 (9):33-34.

FAO. 2002. Land tenure and Rural Development. FAO Land Tenure Studies 3. Rome: FAO.

—. 2005. Global Forest Resources Assessment 2005: Progress towards sustainable forest management. Roma: Food and Agricultural Organization. Report no.

Farthing, Linda, and Benjamin Kohl. 2005. Conflicting Agendas: The Politics of Development Aid in Drug-Producing Areas. *Development Policy Review* 23 (2):183-198.

Fawcett, PH. 1910. Explorations in Bolivia. *Geographical Journal* 24:513-529.

Faye, J. 2008. Land and Decentralisation in Senegal. London: IIED.

FDRE. 1995. The Constitution of the Federal Democratic Republic of Ethiopia: August, Addis Ababa. Federal Democratic Republic of Ethiopia.

—. 2005a. Expropriation of Landholdings for Public Purposes and Payment of Compensation Proclamation: Addis Ababa: Federal Democratic Republic of Ethiopia.

—. 2005b. Rural Land Administration and Land Use Proclamation,, edited by A. Ababa: Federal Democratic Republic of Ethiopia.

Feder, G., T. Onchan, Y. Chalamwong, and C Hongladarom. 1988. *Land Policies and Farm Productivity in Thailand*. Baltimore / London: John Hopkins University Press.

Field, E. 2006. Entitled to work: Urban property rights and labor supply in Peru: Working Paper.

Field, M.J. 1948. *Akim - Kotoku: an Oman of the Gold Coast*. London Crown Agents.

Fitzpatrick, Daniel. 1999. Beyond Dualism: Land Acquisition and Law in Indonesia. In *Indonesia, Law and Society*, edited by T. Lindsey. Sydney: the Federation Press.

—. 2005. 'Best practice' options for the legal recognition of customary tenure. *Development and Change* 36 (3):449-475.

Fjeldstad, O.-H., G. Geisler, S. Nangulah, K. Nygaard, A. Pomuti, A. Shifotoka, and G. van Rooy. 2005. Local governance, urban poverty and service delivery in Namibia. In *Paper no. 12*: Chr. Michelsen Institute.

Foley, Michael W. 1995. Privatizing the Countryside: The Mexican Peasant Movement and Neoliberal Reform. *Latin American Perspectives* Issue 84, 22 (1):59-76.

Foucher, V. 2003. Pas d'alternance en Casamance? Le nouveau pouvoir sénégalais face à la revendication séparatiste casamançaise. *Politique Africaine* 91:101-119.

Fox, Jonathan. 1993. *The Politics of Food in Mexico: State Power and Social Mobilization*. Ithaca, London: Cornell University Press.

Franco, Jennifer. 2005. Making Property Rights Accessible: Social Movements and Legal Innovation in the Philippines. Brighton: IDS Working Paper 244, Institute of Development Studies, University of Sussex.

Frayne, B., and W. Pendleton. 2002. Mobile Namibia: Migration trends and attitudes: Migration policy series no. 27, The Southern African Migration Project.

Fu, Jing. 2006. *Gov't pays Residents for Wrongful Arrest*, June 3 2004 [cited 20 May 2006]. Available from http://www.chinadaily.com.cn/english/doc/2004-06/03/content_335955.htm.

Fuller, B. 2006. Improving tenure security for the rural poor - Namibia country case study: FAO Legal Empowerment of the Poor Working Paper no. 6.

Fundación Tierra. 2004. Fundación Tierra in Bolivia: 12 Years Promoting Rural Development, 1991-2003. La Paz: Fundación Tierra.

—. 2007. Con los pies en la tierra: Un año de Revolución Agraria en Bolivia. La Paz: Fundación Tierra, Observatorio de la Revolución Agraria.

Gadiaga, M. 1984. L'autorisation de construire en droit sénégalais. *Revue des Institutions Politiques et Administratives du Sénégal (RIPAS)* 10 (avril-juin):518-585.

Galeana, Fernandos. 2004. Who wants Credit? Explaining the Demand for Land Titling in Mexico. *SURJ* Spring 16-21.

Galiani, S., and E. Schargrodsky. 2004. Effects of land titling on child health and education: IDB Research Network Working Paper No. R-491.

Galvan, D.C. 2004. *The State Must Be Our Master of Fire: How peasants craft culturally sustainable development in Senegal*. Berkeley: University of California Press.

—. 2007. 'The social reproduction of community-based development: Syncretism and sustainability in a Senegalese farmers' association. *Journal of Modern African Studies* 45 (1):61-88.

Gao, Hongjun. 2000. Zhongguo Gongmin Quanli Yishi de Yanjin (The Awakening of Rights Consciousness Among Chinese Citizens). In *Towards a Society of Rights, research in the development of citizen's rights in China (Zou xiang Quanli de Shidai, Zhongguo Gongmin Quanli Fazhan Yanjiu)*, edited by Y. Xia. Beijing: Falü Chubanshe.

García Linera, Alvaro, Marxa Chávez León, and Patricia Costas Monje. 2004. Sociología de los movimientos sociales en Bolivia; Estructuras de movilización, repertorios culturales y acción política. La Paz: Diakonía, Oxfam.

Gates, Marilyns. 1993. *In Default: Peasants, the Debt Crisis, and the Agricultural Challenge in Mexico*. Boulder, CO, Oxford: Westview Press.

Gensheng, Zhang. 2001. Rural Reform in China: Haitian Publishing.

Gerschenberg, Irving. 1971. Customary land tenure as a constraint on agricultural development: a re-evaluation. *East African Journal of Rural Development* 4 (1):51-62.

Giarracca, Norma. 2001. ¿Una nueva ruralidad en América Latina? Buenos Aires: CLACSO.

Gilbert, Alan. 2002. On the mystery of capital and the myths of Hernando de Soto: What difference does legal title make? *International Development Planning Review* 24 (1):1-19.

Gledhill, John. 1995. *Neoliberalism, Transnationalization and Rural Poverty; A Case Study of Michoacán, Mexico*. Boulder, San Francisco, Oxford: Westview Press.

Gledhill, John 1997. Fantasy and Reality in Restructuring Mexico's Land Reform. In 'Modern Mexico', Annual Meeting of the Society for Latin American Studies. St. Andrews, Scotland.

Gobierno del Estado de México. 2003. Plan Municipal de Desarrollo Urbano de Tultepec. Estado de México, Toluca: Secretaría de Desarrollo Urbano y Vivienda.

Golan, E. H. 1990. Land Tenure Reform in Senegal: An economic study from the peanut bassin. Madison, Wisconsin: Land Tenure Center. Research Paper 1001.

Gold, J., A. Muller, and D. Mitlin. 2001. The principles of local agenda 21 in Windhoek: Collective action and the urban poor. In *Working Paper Series on urban environmental action plans and local agenda 21*: Paper no. 9.

Gollás, Manuel. 2003. Breve relato de cincuenta años de política económica. In *Una historia contemporánea de México, Tomo 1: transformaciones y permanencies*, edited by Ilán Bizberg and L. Meyer. Mexico: Oceano.

Golub, Stephen. 2000. Nonlawyers as Legal Resources for their Communities. In *Many Roads to Justice, The Law Related Work of Ford Foundation Grantees Around the World*, edited by M. McClymont and S. Golub. Washington: Ford Foundation.

—. 2003. Beyond Rule of Law Orthodoxy: The Legal Empowerment Alternative. New York: Working Papers No. 41. Carnegie Endowment for International Peace.

—. 2006. The Legal Empowerment Alternative. In *Promoting the Rule of Law Abroad, In Search of Knowledge*, edited by T. Carothers. Washington D.C.: Carnegie Endowment for International Peace.

Golub, Stephen, and Mary McClymont. 2000. Introduction: A Guide to This Volume. In *Many Roads to Justice, The Law Related Work of the For Foundation Grantees Around the World*, edited by M. McClymont and S. Golub. Washington: Ford Foundation.

Gómez Cruz, Manuel Ángel, and Rita Schwentesius Rindermann. 2003. TLCAN y sector agroalimentario: 10 años de experiencia. www.rimisp.org/boletines.

Goodale, Mark R. G., and Per Kare Sky. 2000. A comparative Study of Land Tenure, Property Boundaries, and Dispute Resolution: Examples from Bolivia and Norway. Madison: University of Wisconsin, Land Tenure Center.

Gordillo, Gustavo. 1992. *Más allá de Zapata: Por una reforma campesina*. Mexico: Cal y Arena.

Gotkowitz, Laura. 2003. Revisiting the Rural Roots of the Revolution. In *Proclaiming Revolution; Bolivia in Comparative Perspective*, edited by Grindle, Merilee and P. Domingo. London, Cambridge, Mass.: Institute for Latin American Studies, University of London, and David Rockefeller Center for Latin American Studies, Harvard University.

Gough, Katherine V., and Paul W.K. Yankson. 2000. Land markets in African cities: the case of peri-urban Accra, Ghana. *Urban Studies* 37 (13):1485-1500.

Grant, D. 2004. Institutional Arrangements Review, Land Sector, Ghana. Accra: Ministry of Lands and Forestry.

Gready, Paul, and Jonathan Ensor. 2005. Introduction. In *Reinventing Development, Translating Rights-Based Approaches from Theory into Practice*, edited by P. Gready and J. Ensor. London: Zed Books.

Guardia B., Fernando. 2004. La vivienda de los pobres: habitat y marginalidad. Cochabamba: Academia Nacional de Ciencias, Embajada de España, Colegio de Arquitectos de Bolivia, COBOCE/Opinión.

Guigou, B, G Pontié, and A Lericollais. 1998. La gestion foncière en pays sereer siin (Sénégal). In *Quelles Politiques Foncières pour l'Afrique Rurale? Réconcilier pratiques, légitimité et légalité*, edited by P. Lavigne Delville. Paris: Karthala.

Guo, Xiaolin. 2001a. Land Expropriation and Rural Conflict in China. *The China Quarterly* 166 (June):422-439.

—. 2001b. Land Expropriation and Rural Conflicts in China. *China Quarterly* 166 (June):422-439.

Gwartney, T. *Estimating Land Values*. Henry George Institute 2008 [cited 31 March 2008]. Available from http://www.henrygeorge.org/ted.htm.

Gyasi, E.A. 1992. State Expropriation of Land for a Plantation and its Impact on Peasants in Ghana. In *Indigenous Land Rights in Commonwealth Countries, Proceedings of a Commonwealth Geographical Bureau Workshop*, edited by G. Cant, J. Overton and E. Pawson: Christchurch: Commonwealth Geographical Bureau.

—. 1994. The Adaptability of African Communal Land Tenure to Economic Opportunity: The example of land acquisition for oil palm farming in Ghana. *Africa* 64 (3):391-405.

Hailey, Lord. 1943. The Colonies and the Atlantic Charter. *Journal of the Royal Central Asian Society* 30:233-246.

Hale, Charles R. 2002. Does Multiculturalism Menace? Governance, Cultural Rights and the Politics of Identity in Guatemala. *Journal of Latin American Studies* 34: 485-524.

—. 2004. Rethinking Indigenous Politics in the Era of the Índio Permitido. In *NACLA Report on the Americas*.

Hammond, Daniel N.A. 2005. Protection of land rights and relations between state and customary authorities in Kumasi and Wa. Paper read at Workshop on Adjudication of Land Disputes, Legal Pluralism and the Protection of Land Rights in Ghana and Cote d'Ivoire, 17-18 February, 2005, at London.

Hardjono, J. 1987. *Land, Labour and Livelihood in a West Java Village*. Yogyakarta: Gadjah Mada University Press.

—. 1999. A Social Assessment of the Land Certificate Program, the Indonesian Land Administration Project, Unpublished report prepared for the World Bank, Jakarta.

Hardjosudarmo, S. 1970. *Masalah Tanah di Indonesia: Suatu Studi Tentang Pelaksanaan Land Reform di Djawa dan Madura (Land Problems in Indonesia: A Study of the Land Reform Implementation in Java and Madura)*. Djakarta: Bhratara.

Harring, S.L. 2004. Indigenous land rights and land reform in Namibia. In *Indigenous people's rights in Southern Africa*, edited by R. Hitchcock and D. Vinding. Copenhagen IWGIA.

Harring, S.L., and W. Odendaal. 2006. Our land they took - San rights under threat in Namibia. Windhoek: Legal Assistance Centre.

Harsono, B. 1997. *Hukum Agraria Indonesia. Sejarah Pembentukan Undang-undang Pokok Agraria, Isi dan Pelaksanaannya*. Jakarta: Djambatan.

Harsono, B. 2005. *Hukum Agraria Indonesia, Sejarah Pembentukan Undang-Undang Pokok Agraria, Isi dan Pelaksanaannya*. Vol. Jilid I, Hukum Tanah Nasional. Jakarta: Penerbit Djambatan.

Hayford, J.E.C. 1970. *Gold Coast Native Institutions: With Thoughts upon a Healthy Imperial Policy for the Gold Coast and Ashanti*. London: Frank Cass & Co. Ltd. Original edition, 1903.

Heath, John Richard. 1990. Enhancing the Contribution of Land Reform to Mexican Agricultural Development. Washington: The World Bank, WPS 285.

Helland, Johan. 2006. Land Tenure in the Pastoral Areas of Ethiopia. In *International Workshop on Property Rights, Collective Action and Poverty Reduction in Pastoral Areas of Ethiopia*. Addis Ababa: 30-31 October.

Heltberg, R. 2002. Property Rights and Natural Resource Management in Developing Countries. *Journal of Economic Surveys* 16.

Hendricks, F.T. 1990. The pillars of apartheid - Land tenure, rural planning and the chieftaincy. Uppsala: University of Uppsala.

Hernáiz, I, and D. Pacheco. 2000. La Ley INRA en el Espejo de la Historia. La Paz, Bolivia: Fundación TIERRA.

Hernáiz, I., D. Pacheco, R. Guerrero, and H. Miranda. 2001. Análisis Critico del Proceso de Saneamiento en el Departamento de Chuquisaca. La Paz: Fundación TIERRA.

Heryani, E, and C Grant. 2004. Land Administration in Indonesia. In *3rd FIG Regional Conference*. Jakarta.

Hesseling, G. 1983. *Le Droit Foncier au Sénégal: l'Impact de la réforme foncière en Basse Casamance*. Leiden: African Studies Center.

—. 1986. Le droit foncier dans une situation semi-urbaine. Le cas de Ziguinchor. In *Espaces Disputés en Afrique Noire. Pratiques foncières locales*, edited by B. Crousse, E. Le Bris and E. Le Roy. Paris: Karthala.

—. 1990/91. Urban land conflicts and the administration of justice in Ziguinchor, Senegal. *Netherlands Review of Development Studies* 3:13-30.

—. 1991. Les citadins et le droit à la ville: Des stratégies diversifiées. In *L'Appropriation de la Terre en Afrique Noire. Manuel d'analyse, de décision et de gestion foncières*, edited by E. Le Bris, E. Le Roy and P. Mathieu. Paris: Karthala.

—. 1992. *Pratiques Foncières à l'Ombre du Droit. L'application du droit foncier urbain à Ziguinchor, Senegal*. Leiden: African Studies Center.

Hesseling, G, and M. B Ba. 1994. Le Foncier et la Gestion des Ressources Naturelles au Sahel: Expériences, contraintes et perspectives. Synthèse régionale. Paris: CILSS/Club.

Hewes, L.I. 1995. *Japan - Land and Men: An account of the Japanese land reform program 1945-51*. Ames: The Iowa State College Press.

Hill, Polly. 1956. *The Gold Coast Cocoa Farmer*. London: Oxford University Press.

—. 1963. *The Migrant Cocoa-Farmers of Southern Ghana. A study in Rural Capitalism*. Cambridge: Cambridge University Press.

Hindley, Jane. 1996. Towards a Pluricultural Nation: The Limits of Indigenismo and Article 4. In *Dismantling the Mexican State?*, edited by N. C. Rob Aitken, Garreth A. Jones and David E. Stansfield. Houndmills, Basingstoke: Macmillan Press.

Hinton, W. 1972. *Fanshen, A Documentary of Revolution in a Chinese Village*. Victoria, Australia: Pelican Books.

Ho, Peter. 2001. Who Owns China's Land? Policies, Property Rights and Deliberate Institutional Ambiguity. *China Quarterly* 166 (June):394-421.

—. 2003. Contesting Rural Spaces: Land Disputes and Customary Tenure in China. In *Chinese Society: Change Conflict and Resistance*, edited by E. Perry and M. Selden. London: Routledge.

Hoben, Allan. 1973. *Land Tenure among the Amhara of Ethiopia*. Chicago: University of Chicago Press.

Hoekema, André J. 2003. Rechtspluralisme en interlegaliteit. naugural Lecture, Vossiuspers UvA, Amsterdam.

—. 2006. A New Codified Future for Local Resource Tenure? In *Agua y derecho: Políticas hídricas, derechos consuetudinarios e identidades locales*, edited by R. Boelens. Wageningen, Lima: WALIR, IEP.

Holleman, J.F., ed. 1981. *Van Vollenhoven on Indonesian Adat Law*. The Hague: Martinus Nijhoff.

Home, Robert, and Hilary Lim, eds. 2004. *Demystifying the Mystery of Capital: Land Tenure and Poverty in Africa and the Caribbean*. London: Glasshouse Press.

Howard, R. 1978. *Colonialism and Underdevelopment in Ghana*. London: Croom Helm.

Huang, Y. 1996. Central-Local relations in China During the reform Era: The Economic and Institutional Dimensions. *Word Development* 24 (4):655-672.

Hueber, Sandra, and Chris de Veer. 2001. Urban spatial management in Kumasi. In *The Fate of the Tree: Planning and Managing the Development of Kumasi, Ghana*, edited by K. K. Adarkwa and J. Post. Accra: Woeli Publishing Services.

Human Rights Watch. 2002. *Dangerous Mediation, China's Campaign Against Falungong*. New York: Human Rights Watch.

Hüsken, F. 1979. Landlords, sharecroppers and agricultural laborers: Changing labor relations in rural Java. *Journal of Contemporary Asia* (9):140-151.

Hylton, Forrest. 2003. Tierra Común: caciques, artesanos e intelectuales radicales y la rebelión de Chayanta. In *Cuatro momentos de insurgencia indígena. Ya es otro tiempo el presente*, edited by F. Hylton, F. Patzi, S. Serulnikov and S. Thomson. La Paz: Muela del Diablo.

IADB. 2003. Bolivia: Land Regularization and Legal Cadastre Program (BO-0221) Loan Proposal. Washington: Inter-American Development Bank.

IIED. 2006. Innovation in Securing Land Rights in Africa: Lessons from experience. Briefing Paper. London: IIED.

ILD. n.d. Evaluación preliminary de la economía extralegal en 12 países de Latinoamérica y el Caribe; Reporte de la investigación en Bolivia. Lima: Instituto Libertad y Democracia.

INRA. 2005. Estado del Proceso de Saneamiento, Mayo 2005. La Paz: Instituto Nacional de Reforma Agraria.

Instituto Nacional de Estadística. 2003. Bolivia: Características sociodemográficas de la población indígena, edited by Ministerio de Hacienda: República de Bolivia, La Paz.

International Land Coalition. 2006. An Analysis of the Land Policies of Selected International Development Agencies. A working paper of the International Land Coalition.

Iracheta, A. 1989. Diez años de planeación del suelo en la Zona Metropolitana de la Ciudad de México. In *Una Década de Planeaci´n Urbano-Regional en México, 1978-1988*, edited by G. Garza. México: El Colegio de México.

Jahiel, A.R. 1997. The Contradictory Impact of Reform on Environmental Protection in China. *China Quarterly* 149:81-103.

—. 1998 (reprinted in 2000). The Organization of Environmental Protection in China. In *Managing the Chinese Environment*, edited by R. L. Edmonds. Oxford: Oxford University Press.

Jansen, K., and E. Roquas. 1998. Modernizing Insecurity: The Land Titling Project in Honduras. *Development and Change* 29:81-106.

Joireman, Sandra. 2001. *Property Rights and Political Development in Ethiopia and Eritrea 1941-1974*. Oxford: James Currey.

Jones, B.T., and A.W. Mosimane. 2000. Empowering communities to manage natural resources: Where does the new power lie? In *Empowering communities to manage natural resources: Case studies from Southern Africa*, edited by S. Shackelton and B. Campbell. Lilongwe, Malawi: SADC Wildlife Sector - Natural Resources Management Programme.

Jones, Gareth. 1996. Dismantling the Ejido: A Lesson in Controlled Pluralism. In *Dismantling the Mexican State?*, edited by Rob Aitken, Nikki Craske, Garreth A. Jones and D. E. Stansfield. Houndmills, Basingstoke: Macmillan Press.

Juma, S.Y., and S.F. Christensen. 2001. Bringing the extra-legal settlers under the register - The Namibia challenge. Paper read at Proceedings of the International conference on spatial information for sustainable development, 2-5 October 2001, at Nairobi, Kenya.

Juul, Kristine, and Christian Lund. 2002. *Negotiating Property in Africa*. Portsmouth: Heinemann.

Kakujaha Matundu. 2002. Self management of common pool resources among pastoral Ovaherero in semi-arid Eastern Namibia. Working Paper presented at the Ninth Conference of the International Association for the Study of Common Property, Victoria Falls, Zimbabwe.

Kalabamu, F.T. 2000. Land tenure and management reforms in East and Southern Africa - The case of Botswana. *Land Use Policy* 17:305.

Kane, Y. 2008. Legal literacy training in the Thiès Region of Senegal' in Cotula. In *Legal Empowerment in Practice. Using legal tools to secure land rights in Africa*, edited by L. Cotula and P. Mathieu. London: IIED.

Kano, H. 1984. Sistem Pemilikan Tanah dan Masyarakat Desa di Jawa pada Abad XIX. In *Dua Abad Penguasaan Tanah: Pola Penguasaan Tanah Pertanian di Jawa dari Masa ke Masa*, edited by S. M. P. Tjondronegoro and G.Wiradi. Jakarta: Yayasan Obor Indonesia.

Kasanga, Kasim. 1996. Land tenure, resource access and decentralisation: The political economy of land tenure in Ghana. In *Managing Land Tenure and Resource Access in West Africa: Proceedings of a Regional Workshop held at Gorée, Sénégal, November 18-22, 1996*, edited by Ministère de la Coopération, Overseas Development Administration, L'Université de Saint Louis, GRET and IIED. London: IIED.

—. 2000a. Changes in land tenure. Paper read at Final Workshop of the Kumasi Natural Resources Management Research, 9-11 February 2000, at Kumasi.

—. 2000b. Land administration reforms and social differentiation. A case study of Ghana's Lands Commission. In *International Workshop on the Rule of Law and Development*. Brighton.

Kasanga, Kasim, Jeff Cochrane, Rudith King, and Michael Roth. 1996. Land Markets and Legal Contradictions in the Peri-Urban Area of Accra Ghana: Informant Interviews and

Secondary Data Investigations. LTC Research Paper 127. Madison, Kumasi: Land Tenure Center.

Kasanga, Kasim, and Nii Ashie Kotey. 2001. *Land Management in Ghana: Building on Tradition and Modernity*. London: IIED.

Kasanga, Kasim, and Gordon R. Woodman. 2004. Ghana: Local law making and land conversion in Kumasi, Ashanti. In *Local Land Law and Globalization: A Comparative Study of Peri-Urban Areas in Benin, Ghana and Tanzania.*, edited by G. R. Woodman, U. Wanitzek and H. Sippel. Münster: Lit Verlag.

Katon, B, Anna Knox, and RM-. Dick. 2001. Collective Action, Property Rights, and Devolution of Natural Resource Management: Policy Brief CAPRI (System Wide Program on Collective Action and Property Rights) 2.

Katz, Friedrich. 1996. The Agrarian Policies and Ideas of the Revolutionary Mexican Factions Led by Emiliano Zapata, Pancho Villa, and Venustiano Carranza. In *Reforming Mexico's Agrarian Reform*, edited by Laura Randall. Armonk NY, London: M.E. Sharpe.

Kay, Cristóbal. 2005. Pobreza y estrategias de desarrollo rural en Bolivia: ¿Está impulsando la ENDAR las capacidades campesinas? *Debate Agrario* No. 38:109-139.

Kay, Cristóbal, and Miguel Urioste. 2007. Bolivia's Unfinished Agrarian Reform: Rural Poverty and Development Policies. In *Land, Poverty and Livelihoods in an Era of Globalization: Perspectives from Developing and Transition Countries*, edited by Akram-Lodhi, A. Haroon, S. M. Borras Jr and C. Kay. London and New York: Routledge.

Ki-Zerbo, F. 1997. *Les Sources du Droit chez les Diola du Sénégal*. Paris: Karthala.

Kimble, David. 1963. *A political history of Ghana: the rise of Gold Coast nationalism, 1850-1928.* Oxford: Clarendon Press.

Klein, Herbert S. 2003. *A Concise History of Bolivia*. Cambridge: Cambridge University Press.

Knetsch, J. 1993. Land Use: Values, Controls, and Compensation. In *Law and Economic Development: Cases and Materials from Southeast Asia.*

Knight, Alan. 1996. Salinas and Social Liberalism in Historical Context. In *Dismantling the Mexican State?*, edited by N. C. Rob Aitken, Garreth A. Jones and David E. Stansfield. Houndmills, Basingstoke: Macmillan Press.

Kofi-Sackey, H. W. 1983. Chieftaincy, law and custom in Asante, Ghana. *Jahrbuch für Afrikanisches Recht* 4:65-79.

Kohl, Benjamin H., and Linda C. Farthing. 2006. *Impasse in Bolivia; Neoliberal Hegemony and Popular Resistance*. London and New York: ZED Books.

Konings, Piet. 1986. *The state and rural class formation in Ghana: a comparative analysis, Monographs from the African Studies Centre, Leiden* London [etc.] Routledge & Kegan Paul.

Kotey, Nii Ashie. 1996. The 1992 Constitution and compulsory acquisition of land in Ghana: Opening new vistas? In *Managing Land Tenure and Resource Access in West Africa: Proceedings of a Regional Workshop held at Gorée, Sénégal, November 18-22, 1996*, edited by Ministère de la Coopération, Overseas Development Administration, L'Université de Saint Louis, GRET and IIED. London: IIED.

Kotey, Nii Ashie, and Marc O. Yeboah. 2003. GTZ Legal Pluralism and Gender Project (Land Law Focal Area). Report of a Study on Peri-Urbanism, Land Relations and Women in Ghana: GTZ.

Kreike, E. 2004. *Re-creating Eden - Land use, environment, and society in Southern Angola and Northern Namibia*. Portsmouth: Heinemann.

Kumado, C.E.K. 1990-1992. Chieftaincy and the law in modern Ghana. *University of Ghana Law Journal* XVIII:194-216.

Kung, James, and Shouying Liu. 1996. Property Rights and Land Tenure Organizations in Rural China: An Empirical Study of Institutions and Institutional Change in Transitional Economies.

LAC. 1999. Proposals for law reform on the recognition of customary marriages. In *Policy Paper*. Windhoek, Namibia: Legal Assistance Centre.

—. 2003. Guide to the Communal Land Reform Act, Act no. 5 of 2002. In *Policy Paper*. Windhoek, Namibia: Legal Assistance Centre.

—. 2005a. A place we want to call our own: A study on land tenure policy and securing housing rights in Namibia. Windhoek: Legal Assistance Centre.

—. 2005b. A study on land tenure policy and securing housing rights in Namibia. In *Policy Paper*. Windhoek, Namibia: Legal Assistance Centre.

Lampton, D.M., ed. 1987. *Policy Implementation in post-Mao China*. Berkeley: University of California Press.

Lanjouw, Jean O., and Philip I. Levy. 2002. Untitled: A study of formal and informal property rights in urban Ecuador. *The Economic Journal* 112 (October):986-1019.

Larbi, W. O. 1996. Spatial planning and urban fragmentation in Accra. *Third World Planning Review* 18:193-214.

Larbi, W.O., E. Odoi-Yemo, and L. Darko. *Developing a geographic information system for land management in Ghana* (internet). GTZ 1998 [cited].

Lardy, N. 1986. Agricultural Reforms in China. *Journal of International Affairs* 39 (2).

Lavaud, Jean-Pierre. 1991. L'instablité politique de l'Amérique latine: Le cas de la Bolivie. Paris: L'Harmattan, IHEAL.

Lavigne Delville, Ph. 1999. Harmonising Formal Law and Customary Land Rights in French-speaking West Africa. London: IIED.

—. 2000. Harmonising formal law and customary land rights in French-speaking West Africa. In *Evolving Land rights, Policy and Tenure in Africa*, edited by C. Toulmin and J. Quan. London: DFID/IIED/NRI.

—. 2003. When farmers use 'pieces of paper' to record their land transactions in Francophone rural Africa: insights into the dynamics of institutional innovation. In *Securing Land Rights in Africa*, edited by T. A. Benjaminsen and C. Lund London: Frank Cass.

Lavigne Delville, Ph., C. Toulmin, J.-P. Colin, and J.-P. Chauveau. 2002. *Negotiating access to land in West Africa: a synthesis of findings from research on derived rights to land Land tenure and resource access in West Africa* London: IIED (International Institute for Environment and Development).

Lawrence, J.C.D., and H.S. Mann. 1966. FAO Land Policy Project (Ethiopia). In *Ethiopia Observer IX, 4:286-336*.

Le Bris, E, A Osmont, A Marie, and A Sinou. 1987. Famille et Résidence dans les Villes Africaines. Paris: L'Harmattan.

Le Roy, Etienne. 1985. Local law in black Africa: contemporary experiences of folk law facing state and capital in Senegal and some other countries. In *People's law and state law, the Bellagio papers*, edited by A. Allott and G. R. Woodman. Dordrecht: Foris Publications.

Leduka, R.C. 2000. The role of the state, law and urban social actors in illegal urban development in Maseru, Lesotho. Unpublished PhD Dissertation, Cardiff: University of Wales.

Legorreta, J. 1994. Efectos Ambientales de la Expansión de la Ciudad de México. México: Centro de Ecodesarrollo.

Lenin, Vladimir I. 1979. El desarrollo de capitalismo en Rusia; El proceso de la formación del mercado interior para la gran industria. Moscow: Progreso.

Lewis, Jessa. 2002. Agrarian Change and Privatization of Ejido Land in Northern Mexico. *Journal of Agrarian Change* 2 (3):401-420.

Li, Changping. 2002a. *Wo Xiang Zongli Shuo Shihua (I tell the Truth to the Prime Minister)* Beijing: Guangming Ribao Chubanshe.

Li, Guo, Scott Rozelle, and Loren Brandt. 1998. Tenure, land rights, and farmer investment incentives in China. *Agricultural Economics* 19:63-71.

Li, Lianjiang. 2002b. The Politics of Introducing Direct Township Elections in China. *China Quarterly* 170:704-723.

Li, Meixian. 2004. China's Compliance with WTO Requirements Will Improve the Efficiency and Effective Implementation of Environmental Laws in China. *Temple International and Comparative Law Journal* 18:155-174.

Lieberthal, K. 1992. Introduction: The "Fragmented Authoritarianism" Model and Its Limitations. In *Bureaucracy, Politics, and Decision Making in Post-Mao China*, edited by K. G. Lieberthal and D. M. Lampton. Berkely: University of California Press.

—. 1995. *Governing China, From Revolution through Reform*. New York: W.W.Norton & Company, Inc.

Lieberthal, K., and M. Oksenberg. 1988. *Policy Making in China, Leaders, Structures and Processes*. Princeton: Princeton University Press.

Liu, Silong. 2000a. Obstacles of the Environmental Law Enforcement System and their Countermeasures (Huanjing Zhifa Tizhi Zhuangai ji qi Xiaochu Duice). *Environmental Protection* (1):3-4.

Liu, Yawei. 2000b. Consequences of Villager Committee Elections in China, Better Local Governance or Consolidation of State Power. *China Perspectives* 31 (September-October):19-69.

Lo, M. 2006. 'Re-conceptualizing civil society: The debate continues with specific reference to contemporary Senegal. *African and Asian Studies* 5 (1):91-117.

Loayza Caero, Román. 2000. Movimiento Campesino, 1996-1998. La Paz: Fondo Editorial de los Diputados.

Löffler, U. 1996. Rural Tenure Developments in Indonesia. In *Study for the Guiding Principles: Land tenure in development cooperation*. Eschborn: GTZ.

Lohmar, Byran. 2006. Feeling for Stones But Not Crossing the River: China's Rural Land Tenure After twenty Years of Reform. *The Chinese Economy* 39 (4):pp. 85-102.

Louw, O. 2003. Exploring the culture of non-payment in post-apartheid South Africa. Doctoral Thesis, Lund University.

Lund, Christian. 1998. Struggles for Land and Political Power on the Politicization of Land Tenure and Disputes in Niger. *Journal of Legal Pluralism* 40:1-22.

—. 2000. African Land Tenure: Questioning Basic Assumptions. London: IIED.

—. 2006. Who owns Bolgatanga? A story of inconclusive encounters. In *Land and the Politics of Belonging in West Africa*, edited by R. Kuba and C. Lentz. Leiden, Boston: Brill.

Luo, Pinghan. 2003. *Gongshe! Gongshe! Nongcun Renmin Gongsheshi (Commune! Commune! A History of Farmers Communes)*. Fuzhou: Fujian Renmin Chubanshe.

Ma, X., and L. Ortolano. 2000. *Environmental Regulation in China*. Landham: Rowman & Littlefield Publishing Group.

Mackinlay, Horacio, and Juan de la Fuente. 1996. La nueva legislación rural en México. *Debate Agrario*, 73-95.

Macmillan, W.M. 1946. African Development. In *Europe and West Africa*, edited by C. K. Meek, W. M. Macmillan and E. R. J. Hussey. London: Macmillan.

MACPIO. 2001. Pueblos indígenas y originarios de Bolivia; Diagnóstico nacional. La Paz: Ministerio de Asuntos Campesinos, Pueblos Indígenas y Originarios.

Manion, Melanie. 1996. The Electoral Connection in the Chinese Countryside. *The American Political Science Review* 90 (4):736-748.

Manji, A. 2006a. Legal Paradigms in Contemporary Land Reform. *Commonwealth & Comparative Politics* 44:151-165.

—. 2006b. *The Politics of Land Reform in Africa: From communal tenure to free markets*. London: Zed Books.

Manning, Daniel S. 1999. The Role of Legal Services Organizations in Attacking Poverty. Washington, D.C: World Bank.

Marcos Ezra. 1990. Population Issues in Rural Development. In *Ethiopia: Options for Rural Development*, edited by S. Pausewang. London: Zed Press.

Marquardt, Mark 2006. Global Experiences in Land Registration and Titling, edited by Solomon et al.

Martínez, José A. 2000. Atlas Territorios Indígenas en Bolivia: Situación de las Tierras Comunitarias de Origen (TCO's) y proceso de titulación. La Paz: CPTI, CIDOB, Plural Editores.

Martínez Saldaña, Tomás. 1991. Agricultura y Estado en México, Siglo XX. In *La agricultura en tierras mexicanas desde sus orígenes hasta nuestros días*, edited by Teresa Rojas. Mexico: Grijalbo.

Maxwell, Daniel, W. Odame Larbi, G.M. Lamptey, S. Zakariah, and Margaret Armar-Klemesu. 1998. Farming in the Shadow of the City: Changes in Land Rights and Livelihoods in Peri-Urban Accra. Ottawa: The International Development Research Centre.

McCaskie, T.C. 1992. Review article. Empire state: Asante and the historians. *Journal of African History* 33:467-476.

—. 1995. *State and Society in Pre-colonial Asante*. Cambridge: Cambridge University Press.

—. 2000a. *Asante Identities: History and Modernity in an African Village 1850-1950*. Edinburgh: Edinburgh University Press.

—. 2000b. The consuming passions of Kwame Boakye: an essay on agency and identity in Asante history. *Journal of African Cultural Studies* 13 (1):43-62.

MDS. 2005. Politicas de tierras para el desarrollo sostenible y la conservación. La Paz, Bolivia: Viceministerio de Tierras-Ministerio de Desarrollo Sostenible. Report no.

Meinzen-Dick, R.S., and R. Pradhan. 2002. Legal Pluralism and Dynamic Property Rights. Washington, D.C: CAPRI Report no.

Melber, H. 2005. Land and politics in Namibia. *Review of African Political Economy* 103.

Méndez Vedia, Javier. 2007. Interview with Pedro Nuni Caiti: 'There is a Gap there, in the Dark, to Move Forward'. *Indigenous Affairs* 1-2:72-75.

Merry, Sally Engle. 1988. Legal pluralism. *Law & Society Review* 22 (5):869-896.

Merz, Joaquín, and Oscar Calizaya. 1999. Reivindicando un derecho histórico: Titulación de Tierras Comunitarias de Origen (TCO) en beneficio de las comunidades campesinas del Altiplano Sud. *Artículo Primero* Año 3 (No. 6):47-62.

Michelson, Ethan. 2003. Jiufen Yu Falü Xuqiu: Yi Beijing de Diaocha Wei Li (Disputes and Legal Demand: Taking a Beijing Survey as a Case). *Jiangsu Shehui Kexue [Jiangsu Social Science]* (1):72-80.

—. 2006. The Practice of Law as an Obstacle to Justice: Chinese Lawyers at Work. *Law & Society Review* 40 (1):1-38.

Migot-Adholla, Shem E., and John W. Bruce. 1994. Introduction: Are indigenous African tenure systems insecure? In *Searching for Land Tenure Security in Africa*, edited by J. W. Bruce and S. E. Migot-Adholla. Dubuque: Kendall/Hunt Publishing Company.

Migot-Adholla, Shem E., Peter Hazell, Benoit Blarel, and Frank Place. 1993. Indigenous land rights systems in sub-Saharan Africa, a constraint on productivity? In *The Economics of Rural Organization: Theory, Practice and Policy*, edited by K. Hoff, A. Braverman and J. E. Stiglitz. New York: Oxford University Press.

Miller, GJ. 1992. *Managerial Dilemmas*. Cambridge: Cambridge University Press.

Ministerio de Asuntos Campesinos. 1953. Decretos Ley Nos. 03464 y 03471 de Reforma Agraria en Bolivia. La Paz: Ministerio de Asuntos Campesinos, República de Bolivia.

Ministerio de Desarrollo Económico. 2005a. Programa Pro-Vivienda: Proyecto piloto de regularización del derecho propietario urbano. La Paz: Ministerio de Desarrollo Económico.

—. 2005b. Sistema nacional de ciudades y bases para la política nacional de desarrollo urbano y asentamientos humanos. La Paz: Ministerio de Desarrollo Económico, Dirección General de Desarrollo Urbano y Vivienda (Documento de Trabajo).

Ministry of Forestry. 2008. Eksekutif Data Strategis Kehutanan 2007. Jakarta.

Ministry of Lands and Forestry. 1999. National Land Policy. Accra: Ministry of Lands and Forestry.

—. 2003. Implementation Manual for Land Administration Project (LAP-1) (2003-2008).

Mitiku Haile, Wray Witten, Kinfe Abraha, Sintayo Fissha, Adane Kebede, Getahun Kassa, and Getachew Reda. 2005. Land Registration in Tigray, Northern Ethiopia. London: IIED.

MLR. 1999. China Land & Resources Almanac, edited by The Ministry of Land and Resources.

MLRA. 1968. A Proclamation to Provide for the Regulation of Agricultural Tenancy Relationships (Draft): Ministry of Land Reform and Administration, Addis Ababa, July.

—. 1972. Policy of the Imperial Ethiopian Government on Agricultural Land Tenure (Draft): Addis Ababa, Ministry of Land Reform and Administration, August.

MOFED. 2005. (Ministry of Finance and Economic Development). Ethiopia: Building on Progress: A Plan for Accelerated and Sustained Development to End Poverty (PASDEP). Addis Ababa: MOFED.

Mohar Ponce, Alejandro. n.d. La nueva institucionalidad rural: El caso de México. FAO-Centro de Estudios para la Reforma del Estado.

Moise, Edwin. 1983. Land Reform in China and Vietnam. Chapel Hill: University of North Carolina Press.

Molina, Ramiro, and Xavier Albó. 2006. Gama étnica y lingüística de la población boliviana. La Paz: PNUD.

Monimart, M. 1993. Femmes du Sahel. Paris: Karthala.

Monnier, L., and Y. Droz, eds. 2004. Côté Jardin, Côté Cour: Anthropologie de la Maison Africaine. Paris/Genève: Presses Universitaires de France/ Nouveaux Cahiers de l'IUED.

Moore, Barrington. 1966. Social Origins of Dictatorship and Democracy. Lord and Peasant in the Making of the Modern World. Harmondsworth: Penguin Books.

Moore, Sally Falk. 1998. Changing African land tenure: Reflections on the incapacities of the state. European Journal of Development Research 10 (2):33-49.

Mortimer, R. 1972. The Indonesian Communist Party and Land Reform 1959-1965. Vol. No. 1, Monash Papers on Southeast Asia. Sydney: Centre of Southeast Asian Studies, Monash University.

Murra, John V. 1980. La organización económica del Estado inca. Mexico: Siglo XXI (segunda edición en español).

Muthoni Wanyeki, L. 2003. Women and Land in Africa. Culture, religion and realizing women's rights. London/New York/Cape Town: Zed Books/David Philips Publishers.

Mwangi, Esther. 2006. Land Rights for African Development. From Knowledge to Action. In CAPRi Policy Briefs. Washington, D.C.: CGIAR CAPRi.

Nader, Laura, and Harry F. Todd Jr. 1978. The Disputing Process: Law in Ten Societies. New York: Columbia University Press.

Ng'weno, B. 2000. On Titling Collective Property, Participation, and Natural Resource Management: Implementing Indigenous and Afro-Colombian Demands: A Review of Bank Experience in Colombia. Washington, D.C.: The World Bank. Report no.

Niang, M. 2004. La politique foncière au Sénégal: Quelles perspectives pour les organisations paysannes? In Participation Paysanne et Développement Rural au Sénégal, edited by M. Niang. Dakar: Codesria.

Niang, T, and S.D Dieng. 2004. Land Tenure and Family Farming in Africa: With special reference to Senegal. London: IIED.

Niessen, N.J.A.P.B. 1999. Municipal Government in Indonesia, Policy, Law, and Practice of Decentralization and Urban Spatial Planning, Research School CNWS, School of Asian, African and Amerindian Studies, Leiden University, Leiden.

Nkonya, L., and R. Meinzen-Dick. 2005. Understanding legal pluralism in water rights: lessons from Africa and Asia. In *International workshop on 'African Water Laws: Plural Legislative Frameworks for Rural Water Management in Africa'*. Johannesburg, South Africa.

NPC Legal Committee. 1998. Guanyu Zhonghuarenmingongheguotudiguanlifa (Xiuding Caoan) Chubu Shenyi Qingkuang de Huibao (Report on the First Review of the PRC Land Management Act Draft Amendment). In *Zhonghua Renmin Gongheguo Tudi Guanlifa Shiyi (Commentary on the Prc Land Management Act)*, edited by NPC-SC Legal Affairs Office. Beijing: Falü Chubanshe.

NPC SC Legal Affairs Office, ed. 2002. *Zhonghua Renmin Gongheguo Nongcun Tudi Chengbaofa Zhiyi (Commentary to the PRC Rural Land Contract Law)*. Beijing: Falü Chubanshe.

NRI (Natural Resources Institute), and UST (University of Science and Technology). 1997. Kumasi Natural Resource Management Research Project, Inception Report. Chatham: NRI.

Nugent, Paul. 1994. An abandoned project? The nuances of chieftaincy, development and history in Ghana's Volta Region. Paper read at Conference on 'The contribution of traditional authority to development, human rights and environmental protection', September 2-6, at Legon.

Nuijten, Monique. 1998. In the Name of the Land: Organization, Transnationalism, and the Culture of the State in a Mexican Ejido (thesis), Landbouw Unviersiteit Wageningen, Wageningen.

Nyamu-Musembi, C. 2006. Breathing Life into Dead Theories about Property Rights: de Soto and land relation in rural Africa. Brighton: IDS, University of Sussex.

O'Brien, Kevin J. 1994. Villagers' Committees, Implementing Political Reform in China's Villages. *The Australian Journal of Chinese Affairs* 0 (32):33-59.

—. 1996. Rightful Resistance. *World Politics* 49 (1):31-55.

O'Brien, Kevin J., and Lianjiang Li. 1995. The Politics of Lodging Complaints in Rural China. *China Quarterly*:756-783.

—. 2000. Accomodating "Democracy" in a One-Party State: Introducing Village Elections in China. *China Quarterly* 162 (June):465-489.

Obeng, Ernest E. 1988. *Ancient Ashanti Chieftaincy*. Tema: Ghana Publishing Corporation.

Odeneho Gyapong Ababio II. 2003. Welcome address. Paper read at Conference on African traditional leaders, August 3, 2003, at Kumasi.

Oduro-Kwarteng, Stephen. 2003. Environmental Implications of Indiscipline in the Land Market: A Case Study of the Kumasi Metropolis, Draft December 2003, Institute of mining and mineral engineering, Kwame Nkrumah University of Science and Technology, Kumasi.

Offen, KH. 2003. The Territorial Turn: Making Black Territories in Pacific Colombia. *Journal of Latin American Geography* 2:43-73.

Okali, Christine 1983. *Cocoa and kinship in Ghana: the matrilineal Akan of Ghana*. London; Boston: Kegan Paul International

Okoth-Ogendo, H.W.O. 1976. African land tenure reform. In *Agricultural Development in Kenya: An Economic Assessment*, edited by J. Heyer, J. K. Maitha and W. M. Senga. Nairobi: Oxford University Press.

Olinto, Pedro, Klaus Deininger, and Benjamin Davis. 2000. Land Market Liberalization and the Access to Land by the Rural Poor. In *Panel Data Evidence of the Impact of the Mexican Ejido Reform*. Washington: World Bank, Basis Working Paper.

Ollennu, N.A. 1962. *Principles of Customary Land Law in Ghana*. London: Sweet & Maxwell.

—. 1967. Aspects of land tenure. In *A Study of Contemporary Ghana. Volume two: Some Aspects of Social Structure*, edited by Birmingham, Neustadt and Omaboe. London: George Allen & Unwin Ltd.

Onchan, T, Y Chalamwong, G. D McColl, F. J Murray, and S Aungsumalin. 1990. Socio-Economic Evaluation of the Land Titling Project: Main report of the case studies. Kasetsart: Center for Applied Economics Research, Faculty of Economics and Business Administration, Kasetsart University.

Oomen, Barbara. 2002. Chiefs! Law, Power and Culture in Contemporary South Africa. Dissertation, Leiden University.

Ostrom, Elinor. 1999. Private and Common Property Rights. In *Encyclopedia of Law and Economics*, edited by B. Bouckaert and G. De Geest. Gent: Edward Elgar Publishing Limited.

—. 2005. *Understanding Institutional Diversity*. Princeton and Oxford: Princeton University Press.

Ostrom, Elinor, CC. Gibson, S. Shivakumar, and K. Andersson. 2001. Aid, Incentive and Sustainability: An Institutional Analysis of Development Cooperation. Stockholm: SIDA. Report no.

Otero, Gerardo. 2004. Adiós al campesinado? Democracia y formación política de las clases en el México Rural. Mexico: Universidad de Zacatecas, Simon Fraser University, Miguel Ángel Porrúa.

Otto, J.M. 2004. The mystery of legal failure? A critical, comparative examination of the potential of legalisation of land assets in developing countries for achieving real legal certainty. Research proposal. Leiden: Van Vollenhoven Institute for Law, Governance and Development.

—. 2009, forthcoming. Rule of law promotion, land tenure and poverty alleviation: Questioning the assumptions of Hernando de Soto *Hague Journal on the Rule of Law* 1.

Ouédraogo, R.S., J.-P. Sawadogo, V. Stamm, and T. Thombiano. 1996. Tenure, agricultural practices and land productivity in Burkina Faso: some recent empirical results. *Land Use Policy* 13 (3):229-232.

Pacheco, Diego. 2007. An Institutional Analysis of Decentralization and Indigenous Timber Management in Bolivia's Lowlands. Bloomington, Indiana, USA: Indiana University.

Pacheco, Diego, and Walter Valda. 2003. La tierra en los valles de Bolivia: Apuntes para la toma de decisiones. La Paz: Fundación Tierra.

Pakleppa, R. 2004. Civil rights in legislation and practice: A case study from Tsumkwe District West, Namibia. In *Indigenous people's rights in Southern Africa*, edited by R. Hitchcock and D. Vinding. Copenhagen: IWGIA.

Palmer, Robin. 2000. Land policy in Africa: Lessons from recent policy and implementation processes. In *Evolving Land Rights, Policy and Tenure in Africa*, edited by C. Toulmin and J. Quan. London: DFID/IIED/NRI.

Parlindungan, A.P. 1989. *Hak Pengelolaan menurut Sistem UUPA*. Bandung: Mandar Maju.

Pastor, Robert, and Qingshan Tan. 2000. The Meaning of China's Village Elections. *China Quarterly*:490-312.

Pausewang, S., K. Tronvoll, and L. Aalen. 2002. *Ethiopia since the Derg. A Decade of Democratic Pretension and Performance*. London: Zed Press.

Payne, Geoffrey. 2000. Urban land tenure policy options: Titles or rights? In *Paper presented at the World Bank Urban Forum* Virginia, USA.

—. 2001. Urban land tenure policy options: Titles or rights? *Habitat International* 25:415-429.

Peerenboom, R. 2002a. *China's Long March toward the Rule of Law*. Cambridge: Cambridge University Press.

—. 2002b. Law Enforcement and the Legal Profession in China. In *Implementation of Law in the People's Republic of China*, edited by J. Chen, Y. Li and J. M. Otto. New York: Kluwer Law International.

—. 2006. The Dynamics and Politics of Legal Reform in China. In *Law Reform in Developing and Transitional States*, edited by T. Lindsey. New York: Routledge.

Pei, Minxin. 1997. Citizens v. Mandarins: Administrative Litigation in China. *The China Quarterly* 152:832-862.

Pélissier, P. 1996. *Les Paysans du Sénégal. Les civilisations agraires du Cayor à la Casamance.* Saint-Yrieix: Imprimerie Frabrègue.

Pemerintah Kota Bandung. 2004a. Kajian Sistem Perijinan di Kota Bandung. Bandung: Kantor Litbang & PT HEGAR DAYA.

—. 2004b. Rencana Tata Ruang Wilayah Kota Bandung 2013, Buku Rencana. Bandung: Badan Perencanaan Pembangunan Daerah Kota Bandung.

Peng, Xizhe. 1987. Demographic Consequences of the Great Leap Forward in China's Provinces. *Population and Development Review* 13 (4):639.

Perez, R. 1996. Monte Verde: Territorio Indígena. *Artículo Primero: Revista de Debate Social y Jurídico*:p. 36-62.

Peters, Pauline E. 2002. The limits of negotiability: Security, equity and class formation in Africa's legal systems. In *Negotiating Property in Africa*, edited by K. Juul and C. Lund. Portsmouth: Heinemann.

Phan, Pamela N. 2005. Enriching the Land or the Political Elite? Lessons from China on Democratization of the Urban Renewal Process. *Pacific Rim Law and Policy Journal* 14 (June):607-656.

Place, F., M. Roth, and P. Hazell. 1994. Land Tenure Security and Agricultural Performance in Africa: Overview of Research Methodology. In *Searching for Land Tenure Security in Africa*, edited by J. W. Bruce and S. E. Migot-Adholla. Dubuque: Kendall/Hunt Publishing Company.

Platt, Tristan. 1982. Estado boliviano y ayllu andino; tierra y tributo en el Norte de Potosí. Lima: IEP.

Platteau, J P. 1996. The evolutionary theory of land rights as applied to Sub-Saharan Africa: A critical assessment. *Development and Change* 27 (1):29-86.

—. 2000. Does Africa need land reform? In *Evolving Land Rights, Policy and Tenure in Africa*, edited by C. Toulmin and J. Quan. London: DFID/IIED/NRI.

PNUD. 2004. Informe de desarrollo humano en Santa Cruz. La Paz: PNUD.

Pogucki, R.J.H. 1962. The main principles of rural land tenure. In *Agriculture and Land Use in Ghana*, edited by B. Wills. London, Accra, New York: Oxford University Press.

Prill-Brett, J. 1994. Indigenous Land Rights and Legal Pluralism among Philippine Highlanders. *Law & Society Review* 28:681-698.

Procuraduría Agraria. 1998. *Legislación Agraria*. Vol. Fourth edition, fourth printing. Mexico: Procuraduría Agraria.

—. 2004a. Ejido tipo 2004. México: Procuraduría Agraria.

—. 2004b. La aportación de tierras ejidales parceladas y de uso común al desarrollo urbano. México: Procuraduría Agraria.

—. 2004c. Los posesionarios: nuevos sujetos agrarios. México.

—. 2004d. Tendencias del campo mexicano 2004. México: Procuraduría Agraria.

Prosterman, Roy, Tim Hanstad, and Li Ping. 1994. Land Reform in China: The Two-Field System in Pingdu: RDI Reports on Foreign Aid and Development.

—. 1998. Large-Scale Farming in China: An Appropriate Policy? *Journal of Contemporary Asia* 28 (74):74.

Prosterman, Roy, Brian Schwarzwalder, and Ye Jianping. 2000. Implementation of 30-Year Land Use Rights for Farmers Under China's 1998 Land Management Law: An Analysis and Recommendations Based on a 17-Province Survey. *Pacific Rim Law and Policy Journal* 9:507.

Qinghe, Huang. 1992. Review and Current Issues on the Rural Land Policy in China. In *Proceedings of the International Symposium on Rural Land Issues in China.*

Quan, Julian. 2000. Land tenure, economic growth and poverty in sub-Saharan Africa. In *Evolving Land Rights, Policy and Tenure in Africa*, edited by C. Toulmin and J. Quan. London: DFID/IIED/NRI.

Quintana, R. D., L. Concheiro Bórquez, and R. Pérez Avilés. 1998. Peasant Logic, Agrarian Policy, Land Mobility, and Land Markets in Mexico, Working Paper # 21. Madison: North America Series, Land Tenure Center, University of Wisconsin.

Quintana, S., and M. Víctor. 2003. La amarga experiencia mexicana en el agro. El circulo vicioso del Tratado de Libre Comercio de América del Norte. www.rimisp.org/boletines.

Rada Vélez, Alfredo. 2003. Demandas territoriales indígenas en la región andina. *Artículo Primero* Año VII (No. 14):365-377.

Rajagukguk, E. 1988. Agrarian Law, Land Tenure and Subsistence in Java: Case Study of the Villages of Sukoharjo and Megayu: University of Washington [Unpublished PhD Thesis].

Rakodi, C., S, and C.R. Leduka. 2005. Informal land delivery processes and access to land for the poor: A comparative study of six African cities: Birmingham University Working Paper.

Ramirez, Alejandro. 2006. Mexico. In *Indigenous Peoples, Poverty and Human Development in Latin America*, edited by Gillette Hall and H. A. Patrinos. Houndmills, Basingstoke, Hampshire, New York: Palgrave McMillan.

Ranger, T. 1993. The Invention of Tradition Revisited: The Case of Colonial Africa. In *Legitimacy and the State in Twentieth-Century Africa: Essays in Honour of A.H. Kirk-Greene*, edited by T. Ranger and O. Vaughan. Oxford: MacMillan Press.

Rathbone, Richard. 1993. *Murder and Politics in Colonial Ghana*. New haven and London: Yale University Press.

—. 1996. Defining Akyemfo: The construction of citizenship in Akyem Abuakwa, Ghana, 1700-1939. *Africa* 66 (4):506-525.

—. 2000. *Nkrumah & the Chiefs. The Politics of Chieftaincy in Ghana 1951-60*. Oxford: James Currey.

Ravenholt, A. 1981. Rural Mobilization for Modernization in South Korea. In *The Politics of Agrarian Change in Asia and Latin America*, edited by H. Handelman. Bloomington: Indiana University Press.

Ray, D.I. 1992. Contemporary Asante chieftaincy: characteristics and development. In *An African Commitment: Papers in Honour of Peter Lewis Shinnie*, edited by J. Sterner and N. Davis. Calgary: University of Calgary Press.

—. 1996. Divided sovereignty: traditional authority and the state in Ghana. *Journal of Legal Pluralism* 37/38:181-202.

Reerink, G.O. Forthcoming. Land Tenure Security for Indonesia's Urban Poor, a Socio-Legal Study in the Kampongs of Post-New Order Bandung, Leiden University, Leiden.

Registro Agrario Nacional. 2005 [cited 28-09-05]. Available from www.ran.gob mx/archivos/PROCEDE/procede4.html.

Republic of Namibia. 2001a. 2001 Census Results, edited by National Planning Commission.

—. 2001b. Epidemiological Report on HIV/AIDS for the Year 2000, edited by Ministry of Health and Social Services.

—. 2006a. Follow-up on the Declaration of Commitment on HIV/AIDS - Namibia Country Report, edited by Ministry of Health and Social Services.

—. 2006b. Namibia Household Income and Expenditure Survey 2003/2004, edited by National Planning Commission.

República de Bolivia. 1996. *Ley del Servicio Nacional de Reforma Agraria, Ley No 1715, Ley de 18 de octubre de 1996*. Oruro: Sonqoy Editores.

République du Sénégal. 1980. Livre Blanc tome I et II Ziguinchor: Plan directeur d'urba-
    nisme, edited by Ministère de l'Urbanisme de l'Habitat et de l'Environnement. Dakar:
    SONED.
—. 1991. *Plan Directeur d'Urbanisme de Ziguinchor. Rapport de présentation.* Dakar: SONED
    Afrique.
—. 2003. Le Recueil des Textes de la Décentralisation. Dakar: La Sénégalaise de l'Imprim-
    erie.
Ribot, J. 1999. Decentralization, participation and accountability in Sahelian forestry: Legal
    instruments of political-administrative control. *Africa* 69 (1).
Rieger, Th., F Djalal, E. St. Pamuncak, R Ramon, and B Soewardi. 2001. Decentralising In-
    donesia's Land Administration System: Are local governments and land offices ready?
    Evidence from 27 districts. Final report. Jakarta: COMO GmbH/PT COMO Konsultindo.
Rivera Cusicanqui, Silvia. 2003. Oprimidos pero no vencidos: Luchas del campesinado ay-
    mara y quechwa 1900-1980 (con prefacio de la autora, 2003). La Paz: Aruwiyiri, Yachay-
    wasi.
Rivera Cusicanqui, Silvia, and Equipo Thoa. 1992. Ayllus y proyectos de desarrollo en el
    norte de Potosí. La Paz: Ediciones Aruwiyiri.
Robles Berlanga, Héctor. 2000. Propiedad de la tierra y población indígena. *Estudios Agrar-
    ios,* 123-147.
—. 2003. Tendencias del campo mexicano a la luz del Programa de Certificación de los De-
    rechos Ejidales (Procede). In *Políticas y regulaciones agrarias; Dinámicas de poder y juegos
    de actors en torno a la tenencia de la tierra,* edited by Éric Léonard, André Quesnel and E.
    Velázquez. Mexico: CIESAS, Miguel Ángel Porrúa.
Roland, Gérard. 2000. *Transition and Economics: Politics, Markets and Firms.* Cambridge:
    Cambridge University Press.
Romero Bonifaz, Carlos. 2001. El proceso agrario, los conflictos, el debate y las perspectivas.
    Artículo Primero, 215-232.
—. 2003. La Reforma Agraria en las tierras bajas de Bolivia. *Artículo Primero* Año VII (No.
    14):53-83.
Rubio, Blanca. 1999. Globalización, reestructuración productiva en la agricultura latinoamer-
    icana y vía campesina 1970-1995: Cuadernos Agrarios, nueva época,.
Runsheng, Du. 2003. *Zhongguo Nongcun Zhidu Bianqiang.* Vol. 38. Chengdu: Sichuan Peo-
    ple's Publishing.
Rural Development Institute. 2002. China Adopts Rural Land Contracting Law: A Break-
    through for Farmers' Land-Tenure Rights. *Monthly News and Notes.*
Sadjarwo. 1978. Land Reform Indonesia dalam rangka pembangunan pertanian dan pedes-
    aan. In *Seminar Hukum Pertanian.* Jakarta: Pusat Pembinaan Sumber Daya Manusia.
Safitri, M.A. 1997. Kebudayaan Birokrasi dan Pengelolaan Hutan: Kajian Perbandingan di
    Provinsi Lampung dan Kalimantan Timur: Department of Anthropology, University of
    Indonesia [Unpublished Master Thesis].
Safitri, M.A., J. Bangun, and B. Philippus. 1999. Kebijakan Penetapan Hutan dan Implikasi-
    nya pada Pengelolaan Hutan di Indonesia. Jakarta: Program Penelitian dan Pengemban-
    gan Antropologi Ekologi Universitas Indonesia.
Salvatierra G., Hugo. 1996. Ley INRA entre la realidad del latifundio y la necesidad del cam-
    bio social en el mundo agrario boliviano. *Artículo Primero,* 73-77.
Sarbah, J.M. 1968. *Fanti Customary Laws. A brief Introduction to the Principles of the Native
    Laws and Customs of the Fanti and Akan Districts of the Gold Coast with a Report of some
    Cases thereon Decided in the Law Courts.* Third edition ed. London: Frank Cass.
SBS. 1980, 1984. National Economic & Social Development Bulletin: State Bureau of Statis-
    tics (SBS).
—. n.d. Compilation of 50-Year Statistical Information of New China: State Bureau of Statis-
    tics.

Schoonmaker Freudenberger, K. 1991. Mbegué: The disingenuous destruction of a Sahelian forest. *Development Anthropological Network: Bulletin of the Institute for Development Anthropology* 9 (2):1-12.

Schoonmaker Freudenberger, M. 1990. World Bank Mission on Land Tenure in Senegal. Draft. Madison, Wisconsin: Land Tenure Center.

—. 1992. Land Tenure, Local Institutions and Natural resources in Senegal. Preliminary draft. Madison, Wisconsin: Land tenure Center.

Schwarzwalder, Brian, Roy Prosterman, Jianping Ye, Jeffrey Riedinger, and Ping Li. 2002. An Update On China's Rural Land Tenure Reforms: Analysis and Recommendations Based on a Seventeen-Province Survey. *Columbia Journal of Asian Law* 16 (1):141-225.

Scott, J. 1985. *Weapons of the Weak: Everyday forms of Peasant Resistance.* New Haven: Yale University Press.

—. 1998. *Seeing Like a State: How Certain Schemes to Improve the Human Condition Have Failed.* New Haven: Yale University Press.

Secretaría de la Reforma Agraria. 1991. Acta de Asamblea General Extraordinario de Ejidatarios, que se celebra por segunda convocatoria, en el poblado denominado "Santiago Teyahualco", municipio de Tultepec, Estado de México, con motivo de la nueva investigación general de usufructo parcelario ejidal. In *Ejido Santiago Tuyahualco, Tultepec, Estado de México, Delegación Agraria en el Estado Promotoría No. 12, 16/10/1991.*

—. 1998. La transformación agraria; origen, evolución, retos, testimonios. Mexico: Secretaria de la Reforma Agraria.

—. 2006. Informe Nacional 1992-2005, México, Report presented at the Conferencia Internacional sobre Reforma Agraria y Desarrollo Rural, del 6 a 10 de marzo de 2006, at Porto Alegre, Río Grande del Sur, Brasil.

Secretaria de Reforma Agraria. 1998. La transformación agraria; origen, evolución, retos, testimonios. Mexico: Secretaria de la Reforma Agraria.

Senghor, L.S. 1960. Rapport sur la voie du socialisme. Dakar.

Sherbourne, R. 2004. A rich man's hobby. In *Who should own the land: Analysis and views on land reform and the land question in Namibia and South Africa,* edited by J. Hunter. Windhoek: Konrad Adenauer Stiftung and Namibian Institute for Democracy.

Shi, Tianjian. 1999. Village Committee Elections in China: Institutionalist Tactics for Democracy. *World Politics* 51 (3):385-412.

Shipton, P., and M. Goheen. 1992. Introduction. Understanding African land holding: Power, wealth and meaning. *Africa* 62 (3):307-325.

Silva Herzog, Jesús. 1959. El agrarismo mexicano y la reforma agraria: Exposición y crítica. Mexico, Buenos Aires: Fondo de Cultura Económica.

Simon, Joel. 1997. *Endangered Mexico: An Environment on the Edge.* London: Latin America Bureau.

Sinkule, J.B., and L. Ortolano. 1995. *Implementing Environmental Policy in China.* Westport: Praeger.

Skidmore, Thomas, and Peter H. Smith. 1997. *Modern Latin America. Fourth edition.* New York, Oxford: Oxford University Press.

Slaats, H. 1997. Evolutionary Change in Indonesian Land Law, Traditional (Adat) Perspectives. Land administration Project - part C, Topic Cycle 4. Jakarta: National Development Planning Agency/National Land Agency.

—. 1999. Land Titling and Customary Rights: Comparing land registration projects in Thailand and Indonesia. In *Property Rights and Economic Development, Land and Natural Resources in Southeast Asia and Oceania,* edited by T. Van Meijl and F. Von Benda-Beckmann. London, New York: Kegan Paul International.

Soehendera, D. 2005. Masalah Sertifikasi Tanah Orang Miskin di Jakarta: Studi Kasus di Kampung Rawa, Departmen Antropologi, Universitas Indonesia, Jakarta.

Soen, Sie Kwat. 1968. Prospects for Agricultural Development in Indonesia, with Special Re-
    ference to Java, Centre for Agricultural Publications and Documentation, Wageningen
    University, Wageningen.
Soetiknjo, I. 1983. *Politik Agraria Nasional*. Jogyakarta: Gadjah Mada University Press.
Soloago, Isidro. 2003. Mexico Policy Paper. In *Roles of Agriculture Project International Confer-
    ence*. Rome: FAO/ESA.
Solomom Bekure, Gizachew Abegaz, Lennart Frej, and Solomon Abebe, eds. 2006. *Standar-
    dization of Land Registration and Cadastral Surveying Methodologies: Experiences in Ethio-
    pia*. Addis Ababa: Ethiopia Land Tenure and Administration Program (ELTAP).
Solomon Abebe. 2006. Land Registration Systems in Ethiopia. Comparative Analysis of Am-
    hara, Oromia, SNNP and Tigray Regional States: USAID
Solón, Pablo. 1995. La tierra prometida; Un aporte al debate sobre las moidificaciones a la
    legislación agraria. La Paz: CEDOIN.
Spence, J.D. 1990. *The Search for Modern China*. New York: Norton.
Stahl, Michael. 1974. *Ethiopia: Political Contradictions in Agricultural Development*. Stockholm:
    Raben.
Statistics Bureau. n.d. Analytical Report on 50 Years of New China: Part Sixteen: China State
    Statistics Bureau.
Stephen, Lynns. 2002. *Zapata Lives! Histories and Cultural Politics in Southern Mexico*. Berke-
    ley, Los Angeles, London: University of California Press.
Subrahmanyan, Arjun. 2004. Land Use in China: the impact of the economic revolution.
    China Law & Practice November.
Sullivan, S. 2002. How sustainable is the communalizing discourse of the New Conserva-
    tion? The masking of difference, inequality and aspiration in the fledgling conservancies
    of Namibia. In *Conservation and Mobile Indigenous Peoples: Displacement, Forced Settle-
    ment and Sustainable Development*, edited by D. Chatty and M. Colchester. New York and
    Oxford: Berghan Books.
Sumardjono, M.S.W. 2008. *Tanah dalam Perspektif Hak Ekonomi, Sosial dan Budaya*. Jakarta:
    Kompas.
Suzman, J. 2002. Report: Minorities in Independent Namibia: Minorities Rights Group In-
    ternational.
Sylla, O. 2004. What does the future hold for Senegalese farmers? *Haramata* 47 (Novem-
    ber):16-19.
Sypkens Smit, M.P. 1976. *Een Systeem van Nivellering van Ongelijkheid in Landbezit: Landleen-
    relaties in Basse-Casamance (Senegal)*. Den Haag: Stichting Werkgroep Studiereizen Ont-
    wikkelingslanden.
Szalachman R., Raquel. 1999. Un perrfil de deficit de vivienda en Bolivia, 1992. Santiago de
    Chile: CEPAL.
Tall, S.M, and A Tine. 2002. 'Farmer participation in land-use negotiations in Thiès Region,
    Senegal. In *Local Government and Participation, PLA (Participatory Learning and Action)
    Notes 44*, edited by A. Inglis and C. Hesse. London: IIED.
Tamburini, L., and AC. Betancur. 2003. Monte Verde. *Artículo Primero* VII:227-267.
Tan, Minghongs. 2005. Urban Land Expansion and Arable Land Loss in China-A Case Study
    of Beijing-Tianjin-Hebei Region. *Land Use Policy* 22:187-196.
Tan, S. F, and B Guèye. 2005. Portraits of Family Farming in West Africa. London: IIED. Is-
    sue Paper 134.
Tang, Shui-Yan, Carlos W. H. Lo, Kai-Chee Cheung, and Jack Man-Keung Lo. 1997. Institu-
    tional Constraints on Environmental Management in Urban China: Environmental Im-
    pact Assessment in Guangzhou and Shanghai. *China Quarterly* (152):863-74.
Tapia Garcia, C. 2004. Land reform in Namibia: Economic versus socio-political rationale.

Taylor, Veronica. 2007. The Law Reform Olympics, Measuring the Effects of Law Reform in Transition Economies. In *Law Reform in Developing and Transitional States*, edited by T. Lindsey. New York: Routledge.

Tegegne Gebre-Egziabher, and Kassahun Berhanu. 2006. Decentralization in Ethiopia: Literature Review. Addis Ababa: Unpublished paper, Forum for Social Studies.

Tellez, Luis. 1994. La modernización del sector agropecuario y forestal. México: Fondo de Cultura Económica.

Ter Haar, B. 1939. *Beginselen en Stelsel van het Adatrecht*. Groningen/Batavia: J.B. Wolters.

Terceros Cuéllar, Elva. 2004. De la utopia indígena al desencanto; Reconocimiento estatal de los derechos territoriales indígenas. Santa Cruz: CEJIS.

The Smeru Research Team. 2002. An Impact Evaluation of Systematic Land Titling under the Land Administration Project (LAP). Jakarta: Smeru Research Institute.

Thiesenhusen, William C. 1995. *Broken Promises; Agrarian Reform and the Latin American Campesino*. Boulder, San Francisco, Oxford: Westview Press.

Thomas, L-V. 1959. *Les Diolas: Essai d'analyse fonctionnelle sur une population de Basse-Casamance*. Dakar: IFAN (2 volumes).

—. 1968. Les Diola. Points de vue sur le présent et l'avenir d'une ethnie Sénégalaise. *Revue de Psychologie des Peuples* 23 (3):244-275.

Ticona Alejo, Esteban. 2000. Organización y liderazgo aymara, 1979-1996. La Paz: Universidad de la Cordillera, AGRUCO.

Ticona Alejo, Esteban, and Xavier Albó Corrons. 1997. La lucha por el poder comunal (Jesús de Machaqa: la marca rebelde vol. 3). La Paz: CEDOIN, CIPCA.

Ticona Alejo, Esteban, Gonzalo Rojas Ortuste, and Xavier Albó Corrons. 1995. Votos y wiphalas; campesinos y pueblos originarios en democracia. La Paz: Fundación Milenio, CIPCA.

Tjondronegoro, S.M.P. 2003. Land Policies in Indonesia: EASRD Working Paper.

Toulmin, Camilla, Philippe Lavigne Delville, and Samba Traoré. 2002. Introduction. In *The Dynamics of Resource Tenure in West Africa*, edited by C. Toulmin, P. Lavigne Delville and S. Traoré. London: IIED.

Toulmin, Camilla, and Judy Longbottom. 2001. West African Land: Rights, Poverty & Growth. London: IIED.

Toulmin, Camilla, and Julian Quan. 2000a. Evolving land rights, tenure and policy in sub-Saharan Africa. In *Evolving Land Rights, Policy and Tenure in Africa*, edited by C. Toulmin and J. Quan. London: DFID/IIED/NRI.

—, eds. 2000b. *Evolving Land Rights, Policy and Tenure in Africa*. London: DFID/IIED/NRI.

Touré, O, and S. M Seck. 2005. Family and Commercial Farming in the Niayes Area of Senegal. London: IIED.

Tribunal Superior Agrario. 2005. Síntesis de la Actividad Jurisdiccional. www.tribunalesagrarios.gob.mx/Act_juris/jul21-may312005.htm.

Tribunal Unitario Agrario Décimo Distrito. 1993. Sentencia Juicio de Privación de Derechos Agrarios numero IUA/10D10./74/92. Poblado Santiago Teyahualco, Tultepec, México.

Trincaz, P. X. 1984. Colonisation et Régionalisme. Ziguinchor en Casamance. Paris: Editions de l'ORSTOM (Travaux et Documents no.172).

Turner, J. 1968. 'Housing priorities, settlement patterns and urban development in modernizing countries. *AIP Journal* (November):354-363.

Tvedten, I., and A. Pomuti. 1995. Urbanisation and urban policies in Namibia: University of Namibia SSD Discussion Paper no. 10.

Twyman, C., A. Dougill, D. Sporton, and D. Thomas. 2001. Community fencing in open rangelands: Self-empowerment in Eastern Namibia. *Review of African Political Economy* No 87.

Ubink, Janine M. 2002-2004. Courts and peri-urban practice: Customary land law in Ghana. *University of Ghana Law Journal* XXII:25-77.

—. 2006. Land, Chiefs and Custom in Peri-Urban Ghana. In *International Conference on Land, Poverty, Social Practice and Development*. The Hague: ISS and ICCO.

—. 2007a. Customary tenure security: Wishful policy thinking or reality? A case from peri-urban Ghana. *Journal of African Law* 51 (2):215-248.

—. 2007b. Traditional authority revisited: Popular perceptions of chiefs and chieftaincy in peri-urban Kumasi, Ghana. *Journal of Legal Pluralism* 55:123-161.

—. 2008. *In the Land of the Chiefs: Customary Law, Land Conflicts, and the Role of the State in Peri-urban Ghana, Law, Governance and Development*. Leiden: Leiden University Press.

—. 2008, in press. Land, chiefs and custom in peri-urban Ghana: Traditional governance in an environment of legal and institutional pluralism. In *The Governance of Legal Pluralism*, edited by W. Zips and M. Weilenmann. Münster: Lit Verlag.

Ubink, Janine M., and Julian F. Quan. 2008. How to combine tradition and modernity? Regulating customary land management in Ghana. *Land Use Policy* 25:198-213.

UN Habitat. 2004. Global Campaign for Secure Tenure. A tool for advocating the provision of adequate shelter for the urban poor. Concept paper, 2nd edition. Nairobi: UN Habitat.

—. 2005. Land tenure, housing rights and gender - National and urban framework. Namibia.

UNAIDS. 2006. Report on the Global Aids Epidemic 2006.

UNDP. 1999. Namibia human development report 1998.

—. 2004a. Access to Justice, Practice Note: UNDP. http://europeandcis.undp.org/files/uploads/HR/mat%20PracticeNote_AccessToJustice.pdf.

—. 2004b. Human development report 2004.

Urioste, Miguel. 2003. La Reforma Agraria Abandonada: Valles y altiplano. In *Artículo Primero*. Santa Cruz: CEJIS.

Urioste, Miguel, Rossana Barragán, and Gonzalo Colque. 2007. Los nietos de la Reforma Agraria: Tierra y comunidad en el altiplano de Bolivia. La Paz: Fundación Tierra-CIPCA.

Urioste, Miguel, and Diego Pacheco. 2000. Land Market in a New Context: the INRA Law in Bolivia. In *Current Land Policy in Latin America; Regulating Land Tenure under Neo-Liberalism*, edited by A. Zoomers and G. Van der Haar. Amsterdam, Frankfurt/Main: KIT, Iberoamericana/Vervuert Verlag.

USAID. 2004. Ethiopia Land Policy and Administration Assessment. Final Report., edited by Submitted by ARD. Burlington, Vt, USA: USAID

—. 2006a. Papers of the In *National Conference on Standardization of Rural Land Registration and Cadastral Surveying Methodologies*. Addis Ababa: ELTAP.

—. 2006b. Public Information and Awareness (PIA) Strategy and Action Plan, edited by ELTAP and Coordination Unit. Addis Ababa.

Utrecht, E. 1976. Political mobilization of peasants in Indonesia. *Journal of Contemporary Asia* (3).

Vadillo, Alcido. 1997. Constitución Política del Estado y pueblos indígenas: Bolivia, país de mayoría indígena. In *Derecho indígena,*, edited by M. Ggómez. Mexico: Instituto Nacional Indigenista, Asociación Mexicana para las Naciones Unidas A.C.

Van Cott, Donna Lee. 2000a. *The Friendly Liquidation of the Past: The Politics of Diversity in Latin America*. Pittsburgh: University of Pittsburgh Press.

—. 2000b. Review: A Political Analysis of Legal Pluralism in Bolivia and Colombia. *Journal of Latin American Studies* 32:207-234.

—. 2005. *From Movements to Parties in Latin America: The Evolution of Ethnic Politics*. New York: Cambridge University Press.

Van de Sandt, J. 2003. Communal Resource Tenure and the Quest for Indigenous Autonomy: On State Law and Ethnic Reorganization in Two Colombian Resguardos. *Journal of Legal Pluralism* 48:125-162.

Van den Brink, Rogier, Glen Thomas, Hans Binswanger, John Bruce, and Frank Byamu-
gisha. 2006. Consensus, Confusion and Controversy. Selected land reform issues in
sub-Saharan Africa. World Bank working paper No. 71. Washington: The World Bank.

Van der Klei, J. M. 1979. Anciens et nouveaux droits fonciers chez les Diola au Sénégal et
leurs conséquences pour la répartition des terres. *African Perspectives* 1.

—. 1989. Trekarbeid en de Roep van het Heilige Bos, Vrije Universiteit, Amsterdam.

Van der Ploeg, Jan D. 1990. *Labour, Markets and Agricultural Production.* Boulder: Westview
Press.

Van Rooij, B. 2006a. Implementation of Chinese Environmental Law: Regular Enforcement
and Political Campaigns. *Development and Change* 37 (1):57-74.

—. 2006b. *Regulating Land and Pollution in China, Lawmaking, Compliance, and Enforcement;
Theory and Cases.* Leiden: Leiden University Press.

Van Rouveroy van Nieuwaal, E.A.B. 1987. Chiefs and African states: Some introductory
notes and an extensive bibliography on African chieftaincy. *Journal of Legal Pluralism* 25/
26:1-46.

—. 1996. States and chiefs: Are chiefs mere puppets? *Journal of Legal Pluralism* 37-38:39-78.

Van Vollenhoven, Cornelis. 1918. *Het Adatrecht van Nederlans-Indië. Vol. I.* Leiden: Brill.

Vandergeest, P., and N.L. Peluso. 2006. Empires of Forestry: Professional Forestry and State
Power in Southeast Asia, Part 1. *Environment and History* 12:31-64.

Varley, Ann. 1985. Urbanisation and agrarian law: The case of Mexico City. *Bulletin of Latin
American Research* 4 (1):1-16.

—. 1989. Relaciones entre la regularización de la tenencia de la tierra y mejoras en la vivienda: el caso de la ciudad de México. *Revista Interamericana de Planificación* xxi (86).

—. 2002. Private or public: Debating the meaning of tenure legalization. *International Journal of Urban and Regional Research* 26 (3):449-61.

Verdier, R. 1971. L'ancien droit et le nouveau droit foncier de l'Afrique noire face au développement. In *Le Droit à la Terre en Afrique.* Paris: Maisonneuve.

Verlinden, A., and A.S. Kruger. 2007. Changing grazing systems in Central North Namibia.
Land Degradation & Development 18:179.

Villanueva I. Arturo D. 2004. Pueblos indígenas y conflictos de tierras: El caso de la CIRA-
BO y la III Marcha por la Tierra, el Territorio y los Recursos Naturales. La Paz: Fundación Tierra.

Von Benda-Beckmann, Franz. 1979. *Property in Social Continuity: Continuity and change in
the maintenance of property relationships through time in Minangkabau, West Sumatra.* The
Hague: Nijhoff.

Von Benda-Beckmann, K, M. De Bruijn, H. Van Dijk, G Hesseling, and L. Res. 1997. Rights
of Women to the Natural Resources Land and Water. The Hague: Ministry of Foreign
Affairs.

Von Trotha, Trutz 1996. From administrative to civil chieftaincy: Some problems and prospects of African chieftaincy. *Journal of Legal Pluralism* 37/38:79-108.

Walijatun, D, and C Grant. 1996. Land Registration Reform in Indonesia. Paper read at Proceedings of International Conference on Land Tenure and Administration in Developing
Countries, at Jakarta.

Walinsky, Louis J., ed. 1977. *Agrarian Reform as Unfinished Business: The selected papers of Wolf
Ladejinski.* New York: Oxford University Press.

Walker, Charles. 1999. *Smoldering Ashes; Cuzco and the Creation of Republican Peru, 1780-
1840.* Durham and London: Duke University Press.

Wang, Liming. 2006. Rural Land Ownership Reform in China's Property Law. *Front. Law
China* 3:311-328.

Wang, Shengming, ed. 2007. *Zhonghua Renmin Gonghe Guo Wuquanfa Jiedu (Understanding
the PRC Property Law).* Beijing: Zhongguo Fazhi Chuban She.

Wanjohi, M.W. 2007. Investigating the effects of property rights formalisation on property markets in informal settlements: The case of Dar es Salaam City, Tanzania, Master thesis submitted to the International Institute for Geo-information Science and Earth Observation, The Netherlands.

Watts, M. 1994. Life under Contract: Contract farming, agrarian restructuring, and flexible accumulation. In *Living under Contract: Contract farming and agrarian transformation in sub-Saharan Africa*, edited by P. Little and M. Watts. Madison: University of Wisconsin Press.

Weaver, L.C., and P. Skyer. 2003. Conservancies: Integrating wildlife land-use options into the livelihood, development, and conservation strategies of Namibian communities. Paper presented at the 5th World Parks Congress, Durban.

Wehrmann, B. 2002. The easiest way to make money is to sell land! Land conflicts in the peri-urban area of Accra, Ghana. *Trialog. Journal for Planning and Building in the Third World* 74 (3):26-32.

Weigeln-Schwidrizik, Susanne. 2003. *Trauma and Memory: The case of the Great Famine in the People's Republic of China (1959-1961).* Leiden: Brill Academic Publishers.

Werner, W. 1993. A brief history of land dispossession in Namibia. *Journal of Southern African Studies* 19:1.

—. 2003. Land reform in Namibia: Motor or obstacle of democratic development. Paper presented at the Friedrich Ebert Foundation, Berlin.

Werner, W., and P. Vigne. 2000. Resettlement co-operatives in Namibia: Past and future. Windhoek: Ministry of Agriculture, Water and Rural Development, and The Namibian Economic Policy Research Unit.

Wetterhall, Hans. 1972. Government Land in Ethiopia. Addis Ababa: Imperial Ethiopian Government, Ministry of Land Reform and Administration.

White, A., and A. Martin. 2002. Who owns the world's forests? Forest Tenure and Public Forests in Transition. Washington, D.C.: Forest Trends and CIFOR. Report no.

Wolf, Eric. 1973. *Peasant Wars of the Twentieth Century.* New York, Hagerstown, San Francisco, London: Harper Torchbooks.

Wollenberg, E., B. Belcher, D. Sheil, S. Dewi, and M. Moeliono. 2004. Why are forest areas relevant to reducing poverty in Indonesia? CIFOR Governance Brief No. 4(E). Bogor Barat CIFOR

Womack Jr., John. 1970. *Zapata and the Mexican Revolution.* New York: Vintage Books.

Woodman, Gordon R. 1996. *Customary Land Law in the Ghanaian Courts.* Accra: Ghana Universities Press.

Woodruff, Christopher. 2001. Review of de Soto's *The Mystery of Capital. Journal of Economic Literature* XXXIX (December 2001):1215-1223.

World Bank. 1973. Agricultural Sector Review, Ethiopia. Washington, D.C: Vols I-III. Report No. PA-143a, World Bank.

—. 1994. Staff Appraisal Report Indonesia Land Administration Project. Washington D.C.: World Bank.

—. 1995. Bolivia, National Land Administration Project. Washington: The World Bank.

—. 1997. Mexico Ejido Reform, Avenues of Adjustment - Five Years Later, Main Report. Washington: World Bank, Environmentally and Socially Sustainable Development Sector Management Unit, Mexico Country Management Unit, Latin America and the Caribbean Region.

—. 1998. México Ejido Reform: Avenues of Adjustment - Five Years Later. Main Report, Decision Draft. Washington: World Bank.

—. 2003a. Cities in Transition: Urban Sector Review in an Era of Decentralization in Indonesia. Washington D.C.: World Bank.

—. 2003b. Ghana Land Administration Project. Washington D.C.: World Bank.

—. 2003c. Implementation Completion Report No. 25637.

—. 2003d. Land Policies for Growth and Poverty Reduction. Washington D.C.: World Bank.

—. 2004a. Customary Land Titling in Vietnam East Asia and Pacific Region. Washington, D.C.: The World Bank, Report no.

—. 2004b. Project Appraisal Document Land Management and Policy Development Project. Washington D.C.: World Bank.

—. 2005. Rural Land Policy in Ethiopia. Aide Memoire. Addis Ababa: World Bank.

—. 2006. National Land Administration Project. Washington, D.C.: The World Bank. Report no.

Xiang, Wu. 2001. Zhongguo Nongcun Gaige Shilu (Records of China's Rural Reforms). Hangzhou: Zhejiang Renmin Chubanshe.

Xiao, Guangwen. 2003. Woguo Nongcun Jiti Tudi Zhengyong Zhidu de Quexian jiqi wanshan (Problems and Sollutions of China's Collective land requisitioning System). In *Nongcun Tudi Falüzhidu Yanjiu, Tianye Diaocha Jiedu (Research in the Village Land Legal System, an Analysis on the Basis of Fieldwork)*, edited by X. e. a. Chen. Beijing: Zhongguo Zhengfa Daxue Chubanshe.

Xinhua News Agency. 2003. Economic Statistical Data: Citizen Consumption Level and Index.

—. 2007. *Lawmaker: Property Law May Serve as Umbrella to Farmers'Land* 2007 [cited 8 June 2007]. Available from http://www.china.org.cn/english/2007rh/202212.htm.

Xu, Wang. 1997. Mutual Empowerment of State and Peasantry: Grassroots Democracy in Rural China. *Word Development* 35 (9):1431-1442.

Yang, Yijie. 2003. Zhongguo Nongdiquan Jiben Wenti, Zhongguo Jiti nongdi quanli tixi de xingcheng yu tuozhan (Fundamental Problems of Rural Land Rights in China, The Formation and Development of Collective Rural Land Rights). Bejing: Zhongguo Haiguan Chubanshe.

Yashar, Deborah J. 2005. *Contesting Citizenship in Latin America; The Rise of Indigenous Movements and the Postliberal Challenge*. Cambridge, New York: Cambridge University Press.

Ye, Hongling. 2004. Zui Yange de Gengdi Baohu Zhidu Shi Shenmo, Cong Bashi Nian de Tudi Guanlishi Kan Woguo Tudi Guanli Tizhi, Zhengce Fazhan Bianhua Yu Hexin Qushi (What is the Strictest System to Protect Arable Land, Looking at Developments, Changes and Core Trends in China's Land Management System and Policies from an Historical Perspective from the 1980s). *Zhongguo Tudi* 2004 (1~2):4-10.

Young, Linda Wilcox. 1995. Free Trade or Fair Trade? NAFTA and Agricultural Labor. *Latin American Perspectives* Issue 84, 22 (1):49-58.

Young, W. 2004. *Sold Out! The True Cost of Supermarket Shopping*. London: Vision Paperbacks.

Zepeda, Guillermo. 1999. La disputa por la tierra: los tribunales agrarios en México. www. pa.gob.mx/publica/rev_11/Zepeda.pdf.

—. 2000. Transformación agraria: Los derechos de propiedad en el campo mexicano bajo el nuevo marco institucional: Mexico CIOAC, Miguel Ángel Porrúa.

Zevenbergen, J.A. 2002. *Systems of Land Registration: Aspects and Effects*. Delft: Nederlandse Commissie voor Geodesie.

Zhang, H., X.F. Li, and X.M. Shao. 2006. Impacts of China's Rural Land Policy and Administration on Rural Economy and Grain Production. *Review of Policy Research* 23 (2):615.

Zhang, Tingwei. 2002. Decentralization, Localization and the Emergence of Quasi Participatory Decision Making in Ubran Development in Shanghai. *International Planning Studies* 7:303-305.

Zhao, Junshui. 2003. Ziboshi Zhengdi Buchang Anzhi Fangshi Diaoyan (Research on the Method of Land Acuiqition Allocation in Zibo Municipality). *Zhongguo Tudi* 2003 (10):39-40.

Zheng, S. 1997. *Party vs. State in Post-1949 China, The Institutional Dilemma*. Cambridge: Cambridge University Press.

Zhu, Keliang, Roy Prosterman, Jianping Ye, Ping Li, Jeffrey Riedinger, and Yiwen Ouyang. 2006. The Rural Land Question in China: Analysis and Recommendations Based on a 17-province Survey in 2005. *New York University Journal of International Law & Politics* Forthcoming.

Zhu, Xiaoyang. 2003. *Zuoguo yu Chengfa, Xiaocun Gushi 1931-1997 (Crime and Punishment, Stories from Xiaocun 1931-1997)*. Tianjin: Tianjin Guji Chubanshe.

Zoomers, Annelies. 1998. Titulando tierras en los Andes bolivianos: Las implicacias de la Ley INRA en Chuquisaca y Potosí. In *Estrategias campesinas en el Surandino de Bolivia*, edited by A. Zoomers. Amsterdam, La Paz: KIT, CEDLA, CID, Plural Editores.

Zweig, David. 2000. The 'Externalities of Development': Can New Political Institutions Manage Rural Conflict? In *Chinese Society: Change, Conflict, and Resistance*, edited by Elizabeth J. Perry and M. Selden. London: Routledge.

List of Contributors

Kojo Sebastian Amanor, Institute of African Studies, University of Ghana, Ghana

Willem Assies, Van Vollenhoven Institute for Law, Governance and Development, Leiden University, the Netherlands

Emilio Duhau, Departamento de Sociología, Universidad Autónoma Metropolitana, Azcapotzalco, Mexico

John Eichelsheim, IDEE-Casamance, Senegal

Nurul Elmiyah, Faculty of Law, University of Indonesia, Indonesia

Gerti Hesseling, Africa Study Centre Leiden and Utrecht University, the Netherlands

André Hoekema, Faculty of Law, University of Amsterdam, the Netherlands

Marco Lankhorst, University of Amsterdam / Independent legal consultant, the Netherlands

Diego Pacheco, Public Policy, Indiana University, USA

Li Ping, Rural Development Institute, Beijing, China

Roy Prosterman, Rural Development Institute, Seattle, USA

Dessalegn Rahmato, Forum for Social Studies, Ethiopia

Erman Rajagukguk, Faculty of Law, University of Indonesia, Indonesia

Gustaaf Reerink, Van Vollenhoven Institute for Law, Governance and Development, Leiden University, the Netherlands

Benjamin van Rooij, Van Vollenhoven Institute for Law, Governance and Development, Leiden University, the Netherlands

Akhmad Safik, Faculty of Law, University of Indonesia, Indonesia

Myrna A. Safitri, Ecological Anthropology Research & Development Program, University of Indonesia, Indonesia

Herman Slaats, Institute for Folk Law, Radboud University Nijmegen, the Netherlands

Janine Ubink, Van Vollenhoven Institute for Law, Governance and Development, Leiden University, the Netherlands

Muriël Veldman, Dutch Ministry of Housing and Environmental Affairs, the Netherlands

Wu Jian, School of Urban and Environment Studies of Peking University, China

Ye Jianping, Department of Land & Real Estate, Renmin University, China

Index